New Standard Encyclopedia

a (A to And)

New Standard Encyclopedia

VOLUME ONE
(A to And)

 Standard Educational Corporation

CHICAGO
1985

Library of Congress Cataloging in Publication Data

Main entry under title:

New standard encyclopedia.

   Includes bibliographies.
   1. Encyclopedias and dictionaries.   I. Standard
Educational Corporation.
AE5.N64   1985   031   84-245
ISBN   0-87392-190-9 (set)   AACR2

Foreword

NEW STANDARD ENCYCLOPEDIA is designed to provide as much information of interest to the general reader as is possible within an illustrated set selling for a moderate price. Although children as young as nine or ten can understand much of the material, the content is not juvenile and the level of detail is sufficient for basic reference use by persons of any age. For school assignments of younger readers and for everyday use by adults, NEW STANDARD ENCYCLOPEDIA itself is usually adequate. For advanced students and for adults who need detailed information, this encyclopedia serves as a general source to consult before seeking out more specialized and advanced works.

For suggestions on how to make the most use of this encyclopedia, see pages vii-ix.

Since each article is the work of several persons, the articles are not signed. Most of the articles are written by members of the encyclopedia's editorial staff. (See pages x-xi.) Staff members are qualified in their fields by education and experience and are trained in the techniques of encyclopedia writing. Their material, after being checked, edited, and rechecked by other staff members, is submitted to one or more of the authorities listed on pages xii-xxxiv.

Each article published has been reviewed by five or more persons. At least one of these is a recognized authority in the field being covered. This authority, called an *authenticator,* assumes responsibility for accuracy; often several authenticators will review all or part of a given article. The other reviewers are specialists concerned with style, illustration, and other technical matters; the goal of each is to insure clarity.

Statistics come from primary sources or from government or United Nations agencies. With few exceptions, statistical sources are cited for graphs and tables, and dates are given. An appendix in the back of the last volume indicates the years and types of data used for population figures.

Metric equivalents, when given in the text, are generally not exact conversions but are rounded up or down to express approximately the same degree of exactness as the accompanying U.S. Customary units. For example, "about 75 miles" becomes "120 km" rather than "121 km" or "120.675 km." A similar policy holds when the source for the measurement used metric units—the U.S. unit is rounded to about the same degree of exactness as the metric one. The purpose of this rounding is to avoid making approximate figures in one system look like exact ones in the other. As a result of this policy, however, some inconsistencies may occur, especially when comparing exact measurements with approximate ones.

Revision is continuous rather than periodic. Three procedures operate simultaneously: (1) Each year up to 40 per cent of the pages throughout the encyclopedia are revised, entirely or partially. Maps, tables, and articles on contemporary subjects are under constant review and are revised whenever significant new information becomes available. Graphs, bibliographies, and statistics are reviewed for revision at least once every four or five years. (2) Each year major sections within volumes are completely revised; all material is reevaluated and many articles are rewritten or reillustrated to assure a contemporary approach to the subjects involved. (3) In a program of "area" revision, all related articles are examined periodically as a unit.

Suggestions on How to Use New Standard Encyclopedia

NEW STANDARD ENCYCLOPEDIA can be useful to you in many ways. Use it to look up quick reference questions such as "When did Alaska become a state?" and "Where is the Baseball Hall of Fame?" Use it to study or write a report on broad subjects such as American colonial life or the history of the airplane. And use it for the pleasure and profit that come from just browsing.

When all you want at the moment is the meaning of a word, the reference work to consult is a dictionary rather than an encyclopedia. When you want to learn to solve algebra problems or play bridge or knit a sweater, consult textbooks and how-to-do-it manuals. NEW STANDARD ENCYCLOPEDIA supplements but does not try to take the place of such works.

Finding What You Want Quickly

Arrangement of Entries is alphabetical, in a word-by-word rather than letter-by-letter system.

Example: AIR WARFARE comes before AIRBORNE TROOPS because "Air" precedes "Airborne" in alphabetical sequence. Similarly NEW ZEALAND comes before NEWARK; NORTH WEST COMPANY comes before NORTHAMPTON.

When several headings have the same first word, they are arranged by the second word of each (unless the normal word order has been inverted, as in the case of AIR, LIQUID for LIQUID AIR).

Example: ANGEL; ANGEL FALLS; ANGEL OF THE CRIMEA. But note the order when an entry is inverted: AIR; AIR, LIQUID; AIR ACADEMY.

Words connected by a hyphen are treated as a single word, not separate words.

Example: ANTI-MASONIC PARTY comes after ANTILLES (as though the spelling were "Antimasonic").

Names beginning with "Mc" are alphabetized as though spelled "Mac."

Example: MCADAM; MACADAMIA; MCADOO; MACARONI; MACARTHUR.

Family names or place names beginning with "St."—such as St. Clair, Arthur, and St. Augustine (the city)—are alphabetized as though spelled "Saint."

When two or more subjects have the same heading they are placed in this order: (1) persons; (2) places; and (3) things or ideas. In alphabetizing, only the family name of a person is considered.

> *Example:* Anderson, Sherwood, comes before Anderson (Indiana).

Persons with the same last name are listed in alphabetical order by first name. Titles are disregarded.

> *Example:* Jones, Casey; Jones, Sir Edward Burne; Jones, Elizabeth Orton.

When two persons have identical full names, the one born earlier is listed first.

When two places have the same name, they are listed in alphabetical order by country or state.

> *Example:* Aberdeen (Scotland) comes before Aberdeen (South Dakota).

Guide Words are titles placed at the top of pages to help you find articles quickly. They tell you whether the article you are looking for is on a particular page. When there are two titles, the first tells you the first new heading on the page; the second tells you the last new heading on that page.

> *Example:* On the page that has the guide words AARD-WOLF—ABACUS, you will find all the headings—Aarhus and Aaron, for instance—that fall alphabetically between Aardwolf and Abacus.

Subtitles divide articles into sections and other divisions to help you pick specific information out of a long article. Center and side headings show major and minor aspects of a broad subject.

Cross References help you find information by directing you to the proper title or lead you to articles that have additional information. This encyclopedia has three kinds of cross references:

> (1) "See" cross references. These are listed alphabetically as entry titles. They lead you to information treated under another title:
>
> *Examples:*
> Abyssinia. See Ethiopia.
> Adelphi University. See Universities and Colleges (table).
> Aileron. See Airplane, section "Parts of an Airplane," subtitle *Wings*.
> Airedale. See Dog, subtitle *Breeds of Dogs:* Terriers.
> American Literature. See Literature, American.

(2) "See also" cross references. These are within articles or at the end of an article. They lead you to additional information.

Example: At the end of the article ABEL is a "See also" reference to CAIN.

(3) "For further information, see:" references. These are within or at the end of articles on major subjects such as Africa, Airplane, Alabama, and Astronomy. They give lists of the articles in this encyclopedia that are related to the subject. Many of these lists are arranged by topic, so that they may serve as study guides or outlines.

Other Study Aids

Pronunciation is given for key title words that readers are likely to find difficult or confusing. A pronunciation guide is at the front of each volume, facing the first page of text.

Visual Aids. Photographs, drawings, diagrams, charts, and maps are selected or prepared to supplement the text. Full-color reproductions of paintings and photographs are placed with the articles they illustrate.

Tables and Lists. Examples of tables are those for automobile racing champions, chemical elements, Nobel Prize winners, and universities and colleges. Examples of lists and glossaries are those for terms used in architecture and in painting.

Bibliographies at the end of major articles serve readers who wish to study a subject further. The books listed are available at most public or school libraries. Often, as in AFRICA, a special listing is included of materials aimed at younger readers (primarily those in grades 4-8).

Organizations. Articles on a field or activity (for example, Accounting and Advertising) often give information about associations closely connected with it.

Editorial Staff

Most of the writing is done by the editorial staff. These writers are specialists both in the fields they cover and in the techniques of encyclopedia writing. Certain staff members also edit manuscripts written by outside contributors; do research; plan, procure, and produce visual aids; and handle the technical chores of book production.

EDITOR IN CHIEF Douglas W. Downey, M.S.

LIBRARIAN David E. King, M.A.L.S.

COPY EDITOR Herwart G. Birg, M.A.

SENIOR EDITORS

Irene Ferguson, B.A.
Margaret G. Franson, M.A.
Robert D. Pruter, M.A.
Robert J. Schlueter, M.A.

ASSOCIATE EDITORS

Sarah M. Aldridge, B.A.
Christine A. Beuoy, B.A.
Megan A. Devlin, B.A.
David C. Hayes, B.A.
Caren S. Koning
Gloria F. Price, B.A.

SENIOR CARTOGRAPHER

Gerald E. Keefe, B.A.

DIRECTOR OF SPECIAL RESEARCH

Alice Rosler, PH.D.

MANAGER, DATA PROCESSING

Louis Gineris, B.S.

EDITORIAL SECRETARY

Lona M. Kirk

LIBRARY ASSISTANT

Suzanne Somos

CONTRIBUTING EDITORS

Dorothy Bakich, B.S.
David G. Buehne, B.A.
Jean Caldwell, B.S.E.
Suzanne Cooke, B.A.
M. Eleanor Gross, B.A.
Janet L. Hale, B.A.
Ignacio Huidobro, M.A.
Linda T. Kase, B.A.
Agnes K. Lavnick, B.A.
Russell Lembke, PH.D.
Leo Macarow, M.A., M.S.
Charles A. Malefyt, A.B.
Julian May
Ralph Miller, PH.B.
Kay Mitchell, M.S.
Floyd Mulkey, A.M.
Dorothy Nolan, B.A.
Arlene Ohlhaber, B.S.
Mary Lee Oliva, B.A.
Kenneth W. Perkins, B.A.
Kenyon Roberts, LL.B.
Linda Sawyers, B.A.
Monica Schneider, M.L.S.
Mary Shank
Georgia K. Sisson, M.ED.
Orville R. Snapp, B.S.
Harriet Thompson, B.A.
Susan W. Tranquilla, B.A.
Karin Wisiol, B.A.
Mary Beth Zielinski, B.S.

Contributors, Consultants, Advisers, and Authenticators

John I. Goodlad, Ph.D., L.H.D., LL.D, D.Ed.
Professor of Education and Former Dean,
Graduate School of Education,
University of California, Los Angeles
CHAIRMAN, NEW STANDARD ENCYCLOPEDIA
EDITORIAL ADVISORY GROUP

Each newly prepared or substantially revised article is submitted to an authority in the field it covers. These authorities may also advise the editors on coverage and assist in specific research problems. In addition, outside authorities are sometimes used to draft articles of a specialized nature. These persons are listed below and on the pages that follow; their names are followed by the titles of the articles on which they worked or the areas in which they served as authors, reviewers, or advisers. (Area designations are printed in italics.) Positions are generally those held at the time the contributions were made.

The editors gratefully acknowledge the additional assistance provided by numerous libraries, museums, universities, government agencies, local chambers of commerce, and industrial corporations.

Lawrence O. Aasen
Executive Secretary, Better Vision Institute, Inc., New York, N.Y.
EYEGLASSES (in part)

Nathaniel Abelson
Map Librarian, United Nations.
FLAG (in part)

Eva Adams
Director, Bureau of the Mint, United States Department of the Treasury, Washington, D.C.
MINT

Alex E. Alden
Staff Engineer, Society of Motion Picture and Television Engineers, New York, N.Y.
MOTION PICTURES (in part)

Ampex Corporation
Audio Engineering Staff, Redwood City, California.
TAPE RECORDER (in part)

M. O. Anderson
Superintendent, Independence National Historical Park, Philadelphia, Pennsylvania.
LIBERTY BELL

Rodney C. Anderson
Assistant Director, Public Relations Division, The American Legion, Indianapolis, Indiana.
AMERICAN LEGION

Ralph L. Andreano, Ph.D.
Professor of Economics, University of Wisconsin. Author of *New Views on American Economic Development; An Economist's Handbook; American Colonial Economic History.* Coauthor of *A History of the American Petroleum Industry.* Editor of *Economic Impact of the American Civil War; Explorations in Entrepreneurial History; The New Economic History.*
ECONOMICS

J. Cutler Andrews, Ph.D.
Late Professor of History, Chatham College. Author of *The North Reports the Civil War; The South Reports the Civil War.*
CIVIL WAR, AMERICAN

Nick P. Apple, Lieutenant Colonel, U.S.A.F.
Air Force Office of Public Affairs, U.S. Air Force, Arlington, Virginia.
AIR FORCE, UNITED STATES

Clint Archer
Public Affairs Department, E.I. Du Pont de Nemours & Co., Wilmington, Delaware.
DU PONT COMPANY

Neil A. Armstrong
Professor of Aerospace Engineering, University of Cincinnati. Former astronaut; first man on the moon.
SPACE EXPLORATION

John B. Ascher
Late Captain, Chicago Police Department.
CRIME (in part)

John A. Aseltine, Ph.D.
Manager, Mission Trajectory Control Program and Assistant Manager for Houston Operations, TRW Systems, Houston, Texas. Author of *Transform Method in Linear System Analysis.* Editor, *Peaceful Uses of Automation in Outer Space.* American Executive Editor, *Automatica—International Journal of Automatic Control and Automation.*
AUTOMATION

Frederick J. Ashley
Public Relations Counsel, Museum of Science and Industry, Chicago, Illinois.
MUSEUM OF SCIENCE AND INDUSTRY

Walter E. Ashley
Office of Reports, The Ford Foundation, New York, N.Y.
FORD FOUNDATION

Robert H. Atkinson
Superintendent, Hot Springs National Park, Arkansas.
HOT SPRINGS NATIONAL PARK

Bill AuCoin
Johnson Motors, Waukegan, Illinois.
SNOWMOBILE

Herbert R. Axelrod, Ph.D.
President and Editor, T.F.H. Publications, Inc. Author of *Axelrod's Tropical Fish Book.* Coauthor of *Handbook of Tropical Aquarium Fishes; Salt-water Aquarium Fishes; Exotic Tropical Fishes.*
TROPICAL FISH

André Bachand
Adjoint au Recteur et Directeur des Relations Extérieures, Université de Montréal.
MONTREAL, UNIVERSITY OF

Martin A. Bacheller
Editor in Chief, Hammond Inc., Maplewood, New Jersey.
MAP

Vinton W. Bacon
Former General Superintendent, Metropolitan Sanitary District of Chicago.
SEWAGE

Stanley F. Bailey, Ph.D.
Professor of Entomology, University of California, Santa Cruz.
ENTOMOLOGY

William Avery Baker
Naval architect; Curator, Francis Russell Hart Nautical Museum, Massachusetts Institute of Technology. Author of *Colonial Vessels; The Engine Powered Vessel; Sloops and Shallops*
SHIP

James P. Banks
Manager, Public Relations, Goodyear Aircraft Corporation, Akron, Ohio.
DIRIGIBLE

B. Devereux Barker III
Associate Editor, *Yachting.*
SAILING

H. Arnold Barton, Ph.D.
Department of History, Southern Illinois University at Carbondale.
SWEDEN (history)

Don Bates
National Association of Social Workers, Inc., New York, N.Y.
SOCIAL WORK

James W. Batten, Ph.D.
Chairman, Department of Secondary Education, East Carolina University. Coauthor of *Soils: Their Nature, Classes, Distribution, Uses, and Care.*
SOIL; SOIL CONSERVATION

W. W. Bauer, M.D., LL.D.
Late Consultant in Personal and Community Health, and Director of Health Education, American Medical Association. Editor of *Today's Health Guide.* Author of *Moving into Manhood;* "Health for Today" column. Coauthor of *The Way to Womanhood; These Are Your Children.*
MEDICINE

Annette Kar Baxter, Ph.D.
Professor of History, Barnard College.
WOMEN'S RIGHTS

Mrs. Margaret C. Bayldon
National League for Nursing, Inc., New York, N.Y.
NURSING

Hayes Beall
Former Director, Educational Services, The Cooperative League of the U.S.A., Chicago, Illinois.
COOPERATIVE

James M. Beall
Public Information Coordinator, National Weather Service, United States Department of Commerce, Washington, D.C.
WEATHER SERVICE, NATIONAL

V. F. Beliajus
Publisher, *Viltis* (magazine), Denver, Colorado.
FOLK MUSIC

Bette Benedict
Creative Playthings, Inc., Princeton, New Jersey.
TOY

Donald E. Bevan
Associate Dean, College of Fisheries, University of Washington.
SALMON

Edward Bevilacqua, Ph.D.
Research Scientist, United States Rubber Company, New York, N.Y.
RUBBER (in part)

Hugh M. Beville, Jr.
Vice President for Planning, National Broadcasting Co., Inc., New York, N.Y.
TELEVISION (history)

Ray Allen Billington, Ph.D., LL.D.
Senior Research Associate, Henry E. Huntington Library, San Marino, California. Author of *Westward Expansion: History of the American Frontier; Frederick Jackson Turner.* Editor of *Westward Movement in the United States;* "Histories of the American Frontier" Series. Coeditor of *The Making of American Democracy.*
WESTWARD MOVEMENT

Eric M. Bishop
Public Information Counsel, American Dental Association, Washington, D.C.
FLUORIDATION

George I. Blanksten, Ph.D.
Professor and Chairman, Department of Political Science, Northwestern University. Author of *Ecuador: Constitutions and Caudillos; Perón's Argentina; The United States' Role in Latin America.*
LATIN AMERICA

Mildred Bond
National Association for the Advancement of Colored People, New York, N.Y.
SPINGARN MEDAL

Arna Bontemps, A.M.
Late Writer in Residence, Fisk University, and Director, Afro-American Program, Yale University. Author of *The Story of the Negro; Famous Negro Athletes; The Story of George Washington Carver; Frederick Douglass; One Hundred Years of Negro Freedom.* Coauthor of *They Seek a City.* Editor of *American Negro Poetry; Great Slave Narratives.*
BLACK AMERICANS

Palmer C. Boothby
President, Jahn & Ollier Engraving Company, Chicago, Illinois.
PHOTOENGRAVING (in part)

Don Booz
Public Relations Counselor, Reorganized Church of Jesus Christ of Latter Day Saints, Independence, Missouri.
LATTER DAY SAINTS, REORGANIZED CHURCH OF JESUS CHRIST OF

Robert Borchardt
Press Secretary, Embassy of the Federal Republic of Germany, Washington, D.C.
BERLIN (in part)

Christy Borth
Automotive Historian. Author of *Pioneers of Plenty; True Steel; Masters of Mass Production.*
AUTOMOBILE (history)

Robert E. Brader
Underwriters' Laboratories, Inc., Northbrook, Illinois.
FIRE PROTECTION

William P. Braker, M.S.
Director, John G. Shedd Aquarium, Chicago, Illinois.
AQUARIUM

Jack Brannan
Financial Communications, The LTV Corporation, Dallas, Texas.
LTV CORPORATION

Robert Branner, Ph.D.
Late Professor of Art History and Archaeology, Columbia University. Editor, *Journal of the Society of Architectural Historians.* Author of *Gothic Architecture; Burgundian Gothic Architecture; La Cathédrale de Bourges.*
ARCHITECTURE

Vincent B. Bray
Corporate Communications, Metropolitan Life Insurance Company, New York, N.Y.
METROPOLITAN LIFE INSURANCE COMPANY

William Bridges
Editor and Curator of Publications, New York Zoological Society, Bronx Park, New York.
NEW YORK ZOOLOGICAL PARK

George R. Brooks
Director, Missouri Historical Society, St. Louis, Missouri.
ST. LOUIS (history)

S. C. Brophy
Peoples Gas, Light, and Coke Company, Chicago, Illinois.
GAS METER

David R. Brower
President, Friends of the Earth; Vice President, John Muir Institution for Environmental Studies; Former Executive Director, Sierra Club. Author of *Not Man Apart; Song of the Earth Spirit.* Editor of *Wilderness: America's Living Heritage.*
CONSERVATION (in part)

Dorothy E. Brown
Public Communications, Gulf Oil Corporation, Pittsburgh, Pennsylvania.
GULF OIL CORPORATION

Paul W. Brown
Minnesota Mining & Manufacturing Company, St. Paul, Minnesota.
GLUES AND ADHESIVES (in part)

Perry E. Brown
Superintendent, Mammoth Cave National Park, Kentucky.
MAMMOTH CAVE NATIONAL PARK

Vernon L. Brown
Researcher, The Coin and Currency Institute, Inc., New York, N.Y., Former Curator of Chase Museum of Moneys of the World.
COIN; MONEY (in part); NUMISMATICS

William L. Browne
Director of Public Relations, National Institute of Drycleaning, Silver Spring, Maryland.
DRY CLEANING

W. B. Brummitt
Manager, Historical Projects, Eastman Kodak Company, Rochester, New York.
EASTMAN, GEORGE

Anne T. Bruno
Director, National News Bureau, Girl Scouts of the U.S.A., New York, N.Y.
LOW, JULIETTE GORDON

Helen Duprey Bullock
Director, Department of Information, National Trust for Historic Preservation, Washington, D.C.
NATIONAL TRUST FOR HISTORIC PRESERVATION

Ray Burch
Schwinn Bicycle Co., Chicago, Illinois.
BICYCLE

Bill Burk
Vice President, Public Relations, Atchison, Topeka and Santa Fe Railway Co., Chicago, Illinois.
ATCHISON, TOPEKA AND SANTA FE RAILWAY CO.

John R. Burkhart
National Council of the Young Men's Christian Associations of the United States of America, New York, N.Y.
WILLIAMS, GEORGE

Bernice L. Bursley
Creative Services, Department of Public Relations, General Mills, Inc., Minneapolis, Minnesota.
FLOUR (in part); GENERAL MILLS, INC.

Virginia Burton
Assistant Curator, Department of Egyptian Art, Metropolitan Museum of Art, New York, N.Y.
ARCHEOLOGY (in part)

William Bushell
Late Educational Representative and Editor of *Outdoor in Illinois,* Department of Conservation, State of Illinois, Springfield, Illinois.
ILLINOIS (in part)

Joyce Busher
Office of Communications, National Council of the Young Men's Christian Association of the United States of America, New York, N.Y.
YOUNG MEN'S CHRISTIAN ASSOCIATION

Grant I. Butterbaugh, Ph.D.
Late Professor of Statistics, College of Business Administration, University of Washington.
BUSINESS; INDUSTRY; ECONOMICS

John E. Byrne
Deputy Assistant Administrator, General Services Administration, Washington, D.C.
GENERAL SERVICES ADMINISTRATION

Fred R. Cagle, Ph.D.
Professor and Chairman, Department of Zoology, Tulane University. Coauthor of *Vertebrates of the United States.*
ZOOLOGY

Martin Caidin
Author; Consultant on Aviation and Space Medicine. Author of *The Astronauts; Rendezvous in Space; Man-in-Space Dictionary; Hydrospace;* etc.
SPACE EXPLORATION (in part)

William A. Calder, Ph.D.
Professor of Physics and Astronomy, Director of the Bradley Observatory, Agnes Scott College.
ASTRONOMY

Mary S. Calderone, M.D.
Executive Director, Sex Information and Education Council of the United States, New York, N.Y.
SEX EDUCATION

John L. Callahan
Vice President, Permacel-Lepage's Inc., New Brunswick, New Jersey.
GLUES AND ADHESIVES (in part)

George G. Cameron, Ph.D.
Professor and Chairman, Department of Near Eastern Languages and Literatures, University of Michigan. Author of *History of Early Iran; Persepolis Treasury Tablets.*
DARIUS (in part)

Dayton W. Canaday
Director, South Dakota State Historical Society, Pierre, South Dakota.
SOUTH DAKOTA (history)

Joanna A. Carey
Bureau of Public Information, American Dental Association, Chicago, Illinois.
TOOTHPASTE AND TOOTH POWDER

A. E. Carlson, Commander, U.S.C.G.
Public Information Division, U.S. Coast Guard, Washington, D.C.
COAST GUARD, UNITED STATES

Robert C. Carmody
Assistant Secretary, Copper & Brass Research Association, New York, N.Y.
COPPER (in part)

Archie Carr, Ph.D.
Graduate Research Professor, Department of Zoology, University of Florida; Research Associate, American Museum of Natural History. Author of *Handbook of Turtles; The Reptiles; So Excellent a Fishe: a Natural History of Sea Turtles.*
TURTLE

F. James Carr
Xerox Corporation, Rochester, New York.
DUPLICATING AND COPYING MACHINES (in part)

William Casagrande
Public Information Representative, Sperry Gyroscope Company, Great Neck, New York.
GYROSCOPE (in part)

Homero Castillo, Ph.D.
Professor of Spanish, University of California, Davis. Editor, *Relatos Humoristicos.* Coauthor of *Bibliography of the Chilean Novel.*
LITERATURE, SPANISH

B. J. Chandler, Ed.D.
Dean, School of Education, Northwestern University. Author of *Education and the Teacher.* Editor of *Research Seminar in Teacher Education.*
TEACHING

Perkins P. K. Chang, Ph.D.
Director of Research, International Sugar Research Foundation, Inc., Bethesda, Maryland.
SUGAR

Sen-dou Chang, Ph.D.
Associate Professor of Geography, San Fernando Valley State College.
CHINA (in part)

F. W. Chapin
Chief, Office of Industrial Relations, Bureau of Engraving and Printing, Treasury Department, Washington, D.C.
ENGRAVING AND PRINTING, BUREAU OF

Jim C. Chapralis
President, PanAngling Travel Service; Editor of *The PanAngler.*
FISHING

Sheldon Cheney
Author of *Sculpture of the World: A History.*
SCULPTURE (history)

Jess Chernak
Secretary, Fur Information and Fashion Council, Inc., New York, N.Y.
FUR

Louis Cheskin
Director, Color Research Institute, Chicago, Illinois. Author of *Color for Profit; Colors: What They Can Do for You; How to Color-tune Your Home.*
COLOR (in part)

G. Wallace Chessman, Ph.D.
Professor of History, Denison University. Author of *Theodore Roosevelt and the Politics of Power; Governor Theodore Roosevelt: The Albany Apprenticeship, 1898-1900.*
ROOSEVELT, THEODORE

Mike Ciccarelli
Polaroid Corporation, Cambridge, Massachusetts.
PHOTOGRAPHY (in part)

Phil Clark
The New York Botanical Garden, Bronx Park, New York.
NEW YORK BOTANICAL GARDEN

Albert C. Claus, Ph.D.
Assistant Professor of Physics, Loyola University, Chicago.
PHYSICS

Rudolf A. Clemen, Jr.
Information Research Specialist, American Red Cross, Washington, D.C.
RED CROSS

Audrey F. Clough
Communications Editor, National Office, Boy Scouts of America, Irving, Texas.
BOY SCOUTS

Fred A. Clough
Director of Public Relations, Oxford Paper Company, Portland, Maine.
PAPER (in part)

Paul H. Clyde, Ph.D.
Professor of History, Duke University. Author of *Japan's Pacific Mandate; The Far East: a History of the Impact of the West on Eastern Asia.* Editor of *United States Policy Toward China.*
ASIATIC HISTORY

William C. Cobb
Office of Publications, The Rockefeller Foundation, New York, N.Y.
ROCKEFELLER FOUNDATION

Charles Cogen
President, American Federation of Teachers, Chicago, Illinois.
AMERICAN FEDERATION OF TEACHERS

Richard Cohen
Public Relations Director, American Jewish Congress, New York, N.Y.
AMERICAN JEWISH CONGRESS

Alice Colgan
Curtis Institute of Music.
CURTIS INSTITUTE OF MUSIC

Joel Colton, Ph.D.
Professor of History, Duke University. Coauthor of *A History of the Modern World.*
EUROPEAN HISTORY

Mrs. Del Commisso
Editorial Service Bureau, Eastman Kodak Company, Rochester, New York.
PHOTOGRAPHY (in part)

Mrs. A. Carl Competello
Executive Director, The Eye-Bank for Sight Restoration, Inc., New York, N.Y.
EYE-BANK FOR SIGHT RESTORATION, INC.

Richard W. Conklin
Director of Information Services, University of Notre Dame, Notre Dame, Indiana.
NOTRE DAME, UNIVERSITY OF

Paul H. Connelley
Research Department, United Brotherhood of Carpenters and Joiners of America, Indianapolis, Indiana.
CARPENTRY

Howard L. Conover
Executive Vice President, Schulmerich Carillons, Inc., Sellersville, Pennsylvania.
BELL; CARILLON; CHIME

H. E. Conrad
Assistant District Director, Wire Division, U.S. Steel Corporation, Pittsburgh, Pennsylvania.
NAIL

Continental Arms Corporation
New York, N.Y.
SHOTGUN

John A. L. Cooke, Ph.D.
Associate Curator, Arachnida, Department of Entomology, American Museum of Natural History, New York, N.Y.
SPIDER

W. H. Corbett
Chief Engineer, Atomizer Division, The De Vilbiss Co., Somerset, Pennsylvania.
ATOMIZER

Fred P. Corey
Executive Vice President, National Apple Institute, Washington, D.C.
APPLE (in part)

Carl Cotton
Department of Exhibition, Field Museum of Natural History, Chicago, Illinois.
TAXIDERMY

Leonard S. Cottrell, Jr.
Social Psychologist and Secretary, Russell Sage Foundation, New York, N.Y.
RUSSELL SAGE FOUNDATION

J. E. Council
Customer Relations Manager, Hershey Chocolate Corporation, Hershey, Pennsylvania.
HERSHEY, MILTON SNAVELY

Rufus F. Cox, Ph.D.
Professor Emeritus, Department of Animal Husbandry, Kansas State University.
AGRICULTURE

Robert E. Cramer, Ph.D.
Professor and Chairman, Department of Geography, East Carolina College. Author of *Manufacturing Structure of the Cicero District, Metropolitan Chicago; A Workbook in Essentials of Cartography and Mapping.*
GEOGRAPHY

James T. Crow
Editor, *Road & Track.*
AUTOMOBILE RACING

Thomas I. Crowell, Ph.D.
Professor of Chemistry, Cobb Chemical Laboratory, Department of Chemistry, University of Virginia.
OIL

Richard N. Current, Ph.D.
Distinguished Professor of American History, University of North Carolina. Author of *Lincoln and The First Shot; The Lincoln Nobody Knows; The Political Thoughts of Abraham Lincoln; Essentials of American History.*
LINCOLN, ABRAHAM

Edward Harvey Cushing, M.D., Captain, M.C., U.S.N.R.
Former Deputy Assistant Secretary of Defense (Health and Medical), U.S. Department of Defense, Washington, D.C.
MEDICAL SERVICES, U.S. ARMED FORCES

Eric H. Davidson, Ph.D.
Assistant Professor of Cell Biology, Rockefeller University. Author of *Gene Activity in Early Development.*
CELL

David S. Davies
Regional Program Presentation Coordinator, Alliance for Progress, Agency for International Development, Department of State, Washington, D.C.
ALLIANCE FOR PROGRESS

Bertram H. Davis
Deputy General Secretary, American Association of University Professors, Washington, D.C.
AMERICAN ASSOCIATION OF UNIVERSITY PROFESSORS

Will B. Davis, C.S.B.
Late Manager, Committees on Publication, The First Church of Christ, Scientist; Boston, Massachusetts.
CHRISTIAN SCIENCE; EDDY, MARY BAKER

Darrel deChaby
Media Relations Officer, National Endowment for the Humanities, Washington, D.C.
NATIONAL FOUNDATION FOR THE ARTS AND THE HUMANITIES

Edward S. Deevey, Jr., Ph.D.
Professor of Biology, Osborn Memorial Laboratories, Yale University.
POPULATION

Walter S. DeForest, Lieutenant Colonel, U.S.M.C.
Division of Public Affairs, U.S. Marine Corps, Washington, D.C.
MARINE CORPS, UNITED STATES

F. Donald DeLong
First Vice President and Midwest Regional Manager, Shearson, Hammill & Co., Chicago, Illinois.
STOCK; STOCK EXCHANGE

William H. Depperman
Link-Belt Company, Chicago, Illinois.
BEARING

E. C. Derryberry, Major, U.S.A.F.
U.S. Air Force Midwest Office of Information, Chicago, Illinois.
DEFENSE, AIR

Ann M. DeSandis
Information Services Director, Junior League.
JUNIOR LEAGUE

H. Thomas Dewhirst
Secretary, Israelite House of David, Benton Harbor, Michigan.
DAVID, HOUSE OF

Ralph E. Dimmick
Special Assistant to the Secretary General, Organization of American States, Pan American Union, Washington, D.C.
ORGANIZATION OF AMERICAN STATES

H. T. Dinkelkamp
Director of Engineering, Stewart-Warner Corporation, Chicago, Illinois.
SPEEDOMETER

Henry S. Distelhorst
Public Relations Council, The Salvation Army, Chicago, Illinois.
BOOTH (family)

Gordon B. Dodds, Ph.D.
Professor of History, Portland State University. Author of *Salmon King of Oregon; Hiram Martin Chittenden: His Public Career.* Editor of *Pygmy Monopolist: the Life and Doings of R. D. Hume.*
U.S. HISTORY

Robert H. Dodds, C.E., M.S.J.
Development Engineer, Lockwood, Kessler & Bartlett, Inc., Syosset, New York.
CIVIL ENGINEERING

Milton B. Dolinger
Director of Public Relations, Chessie System, Cleveland, Ohio.
BALTIMORE AND OHIO RAILROAD

L. A. Donaldson
Grand Secretary, Benevolent and Protective Order of Elks, Chicago, Illinois.
ELKS, BENEVOLENT AND PROTECTIVE ORDER OF

Robert B. Downs, M.S., L.S.D.
Former Dean of Library Administration, University of Illinois. Author of *The Story of Books; American Library Resources; Books that Changed the World; Molders of the Modern Mind; Famous Books, Ancient and Medieval; Books that Changed America; Famous American Books; British Library Resources.* Coauthor of *How to Do Library Research.*
POLICY PLANNING

Alan Drattell
Publications Division, United States Postal Service, Washington, D.C.
POST OFFICE

Laura Dru
Records and Archives, Madame Tussaud's Ltd., London.
TUSSAUD, MARIE

Crozet J. Duplantier
Director, University Relations, Tulane University.
TULANE UNIVERSITY OF LOUISIANA

Eugene M. Dutchak, Lieutenant Colonel, Armor
Editor of *Armor, the Magazine of Mobile Warfare.*
TANK

Don Dutcher
Public Affairs Department, Western Union Corporation, Upper Saddle River, New Jersey.
WESTERN UNION CORPORATION

Jefferson C. Dykes
Deputy Administrator, Field Services, Soil Conservation Service, U.S. Department of Agriculture, Washington, D.C.
CONSERVATION (in part)

J. H. Easley
Assistant General Manager, Rock Hill Printing and Finishing Company, Rock Hill, South Carolina.
PRINTING, TEXTILE

Clement Eaton, Ph.D.
Department of History, University of Kentucky. Author of *Freedom of Thought in the Old South; History of the Southern Confederacy; Growth of Southern Civilization.*
SOUTH, THE

Charles H. V. Ebert, Ph.D.
Associate Professor of Geography, University of Buffalo.
GEOGRAPHY

Marion Edman, Ph.D.
Professor of Elementary Education and English Education, Wayne State University. Author of *Self-Image of Primary School Teachers.* Coauthor of "Reading for Enjoyment" Series.
EDUCATION; CHILDREN'S LITERATURE

Floyd H. Egan
Former Vice President, Central National Bank, Chicago, Illinois.
BANKS AND BANKING (in part)

William J. Ellena
Associate Secretary, American Association of School Administrators, Washington, D.C.
AMERICAN ASSOCIATION OF SCHOOL ADMINISTRATORS

Russell Z. Eller
Sunkist Growers, Los Angeles, California.
ORANGE (in part)

James C. Elliott, Major, U.S.A.F.
Deputy Chief, Office of Public Relations, National Guard Bureau, Washington, D.C.
NATIONAL GUARD

L. Tuffly Ellis
Assistant Director, Texas State Historical Association, Austin, Texas.
TEXAS (history)

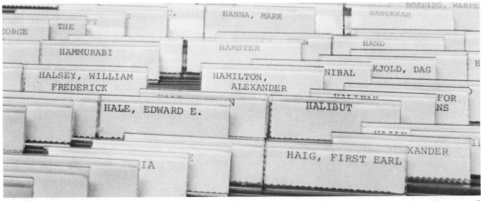

Alfred E. Emerson, Ph.D., Sc.D.
Emeritus Professor of Zoology, University of Chicago. Author of *Impact of Darwin on Biology; Distribution of Termites;* etc. Coauthor of *Principles of Animal Ecology.*
ZOOLOGY

Russell C. Engberg
Former Chief, Research and Information Division, Farm Credit Administration, Washington, D.C.
FARM CREDIT ADMINISTRATION

Philip H. Erbes
Vice President and Secretary, Wm. Wrigley Jr. Company, Chicago, Illinois.
CHEWING GUM

J. F. Estes
President, Haeger Potteries, Inc., Dundee, Illinois.
POTTERY AND PORCELAIN (in part)

Ernest Evans
Director, British Columbia Travel Bureau, Victoria, British Columbia.
BRITISH COLUMBIA (in part)

M. M. Ewen
Supreme Secretary, Knights of Pythias, Chicago, Illinois.
KNIGHTS OF PYTHIAS

John C. Ewers, M.A.
Senior Ethnologist, National Museum of Natural History, Smithsonian Institution, Washington, D.C. Author of *Blackfeet: Raiders on the Northwestern Plains.* Coauthor of *Indians of the Plains.* Editor of *Adventures of Zenas Leonard, Fur Trader,* by Zenas Leonard; *Five Indian Tribes of the Upper Missouri,* by Edwin T. Denig.
INDIANS, AMERICAN

David W. Eyre
Castle & Cooke, Inc., Honolulu, Hawaii.
PINEAPPLE

Noah D. Fabricant, M.D., M.S.
Late Clinical Assistant Professor of Otolaryngology, University of Illinois College of Medicine. Author of *Headaches: What Causes Them, How to Get Relief.* Coauthor of *The Dangerous Cold: Its Cures and Complications.* Editor of *Doctors and Patients; Why We Became Doctors.* Editor, *Medical Digest; Otolaryngology.*
MEDICINE

Agnes Fahy
Science Writer, National Tuberculosis & Respiratory Disease Association.
TUBERCULOSIS

Philip A. Farris, Major, U.S.A.
Assistant Information Officer, United States Military Academy.
UNITED STATES SERVICE ACADEMIES (in part)

Carole Feil
Public Information Office, Underwriters Laboratories, Incorporated, Northbrook, Illinois.
UNDERWRITERS LABORATORIES, INCORPORATED

Andrew A. Fejer, Ph.D.
Professor of Mechanical Engineering and Director of Mechanical and Aerospace Engineering, Illinois Institute of Technology.
ENGINEERING

Dave Feldman
Turf Editor, Chicago *Sun-Times.*
HORSE RACING

Ben R. Fern, Major, U.S.A.F.
Chief, Magazine and Book Branch, Office of the Assistant Secretary of Defense (Public Affairs), Washington, D.C.
DEFENSE, U.S. DEPARTMENT OF

Ogden W. Fields
Executive Secretary, National Labor Relations Board, Washington, D.C.
NATIONAL LABOR RELATIONS BOARD

Raymond C. Fingado
Chairman, Richmondtown Restoration Planning Committee, Richmondtown, Staten Island, New York.
RICHMONDTOWN

Arlene Flom
Information Services, Communication Division, Blue Cross and Blue Shield Association, Chicago, Illinois.
BLUE CROSS-BLUE SHIELD

M. H. Floto
Manager, Carnegie Hero Fund Commission, Pittsburgh, Pennsylvania.
CARNEGIE HERO FUND COMMISSION

Stanley A. Flower
Consumer and Marketing Service, U.S. Department of Agriculture, Washington, D.C.
SCHOOL LUNCH PROGRAM

David W. Foley, A.M.L.S.
Chief Librarian, University of Manitoba.
CANADA

Robert B. Ford
Corporate Relations Division, Carrier Corporation, Syracuse, New York.
AIR CONDITIONING

Bill Foreman
National Cotton Council of America, Memphis, Tennessee.
COTTON

Brian M. Forster
Director, Public Information, American Veterinary Medical Association, Chicago, Illinois.
VETERINARY MEDICINE AND SURGERY

Newell H. Foster
Superintendent, Statue of Liberty National Monument, New York, N.Y.
LIBERTY, STATUE OF

William S. Foster
Editor, *American City.*
CITY

Leo G. Fradenburg, Colonel, U.S.A.F.
Air University, United States Air Force, Maxwell Air Force Base, Alabama.
AIR UNIVERSITY

Gail A. Frekleton
Corporate Communications, Eastman Kodak Company, Rochester, New York.
EASTMAN KODAK COMPANY

Rudolph H. Friedrich, D.D.S.
Former Secretary, Council on Dental Health, American Dental Association, Chicago, Illinois.
DENTISTRY

R. J. Fritz
Supervisor of Community Relations, Cummins Engine Company, Inc., Columbus, Indiana.
DIESEL ENGINE (in part)

Harvey R. Fuller
The Fuller Brush Company, Hartford, Connecticut.
FULLER, ALFRED CARL

Dave Fultz, Ph.D.
Professor of Meteorology, University of Chicago.
WEATHER

Mary Gaither, Ph.D.
Professor of English, Indiana University. Author of *Comparative Literature: Method and Perspective.*
WORLD LITERATURE

David Gander
Senior Editor, *Sierra,* Sierra Club, San Francisco, California.
SIERRA CLUB

Curtis B. Gans
Director of Information, Americans for Democratic Action, Washington, D.C.
AMERICANS FOR DEMOCRATIC ACTION

Larry Gara, Ph.D.
Chairman, Department of History and Government, Wilmington College. Author of *Short History of Wisconsin.*
WISCONSIN (history)

Paul E. Garber
Assistant Director, Education and Information Services, National Air Museum, Smithsonian Institution.
AIRPLANE (history); WRIGHT, WILBUR AND ORVILLE

Peter J. Gariti
A. B. Dick Company, Chicago, Illinois.
DUPLICATING AND COPYING MACHINES (in part)

Maxwell R. Garret
Head Fencing Coach, University of Illinois. Author of *Fencing; How to Improve Your Fencing.*
FENCING

Jonathan Garst, Ph.D.
Agricultural Consultant. Author of *No Need for Hunger.*
AGRICULTURE (in part)

E. Howard Gatewood
Executive Vice President, Fine Hardwoods Association, Chicago, Illinois.
WOOD (in part)

E. W. Gaumnitz, Ph.D.
Executive Secretary, National Cheese Institute, Inc., Chicago, Illinois; Executive Secretary, American Butter Institute, Inc., Chicago, Illinois.
BUTTER; BUTTERFAT; CHEESE

Nigel Gaydon
Former Director, British Information Services, Chicago, Illinois.
CRICKET (game)

Ralph J. Gentles
Public Relations Director, Optimist International, St. Louis, Missouri.
OPTIMIST INTERNATIONAL

J. Sullivan Gibson, Ph.D.
Late Associate Professor of Geography, University of North Carolina at Chapel Hill, and Geographer, Indiana State University. Coauthor of *Soils: Their Nature, Classes, Distribution, Uses, and Care.*
GEOGRAPHY AND GEOLOGY

Mrs. Stanley Gibson
Secretary-Treasurer, The American Cat Association, Inc., Evanston, Illinois.
CAT (in part)

The Rev. Gerald W. Gillette
Research Historian, The Presbyterian Historical Society, Philadelphia, Pennsylvania.
PRESBYTERIANS

George O. Gillingham
Chief, Office of Reports and Information, Federal Communications Commission, Washington, D.C.
FEDERAL COMMUNICATIONS COMMISSION

Henry L. Giordano
Commissioner of Narcotics, United States Department of the Treasury, Washington, D.C.
OPIUM

Jean Glasscock
Director, Office of Publicity, Wellesley College.
WELLESLEY COLLEGE

Kneeland A. Godfrey, Jr.
Director of Information, American Association for the Advancement of Science, Washington, D.C.
AMERICAN ASSOCIATION FOR THE ADVANCEMENT OF SCIENCE

Eileen J. Golab
News Bureau, United Airlines, Chicago, Illinois.
UNITED AIRLINES

Hannah L. Goldberg
Executive Director, Hadassah, New York, N.Y.
HADASSAH

Lucy Goldthwaite
Editor, The Arthritis Foundation, New York, N.Y.
ARTHRITIS FOUNDATION

Henry M. Goodkind, F.R.P.S.L.
Editor, The Collectors Club of New York, New York.
PHILATELY

B. F. Goodrich Company
Tire Technical Department, Akron, Ohio.
TIRE (in part)

Howard Gotthardt
Manager, Advertising and Public Relations, Otis Elevator Company, New York, N.Y.
OTIS, ELISHA GRAVES

Jerald E. Gould
Regional Manager, The Western Union Telegraph Company, Chicago, Illinois.
CABLE, ELECTRIC (in part)

W. Parks Grant, Ph.D.
Professor of Music Education, University of Mississippi. Author of *Music for Elementary Teachers; Handbook of Music Terms.*
MUSIC

David Graubart, D.D., Ph.D.
Presiding Rabbi of the Bet Din of the Chicago Region of the Rabbinical Assembly; Professor of Rabbinic Literature, College of Jewish Studies, Chicago, Illinois. Coeditor, *Jewish Family Bible.*
JEWS; JUDAISM

Amos F. Gregory
Secretary, The Kresge Foundation, Detroit, Michigan.
KRESGE FOUNDATION

George B. Griffenhagen
Director, Division of Communications, American Pharmaceutical Association, Washington, D.C.
PHARMACY

Albert A. Grigarick, Jr., Ph.D.
Associate Professor of Entomology, University of California, Davis.
ENTOMOLOGY

E. C. Grimm
Editorial Committee, Aluminum Company of America, Pittsburgh, Pennsylvania.
ALUMINUM (in part)

Peter Griskivich
Assistant Director, Committee on Public Affairs, American Petroleum Institute, New York, N.Y.
GASOLINE; PETROLEUM

Harry A. Grove
Brunswick Corporation, Chicago, Illinois.
BOWLING (equipment)

Wayne C. Grover
Archivist of the United States, National Archives and Records Service, General Services Administration, Washington, D.C.
NATIONAL ARCHIVES

R. G. Gulian
Corporate Communications, Union Carbide Corp., New York, N.Y.
UNION CARBIDE CORPORATION

Edwin Guthman
Special Assistant for Public Information, Department of Justice, Washington, D.C.
JUSTICE, U.S. DEPARTMENT OF

Mary Ann Guyol
Public Relations, League of Women Voters, Washington, D.C.
LEAGUE OF WOMEN VOTERS OF THE UNITED STATES

Fritz Haas, Ph.D.
Conchologist, Field Museum of Natural History, Chicago, Illinois.
SNAIL

Mohammed Habib
Press Attaché, Egyptian Embassy, Washington, D.C.
CAIRO

Lawrence C. Hadley
Management Assistant, Yellowstone National Park, Yellowstone Park, Wyoming.
YELLOWSTONE NATIONAL PARK

Spencer Hagen
Hammond Organ Company, Chicago, Illinois.
ORGAN (in part)

Mary Janice Hale, Lieutenant Colonel, U.S.M.C.
Executive Secretary to the Defense Advisory Committee on Women in the Services, Office of the Assistant Secretary of Defense (Manpower), Washington, D.C.
WOMEN IN THE ARMED FORCES OF THE UNITED STATES

Charles T. Haley, Sr.
Director of Public Relations, Hampton Institute, Hampton, Virginia.
HAMPTON INSTITUTE

Ruth C. Hall, Ph.D.
Late Professor and Director, School of Home Economics, University of Arizona.
HOME ECONOMICS

John D. Hallenberg
Power Use Section, Electric Utility Sales Department, Westinghouse Electric Corporation, East Pittsburgh, Pennsylvania.
ELECTRICAL EQUIPMENT

Charles L. Hamilton, Ph.D.
Associate Professor, Department of History, Simon Fraser University, Burnaby, British Columbia.
SCOTLAND (culture and history)

Stanley Hamilton
Director, Publications Staff, U.S. Department of Transportation, Washington, D.C.
TRANSPORTATION, U.S. DEPARTMENT OF

Mikiso Hane, Ph.D.
Associate Professor of History, Knox College. Author of *Japan: a Historical Survey.*
ASIATIC HISTORY

Gil Hanesworth
Executive Secretary, National Archery Association, Chicago, Illinois.
ARCHERY

Jack Hank
Director of Public Relations, Lions International, Chicago, Illinois.
LIONS INTERNATIONAL

Alfred Harbage, Ph.D.
Cabot Professor of English Literature, Harvard University. Author of *William Shakespeare: A Reader's Guide; Conceptions of Shakespeare.* General editor, Pelican editions of Shakespeare.
SHAKESPEARE, WILLIAM

Covington Hardee, A.B., LL.B.
Partner, New York law firm of Hardee Barovick Konecky & Gaines. Former Professor of Law, Harvard University.
LAW

Russell Harder
Department of the Army, Division of Engineering, Chicago, Illinois.
CANAL (in part)

Richard E. Harkins
Director of Public Relations, The International Supreme Council, Order of DeMolay, Kansas City, Missouri.
DEMOLAY, ORDER OF

Robert J. Harlow, Commander, U.S.N.
Department of English, History, and Government, U.S. Naval Academy.
NAVIGATION

Thomas E. Harmening
Assistant News Director, Burlington Northern, St. Paul, Minnesota.
BURLINGTON NORTHERN

H. P. Hart
U.S. Merchant Marine Academy.
MERCHANT MARINE ACADEMY, U.S.

Kay N. Hart
San Antonio Conservation Society, San Antonio, Texas.
SAN ANTONIO (history)

Patricia L. Hartwell
Director of Public Information, United Nations Children's Fund, United Nations, New York.
UNITED NATIONS CHILDREN'S FUND

Jess Hassell
Assistant to the Director, California Foods Research Institute, San Francisco, California.
OLIVE

Warren W. Hassler, Ph.D.
Associate Professor of History, Pennsylvania State University. Author of *General George B. McClellan: Shield of the Union; Commanders of the Army of the Potomac.*
UNITED STATES HISTORY

Anthony Haswell
Founder and former Chairman, National Association of Railroad Passengers and RAIL Foundation, Washington, D.C.
RAILWAY; RAILWAY, INTERURBAN

Enid A. Haupt
Former Editor in Chief, *Seventeen.* Author of *The Seventeen Book of Etiquette and Entertainment; Seventeen Book of Young Living.*
ADDRESS, FORMS OF; ETIQUETTE

Dwight Havens
Manager, Local Chamber of Commerce Service Department, Chamber of Commerce of the United States, Washington, D.C.
CHAMBER OF COMMERCE (in part)

William E. Hawkins
Magazine Publicity Manager, United Airlines, Chicago, Illinois.
AIRLINE (in part)

D. J. Hawthorne
President, General Time Corporation, New York, N.Y.
CLOCK (in part)

Allen Hayman, Ph.D.
Associate Professor of English, Purdue University. Director, NDEA English Institute. Advisory Editor of *Modern Fiction Studies.*
ENGLISH AND AMERICAN LITERATURE THROUGH THE 19TH CENTURY

Philip A. Hazelton
Law Librarian, New Hampshire State Library, Concord, New Hampshire.
NEW HAMPSHIRE (history)

Grant W. Heath
Information Service, The Church of Jesus Christ of Latter-day Saints, Salt Lake City, Utah.
MORMONS

Lucille Hecht
Editor and Publicity Director, Altrusa International, Inc., Chicago, Illinois.
ALTRUSA INTERNATIONAL, INC.

Leonard A. Hehner
Director of Advertising and Sales Promotion, Venus Pen and Pencil Corporation, New York, N.Y.
PEN; PENCIL

Hyman Heimowitz
Executive Secretary, Trading Stamp Institute of America, Inc., New York, N.Y.
TRADING STAMPS

Cornelius W. Heine
Chief, Division of Public Use and Interpretation, National Park Service, National Capital Parks, United States Department of the Interior, Washington, D.C.
LINCOLN MEMORIAL; WHITE HOUSE

Stanley Herbertt
Ballet Arts Academy, Clayton, Missouri.
BALLET

J. Robert Herbin
Publications Service, Office of Public Information, United Nations, New York, N.Y.
UNITED NATIONS

William B. Hesseltine, Ph.D.
Late Professor of History, University of Wisconsin. Author of *Civil War Prisons; Confederate Leaders in the New South; Lincoln and the War Governors; Lincoln's Plan of Reconstruction; Rise and Fall of Third Parties; Syllabus of United States History; Third-Party Movements in the United States; Ulysses S. Grant: Politician.* Coauthor of *The South in American History; The Blue and the Gray on the Nile.* Editor of *The Tragic Conflict: the Civil War and Reconstruction.*
UNITED STATES HISTORY

M. Carol Hetzell
Associate Director, Public Relations, Seventh-day Adventist Church, Washington, D.C.
SEVENTH-DAY ADVENTIST CHURCH

Philip Hiaring
Wine Institute, San Francisco, California.
WINE

George W. Hickman, Jr., Major General, U.S.A.
The Judge Advocate General, Department of the Army, Washington, D.C.
COURT-MARTIAL

Elmer Higgins
Former Chief Fisheries Biologist, Bureau of Commercial Fisheries, United States Department of the Interior, Washington, D.C.
FISHERIES

Richard M. Highsmith, Jr., Ph.D.
Professor and Chairman, Department of Geography, School of Humanities and Social Sciences, Oregon State University. Coauthor of *Geography of Commodity Production; Case Studies in World Geography; World Regional Geography; Conservation in the United States.* Editor of *Atlas of the Pacific Northwest.*
AGRICULTURE (in part)

Helen-Anne Hilker
Information Officer, The Library of Congress, Washington, D.C.
LIBRARY OF CONGRESS

Jacob I. Hirsch, M.D.
Practicing Physician, Forest Hills, N.Y.
BABY (in part)

Philip K. Hitti, Ph.D.
Professor of Semitic Languages and Chairman, Department of Oriental Languages, Princeton University. Author of *The Arabs: a Short History; History of the Arabs; The Near East in History; Islam and the West; Islam: a Way of Life.*
ARABIA (history); ISLAM (history); ISLAMIC CULTURE

Verna Hobson
Secretary to the Director, Institute for Advanced Study.
INSTITUTE FOR ADVANCED STUDY

Bert Hochman
News Bureau Manager, Lever Brothers Company, New York, N.Y.
LEVERHULME, VISCOUNT

Frederick J. Hoffman, Ph.D.
Late Distinguished Professor of English, University of Wisconsin—Milwaukee. Author of *Samuel Beckett; Freudianism and the Literary Mind; The Twenties: American Writing in the Postwar Decade; William Faulkner; The Modern American Novel, 1900-1950; Marginal Manners.*
20TH-CENTURY AMERICAN AND ENGLISH LITERATURE

George W. Hoffman, Ph.D.
Professor of Geography, University of Texas. Author of *The Balkans in Transition; Regional Development Strategy in Southwest Europe.* Coauthor of *Yugoslavia and the New Communism; Geography of Europe;* "Europe Geography Series"; "Steck-Vaughn Geography Work-Text Series." Editor of *Eastern Europe: Essays in Geographical Problems.*
EUROPEAN GEOGRAPHY

Marcia F. Holabird
Museum Education Department, The Art Institute of Chicago.
ART

Horace Holley
Late Secretary, National Spiritual Assembly of the Bahá'ís of the United States, Wilmette, Illinois. Author of *The Modern Social Religion; Religion for Mankind.*
BAHÁ'Í FAITH

Daniel W. Hollis, Ph.D.
Department of History, University of South Carolina.
SOUTH CAROLINA (history)

Ruth Holman
Public Relations, American Carpet Institute, New York, N.Y.
RUGS AND CARPETS

James C. Holzman, Captain, Chicago Police Department
POLICE (in part)

Frank R. Hood
Director, Information Service, Veterans Administration, Washington, D.C.
VETERANS ADMINISTRATION

Marjorie S. Hooper
Editor, American Printing House for the Blind, Inc., Louisville, Kentucky.
AMERICAN PRINTING HOUSE FOR THE BLIND, INC.

Colburn E. Hooton
Assistant Director of Student Activities, National Honor Society, Washington, D.C.
NATIONAL HONOR SOCIETY

J. Edgar Hoover
Late Director, Federal Bureau of Investigation, Department of Justice, Washington, D.C.
FINGERPRINT IDENTIFICATION

John E. Hoover, Colonel, U.S. Army
Office of the Assistant Chief of Staff for Communications-Electronics, Department of the Army, Washington, D.C.
SIGNAL CORPS

Robert J. Hoover
Manager, Public Information, The
Maytag Company, Newton, Iowa.
WASHING MACHINE

Francis Houghton
Vice President and Copy Manager,
Ogilvy, Benson & Mather Inc., New
York, N.Y.
ADVERTISING (in part)

Richard A. Howard
Director, The Arnold Arboretum,
Harvard University.
ARNOLD ARBORETUM

Robert West Howard
Author of *The Great Iron Trail; The
Race West; The Wagonmen; The
Horse in the New World; Flag of the
Dreadful Bear.* Editor and coauthor
of *This Is the West; Hoofbeats of Des-
tiny.*
CATTLE; COWBOY

A. R. Huband
Secretary, Canadian Committee,
Hudson's Bay Company, Winnipeg,
Manitoba.
HUDSON'S BAY COMPANY

David S. Hugg
Administrative Assistant, Delaware
State Development Department,
Dover, Delaware.
DELAWARE (in part)

Fred Hulburd
Victor Comptometer Corporation,
Chicago, Illinois.
CALCULATING MACHINE

J. Stewart Hunter
Assistant to the Surgeon General and
Chief, Office of Information and Pub-
lications, U.S. Public Health Service,
Washington, D.C.
PUBLIC HEALTH SERVICE

Elizabeth B. Hurlock, Ph.D.
Professor, Graduate School of Ed-
ucation, University of Pennsylvania.
Author of *Adolescent Development;
Child Development; Child Growth
and Development; Developmental
Psychology; Guideposts to Growing
Up.* Former Child Training Editor,
Today's Health; Syndicated Newspa-
per Column, "As We Live."
ADOLESCENCE; BABY (in part); CHILD
DEVELOPMENT

Jessie Hutton
Director of Sewing Education, The
Singer Company, New York, N.Y.
SEWING MACHINE; SINGER, ISAAC M.

Ruth Hyatt, B.S.
Former Librarian, Farmington Public
Library, Farmington, Connecticut.
POLICY PLANNING

C. P. Idyll, Ph.D.
Fishery and Research Adviser, Food
and Agricultural Organization, United Nations, Rome, Italy; formerly
Chairman, Division of Fishery Sciences, Institute of Marine Science,
University of Miami. Author of
*Abyss: the Deep Sea and the Crea-
tures That Live in It; The Sea
Against Hunger.* Editor of *Exploring
the Ocean World.* Contributing Editor, *Sea Frontiers.*
FISH

Paul B. Ingham
Press Relations Manager, The Yale &
Towne Manufacturing Company,
New York, N.Y.
LOCK

George M. Ireland
Director of Athletics, Loyola Univer-
sity, Chicago.
BASKETBALL

Jack Jackson
Director of Public Relations, National
Grange, Washington, D.C.
GRANGE, NATIONAL

George H. Jacobson, M.M., Ph.D.
Professor of Music Education and
Theory; Chairman of the Division of
Music and Art, The College of Em-
poria.
MUSIC

Robert E. Jagoda
National Carbon Company Division
of Union Carbide Corporation, New
York, N.Y.
BATTERY, ELECTRIC (in part)

D. R. James
American Iron and Steel Institute,
New York, N.Y.
IRON AND STEEL (in part)

Viola L. James, A.M.
Former Director, Instructional Re-
sources and Media, Glenbrook North
High School, Northbrook, Illinois.
POLICY PLANNING

William W. James, Lieutenant Colonel, U.S.A.F.
Director, Public Information, North American Aerospace Defense Command, Colorado Springs, Colorado.
NORTH AMERICAN AEROSPACE DEFENSE COMMAND

Paul Jans, M.S.W.
Director, Hull House Association, Chicago, Illinois.
ADDAMS, JANE

Wallace F. Janssen
Director, Division of Public Information, Food and Drug Administration, Washington, D.C.
FOOD AND DRUG ADMINISTRATION

James W. Jardine
Commissioner, Department of Water and Sewers, City of Chicago, Chicago, Illinois.
WATER SUPPLY

Walter C. Jerige
Executive Vice President, American Turkish Society, Inc., New York, N.Y.
TURKEY (in part)

Connie Johnson
Associate Editor, *Skin Diver Magazine.*
DIVING (in part)

Edward C. Johnson
Johnson Mortuary, Chicago, Illinois.
EMBALMING

Granville B. Johnson, Ph.D.
Late Professor of Educational Psychology, University of South Alabama.
PSYCHOLOGY

Jeanette Ninas Johnson
Executive Secretary, Alexander Graham Bell Association for the Deaf, Inc.; Editor, *The Volta Review,* Washington, D.C.
DEAFNESS (in part)

Mary Johnson
Contributing Editor, *Woman's Day* (sewing). Author of *Sew for Your Children; Sewing the Easy Way; Mary Johnson's Guide to Altering and Restyling Ready-Made Clothes; The Easier Way to Sew for Your Family.*
SEWING

Robert I. Johnson
Director, Kansas City Museum of History and Science, Missouri. Former Director, Adler Planetarium and Astronomical Museum, Chicago, Illinois. Author of *Astronomy: Our Solar System and Beyond; Galaxy Model Study Guide; The Story of the Moon.*
ASTRONOMY (star maps)

Woodrow Johnson
Pitney-Bowes Inc., Stamford, Connecticut.
POSTAGE METER

Fred T. Johnston
Superintendent, Hawaii Volcanoes National Park, Hawaii.
HAWAII VOLCANOES NATIONAL PARK

Edgar B. Johnwick, M.D.
Medical Director, Medical Officer in Charge, U.S. Public Health Service Hospital, Carville, Louisiana.
HANSEN'S DISEASE

Gladys W. Jones
General Secretary, Quota International, Incorporated, Washington, D.C.
QUOTA INTERNATIONAL, INCORPORATED

Louis Joughin
Associate Secretary, American Association of University Professors, Washington, D.C.
ACADEMIC FREEDOM

Walter E. Kaegi, Jr., Ph.D.
Professor of History, University of Chicago. Author of *Byzantium and the Decline of the Roman Empire.*
BYZANTINE EMPIRE

Donald Kagan, Ph.D.
Professor of History and Classics, Yale University. Author of *The Outbreak of the Peloponnesian War.* Editor of *The Decline and Fall of the Roman Empire in the West; Readings in Greek Political Thought; Problems in Ancient History; Botsford and Robinson's Hellenic History.* Coeditor of *Great Issues in Western Civilization.*
ANCIENT HISTORY

Robert B. Kane, Ph.D.
Associate Professor of Mathematics and Education, Purdue University.
MATHEMATICS

Paul Kaplowitz, LL.B.
Chairman, United States Tariff Commission, Washington, D.C.
TARIFF

John S. Karling, Ph.D., F.R.S.A.
Professor Emeritus of Biological Sciences, Purdue University. Author of *Synchytrium.*
BIOLOGY

Edward W. Kase, Ph.D.
Assistant Professor of History, Loyola University, Chicago.
EGYPT, ANCIENT

Matt J. Kaufman
Marketing and Public Relations, Outboard Boating Club of America, Chicago, Illinois.
OUTBOARD MOTOR

Sam Kaufman
Director, Publicity Division, CARE, New York, N.Y.
CARE

Andreas M. Kazamias, Ph.D.
Professor of Educational Policy Studies, School of Education, University of Wisconsin. Author of *Politics and Secondary Education in England.* Coauthor of *Tradition and Change in Education.*
EDUCATION (in part)

John Kearney
Sculptor and Director, Contemporary Art Workshop, Chicago, Illinois.
SCULPTURE (techniques)

Frances X. Kelly
Press Officer, National Park Service, United States Department of the Interior, Washington, D.C.
NATIONAL HISTORIC LANDMARK; NATURAL LANDMARKS

Druzilla C. Kent, Ph.D.
Late Professor of Home Economics Education, Southern Illinois University.
HOME ECONOMICS

Susan Kenyon
Public Relations, The National PTA, Chicago, Illinois.
PARENT-TEACHER ASSOCIATION, NATIONAL

Gordon Kidd
Director of Publications, United Fruit Company, New York, N.Y.
BANANA

William F. Kieffer, Ph.D.
Professor of Chemistry, The College of Wooster. Editor, *Journal of Chemical Education.*
CHEMISTRY

Martin Kilpatrick, Ph.D.
Senior Chemist Emeritus, Argonne National Laboratory; Emeritus Professor and Chairman, Department of Chemistry, Illinois Institute of Technology.
CHEMISTRY

Thomas L. Kimball
Executive Director, National Wildlife Federation, Washington, D.C.
NATIONAL WILDLIFE FEDERATION

Edna King
Office of Public Information, United States Information Agency, Washington, D.C.
MURROW, EDWARD R.

Charles Kirby
Vice President for Research, Threads —Inc., Gastonia, North Carolina
THREAD

David P. Kirby, Ph.D.
Professor of History, University of Liverpool.
ANGLO-SAXONS; ENGLAND (early history); JUTES; SAXONS

Don Kirkendall
Manager, Advertising and Sales Promotion, Electro-Voice Incorporated, Buchanan, Michigan.
LOUDSPEAKER

Gail W. Knapp
Issue Management, Kennecott Copper Corporation, Stamford, Connecticut.
KENNECOTT COPPER CORPORATION

Richard G. Knox
Portland Cement Association, Chicago, Illinois.
CEMENT

A. W. Koehler, M.E.
Secretary-Manager, National Association of Motor Bus Operators, Washington, D.C.
BUS

Arthur L. Koop
Mergenthaler Linotype Company, Brooklyn, New York.
TYPE AND TYPE COMPOSITION (in part)

Gerhard Krapf
Music Division, Northwest Missouri State College. Author of *Liturgical Organ Playing; Organ Vespers.*
MUSIC

Alex E. Krill, M.D.
Late Professor of Ophthalmology, Pritzker School of Medicine, University of Chicago. Author of *Hereditary Retinal and Choroidal Diseases.*
EYE (in part); *OPHTHALMOLOGY*

Bob Kruse
Director of Youth Activities, The American Legion, Indianapolis, Indiana.
BOYS STATE

The Rev. Gyomay M. Kubose
Chicago Buddhist Church, Chicago, Illinois.
BUDDHA; BUDDHISM

Dennis C. Kurjack
Acting Superintendent, Independence National Historical Park, Philadelphia, Pennsylvania.
INDEPENDENCE HALL

Matthew C. Kurtz
Secretary, National Association of Hosiery Manufacturers, New York, N.Y.
HOSIERY

Stephen G. Kurtz, Ph.D.
Principal, The Phillips Exeter Academy. Author of *The Presidency of John Adams.* Editor of *Federalists: Creators and Critics of Union, 1780-1801.* Coeditor of *Essays on the American Revolution.*
ADAMS, JOHN; ADAMS, JOHN QUINCY

John P. Kushnerick
Editor of *Motor Age,* Chilton Publications, Philadelphia.
AUTOMOBILE (in part)

Robert T. Lagemann, Ph.D., D.Sc.
Landon C. Garland Professor of Physics and Dean of the Graduate School, Vanderbilt University. Author of *Physical Science; Experimental Physical Science.* Coauthor of *Physics for the Space Age.*
PHYSICS

David Laine
Secretary, Open Die Forging Institute, Inc., New York, N.Y.
FORGING

Sam M. Lambert
Director, Research Division, National Education Association of the United States, Washington, D.C.
NATIONAL EDUCATION ASSOCIATION OF THE UNITED STATES

Clayton H. Lange
Manager, Public Relations, The Sherwin-Williams Company, Cleveland, Ohio.
LACQUER; PAINT; VARNISH

George P. Larrick
Late Commissioner of Food and Drugs, Food and Drug Administration, Washington, D.C.
ADULTERATION

Alexander S. Lawson
Professor, School of Printing, Rochester Institute of Technology.
TYPE AND TYPE COMPOSITION (in part)

Clemewell Lay
Co-Headmistress, Emma Willard School, Troy, New York.
WILLARD, EMMA

F. C. Layng
Vice President and Secretary, Talon, Inc., Meadville, Pennsylvania.
ZIPPER

Paul R. Leach, Jr.
E. I. du Pont de Nemours & Co., Wilmington, Delaware.
TEFLON

Louis S. B. Leakey, Ph.D., F.R.A.I.
Late Honorary Director of the National Centre of Pre-History and Paleontology, and Former Curator of the Coryndon Memorial Museum, Nairobi, Kenya. Author of *Adam's Ancestors; Olduvai Gorge.* Coauthor of *Unveiling Man's Origins.*
ARCHEOLOGY (in part)

Chapin R. Leinbach
Information Services, Air Transport Association of America, Washington, D.C.
AIRLINE (in part)

Helga Lende
Coordinator of Publications, American Foundation for the Blind, Inc., New York, N.Y.
BLINDNESS (in part)

Art Lentz
United States Olympic Committee, New York, N.Y.
OLYMPIC GAMES

Don Eric Levine, Ph.D.
Department of Comparative Literature, University of Massachusetts.
LITERARY CRITICISM

Jason L. Levine
News Editor, American Automobile Association, Washington, D.C.
AMERICAN AUTOMOBILE ASSOCIATION

David Levinson, Jr.
Member, Illinois Bar. Arbitrator, Illinois Industrial Commission, Chicago, Illinois.
LAW

Raphael Levy
Director of Publicity, United Jewish Appeal, New York, N.Y.
UNITED JEWISH APPEAL

Harold R. Lewis
Director of Information, United States Department of Agriculture, Washington, D.C.
AGRICULTURE, U.S. DEPARTMENT OF

Winston B. Lewis, Ph.D.
Associate Professor, Department of English, History, and Government, U.S. Naval Academy.
MILITARY HISTORY

Paul S. Lietz, Ph.D.
Professor and Chairman, Department of History, Loyola University, Chicago.
ROMAN CATHOLIC CHURCH

Arthur V. Linden
Director of Educational Studies, Licensed Beverage Industries, Inc., New York, N.Y.
WHISKEY

Arthur S. Link, Ph.D.
Edwards Professor of American History, Princeton University. Editor of *The Papers of Woodrow Wilson.*
WILSON, WOODROW

George E. Linton, Ph.D.
Professor Emeritus, Fashion Institute, New York City; Textile Editor, *American Fabrics Magazine.* Author of *Applied Basic Textiles; The Modern Textile Dictionary; Natural and Man-made Textile Fibers.*
TEXTILE

Dorothy Hale Litchfield
Head, Print and Picture Department, Free Library of Philadelphia.
BANK OF THE UNITED STATES

Leroy E. Loemker, Ph.D., LL.D.
Charles Howard Candler Professor of
Philosophy (Emeritus), Emory University. Author of *Struggle for Synthesis: the 17th-century Background
of Leibniz's Synthesis of Order and
Freedom.* Editor of *Gottfried Wilhelm
von Leibniz: Philosophical Papers
and Letters.*
PHILOSOPHY AND RELIGION

Frederick M. Logan, M.A.
Professor and Former Chairman, De-
partment of Art and Art Education,
University of Wisconsin. Author of
Growth of Art in American Schools.
ART

Herschel C. Logan
Contributing Editor, *The American
Rifleman,* Salina, Kansas. Author of
Underhammer Guns.
RIFLE

E. B. Long
Civil War Research Consultant, Dou-
bleday & Company. Coauthor of *The
Civil War.* Director of Research for
*The Centennial History of the Civil
War* by Bruce Catton. Editor, *Ulysses
S. Grant, Personal Memoirs.*
AMERICAN CIVIL WAR

Winifred R. Long
National Catholic Educational Associ-
ation, Washington, D.C.
NATIONAL CATHOLIC EDUCATIONAL
ASSOCIATION

E. A. Loughran
Associate Commissioner, Manage-
ment, Immigration and Naturaliza-
tion Service, Department of Justice,
Washington, D.C.
IMMIGRATION AND NATURALIZATION
SERVICE

Jayne Lowell
Publications Director, Chicago Metro-
politan Council, Camp Fire, Inc.,
Chicago, Illinois.
CAMP FIRE

John N. Luft
Manager, Federal Crop Insurance
Corporation, United States Depart-
ment of Agriculture, Washington,
D.C.
FEDERAL CROP INSURANCE CORPORA-
TION

Morten Lund
General Editor, *Ski Magazine.* Au-
thor of *The Skier's Bible.*
SKIING

S. E. Torsten Lund, Ph.D.
Former Associate Professor and As-
sistant Dean, School of Education,
University of California, Berkeley.
POLICY PLANNING

Roger Lyons
Carnegie Endowment for Internation-
al Peace, New York, N.Y.
CARNEGIE ENDOWMENT FOR INTER-
NATIONAL PEACE

Osamu Mabuchi, Ph.D.
Sony Corporation of America, Long
Island City, N.Y.
TAPE RECORDER (in part)

Robert M. McBride
Director, Research and Publications,
and Editor of *Tennessee Historical
Quarterly,* Tennessee State Library
and Archives, Nashville, Tennessee.
TENNESSEE (history)

Dean McCarty
Technologist, Extension Horticulture,
University of California, Riverside.
ORANGE (in part)

M. McCaskill, Ph.D.
Professor of Geography, University of
Canterbury, Christchurch, New Zea-
land.
NEW ZEALAND (in part)

Wesley McCune
National Farmers Union, Denver,
Colorado.
FARMERS EDUCATIONAL AND COOPER-
ATIVE UNION OF AMERICA

Lee C. McDonald, Ph.D.
Dean and Professor of Government,
Pomona College. Author of *Western
Political Theory.* Coauthor of *Myth,
Religion and Politics.*
GOVERNMENT

Maurice J. McDonald
Assistant Chief of Publications, Pub-
lic Affairs Division, Information Staff,
Agency for International Develop-
ment, Department of State, Washing-
ton, D.C.
AGENCY FOR INTERNATIONAL DEVEL-
OPMENT

Thomas E. McDonough, Sr., Sc.D.
Consultant, Physical Education and
Athletics, Georgia Department of Ed-
ucation.
PHYSICAL EDUCATION; RECREATION

James C. MacFarland, Colonel,
U.S.A.
Chief, Memorial Division, Office of
the Chief of Support Services, United
States Department of the Army,
Washington, D.C.
NATIONAL CEMETERY

John W. McFarlane
Editorial Manager, Publications Service, Eastman Kodak Company, Rochester, N.Y.
CAMERA (in part)

Charles McGaw
Chairman, Goodman School of Drama, The Art Institute of Chicago. Author of *Acting Is Believing: a Basic Method.*
ACTING

John L. McGehee
Director, Public Relations Department, Kiwanis International, Chicago, Illinois.
KIWANIS INTERNATIONAL

R. M. MacIntosh
Manager, Tin Research Institute, Inc., Columbus, Ohio.
TIN

Hugh McKinley
Amateur Trapshooting Association, Vandalia, Ohio.
TRAPSHOOTING AND SKEET SHOOTING (in part)

Robert H. McKowen
Armstrong Cork Company, Lancaster, Pennsylvania.
CORK

H. G. MacPherson, Ph.D.
Deputy Director, Oak Ridge National Laboratory, Oak Ridge, Tennessee.
ATOM; ATOMIC ENERGY

E. M. Maguire
Manager, Consumer Service Department, Thomas J. Lipton, Inc., Hoboken, New Jersey.
LIPTON, SIR THOMAS JOHNSTONE

Agnes L. Maher
Press Assistant, Office of Information, International Bank for Reconstruction and Development, Washington, D.C.
INTERNATIONAL BANK FOR RECONSTRUCTION AND DEVELOPMENT

Robert Maidment, D.Ed.
President, Educatalysts; former Associate Professor and Associate Dean, School of Education, Northwestern University; former principal, Glenbrook North High School, Northbrook, Illinois.
SECONDARY EDUCATION

Gregory Malak
Curator, Will Rogers Memorial, Claremore, Oklahoma.
ROGERS, WILL

Reynold W. Malmer
American Optometric Association, St. Louis, Missouri.
EYEGLASSES (in part)

Helen Manasian
Manager, Trade Publicity, National Broadcasting Company, New York, N.Y.
NATIONAL BROADCASTING COMPANY

Robert Markus
Sports Columnist, The Chicago *Tribune.*
BASEBALL

Alpheus Thomas Mason, Ph.D., LL.D.
McCormick Professor of Jurisprudence, Princeton University. Author of *William Howard Taft: Chief Justice.* Coauthor of *American Constitutional Law; The Supreme Court.*
TAFT, WILLIAM HOWARD; SUPREME COURT OF THE UNITED STATES

John E. Matthews
Executive Creative Director, Leo Burnett Company, Inc., Chicago, Illinois.
ADVERTISING (in part)

R. M. May
Service Manager, Westclox, Division of General Time Corporation, LaSalle, Illinois.
CLOCK (in part)

Alfred Max Mayer, Ph.D.
Department of Biology, Hebrew University, Jerusalem. Coauthor of *Germination of Seeds.*
SEED

Jane Gould Mayer
National Secretary, American Legion Auxiliary, Indianapolis, Indiana.
GIRLS STATE

R. L. Mead, Lieutenant (j.g.), U.S.C.G.R.
Public Information Officer, United States Coast Guard Academy.
UNITED STATES COAST GUARD ACADEMY

Sylvia Earle Mead, Ph.D.
Marine biologist, aquanaut, and team leader of *Tektite II.*
DIVING (in part); SUBMERSIBLE; UNDERWATER HABITAT

Charles T. Meadow
Author of *The Analysis of Information Systems; The Story of Computers.*
COMPUTER

Roy W. Menninger, M.D.
President, the Menninger Foundation, Topeka, Kansas.
MENNINGER FOUNDATION

George H. Merriam
Director of Admissions, Clark University.
CLARK UNIVERSITY

Frederick S. Merritt
Associate Editor, *Engineering News-Record.* Author of *Building Construction Handbook; Mathematics Manual.*
BUILDING CONSTRUCTION

Alberta L. Meyer
Executive Secretary, Association for Childhood Education International, Washington, D.C.
ASSOCIATION FOR CHILDHOOD EDUCATION INTERNATIONAL

Carl F. Meyer
Technical Press and Customer Publications, Allis-Chalmers, Milwaukee, Wisconsin.
TRACTOR (in part)

Werner P. Meyer
Assistant to the Director, Research Communications, State Experiment Stations Division, Agricultural Research Service, United States Department of Agriculture, Washington, D.C.
EXPERIMENT STATION

Gordon E. Michalson
Professor of Historical Theology, Garrett Biblical Institute, Evanston, Illinois.
METHODISTS

John Middleton, Ph.D.
Professor of African Anthropology, University of London. Author of *The Lugbara of Uganda; Lugbara Religion.* Coauthor of *Zanzibar: Its Society and Its Politics.* Coeditor of *Tribes Without Rulers: Studies in African Segmentary Systems; Witchcraft and Sorcery in East Africa.*
AFRICA

David B. Miller, Ph.D.
Department of History, Roosevelt University.
STALIN, JOSEPH

Edward S. Miller
Vice President, Sherwood Electronic Laboratories, Inc., Chicago, Illinois.
AMPLIFIER

J. A. Miller
Executive Secretary-Treasurer, Opticians Association of America, Washington, D.C.
EYEGLASSES (in part)

James N. Miller
Information Division, Agricultural Stabilization and Conservation Service, U.S. Department of Agriculture, Washington D.C.
PRICE SUPPORTS (in part)

James R. Miller
Director, News Bureau, California Institute of Technology.
CALIFORNIA INSTITUTE OF TECHNOLOGY

R. D. Miller
Bates Manufacturing Company, Orange, New Jersey.
NUMBERING MACHINE

Robert R. Miller, Ph.D.
Professor of Zoology and Curator of Fishes, Museum of Zoology, University of Michigan.
TROUT

Harry Milt
Director, Public Relations, National Association for Mental Health, Inc., New York, N.Y.
NATIONAL ASSOCIATION FOR MENTAL HEALTH

Glenn O. Mittelstadt
Harley-Davidson Motor Company, Milwaukee, Wisconsin.
MOTORCYCLE

Margaret L. Mohler
Executive Secretary, P.E.O. Sisterhood, Des Moines, Iowa.
P.E.O. SISTERHOOD

Charles F. Moore, Jr.
Vice President, Ford Motor Company, Dearborn, Michigan.
FORD (family)

Wallace S. Moreland
Director of Public Relations, Rutgers, The State University of New Jersey.
RUTGERS UNIVERSITY

Charles O. Morgret
Manager, Public and Special Services, Public Relations Department, Association of American Railroads, Washington, D.C.
RAILWAY (in part)

Edouard Morot-Sir
Cultural Counselor, Representative in the United States of French Universities, French Embassy, New York, N.Y.
INSTITUTE OF FRANCE

Ellsworth H. Morse, Jr.
Director, Accounting and Auditing Policy Staff, United States General Accounting Office, Washington, D.C.
GENERAL ACCOUNTING OFFICE

J. M. Moseley
Director of Agricultural Research, American Tobacco Company, Richmond, Virginia.
TOBACCO (in part)

Charles C. Moskos, Jr., Ph.D.
Chairman, Department of Sociology, Northwestern University.
SOCIETY; SOCIOLOGY

Jim Mott
Assistant Director, Sports Information, University of Wisconsin.
ROWING

Roy Moyer
Director, American Federation of Arts, New York, N.Y.
AMERICAN FEDERATION OF ARTS

Malcolm R. Murlless
Director of Research and Development, A.S.R. Products Corporation, Staunton, Virginia.
CUTLERY

Robert W. Murphy
Merchandise Manager, The Boye Needle Company, Chicago, Illinois.
NEEDLE

Calvin Clyde Murray, Ph.D.
Professor of Agronomy and Dean and Coordinator, College of Agriculture, University of Georgia.
AGRONOMY

Marian Murray
Former Director of Public Relations, John and Mable Ringling Museum of Art, Sarasota, Florida. Author of *Circus! From Rome to Ringling; Children of the Big Top; Here Comes the Circus; Sarasota, the Circus City.*
CIRCUS

National Safety Council
Public Information Department, Chicago, Illinois.
SAFETY

Lewis Edwin Neff
Governor General, General Society of Mayflower Descendants, Plymouth, Massachusetts.
MAYFLOWER DESCENDANTS, GENERAL SOCIETY OF

Ralph C. Neill
Director, Public Relations Department, International Convention of Christian Churches (Disciples of Christ), Indianapolis, Indiana.
DISCIPLES OF CHRIST

Donald D. Nelson, Ph.D.
Associate Professor of Animal Science, California State University, Fresno.
HORSE

W. B. Nelson
Wallpaper Division, Imperial Color Chemical & Paper, Glens Falls, New York.
WALLPAPER

Frank R. Neu
Director, Public Relations Division, American Dairy Association, Chicago, Illinois.
MILK (in part)

Barbara E. Neuhaus, O.T.R.
Educational Consultant in Recruitment, American Occupational Therapy Association, New York, N.Y.
OCCUPATIONAL THERAPY

A. L. Newman
Deputy Director of Information, United States Department of the Interior, Washington, D.C.
INTERIOR, U.S. DEPARTMENT OF THE

Ross F. Nigrelli, Ph.D.
Director, New York Aquarium and the Osborn Laboratories of Marine Sciences.
SEAL

M. Nikolic
Yugoslav Consul, Chicago, Illinois.
YUGOSLAVIA

Emlin E. North, Jr.
Director of Information Services, The Menninger Foundation, Topeka, Kansas.
MENNINGER (family)

Ernest A. Norwig
Administrative Assistant to the Commissioner of Patents, Patent Office, United States Department of Commerce, Washington, D.C.
PATENT OFFICE

Jens Nyholm, M.A.
University Librarian, Northwestern University, Author of *Portal til Amerika.*
LITERATURE, DANISH

George O'Connell
Director, News Service, Dartmouth College.
DARTMOUTH COLLEGE

William J. O'Donnell
News Chief, Public Relations Office, National Aeronautics and Space Administration, Washington, D.C.
NATIONAL AERONAUTICS AND SPACE ADMINISTRATION

Felix J. Oinas, Ph.D.
Professor of Slavic Languages and Literatures and Associate Professor of Uralic and Altaic Studies, Indiana University. Author of *The Development of Some Post-positional Cases.* Editor, *Language Teaching Today.*
LITERATURE, FINNISH

Richard Orr
Farm and Garden Editor, Chicago *Tribune.*
GARDENING AND LANDSCAPING

Clifford D. Owsley
Chief, Special Reports, Press and Writing Services, Division of Information and Education, Forest Service, United States Department of Agriculture, Washington, D.C.
FOREST SERVICE, UNITED STATES

Roland D. Paine, Jr.
Public Information Officer, National Science Foundation, Washington, D.C.
NATIONAL SCIENCE FOUNDATION

Sidney Painter, Ph.D.
Late Professor of History, Johns Hopkins University. Author of *Feudalism and Liberty: Articles and Addresses; French Chivalry; History of the Middle Ages; Mediaeval Society; The Reign of King John; The Rise of the Feudal Monarchies; Studies in the History of the English Feudal Barony.* Coauthor, *The Past That Lives Today.*
EUROPEAN HISTORY

Eva Pantzari
Teacher of Classics and History, Kilkis (Greece) High School for Girls.
LITERATURE, GREEK (in part)

R. A. Pape
Merchandising Manager, Plumbing Products, Crane Company, Johnstown, Pennsylvania.
PLUMBING

George F. Papenfuss, Ph.D.
Professor of Botany, University of California, Berkeley.
ALGAE

Alfred Parker
Executive Director, Tax Foundation, Inc., New York, N.Y.
TAXATION

James A. Parker
Office of Information, U.S. Department of the Treasury, Washington, D.C.
TREASURY, U.S. DEPARTMENT OF THE

Robert H. Parrish
Director of Institutional Public Relations, Illinois Institute of Technology.
ILLINOIS INSTITUTE OF TECHNOLOGY

William S. Pascoe, Captain, U.S.N.
Public Information Officer, Selective Service System, Washington, D.C.
SELECTIVE SERVICE SYSTEM

Clarissa M. H. Patterson
Chairman, Department of Secretarial and Office Education, Bryant College.
SHORTHAND

Clifford W. Patton
Director, Office of Information, Federal Home Loan Bank Board, Washington, D.C.
FEDERAL HOME LOAN BANK BOARD

Mario Pei, Ph.D.
Professor of Romance Philology, Columbia University. Author of *The World's Chief Languages; The Story of Language; The Story of the English Language; All About Language.* Coauthor of *A Dictionary of Linguistics; Language for Everybody; One Language for the World; The Families of Words; Invitation to Linguistics.* Associate Editor, *Modern Language Journal; Symposium; Romanic Review.* Former Consultant to U.S. Army Language School. Compiler and Director, "World Language Series."
ALPHABET; LANGUAGE

Mary Ellis Peltz
Archivist, Metropolitan Opera Association. Founder and Former Editor, *Opera News.* Author of *Behind the Gold Curtain; The Magic of Opera.* Editor, *Opera Lover's Companion; Introduction to Opera.*
OPERA

Bartlett Peterson
General Secretary, General Council of the Assemblies of God, Springfield, Missouri.
ASSEMBLIES OF GOD

Owen Peterson, Ph.D.
Former Executive Secretary, Speech Association of America, Louisiana State University.
DEBATE

Shailer Peterson, Ph.D.
Dean, College of Dentistry, University of Tennessee. Former Secretary to Council on Dental Health and Assistant Secretary of Educational Affairs, American Dental Association.
BLACK, GREENE VARDIMAN

Dale Phalen
Executive Director, Samuel S. Fels Fund, Philadelphia, Pennsylvania.
FELS FUND

Rutherford T. Phillips
Executive Director, The American Humane Association, Denver, Colorado.
HUMANE SOCIETIES

Mary Brooks Picken
Coauthor of *Needlepoint for Everyone; Needlepoint Made Easy.* Editor of *The Fashion Dictionary: Fabric, Sewing and Press as Expressed in the Language of Fashion.*
DRESS

Helen C. Pidgeon
National News Bureau, Public Relations Department, Girl Scouts of the U.S.A., New York, N.Y.
GIRL GUIDES; GIRL SCOUTS

Harry W. Pierson
Director, News Bureau, United States Savings and Loan League, Chicago, Illinois.
SAVINGS AND LOAN ASSOCIATION

Jane Pinkerton
Director of Communications, National Board of the Young Women's Christian Association of the U.S.A., New York, N.Y.
YOUNG WOMEN'S CHRISTIAN ASSOCIATION

William M. Pinkerton
University News Office, Harvard University.
HARVARD UNIVERSITY

Jean M. Pinkley
Chief Park Archeologist, Mesa Verde National Park, Colorado.
MESA VERDE NATIONAL PARK

Robert A. Placek
Public Relations Department, Rotary International, Evanston, Illinois.
ROTARY INTERNATIONAL

Bruce Pluckhahn
Manager, Public Relations Department, American Bowling Congress, Milwaukee, Wisconsin.
BOWLING (in part)

Stephen H. Poe
Chief, Technical Information Bureau, Office of Assistant Commissioner and Chief Engineer, Bureau of Reclamation, United States Department of the Interior, Denver, Colorado.
HOOVER DAM

Frederik Pohl
Editor, Galaxy Publishing Corporation, New York, N.Y.
SCIENCE FICTION

Lynn Poole
Director, Public Relations, The Johns Hopkins University.
JOHNS HOPKINS UNIVERSITY

Charles W. Porter III
Chief Historian, National Park Service, United States Department of the Interior, Washington, D.C.
NATIONAL PARKS

Willis Hubert Porter
Associate General Secretary, American Baptist Convention, New York, N.Y.
BAPTISTS (in part)

Bernard Postal
Director, Public Information, National Jewish Welfare Board, New York, N.Y.
JEWISH COMMUNITY CENTER; JEWISH WELFARE BOARD, NATIONAL

John Mason Potter
Director, News Bureau, Cornell University.
CORNELL UNIVERSITY

Carl J. Potthoff, M.D., M.P.H.
Professor Emeritus of Medical and Educational Administration, University of Nebraska College of Medicine. Fellow, American College of Preventive Medicine. Author of *American Red Cross First Aid Textbook* and *First Aid Textbook for Juniors.* Former columnist, *American Journal of Public Health; Today's Health.*
MEDICINE

John R. Powers, Jr.
Vice President, Daisy Manufacturing Company, Rogers, Arkansas.
AIR AND GAS GUNS

Paul Prikos
Prikos & Becker Tool Company, Chicago, Illinois.
DIE (in part)

Hugo Pruter, M.Div., M.A.
Presiding Bishop, Christ Catholic Church, Chicago, Illinois. Author of *A History of the Old Catholic Church* and coauthor of *Source Book of Old Catholicism.*
OLD CATHOLICS

George B. Rabb, Ph.D.
Associate Director of Research and Education, Chicago Zoological Park (Brookfield Zoo).
ZOOLOGY

William H. Radebaugh
Public Relations Department, E. I. du Pont de Nemours & Company, Incorporated, Wilmington, Delaware.
DACRON; NYLON

Joan Rahn, Ph.D.
Former Assistant Professor of Biology, Lake Forest College. Author of *Seeing What Plants Do; How Plants Travel.*
BIOLOGY

M. J. Randleman
Office of the Secretary, Contest Board, National Aeronautic Association, Washington, D.C.
BALLOON (in part)

Edward J. Reardon
Manager, Press Relations, Public Information Bureau, American Gas Association, New York, N.Y.
GAS

Thetis Reavis
Vice President/Public Affairs, Foreign Policy Association, New York, N.Y.
FOREIGN POLICY ASSOCIATION

Glenn A. Reece
General Secretary, The Five Years Meeting of Friends, Richmond, Indiana.
FRIENDS, SOCIETY OF

M. P. Reed
Publicity Manager, United States Gypsum Company, Chicago, Illinois.
WALLBOARD

Walter O. Reed
Director of Public Relations, National Automatic Merchandising Association, Chicago, Illinois.
VENDING MACHINES

Walter Reeves
Director of Public Relations, Oberlin College.
OBERLIN COLLEGE

Jay Reid
Information Officer, International Monetary Fund, Washington, D.C.
INTERNATIONAL MONETARY FUND

J. F. Reilly
National Bureau of Standards, United States Department of Commerce, Washington, D.C.
NATIONAL BUREAU OF STANDARDS

John L. Reith
Department of Research and Transport Economics, American Trucking Associations, Inc., Washington, D.C.
TRUCK

John J. Renard
Sales Manager, Anchor Hocking Glass Corporation, Lancaster, Ohio.
BOTTLE

Roberto Rendueles
Chief, Information Office, Pan American Sanitary Bureau, Regional Office of the World Health Organization, Washington, D.C.
WORLD HEALTH ORGANIZATION

Donald W. Reynolds
Late President, Reynolds Brothers Orchards, Sturgeon Bay, Wisconsin.
CHERRY

D. F. Rhebergen
Supervisor, Videotape Engineering, ABC-TV, Central Division, Chicago.
TAPE RECORDER (in part); TELEVISION (in part)

Lawrence Rieser
Development Director, Hull House Association, Chicago, Illinois.
HULL HOUSE

Phyllis Rike
Assistant Secretary, International Society of Christian Endeavor, Columbus, Ohio.
CHRISTIAN ENDEAVOR

Irving Rimer
Vice President for Public Information, American Cancer Society, New York, N.Y.
AMERICAN CANCER SOCIETY

Charles R. Ritcheson, D.Phil.
Colin Rhys Lovell Professor of British History, University of Southern California. Author of *British Politics and the American Revolution; Aftermath of Revolution: British Policy Toward the U.S., 1783-1795.*
EUROPEAN HISTORY

Donald E. Roberts, Captain, U.S.A.F.
Information, Officer, United States Air Force Academy.
UNITED STATES SERVICE ACADEMIES (in part)

Francis Robinson
Public Relations, Metropolitan Opera Association, Inc., New York, N.Y.
METROPOLITAN OPERA ASSOCIATION, INC.

James K. Robinson, Ph.D.
Professor of English, University of Cincinnati. Coauthor of *A College Book of Modern Verse; A College Book of Modern Fiction.*
WORLD LITERATURE

Paul Minnich Robinson, D.D., LL.D.
President, Bethany Theological Seminary, Oak Brook, Illinois.
DUNKERS

William Roetzheim
Director of Athletics, University of Illinois, Chicago. Former President, United States Gymnastics Federation. Gymnastics Judge, 1976 Olympic Games.
GYMNASTICS

Lee Romich
Publicity Director, American Youth Hostels, New York, N.Y.
HOSTEL

Ernest J. Roscoe, Ph.D.
Field Museum of Natural History, Chicago, Illinois.
LEECH (illustration)

Claybourne B. Ross
General Manager, Rice Council, Houston, Texas.
RICE

Evangelos V. Rousos
Former Secretary of the Greek Consulate, Chicago, Illinois.
LITERATURE, GREEK (in part)

A. Prescott Rowe
Assistant Director of Information Services, Washington and Lee University.
WASHINGTON AND LEE UNIVERSITY

Abe Rubin, D.S.C.
Former Secretary and Editor, American Podiatry Association, Washington, D.C.
PODIATRY

Edward Rudnick
Assistant Commissioner, Immigration and Naturalization Service, United States Department of Justice, Washington, D.C.
NATURALIZATION

Robert T. Rudulph
U.S. Table Tennis Association, Orlando, Florida.
TABLE TENNIS

Ronald S. Ryner
Regional Director, Structural Clay Products Institute, Chicago, Illinois.
BRICK

Martha C. Sager, Ph.D.
Director, Institutes for Environmental Systems Analysis, College of Continuing Education, The American University.
ECOLOGY

Perry J. Sandell
Director, Bureau of Dental Health Education, American Dental Association, Chicago, Illinois.
TEETH

Joseph Sander
President, Sander Wood Engraving Company, Chicago, Illinois.
ENGRAVING (in part)

Sam H. Saran
Director of Public Relations and Publications, Northwestern University.
NORTHWESTERN UNIVERSITY

George M. Saunders
Imperial Recorder, The Imperial Council of the Ancient Arabic Order, Nobles of the Mystic Shrine for North America.
SHRINERS

Roland Sawyer
Special Assistant to the Board of Directors, Export-Import Bank of Washington, Washington, D.C.
EXPORT-IMPORT BANK OF WASHINGTON

W. B. Sayers
Director of Research, American Forest Institute, Washington, D.C.
FOREST (in part); LUMBERING (in part)

John T. Saywell, Ph.D.
Professor of History and Dean, Faculty of Arts and Science, York University, Toronto. Author of *Office of the Lieutenant-Governor; How Are We Governed?; Nation and Province; Quebec 70: a Documentary Narrative.* Coauthor of *The Modern Era.* Editor of *Canadian Annual Review of Politics and Public Affairs.*
CANADA

Julian Scheer
Assistant Administrator for Public Affairs, National Aeronautics and Space Administration, Washington, D.C.
ASTRONAUT

William A. Scherff
Sales Promotion Manager, Plymouth Cordage Company, Plymouth, Massachusetts.
KNOTS, HITCHES, AND SPLICES; ROPE

Raymond H. Schmandt, Ph.D.
Professor of History, St. Joseph's College, Philadelphia. Coauthor of *History of the Catholic Church; Leo XIII and the Modern World; Europe and Asia.* Editor of *The Popes Through History.*
ROMAN CATHOLIC CHURCH

John N. Schmidt
Attorney-at-law, Rockford, Illinois.
LAW

Marci R. Schneider
Public Affairs, Board of Governors of the Federal Reserve System, Washington, D.C.
BANKS AND BANKING (Federal Reserve System)

Patricia Q. Schoeni
Writer-Editor, National Clearinghouse for Smoking and Health, Public Health Service, U.S. Department of Health and Human Services, Arlington, Virginia.
TOBACCO (in part)

Philip W. Schulte
Chief, Public Information Office, United States Civil Service Commission, Washington, D.C.
CIVIL SERVICE

Trudi Schutz
Public Information Director, American Civil Liberties Union, New York, N.Y.
AMERICAN CIVIL LIBERTIES UNION

Robert E. Schwarm
Chairman, Education Committee, National Association of Printing Ink Makers, Inc., New York, N.Y.; The Schwarm and Jacobus Company, Cincinnati, Ohio.
INK

W. M. Schwarz, Ph.D.
Associate Professor of Physics, Union College. Author of *Intermediate Electromagnetic Theory.*
PHYSICS

Howard Scott
Director-in-chief, Technocracy, Inc., Rushland, Pennsylvania.
TECHNOCRACY

William Henry Sebrell, Jr., M.D., Sc.D.
Director, Institute of Human Nutrition, Columbia University; Medical Director, Weight Watchers International. Author of *Food and Nutrition*. Coeditor of *The Vitamins: Chemistry, Physiology, Pathology, Methods*.
FOOD AND NUTRITION

Julius Segal, Ph.D.
Chief, Program Analysis and Evaluation Branch, U.S. National Institute of Mental Health, Bethesda, Maryland. Coauthor of *Sleep; Insomnia: The Guide for Troubled Sleepers*.
SLEEP

Marshall Sewell
Manager, Publications & Films, United States Rubber Company, New York, N.Y.
RUBBER (in part)

R. T. Shafer
Air Brake Division, Westinghouse Air Brake Company, Wilmerding, Pennsylvania.
BRAKE (in part)

Max C. Shank, Ph.D.
Professor, Department of Biological Sciences, University of Illinois, Chicago.
ZOOLOGY

James A. Shannon, M.D.
Director, National Institutes of Health, U.S. Public Health Service, Bethesda, Maryland.
NATIONAL INSTITUTES OF HEALTH

Charles B. Shaw, Colonel, U.S.A.
Officer in Charge, American Battle Monuments Commission, Washington, D.C.
AMERICAN BATTLE MONUMENTS COMMISSION

Elizabeth Shaw
Director, Department of Public Information, Museum of Modern Art, New York, N.Y.
MUSEUM OF MODERN ART

Leon Shechter
Director, Applications R & D, Plastics Division, Union Carbide Corporation, Bound Brook, New Jersey.
PLASTICS (in part)

Ira Sherman
Public Information Director, American Heart Association, Inc., New York, N.Y.
AMERICAN HEART ASSOCIATION

William S. Shields, Ph.D.
Senior Professor and Dean of Admissions, United States Naval Academy.
UNITED STATES SERVICE ACADEMIES (in part)

Charles B. Shuman
President, American Farm Bureau Federation, Chicago, Illinois.
AMERICAN FARM BUREAU FEDERATION

Bernard Simon
Public Relations Director, B'nai B'rith, Washington, D.C.
B'NAI B'RITH

K. L. Sinclair
Secretary-Treasurer, American Lawn Bowling Association, Los Angeles, California.
LAWN BOWLING

Kenneth Singer, D.M.
Dean, National College of Naprapathy, Chicago, Illinois.
NAPRAPATHY

Paul A. Siple, Ph.D., D.Sc.
Late Scientific Attaché, Embassy of the United States of America, Canberra, Australia. Military Geographer; Member, Byrd Expeditions to the Antarctic. Author of *90° South: the Story of the American South Pole Expedition; Climatic Design Control for Housing; Mechanics of Polar Motion and Continental Drift*.
ANTARCTICA

Frank Skidmore
Director of Industry Relations, Associated Equipment Distributors, Oak Brook, Illinois.
POWER SHOVELS AND CRANES

Knud Skrivergaard
Assistant Press Attaché, Danish Information Office, New York, N.Y.
DENMARK (in part)

Jerry L. Sloan
Director, Corporate Information, Ford Motor Company, Dearborn, Michigan.
FORD MOTOR COMPANY

Melvin Sloan
Professor, Department of Cinema, University of Southern California.
MOTION PICTURES

Alexander H. Smith, Ph.D.
Professor of Botany, University of Michigan. Author of *Mushroom Hunter's Field Guide; Puffballs and Their Allies in Michigan*.
MUSHROOM

G. Kerry Smith
Executive Secretary, Association for Higher Education, Washington, D.C.
ASSOCIATION FOR HIGHER EDUCATION

Rhea Marsh Smith, Ph.D.
Professor of History, Rollins College. Author of *Spain: A Modern History*.
SPAIN (history); SPANISH CIVIL WAR

Willard A. Smith, Ph.D.
Late Professor of History, University of Toledo.
EUROPEAN HISTORY

Jean Sonnhalter
Department of Public Relations, Firestone Tire & Rubber Company, Akron, Ohio.
FIRESTONE, HARVEY S.

Luis Amorim de Sousa
Press Counsellor, Portuguese Embassy, Washington, D.C.
PORTUGAL

Leonard Spacek, C.P.A.
Managing Partner, Arthur Andersen & Co., Chicago, Illinois.
ACCOUNTING

Virginia Spaeth, M.S.
Department of Biological Sciences, University of Illinois, Chicago.
TERMITE

Don Spagnolo
National Executive Director, American Veterans of World War II and Korea, Washington, D.C.
AMVETS

Meno Spann, Ph.D.
Associate Professor of German, Northwestern University. Coauthor of *Deutsche Denker und Forscher; Deutsch für Amerikaner; Cultural Graded Readers*. Author of *Heine*.
LITERATURE, GERMAN

Eugene Speakman
P. R. Mallory & Company, Inc., Indianapolis, Indiana.
BATTERY, ELECTRIC (in part)

Leonard Spector
Associate Professor of Biochemistry,
Rockefeller University.
ADENOSINE TRIPHOSPHATE

Robert M. Sperling
The Wicks Organ Company, Highland, Illinois.
ORGAN (in part)

James H. Stack
Director, Public, Professional, and
Member Relations Division, American Chemical Society, Washington,
D.C.
AMERICAN CHEMICAL SOCIETY

William T. Stafford, Ph.D.
Associate Professor of English, Purdue University. Editor of *Melville's
Billy Budd and the Critics; James's
Daisy Miller; Twentieth Century
American Writing; Emerson and the
James Family.*
ENGLISH LITERATURE

Irwin Stambler
Associate Editor, *Space/Aeronautics.*
Author of *Orbiting Stations; Find a
Career in Aviation; Space Ship: the
Story of the X-15; The Battle for
Inner Space; Project Gemini; Project
Mariner; Build the Unknown.*
AIRPLANE (in part)

Carl W. Starner
Black & Decker Manufacturing Company, Towson, Maryland.
SAW

Ralph Stauber
Chief, Agricultural Price Statistics
Branch, Statistical Reporting Service,
United States Department of Agriculture, Washington, D.C.
PRICE SUPPORTS (in part)

Andrew D. Staursky
Director, Public Relations, United
States Steel Corporation, Pittsburgh,
Pennsylvania.
UNITED STATES STEEL CORPORATION

Floyd E. Stayton
Acting Superintendent, Haskell Institute, Lawrence, Kansas.
HASKELL INSTITUTE

Thomas J. Stebbins
Director, Submarine Force Library &
Museum, Naval Submarine Base,
New London, Groton, Connecticut.
SUBMARINE

Alfred Steinberg
Author of *The Bosses;* "Lives to Remember" series; *Man from Missouri:
Life and Times of Harry S. Truman;
The First Ten: The Founding Presidents and Their Administrations.*
TRUMAN, HARRY S.

Wendell H. Stephenson, Ph.D.,
LL.D.
Professor of History, University of
Oregon. Author of *A Basic History of
the Old South; Southern History in
the Making.* Coeditor of *A History of
the South.*
TAYLOR, ZACHARY

William L. Stern, Ph.D.
Professor of Botany, University of
Maryland. Editor of *Plant Science
Bulletin; Economic Botany; Biotropica.*
BOTANY

Gilbert Stewart, Jr.
Assistant Director of Information,
Tennessee Valley Authority, Knoxville, Tennessee.
TENNESSEE VALLEY AUTHORITY

Leonard Stoller
Advertising Manager, Givaudan-Delawanna, Inc., New York, N.Y.
PERFUME

Elsbeth Strathern
Director of Public Relations and Editor of *The Zontian,* Zonta International, Chicago, Illinois.
ZONTA INTERNATIONAL

John W. Stratton
Management Assistant, Yosemite National Park, California.
YOSEMITE NATIONAL PARK

Donald B. Straus
President, American Arbitration Association, New York, N.Y.
ARBITRATION (in part)

Felix Streyckmans
Information Director, The Izaak Walton League of America, Arlington,
Virginia.
IZAAK WALTON LEAGUE OF AMERICA

A. W. von Struve
Public Information Office, Bureau of
the Census, U.S. Department of
Commerce, Washington, D.C.
CENSUS

Erwin van Swol
Office of Public Information, United
States Information Agency, Washington, D.C.
VOICE OF AMERICA

Ann Tannyhill
Associate Public Relations Director,
National Urban League, Inc., New
York, N.Y.
NATIONAL URBAN LEAGUE

Earl W. Taylor
Grand Secretary, Grand Lodge of
Massachusetts.
MASONS

Richard J. Tedesco
Public Relations Assistant, New York Life Insurance Company, New York, N.Y.
NEW YORK LIFE INSURANCE COMPANY

Ernest W. Tedlock, Jr., Ph.D.
Professor of English, University of New Mexico. Author of *D. H. Lawrence: Artist and Rebel.* Editor of *D. H. Lawrence's Sons and Lovers: Sources and Criticism; Dylan Thomas, the Legend and the Poet.* Coeditor of *Steinbeck and His Critics.*
20TH-CENTURY ENGLISH AND AMERICAN LITERATURE

Ruth Teiser
Writer on Western subjects. Interviewer, Regional Oral History Office, University of California, Berkeley.
SAN FRANCISCO (history)

Teletype Corporation
Skokie, Illinois.
TELETYPEWRITER

Joseph P. Templeton
Secretary, The Joseph Dixon Crucible Company, Jersey City, New Jersey.
DIXON, JOSEPH

Leonard B. Tennyson
Information Consultant, Information Service, The European Community, Washington, D.C.
EUROPEAN COMMUNITY

A. F. Tesi
Celanese Fibers Company, Charlotte, North Carolina.
RAYON AND ACETATE (in part)

Lloyd Thiel, O.F.M.
Provincial Minister, the Province of St. Joseph of the Capuchin Order, Detroit, Michigan.
CAPUCHINS

Charles J. Thill, M.D.
Practicing Physician, Chicago, Illinois.
GLAND

Betty Thompson
Public Relations, United States Conference for the World Council of Churches, New York, N.Y.
WORLD COUNCIL OF CHURCHES

E. Bruce Thompson, Ph.D.
Professor of History, Baylor University. Author of *Matthew Hale Carpenter, Webster of the West.* Coauthor of *Church and State in Religion, History, and Constitutional Law.*
UNITED STATES HISTORY

Harry C. Thomson, Ph.D.
Former Chief Historian, Army Ordnance Corps, Washington, D.C.
MILITARY HISTORY

Patricia Thrash, Ph.D.
Dean of Women, Northwestern University.
EDUCATORS

Mrs. Fred J. Tooze
President, National Woman's Christian Temperance Union, Evanston, Illinois.
WOMAN'S CHRISTIAN TEMPERANCE UNION

Frederick Tough
Pan-American Coffee Bureau, New York, N.Y.
COFFEE (in part)

Lawrence Phelps Tower
President, United States Flag Foundation, Inc., New York, N.Y.
FLAG (in part)

Clive Toye
Chairman, Promotion and Publicity Committee, U.S. Soccer Football Association, New York, N.Y.
SOCCER

M. M. Tozier
Information Officer, Bureau of Indian Affairs, United States Department of the Interior, Washington, D.C.
INDIAN AFFAIRS, BUREAU OF

H. C. Traute, Jr.
Diamond Match Division, Diamond National Corporation, New York, N.Y.
MATCHES

Melvin A. Traylor
Associate Curator of Birds, Field Museum of Natural History, Chicago, Illinois.
BIRD (in part)

Carson B. Trenor
Morton International, Inc.
SALT, COMMON

C. V. Truax
Public Relations, The National Cash Register Company, Dayton, Ohio.
PATTERSON, JOHN HENRY

Gilbert Twiss
Editorial Staff, Chicago *Tribune.*
NEWSPAPER (in part)

Felix R. Tyroler
Executive Secretary, National Tulip Society, New York, N.Y.
TULIP

Frank Uhlig, Jr.
Faculty member, Center for Naval Warfare Studies, U.S. Naval War College, Newport, Rhode Island. Editor, Naval War College *Review.* Former editor, *Naval Review.*
NAVAL ARTICLES

Stephen Ullmann, Ph.D.
Professor of Romance Languages, Oxford University. Author of *The Principles of Semantics; Semantics: an Introduction to the Science of Meaning; Language and Style.*
SEMANTICS

Rabbi Jerome Unger
Former Executive Director, American Zionist Council, New York, N.Y.
ZIONISM

Anna C. Urband
Office of Information, Department of the Navy, Washington, D.C.
NAVY, UNITED STATES

James H. Van Alen
President, National Lawn Tennis Hall of Fame and Tennis Museum, Inc., Newport, Rhode Island.
TENNIS

Calvin A. Vander Werf, Ph.D.
Professor of Chemistry, University of Kansas. Author of *Acids, Bases, and the Chemistry of the Covalent Bond.* Coauthor of *College Chemistry: a Systematic Approach.*
CHEMISTRY

George Vass
Author of *The Chicago Black Hawks Story.*
HOCKEY

Richard N. Vaughan
Manager, Public Relations Department, American Institute of Laundering, Joliet, Illinois.
LAUNDRY

James T. Veeder
Director, Information Service, National 4-H Service Committee Inc., Chicago, Illinois.
FOUR-H CLUBS

John A. Vieg, Ph.D.
Professor of Government, Pomona College and Claremont Graduate School. Author of *Progress versus Utopia.* Coauthor of *Elements of Public Administration; Our Needy Aged; The Government and Politics of California; California Local Finance; California People and Their Government.*
GOVERNMENT

Becky Vining
Information Office, Future Farmers of America, Alexandria, Virginia.
FUTURE FARMERS OF AMERICA

Iris Vinton
Director, Publications, Boys' Clubs of America, New York, N.Y.
BOYS' CLUBS OF AMERICA

Judy Vodicka
Communications Division, American Medical Association, Chicago, Illinois.
AMERICAN MEDICAL ASSOCIATION

Harold A. Vogel
Regional Representative, Food and Agriculture Organization of the United Nations, North American Regional Office, Washington, D.C.
FOOD AND AGRICULTURE ORGANIZATION OF THE UNITED NATIONS

Don Lester Waage
Assistant to the Board, Federal Deposit Insurance Corporation, Washington, D.C.
FEDERAL DEPOSIT INSURANCE CORPORATION

Selman A. Waksman, Ph.D., D.Sc.
Late Professor of Microbiology, Institute of Microbiology, Rutgers, The State University of New Jersey. Nobel Laureate in Physiology/Medicine. Author of *The Actinomycetes; Guide to the Actinomycetes and Their Antibiotics; Conquest of Tuberculosis; Neomycin; Soil Microbiology; My Life With the Microbes; Streptomycin, Its Nature and Application.*
ANTIBIOTICS

Ernest P. Walker
Late Assistant Director, National Zoological Park, Washington, D.C. Senior Author of *Mammals of the World.*
ANIMAL

Charles P. Wall
Resident Director, Mount Vernon Ladies' Association of the Union, Mount Vernon, Virginia.
MOUNT VERNON

Laura S. Wallace
International Order of Job's Daughters, Silver Spring, Maryland.
JOB'S DAUGHTERS, INTERNATIONAL ORDER OF

James J. Walsh, Ph.D.
Faculty of Philosophy, Columbia University.
SCHOLASTICISM

Warren B. Walsh, Ph.D.
Professor of Russian History and Chairman, Department of History, Syracuse University. Author of *Russia: a Handbook; Russia and the Soviet Union.* Editor of *Readings in Russian History.* Editor, *Russian Review.*
UNION OF SOVIET SOCIALIST REPUBLICS (history)

Beryl Walter
Director, Consumer Services, Tea Council of the United States, New York, N.Y.
TEA (in part)

Robert G. Ward
The Wool Bureau, New York, N.Y.
WOOL

Russel Ward
Associate Professor of History, University of New England, New South Wales. Author of *The Australian Legend; Australia.*
AUSTRALIA (in part)

John W. Warner, Jr.
Assistant to the Director, United States Secret Service, Washington, D.C.
SECRET SERVICE, UNITED STATES

Leonard Warner
Director, Department of Agriculture, Appleton Vocational School for Adult Education, Appleton, Wisconsin.
PLOW

William G. Watson
Grand Secretary, Fraternal Order of Eagles, Zanesville, Ohio.
EAGLES, FRATERNAL ORDER OF

Harold H. Watts, Ph.D.
Professor of English, Purdue University. Author of *The Modern Reader's Guide to the Bible; The Modern Reader's Guide to Religions; Ezra Pound and the Cantos.*
ENGLISH LITERATURE

William H. Watts
Western Union Telegraph Co., New York, N.Y.
TELEGRAPHY (in part)

Sam P. Weems
Superintendent, Blue Ridge Parkway, National Park Service, U.S. Department of the Interior, Roanoke, Virginia.
BLUE RIDGE PARKWAY

Rt. Rev. Msgr. Nicholas H. Wegner
Director, Father Flanagan's Boys' Home, Boys Town, Nebraska.
BOYS TOWN

Bretta Weiss
National Director, American Montessori Society, New York, N.Y.
MONTESSORI METHOD

Ellis Weitzman, Ph.D.
Professor and Chairman, Department of Psychology, American University. Author of *Growing Up Socially.* Coauthor of *Constructing Classroom Examinations; Guiding Children's Social Growth.*
TESTING

Edward Wellin, Ph.D.
Professor of Anthropology, University of Wisconsin—Milwaukee.
ANTHROPOLOGY

George S. Wells
Editor-in-chief, *Camping Guide Magazine.*
CAMPS AND CAMPING

Sara Wentworth
Corporate Information, CBS Inc., New York, N.Y.
CBS INC.

Irwin Werner
General Manager, Intaglio Service Corporation, Chicago, Illinois.
PHOTOENGRAVING (in part)

George Werntz, Jr.
Executive Vice President and Secretary, The Seeing Eye, Inc., Morristown, New Jersey.
BLINDNESS (in part)

Jeffry S. Wetrich
The Watchmakers of Switzerland Information Center, Inc., New York, N.Y.
WATCH (in part)

John N. Wheelock
Executive Director, Federal Trade Commission, Washington, D.C.
FEDERAL TRADE COMMISSION

George W. White
National Skeet Shooting Association, Dallas, Texas.
TRAPSHOOTING AND SKEET SHOOTING (in part)

Thomas D. White, LL.D., General, U.S.A.F. (Ret.)
Late Chief of Staff, United States Air Force; Contributing Editor, *Newsweek.*
AIR FORCE

Alvin D. Whitley
Public Information Office, Armed Forces Staff College, Norfolk, Virginia.
ARMED FORCES STAFF COLLEGE

John Wight
Language Research, Inc., Cambridge, Massachusetts.
BASIC ENGLISH

Philip R. Wikelund, Ph.D.
Associate Professor of English, Indiana University.
LANGUAGE ARTS

R. A. Wilgus
Protection Marketing Manager, Diebold, Inc., Canton, Ohio.
SAFE

Joan Willard
Assistant Director of Public Relations, United Service Organizations, Inc., New York, N.Y.
UNITED SERVICE ORGANIZATIONS

Edward L. Wilson
Managing Director, Mobile Homes Manufacturers Association, Chicago, Illinois.
MOBILE HOMES AND TRAVEL TRAILERS

Logan Wilson
President, American Council on Education, Washington, D.C.
ACADEMIC DRESS

Orlando W. Wilson
Former Superintendent of Police, Chicago, Illinois. Late Professor of Police Administration and Dean, School of Criminology, University of California, Berkeley. Author of *Police Administration; Police Planning.*
POLICE (in part)

Helen Wing
Author and Composer, Chicago, Illinois.
MUSIC (in part)

Bernard R. Winter
Tool and Die Institute, Chicago, Illinois.
DIE (in part)

Lois Winterberg
National Federation of Music Clubs, Chicago, Illinois.
NATIONAL FEDERATION OF MUSIC CLUBS

Eileen M. Wirth
Public Relations, Union Pacific Railroad Company, Omaha, Nebraska.
UNION PACIFIC RAILROAD

Harry H. Wolff
Field Officer, Fire Prevention Department, Western Actuarial Bureau, Chicago, Illinois.
FIRE DEPARTMENT

Harry Woolf, Ph.D.
Chairman, Department of the History of Science, Johns Hopkins University.
SCIENCE

F. L. Wormald
Vice President, Association of American Colleges, Washington, D.C.
ASSOCIATION OF AMERICAN COLLEGES

B. C. Yates
Superintendent, Kennesaw Mountain National Battlefield Park, Marietta, Georgia.
CIVIL WAR, AMERICAN (in part)

Howard N. Yates
Executive Vice President, Colorado State Chamber of Commerce, Denver.
COLORADO (in part)

Burton L. Youngman
Director of Research, Insurance Information Institute, New York, N.Y.
INSURANCE (in part)

William R. Yowell
President, Chicago Mountaineering Club, Chicago, Illinois.
MOUNTAIN CLIMBING

Albert J. Zack
Director, Department of Public Relations, American Federation of Labor and Congress of Industrial Organizations, Washington, D.C.
AMERICAN FEDERATION OF LABOR AND CONGRESS OF INDUSTRIAL ORGANIZATIONS

Tony Zale
World Middleweight Champion, 1941-48; Director of Park District Boxing Program, Chicago, Illinois.
BOXING

Lewis E. Zender
District Director, Public Relations, United States Steel Corporation, Cleveland, Ohio.
WIRE

John I. Zerbe
Manager, Education Services Department, National Lumber Manufacturers Association, Washington, D.C.
WOOD (in part)

Mary Hart Zink
Assistant Professor of Mathematics, Elmhurst College.
GEOMETRY

Molly Zwerling
National Public Relations, Junior Achievement Inc., Stamford, Connecticut.
JUNIOR ACHIEVEMENT, INC.

Photos in this section: Page vi, John Von Dorn; Page viii, D. W. Downey; Page xii, courtesy John I. Goodlad. All others are NEW STANDARD photos showing various aspects of the work involved in compiling, revising, and editing NEW STANDARD ENCYCLOPEDIA.

The type for NEW STANDARD ENCYCLOPEDIA is set electronically using the Linotron 606 typographic system. The basic text typeface is Old Style No. 7. Other text typefaces are Spartan bold, medium, and demibold; and Helvetica regular and medium.

Typography by Black Dot Typographers, Crystal Lake and Freeport, Illinois. Color separations by Black Dot Color, Crystal Lake, Illinois, and others. Printing and binding by Von Hoffmann Press, Inc., St. Louis and Jefferson City, Missouri.

Pronunciation Guide

Letters with their pronunciation markings are pronounced as follows:

ā as in āte	ă as in ănt	á as in fást
â as in vâcation	ă̇ as in ă̇bhor	ȧ as in ȧbandon
â as in râre	ä as in färm	

ē as in ēven	ê as in crêation	ĕ as in parĕnt
ẹ̄ as in fẹ̄ar	ĕ as in sĕlf	ẽ as in farmẽr

ī as in īre	ĭ as in ĭnk	ĭ as in qualĭty

ō as in ōver	ŏ as in pŏcket	o͞o as in po͞ol
o̊ as in o̊blige	ŏ̇ as in ŏ̇ccur	o͝o as in wo͝ol
ô as in ôrgan	ô̇ as in ô̇ff	

ū as in redūce	û as in occûr	ŭ as in sŭppose
u̇ as in su̇perior	ŭ as in cŭp	ü as in the French menü

th as in three; t̶h̶ as in these
ᴋ German ch sound as in ach (äᴋ)
ɴ as in the French bon (bôɴ); the n is silent and the preceding vowel is nasalized

Syllables are separated by an accent mark (′ or ′) or hyphen (-). The mark ′ is placed after a syllable with primary accent, and the mark ′ after a syllable with lighter, or secondary, accent, Example: prȯ-nŭn′sĭ-ā′shŭn.

A vowel that is not pronounced is replaced by an apostrophe(′), as in fasten (fȧs″n).

A consonant that is pronounced very lightly is enclosed by brackets, as in Hampshire (hăm[p]′shĭr).

Weights and Measures

Weights and measures are generally given in units of the U.S. Customary System. Rough conversions into metric units may be made as follows:

Inches × 25 = Millimeters	Ounces (weight) × 28 = Grams
Feet × 30 = Centimeters	Pounds × 0.45 = Kilograms
Feet × 0.3 = Meters	Short Tons × 0.9 = Metric Tons
Yards × 0.9 = Meters	Ounces (liquid) × 30 = Milliliters
Miles × 1.6 = Kilometers	Pints × 0.47 = Liters
Square Miles × 2.6 = Square Kilometers	Quarts × 0.95 = Liters
Acres × 0.4 = Hectares	Gallons × 3.8 = Liters

An exact conversion of degrees Fahrenheit to degrees Celsius is obtained as follows: (Degrees Fahrenheit − 32) × 5/9 = Degrees Celsius

For additional and more accurate conversion factors, see WEIGHTS AND MEASURES.

K	A	A
1000 B.C. PHOENICIAN	800 B.C. WESTERN GREEK	50 A.D. LATIN

A a	*A a*
MODERN ROMAN (Bodoni)	MODERN ITALIC (Bodoni)

A, the first letter of the English alphabet. It was originally a consonant in the ancient Semitic alphabets. The name of the letter was *'aleph,* which meant "ox"; the symbol may have been adopted from the Egyptian hieroglyph for "ox." The Phoenician version above could be considered a profile of the animal's head. The Greeks did not need the consonant *'aleph* to write their language. When they adopted one of the Semitic alphabets (probably the Phoenician), they changed *'aleph* into the vowel *alpha,* with the sound of A as in "far." The symbol was turned so the "horns" pointed downward. The letter kept the same form and same sound in the Latin and Old English alphabets.

In modern English A has many sounds, as in "fate," "fat," "fare," "far," and "fall." The combination AE is usually pronounced as in "aesthetics," but occasionally as in "Aesop." AI or AY generally has a sound as in "sail" and "say," but sometimes as in "said," "aye," and "quay." The usual sound of AU and AW is as in "auto" and "saw." EA is pronounced as in "heat," "hear," "heart," "pear," and "pearl"; OA as in "oats" and "board."

A is the sixth musical note, or *la,* in the scale of C. "Class A" and "Grade A" are used to designate the best quality. In an alphabetical school grading system, A is the highest mark. The indefinite article "a" is one of two one-letter words in the English language (the other being "I").

A & P Company, the popular name of The Great Atlantic and Pacific Tea Company, one of the largest food store chains in the United States. The A & P has more than 1,000 stores in the United States and Canada. They are mainly concentrated along the East Coast of the United States.

The A & P was founded in New York City about 1860. George Huntington Hartford (1833-1917) is generally regarded as the founder. Only tea was sold at first; soon coffee and spices were added. About 1870 the company began to branch out, and gradually it added a full line of groceries. The Hartford family controlled the A & P until late 1958, when the company became a publicly owned corporation. Headquarters are in Montvale, New Jersey.

À Becket, Thomas. See BECKET, THOMAS.

A.D. See CHRONOLOGY.

À Kempis, Thomas. See KEMPIS, THOMAS À.

AA. See ALCOHOLICS ANONYMOUS.

AAA. See AMERICAN AUTOMOBILE ASSOCIATION.

AAA. See ANTIAIRCRAFT WEAPONS.

AAAS. See AMERICAN ASSOCIATION FOR THE ADVANCEMENT OF SCIENCE.

Aachen, ä'kĕn, West Germany, a city in the state of North Rhine-Westphalia. The city limits on the west follow the national border at the junction of the Belgian and Netherlands frontiers. The city is about 40 miles (64 km) west of Cologne. Aachen is the German name; the old French name, Aix-la-Chapelle, is frequently used in history. Aachen is associated with Charlemagne, and is one of the historic cities of Europe. It is famous for its hot sulfur springs.

Aachen is an industrial and railway center. Coal is mined in the vicinity. Industrial products include machinery, textiles, glass, and rubber tires.

The chief landmark is the imperial cathedral, the core of which—called the Octagon—was built by Charlemagne about 800. In this cathedral are Charlemagne's tomb and his royal marble chair, on which Holy Roman emperors were crowned until 1531. Adjoining the cathedral is the Gothic town hall, built 1300-50 on the foundations of the royal palace. In the market place in

Field Museum of Natural History
Aardvark

front of the town hall is a statue of Charlemagne. The Rhenish Westphalian Technical College is in Aachen.

In the first century A.D. the Romans used the hot springs for a health resort, which they called Aquae Grani or Aquisgranum. Charlemagne built a palace, magnificent for the time, in Aachen. In the 17th and 18th centuries the city's hot springs became the "Spa of Kings," and several international congresses were held there. The French held Aachen 1792-1815, then the Congress of Vienna gave it to Prussia. In 1944 during World War II United States troops captured Aachen. Most of the buildings were damaged or destroyed but were rebuilt and restored after the war. The cathedral was not badly damaged.

Population: 243,282.

See also AIX-LA-CHAPELLE, CONGRESS OF; AIX-LA-CHAPELLE, TREATIES OF.

Aalborg, ôl'bôrg, Denmark, a seaport and one of the nation's largest cities. It is the seat of Aalborg County. Aalborg is in northern Jutland near the eastern end of Lim Fjord, a strait connecting the Kattegat and the North Sea. The city is about 140 miles (225 km) northwest of Copenhagen. Aalborg is a regional center of transportation, commerce, and manufacturing. Products include cement, textiles, liquor, ships, and tobacco items. Nearby is Rebild National Park, a gift to Denmark from Danes who emigrated to the United States.

The site of Aalborg was settled by Vikings in the eighth century. Aalborg was chartered as a city in 1342. It became a leading port and commercial center late in the 19th century with the beginning of industrialization in Denmark.

Population: 154,074.

Aalto, äl'tŏ, **Alvar** (1898-1976), a Finnish architect and furniture designer. His functional, irregularly shaped buildings harmonize in both form and material with the natural environment. Among his many works are National Pensions Institute, House of Culture, and Finlandia House—all in Helsinki—and Baker House, a dormitory at Massachusetts Institute of Technology. He also designed the furniture and lighting fixtures for many of his buildings. Aalto was born in central Finland and studied in Helsinki.

Aardvark, ärd'värk', an African mammal. The name means "earth pig" in Afrikaans. Aardvarks live in burrows in open country south of the Sahara wherever termites, their main food, are numerous. An aardvark grows to 4½ to 7 feet (1.4-2.1 m) long, including the muscular, 2-foot (60-cm) tail, and is about 2 feet tall at the shoulder. It weighs between 110 and 155 pounds (50-70 kg). The aardvark has a long, narrow head, long ears, and a blunt snout. Its strong front legs have large, sharp claws, with which it digs rapidly. The coat has coarse gray or black hair.

The aardvark hunts at night. It locates termites by scent and by listening for them. It digs into termite nests or gathers up marching termites with its sticky tongue.

The Cathedral at Aachen
German Tourist Information Office

The female aardvark gives birth to one young each year. Aardvarks are hunted by some Africans for their meat and skins, and are becoming scarce.

The aardvark is the sole member of the order Tubulidentata (tubule-toothed, referring to the animal's columnar teeth). The single living species of aardvark is *Orycteropus afer.*

Aardwolf, ärd'wŏŏlf', a rare, doglike mammal that lives in burrows in the open country of southern and eastern Africa. The aardwolf (meaning "earth wolf" in Afrikaans) is related to the hyena. Its length is from 2½ to 3½ feet (75-105 cm), including the 8- to 12-inch (20- to 30-cm) bushy tail. The head is small compared to the long neck, and the ears and nose are pointed. The aardwolf has a yellow-gray coat, black feet, narrow black stripes across the back, and a crest along the back and neck. Aardwolves eat termites and insect larvae, which they hunt at night by scent. The females bear from one to four young each spring.

The aardwolf is *Proteles cristatus,* the single species of its genus. It belongs to the hyena family, Hyaenidae.

Aarhus, ôr'hōōs', Denmark's second largest city. It is a seaport and the capital of Aarhus County. The city lies on the eastern coast of Jutland on Aarhus Bay, an inlet of Kattegat Strait, and is 112 miles (180 km) northwest of Copenhagen. Products include soap, margarine, machinery, refrigerators, beer, telephones, and processed foods. The University of Aarhus is here. The Old Town Museum is a reproduction of a 16th- or 17th-century Danish town, for which more than 50 original buildings were moved in from all parts of Denmark. The first settlers were Vikings of the eighth century.

Population: 245,174.

Aaron, âr'ŭn, in the Bible, the elder brother of Moses. He was a leader in the Exodus from Egypt, and the founder of the Jewish priesthood. Before the Exodus he was Moses' spokesman before Pharaoh. While Moses was on Mount Sinai receiving the Ten Commandments, Aaron made a golden calf for his people to worship. (See MOSES, subtitle *The Ten Commandments and the Covenant.*) He died on Mount Hor before the Israelites entered Canaan.

Aaron, Henry Louis (Hank) (1934-   ), a United States baseball player. His career total of 755 home runs made him the most prolific home-run hitter of all time. He had 3,771 hits during his career, set the record for total RBI's (runs batted in), and participated in 24 All-Star games. Aaron, an outfielder, played with the Braves in Milwaukee (1954-64) and Atlanta (1965-74) and with the Milwaukee Brewers (1975-76).

Aaron was born in Mobile, Alabama. He played his first professional ball game in 1952 with the Indianapolis Clowns of the Negro American League. The Braves bought his contract and he played two years of minor league ball before joining the team. He broke Babe Ruth's lifetime record of 714 home runs in 1974. (For a picture of this event, see BASEBALL, section titled *Some Baseball Terms*). He retired in 1976.

AASA. See AMERICAN ASSOCIATION OF SCHOOL ADMINISTRATORS.

AAU. See AMATEUR ATHLETIC UNION OF THE UNITED STATES.

AAUW. See AMERICAN ASSOCIATION OF UNIVERSITY WOMEN.

Abaca. See MANILA (fiber).

Abacus, ăb'á-kŭs, a calculating device of ancient origin. In its modern form, the abacus consists of a rectangular frame that can be held in the hand. In this frame are several fixed rods strung with movable beads or other counters.

The abacus is widely used in Japan, China, and other Asian countries, as well as in European Russia. In the United States, it is sometimes used as a teaching tool in elementary grades.

How the Abacus Is Used

There are several forms of abaci (or abacuses) in use. The most common form is divided by a crossbar into two rectangular sections. There are seven beads on each rod—two on one side of the crossbar and five on the other. The abacus is held so that the pairs of beads are above the bar and the groups of five below. The beads on the rod at the extreme right represent units, those on the next rod represent tens, those on the next rod represent hundreds, etc. Each bead above the crossbar represents five times the value of a bead below the crossbar. Numbers are indicated by moving beads to the crossbar, as shown in the accompanying diagrams.

The procedure for adding two numbers is shown in the diagrams. Subtraction is the opposite of addition; that is, beads are taken away from a number set at the crossbar instead of being moved to the crossbar. A

How an ⬭ABACUS⬮ Works

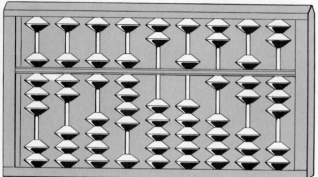

Beads on the first rod at right represent units; those on the second rod, tens; next rod, hundreds, etc. To be counted, the beads must be next to the middle crossbar; the beads above this bar count 5; those below, 1. The number shown here is 876,905,173.

Example: Add 86 to 173

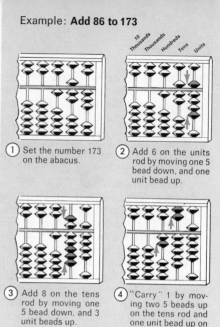

1. Set the number 173 on the abacus.

2. Add 6 on the units rod by moving one 5 bead down, and one unit bead up.

3. Add 8 on the tens rod by moving one 5 bead down, and 3 unit beads up.

4. "Carry" 1 by moving two 5 beads up on the tens rod and one unit bead up on the hundreds rod.

The answer, 259, is now set on the abacus.

---

skilled abacus operator can easily keep pace with a person using an electronic calculator in problems of addition and subtraction. Multiplication and division are more time-consuming, because they are performed by repeated addition and subtraction.

History

The abacus, in one form or another, was used in all the civilizations of antiquity. The earliest form, used several thousand years before Christ, was a dust-covered tablet on which people drew figures. (The term "abacus" comes from *abax*, a Greek word thought to be derived from an older Semitic word meaning "dust.")

The dust-covered tablet was developed into a ruled table upon which movable disks were arranged in lines. The frame containing fixed rods and movable beads is known to have been used by the Chinese as early as the 12th century, but is believed to have originated in central or western Asia rather than in China itself.

Abadan, ä'bä-dän', Iran, a city in Khuzistan province, about 410 miles (660 km) south-southwest of Teheran. It is on an island in the Shatt al Arab River, near the head of the Persian Gulf. Abadan is a major oil port in Iran, and the terminus of pipelines from nearby oil fields. The city is one of the largest oil refining centers in the world. For centuries an unimportant village, Abadan

A-4

became prominent after oil was discovered in neighboring regions in 1908.

Population: 296,081.

Abalone, ăb'á-lō'nĕ, a marine snail. It is also called ear shell and ormer. Abalones are distantly related to limpets. They live in warm areas of the Pacific Ocean, in the Indian Ocean, and on Europe's coasts.

An abalone's shell is roughly ear-shaped and has a row of three to eight small holes near one edge. It grows to a length of more than 12 inches (30 cm). The shell is lined with a pearly layer and is used to make mother-of-pearl buttons and ornaments.

An abalone clings with its powerful foot to rocks either in the surf or at depths of about 60 feet (18 m). It eats seaweed and microscopic algae. If cooked until tender, the foot is delicious to eat. Fishing for abalones is strictly regulated in California, the only state in the United States where they are found.

There are about 100 species of abalones in the abalone family, Haliotidae. The three most common California species are: the red abalone, *Haliotus rufescens;* the green, or blue, abalone, *H. fulgens;* and the black abalone, *H. cracherodii.*

Abandonment, á-băn'dŭn-mĕnt, in law, the voluntary giving up of property or of certain rights. A person may give up personal property by discarding it and not reclaiming it. Anyone then may appropriate the property. Real property, such as land, however, is not subject to legal abandonment.

Abandonment also means the desertion of family. The abandonment of a child by a parent is a crime. Abandoment of a wife or husband may be a ground for divorce.

Abattoir. See MEAT PACKING, subtitle *The Packinghouse.*

Abbas I. See PERSIA, subtitle *Persia as an Independent State.*

Abbasid Caliphate, ăb′*a*-sĭd, the third caliphate of the Moslem community, 750-1258. See CALIPH.

Abbe, ăb′ĕ, **Cleveland** (1838-1916), a United States meteorologist, often called the "father of the Weather Bureau." As director of the Cincinnati Observatory, 1868-73, Abbe issued daily weather reports, which led to the federal government's establishment of a national weather service. He joined the newly organized Weather Service in 1871, serving as a meteorologist until 1916. Abbe was influential in securing the adoption of standard time zones. He was born in New York City and graduated from New York Free Academy (later City University of New York).

Abbe, äb′ĕ, **Ernst** (1840-1905), a German physicist and industrialist noted for his researches in optics (the study of light). Abbe improved the quality of optical glass and developed new optical instruments, including the Abbe refractometer. He became director of research at the optical works of Carl Zeiss in 1866 and helped make the firm world famous. After Zeiss's death in 1888, Abbe became sole owner and introduced many advanced labor policies. He taught at the University of Jena and was director of its observatories, 1878-89.

Abbé Prévost. See PRÉVOST D'EXILES, ANTOINE FRANÇOIS.

Abbess. See ABBOT.

Abbey, Edwin Austin (1852-1911), a United States illustrator and painter. His pen-and-ink drawings of 17th- and 18th-century British life brought him fame. He illustrated *She Stoops to Conquer* (1886) and *Old Songs* (1889) and many Shakespeare plays.

Abbey was born in Philadelphia. After attending the Pennsylvania Academy of Fine Arts, he began his career as an illustrator for *Harper's Weekly.* In 1878 he settled in England. Abbey was elected to the Royal Academy in 1898 and to the National Academy in 1902.

His many historical paintings include the mural

Yale University Art Gallery
Edwin Austin Abbey's illustration of *King Lear,* Act III, Scene IV. The pen-and-ink drawing, done in 1902, shows King Lear, near madness, approaching Edgar, disguised as a madman, while wandering on the heath during a storm. At the right are the Earl of Kent and the frightened Fool.

decoration *The Quest of the Holy Grail* in the Boston Public Library.

See also REVOLUTIONARY WAR, AMERICAN (illustration).

Abbey. See ABBOT; MONASTICISM, subtitle *Monastic Life:* A Monastery.

Abbey Theatre, the national theater of Ireland, located in Dublin. It won worldwide attention for the plays introduced there and for its acting company, which frequently went on foreign tours. The Abbey players toured the United States four times between 1911 and 1938. Dudley Digges, Barry Fitzgerald, Arthur Shields, and Sara Allgood were prominent in the acting company. Among the playwrights who won reputations at the Abbey were Sean O'Casey, J. M. Synge, Padraic Colum, Lady Gregory, W. B. Yeats, and Lord Dunsany.

W. B. Yeats and others organized the Irish Literary Theatre Society in 1899. Its name later was changed to Irish National Theatre Society. The society played a lead-

Consulate General of Ireland

New Abbey Theatre in Dublin

ing role in the Irish Literary Revival. In 1904 Annie E. F. Horniman, an English theater manager, gave the society financial aid and granted it free use of the Abbey Theatre. The playhouse was bought for the society by public subscription in 1910. It later received a government subsidy. In 1951 the theater burned down and the company was housed in the Queens theater, a former variety house, until it occupied a new-built playhouse in 1966.

Abbot, Charles Greeley (1872-1973), a United States astrophysicist and authority on solar radiation. As director of the Smithsonian Astrophysical Observatory, 1907-44, Abbot studied the influence of solar radiation on climate and weather cycles. He perfected instruments for measuring radiation. With Samuel P. Langley, he mapped the infrared spectrum. Abbot was secretary of the Smithsonian Institution from 1928 until 1944, when he became research associate. He was born in Wilton, New Hampshire, and was graduated from Massachusetts Institute of Technology.

His writings include *The Sun* (1911) and *The Earth and the Stars* (1925, revised edition 1946).

Abbot, the head of an abbey for men. The head of an abbey for women is an abbess. An abbey is the name for a monastery or convent in certain religious orders. It often has subordinate units called priories. A priory is headed by a prior or prioress, who ranks below an abbot or abbess. In a few orders, however, a priory is an independent monastery or convent.

The abbot is elected, normally for life, by the monks of the abbey. He must be a priest and at least 30 years old. The abbot is ruler, teacher, and spiritual father of his monks, who owe him complete obedience. Most abbots are exempt from the jurisdiction of the bishops of their dioceses. Abbots rank next after bishops in the church hierarchy and have the right to vote in some church councils.

In the early years of monasticism the term "abbot" was applied to any monk noted for piety, but soon it was restricted to the head

of an abbey. The first abbots were laymen, but after the seventh century most of them were priests. In 826 a council restricted the office to ordained priests. As many abbeys grew in wealth some fell into the hands of abbots *in commendam* (in trust), who were often laymen. These lay abbots did not perform the duties but took the major part of the revenues. Attempts were made to end this abuse in the 10th century, but it developed again in the 13th and 14th centuries, and continued in France until the French Revolution of 1789.

See also MONASTICISM.

Abbott, the family name of two United States authors, father and son.

Jacob Abbott (1803-1879) was known chiefly for his 28 *Rollo* books, begun in 1834. These describe the imaginary adventures of a model American boy at home and abroad. Abbott wrote and edited about 200 fiction and history books designed to instruct youth in morals. He also wrote books with his brother, John Stevens Cabot Abbott (1805-1887), an author of popular histories and biographies. Jacob Abbott was born in Hallowell, Maine. After graduation from Bowdoin College, he studied at Andover Theological Seminary. He then taught natural philosophy and mathematics at Amherst College until he founded the Mount Vernon School for Girls in 1829. In 1833 he became a Congregational pastor. His writing success began with *The Young Christian* (1832).

Lyman Abbott (1835-1922), the son, was born in Roxbury, Massachusetts. He left his law practice in 1860 to become a Congregational clergyman. In 1881 he succeeded Henry Ward Beecher as editor of *The Christian Union* (later *The Outlook*), and after Beecher's death in 1887 he took his place as pastor of Plymouth Congregational Church. Abbott, a liberal, wrote *Theology of an Evolutionist* (1897) and other books.

Abbott, Grace (1878-1939), a United States social worker especially interested in child welfare. She was born in Grand Island, Nebraska, and was graduated from Grand Island College and the University of Chicago. While a resident at Hull House in Chicago, she headed the Immigrants' Protective League. From 1921 to 1934 she was chief of the U.S. Children's Bureau, following which she was professor of public welfare administration at the University of Chicago School of Social Service Administration from 1934 until her death. Her books include *The Immigrant and the Community* (1917) and *The Child and the State* (2 volumes, 1938).

Edith Abbott (1876-1957), her sister, was dean of the University of Chicago School of Social Service Administration from 1924 to 1942. She wrote *Women in Industry* (1910).

Abbott, Jacob. See ABBOTT (family).

Abbott, Sir **John Joseph Caldwell** (1821-1893), a Canadian statesman. A Conservative, Abbott was prime minister of Canada, 1891-92. He was born in St. Andrews, Lower Canada (now Quebec). He studied law at McGill University, and was its dean of law, 1855-80. During 1859-74 and 1880-93 Abbott served in the Legislative Assembly and then in the House of Commons. He was appointed to the Dominion Senate in 1887. Later that year he became minister without portfolio in Sir John A. Macdonald's cabinet. Abbott was knighted in 1892.

Abbott, John Stevens Cabot. See ABBOTT (Jacob Abbott).

Abbott, Lyman. See ABBOTT (family).

Abbreviation, ă-brē'vĭ-ā'shŭn, a short, incomplete form of a word or name used in writing or in speaking to save space or effort. Generally, a word is abbreviated only if it contains at least four letters. Abbreviations are widely used in informal or technical writing, but in formal or literary writing they are considered inappropriate, with certain exceptions. Among these exceptions are titles of address such as *Mr.* and *Dr.,* and academic or honorary degrees such as *B.A.* and *LL.D.* Oral abbreviations are a form of slang; examples are *math, gym,* and *exams.*

Lists of common abbreviations are found in most dictionaries, and special lists are printed in textbooks and other works in specialized fields.

Written Abbreviations

The simplest form of written abbreviation is one in which the latter part of the word is omitted and the omission indicated by a period—for example, *pres.* for president. Sometimes all but the initial letter is omitted —as in *S.* for south. A single-letter abbreviation is usually written as a capital. When a simple abbreviation is read aloud, the full word is pronounced.

Multiword Names and Phrases. Organization, agency, and company names of more than two words are often written in abbreviated form by using the initial letter of each word—*YMCA* (Young Men's Christian Association), *PTA* (Parent-Teacher Association), *IBM* (International Business Machines [Corporation]), and *FBI* (Federal Bureau of Investigation). The tendency is to omit periods in names of organizations. When a place name of several words is abbreviated to initial letters, however, periods are used—*U.S.A., N.Y.,* and *D.C.* The periods are retained also in academic and professional degrees and titles—*B.A., M.D.,* and *J.D.*

Generally, an initial-letters abbreviation is spoken exactly as written—for example, "F-B-I." However, if there are more than three letters and they form a pronounceable word, the tendency is to pronounce the abbreviation as a word. For example, *UNESCO* (United Nations Educational, Scientific and Cultural Organization) is pronounced "ū-nĕs'kō." In military usage, especially, there is a tendency to make words of abbreviations, such as the *WAC's* (wăks) and *NATO* (nā'tō). In some cases extra letters are included with the initial letters so that a word will be formed, as in *CINCPAC* (sĭnk'păk) for Commander in Chief, Pacific.

The abbreviations of many commonly used expressions are more widely known than the expressions themselves—*C.O.D.* (cash on delivery), *I.Q.* (intelligence quotient), and *f.o.b.* (free on board [a ship or train that had conveyed the merchandise to market], meaning that the buyer pays no extra transportation charges).

Contractions. Another way of abbreviating a word is to form a *contraction,* leaving out various letters in the body of the word, but usually retaining the last letter. The omission may be indicated by an apostrophe, or a period may be used to identify the word as an abbreviation—*nat'l* or *natl.* for national, *att'n* or *attn.* for attention, *mfg.* for manufacturing, and *Ga.* for Georgia. A contraction is usually read as the word or phrase it represents in English, even though it may have been formed from foreign words. (See the discussion in this article on *Foreign Abbreviations in English.*)

Plural Forms. An English abbreviation is made plural by adding an *s* (*pars.* for paragraphs, *qts.* for quarts) or by the Latin method of doubling the letter (*pp.* for pages).

Foreign Abbreviations in English. Some commonly used abbreviations are short forms of Latin words, but are normally translated into English when read aloud. These include *i.e.* for *id est,* translated "that is"; *e.g.* for *exempli gratia,* "for example"; and *lb.* for *libra,* "pound." An abbreviation from the early Christian Era is *X* for Christ, which in the Greek alphabet has the initial letter *chi,* written *X.* This abbreviation survives in "Xmas."

Technical Abbreviations

All units of measurement with names of more than three letters have abbreviations that are used in technical writing and sometimes in informal, nontechnical writing. Examples include *hr.* and *min., mo.* and *wk., gal.* and *oz.,* and *mph.* The capacity of an air conditioner is commonly stated in *Btu's* and that of an electric motor in *hp* and *rpm's.*

Every professional activity, especially in the scientific fields, has abbreviations unique to its own literature. In many fields symbols are used in place of or in addition to abbreviations. For an example, see CHEMISTRY, section "The Fundamentals of Chemistry," subtitle *Chemical Symbols, Formulas, and Equations:* Symbols; and the symbol column in the table *The Chemical Elements.* For examples of symbols international in use, see SYMBOL.

Oral Abbreviations

There is a tendency in everyday speech to shorten commonly used words. The coffee in the percolator *perks;* a person turns on the *TV* to see the *ball game* (for baseball game). By usage some oral abbreviations become established as words—for example, *bus* (from omnibus), *pop* (from soda pop), *plane, flu* (from influenza), and *phone.* Another type of oral abbreviation is the contraction of some negative verb forms, which are written informally as they are pronounced—*can't, didn't,* and *wasn't.*

Nicknames. In everyday speech a given name is frequently reduced to a short form that in time becomes recognized as a nickname. Often the familiar form is a simple abbreviation, although there may be a slight change of spelling—for example, Mike for Michael. When changes are more extensive, as in Peg for Margaret, or Dick for Richard, the nickname is a *derivation* (outgrowth) rather than an abbreviation.

A nickname may also be a *diminutive—* an abbreviation or other short form with a new ending denoting familiarity and affection—such as Danny for Daniel, or Ginny for Virginia.

History

In the pre-Christian era the Greeks and Romans used abbreviations freely in inscriptions carved in stone or painted on pottery, as well as in business and government records and legal documents. In literary manuscripts, however, generally only proper names and numerals were abbreviated. The usual method of writing an abbreviation was to use the first letter or letters of a word and put a horizontal bar above them or place the last included letter above the line. For example, *senatus* (senate) might be abbreviated as $\overline{sen}$ or se^n.

In about 63 B.C. Marcus Tullius Tiro, a scribe for Cicero, devised a complete system of shorthand, composed of some 500 abbreviations and symbols. The Tironian Notes were used for more than 1,000 years, and one of the symbols, the ampersand (&), is still in use.

During the Middle Ages abbreviations and contractions were used more and more freely in both Latin and Byzantine manuscripts. The practice of abbreviating in literary works declined after printing was introduced in the 15th century, but continued in handwritten matter. The identifying horizontal bar was replaced by a concluding colon, and finally by a period.

In the late 18th and early 19th centuries, the complimentary close of a letter, customarily very long, was often abbreviated. Examples include "yr. mo. ob. serv. (your most obedient servant), Th: Jefferson," and, on a letter written by John Tyler, "Yrs &c." The old Latin custom of placing the last letter of an abbreviation above the line was adapted to contractions in titles such as Maj^r, and Brig^{dr}, as well as in given names. For examples, see AUTOGRAPH for signatures of signers of the Declaration of Inde-

Dictionaries of Abbreviations

Buttress, F. A. *World Guide to Abbreviations of Organizations,* 5th edition (Gale, 1975).

Crowley, E. T., editor. *Acronyms, Initialisms, and Abbreviations Dictionary,* 6th edition (3 volumes; Gale, 1978-80).

DeSola, Ralph. *Abbreviations Dictionary,* 5th edition (Elsevier North-Holland, 1977).

Paxton, John, editor. *Dictionary of Abbreviations* (Rowman & Littlefield, 1973).

pendence, and UNITED STATES CONSTITU-
TION for the signers of the Constitution.

For some abbreviations in common use,
see COMPASS, box *Points of the Compass;*
DEGREE; UNITED STATES, table *States of
the United States;* WEIGHTS AND MEAS-
URES, *Tables of Weights and Measures.*

ABC. See AMERICAN BROADCASTING
COMPANIES, INC.

ABC Powers, a short term for three
principal nations of South America—
Argentina, Brazil, and Chile. The term was
first used in 1914 when the three countries
mediated the dispute between the United
States and Mexico that followed the occupation of Veracruz by U.S. Marines. In 1915
the three nations signed the ABC Treaty, an
agreement to arbitrate their disputes.

Abd-el-Krim, ăb'dĕl-krĭm' (1880?-1963),
a Moorish chieftain, leader of the Riff tribes
in Morocco. His revolt against Spanish rule
in Morocco was successful during 1921-24.
Then his forces attacked the French Zone,
but were defeated in 1926 by combined
Spanish and French armies. Although exiled
for more than 20 years on the island of
Réunion, Abd-el-Krim remained a national
hero. In 1947 he fled to Egypt, becoming a
leader of the North African nationalist
movement. His exploits in Morocco inspired
Sigmund Romberg's operetta *The Desert
Song* (1926).

Abdias. See OBADIAH.

Abdication, ăb'dĭ-kā'shŭn, the formal
surrender of sovereign authority by a ruler,
usually a monarch. A number of monarchs
have abdicated. A few have surrendered
their authority voluntarily, but most were
forced to abdicate. Voluntary abdications
often occur for reasons of age or health;
involuntary abdications result from a defeat
in war, a rivalry for power, or a general
dissatisfaction with the monarch's rule. In
some cases, a ruler has abdicated in favor of
a son or another member of the family in the
hope of later returning to power.

Voluntary royal abdications include:

Diocletian, Roman Emperor 305
Charles V, Holy Roman Emperor 1556
Christina, Queen of Sweden 1654
Edward VIII, King of Great Britain 1936
Wilhelmina, Queen of the Netherlands 1948
Charlotte, Grand Duchess of Luxembourg . . . 1964
Juliana, Queen of the Netherlands 1980

Involuntary royal abdications include:

Napoleon I, Emperor of France . . . . 1814 & 1815
Charles X, King of France 1830

Pedro I, Emperor of Brazil 1831
Louis Philippe, King of France 1848
Isabella II, Queen of Spain 1870
Nicholas II, Czar of Russia 1917
William II, Emperor of Germany 1918
Constantine I, King of Greece 1922
Leopold III, King of Belgium 1951
Farouk, King of Egypt 1952
Saud Ibn, King of Saudi Arabia 1964
Idris, King of Libya 1969

Abdomen, ăb'dō-mĕn; ăb-dō'mĕn, in
mammals, including man, a cavity in which
are found the digestive organs; the spleen;
kidneys; bladder; and, in the female, the
reproductive organs. In most other animals,
the abdomen contains only the digestive
organs. In insects and several kinds of
arthropods (animals having jointed legs), the
term refers to the posterior section of the
body. The rest of this article is concerned
with the abdomen of mammals.

The abdomen, commonly called the belly,
has the diaphragm for its upper boundary
and the pelvis for its lower boundary. The
front wall of the cavity is formed by solid
layers of muscles called the abdominal muscles. The posterior wall is formed by the
spine and the muscles of the back. A thin
membrane, the *peritoneum,* lines the abdomen.

The upper section of the abdominal cavity
contains the liver, gall bladder, pancreas,
stomach, spleen, and a portion of the large
intestine. The central portion of the cavity
contains the small intestine, and behind this
the kidneys and ureters. The large intestine
lies at the sides. The lower, or pelvic, region
of the abdomen encloses the bladder and the
female reproductive organs.

Abduction, ăb-dŭk'shŭn, in law, the act
of removing a person by force or by fraud

Organs of the Abdomen

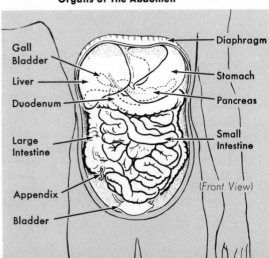

Gall Bladder

Liver

Duodenum

Large Intestine

Appendix

Bladder

Diaphragm

Stomach

Pancreas

Small Intestine

(Front View)

from the protection or custody of a husband, parent, or legal guardian. The term may be used as a synonym for kidnapping, but is usually limited to the taking away of a woman for marriage or immoral purposes. The crime is variously defined under state laws. The taking, or enticing, away of a woman even when she is willing is abduction if she is below the age of consent, usually 18.

See also KIDNAPPING.

Abdul Hamid II, äb′dül-hä-mēd′ (1842-1918), sultan of Turkey, 1876-1909, and the last absolute monarch of the Ottoman Empire. He succeeded his brother who had been deposed by the liberals later known as the Young Turks. Abdul Hamid was forced to approve a constitution, but the war with Russia, 1877-78, gave him the opportunity to regain absolute authority. In 1908 he was forced to restore constitutional government, and the next year he was deposed.

Abdul-Jabbar, Kareem (1947-   ), a professional basketball player, considered one of the greatest centers in the history of the game. Abdul-Jabbar, 7′ 2″ tall, was drafted by the Milwaukee Bucks of the National Basketball Association in 1969 and led the team to its first championship in 1971. In 1975 he was traded to the Los Angeles Lakers in exchange for five players.

Abdul-Jabbar was born Ferdinand Lewis Alcindor in New York City. He changed his name in 1971 when he became a member of a black Islamic sect. He gained national fame as a high school player at Power Memorial in New York. In college, Abdul-Jabbar led the University of California at Los Angeles (UCLA) to three national championships (1967-68-69). For photo, see BEARD.

Abel, ā′bĕl, in the Bible, the second son of Adam and Eve, and brother of Cain. Abel was a shepherd, Cain a farmer. Each brought offerings to the Lord: Cain the first fruits of the ground, Abel the first-born of the flock. God accepted Abel's offerings but rejected Cain's. In a jealous rage Cain killed his brother (Genesis 4:1-8). The story reflects the belief of nomads that God preferred herding to farming.

See also CAIN.

Abel, Sir **Frederick Augustus** (1827-1902), a British chemist. He was an authority on explosives. With Sir James Dewar, Abel invented cordite, a smokeless gunpowder, in 1889. He developed the Abel tester

for determining the flash point of petroleum. From 1854 to 1888, Abel was chemist to the British War Department. He was created a baronet in 1893.

Abelard, ăb′ĕ-lärd, **Peter** (*French: Pierre Abélard,* à′bā′lär′) (1079-1142), a French philosopher and theologian. A keen and bold thinker, he was one of the most brilliant of the medieval Schoolmen, or Scholastics. Through his insistence on the need for reason and proof Abelard helped pave the way for scientific and rational methods in philosophy and theology. His popular fame, however, sprang not from his scholarly achievements, but from his tragic love affair with Héloïse.

Abelard was born near Nantes, eldest son of a Breton noble. Renouncing his birthright, he went to Paris and studied philosophy. The school he later founded in the Abbey of Ste. Geneviève eventually developed into the University of Paris. In 1113 he studied theology under Anselm of Laon. Abelard disagreed with him, as he did with most of his other teachers.

Abelard and Héloïse

Fulbert, canon of Notre Dame, engaged Abelard as a tutor for his beautiful and talented niece Héloïse (1101?-1164). They fell in love and ran away together. After a son, Astrolabus, was born to them, Abelard and Héloïse were married. However, Fulbert, incensed at the relationship, hired ruffians to attack and castrate Abelard, who then took refuge in a monastery at St. Denis. Héloïse became a nun in the convent of St. Argenteuil. The love letters they exchanged survive as classics of literature.

Abelard began lecturing on theology again, often disputing official church doctrine. In 1121 he was denounced by the synod of Soissons and compelled to burn his book on the Trinity. Saint Bernard of Clairvaux became his relentless opponent. Abelard fled to Nogent-sur-Seine. His loyal students followed him and built for him the Oratory of the Paraclete (Holy Spirit or Comforter). Later he gave the Paraclete to Héloïse to house a sisterhood she had organized.

Bernard managed to have Abelard condemned by the Council of Sens in 1141 and by Pope Innocent II a year later. Abelard set out for Rome to plead his cause, but was taken ill and died at St. Marcel. He was buried at the Paraclete. Upon her death in

1164 Héloïse was buried beside him. In 1817 their remains were entombed together in the Père Lachaise cemetery in Paris.

Abelard's writings include *Sic et Non* ("Yes and No"), an objective account of theological controversies; a series of commentaries on Aristotle's logical writings; and *Historia Calamitatum Mearum* ("The Story of My Misfortunes").

Abenaki. See ABNAKI INDIANS.

Abercromby, ăb'ĕr-krŏm'bĭ, **James** (1706-1781), a British general. Abercromby assumed command of British and colonial forces in America in March, 1758, during the French and Indian War. At Ticonderoga in July, 1758, he led a bloody but unsuccessful attack against a smaller French force under Montcalm. He was then relieved of his command and recalled to England.

Abercromby was born in Scotland. He entered upon a career in the army and served as a member of Parliament, 1734-54. He was sent to America in 1756 as second in command to Lord Loudoun.

Abercromby, Sir **Ralph** (1734-1801), a British general. He was noted for having restored discipline and military effectiveness to the army. Abercromby joined the army in 1756 and served in the Seven Years' War. He was a member of Parliament, 1774-80. His generalship during the campaign in Flanders, 1794-95, gained him the admiration of the army. Abercromby led the British troops that captured the West Indies, 1795-96. Commanding the British Mediterranean expedition, he conducted a brilliant amphibious assault at Abukir Bay in March, 1801, after which he defeated the French at Alexandria. He was mortally wounded in the battle.

Aberdeen, ăb'ĕr-dēn', George Hamilton Gordon, Fourth **Earl of** (1784-1860), a British statesman. He was prime minister, 1852-55. Although successful in domestic affairs, the Aberdeen ministry was forced into the disastrous Crimean War. As foreign secretary under Sir Robert Peel, 1841-46, Aberdeen improved relations with France, ended the Anglo-Chinese (Opium) War, and through the Webster-Ashburton and Oregon treaties peacefully settled disputes between Great Britain and the United States.

Aberdeen, John Campbell Gordon, Seventh **Earl of** (1847-1934), a British administrator, the grandson of the fourth Earl. From 1893 to 1898, Aberdeen was governor general of Canada. Both he and his wife were active in social welfare work in Cana-

da. Aberdeen served as lord lieutenant of Ireland in 1886 and from 1905 to 1915. In 1915 he was created the first Marquess of Aberdeen and Temair.

Aberdeen, ăb'ĕr-dēn'; ăb'ĕr-dēn, Scotland, a city on the North Sea. It lies at the mouths of the Dee and Don rivers, 90 miles (145 km) north-northeast of Edinburgh. Aberdeen is often called the Granite City because of its many fine granite buildings made of stone from nearby quarries.

Aberdeen is the shipping and commercial center of northern Scotland, partly because of its excellent harbor and port. Many petroleum companies use Aberdeen as the operational center for the development of North Sea oil. From the city's factories and mills come textiles, paper, Scotch whisky, and polished granite. Its shipbuilding industry serves mainly the fishing fleet, which has long been one of the largest in Great Britain. Many industries are based on the processing of fish and of farm products. Aberdeen Angus, originally bred in the Aberdeen area, is an internationally known breed of cattle. Many tourists are attracted by Aberdeen's old buildings, resorts, and beaches.

The University of Aberdeen was formed in 1860 by the union of King's College (founded 1494) and Marischal College (1593). The city's art gallery has a large collection of 19th- and 20th- century paintings and sculptures. The Cathedral of St. Machar (completed 1498), built upon the remains of a sixth-century Norman church, is probably the most impressive church in the city.

Little is known of Aberdeen until 1179, when it was made a royal burgh. The city was twice burned by Edward III of England early in the 14th century and was plundered by the Earl of Montrose, a Scottish soldier, in 1644 during the Great Rebellion. Aberdeen's chief periods of growth and prosperity came with its industrialization in the 19th century and with the development of North Sea oil in the 1970's.

Population: 208,569.

Aberdeen, South Dakota, the seat of Brown County. It is 117 miles (188 km) northeast of Pierre. Products include automobile parts, tools, and computer components. Aberdeen is an agricultural marketing center. Northern State College is here.

Aberdeen was founded in 1881 with the coming of the Milwaukee Road railway and

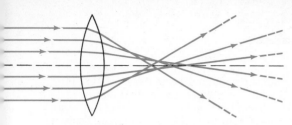

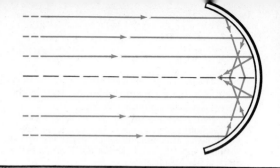

Spherical Aberration in a convex lens, at left, and in a spherical concave mirror, at right. Rays of light striking near the edges of the lens or mirror are brought to focus closer to the lens or mirror than are the central rays.

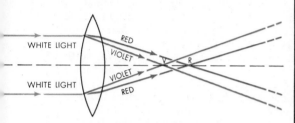

Chromatic Aberration in a convex lens. When rays of white light (which contains all colors) strike the lens, violet light is refracted more than red light.

was named after Aberdeen, Scotland. It was incorporated as a town in 1882 and chartered as a city in 1883. The Fischer quintuplets—the first surviving quintuplets to be born in the United States—were born here in 1963. Aberdeen has the commission form of government.

Population: 25,851.

Aberdeen Angus. See CATTLE, subtitle *Breeds of Beef Cattle: Aberdeen Angus.*

Aberration, ăb'ĕr-ā'shŭn, in optics, a condition that causes blurring, loss of clearness, or distortion of shape in the images formed by lenses or curved mirrors. Although it is impossible to produce a telescope, microscope, camera lens, or other optical device that is free from aberrations, optical engineers can eliminate or reduce most of these effects by careful design. The two most familiar types of aberration are *chromatic aberration* and *spherical aberration.*

Distortion in a lens. In this type of aberration, the image of a square object, shown at the left, assumes the shape of either a pincushion, center, or a barrel, right.

Chromatic aberration occurs when a ray of light containing more than one color (for example, a ray of white light) is spread out slightly by refraction when it passes through a lens. (See REFRACTION.) The resulting image is surrounded by blurred, colored fringes. Chromatic aberration does not occur in images formed by mirrors. The absence of this type of aberration is one of the most important advantages of the reflecting telescope over the refracting.

Spherical aberration occurs when light rays striking near the edges of a lens or curved mirror are brought to a focus closer to the lens or mirror than are the central rays. The result is that the image of a point appears as a small disk.

Other aberrations, known as *coma, astigmatism, curvature of field,* and *distortion,* can also occur when the source of the image, or any part of the source, is not on the optical axis of the lens or mirror.

Aberration of Light, a phenomenon in which a star or other celestial body, as viewed from the earth, appears to be slightly displaced from its true position. This phenomenon, which was first explained by the English astronomer James Bradley in 1729, occurs because (1) the earth is constantly moving in its orbit around the sun and (2) light travels through space at a finite speed (about 186,000 miles per second [300,000 km/s]). If the earth were stationary, or if light traveled through space instantaneously, the aberration phenomenon would not exist.

The traces left by raindrops on the side windows of a moving automobile provide an analogy to the aberration of light. Even if the rain is coming straight down, the traces will be at an angle.

Abidjan, ăb'ĭ-jän', Ivory Coast, the nation's capital, largest city, and chief port. It lies on Ebrié Lagoon, an inlet of the Gulf of Guinea. Abidjan is the country's leading commercial, industrial, and transportation center. Industries include oil refining, textile milling, food processing, and automobile assembling. The University of Abidjan and a national museum of art and ethnology are here. The city first gained importance after 1903 as the southern terminus of the nation's only railway. It was made the capital in 1935. Completion of the Vridi Canal in 1950, enabling deep-draft vessels to enter Abidjan's harbor, contributed greatly to the city's growth.

Population: 555,000.

Abilene, ăb'ĭ-lēn, Kansas, the seat of Dickinson County, in the northeastern part of the state. Abilene has several manufacturing industries but is primarily a marketing and transportation center for locally raised grain and livestock. The Eisenhower Center —which includes President Dwight D. Eisenhower's boyhood home, his grave, and a library and museum—is here. Abilene was settled in 1858 and became the terminus of the Kansas Pacific Railroad in 1867 and the railhead for cattle driven northward over the Chisholm Trail. The city was incorporated in 1869. "Wild Bill" Hickok served as marshal in 1871.

Population: 6,572.

Abilene, Texas, the seat of Taylor County. It is 150 miles (240 km) west-southwest of Fort Worth. Abilene is a processing and marketing center for the surrounding farming, ranching, and oil-producing region. Products include appliances, plumbing fixtures, band instruments, and components for the aerospace industry. McMurry College, Abilene Christian University, and Hardin-Simmons University are here.

In 1881 the site of Abilene became the terminus of the Texas and Pacific Railway. The city was founded in 1882 by a group of landowners and named after Abilene, Kansas. It owes its growth to the presence of the railway, the discovery of oil in the area, and the establishment nearby in 1941 of Camp Barkeley, now Dyess Air Force Base. Abilene has the council-manager form of government.

Population: 98,315.

Abilene Christian University. See UNIVERSITIES AND COLLEGES (table).

Abimelech, ȧ-bĭm'ē-lĕk, the name of two early Biblical figures. The first was a Philistine king of Gerar who had friendly dealings with Abraham and Isaac (Genesis 21:22-34; 26:26-31). The later Abimelech was a Hebrew judge, the son of Gideon, or Jerubbaal

(Judges 9). His career was bloody, beginning with the murder of his 70 half brothers. His own life ended violently.

ABM. See MISSILES AND ROCKETS, section "Military Missiles," subtitle *ABM System.*

Abnaki (or **Abenaki) Indians,** ăb-nä'ki, a group of related Algonquian-speaking tribes. Originally, they were divided into two branches. The eastern Abnaki, which included the Kennebec and Penobscot tribes, were located along the Maine coast and were principally a fishing people. The western Abnaki, which included the Winnipesaukee and Pennacook, lived in New Hampshire, Vermont, Massachusetts, and Quebec, and were mainly hunters and farmers. In the 1700's, the Abnaki joined with the Malecite, Passamaquoddy, and Micmac tribes to form the Abnaki Confederacy, which became allied with the French. Most Abnaki were driven into Canada by the British.

There are about 1,000 Abnaki, mainly Penobscots, on the Penobscot reservation in Maine, and about 1,000 descendants of western and eastern Abnaki tribes in Quebec. The latter are sometimes called the St. Francis Indians.

Abnormal Psychology. See PSYCHOLOGY, subtitle *Branches of Psychology* (Clinical Psychology).

Abo. See TURKU.

Abolitionist, ăb'ō-lĭsh'ŭn-ĭst, in United States history, a person who urged the immediate freeing of the slaves regardless of the Constitution, laws, or property rights. Quakers, notably Benjamin Lundy, began antislavery societies in 1815, but the abolition movement did not become nationally important until the founding in 1831 of *The Liberator* by William Lloyd Garrison. The Nat Turner insurrection in Virginia the same year caused immediate reaction in the South, which became united against all antislavery proposals. In the North also abolitionists met with denunciation and violence. A mob in Alton, Illinois, killed Elijah P. Lovejoy, an abolitionist editor. Nevertheless the movement grew rapidly.

Garrison opposed action as a political party and avoided alignment with other antislavery groups. A faction rejecting his leadership formed the Liberty party, which ran James G. Birney for President in 1840 and 1844. It then merged with the Free Soil party, which opposed the extension of slavery, but did not try to abolish it.

Abolitionist leaders included Wendell Phillips, lawyer; John Greenleaf Whittier, poet; Henry Ward Beecher, Theodore Parker, and Theodore Weld, preachers; Angelina Grimké, who became Mrs. Weld; and her sister Sarah Grimké.

Abolitionists were outraged by passage of the Fugitive Slave Law of 1850 and became active in the "underground railroad" to smuggle runaway slaves to freedom. Most abolitionists supported the Republican party when it was formed, but many were unhappy over the moderate proposals of its early platforms. Garrison was ready to end the abolition movement in 1865, but Phillips kept it alive until 1870, when its purposes seemed to be achieved by passage of the 15th Amendment to the Constitution.

For further information, see:

Biographies

BEECHER, HENRY W.	PARKER, THEODORE
BIRNEY, JAMES G.	PHILLIPS, WENDELL
BROWN, JOHN	SUMNER, CHARLES
DOUGLASS, FREDERICK	TAPPAN (family)
GARRISON, WILLIAM L.	TURNER, NAT
LOVEJOY (family)	WHITTIER, JOHN G.
LUNDY, BENJAMIN	

Miscellaneous

COMPROMISE OF 1850	LIBERTY PARTY
FREE SOIL PARTY	UNDERGROUND RAILROAD

Abomasum. See RUMINANT.

A-bomb. See NUCLEAR WEAPONS.

Abominable Snowman. See YETI.

Aborigine, an original inhabitant of a country. See AUSTRALIAN ABORIGINES; ESKIMO; INDIANS, AMERICAN.

Abortion, á-bôr'shŭn, the forcing out of the incompletely developed embryo or fetus

The Sacrifice of Abraham, oil on canvas by Giovanni Domenico Tiepolo (1727-1804), son of the Venetian painter Giovanni Battista Tiepolo.
Metropolitan Museum of Art, Purchase, 1871

from the mother's uterus, or womb. An abortion ends a pregnancy before the fetus or embryo is able to live outside the uterus. In *complete abortion* the tissues surrounding the embryo or fetus are also expelled. Abortion can occur in a pregnant woman between the time the fertilized egg attaches itself to the wall of the uterus and the time the fetus is 28 weeks old. (After the fetus is 28 weeks old, it may survive outside the uterus.)

A naturally occurring abortion is called a *spontaneous abortion* or, commonly, a *miscarriage.* It usually occurs because the uterus has rejected an abnormal embryo or fetus. Sometimes spontaneous abortion is the result of the mother's having an injury, a disease, or a deficiency of certain hormones.

An *induced abortion* is one that is caused deliberately. It is called a *therapeutic abortion* when it is performed by a physician because the life or health of the mother would be endangered if the pregnancy were to continue. Abortions for any other reason long were illegal in most of the United States. However, a 1973 decision of the U.S. Supreme Court held that the right of privacy covered a woman's right to end an unwanted pregnancy in the early stages. Induced abortions are also legal in a number of other countries, where they are often considered birth-control measures.

Aboukir (or **Abukir**) **Bay.** See NILE, BATTLE OF THE.

Abraham, ā'brá-hăm, or **Abram,** ā'brăm, in the Bible, the traditional forefather of the Hebrews and of the Ishmaelites and other Arab tribes. His narrative is found in Genesis 11:26 to 25:18. He was first known as Abram, which means "exalted father," until God called him Abraham, "father of many nations." He was the first of the three Hebrew patriarchs, the others being his son Isaac and his grandson Jacob. Abraham discarded idol worship and became the father of Jewish monotheism. Three great religions—Judaism, Christianity, and Islam—trace their origin to him.

The narratives about Abraham were Hebrew traditions for centuries before they were put into writing. He was a folk hero about whom clustered many legends, but he was certainly a historical character. He probably lived about the 14th century B.C. The details of the Biblical stories fit in well with historians' findings about this period in Babylonia and the Middle East.

A-14

Abraham was a man of faith who submitted himself completely to God's will. A native of Ur of the Chaldees, later a resident of Haran, he heeded the call of God to leave Babylonia to go "unto a land that I will show you" (Genesis 12:1).

Abraham left his native land with his wife Sarah (or Sarai, the original form) and his nephew Lot. At the age of 75 he gave up his settled life and became a nomad in the Negev, the desert region of southern Canaan. God promised that this land would be given to his descendants. Later, even though Abraham and Sarah had no children, God renewed His promise and assured him that the land would be given to his descendants. This promise was called a covenant, or agreement. Finally, Isaac was born as the child of promise although Sarah was advanced in years.

Abraham had other sons. By Hagar, Sarah's Egyptian maid, he had Ishmael, who became the forefather of the Ishmaelites. By Keturah he had six sons, from whom sprang other Arab tribes. Abraham died at the age of 175 and was buried in a cave near the site of Hebron in southern Canaan.

Judaism regards Abraham as the father of the Jewish people. Christianity looks upon Abraham as its spiritual ancestor on account of his faith. His readiness to offer his son Isaac as a human sacrifice became the model of perfect submission to the will of God. Moslems believe that Abraham and Ishmael built the shrine of the Kaaba in Mecca, and assert that since Abraham was a man who submitted himself completely to God he was one of them.

See also ISAAC; ISHMAEL; JACOB; LOT; UR.

Abraham, Plains of. See QUEBEC, BATTLE OF.

Abraham Lincoln Birthplace National Historic Site. See NATIONAL PARKS, section "United States."

Abrasive, ăb-rā′sĭv, a hard substance used to grind, cut, or polish another substance that is either softer (the usual case) or equally hard. Abrasives are contained in sandpaper, steel wool, household cleanser, knife sharpeners, and toothpaste. Nearly all manufactured products depend upon the use of abrasives in one way or another for their manufacture.

Abrasive Materials

Materials used as abrasives are either synthetic (man-made) or formed from natural minerals and stones. Natural abrasives include diamond, corundum, emery, sand, garnet, tripoli, pumice, and talc.

Synthetic abrasives, produced in high-temperature electric furnaces, are used more extensively than natural abrasives. Important synthetic abrasives are silicon carbide, which does not occur in nature, and artificial corundum. Diamond, the hardest natural substance, has been produced synthetically since 1955.

The effectiveness of an abrasive depends upon its hardness. Among means used to specify the hardness of abrasives is the *Mohs scale,* in which substances are assigned numbers from 1 to 10 (softest to hardest), depending on their hardness. (See HARDNESS.) Diamond has a value of 10 on this scale. Some important abrasives, their hardness, and their uses are given in the accompanying table.

Uses of Abrasives

Abrasives are used in the form of powders (as in polishes and household cleansers), shaped solid pieces (to form tools and other implements), fine shavings (as in steel wool), and grains of various sizes. Abrasive grains can be used loose, as in sandblasting; in coatings on cloth or paper, as in sandpaper; and bonded together to form grinding wheels.

Abrasive grinding wheels range in size from tiny devices used by dentists to huge pulpstones six feet in diameter, used in the paper industry to grind logs into pulp. Narrow high-speed wheels are used as saws to cut steel and other metals. Grinding wheels shaped from natural stones are called *grindstones.* Most grinding wheels are made from abrasive grains that have been mixed with a bonding agent (for example, a ceramic, shellac, or rubber), pressed into the desired

Action of an Abrasive Grinding Wheel. In grinding, thousands of abrasive grains on the face of the wheel cut chips from the material being ground. The abrasive grains are bonded together with rubber, shellac, or some other material.

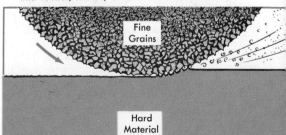

Fine Grains

Hard Material

SOME IMPORTANT ABRASIVES

NAME	CHEMICAL COMPOSITION	ORIGIN	MOHS HARDNESS	TYPICAL USES
Diamond	Carbon, C	Natural and Synthetic	10	Grinding wheels; tips for earth drills; cutting and polishing of diamonds and other gem stones
Borazon	Boron nitride, BN	Synthetic	about 10	Cutting and polishing of hardest materials
Silicon carbide	Silicon carbide, SiC	Synthetic	9.5	Grinding and cutting of metals; shaping of metals, alloys, marble, and glass
Corundum	Alumina, Al_2O_3	Natural and Synthetic	9	Grinding wheels; ceramic cutting tools; whetstones
Emery	Impure alumina, Al_2O_3, with magnetite or other iron-containing minerals	Natural	7-9	Grinding and polishing of metals, lenses, and prisms; dental grinding wheels
Sand	Quartz, SiO_2, and other minerals	Natural	7*	Etching and cleaning of glass and stone surfaces (sandblasting); sandpaper
Garnet	Mineral silicate, $X_3Y_2(SiO_4)_3$†	Natural	6.5-7.5	Coated abrasives (garnet paper); cutting and grinding of stones; lens grinding
Tripoli	Mainly silica, SiO_2	Natural	‡	Scouring soaps and powders; fine polishing
Pumice	Mainly silica, SiO_2, and alumina, Al_2O_3	Natural	6	Scouring powders; hand soaps; toothpastes and tooth powders
Talc	Hydrated magnesium silicate, $Mg_3Si_4O_{10}(OH)_2$	Natural	1	Polishing of barley, rice, and peanuts; polishing of turned wooden articles, such as knife handles

*Quartz
†$X = Fe''$, Mn'', Mg, or Ca; $Y = Al$, Fe''', Ti, or Cr'''
‡Varies widely, depending on exact composition

size and shape, and heated in a furnace. (See also GRINDING.)

The diamond used as an abrasive, called *black diamond, bort,* or *carbonado,* is not of gem quality, but is nevertheless very expensive compared to other abrasives. It is used in the form of crystals, chips, grains, and powder. Powdered diamond, natural or synthetic, is used to cut diamond stones. The stones are cut by a thin metallic disk that is constantly dipped in powdered diamond and oil while revolving at high speed. Borazon, a special form of boron nitride created by the General Electric Company in 1957, is the only other substance that is hard enough to cut diamonds.

History of Abrasives

Natural minerals and stones were used by man thousands of years ago to polish crude tools and weapons. Drawings in ancient Egyptian tombs show the polishing of jewelry and vases with abrasives. Until the 19th century, grindstones and whetstones were the only tools available that were made from abrasive materials. By 1825, bonded abrasive grinding wheels were in use in the East Indies. The wheels, made from grains of natural corundum bonded together with gum from trees, were used for gem cutting.

Silicon carbide, the first important synthetic abrasive, was created in 1891 by the United States inventor Edward Goodrich Acheson. Since then, synthetic abrasives have largely replaced natural abrasives.

See also BORAZON; CORUNDUM; DIAMOND; EMERY; GARNET; PUMICE; SAND; SANDBLASTING; TALC; WHETSTONE.

Abruzzi, ä-brōōt′tsĕ, Luigi Amedeo, **Duke of the** (1873-1933), an Italian naval officer and explorer, noted for his mountain-climbing expeditions. Abruzzi was born in Madrid, when his father, the son of King

Victor Emmanuel II of Italy, ruled as King Amadeo I of Spain, 1870-73.

In 1897 Abruzzi was the first to climb 18,008-foot Mount St. Elias in Alaska. His expedition to the North Pole (1899-1900) reached a record north latitude of

Wide World
Duke of the Abruzzi

86° 34' in Franz Josef Land. Abruzzi did not share in this feat, having remained at a base camp because of severe frostbite.

Abruzzi explored and mapped the Ruwenzori Range in East Africa in 1906. In 1909 he set an altitude record, reaching 24,600 feet on Mount Godwin Austen in the Himalayas. During World War I, Abruzzi commanded the Italian navy, 1914-17. After the war, he explored and colonized in East Africa.

Absalom, ăb′sȧ-lŏm, in the Bible, the third son of David, King of Israel. He was handsome and noted for his long hair. Absalom killed his half-brother Amnon for violating his sister Tamar, and had to flee. He returned three years later and organized a revolt against his father. Successful at first, Absalom was later beaten in battle. The defeated prince fled through the woods on a mule but his hair became entangled in a tree. There he was killed by Joab, David's commander, in spite of the king's orders not to harm the youth. David's grief was profound. The story is told in II Samuel 13-18.

Absaroke. See CROW INDIANS.

Abscess, ăb′sĕs, a pus-filled cavity in the body around which redness and swelling usually occur. (Pus is a light-colored, opaque liquid composed primarily of germs, dead cells, and infection-fighting white blood cells.) Abscesses are usually caused by bacteria, but they may also be caused by fungi, amoebas, other parasites, and cysts. Often painful and dangerous, abscesses can occur in any region of the body. Those located near the surface of the skin and forming a single pus cavity and a single tract to the surface are called *furuncles,* or *boils.* Those located near the skin and having several connected cavities and tracts are called *carbuncles.*

In the formation of boils and carbuncles, bacteria or other germs enter hair follicles,

sweat glands, or shallow wounds; in the formation of deeper abscesses, they enter deeper tissues. The germs destroy tissue in an area. In defense, the body sends white blood cells to the area and walls off the site of infection. A walled cavity, containing pus, forms. In boils and carbuncles, the pus cavity usually works its way to the surface of the skin and forms a whitish point containing pus. The cavity may burst and drain, or the pus may eventually be resorbed by the body. Deep abscesses are usually too far below the surface to come to a point on the skin and drain.

As the germs of an abscess destroy new tissue, the abscess spreads from one area to another. If the germs enter the bloodstream, serious, widespread infection results.

An abscess should be treated by a physician. He may prescribe antibiotics or other medicines and open and drain the abscess or remove it surgically.

Absentee Landlord, a person who owns, and receives income from, property that is in a country or district in which he does not live. Absenteeism of landlords occurred in Europe when it was the custom for the nobility to live at the king's court. The agent who managed a noble's property did little or nothing for the peasants who rented the land. In France the poverty of the tenant farmers was one cause of the French Revolution.

Absenteeism was a particular problem in Ireland in the 18th and 19th centuries, when most farms were owned by landlords living in England. Not only did the peasants suffer from the harsh treatment of the agents, but the country suffered because of the vast sums of money being drained out of it. The evils of absenteeism began to be remedied by the Land Acts of 1870 and 1881, but were still a major cause of the Irish demand for home rule, which led eventually to independence.

See also BOYCOTT (concluding paragraph).

Absentee Voting. See VOTING, subtitle *Voting in the United States.*

Absinthe, ăb′sĭnth, a green liqueur flavored with the bitter oil from the dried leaves and tops of the common wormwood, an herb. Other ingredients of this alcoholic beverage are the oils of peppermint, angelica, anise, and cinnamon. If taken in excess, absinthe causes weakness and mental disturbances, which may develop into convulsions, paralysis, and mental illness. Because absinthe has these effects, its importation to the United States was outlawed in 1912. Its manufacture in France was prohibited in 1915.

Absolute Zero. See HEAT, subtitle *Heat and Temperature:* Absolute Zero.

Absorption, ăb-sôrp′shŭn, the process by which matter or radiant energy is taken up internally, or assimilated, by a substance. Matter that is absorbed can be gaseous, liquid, or solid. Radiant energy includes light, heat, X rays, ultraviolet rays, radio waves, and sound.

Adsorption, a related phenomenon, is sometimes confused with absorption. Adsorption is the process by which a substance attracts and holds particles of another substance on its surface. Absorption always involves internal penetration of a substance, whereas adsorption involves surface retention only. (See ADSORPTION.)

Absorption of Matter

Many examples of the absorption of matter occur in everyday experience. A readily observed example is provided by a sponge. It is a porous solid that will absorb water and other liquids.

In animals and plants, the absorption of matter is of vital importance. Digested food in the small intestine is absorbed by the blood stream and distributed to all parts of the body. Plant roots absorb water and nutrients from soil, and leaves absorb oxygen and carbon dioxide from air.

Geometric Abstraction. Piet Mondrian's *Broadway Boogie Woogie,* oil on canvas, 50 by 50 inches, painted in 1942-43.
Museum of Modern Art

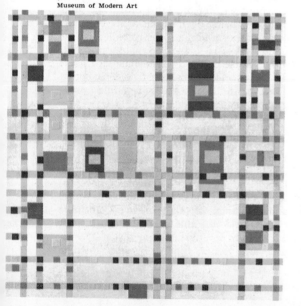

The production of atomic energy in nuclear reactors depends on the fact that atomic particles called *neutrons* are absorbed by atoms of uranium. The absorbed neutrons then cause the uranium atoms to *fission,* or split, and in the process of splitting the uranium atoms release energy together with additional neutrons.

Absorption of Radiant Energy

Radiant energy that strikes a substance can be absorbed, transmitted, or reflected. (See REFLECTION.) The radiant energy that is absorbed by a substance is converted into heat or some other form of energy. The amount of energy absorbed depends on the physical nature of the substance and the character of the radiant energy. A mirror reflects most of the light that shines on it, while most of the light that strikes an untinted glass window is transmitted through the window. Charcoal and soot, on the other hand, absorb virtually all light that strikes them.

The earth's atmosphere absorbs part of the energy radiated by the sun and thus prevents this energy from reaching the earth's surface. If this atmospheric absorption did not occur, life probably could not exist on earth. This is because the atmosphere absorbs ultraviolet rays, some of which are known to be lethal to both animals and plants. Light from distant stars is absorbed both by the atmosphere and by interstellar gas and dust.

The color of an object that is not self-luminous is determined by the wavelengths of light that the object absorbs, transmits, and reflects. (See COLOR, subtitles *Color and Light* and *Color and Objects.*)

All materials used in building construction absorb sound waves to a certain extent; those that are designed to absorb a large percentage of sound waves are known as *acoustical materials.* Such materials are usually lightweight, porous, flexible, or compressible. Gypsum plaster and perforated cellulose-fiber tile are among the common acoustical materials.

Absorption Spectrum. See SPECTRUM.

Abstract Art, a general term for paintings and sculptures that do not represent natural forms realistically. It is sometimes called *nonobjective, nonrepresentational,* and *nonfigurative* art. Instead of creating an illusion of reality, the abstract artist stresses shape, line, color, texture, or design.

Abstract Expressionism. Jackson Pollock's *Autumn Rhythm*, 105 by 207 inches, painted in 1950.

Abstract art is a complex of many different styles. It may contain elements of Cubism, Expressionism, or other styles. Some painters and sculptors, such as Picasso and Alberto Giacometti, use natural forms but simplify and distort them. (For examples, see PAINTING, illustration of Picasso's *Night Fishing at Antibes;* GIACOMETTI, ALBERTO, illustration *City Square.*) Abstract art that is completely unrelated to natural forms falls into two major divisions—*geometric abstraction* and *Abstract Expressionism.*

Piet Mondrian, a major geometric abstract painter, used rectangles and squares in *Broadway Boogie Woogie* and other works. Geometric abstract sculptors, such as Moholy-Nagy and Naum Gabo, are often called *Constructivists.* (See CONSTRUCTIVISM.)

Opposed to the precision and balance of geometric abstraction is the highly emotional school of Abstract Expressionism. Vasily Kandinsky, Willem de Kooning, and others often used broad brush strokes and intense colors in their paintings. (See PAINTING, illustration of Kandinsky's *Improvisation Number 30.*) Jackson Pollock, probably the best-known Abstract Expressionist in the United States, dripped and flung paint on his canvases. This style and technique is often called *action painting.*

There is much disagreement about the beginnings of abstract art. Some art historians credit Kandinsky with painting the first completely abstract work in 1910. Others point out that John Marin of the United States painted an abstract work—*Weehawken Sequence #7*—in 1903.

For biographies, see:

ARP, JEAN	GIACOMETTI, ALBERTO
DE KOONING, WILLEM	GORKY, ARSHILE
DOESBURG, THEO VAN	GOTTLIEB, ADOLPH
DOVE, ARTHUR	HARTLEY, MARSDEN
GABO, NAUM	HOFMANN, HANS
KANDINSKY, VASILY	O'KEEFFE, GEORGIA
MARIN, JOHN	PICASSO, PABLO
MOHOLY-NAGY, LASZLO	POLLOCK, JACKSON
MONDRIAN, PIET	STAËL, NICHOLAS DE
MOTHERWELL, ROBERT	STILL, CLYFFORD
NOGUCHI, ISAMU	

Abstract of Title, a summary that gives the essential facts of all deeds, mortgages, releases, or other transactions affecting the title or legal right to a tract of land. A complete abstract states how the original owner came into possession, and describes all transfers to the present time. It also shows what taxes, if any, remain unpaid, and whether any judgments or other obligations exist that weaken the title.

An abstract is generally compiled from public records, but the original instruments (such as deeds, mortgages, judgments, probates, and the like) may be examined. Ordinarily the seller of a property is expected to furnish such an abstract for the inspection of the buyer, but usually he is under no legal obligation to do so. Most abstracts are drawn up by title companies or individual lawyers.

See also DEED; TITLE (in law).

Abu Dhabi. See UNITED ARAB EMIRATES.

Abu Simbel Temples. See ASWAN DAM.

Abu-Bakr, á-boo'băk'ĕr (573-634), the first caliph of Islam. He was the father-in-law of the prophet Mohammed. As Mohammed's most trusted follower, abu-Bakr succeeded to the leadership of Islam after the prophet's death.

During abu-Bakr's reign, 632-34, Palestine was conquered. Abu-Bakr chose Omar to be his successor.

Abukir Bay. See NILE, BATTLE OF THE.

Abul Kasim Mansur. See SHAH NAMAH.

Abutilon. See FLOWERING MAPLE.

Chicago Natural History Museum
Acacia. The Australian blackwood, one of the 450 species of acacias, is grown in California. Blackwood lumber is commercially important.

Acacia, *á-kā'shá*, a large genus of tropical and subtropical trees and shrubs belonging to the pea family. Acacias are found throughout the world in warm, dry areas. Many native North American acacias are known as *catclaw;* several Australian species are called *wattle.*

Acacias vary in height from about 6 feet to 60 feet. Most have featherlike or fernlike leaves, but many Australian species have flattened leaf stalks rather than leaves. In general, the leaflets are narrow and pointed, and most are less than two inches long. Acacias frequently bear thorns. The flowers are small and usually grow in globular or elongated clusters less than one inch long. They vary in color from a light, whitish yellow to a deep orange. Seeds grow in beanlike pods.

Acacias are widely raised as ornamental shrubs. The Australian blackwood is an important lumber tree. Catechu, a brown dye and a medicine, is extracted from the heartwood of the catechu acacia. Tannin, for tanning leather, is made from the powdered bark of the black wattle, the golden wattle, and other acacias. The dried sap of gum arabic trees is gum arabic, used chiefly in mucilage. (See GUM ARABIC.)

A fragrant oil, called acacia, or cassie, is extracted from the blossoms of the sweet acacia, or cassie, and is used in perfumes. The babul is one of the trees on which the lac insect lives. Shellac is made from the secretions of this insect. (See LAC.) Certain species of ants hollow out the large thorns of bull-horn acacias and live in them.

The 450 species in the *Acacia* genus belong to the pea family, Leguminosae. The true catclaw is *A. greggii;* the blackwood, *A. melanoxylon;* the catechu, *A. catechu;* the black wattle, *A. decurrens;* the golden wattle, *A. pycnantha;* the sweet acacia, *A. farnesiana;* and the true bull-horn, *A. cornigera. A. arabica* is the babul and is one of the gum arabic trees. *A. senegal* is another gum arabic tree.

Academic Degree. See DEGREE.

Academic Dress, the costume worn on certain occasions in colleges and universities by students, holders of degrees, faculty members, and members of governing bodies. The costume consists of gown, cap, and, usually, hood. Differences in the costume indicate the wearer's academic degree—bachelor's, master's, or doctor's—and his field. (A costume similar to the bachelor's, without hood or indication of field, is commonly worn by graduating high school seniors.)

Abydos, *á-bī'dŏs*, an ancient Greek town in Asia Minor at the narrowest part of the Hellespont, opposite Sestos. It was founded in the sixth century B.C. by the city-state of Miletus in Ionia. A natural crossing point, Abydos was the site of Xerxes' bridge of boats when the Persian army marched against Greece in 480 B.C. The army of Alexander the Great crossed there also on the way to its conquests. Abydos was an important community until the decline of the Byzantine Empire. The nearby Turkish town of Canakkale replaced it.

There are several legends about Abydos. One is the story of Hero and Leander. (See HERO AND LEANDER.) Another tells of the men of the town, besieged by the brutal Philip V of Macedon in 200 B.C., killing their wives and children and then themselves to avoid capture.

Abyla. See HERCULES, PILLARS OF.

Abyssinia. See ETHIOPIA.

Abyssinian Cat. See CAT, subtitle *The Domestic Cat: Breeds (Short-haired Cats).*

AC. See ELECTRICITY, subtitle *The Nature of Electricity: Currents.*

Academic dress is worn in academic processions and during baccalaureate services and commencement exercises. The processions are held as part of commencement exercises, for the inauguration of a president or chancellor of a college or university, and on other ceremonial occasions. In some foreign universities students wear academic dress when attending lectures.

Academic Costume Code

The Academic Costume Code, worked out by the Committee on Academic Costumes and Ceremonies of the American Council on Education, is recognized by nearly all degree-granting institutions in the United States. The Intercollegiate Bureau of Academic Costume, established to provide information and guidance on matters of academic dress, is affiliated with the firm of Cotrell and Leonard of Albany, New York.

Gowns are black, with certain exceptions. (Some institutions grant an associate degree for a two-year college course. The Academic Costume Code recommends that the gown for such a degree be a lighter color, such as gray.) The gown for the bachelor's degree has pointed sleeves and is designed to be worn closed. The master's gown has oblong sleeves and is so designed that it may be worn open or closed. The doctor's gown has bell-shaped sleeves and may be worn open or closed. Cotton poplin or similar material is used for the bachelor's and master's gowns, and rayon or silk ribbed material for the doctor's.

Trimmings are not used for the bachelor's and master's gowns. The doctor's gown is faced down the front with velvet and with three bars of the same material across the sleeves. The velvet may be black or the color appropriate to the subject field. Each subject has its own color. Pink, for example, indicates music; golden yellow stands for science; and light blue is assigned to education.

Caps generally are in the form of mortarboards, but women are sometimes permitted to wear soft square-topped caps. Caps are always black. A long tassel—black or of an appropriate color—is fastened to the top of the cap at the middle. The doctor's cap may have a gold tassel. There is no prescribed position for the tassel, although some institutions require candidates for degrees to wear the tassels on the right before degrees are conferred and to shift them to the left as the degrees are awarded.

Bachelor's. The gown has pointed sleeves. The hood lining (here, red) is in the official color of the degree-conferring institution. The color of the hood edging represents the field of learning (pink is for Music).

Master's. The gown has oblong sleeves. (The hood's golden-yellow edging represents Science.)

Doctor's. The gown has bell-shaped sleeves. The facing of the gown and the sleeve bars are of velvet. (Light blue represents Education, also indicated by the color of the cap's tassel.)

Hoods are ornamental scarves worn around the neck and over the gown. The hood is usually made of the same material as the gown. It is always black, but is lined with the official colors of the institution granting the degree, and may be edged with velvet or velveteen of the color appropriate to the subject field. The width of the edging indicates the degree: 2 inches for the bachelor's, 3 inches for the master's, and 5 inches for the doctor's.

The hood for the bachelor's degree is 3 feet long; that for the master's, 3½ feet; and that for the doctor's, 4 feet.

At many large institutions it is customary for the hood not to be worn by those receiving the bachelor's degree.

History of Academic Dress

Academic dress probably had an ecclesiastical origin. The medieval scholar was usually connected with the church and had to wear the proper gown. In England academic gowns were worn at Oxford and Cambridge before 1350.

Academic dress was used in American colleges during the early colonial period. In 1893 an intercollegiate commission was appointed to draft a uniform code. In 1895 the commission presented the Intercollegiate Code, which was accepted by almost all colleges and universities in the United States. In 1932 the American Council on Education appointed a commission to study the code. Very few changes were made. In 1959 the Committee on Academic Costumes and Ceremonies of the American Council on Education reviewed the code and made a number of changes.

Academic Freedom, the right of teachers, especially in colleges and universities, to seek knowledge and present their findings without interference. A related right is that of tenure—the right to hold an academic job as long as the teacher or researcher continues to do competent and ethical work in the opinion of qualified professional colleagues.

Academic freedom is based on the principle that the function of an institution of higher learning is to increase and preserve knowledge, evaluate it, and impart it to others. For the institution to perform this function its scholars must be free to hold and express unpopular or even mistaken views, for it is only through an open exchange of varying points of view that ideas can be tested and knowledge advanced.

A-22

Conflicting interpretations of the limits and obligations of academic freedom have led to disputes between teachers and the governing boards of educational institutions. In some states teachers in public institutions are required to sign loyalty oaths, swearing that they do not advocate violent overthrow of the government and do not belong to subversive organizations. Various pressure groups attempt to influence the content of courses and instructors' selection of books.

For a leading organization in the effort to safeguard academic freedom, see AMERICAN ASSOCIATION OF UNIVERSITY PROFESSORS.

The Development of Academic Freedom in the United States, by Richard Hofstadter and Walter P. Metzger (Columbia, 1955), is a study prepared for the American Academic Freedom Project at Columbia University.

Académie Française. See FRENCH ACADEMY.

Academy, a society of learned persons formed to encourage and promote arts and sciences or some branch of the arts or sciences. (Academy also may mean a secondary school or an institution of higher learning, such as a military academy or an academy of art or music, but in that meaning will not be considered in this article.) A learned society may be known as an academy, society, association, or institute. A professional association is a learned society and is sometimes called an academy. More often, however, an academy is an honorary society with a rather broad field of scholarly interest, with membership by invitation only.

History of Academies

In Athens the Greek philosopher Plato (427?-347 B.C.) conducted a school known as the Academy, named after the grove where the classes were held. His successors continued to use the name. The Greek Academy remained in existence for about eight centuries, and "academy" came to mean any scholarly institution.

In the late 13th and early 14th centuries a number of societies were formed in southern France and in Italy for the cultivation of poetry. The Academy of Floral Games, begun by French troubadours in 1323, still makes literary awards. In Italy, where many Greek scholars took refuge after the fall of the Byzantine Empire, the society devoted to classical learning originated. One of these was the Platonic Academy, founded in 1442 in Florence by Cosimo de' Medici for the study of Greek literature. Later it turned to the study of the Italian language. Other early academies in Italy, Germany, France, and Spain were also concerned with purification of the national language; some of them published dictionaries.

The study of classical literature gave way to the study of contemporary literature, and then interest turned to science. In the 17th century academies of science were established in Germany, England, and France under the sponsorship of monarchs or nobles. Four of the academies now included in the Institute of France were begun in the 1600's, and England's Royal Society was founded in 1662.

The first learned society in America was the American Philosophical Society, founded by Benjamin Franklin in 1743. In the 19th century national academies were established in most nations of Europe that did not yet have them, as well as in many countries in other parts of the world.

Academy of Natural Sciences of Philadelphia
Children's Nature Museum is a special feature of the Academy of Natural Sciences of Philadelphia.

For articles on some noted academies, see:

Academy Award. See MOTION PICTURES, section "History of Motion Pictures," subtitle *Organizations:* Academy of Motion Picture Arts and Sciences; also table titled *Motion Picture Academy Awards.*

Academy of Motion Picture Arts and Sciences. See MOTION PICTURES, same subtitles as above.

Academy of Natural Sciences of Philadelphia, a private institution for research and education in natural history. In the academy's museum are exhibits showing mammals in their natural habitats, and exhibits of birds, minerals, and fossils. The natural history reference library has 180,000 volumes. The academy carries on research in taxonomy, ecology, and limnology, and conducts field expeditions. Educational services include museum classes, lectures, films, and other programs for youth and adults. The academy was founded in 1812.

Acadia, á-kā′dĭ-á *(French:* **Acadie,** á′ká′dē′), a former French colony along the Atlantic coast of North America. The area has become the Canadian provinces of Nova Scotia and New Brunswick, but at one time included part of what is now Maine. For more than a century, this region was involved in the Anglo-French struggle for control of North America.

The first settlement was made at Port Royal by the French under Samuel de Champlain, the Sieur de Monts, and Jean de Biencourt de Poutrincourt in 1605. In 1613 Samuel Argall, an English adventurer, set fire to the town and carried off several of its inhabitants. In 1621 Acadia was claimed by the English, on the basis of the 15th-century explorations of John Cabot, and named Nova Scotia. The colony was ceded back to France in 1632, and French colonization was renewed. Warfare between the English and French continued, however, and in

A-23

Field Museum of Natural History
Acanthus

1710 the British took possession of Acadia. This conquest was confirmed by the Treaty of Utrecht (1713). The French government then attempted, unsuccessfully, to persuade the Acadians to move to nearby Cape Breton Island, which remained under French control.

The peaceful, hard-working, religious French Acadians tried to remain neutral in the continuing wars between France and Great Britain. Their number, about 1,800 in 1713, had increased to about 10,000 by 1750. The British feared that the Acadians would support France and encourage the Indians to help the French. In 1755 the Acadians were directed to take an oath of allegiance to Britain, but refused. They were then ordered expelled.

Longfellow's poem *Evangeline* is based on the story of the Acadian deportation. Some 6,000 Acadians were shipped off to British colonies to the south. Families were separated; homes were burned. Enduring much hardship, many found their way to Louisiana, where their descendants, the "Cajuns," still live. Other Acadians drifted back to Canada and some returned to France.

See also EVANGELINE; NOVA SCOTIA, subtitle *History:* French-English Rivalry.

Acadia National Park. See NATIONAL PARKS, section "United States."

Acanthus, *à*-kăn′thŭs, the name of a genus of herbaceous plants native to southern Europe. There are 20 species. Acanthuses are raised as ornamental plants because of their large, deeply toothed leaves and tall spikes of white, pink, red, or lilac-colored blossoms. They are perennials but do not survive winter temperatures below 20° F. (−7° C.). Some species have spiny leaves. In the United States, a widely raised acanthus is the bear's breech, which reaches a height of two feet (60 cm). It has large, hairy leaves and showy flower spikes.

The bear's breech is *Acanthus mollis* of the acanthus family, Acanthaceae.

In architecture, the leaves that adorn the capital (top) of the Corinthian column are copied from the soft-leaved acanthus. The acanthus-leaf design was a favorite ornamentation for the capital not only in Greek, but also in Roman, Byzantine, and Romanesque architecture. In the rinceau pattern of the Renaissance, used for borders and pilasters, acanthus leaves were combined with scrolls.

See also ARCHITECTURE, illustration titled *Greek Orders.*

Acapulco, ä′kä-pōōl′kŏ (full name, **Acapulco de Juárez,** thå hwä′räs), Mexico, a city and seaport in Guerrero State. It is about 185 miles (300 km) south-southwest of Mexico City. Much of Acapulco is perched on high, rocky cliffs overlooking scenic coves and beaches of Acapulco Bay, an inlet of the Pacific Ocean. The city is an internationally famous seaside resort with luxurious hotels and glittering nightclubs. It is also a shipping point for coffee, sugar, cotton, and hides.

Acapulco is the oldest port on the North American Pacific coast. Founded by Spanish explorers in the middle of the 16th century, it served as the chief port for trade between Asia and the New World for almost 300 years. The city has several times suffered severe damage from earthquakes and hurricanes.

Population: 421,088.

Accad. See AKKADIANS.

Acceleration. See VELOCITY, subtitle *Acceleration.*

Accelerator, Nuclear. See ATOM SMASHER; BETATRON; BEVATRON; COSMOTRON; CYCLOTRON; VAN DE GRAAFF GENERATOR.

Accent, ăk′sĕnt, an emphasis or stress placed upon certain syllables in a word, a group of words, or a line of verse. If more than one syllable in a word is accented, the strongest is called the *primary* accent. Others are *secondary.* In rendering some foreign words into English, all syllables are accented equally. The method used in this encyclopedia to indicate pronunciation employs two types of accent marks following accented syllables: ' indicates the primary accent; ' indicates the secondary accent. In words with only one accented syllable, ' rather than ' is used.

In Latin, Spanish, and some other languages, the accent is fixed by rule on a specific syllable. In English, the accent is not rigidly fixed, but it has a tendency toward the first syllable, as in actual, ăk'tŭ-ăl. The accent often shifts when prefixes or suffixes are used. In the word *actuality*, ăk'tŭ-ăl'i-tĭ, for example, the primary accent is on the third syllable and the secondary on the first.

Changing the accent may give words different meanings as well as different pronunciation. For example:

I *present*, prĕ-zĕnt', you with this diploma. (verb)

Tom is *present*, prĕz'ĕnt, today. (adjective)

The irregular accenting of English words permits a variety of poetic forms—since rhythm depends upon the pattern of accented and unaccented syllables.

See also MUSIC, subtitle *Elements of Music*: Rhythm; POETRY, subtitle *Rhythm and Meter*.

Acceptance, in commerce, a special form of *draft;* also the act that creates an acceptance. (See DRAFT.) Three parties are usually involved in an acceptance. The party making the draft, usually a seller of goods, is the *drawer*. The party ordered to make payment, usually the buyer, is the *drawee*. The party to whom the payment is to be made, usually a bank, is the *payee*. To accept a draft, the drawee writes on it the word "accepted," the date, and the name of the bank where payment is to be made, and then signs it. These actions constitute the act of acceptance.

When a buyer of goods pays for them in the form of a draft, his acceptance of the draft guarantees to the payee (the seller or the bank handling the transaction) that the drawee will pay according to the terms of the draft. The act of acceptance makes the drawee legally liable for payment.

An unaccepted draft, on the other hand, may be *dishonored* (payment may be refused) by the drawee; the drawer is primarily liable on this type of draft. When parties beginning a business transaction have little or no experience with each other's reliability, acceptance substitutes a bank's reliability for that of the buyer, and makes completion of the transaction more certain.

There are two types of acceptances. The *bank acceptance* is a draft accepted by a bank, trust company, or other party specializing in such activities. It is mostly used in international trade and in dealings with major staple commodities, such as wheat. A *trade acceptance* is a draft sent by the seller with the merchandise to the buyer. It is made out to the seller for the required amount. Upon delivery and inspection of the merchandise, the buyer may remit payment at once or he may accept the draft, making him the drawee. The acceptance is then returned to the seller. In effect, a trade acceptance is a promissory note from the buyer.

Acceptance, in contract law. See CONTRACT.

Accessory, ăk-sĕs'ō-rĭ, in law, a person who is connected with a crime but is not a *principal* (chief actor) in it, and, ordinarily, is not present when the crime is committed. To be an accessory, a person must take an actual part in the crime; just knowing a crime is to be committed—or has been committed—and not doing anything about it does not make a person an accessory.

An *accessory before the fact* helps, encourages, or commands another to commit a crime. An *accessory after the fact* helps the criminal escape, or aids him in some other way, while knowing that he has committed the crime.

In the crime of treason there are no accessories; all persons involved in any way are considered principals and punished as such.

Accident. See SAFETY.

Accidental, in music. See MUSIC, subtitle *Notation of Music*: Pitch.

Accolade. See KNIGHT, subtitle *Training for Knighthood*.

Accommodation. See EYE, subtitle *How the Eyes See*: Focusing.

Accomplice, ă-kŏm'plĭs, in criminal law, a person who takes part with another in a crime either as a principal or accessory. In a criminal trial the general rule is that a defendant cannot be convicted on the unsupported testimony of an accomplice.

See also ACCESSORY.

Accordion, ă-kôr'dĭ-ŭn, a portable reed-wind instrument. It consists of free metal reeds enclosed in two sound boxes that are connected by a large bellows. On the right-hand sound box of the *piano accordion* is a keyboard of about 3½ octaves on which the

© C. E. Pefley, Seattle

Piano Accordion

melody is played. (Small models, designed for beginners, have a range of only two octaves.) Buttons on the left-hand sound box furnish bass tones and chords for accompaniment. By pressing keys and buttons while pushing the bellows, the accordionist opens valves and forces air over the reeds to produce tones. Some professional-model accordions have buttons instead of keys.

The accordion is a solo and accompaniment instrument, and often is used in dance bands. It was developed in the 19th century. Several persons, including F. Buschmann of Berlin (1822) and C. Damian of Vienna (1829), are credited with its invention.

See also CONCERTINA.

Accounting, the recording, classifying, and summarizing of business transactions in terms of money. *Accountants* make up reports and analyze and interpret accounting data for managers and others who must base decisions on them. Recording and classifying, the clerical activities of accounting, are called *bookkeeping,* and are performed by *bookkeepers.* The profession of accounting is sometimes called *accountancy.*

A-26

Types of Accounting

Financial, or **General, Accounting** deals with the financial position of an enterprise and with the results of its operation. Financial position is reported in terms of assets and liabilities; results of operations, in terms of profit and loss. The procedures for compiling these reports are discussed in the article BOOKKEEPING.

Tax Accounting is concerned with determining the taxes owed by individuals, enterprises, and estates and trusts. The means of computing these taxes are established by laws and by rules and regulations under the laws. For taxes based on income, the laws in many cases do not follow the same principles as financial accounting.

Governmental Accounting is concerned with identifying and tracing the use of public funds rather than determining profit. When used for cities and towns it is often called *municipal accounting.* Its principles and procedures differ somewhat from those of financial accounting.

Fiduciary Accounting deals with financial entities held in trust, such as estates and insolvent or bankrupt concerns.

Cost Accounting is concerned with the costs of a particular product, process, job, or division of an organization. Cost accounting provides management with data that can be used in control and planning. It is most frequently used to analyze manufacturing costs, but there is a trend toward increased use of cost accounting and related activities as an aid in controlling distribution and administrative costs.

Auditing is concerned with checking the accuracy, authenticity, and, in some cases, interpretation of accounting records and reports. *Internal auditing* is performed by the employees of the organization; *independent auditing,* by persons or firms hired especially for the task.

Internal auditors provide a continuous check and review of accounting procedures for management. Independent auditors express an opinion as to whether the firm's financial reports present a fair picture of its financial position to others, such as stockholders, government, and creditors. At the same time they provide management with a periodic objective review of accounting procedures.

Management, or **Administrative, Accounting** is a comparatively recent development.

After World War II, management became increasingly aware that accounting data—particularly cost accounting data—are useful in planning, as well as in providing a record of past activities. *Budgetary accounting* is a term sometimes used to describe the use of accounting data in planning.

Systems, or **Systems and Procedures, Activity** is the coordination of accounting procedures with other organizational functions, such as sales and production, to establish an over-all control and planning system for the organization. Systems activity has become much more complex since World War II, when the development of computers made it possible to handle large amounts of data in a short time.

The Accounting Profession

Accountants who provide services for hire are called *public accountants*. They may be individuals or members of a firm.

Certified public accountants (CPA's) are accountants who have met state licensing requirements. The requirements vary from state to state, but CPA's must pass an examination in accounting theory and practice, auditing, and commercial law, and they must fulfill requirements as to education and accounting experience. The equivalent title in Canada and Great Britain is *chartered accountant*.

Regular employees of an organization who do accounting work are called *private accountants*. They may be CPA's. The accounting executive of a medium-sized or large organization is called the *comptroller,* or *controller.* (Both words are pronounced kŏn-trōl'ĕr.) He is usually highly placed in management.

Requirements for most public and private accounting jobs include accounting education beyond the level of high school courses in bookkeeping. Professional accounting courses are offered by many universities, colleges, junior colleges, business schools, and correspondence schools.

Positions with public accounting firms, the federal government, and many other institutions and businesses are restricted, in many cases, to persons who have had substantial college accounting training or its equivalent. Such organizations often require a bachelor's degree in accounting. To become an accounting executive in business or government or attain a high position in public accounting firms it is usually necessary to have a postgraduate degree in accounting, or a CPA license, or both.

The professional association of CPA's is the American Institute of Certified Public Accountants (AICPA), founded in 1887. The AICPA compiles and grades all CPA examinations, and exerts influence on the profession in other ways. *Journal of Accountancy* and *Tax Adviser* are monthly publications. Membership is about 135,000. Headquarters are in New York City.

Books about Accounting

Dyer, M. L. *Practical Bookkeeping for the Small Business* (Contemporary Books, 1976).

Edwards, J. D., and H. A. Black, editors. *The Modern Accountant's Handbook* (Dow Jones-Irwin, 1976).

Istvan, D. F., and C. G. Avery. *Accounting Principles* (Harcourt Brace Jovanovich, 1979).

Myer, J. N. *Accounting for Non-Accountants,* 2nd edition (Hawthorn Books, 1979).

Rosenthal, Lawrence. *Your Future in Accounting Careers* (Richards Rosen Press, 1978).

Accra, ă-krä'; ăk'rá, Ghana, the nation's capital and largest city. It lies on the Gulf of Guinea about 400 miles north of the Equator and near the prime meridian (0° longitude). As in many African capitals, the modern section in Accra, with up-to-date stores, homes, offices, and government buildings, contrasts sharply with older sections.

Consumer goods and light industrial products, such as soap, shoes, furniture, beer, bricks, and metal containers, are manu-

Auditing, a major branch of accounting, includes periodic examinations of a company's books (financial records) to verify their accuracy.

NEW STANDARD Photo

factured. Accra is the industrial and commercial center of Ghana.

Accra's port lacks docking facilities and uses surfboats and lighters for loading and unloading ships. Most of the shipping, however, is carried on through the nearby port at Tema, which was opened in 1962. Accra has a busy international airport and is connected by roads with other parts of the country and with adjoining countries in western Africa. There is railway service inland as far north as Kumasi.

As the nation's cultural center, Accra is the site of a national museum containing exhibits of native art and culture. A number of technical schools are here. The University of Ghana is nearby.

Accra developed early in the 17th century around forts built by Dutch, British, and Danish traders. In 1876, after Britain achieved supremacy in the area, Accra was made capital of the Gold Coast. The city rose as a trading center after 1923, when a railway was completed linking Accra and its agricultural and mining hinterland. It was made the capital of the newly independent country of Ghana in 1957.

Population, including suburbs: 738,498.

Acculturation, ă-kŭl'tŭ-rā'shŭn, the process by which social and economic changes are brought about by continuous first-hand contact between groups with diverse cultures. It especially refers to modifications made in the cultural patterns and economic systems of primitive groups that have been subjected to direct and prolonged contact with groups of more advanced cultures and higher economic standards.

An example of acculturation is the changed cultural and economic patterns of the Central and South American Indians that resulted from their enforced contact with the culture and economy of the Spanish conquistadors. The Roman Catholic missions, which converted Indian aborigines to Christianity and taught them industrial and agricultural skills, contributed greatly to these changes.

Acetanilid, ăs'ĕt-ăn'ĭ-lĭd, a drug used to relieve pain and, occasionally, to reduce fever. It is taken by mouth for pain caused by neuralgia and rheumatism. Pure acetanilid is a white, crystalline powder made by treating aniline (a chemical derived from petroleum or coal tar) with acetic acid. Continued use can lead to poisoning.

A-28

Acetate, ăs'ĕ-tāt, a chemical compound formed by the reaction of acetic acid with either a metal or an alcohol. (See ACETIC ACID.) Metal acetates of commercial importance include lead acetate, used in waterproofing and as a mordant (fixing agent) in dyeing; aluminum acetate, used in embalming fluids; and sodium acetate, used in drugs.

The most important acetates formed from acetic acid and alcohol are cellulose acetate, from which a man-made textile fiber, photographic film, and magnetic-recording tape are made; vinyl acetate, used in plastics, adhesives, and paints; and ethyl acetate, used as a solvent in the manufacture of varnishes and lacquers. The man-made fiber produced from cellulose acetate was officially designated "acetate" by the Federal Trade Commission in 1951; previously it was called "acetate rayon."

Acetates are either salts or esters of acetic acid, CH_3COOH or $HC_2H_3O_2$. In the salts, the terminal hydrogen atom is replaced by a metal ion; in the esters, the terminal hydrogen atom is replaced by an organic radical. The formula for aluminum acetate is $Al(C_2H_3O_2)_3$; that for ethyl acetate is $C_2H_3O_2C_2H_5$.

See also PLASTICS, subtitle *Thermoplastics;* RAYON AND ACETATE.

Acetic Acid, ă-sē'tĭk, a clear, colorless acid with a pungent odor. Acetic acid constitutes 4 per cent or more of vinegar and is responsible for its characteristic odor and sour taste. Pure acetic acid is called *glacial acetic acid* because it becomes an icelike solid when cooled to its freezing point (62° F. [16.7° C.]). In pure form and in concentrated solutions, acetic acid is highly corrosive, and can produce painful burns on the skin.

The most important method for producing acetic acid commercially is the oxidation of ethylene, a hydrocarbon obtained during the refining of petroleum. Acetic acid is used in the production of a number of important chemical compounds, including aspirin (acetylsalicylic acid), acetyl chloride, and a group of substances called *acetates.* (See ACETATE.) It is used as a solvent and a food preservative, in photography, and in the treatment of natural rubber.

Acetic acid was one of the first acids known to man, because of its occurrence in vinegar. Its name is derived from *acetum,* the Latin word for "vinegar" or "sour wine." The German chemist Georg Ernst Stahl isolated glacial acetic acid from vinegar in 1700.

Acetic acid, with chemical formula CH_3COOH (or $HC_2H_3O_2$), is an organic acid belonging to the fatty-acid series. In aqueous solutions it is weakly dissociated.

See also VINEGAR.

Acetone, ăs'ĕ-tōn, an industrially important chemical compound composed of carbon, hydrogen, and oxygen. Acetone is a colorless, highly flammable liquid with an odor resembling that of ether. Most of the acetone used commercially is produced from propylene, a hydrocarbon obtained from the cracking of petroleum.

Acetone is the solvent in certain types of model-airplane glue, and is widely used as an industrial solvent. It dissolves resins, fats, oils, cellulose acetate, and many other substances. It is used in the manufacture of such things as acetic anhydride, an important industrial chemical; acetate fiber, a textile; cordite, an explosive; and chloroform. It is used also in storing acetylene. (See ACETYLENE.)

Acetone is formed in animal metabolism and is excreted in the urine. An excessive amount of acetone in the urine is an indication of diabetes.

Acetone has the chemical formula CH_3COCH_3. It is the simplest and most important of the organic chemicals called *ketones*. (See KETONE.)

Acetylene, ă-sĕt'ĭ-lēn, a colorless, flammable gas. Acetylene is highly reactive, and for this reason is used as the starting material in the production of many important chemicals. When acetylene burns in oxygen, it produces a very hot flame that can cut through the hardest steels.

Acetylene is a poisonous gas about nine-tenths as heavy as air. Pure acetylene is virtually odorless, but the gas usually contains impurities that give it an odor similar to that of garlic. Most acetylene is produced by adding water to calcium carbide, but a considerable amount is made from methane, which occurs in natural gas.

When acetylene is compressed or heated, it becomes highly explosive. It can be stored safely in steel cylinders containing acetone, a liquid chemical that can hold many times its own volume of acetylene. The acetylene is dissolved under pressure in acetone that has been absorbed by a chemically inert (nonreactive) material such as asbestos. Acetylene-lighted buoys contain tanks of acetylene dissolved in acetone.

Acetylene is used to produce vinyl chloride for plastics; neoprene, a synthetic rubber; acrylonitrile, used in synthetic fibers; and vinyl acetate, used in plastics, adhesives, and paints. Acetylene is also used to synthesize vitamin A, an important food supplement. *Acetylene black*, carbon resulting from the incomplete combustion of acetylene, is used in dry-cell batteries.

When acetylene burns in air, a hot and brilliant flame that resembles sunlight is produced. In the *carbide lamp*, water drips onto lumps of calcium carbide to form acetylene. This lamp, which can be fastened to the helmet of a miner, has been widely used

Acetylene Torches. *Left,* high-pressure torch used in welding delivers both acetylene and oxygen under high pressure. *Right,* low-pressure, or injector, torch is used for cutting. In this torch only the oxygen is under high pressure.

Victor Equipment Company

in underground mines as a source of illumination, but it is being replaced by portable electric lamps. Carbide lamps were formerly widely used on autos and bicycles. When acetylene burns in pure oxygen, the flame (called an *oxyacetylene flame*) is less brilliant but much hotter. In the *acetylene torch,* used for the welding and cutting of metals, acetylene is burned in oxygen to produce temperatures in excess of 6000° F.

Acetylene, C_2H_2 or $HC{\equiv}CH$, is an unsaturated aliphatic hydrocarbon. (See HYDROCARBON.) The triple bond makes acetylene highly reactive. The equation for its formation from calcium carbide and water is $CaC_2 + 2H_2O \rightarrow C_2H_2 + Ca\,(OH)_2$.

Acetylsalicilic Acid. See ASPIRIN.

Achaean League. See AETOLIAN LEAGUE AND ACHAEAN LEAGUE.

Achaeans, *à-kē′ănz,* the earliest branch of the ancient Greeks. They were a Greek-speaking, warlike people who migrated into and conquered the Greek peninsula between 2000 and 1700 B.C. Several hundred years later they established close contact with the Minoans on Crete. It is not known if the Achaeans conquered the Minoans, but the final form of writing (known as Linear B) found at Cretan archeological sites has been deciphered as Greek.

The Achaeans adopted Minoan art forms, and built splendid cities. The civilization developed by the Achaeans is called the Mycenaean civilization; the name comes from Mycenae, one of their cities.

Barbaric newcomers, the Dorians, swept down from the north about 1100 B.C. Two branches of the Achaeans, the Aeolians and the Ionians, escaped. Some took refuge in Attica, others migrated to the Aegean islands and the west coast of Asia Minor. A third branch, the Arcadians, were conquered and absorbed by the Dorians.

See also MINOAN CULTURE; MYCENAEAN CIVILIZATION.

Achates, *à-kā′tēz,* in Roman legend, the constant companion of Aeneas in his wanderings after the fall of Troy. He is frequently referred to in Virgil's *Aeneid* as *fidus Achates* (faithful Achates). Figuratively, a trustworthy friend or devoted companion may be called a *fidus Achates.*

Achelous, *äk′ē-lō′ŭs,* in Greek mythology, a river god. He was the son of Oceanus and Tethys, and father of the Sirens. Achelous had the power of assuming various forms. He unsuccessfully fought Hercules

A-30

for the love of Deianira. First he changed himself into a snake; Hercules nearly strangled him. Next he became a bull, but Hercules threw him to the ground and tore off one of his horns. According to one story, naiads (water nymphs) consecrated the horn and gave it to Amalthea as the cornucopia (horn of plenty).

Ashamed after his defeat by Hercules, Achelous threw himself into the nearby river, which thereafter bore his name. The Achelous (modern Greek: Akhelóös) is one of Greece's chief rivers, flowing 130 miles from the central Pindus Mountains southward into the Ionian Sea. Worship of Achelous was widespread throughout Greece, and extended to Sicily. His name frequently was invoked in taking oaths.

See also AMALTHEA.

Acheron, *ăk′ĕr-ŏn,* in Greek mythology, one of the five rivers of Hades, underground abode of the dead. The name means "River of Eternal Woe." The name Acheron is sometimes used for the entire lower world.

The ancients called several rivers Acheron. One of these rises in the Tómaros Mountains of Epirus, Greece, and flows 36 miles to the Ionian Sea. In its upper course it runs through deep gorges and sometimes disappears underground, suggesting to Homer that it led to the underground domain of Hades. Literary references to it are frequent. Milton speaks of it in the second book of *Paradise Lost* as "sad Acheron of sorrow, black and deep." Spenser writes in *The Faerie Queene:*

They pass the bitter waves of Acheron
Where many souls sit wailing woefully.

See also HADES.

Acheson, *ăch′ĕ-s′n,* **Dean** (Gooderham) (1893-1971), a United States statesman and lawyer. Acheson was a principal architect of United States foreign policy in the early post-World War II period. In the administrations of Presidents Roosevelt and Truman he served as assistant secretary of state, 1941-45; under secretary of state, 1945-47; and secretary of state, 1949-53. Acheson played a major role in shaping the Bretton Woods Agreement, the United Na-

Dean Acheson
Wide World

tions, the Japanese peace treaty, and the North Atlantic Treaty Organization. He helped to formulate and carry out the Marshall Plan and the Truman Doctrine.

Acheson was born in Middletown, Connecticut. He was graduated from Yale University, 1915, and Harvard Law School, 1918. He served as private secretary to Louis D. Brandeis, associate justice of the U.S. Supreme Court, 1919-21. Acheson then practiced corporate and international law until 1933, when he was appointed under secretary of the treasury. Resigning later that year in a policy disagreement, he resumed private law practice.

While Acheson was secretary of state, major international crises included the fall of the Nationalist government of China and the Korean Conflict. There was much domestic controversy over the Truman-Acheson foreign policy. However, "containment" of Communist expansion, the cornerstone of this policy, was continued under the Republican Eisenhower administration. Acheson again resumed his law practice in 1953, but remained an influential Democrat and adviser on foreign policy.

His writings include: *A Democrat Looks at His Party* (1955); *A Citizen Looks at Congress* (1957); *Power and Diplomacy* (1958); *Sketches from Life of Men I Have Known* (1961); *Present at the Creation: My Years in the State Department* (1970), winner of the 1970 Pulitzer Prize in history; *Fragments of My Fleece* (1971); *Grapes from Thorns* (1972). *Morning and Noon* (1965) is his autobiography.

Acheson, Edward Goodrich (1856-1931), a United States inventor. Acheson received 69 patents for inventions ranging from carborundum (silicon carbide, an abrasive) in 1891 to the electric resistance furnace in 1896. (See also CARBORUNDUM.)

Acheson was born in Washington, Pennsylvania. Forced to leave school during the financial panic of 1872, he worked at a number of temporary jobs, conducting experiments in his spare time. At 17, Acheson invented a rock-boring machine for use in coal mines. In 1880 he became an assistant to Thomas A. Edison. As Edison's representative, he installed electric lighting in Italy, Belgium, and the Netherlands.

Acheson entered business on his own and in 1884 sold the rights to his anti-induction cable to George Westinghouse. In 1899 he developed a process for the artificial production of pure graphite. A pioneer in colloid chemistry, he produced "Egyptianized clay," a highly plastic clay, and the lubricants Aquadag and Oildag. Acheson founded a number of companies to manufacture his discoveries. One of them, the Acheson Graphite Company, became part of National Carbon Company, a division of Union Carbide Corporation.

A Pathfinder (1910) is his autobiography.

Achievement Tests. See TESTING, subtitle *Achievement Tests.*

Achilles, à-kĭl′lēz, in Greek legend, the bravest of the Greek heroes who fought in the war against Troy. His father was Peleus, king of Phthia, in Thessaly; his mother was Thetis, a Nereid (sea nymph).

When Achilles was a baby, Thetis dipped him in the River Styx to make his body safe from all wounds. Since the water did not touch the heel by which she held him, he was

Achilles Contending with the Rivers, from a drawing by John Flaxman for a 1795 edition of Pope's translation of the *Iliad.* Achilles has pursued the Trojans to the River Scamander, as told in Book XXI. The river itself joins in the fight; two of its waves, with human heads, arms, and chests, are seen on either side of Achilles. The battle ends when the gods intervene.
Ryerson Library,
Art Institute of Chicago

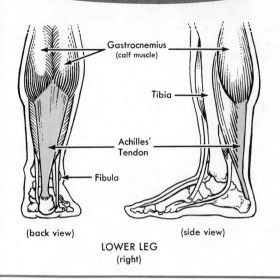

Location of
ACHILLES' TENDON

Gastrocnemius
(calf muscle)

Tibia

Achilles'
Tendon

Fibula

(back view)   (side view)

LOWER LEG
(right)

vulnerable in that spot. The centaur Chiron taught him the manly arts during his boyhood. An oracle told Thetis that Achilles would be slain in the war against Troy. To protect him, she sent him to the court of King Lycomedes of Scyros. There, dressed as a girl, he lived with the women of the court.

The prophet Calchas had informed Ulysses that the Greeks could not win the Trojan War without the help of Achilles. Learning of the whereabouts of Achilles, Ulysses went to Scyros disguised as a peddler. He displayed finery likely to appeal to women, and also a spear and shield. When, as a ruse, Ulysses let out a cry of warning, the women ran, but Achilles seized spear and shield. His identity thus revealed, Achilles then promised to help the Greeks. He led a fleet of 50 ships and an army of Myrmidons to join the Greeks besieging Troy.

After he quarreled with Agamemnon, leader of the Greeks, over a slave girl Agamemnon had taken away from him, Achilles quit the fight to sulk in his tent. Patroclus, his best friend, asked him to lend him his feared helmet and crest so that he might frighten the Trojans with them on the battlefield. Achilles agreed, and Patroclus went into battle wearing the armor of Achilles. He was killed by Hector, son of King Priam of Troy.

To avenge Patroclus, Achilles led his warriors to an attack. He killed Hector, and dragged his body behind a chariot around

A-32

the walls of Troy. When Priam came begging for his son's body to give it proper burial, Achilles consented. Achilles met his predicted death when Paris shot an arrow into his heel, his only vulnerable spot.

Achilles is the main character of Homer's *Iliad,* which is sometimes referred to as *Wrath of Achilles.* Goethe wrote an unfinished work about him called *Achilles* (1797-99).

Achilles' Tendon, the large cord connecting the bone of the heel *(calcaneus)* with the main muscles *(gastrocnemius* and *soleus)* of the calf of the leg. The medical name of the Achilles' tendon is *tendo calcaneus.* When the calf muscles contract, they cause the tendon to pull up the heel and lower the toes. This action enables a person to walk and to stand on tiptoe. The name of the tendon comes from the myth about Achilles' heel.

Acho, Mount. See HERCULES, PILLARS OF.

Acid, ăs'ĭd, a chemical compound that is capable of releasing hydrogen ions (electrically charged hydrogen atoms) for a chemical reaction. All acids contain hydrogen, but not all hydrogen-containing compounds are acids. Most acids also contain oxygen.

Long, chainlike compounds called *nucleic acids* are found in all living cells and are essential to life. *Amino acids,* also found in living organisms, are the "building blocks" of proteins. Other acids, such as sulfuric acid and nitric acid, are of tremendous importance industrially. Sulfuric acid, familiar as the acid in automobile storage batteries, is the largest single product of the chemical industry.

Properties of Acids

At ordinary temperatures, most pure acids are solids. Many, however, are liquids, and a few are gases. Some acids, such as prussic acid (hydrogen cyanide), are deadly poison.

When acids are dissolved in water in sufficiently high concentration they typically have the following properties:

1. They have a sour taste. (The term "acid" is derived from *acidus,* the Latin word for "sour.")
2. They are corrosive.
3. They will turn blue litmus paper red. (See LITMUS.)
4. They will dissolve many metals (for example, iron, tin, and zinc) and at the same time release hydrogen gas.
5. They will conduct an electric current, with the simultaneous liberation of hydrogen gas.

Acids will react with substances called bases (for example, sodium hydroxide) to form *salts* (such as sodium chloride, or table salt). A base is a substance that is capable of accepting hydrogen from another substance; thus it can be considered the opposite of an acid. (See BASE; SALT.)

Structure of Acids

The simplest type of acid has a molecule consisting of one atom of hydrogen and one atom of a nonmetallic element. A molecule of hydrochloric acid, for example, contains one atom of hydrogen and one atom of chlorine. Hydrochloric acid can be obtained by dissolving hydrogen chloride, a gas, in water. Both hydrochloric acid and hydrogen chloride have the chemical formula HCl, H being the symbol for hydrogen and Cl the symbol for chlorine.

Sodium chloride, one of the many chemical compounds classified as a salt, can be formed by combining metallic sodium (Na) with hydrochloric acid. The sodium replaces the hydrogen, as indicated by the chemical equation for this reaction:

$$2 \, Na + 2 \, HCl \rightarrow 2 \, NaCl + H_2$$

Sulfur, nitrogen, carbon, phosphorus, fluorine, and arsenic are among the other common elements that combine with hydrogen, or with hydrogen and oxygen, to form acids. Most of the common acids can be prepared by the reaction of oxides of nonmetals with water. In contrast to hydrochloric acid and other simple acids, some acids contain dozens of atoms in each of their molecules. The largest nucleic-acid molecules each contain millions of atoms.

Organic and Inorganic Acids

Acids, like all chemical compounds, are classified as either organic or inorganic. Organic acids occur in, or can be produced from, animal and vegetable matter. In addition to hydrogen, organic acids always contain carbon and at least one other element.

Nucleic acids and amino acids are organic. Other common organic acids are acetic acid, found in vinegar and cider; citric acid, found in citrus fruits, gooseberries, and currants; tannic acid (tannin), found in oak galls; formic acid, which occurs in insects and plants; lactic acid, a constituent of sour milk; oleic acid, found in animal fats and vegetable oils; and oxalic acid, found in rhubarb, spinach, and other edible plants.

Organic acids are used as food additives, in medicines, in dyeing and bleaching, in the tanning of leather, and in the manufacture of various chemicals.

Inorganic acids, which contain no carbon, are sometimes called *mineral acids*. In order of tonnage produced in the United States, the most important inorganic acids are sulfuric, nitric, phosphoric, and hydrochloric acid. Inorganic acids are used in the manufacture of fertilizers, plastics, explosives, synthetic textiles, paints, dyes, solvents, and many other substances.

Strength of Acids

The ability of an acid to release hydrogen ions is specified by its *strength*. A strong acid (for example, sulfuric or hydrochloric acid) dissociates (breaks up) completely, or nearly completely, into positive and negative ions in a dilute (nonconcentrated) water solution. Only a small percentage of a weak acid (for example, acetic acid), on the other hand, forms ions in solution, the major portion of the acid remaining in the form of molecules. As a general rule, inorganic acids are stronger than organic acids. The formation of positive and negative ions is the reason that an acid in a water solution will conduct electricity.

The strength of an acid is denoted by its "pH." The pH value of a dilute solution is given approximately by the following expression:

$$pH = \log \frac{1}{[H^+]}$$

In this expression $[H^+]$ is a number whose value is determined by the quantity of hydrogen ions per unit volume. The pH of a substance ranges from 0 to 14. Pure water, which is neutral (that is, neither an acid nor a base), has a pH of 7. Substances with pH values of less than 7 are acids, and substances with pH values of more than 7 are bases. Strong acids have pH values near 0, while strong bases have pH values near 14.

Certain *indicators,* such as methyl orange and bromphenol blue, which will change color at a known pH, can be used to find the pH of a solution. Electric meters that give a direct reading of the pH of a solution are also used by chemists.

For further information, see:

Organic Acids

ACETIC ACID	FORMIC ACID	PHENOL
AMINO ACIDS	GALLIC ACID	SALICYLIC ACID
ASPIRIN	LACTIC ACID	TANNIN
CITRIC ACID	NUCLEIC ACIDS	TARTARIC ACID
FATTY ACIDS	OXALIC ACID	

Inorganic Acids

BORIC ACID	PHOSPHORIC ACID
HYDROCHLORIC ACID	SULFURIC ACID
HYDROFLUORIC ACID	
NITRIC ACID	

Related Subjects

BASE	SALT
IONS AND IONIZATION	SOLUTION
LITMUS	

Acid Rain. See POLLUTION (Water).

Acidosis and Alkalosis, ăs′ĭ-dō′sĭs; ăl′kȧ-lō′sĭs. Acidosis is a condition of the body in which the blood and intercellular fluids (fluids between the cells) become less alkaline than normal. (Despite the name, they do not actually become acidic; the body never becomes acid during life.) Alkalosis is the condition in which the blood and intercellular fluids become more alkaline than normal. The kidneys and lungs regulate the degree of alkalinity in the body. Normally, they maintain the blood and intercellular fluids in a slightly alkaline condition. When the kidneys and lungs are unable to regulate the acid-base balance sufficiently, acidosis or alkalosis results.

Acidosis is one symptom of uncontrolled diabetes mellitus, kidney disease, and certain intestinal and lung diseases. Severe acidosis causes heavy breathing, drowsiness, vomiting, coma, and death. Alkalosis is a result of having eaten too much of an alkaline substance (such as certain drugs and poisons), or a symptom of some intestinal ailments and an excessive loss of carbon dioxide through long periods of heavy breathing. Alkalosis can cause severe cramps, muscle spasms, and death.

Acidosis and alkalosis can usually be corrected if promptly treated. Treatment consists of restoring the proper alkaline balance by the administration of solutions by mouth or by injection (intravenous or directly into the abdominal cavity).

Aclinic Line, ȧ-klĭn′ĭk, or **Magnetic Equator,** an imaginary, irregular line circling the earth near the geographical equator. Along the aclinic line, the earth's magnetic field is horizontal. Elsewhere on the earth, the field is inclined toward the earth's surface.

Acne, ăk′nĕ, a disease of the sebaceous, or oil, glands of the skin. *Acne vulgaris,* the most common form, usually begins in adolescence and continues into the 20's. It is more common in boys than girls. Acne usually affects the oil glands of the face, chest, and back.

Acne vulgaris usually begins at puberty when the oil glands enlarge and become more active. The oil glands are located deep within the skin and open to the surface through ducts (usually hair follicles). Acne occurs when *sebum,* the normally oily secretion of the sebaceous glands, combines in a

duct with dead skin cells and bacteria to form a plug called a *comedo* (plural: *comedones*).

A *blackhead* is a type of comedo that occurs at the duct opening, exposing the black pigment that gives it its characteristic color; it is not caused by dirt. A *whitehead* is a type of comedo in which a tiny white cyst or bump forms below the duct opening. Sometimes bacteria in the whitehead break down fats in the sebum, forming fatty acids. These fatty acids irritate the duct, causing the whitehead to rupture and spread its contents into the deeper layers of the skin. This causes inflammation in the form of *papules* (red pimples), *pustules* (pimples with a head), and *nodules* (cysts).

Causes

Acne is caused mainly by the increased production of sebum and testosterone, a male hormone. (Testosterone is produced in both females and males, but to a greater extent in males.) Outbreaks of acne can be triggered by a number of factors, such as the effect of cosmetics on the skin; menstruation; hot, humid weather; stress; pressure on the skin from tight headbands or collars; and certain drugs. Exposure to grease and petroleum oils tends to plug the duct openings, producing comedones. Diet seems to have little effect, although some foods, such as dairy products, nuts, chocolate, cola drinks, and fried foods, do trigger outbreaks in certain individuals.

Treatment

Gentle washing of the affected area two or three times a day with an abrasive cleanser or medicated soap is usually recommended. For mild cases, lotions, creams, or gels containing benzoyl peroxide or a combination of sulfur and resorcinol should then be applied. The sulfur-resorcinol combination dries up existing pimples and promotes peeling. Benzoyl peroxide is the only nonprescription medication that can prevent acne from recurring. It penetrates the sebaceous ducts and kills skin bacteria. It promotes healing of existing comedones and prevents the formation of new ones. It can be very abrasive to the skin and should be used sparingly.

Medical treatment should be obtained for moderate and severe acne vulgaris. A physician may remove comedones and prescribe soaps and drugs. Ultraviolet radiation from a sunlamp is a common treatment used to shrink comedones and promote peeling. Oral antibiotics, such as tetracycline, are often prescribed to inhibit the growth of bacteria in the ducts. Birth control pills help control acne in some women; the estrogen they contain counteracts the effect of the testosterone. A lotion or gel preparation containing vitamin A, or retinoic acid, is the most effective prescription acne medication available. It is applied to the skin's surface and penetrates the follicles, preventing the formation of plugs.

In most cases, complete recovery is slow. Treatment, however, lessens the effects of acne vulgaris and decreases the chances of scarring. Remaining acne scars may gradually disappear or they can be removed by *cryosurgery* or *dermabrasion*. Cryosurgery is a process in which the affected areas of the skin are sprayed with cold Freon. The spray freezes the skin and causes peeling. In dermabrasion, the skin is anesthetized with Freon and then scraped with a wire brush to remove the entire epidermis and part of the dermis. It is only used on individuals with severe scarring.

Other Forms of Acne

Cystic acne is a chronic form of acne. It produces deep pits and scars on the surface of the skin. The only effective treatment is with the prescription drug isotretinoin, which contains 13-cis retinoic acid, a form of vitamin A. Isotretinoin is taken orally. Side effects include severe chapping of the lips and increased levels of cholesterol in the blood.

Acne excoriée may be caused when a person scratches or picks his skin and makes sores. This form of acne is the result of a nervous habit usually due to tension and frustration. Treatment often consists of removing the sources of tension and frustration by altering the patient's way of life and attitudes. Occasionally, psychiatric treatment is necessary.

Acoma, ăk′ō-mȧ, a pueblo (village) on a rock mesa, 357 feet (109 m) in height, 60 miles (100 km) west of the Rio Grande, in Valencia County, New Mexico. It is one of the oldest inhabited places in the United States. Its people are Indians of the Keresan language stock. From ancient times, irrigation has been used in farming lands around the mesa, and some livestock is raised.

Aconcagua, ăk′ŭn-kä′gwȧ, the highest mountain in the Western Hemisphere and one of the highest in the world. It rises 22,834 feet (6,960 m) above sea level in the Andes Mountains of west-central Argentina, near the Chilean border. The snow-clad upper slopes of Aconcagua, rising high above the general level of the surrounding peaks, can be seen from the Pacific coast of Chile, about 80 miles (130 km) away. The summit of Aconcagua was first reached in 1897, by Swiss climbers.

Aconite, ăk′ō-nīt, the name of the genus of plants that includes wolfsbane and monkshood. The drug aconite is extracted from the roots of a few species of this genus. The aconite plants are found in cool areas of the north temperate zone and belong to the buttercup family. A few species are widely raised as ornamental plants. All of the plants of the genus are poisonous.

The aconites are nonwoody perennials that produce showy blossoms and much-divided, palm-shaped leaves. They grow to heights of from one to eight feet (30 to 240 cm). Aconite flowers are irregular, many having a hoodlike upper sepal and four or more flaring lower petals. The flowers of most species are blue or white; a few species, including wolfsbane, have yellow flowers.

Aconites contain the alkaloid *aconitine,* the active ingredient of the drug aconite. Aconite is used to slow heartbeat and breathing, to lessen pain, to reduce fever, and to increase the production of urine. Common monkshood is the main source of the drug. Aconite is no longer widely used in the United States.

The 50 species in the aconite genus belong to the buttercup family, Ranunculaceae. Wolfsbane is *Aconitum lycoctonum;* common monkshood, often called aconite, *A. napellus;* wild monkshood, *A. uncinatum.*

Acorn. See OAK.

Acoustic Mine. See MINE, subtitle *Submarine Mines:* Influence Mines.

Acoustics, ȧ-kōōs′tĭks, the branch of physics that deals with the production, transmission, properties, and effects of sound waves. (See SOUND.) It includes the following areas of study:

Architectural Acoustics is concerned with the behavior of sound waves in enclosed areas such as auditoriums, theaters, recording studios, and churches. Its goal is to achieve the proper conditions for hearing or recording speech and music in such areas. (See INSULATION, subtitle *Sound and Vibration Insulation.*)

Musical Acoustics deals with musical sounds and with the theory and design of musical instruments. (See MUSIC, subtitle *Nature of Musical Sound;* MU-

SICAL INSTRUMENT and references; PITCH, in music.)

Physiological Acoustics deals with hearing and speech. (See DEAFNESS; EAR, subtitle *How the Ear Functions;* LANGUAGE, subtitle *Structure of Language:* Sound; PHONETICS.)

Underwater Acoustics is concerned with the behavior of sound waves in water, especially in seawater. (See OCEAN, subtitle *Transmission of Energy in the Ocean:* Sound; SONAR.)

Electroacoustics deals with methods and devices for converting sound energy into electrical energy or vice versa. It is concerned with the design of such devices as phonographs, tape recorders, microphones, and loudspeakers. (See HIGH FIDELITY; LOUDSPEAKER; MICROPHONE; PHONOGRAPH; TAPE RECORDER.)

Noise Control is concerned with the measurement and reduction of unwanted sound. (See NOISE.)

Ultrasonics is the science of sound waves having frequencies that are beyond the upper limit of normal human hearing. This upper frequency limit is generally taken to be 20,000 hertz (cycles per second). (See ULTRASONICS.)

See also ECHO; INTERFERENCE; OVERTONE; RESONANCE; TUNING FORK; VIBRATION.

Acquired Immune Deficiency Syndrome. See AIDS.

Acre, ä'kĕr (*Hebrew:* **Akko**), Israel, a small city on the northern shore of the Bay of Acre across from Haifa. It dates from at least the 15th century B.C., when it was an important Phoenician port known as Acco (Accho in the Old Testament). It was a rich prize for invading Egyptians, Assyrians, Babylonians, and Israelites. As part of ancient Israel it belonged in turn to the Persian, Seleucid, and Roman empires. In the New Testament it is called Ptolemais.

Acre was taken by Moslem Arabs in 638. In 1104, during the First Crusade, the Christians captured it and named it St. Jean d'Acre. Retaken by the Saracens (Moslems)

Acropolis of Athens. The roofless Parthenon has been partly restored. A portion of the wall and sites of other buildings are also shown.
Raphaelidis: National Tourist Organization of Greece

in 1187, it was besieged for two years during the Third Crusade and recaptured by Richard the Lion-Hearted and Philip II of France in 1191. It was the major Palestinian port of the Crusaders for 100 years, until it fell again to the Saracens.

In the early 16th century the city passed from Egyptian to Ottoman Turkish rule. The Turks defended it successfully against Napoleon in 1799, but lost it to Egypt in 1832-40. It was part of the British mandate of Palestine after World War I, and became part of Israel in 1948. The ancient harbor has gradually filled with silt. There are historic structures and ruins dating back to the Romans and the Crusaders.

Population: about 34,200.

Acre, ā'kĕr, a unit of land measure. An acre is 43,560 square feet (4,047 m²). There are 640 acres in a square mile. A football playing field (with end zones) is about 1⅓ acres. The hectare, a metric unit of land measure, equals 2.471 acres.

The word acre is from the Latin *ager,* which means "field." In England an acre was originally the amount of land a man with a yoke of oxen could plow in a day. Laws of the 13th century and later defined the acre exactly.

Acrea. See BUTTERFLIES AND MOTHS, subtitle *Kinds of Moths:* The Tiger Moths (and illustration.)

Acrobatics. See GYMNASTICS, subtitle *Acrobatics.*

Acromegaly. See GIANT.

Acropolis, á-krŏp'ô-lĭs, in ancient Greece, the name for the high part of a city that was fortified as a citadel. Greek cities were usually built on a hill with the acropolis, containing temples and public buildings, at the summit. The acropolis as well as the city was surrounded by massive walls.

The most noted is the Acropolis of Athens. It is on a rocky, flat-topped hill that rises about 260 feet (80 m) above the city and is about 1,000 feet (300 m) long, east-west, and 400 feet (120 m) wide. The Propylaea, at the west end, forms the entrance. Other noted buildings are the Parthenon and the Erechtheum, known for its Porch of Maidens. Outside the walls to the southeast, scooped out of the rock, is the open-air Theater of Dionysus.

The first kings of Athens built their palaces and temples on the Acropolis. In 480 B.C. the Persians destroyed nearly all the

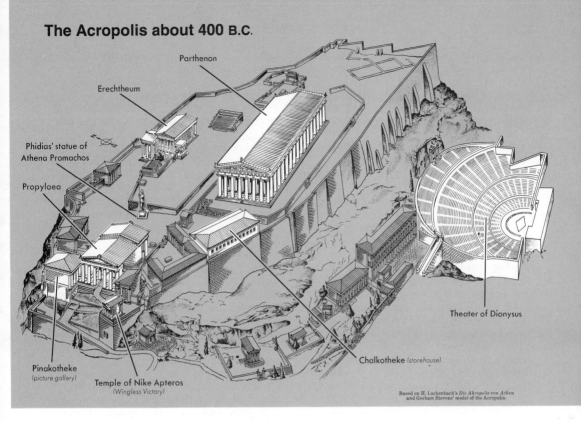

The Acropolis about 400 B.C.

Parthenon

Erechtheum

Phidias' statue of
Athena Promachos

Propylaea

Theater of Dionysus

Chalkotheke (storehouse)

Pinakotheke
(picture gallery)

Temple of Nike Apteros
(Wingless Victory)

Based on H. Luckenbach's *Die Akropolis von Athen*
and Gorham Stevens' model of the Acropolis.

buildings. Reconstruction of the Acropolis was begun in the last half of the fifth century B.C. during the rule of Pericles. The sculptor Phidias supervised much of the work and carved many of the sculptures.

See also ATHENS; ERECHTHEUM; PARTHENON; PERICLES; PHIDIAS.

Acrostic, *à-krŏs′tĭk,* a composition, usually in rhyme, arranged so that certain letters or sets of letters (such as the first, middle, or last) in successive lines spell a word, a group of words, or a name. A *true* acrostic is one in which the first letters form the word, as in this example:

> Here's an acrostic to use as a guide;
> Our hidden word runs along the left side.
> Make up your own, and you'll decide
> Examples look easy—until you've tried!

Acrostic poems were written by several early Latin poets. Among Englishmen who wrote acrostics are the Elizabethan poet John Davies and Charles Lamb. Edgar Allan Poe also wrote acrostics. Acrostic poems ordinarily are not taken seriously as literary efforts, being written mainly for amusement or technical novelty.

A special kind of acrostic is the *abecedarius,* in which the letters form the

alphabet or a section of the alphabet. In the original Hebrew version of the 119th Psalm, for example, the first letters of the divisions form the alphabet.

An acrostic notable in English history formed the word *cabal* from the initial letters of the names of five advisors of Charles II, who were notorious for their intrigues and plots. (See CABAL.)

Acrostics are frequently used in puzzles. A word square that reads the same horizontally and vertically is also called an acrostic. The following is a simple example:

```
L A M B
A L O E
M O R E
B E E T
```

Acrylic Fiber. See SYNTHETIC FIBER, table titled *Common Synthetic Fibers.*

Acrylic Resin. See PLASTICS, subtitle *Thermoplastics:* Acrylics.

Act of . . . A separate article devoted to a legal act is listed by the key word, for example, CHAPULTEPEC, ACT OF.

Act of God, in law, a calamity of nature, such as an earthquake, tornado, or flood. A person cannot be held legally responsible for an act of God, except under provisions of a special contract, such as an insurance contract.

Act of Settlement (1707). See ENGLAND, subtitle *History of England to 1707: The Supremacy of Parliament.*

Act of Supremacy (1534). See REFORMATION, subtitle *Spread of the Reformation: Henry VIII in England.*

Act of Uniformity (1662). See ENGLAND, CHURCH OF, subtitle *History.*

Actaeon, or **Aktaeon.** See DIANA.

ACTH, the abbreviation for *adrenocorticotropic hormone.* This hormone is vital to the functioning of the body and is also used as a drug. It is secreted into the blood by the anterior (front) lobe of the pituitary gland, located on the underside of the brain. ACTH controls the nourishment and function of the cortexes (outer areas) of the adrenal glands. ACTH also stimulates the adrenal cortexes to secrete other hormones (steroids such as hydrocortisone, corticosterone, and aldosterone), which control many vital functions of the body. If a person has no ACTH in his blood, his adrenal cortexes become small and cease to function, and he may die.

ACTH is released into the blood in response to stimuli from the hypothalamus (a part of the brain). The amounts of ACTH and adrenal hormones in the blood also control the amounts of new ACTH secreted into the blood. Acute illness, emotional disturbance, and certain medicines cause increased secretion of ACTH.

As a drug, ACTH is used to maintain the health of the adrenal cortex when the pituitary gland does not produce enough ACTH. It is also used to stimulate the production of adrenal cortex hormones. These steroids lessen the symptoms of several diseases, including arthritis, asthma, and gout. (See CORTISONE.) This drug is also used in tests to diagnose diseases of the adrenal cortex and the pituitary gland.

ACTH was first isolated in 1943, and first synthesized in 1960. For commercial use, it is extracted from the pituitary glands of cattle. Because the drug may have harmful effects, it can be obtained only by prescription. It is administered by injection.

In chemical structure, ACTH is a peptide chain of 39 amino acids. It has a molecular weight of 4,500.

Acting, the art or practice of impersonating a character for an audience. The actor's

A-38

task is to bring to life the character he represents, interpreting the character according to the playwright's description and the director's instructions.

This interpretation, in the case of stage, motion pictures, and television, the actor accomplishes by means of a combination of speaking voice, facial expression, gesture, and other body movements. Voice alone (except for various special sound effects) is used in radio plays. The effects of the pantomimist are achieved by the use of gestures and other body motions, without spoken words. (See also PANTOMIME.)

The Actor's Job

Acting may seem to be an easy and glamorous profession to stagestruck boys and girls. Actually, the work is hard and demanding, the training long and difficult, and the prospects for any considerable success are not great. Very few actors and actresses ever become well-paid, famous stars. Even stars may be without work for long periods while no role is available.

In addition to stars, there are supporting players who have roles of varying importance. Some of these are fairly successful, and sometimes acquire many admirers. Character actors, who specialize in playing elderly or unconventional characters, may enjoy longer careers than do stars. One reason is that stars usually must depend upon and maintain an attractive, youthful appearance.

A *bit* player is one who has only a few lines to speak. Supporting players and even bit players may understudy a star, learning his or her lines, so that they may be able to perform the role if the star is unable to appear. A *walk-on* role is usually without lines and involves merely walking about, or on or off, the stage.

The stars for a play, motion picture, or television show are often chosen on the basis of past performances or "box-office appeal" (popularity with audiences). (The actor's *agent,* who represents him in business affairs, sees to it that producers are kept aware of his client's accomplishments.) Other actors and actresses may be chosen in the same way or through an *audition*—a reading of the script before the director or producer by those interested in the parts being offered. The chances of a beginner being selected for a major role are slim.

Once the casting (selection of actors) is

complete, rehearsals begin. In the theater, these traditionally begin with readings; progress through blocking-out sessions in which the actors learn their movements; and culminate with the dress rehearsal, the final rehearsal prior to performance before the opening-night audience. Sometimes a preview performance is given before an audience prior to the opening night. In motion pictures and taped television dramas, the procedure is somewhat different. For example, scenes are often filmed out of sequence, permitting the actors to concentrate on one scene at a time.

The Actor's Training

In the early days of professional acting it was the ambition of most young apprentices to join a company dominated by some great star and to study and emulate his or her techniques, serving as an understudy if possible. At one time there were many touring and stock companies in which an actor could gain valuable experience, but their numbers decreased after motion pictures won first rank in the entertainment field. "Little theaters" to some extent assumed the role of the stock companies in preparing new talent for the professional stage. (See also LITTLE THEATER.)

Many young actors prepare for the theater in dramatic schools and college dramatic departments. Summer theaters often build an amateur or semiprofessional cast around an out-of-town star whose name has drawing power at the box office. The other members of the cast learn from observing and associating with the star.

History

Acting had its origin in the dim past with communal singing and dancing as part of religious rites. The ancient Greeks established formal rules for acting. Actors wore conventional masks expressing emotions and character traits, and did not rely upon facial changes. Events were described rather than enacted. A chorus of several performers provided a background and also offered comments and explanations. (See also TRAGEDY, subtitle *History*.)

Actors still are called thespians (usually with a humorous inference) after Thespis, a Greek dramatist of the sixth century B.C. He was the first to introduce an actor independent of the chorus. Other actors eventually were added.

In the Greek theater, all the actors were male. A few women appeared on the Roman stage. All-male casts prevailed for the most part, however, until actresses began to appear in Italy in the 16th century. In Shakespeare's plays female roles were taken by boys. Actresses were not seen on the English stage until the Restoration (1660).

With the end of the Roman Empire in 476

Rehearsal for a Play. The diagram on the stage floor guides the actors as they learn the movements that go with their parts. Seated are the actor and actress playing the lead parts. Standing are the director and author of the play.

Inge Morath, Magnum Photos

Student Actors. The experience gained by these students acting in *Hamlet* will help them in their appreciation of drama and literature. Amateur acting also builds confidence and poise. Although many college actors become professionals, few colleges look upon drama departments as acting schools.

A.D., acting suffered a decline. However, there were some traveling troupes of acrobats and mimes (comic pantomimists). In the medieval miracle plays (written for religious instruction) priests were the actors. As these plays became more popular, laymen took the place of priests.

In Shakespeare's time (1564-1616) actors usually were young men of good family, often university students. Acting brought both money and fame of a sort, but for many years actors had a reputation for wild and immoral behavior and were not given general social acceptance. The stigma was gradually lessened after the British actor Henry Irving was knighted in 1895.

The theater of improvisation, in which the actors begin with a bare plot and develop dialogue and action as they go along, without using a script, was advanced by the Italian *commedia dell' arte* in the 16th century. The extemporaneous style of the *commedia dell' arte* had a strong influence on the European theater in the 16th and 17th centuries and enjoyed a revival in the latter half of the 20th century. The Second City players of Chicago and New York took a prominent part in reviving the improvisational method of acting. (See also COMEDY, subtitle *History of Comedy:* Decline and Rebirth.)

Acting has always involved exaggerations of both speech and movement. At first this was made necessary because theaters were outdoors. When roofed theaters became

A-40

more common during the English Restoration, some actors began to adopt more natural tones and motions. Nevertheless, theatrical convention (as well as poor acoustics and noisy audiences) long continued to call for a style of acting that today would be considered excessively flamboyant. Only occasionally were there actors whose emotional intensity and stage presence were powerful enough to permit them to exercise restraint; David Garrick (1717-1779) and Edwin Booth (1833-1893) were notable examples.

As early as 1760, the French writer Denis Diderot was inquiring whether an actor should actually "feel" his part. Should he be deeply involved emotionally—or should he merely simulate the feeling prescribed by the playwright and the director? Duke Georg of Saxe-Meiningen (1826-1914), in directing his court theater, advocated emotional involvement by the actor. His example was followed in the French Théâtre Libre of André Antoine (1857?-1943) and the Moscow Art Theatre of Konstantin Stanislavsky (1863-1938).

A more realistic style of acting was made necessary by the late-19th-century trend toward greater realism in plot, characterization, and dialogue of the written play as well as in the style of stage presentation. Émile Zola advocated a meticulous realism that he called naturalism.

Stanislavsky became especially identified with the naturalistic approach to acting. "In our art you must live the part every moment that you are playing it," he told his actors. He added that it is necessary to "creep into the skin and body" of the character being portrayed. Lee Strasberg, who became director of the Actors' Studio of New York City in 1948, developed there the Stanislavsky method of actor training. It became known simply as "the Method" and exerted an enormous influence on acting in the United States. Marlon Brando's performance in *A Streetcar Named Desire* (1948) was a notable early example of the technique taught by "the Method."

The silent motion picture used a form of pantomime that was generally less conventionalized and more restrained than that required for stage performance; closeups, for example, could convey facial expressions too subtle to be seen by theater audiences. Talking pictures and television embody some of the techniques of both the silent screen and the stage.

Although motion pictures and television can provide more surface realism (authentic settings, for example) than the older forms of dramatic presentation, they do not necessarily bring forth more convincing performances by the actors. The actor's ability to communicate with his audience still depends on the actor, not the medium used.

Actors' Equity Association, New York City, is a trade union that bargains for stage actors. The Screen Actors Guild, Hollywood, California, performs a similar service for motion picture actors. Members of the American Federation of Television and Radio Artists, New York City, are performers on radio and television.

See also DRAMA; MOTION PICTURES, table *Motion Picture Academy Awards;* THEATER.

For biographies of actors and actresses, see:

ADAMS, MAUDE	COWARD, Sir NOEL
ANDERSON, JUDITH	CROSBY, BING
ARLISS, GEORGE	CUSHMAN,
BAILEY, PEARL	CHARLOTTE
BANKHEAD,	DREW (family)
TALLULAH	DUSE, ELEONORA
BARRYMORE (family)	EDDY, NELSON
BERNHARDT, SARAH	EVANS, MAURICE
BOGART, HUMPHREY	FAIRBANKS, DOUGLAS
BOOTH (family)	FIELDS, W. C.
BOUCICAULT, DION	FISKE, MINNIE M.
CAMPBELL, MRS.	FORBES-ROBERTSON,
PATRICK	Sir JOHNSTON
CANTOR, EDDIE	FORREST, EDWIN
CHAPLIN, CHARLIE	GABLE, CLARK
COHAN, GEORGE M.	GARBO, GRETA
COOPER, GARY	GIELGUD, Sir JOHN

GILLETTE, WILLIAM	LUNT, ALFRED, and
GISH, LILLIAN AND	LYNN FONTANNE
DOROTHY	MANSFIELD, RICHARD
GUINNESS, Sir ALEC	MANTELL, ROBERT
GWYN, NELL	MARLOWE, JULIA
HAMPDEN, WALTER	MARX BROTHERS
HAYES, HELEN	MIX, TOM
HEPBURN, KATHARINE	MODJESKA, HELENA
HERNE, JAMES A.	MUNI, PAUL
HOPE, BOB	OLIVIER, Sir
HUSTON (family)	LAURENCE
IRVING, Sir HENRY	O'NEAL, FREDERICK
IVES, BURL	PICKFORD, MARY
JANIS, ELSIE	ROBESON, PAUL
JEFFERSON, JOSEPH	ROGERS, WILL
JOLSON, AL	ROSCIUS, QUINTUS
KAYE, DANNY	RUSSELL, LILLIAN
KEAN, EDMUND	SKINNER (family)
KEENE, LAURA	SOTHERN, E. H.
KELLY, GEORGE	TERRY, Dame ELLEN
KELLY, GRACE	THOMPSON, DENMAN
KEMBLE (family)	THORNDIKE, Dame
LANGTRY, LILY	SYBIL
LAUGHTON, CHARLES	TREE, Sir HERBERT
LAUREL AND HARDY	BEERBOHM
LAWRENCE,	VALENTINO,
GERTRUDE	RUDOLPH
LE GALLIENNE, EVA	WAYNE, JOHN
LEIGH, VIVIEN	WELLES, ORSON
LILLIE, BEATRICE	
LLOYD, HAROLD	

Books about Acting

Kalter, Joanmarie. *Actors on Acting: Performing in Theatre and Film Today* (Sterling, 1979).

Kuritz, Paul. *Playing: an Introduction to Acting* (Prentice-Hall, 1982).

McGaw, C. J., and Gary Blake. *Acting Is Believing: a Basic Method,* 4th edition (Holt, Rinehart & Winston, 1980).

Sandler, Bernard, and Steve Posner. *In Front of the Camera: How to Make It and Survive in Movies and Television* (Dutton, 1981).

Seto, J. R. *The Young Actors' Workbook* (Doubleday, 1979).

For Younger Readers:

Carlson, B. W. *Funny-Bone Dramatics* (Abingdon, 1974).

Actinide Elements, ăk′tĭ-nīd, or **Actinides,** a series of 15 chemical elements (atomic numbers 89 through 103). The series is named after actinium, the first element of the group. The other actinides, in order of increasing atomic number, are thorium, protactinium, uranium, neptunium, plutonium, americium, curium, berkelium, californium, einsteinium, fermium, mendelevium, nobelium, and lawrencium. The actinides with atomic numbers higher than 92 (neptunium through lawrencium) are also called *transuranium elements.* (See CHEMISTRY, *A Periodic Table.*)

All the actinides are radioactive metals. Because of the arrangement of their orbital electrons, they are chemically similar to one another and also to the *lanthanides,* or rare-earth metals. (See RARE EARTHS.)

Thorium, protactinium, uranium, and very small amounts of actinium and plutonium are found in nature. The other actinides, along with most plutonium, are produced artificially in nuclear reactors and particle accelerators. Uranium, plutonium, and thorium are used to produce nuclear energy. Thorium is also used as an alloying agent. Other actinides have applications in nuclear research, medicine, and industry.

See also ACTINIUM; AMERICIUM; BERKELIUM; CALIFORNIUM; CURIUM; EINSTEINIUM; FERMIUM; MENDELEVIUM; NEPTUNIUM; NOBELIUM; PLUTONIUM; PROTACTINIUM; THORIUM; URANIUM.

Actinium, ăk-tĭn′ĭ-ŭm, a radioactive chemical element that occurs in nature in trace amounts as a result of the radioactive decay of uranium and thorium. (See RADIOACTIVITY.) Actinium, a heavy, silver-white metal, is usually prepared artificially by bombarding radium with neutrons in a nuclear reactor. It is the first element of the actinide series. (See ACTINIDE ELEMENTS.) The longest-lived isotope of actinium has a half-life period of about 22 years.

Actinium was discovered in 1899 by the French chemist André Debierne. Its name is derived from a Greek word meaning "ray" in recognition of its radioactivity.

Symbol: Ac. Atomic number: 89. Atomic weight: 227. Specific gravity: 10.07. Melting point: 1922° F. (1050° C.). Boiling point: about 5400° F. (3000° C.). Three actinium isotopes, Ac^{225}, Ac^{227}, and Ac^{228}, occur in nature, and eight others have been produced artificially. Actinium belongs to the actinide series of the Periodic Table and has a valence of +3.

Actinolite. See ASBESTOS, subtitle *Asbestos Minerals;* JADE.

Actinomycosis. See LUMPY JAW.

Actium, ăk′shĭ-ŭm, **Battle of,** a decisive naval engagement fought in 31 B.C. near the promontory of Actium, on the west coast of Greece. Here the forces of Octavian (Augustus) met those of Mark Antony and Cleopatra. Octavian's victory marked the end of the Second Triumvirate and made it possible for him to establish the Roman Empire. Antony's forces, resentful of being expected to fight for Cleopatra, deserted in great numbers. During the battle Cleopatra withdrew her fleet and with it escaped to Egypt. Antony followed her, leaving his fleet to conclude the battle.

A-42

Activated Charcoal. See CHARCOAL, subtitle *Other Types of Charcoal.*

Active Voice. See INFLECTION, subtitle *Conjugation:* Voice.

Acton, ăk′tŭn, of Aldenham, John Emerich Edward Dalberg-Acton, First **Baron** (1834-1902), an English historian. Though he never finished a major work, he was a brilliant scholar who had a strong influence on others. Acton planned the *Cambridge Modern History,* but lived to edit only the first volume. He was a leader of the liberal Roman Catholics who disputed the doctrine of papal infallibility.

Acton was born in Naples, the son of a British nobleman. After studying with a Roman Catholic priest in Munich, he served six years in the House of Commons as a Liberal. In 1869 he was created a baron. He taught history at Cambridge, 1895-1902.

Essays on Freedom and Power (1955) is one of several volumes of lectures and articles published after his death. It contains his oft quoted remark, "Power tends to corrupt and absolute power corrupts absolutely."

Actors' Equity Association. See ACTING (last paragraph).

Actors' Studio. See ACTING, subtitle *History.*

Acts of the Apostles, the fifth book of the New Testament. According to tradition, it was written by Saint Luke. The date of the writing is uncertain, but most scholars favor the period 80-90 A.D.

At the beginning of the book the author states his purpose: to explain to Theophilus (who was perhaps a Roman official friendly to Christianity), and to the world, how Christianity arose and began its sweep across the earth. By this time Christianity appeared to be on the way to becoming a world religion, and some account of its beginning was needed so that it might appeal to cultured and learned people.

The title is misleading, for Acts is not a record of all the original disciples of Jesus. The book gives the early history of Christianity from Christ's ascension outside Jerusalem to Paul's visit in Rome. Chapters 1-12 stress the work of Peter in Judea and nearby lands, mainly among Jews. Chapters 13-28 tell of the far-ranging missionary preaching of Paul, mainly to gentiles (non-Jews).

See also LUKE, Saint; PAUL, Saint; PETER, Saint.

Actuary, a mathematician who specializes in problems related to insurance. Working mainly with statistical and probability mathematics, actuaries determine risks undertaken by insurance companies and compute premium rates that minimize the companies' risks. (See PROBABILITY; STATISTICS.) Rates must be competitive to those charged by other firms for the same protection and must be profitable.

Actuaries also determine dividends paid to policyholders and many other financial matters. The chief actuary has broad financial and operational responsibility, often being a member of top management or company president. Actuaries are also employed in other private industries and in government.

The Society of Actuaries was formed in 1949 by a merger of two professional groups. Headquarters are in Chicago.

Acupuncture, ăk'ŭ-pŭngk'tŭr, a Chinese method of treating disease or producing anesthesia by inserting needles into certain points of the body. Acupuncture has been used in China since about 2,500 B.C. to treat disease, but only since the late 1950's as an anesthetic.

According to ancient Chinese theory, acupuncture works by balancing the body's negative (yin) and positive (yang) life forces, which become unbalanced during disease and pain. The various organs of the body are said to be either yang or yin and the spirit of life flows between yang and yin through a number of channels, called meridians, lying beneath the skin. By inserting needles at designated points along these channels, the balance of yang and yin can be restored. After insertion, the needles are twirled by hand or stimulated electrically. They are made of steel or copper and are of various lengths.

Acupuncture has been viewed by Western physicians with a mixture of enthusiasm and skepticism. Most of them feel that as a means of anesthesia acupuncture techniques are worth serious investigation. How acupuncture works—and there is evidence that it does work for certain patients—has not been explained by modern science, although various theories have been suggested to explain the anesthetic effects. Some physicians say that acupuncture is little more than quackery.

Ad Valorem Duties. See TARIFF, subtitle *National Tariff Systems.*

ADA. See AMERICANS FOR DEMOCRATIC ACTION.

Adagio. See DANCE, THE, subtitle *The Stage Dance:* Twentieth Century.

Adam, Robert. See FURNITURE, subtitle *Period Styles of Furniture:* England.

Adam and Eve, in the Bible story of creation, the first man and woman. Adam in Hebrew means "man," "mankind," and originally probably meant "reddish"; Eve means "life." Both names are symbolic. Genesis sometimes uses the word *Adam* to refer to man in general.

Genesis has two accounts of the creation. In one account man is the crowning act of

Expulsion of Adam and Eve, by Masaccio (1401-1428?), is a fresco in the Carmine church, Florence.
Art Reference Bureau

creation on the sixth day. "So God created man in his own image, in the image of God created he him; male and female created he them" (1:27). In the other account "the Lord God formed man of the dust of the ground, and breathed into his nostrils the breath of life; and man became a living soul" (2:7). Later, God created Eve as a help-meet; he caused a deep sleep to fall upon Adam, took one of his ribs, and from it made a woman.

God placed Adam and Eve in the Garden of Eden, warning them against the tree of knowledge and its forbidden fruit. Enticed by a serpent, Eve ate some of the fruit, and she gave some to Adam, who also ate. Then followed shame and banishment from Eden.

Adam and Eve became the parents of Cain and Abel. After the murder of Abel, and the banishment of Cain, Seth was born. Later there were other sons and daughters. Adam died at the age of 930 (Genesis 5:5).

See also ABEL; CAIN; EDEN.

Adamic, ăd'á-mĭk, **Louis** (1899-1951), a United States author. His interests included the lot of the immigrant in the United States, national and international politics, and labor history.

Adamic was born in an Austrian province now part of Yugoslavia. He came to the United States in 1913, and was naturalized in 1918. *Dynamite* (1931), his first book, is about violence in labor disputes. *Laughing in the Jungle* (1932) is an autobiographical account of his early experiences in the United States. *The Native's Return* (1934) tells of a visit to his birthplace. Adamic died of an apparently self-inflicted gunshot wound.

Other books include: *Two-Way Passage* (1941); *A Nation of Nations* (1945); *Dinner at the White House* (1946); *The Eagle and the Roots* (1952).

Adams, a Massachusetts family of statesmen, scholars, and authors that included two Presidents of the United States. It is considered by many historians to be the most remarkable family in American history. Intellectually gifted and articulate, its members made notable contributions to public life and letters from colonial times to the 20th century.

Samuel Adams by J. S. Copley
City of Boston: Museum of Fine Arts

A-44

Henry Adams (1583?-1646), the founder of the family in America, came from England in 1636. He settled at Mount Wollaston (later called Braintree, now Quincy), Massachusetts, and became a farmer. Two of his great-grandsons were Samuel (1689-1748) and John Adams (1691-1761). One of Samuel's 12 children was the Revolutionary War patriot Samuel Adams (1722-1803). John was the father of the second President of the United States, John Adams (1735-1826).

The eldest son of President Adams, John Quincy Adams (1767-1848), became the sixth President of the United States. John Quincy Adams' son, Charles Francis Adams (1807-1886), served as minister to Great Britain during the Civil War. Three of Charles Francis Adams' sons were historians —Charles Francis (1835-1915), Henry (1838-1918), and Brooks Adams (1848-1927). Their nephew, Charles Francis Adams (1866-1954), was secretary of the navy in the cabinet of President Herbert Hoover.

These men are discussed in this article in chronological order.

Samuel Adams (1722-1803) was an American Revolutionary leader. He was a second cousin of John Adams, second President of the United States. A skilled politician and propagandist, Sam Adams (as he was popularly called), more than any other man, prepared the way for the American Revolution. During the Revolutionary period, he stirred the colonists against Great Britain through writings, speeches, and personal contact. To his opponents, Adams was the "Chief Incendiary," exploiting colonial differences with Britain to advance his own radical ideas. To his supporters, he was the "Firebrand of Independence," dedicated to the cause of American liberty.

Early Career. Sam Adams was born in Boston. He was graduated from Harvard in 1740, receiving a master's degree in 1743. He gave up the study of law to enter business. Unsuccessful in a number of ventures, he became tax collector of Boston in 1756. Adams left this post in 1764, after falling behind in collections. The struggle with Great Britain for colonial rights gave him an opportunity to devote all of his energy to politics, at which he was eminently more effective.

Revolutionary Period. By 1764 Sam Adams was already a leading figure in Bos-

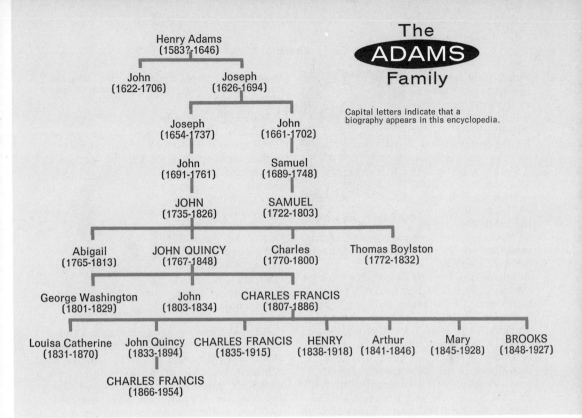

The ADAMS Family

Capital letters indicate that a biography appears in this encyclopedia.

Henry Adams
(1583?-1646)

John
(1622-1706)

Joseph
(1626-1694)

Joseph
(1654-1737)

John
(1661-1702)

John
(1691-1761)

Samuel
(1689-1748)

JOHN
(1735-1826)

SAMUEL
(1722-1803)

Abigail
(1765-1813)

JOHN QUINCY
(1767-1848)

Charles
(1770-1800)

Thomas Boylston
(1772-1832)

George Washington
(1801-1829)

John
(1803-1834)

CHARLES FRANCIS
(1807-1886)

Louisa Catherine
(1831-1870)

John Quincy
(1833-1894)

CHARLES FRANCIS
(1835-1915)

HENRY
(1838-1918)

Arthur
(1841-1846)

Mary
(1845-1928)

BROOKS
(1848-1927)

CHARLES FRANCIS
(1866-1954)

ton politics, having opposed for some years the small group of aristocratic families that virtually ruled Massachusetts. He took a prominent part in the agitation against the Sugar Act of 1764 and the Stamp Act of 1765, protesting "taxation without representation." In 1765 he helped form the Sons of Liberty, a secret revolutionary society. Serving in the Massachusetts legislature, 1765-74, Adams became leader of the radicals and was clerk of the House, 1766-74. Adams stirred up opposition to the Townshend Acts (1767), and was an organizer of the Non-Importation Association in 1768.

During a period of relative calm, 1770-72, Sam Adams kept discontent alive by writing inflammatory newspaper articles. In 1772 he organized the first Committee of Correspondence. He drafted the Boston Declaration of Rights in 1772 and was influential in the agitation that led to the Boston Tea Party. After passage of the Intolerable Acts, 1774, Adams was one of the first to call for a congress of the colonies. He was chosen as a delegate to the First and Second Continental Congresses, 1774-75. An early supporter of separation from Britain, he voted for and signed the Declaration of Independence in 1776.

After Independence. As Adams was more a revolutionary agitator than statesman, his influence declined after American independence was declared. He was a member of the Continental Congress until 1781, serving on the committee that drafted the Articles of Confederation. Although at first opposed to a strong central government, Adams voted for ratification of the Federal Constitution at the Massachusetts Convention of 1788. He was lieutenant governor of Massachusetts, 1789-93, and governor, 1794-97.

See also BOSTON TEA PARTY; COMMITTEES OF CORRESPONDENCE; SONS OF LIBERTY.

John Adams (1735-1826) was the second President and first Vice President of the United States. See ADAMS, JOHN.

John Quincy Adams (1767-1848), the son of John Adams, was the sixth President of the United States. See ADAMS, JOHN QUINCY.

Charles Francis Adams (1807-1886), son of John Quincy Adams, was a statesman and author. As minister to Great Britain, 1861-68, Adams adroitly handled the difficult problems that the Civil War created between Great Britain and the United States, such as the *Trent* affair. He thus helped to prevent Britain from recognizing and giving assistance to the Confederacy. Adams served as one of the United States arbitrators at the Geneva Tribunal that settled the *Alabama* Claims against Great Britain, 1871-72. While on the arbitration board,

Chicago Historical Society
Charles Francis Adams

he was considered as a possible Presidential candidate by the Liberal Republicans for the 1872 election.

Adams was born in Boston. He attended schools in Russia and in England, when his father was United States minister to those countries. In 1825 he was graduated from Harvard. Adams was admitted to the bar in 1829, having studied law in the office of Daniel Webster, but never practiced. He was elected to the Massachusetts legislature as a Whig in 1840 and served until 1845. In 1848 he was the Vice Presidential candidate of the Free Soil party. From 1859 to 1861, Adams served in the U.S. House of Representatives as a Republican. There he led a group that sought to reach an understanding with the South.

Adams edited and published the letters of Abigail Adams (1840-41), *Works of John Adams* (10 volumes, 1850-56), and *Memoirs of John Quincy Adams* (12 volumes, 1874-77).

See also ALABAMA CLAIMS; TRENT AFFAIR.

Charles Francis Adams (1835-1915), son of the first Charles Francis Adams, was a historian and a railroad expert. Adams was born in Boston. After graduation from Harvard in 1856 he studied law in the office of Richard Henry Dana and Francis E. Parker. During the Civil War he served in the Union army, rising to brevet brigadier general.

After the war, Adams studied railroad development and operations. He was named to the Massachusetts Board of Railroad Commissioners in 1869, serving as chairman 1872-79. He wrote *Chapters of Erie and Other Essays* (1871), exposing corruption in railroad finance. Adams was chairman of the government directors of the Union Pacific Railroad, 1878-84, and president of the railroad, 1884-90.

His numerous writings include: *Railroads: Their Origin and Problems* (1878); *Richard Henry*

Dana (1890); *Three Episodes in Massachusetts History* (1892); *Life of Charles Francis Adams* (1900).

Henry (Brooks) **Adams** (1838-1918), son of the first Charles Francis Adams, was a historian and one of the most important authors and original thinkers of his time. Adams analyzed what Darwin's evolutionary theory implied for the future of society. In his dynamic theory of history he concluded that society, instead of moving toward perfection, was subject to dissipation of energy and eventual exhaustion.

Houghton Mifflin
Henry Adams

Adams' *History of the United States During the Administrations of Jefferson and Madison* (9 volumes, 1889-91) remains a definitive analysis of the early years of American democracy. *Mont-Saint-Michel and Chartres* (1913; privately published 1904) is a study of the medieval spirit in architecture and philosophy. His brilliant autobiography, *The Education of Henry Adams* (1918; privately published 1906), was awarded the Pulitzer Prize in 1919. In these two books, Adams contrasts what he considered the unifying effect of religion on life in the 13th century with the disruptive effect of science on the modern mind and society.

Adams was born in Boston and was graduated from Harvard in 1858. After studying in Germany, he was secretary to his father, who was minister to Great Britain, 1861-68. In 1870 Henry Adams became assistant professor of history at Harvard and editor of the *North American Review*. He resigned as editor in 1876 and as professor in 1877 and moved to Washington, D.C., to devote his time to writing. The tragedy of his wife's suicide in 1885 embittered his later years.

Adams' other writings include: *The Life of Albert Gallatin* (1879); *The Works of Albert Gallatin* (3 volumes, 1879); *A Letter to American Teachers of History* (1910); *The Degradation of Democratic Dogma* (1919). *Democracy* (anonymously published in 1880) is a novel.

Brooks Adams (1848-1927), son of the first Charles Francis Adams, was a historian and a critic of society. Adams questioned prevailing attitudes and theories and developed his own theory of the movement of history. He believed that all history is a struggle between concentration and dissipation of energy. His ideas influenced his older brother, Henry Adams, and laid the groundwork for later historians and economists, including Thorstein Veblen, Oswald Spengler, and Charles A. Beard.

Adams' first book, *The Emancipation of Massachusetts* (1887), describes the development of religious freedom in that commonwealth. In his most important work, *Law of Civilization and Decay* (1895), he developed his cyclical interpretation of history. Civilization, he wrote, rose and fell according to the growth and decay of commerce. Adams applied this principle to the course of modern history and foresaw eventual chaos.

Brooks Adams was born in Quincy, Massachusetts. He was graduated from Harvard in 1870 and studied at Harvard Law School. Adams was secretary to his father at the *Alabama* Claims negotiations in Geneva, 1871-72. After practicing law in Boston, 1873-81, Adams, like his brothers Henry and Charles Francis, turned to writing and research.

His other writings include: *America's Economic Supremacy* (1900) ; *The New Empire* (1902) ; *The Theory of Social Revolutions* (1913).

Charles Francis Adams (1866-1954), son of the second John Quincy Adams (1833-1894) and grandson of the first Charles Francis Adams, was a banker and public official. As secretary of the navy, 1929-33, under President Herbert Hoover, Adams helped negotiate the agreements at the London Naval Conference of 1930, which restricted the size and number of naval vessels. He returned to the banking business in 1933. Adams was born in Quincy, Massachusetts, and was graduated from Harvard Law School in 1892. He was mayor of Quincy, 1896-97.

Adams, Abigail Smith. See ADAMS, JOHN.

Adams, Alvin (1804-1877). See EXPRESS COMPANY, subtitle *History of Express Services*.

Adams, Brooks. See ADAMS (family).

Adams, Charles Francis (1807-1886). See ADAMS (family).

Adams, Charles Francis (1835-1915). See ADAMS (family).

Adams, Charles Francis (1866-1954). See ADAMS (family).

Adams, Franklin P. (Pierce) (1881-1960), a United States columnist and humorist who often signed his work F. P. A. His "Conning Tower" column, which appeared in several New York newspapers—beginning with the *Tribune* in 1913 and ending with the *Post* in 1941—contained light verse and witty comment. Adams was a panelist on the popular "Information Please" radio program for about 10 years, beginning in 1938.

Adams was born in Chicago. After graduating from Armour Scientific Academy in 1899, he studied for a year at the University of Michigan. He began his journalistic career in Chicago in 1903, and moved to New York during the next year.

Among his many books are *Tobogganing on Parnassus* (1910) ; *The Diary of Our Own Samuel Pepys* (2 volumes, 1935) ; *Nods and Becks* (1944).

Adams, Henry Brooks. See ADAMS (family).

Adams, Herbert Baxter (1850-1901), a United States historian. Adams was a founder of the American Historical Association and its first secretary, 1884-1900. While professor of history at Johns Hopkins University, 1876-1901, he began the *Johns Hopkins Studies in Historical and Political Science*. It became a model for similar series elsewhere. Adams was born in Shutesbury, Massachusetts. He was graduated from Amherst College in 1872 and received a doctorate from Heidelberg University, Germany, in 1876.

Adams, James Truslow (1878-1949), a United States historian. Adams was an authority on the history of New England and the New England Adamses (to whom he was not related). He was awarded the Pulitzer Prize in history in 1922 for *The Founding of New England* (1921). His works include *The Adams Family* (1930) and *The Epic of America* (1931), an interpretive history of America since the Spanish explorations.

Adams was born in Brooklyn, New York. He was graduated from Brooklyn Polytechnic Institute, 1898, and received an M.A. degree from Yale University, 1900. After 12 years as a successful banker and stock broker, Adams retired in 1912 to study and write history. An army captain in World War I, he later served on special duty at the Paris Peace Conference of 1919.

His other books include: *Revolutionary New England, 1691-1776* (1923); *New England in the*

Republic, 1776-1850 (1926); *Provincial Society, 1690-1763* (1927); *The March of Democracy* (2 volumes, 1932-33); and *Henry Adams* (1933). Adams edited *The Dictionary of American History* (6 volumes, 1940); *The Atlas of American History* (1943); and *Album of American History* (4 volumes, 1944-48). (Both the *Dictionary* and the *Album* added volumes after his death.)

Adams, John (1735-1826), the second President of the United States and the first Vice President. As President, Adams kept the young republic at peace in a time of crisis, avoiding a needless war with France and preventing civil conflict at home. He considered this act of preserving the peace "the most determined and the most successful of my whole life." However, the independent course that Adams followed during the crisis with France divided the Federalist party between those who supported the President and those who supported Alexander Hamilton. This division contributed to Adams' defeat in the election of 1800 and to the eventual downfall of the Federalist party.

Revolutionary leader, statesman, political philosopher, orator, and scholar, Adams was one of the great men of an era that produced many illustrious men. Although not personally popular, he was widely respected for his abilities. That his Presidency was not as successful as were his efforts during the long struggle for independence was due, in part, to his personality. Adams possessed vision, courage, sound judgment, and integrity—but he was also proud, overly sensitive, and short-tempered, unable to engage in the give-and-take necessary for political success.

Early Life

John Adams was born October 30, 1735, on a farm in Braintree (now a part of Quincy), Massachusetts. He was the eldest son of John and Susanna Boylston Adams. After being graduated from Harvard College in 1755, he taught school. He had contemplated a career in the ministry, but then decided to study law. In 1758 he was admitted to the bar. He began to practice in Braintree and soon took an interest in public affairs.

In 1764 Adams married Abigail Smith (1744-1818) of Weymouth. Intelligent, well-read, and resourceful, she assisted and counseled her husband throughout his career. During his long absences in the Revolutionary period, she managed the farm and raised the children. Mrs. Adams was also a prolific letter writer, and her letters have been an important source of social history. The wife of one President and mother of another, she was one of the most prominent women in the early days of the Republic.

Revolutionary Leader, 1765-77

Colonial Agitation. Adams first became identified with the struggle for colonial rights in 1765, when he prepared Braintree's arguments against the Stamp Act. In 1768 he moved to Boston. He was offered the position of advocate-general of the Admiralty Court, but refused the appointment, considering it an attempt to draw him from the patriot cause. Two years later Adams agreed to defend the British soldiers being tried for their part in the Boston Massacre. He risked his career to see that they received a fair trial.

During this period, Adams wrote a number of articles on taxation and other controversial matters. They appeared in the *Boston Gazette* as "A Dissertation on the Canon and Feudal Law." In one of these articles he wrote "Liberty cannot be preserved without a general knowledge among the people."

Adams was elected to the Massachusetts General Court in 1770. After serving a year, he retired to Braintree. The tide of events brought about Adams' return to public life, and he became one of the political leaders of

Gilbert Stuart
National Gallery of Art

the colony, along with his distant cousin Samuel Adams. He approved of the Boston Tea Party, 1773, although he was opposed to mob action. In 1774 Adams denounced the oppressive Boston Port Act.

The Continental Congress. As a delegate to the First Continental Congress, meeting in Philadelphia in 1774, Adams served on committees preparing the petition to the king and the declaration of rights. A leader of the radical faction, he favored stronger action than that finally taken against Great Britain. Returning to Boston, Adams was a member of the Revolutionary Provincial Congress, 1774-75. In a series of newspaper articles under the name "Novanglus," he set forth his views on the dispute with Britain.

Adams returned to Philadelphia in 1775 as a delegate to the Second Continental Congress. He proposed that Congress make the New England militia, already fighting the British, the beginning of a continental army. He nominated George Washington as commander in chief. The appointment of a Virginian was important in gaining support for the cause outside New England.

One of the early advocates of independence, Adams served on the committee drafting a declaration of independence. However, his most important contribution was his vigorous and eloquent championing of the declaration's passage in Congress. Jefferson called Adams "the pillar of its support on the floor of Congress" and "its ablest advocate and defender." Adams remained in Congress until November, 1777, a member of a number of important committees, including the Board of War.

See also CONTINENTAL CONGRESS; DECLARATION OF INDEPENDENCE.

Diplomatic Service, 1777-88

In 1777 Adams was elected commissioner to France to succeed Silas Deane. Returning from France in 1779, he became the principal architect of Massachusetts' first constitution. Later that year, Adams was appointed to negotiate the peace treaty with Great Britain. He arrived in Paris in 1780, but found it difficult to deal with the French, whose intentions he distrusted, and with Benjamin Franklin, who he believed interfered with his efforts.

In 1780 Adams was sent to the United Provinces of the Netherlands, where he obtained a $2,000,000 loan and a treaty of commerce and friendship. He returned to

Henry Francis du Pont Winterthur Museum

American Peace Commissioners at the signing of the Treaty of Paris, 1783, from an unfinished painting by Benjamin West. Seated, from left, John Adams, Benjamin Franklin, and Henry Laurens. Standing, John Jay and Franklin's grandson, William Temple Franklin, secretary to the delegation.

Paris in 1782 to take part in the final negotiations with Britain and made important contributions on the questions of fisheries, boundaries, and debts owed to Loyalists. In 1785 Adams was appointed the first minister to the Court of St. James's. Relations between the United States and Britain were so strained that his position there was far from pleasant, and he resigned in 1788. While in London, Adams wrote the three-volume *Defence of the Constitutions of Government of the United States of America* (1787-88).

Vice President, 1789-97

Shortly after his return to Massachusetts, Adams was elected the first Vice President of the United States, serving during George Washington's two administrations, 1789-97. The vigorous and brilliant Adams felt frustrated in the Vice Presidency, forever in the shadow of Washington. He wrote to his wife that it was the "most insignificant office that ever the invention of man contrived or his imagination conceived." As presiding officer in the Senate, Adams supported the administration and cast tie-breaking votes on some 20 occasions.

President, 1797-1801

John Adams succeeded Washington as President. In the election of 1796, Adams received 71 electoral votes to 68 votes for Thomas Jefferson, his Republican party rival, who became Vice President. This was the only instance in United States history in which election opponents became President and Vice President in the same administration. Adams was further handicapped in the

The Second President

John Adams
1735–1826

Birthplace in Braintree (now Quincy), Massachusetts.

Quincy South Shore Chamber of Commerce

Parents: John and Susanna (Boylston) Adams.

Ancestry: English.

Height: 5 feet 7 inches.

Religion: Unitarian.

Political Party: Federalist.

Family: Adams married Abigail Smith (1744–1818) in 1764. They had five children: Abigail (1765–1813); John Quincy (1767–1848); Susanna (1768–1770); Charles (1770–1800); Thomas Boylston (1772–1832).

Abigail Smith Adams

National Gallery of Art

1735 – Born on October 30.

1755 – Graduated from Harvard College.

1758 – Admitted to the bar in Boston.

1770 – Elected to Massachusetts legislature.

1774 – Chosen delegate to Continental Congress.

1778 – Appointed commissioner to France.

1779 – Serves as member of Massachusetts Constitutional Convention.

1780 – Named minister to the Netherlands.

1783 – Negotiates peace treaty with Great Britain.

1785 – Becomes first minister to Britain.

1788 – Elected Vice President; reelected in 1792.

1796 – Elected President; inaugurated March 4, 1797.

1801 – Retires to home in Quincy, Massachusetts.

1826 – Dies on July 4.

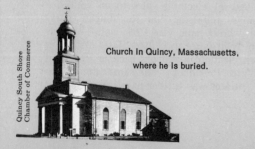

Quincy South Shore Chamber of Commerce

Church in Quincy, Massachusetts, where he is buried.

ADAMS, JOHN

Presidency by the division within the Federalist party, caused by the opposition of Alexander Hamilton.

War Crisis with France. When Adams took office, he was faced by a crisis with France over the role of the United States in the European wars of the French Revolution. Three peace commissioners sent to France in 1797 were rebuffed by the French, who demanded a bribe as the price for recognition. This incident, known as the XYZ Affair, resulted in public support for Adams.

The Hamilton faction favored stirring popular passion against France, hoping that one effect would be the discrediting of the pro-French Jeffersonian Republicans. The President, however, was determined to preserve peace, while attempting to force France to abandon its coercive policy by strengthening the naval and military forces of the United States. This difference of views further divided the Federalists. The Republicans opposed the defense measures.

From 1798 to 1800, an undeclared naval war was waged on the high seas by French and American ships. Adams was informed that the French were willing to reopen negotiations late in 1798. Without advising his cabinet, which he had discovered was under Hamilton's influence, Adams named a new peace mission. In 1800 the commissioners were received by Napoleon Bonaparte, the new leader of the French government, and Treaty of Morfontaine was signed.

See also XYZ Affair.

Alien and Sedition Acts. During the crisis, the Federalists in Congress passed the restrictive Alien and Sedition Acts (1798). They were intended to force foreign agents out of the country and to suppress criticism by Jeffersonian Republicans. Although Adams was not responsible for their enactment, he did not attempt to stop their passage. Under these acts, hundreds of foreign residents fled the country and many critics of Federalist policies were prosecuted. (See also Alien and Sedition Acts.)

Opposition to the acts was expressed in resolutions adopted by the legislatures of Kentucky and Virginia in 1798. They condemned the Alien and Sedition Acts as unconstitutional. The Kentucky resolutions were written, anonymously, by Thomas Jefferson; those of Virginia, by James Madison. (See also Kentucky and Virginia Resolutions.)

A-50

ADAMS, JOHN

Election of 1800. In 1800 the government was moved to Washington, D.C., and Adams became the first occupant of the White House. Mrs. Adams wrote to her daughter that she hung the family wash in the East Room of the yet unfinished building. President Adams' high regard for his wife's views on a number of matters made her one of the most influential First Ladies in history and led to the derisive nicknames "Her Majesty" and "Mrs. President." Adams' opponents called him "His Rotundity," referring to his stature (a stout 5 feet 7 inches) and his aristocratic manner.

Renominated by the Federalists, Adams was defeated by Jefferson in the election of 1800. He lost by only eight electoral votes, despite the waning appeal of the Federalists and the division within the party. Jefferson received 73 electoral votes; Adams, 65. One of Adams' last acts as President was to appoint John Marshall chief justice of the United States.

Later Years

In 1801 Adams retired to his farm in Quincy, Massachusetts. He retained his interest in public affairs and watched with satisfaction the career of his son, John Quincy Adams. In 1818 his wife died, and this loss saddened his remaining years. Throughout their marriage, whenever separated, the Adamses had carried on a remarkable correspondence. Their letters contain vivid descriptions of life in the Revolutionary period and in the early years of the new nation. The letters also reveal the depth of their relationship and the warmth and wit of John Adams, devoted husband and father.

In 1820 Adams was a member of the Second Constitutional Convention of Massachusetts. He lived to see his son, John Quincy, inaugurated as the sixth President of the United States in 1825. On July 4, 1826, John Adams died. His last words were reported to be, "Thomas Jefferson survives." However, his former political opponent and, in their later years, valued friend and correspondent had died a few hours earlier that day, the 50th anniversary of the Declaration of Independence.

John Adams' determination to record and to preserve his thoughts and experiences for succeeding generations has provided a personally revealing and historically informative account of the man and his times. Portions of Adams' diary and autobiography, edited by his grandson Charles Francis Adams, appeared in print during 1850-56. The

During the
Adams Administration
1797–1801

The population of the United States (1800 census) was 5,308,483. There were 16 states in the union during his term of office.

Vice President: Thomas Jefferson*

Cabinet:

Secretary of State	Timothy Pickering*
	John Marshall*
Secretary of the Treasury	Oliver Wolcott (Jr.)
	Samuel Dexter
Secretary of War	James McHenry*
	Samuel Dexter
	Roger Griswold
Attorney General	Charles Lee
	Theophilus Parsons
Postmaster General	Joseph Habersham
Secretary of the Navy	Benjamin Stoddert

*Indicates a separate article in this encyclopedia.

Events in the United States

1797	The Great Revival, a religious movement, begins to sweep the western frontier.
June 26, 1797	Iron plow patented by Charles Newbold of New Jersey.
1798	Eli Whitney introduces the principle of interchangeable parts in manufacturing.
January 8, 1798	11th Amendment to the Constitution becomes effective – one state cannot be sued by citizens of another state.
April 30, 1798	U.S. Navy Department created.
June - July 1798	The restrictive Alien and Sedition Acts become law.
July 16, 1798	U.S. Public Health Service founded as the Marine Health Service.
November 17, 1800	Congress convenes for the first time in new federal capital of Washington, D.C.
February 17, 1801	Electoral college vote tie broken in House of Representatives – Thomas Jefferson chosen President; Aaron Burr, Vice President.

World Events

July 13, 1797	First revolt against Spanish rule in Venezuela breaks out.
October 17, 1797	Treaty of Campo Formio ends unsuccessful first European coalition war against France.
1798	*An Essay on the Principle of Population* by Thomas Malthus is published.
May - June 1798	Irish rebellion against British rule fails.
December 1798	Second coalition (Great Britain, Austria, Russia, Naples, Portugal, and Turkey) formed to battle France.
1798 - 1800	United States and France fight undeclared naval war.
November 10, 1799	Napoleon seizes power in France.
October 1, 1800	Spain forced to return Louisiana to France by secret Treaty of San Ildefonso.
January 1, 1801	Great Britain and Ireland are united as one kingdom.

Painting by G. P. A. Healy
Courtesy White House Historical Association

complete *Diary and Autobiography of John Adams* (4 volumes, edited by Lyman H. Butterfield) was published in 1961.

For further information, see:

Books about John Adams

Brown, R. A. *The Presidency of John Adams* (Regents Press of Kansas, 1975).
Butterfield, L. H., and others, editors. *The Book of Abigail and John: Selected Letters of the Adams Family* (Harvard University, 1975).
East, R. A. *John Adams* (Twayne, 1979).

Adams, John Couch (1819-1892), a British astronomer, one of the discoverers of the planet Neptune. From his study of the planet Uranus, Adams was able to calculate mathematically the existence of Neptune in 1845. Urbain Leverrier made the same discovery independently in 1846. Adams also determined the orbit of the Leonid meteors (swarms of meteors that appear each November) and studied the earth's magnetism and the moon's motions. Adams was professor of astronomy and geometry at Cambridge University, 1858-92.

A-52

Adams, John Quincy (1767-1848), the sixth President of the United States. He was the son of John Adams, the second President. John Quincy Adams served his country not only as President, but as a diplomat, secretary of state, and member of the U.S. House of Representatives. He was the only President's son to obtain the highest office himself, and the only man to serve in the House of Representatives after being President.

Adams' four years as President were the least distinguished of his career. In the critical period of the United States' emergence as a nation, his diplomatic service had been remarkably successful; his achievements as secretary of state under Monroe, brilliant. As President, Adams faced no crises. The period of his administration was notable especially for the conflict of political philosophies and the formation of two parties reflecting the two major points of view. In Congress, where he represented the Northern view, favoring nationalism over states' rights and abolition over the perpetuation of slavery, Adams met his greatest challenge and attained perhaps his greatest victory.

In manner cold and stiff, Adams had a passionate temper and a tongue so cutting that he was feared and resented by many of his associates. His proud and jealous nature, intensity of conviction, and fierce obstinacy made him extremely difficult to deal with, yet he aroused fervent loyalty in his adherents. Adams' unswerving moral rectitude gained the respect even of his enemies. He was five feet, seven inches (1.70 m) tall, and bald from early manhood. His voice was shrill, and in his years in the House of Representatives was prone to crack. Yet his wit was so keen and his arguments so telling that he was known as "old man eloquent."

Early Career

John Quincy Adams was born July 11, 1767, at Braintree (now Quincy), Massachusetts, the second child and eldest son of John and Abigail Adams. He was given schooling at home by his parents until 1778, when he accompanied his father on a mission to France and attended school in Paris. His father's next mission was to the United Provinces of the Netherlands, where John Quincy attended the University of Leiden.

Because of his proficiency in foreign languages, Adams in 1781, at the age of 14, served as private secretary to Francis Dana, minister to Russia. He served also in Paris as his father's secretary during the peace conference that ended the American Revolution in 1783. He shortly returned to the United States, was graduated from Harvard College in 1788, and was admitted to the bar in 1790.

While practicing law in Boston, Adams wrote pamphlets and articles on political matters of the day. On the basis of these writings, President Washington in 1794 appointed him minister to the Netherlands. While on diplomatic missions to London he courted Louisa Catherine Johnson (1775-1852), daughter of the United States consul there. They were married in 1797. In the same year the elder Adams, then President, appointed his son minister to Prussia, where he served until 1801.

Having been abroad while the Federalist and Jeffersonian Republican parties took form, Adams had made no party affiliation. Assuming him to be a Federalist, as was his father, the Massachusetts legislature elected him to the U.S. Senate in 1803. From the beginning Adams proved independent in attitude and action. When he supported President Jefferson's 1807 Embargo Act, his constituents in mercantile Massachusetts were outraged. A special election was held to choose a replacement for him, and Adams resigned in 1808. He returned to his law practice, and continued his teaching, begun in 1806, as professor of oratory and rhetoric at Harvard.

Foreign Service, 1809-17

Adams' support of the Jeffersonian administration had established him as a Republican. In 1809 President Madison appointed him minister to Russia. Adams presented his nation's rights and aims with singular success. His accomplishment in having Baltic ports opened to United States ships and virtually closed to the French was one cause of Napoleon's attack on Russia. The last of the Adamses' four children was born during the Russian sojourn.

During the War of 1812 between Great Britain and the United States, Adams was a member of the United States peace commission that met with the British at Ghent, Belgium, in early 1814. Adams' ready resentment and bad humor contributed to stormy differences among the commission members; he was constantly at odds with Henry Clay over East Coast versus Western

A-53

The Sixth President
John Quincy Adams
1767-1848

Birthplace in Braintree (now Quincy), Massachusetts.

Quincy South Shore Chamber of Commerce

Parents: John and Abigail (Smith) Adams

Ancestry: English

Height: 5 feet 7 inches

Religion: Unitarian

Political Party: Jeffersonian Republican

Family: Adams married Louisa Catherine Johnson (1775-1852) in 1797. They had four children: George Washington (1801-1829); John (1803-1834); Charles Francis (1807-1886); Louisa Catherine (1811-1812).

National Collection of Fine Arts Smithsonian Institution

Louisa Johnson Adams

1767 – Born on July 11.
1788 – Graduated from Harvard College.
1790 – Admitted to the bar.
1794 – Appointed minister to the Netherlands.
1797 – Named minister to Prussia.
1803 – Elected to U.S. Senate from Massachusetts.
1809 – Chosen minister to Russia.
1815 – Appointed minister to Great Britain.
1817 – Becomes secretary of state in cabinet of President Monroe.
1824 – Elected President of the United States; serves 1825-29.
1830 – Elected to U.S. House of Representatives.
1848 – Dies on February 23.

Quincy South Shore Chamber of Commerce

Church in Quincy, Massachusetts, where his body lies.

During the
Adams Administration
1825-1829

The population of the United States (1825 estimate) was 11,252,000. There were 24 states in the Union during his term of office.

Vice President: John C. Calhoun*

Cabinet:

Secretary of State	Henry Clay*
Secretary of the Treasury	Richard Rush*
Secretary of War	James Barbour
	Peter B. Porter*
Attorney General	William Wirt
Postmaster General	John McLean
Secretary of the Navy	Samuel L. Southard

*Indicates a separate article in this encyclopedia.

Events in the United States

1825 – Hudson River School of landscape painting begins to develop.

1825 – New Harmony, Indiana, founded as socialistic community by Robert Owen.

October 26, 1825 – Erie Canal opened to traffic.

1826 – Anti-Masonic Party, earliest third party in American history, organized.

January 24, 1826 – Creek Indians cede most of land in Georgia to the United States.

August 22, 1826 – First overland expedition to California begins, led by Jedediah Smith.

April 14, 1828 – Noah Webster's dictionary published.

May 19, 1828 – High protective tariff passed by Congress; called "tariff of abominations" by the South.

July 4, 1828 – Construction starts on first passenger railway in the United States, the Baltimore and Ohio.

December 19, 1828 – "South Carolina Exposition" by John C. Calhoun sets forth doctrine of nullification.

World Events

September 27, 1825 – World's first railroad, the Stockton and Darlington, opens in Great Britain.

December 26-29, 1825 – Decembrist Revolt of liberal military officers quickly suppressed in Russia.

1825-1828 – Argentine-Brazilian War fought over Uruguay; Uruguay given independence.

June 1826 – First inter-American congress, planned by Bolívar, convenes in Panama.

1827 – Friction match invented by John Walker, an English chemist.

July 6, 1827 – Greek independence proclaimed in Treaty of London.

April 26, 1828 – Russo-Turkish war breaks out.

March 1829 – Catholic Emancipation Bill introduced in British Parliament.

interests. However, in December the commission completed a treaty that Madison called "highly honorable to the nation." (See also GHENT, TREATY OF.) Adams served as minister to Great Britain, 1815-17.

Secretary of State, 1817-25

In 1817 Adams was called home from London by President Monroe to head the State Department. No one could have been better fitted for the post. In domestic politics Adams invariably aroused dissension; in foreign affairs, however, he moved toward his goals with suavity and skill.

United States expansion was threatened by territorial claims of Spain and Great Britain. In 1818 Adams persuaded the British to accept temporary joint ownership of the Oregon country. The next year a treaty, known as the Adams-Onis Treaty, was signed with Spain ceding East and West Florida to the United States, and drawing a boundary line that separated California and Oregon. This was probably Adams' greatest achievement as secretary of state.

After the Spanish treaty was ratified in 1821, the new Latin American republics were recognized by the United States, as advocated by Adams. This was the first step toward formulation of the Monroe Doctrine. Meanwhile, Russia had laid claim to the Pacific coast south of Alaska. In July, 1823, Adams told the Russian minister that "the American continents are no longer subjects for any new European colonial establishments." In December President Monroe incorporated this policy into his message to Congress, thus establishing the doctrine. The next year Adams induced Russia to cede all land south of 54°40′ latitude.

President, 1825-29

Although Adams was considered the natural successor to Monroe, differences within the Republican party resulted in four factions each naming a candidate. The nominees were Adams, Clay, Andrew Jackson, and William H. Crawford. The Federalist party no longer existed.

In the November, 1824, election the popular vote was 153,544 for Jackson, 108,740 for Adams, and less than 50,000 each for Crawford and Clay. Jackson received 99 electoral votes to Adams' 84, Crawford's 41, and Clay's 37. As no candidate had a majority, it was up to the House of Representatives to elect one of the three leading contenders. Clay being eliminated, his support was given to Adams, who favored Clay's "American System" of protective tariffs and internal improvements. Adams became President, with John C. Calhoun as his Vice President. When Adams chose Clay, with whom he had often been at odds, to be his secretary of state, accusations of corrupt bargaining were raised.

President Adams' program called for wide use of federal authority. He favored, besides tariffs and internal improvements, a bank of the United States, national administration of public lands, a national university and observatory, and government expeditions of exploration. Federal highways were constructed during his administration, and financial aid and land grants given to canal companies. A high-tariff law, known as the "tariff of abominations," was passed.

Adams' political opponents—mainly from the West and South, and including Vice President Calhoun—wanted free access to public lands, low tariffs, and a federal government too weak ever to interfere with slavery. They accused Adams of being a "monarchist" seeking to destroy state autonomy, and threatened to nullify the tariff act. Led by Jackson, the states' rights adherents took the name Democratic-Republicans. The Adams-Clay faction became the National Republicans.

Adams himself remained aloof from political maneuvering, and did not build a party organization. With Richard Rush as running mate, he was opposed by Jackson and Calhoun in the 1828 election. Jackson received a popular vote of 647,286 and electoral vote of 178 to Adams' 508,064 and 83.

The Metropolitan Museum of Art

John Quincy Adams in 1847 at the age of 79. He was the earliest President to be photographed. This daguerreotype was taken after his Presidency when he was a member of the House.

Congressman, 1831-48

In 1830 Adams was elected to the House of Representatives. At the time citizens' petitions for the abolition of slavery were being sent in considerable number to members of Congress. Adams began reading the petitions aloud in the House, not because he favored abolition, but because right of petition was guaranteed by the Constitution. Soon Adams was deluged with antislavery petitions, all of which he introduced in Congress. At last, in 1836, Southern congressmen succeeded in passing a resolution that no petition relating to slavery could be presented. This "gag rule" was renewed at every session for the next eight years.

Adams fought the gag rule with every device that he could muster, often holding the floor over the shouted objections of his opponents. His tenacity and ingenuity captured public imagination and created a respect and fondness for him that he had never before known. In 1842 a congressional effort to censure him failed, and in 1844 the gag rule was rescinded.

In 1846 Adams suffered a slight stroke, but recovered and returned to Congress in a few months. On February 21, 1848, he was stricken at his desk in the House chamber. Removed to the adjoining speaker's room, he lingered for two days. He was buried in the family tomb in Quincy.

Adams' diary, begun in boyhood and continued all his life, was edited by his son Charles Francis Adams and published as *Memoirs of John Quincy Adams* in 12 volumes in 1874-77. Seven volumes of miscellaneous writings were published 1913-17.

Books about John Quincy Adams

Bemis, S. F. *John Quincy Adams and the Foundations of American Foreign Policy* (1949; Greenwood Press reprint, 1981).

Hecht, M. B. *John Quincy Adams: a Personal History of an Independent Man* (Macmillan, 1972).

Jones, K. V., editor. *John Quincy Adams, 1767-1848: Chronology, Documents, Bibliographic Aids* (Oceana, 1970).

Shepherd, Jack. *Cannibals of the Heart: a Personal Biography of Louisa Catherine and John Quincy Adams* (McGraw-Hill, 1981).

Adams, Louisa Johnson (1775-1852), wife of President John Quincy Adams. See ADAMS, JOHN QUINCY, subtitle *Early Career.*

Adams, Maude, the stage name of Maude Kiskadden, kĭs-kăd″n (1872-1953), a United States actress. She was especially famous in the title role in J. M. Barrie's *Peter Pan.* Beginning in 1905, she enacted the part more than 1,500 times.

She was born in Salt Lake City, Utah.

Maude Adams as the young deposed emperor in *L'Aiglon,* Rostand's play about Napoleon II. She also played male roles in Peter Pan and Chantecler.
Chicago Historical Society

Her first experience was in juvenile roles in Western theaters. At 16 she joined E. H. Sothern's stock company in New York City. She achieved stardom as Lady Babbie in Barrie's *The Little Minister* (1897). By the time she retired in 1981, she had starred in several other Barrie plays, three Shakespearean roles, Edmond Rostand's *Chantecler,* and other productions. From 1937 to 1945 she was chairman of the drama department at Stephens College in Missouri.

Adams, Roger (1889-1971), a United States organic chemist. Adams improved procedures for identifying new substances and developed new techniques of synthesis. He was one of the first to synthesize Butyn (butacaine), a local anesthetic. Adams was born in Boston. He received his B.A. from Harvard in 1909 and Ph.D. in 1912. He was at the University of Illinois, 1916-57, as professor of organic chemistry from 1919, and as head of the chemistry department from 1926. After World War II, Adams served as scientific adviser to the military governments in Germany and Japan.

Adams, Samuel. See ADAMS (family).

Adams, Samuel Hopkins (1871-1958), a United States author. He was a prolific writer for almost 70 years. Adams' works include novels, biographies, histories, magazine articles, and motion-picture scripts. His novels *Revelry* (1926) and *Canal Town* (1944) and the Warren G. Harding biography *The Incredible Era* (1939) were the most successful. He crusaded against medical quackery in the early 1900's, helping to bring about the enactment of the Pure Food and Drug Act. Adams was born in Dunkirk, New York. After his graduation from Hamilton College in 1891, he was with the New York *Sun,* 1891-1900, and *McClure's Magazine,* 1903-05.

Adams, William (1564?-1620), the first Englishman to enter Japan. In 1598 Adams was engaged as pilot of a fleet of five Dutch vessels bound for the East Indies. The fleet was scattered by storms and Adams landed at Kyushu, Japan, in 1600. The shogun (military governor) Iyeyasu was impressed by Adams' knowledge of ships and navigation and employed him as a shipbuilder and adviser. He promoted Dutch and English trade with Japan and lived there the rest of his life. The Japanese called him Anjin Sama (Mr. Pilot) and gave him an estate in Yokosuka and a pension.

Adams, William Taylor. See OPTIC, OLIVER.

Adam's Apple. See LARYNX.

Adams National Historic Site. See NATIONAL PARKS, section "United States."

Adam's Needle. See YUCCA.

Adams State College. See UNIVERSITIES AND COLLEGES (table).

Adamson Act. See LABOR LEGISLATION, subtitle *In the United States.*

Adana, ä-dä-nä', Turkey, the country's fourth largest city and the capital of Seyhan province. It is on the Seyhan River, about 240 miles (385 km) south-southeast of Ankara. It is an agricultural trading center. Manufactured products include tobacco goods, cotton textiles, processed foods, and agricultural machinery.

Adana was an ancient Hittite town that flourished under the Romans and then declined. The city's vitality was restored under the Moslems, beginning in the late eighth century.

Population: 475,384.

Adaptation, ăd'ăp-tā'shŭn, in biology, the process by which an animal or plant species becomes better suited to its environment. The term is applied also to the results of the process. In both plants and animals, there are structural, functional, and color adaptations, and in animals there are also adaptations in instinctive (unlearned) behavior.

Structural Adaptations. The extensive root systems and the small leaves common to many desert plants are good examples of structural adaptation. Such roots enable the plants to collect more of the available moisture from their dry environment. Small leaves, since they provide little surface area for evaporation, reduce loss of water. The powerful forelegs and out-turned palms of the mole are structural adaptations for burrowing.

Functional Adaptations. The ability to complete its growth cycle in a short growing season is a functional adaptation that enables a plant to survive in northerly latitudes. Another example of functional adaptation is provided by the clothes moth, which has a special enzyme that enables it to digest wool.

Color Adaptations. There are three general types of color adaptation: (1) protective coloration, (2) warning coloration, and (3) mimicry.

Protective coloration enables an animal to blend in with its background. The animal is thus less likely to be seen—and, therefore, less likely to be eaten by its enemies. Protective coloration can also help make it easier for an animal that is hunting to approach its prey.

Warning coloration occurs in certain poisonous or unpleasant-tasting animals. For example, birds will not eat the monarch butterfly because of its unpleasant taste; they are able to recognize it because of its distinctive coloring.

In *mimicry,* a relatively defenseless animal (called the mimic) has a superficial likeness to an animal (called the model) with qualities that cause predators to avoid it. The viceroy butterfly, for example, looks very much like the monarch butterfly, and therefore birds avoid it also.

Behavioral Adaptations. Examples of behavioral adaptation can be readily found in areas where there is a marked seasonal change in the weather. Squirrels store nuts for the winter. Many birds migrate to the south to avoid cold northern winters. Woodchucks hibernate when cold weather arrives and food becomes scarce.

Adaptation and Survival

An environment tends to eliminate plants and animals that are not suited to it. A plant that was not adapted to conserve moisture would soon die in the desert; an animal that stood out from its surroundings would be the most likely to fall prey to its enemies. This process of elimination is called *natural selection.* The phrase "survival of the fittest" refers to natural selection. Natural selection is an important factor in evolution. (See also EVOLUTION, subtitle *How Evolution Takes Place:* Natural Selection.)

An example of adaptation involving natural selection is found in the case of DDT and houseflies. When this insecticide was first used in the early 1940's, almost all the flies subjected to it were killed. Some, however, survived and continued to reproduce. Eventually only this type of resistant fly was left in the areas where DDT was used for a succession of years.

Adaptation is not voluntary, but is based on inherited traits. The diversity of inherited traits is chiefly a result of *mutation.* Mutation is any change in the inherited characteristics of an organism which results in new traits that will be passed on to the organism's descendants. In any given environment, some

A-57

traits will be advantageous and others will not. (In forests, the ability of an animal to climb trees might be an adaptation for survival, but on open grasslands speed would be more advantageous.) The organism that is best suited to its environment is most likely to survive and reproduce, and the traits that are not advantageous tend gradually to be eliminated.

Adaptive Radiation and Convergence

As a result of competition for food and living space, plants and animals tend to spread to as many areas as they can reach and survive in. The evolution from a single group to various forms adapted to different environments and ways of life is called *adaptive radiation.*

An example of adaptive radiation is found among the teleosts (the ray-finned fishes). The primitive or ancestral teleosts were active, elongated fishes of the open waters. From this generalized type evolved more than 20,000 species, able to live in virtually every kind of aquatic environment. Flounders with flattened bodies dwell at the bottom of the ocean, while other teleosts, such as sea horses, have adapted to life among seaweeds and coral reefs.

Groups of organisms that are only distantly related, but which live in the same type of environment, tend to develop structures that are superficially similar, because they are adaptations to the same environment. This similarity of structure evolves through a process called *adaptive convergence.* For example, porpoises, seals, and fishes have all developed streamlined bodies that facilitate their movement in water.

For further examples of adaptation, see ANIMAL, subtitle *Adaptations.* See also BALANCE OF NATURE; ECOLOGY.

Addams, Jane (1860-1935), a United States social worker, reformer, and peace advocate. During her active career of 46 years she made Hull House in Chicago world-famous as a social settlement. An outspoken pacifist, Miss Addams shared the 1931 Nobel Peace Prize with President Nicholas Murray Butler of Columbia University.

Jane Addams was born in Cedarville, Illinois, and was graduated from Rockford College. She began the study of medicine but her health broke down, and for two years she was an invalid. During several years of unhappy indecision she traveled and studied in Europe. She found her purpose when she visited Toynbee Hall, a social settlement in London. In 1889 Jane Addams and Ellen Gates Starr moved into the Hull House mansion, located in one of the worst slum communities of Chicago.

The two women held classes for immigrants, tended the sick, cared for babies, and provided a community center, coffee shop, art gallery, theater, gymnasium, and co-operative boarding club for working girls. They helped the poor with their problems and fought all forms of injustice and cruelty. Miss Addams solicited financial support, added new buildings to her social settlement, and recruited volunteer workers. Her book *Twenty Years at Hull-House* (1910) made her famous. The institution became the leading social settlement in the United States, and a training center for social workers.

Jane Addams was active in Chicago in fighting civic vice and corruption. She campaigned for better working conditions, more protection for working women, for stricter child labor laws, for improvements in public welfare, for playgrounds, and for a juvenile court. She joined in the votes-for-women movement. After World War I broke out in 1914 Miss Addams devoted much effort to obtaining peace. In 1915 she was elected chairman of the new Women's Peace party and was president of the International Con-

Jane Addams and Friends
Hull House Association

gress of Women at The Hague, Netherlands. After the war she became president of the Women's International League for Peace and Freedom.

Her books include: *Democracy and Social Ethics* (1902); *Newer Ideals of Peace* (1907); *The Spirit of Youth and the City Streets* (1909); *The Second Twenty Years at Hull-House* (1930).

See also HULL HOUSE.

Addax, ăd'ăks, an African antelope related to the oryx. Addaxes live in the central and southern parts of the Sahara desert. They grow up to 40 inches (1 m) tall at the shoulder. Large addaxes weigh about 265 pounds (120 kg). Both males and females have a pair of twisted horns, 30 to 40 inches (75-100 cm) long. An addax's coat is light brown and is paler in summer than in winter. The animal has white underparts and facial markings, and a dark forelock. One young is born in winter or early spring.

Addaxes travel through the desert in small herds. They are able to live without drinking water, obtaining the moisture they need from the plants they eat.

The addax is *Addax nasomaculatus* of the cattle family, Bovidae.

Adder, ăd'ẽr, the name of several snakes, including many European vipers and harmless North American snakes. The *common adder* is another name for the common European viper. (See VIPER.) Also called adder is the copperhead. (See COPPERHEAD.) *Puff adder* is a name applied to the true puff adder and to the harmless hognose snake. (See PUFF ADDER; HOGNOSE SNAKE.) The milk snake sometimes is called an adder; the moccasin, the *water adder*. (See MILK SNAKE; MOCCASIN.)

Night adders form a genus of primitive true vipers. These nocturnal snakes live in Africa south of the Sahara. The *death adder* of Australia is a venomous snake that resembles a viper but is related to the cobras and coral snakes.

The four species of night adders form the genus *Causus* of the viper family, Viperidae. The death adder is *Acanthophis antarcticus* of the cobra and coral snake family, Elapidae.

Adder's Tongue. See DOGTOOTH VIOLET.

Addiction. See DRUG, subtitle *The Drug Problem*.

Adding Machine. See CALCULATING MACHINE, subtitle *Adding and Accounting Machines*.

Addax

Addis Ababa, ăd'ĭs ăb'ȧ-bȧ, Ethiopia, the capital of Shoa Province and of the nation. The city is on a high plateau, 8,200 feet (2,500 m) above sea level, and is surrounded by hills and mountains. It is about 1,540 miles (2,480 km) south-southeast of Cairo, Egypt.

Addis Ababa is the cultural, commercial, and administrative center of Ethiopia. Its products include coffee, hides, plywood, textiles, clothing, and cement. The University of Addis Ababa and several technical schools are here. Notable buildings include the palace of Menelik II, National Palace, and Trinity Cathedral.

Addis Ababa, formerly the small village of Phinphinnie, was chosen as the site of the capital in the late 19th century by Menelik II. His wife gave it the name Addis Ababa (Amharic for "new flower"), because of the beautiful flowers found in all parts of the city throughout the year.

Population: 1,196,300.

Addison, ăd'ĭ-s'n, **Joseph** (1672-1719), an English essayist, poet, dramatist, and statesman. Addison and Richard Steele, with whom he frequently collaborated, are credited with developing the light, witty essay found in modern magazines. Addison, a more polished though somewhat less vigorous writer than Steele, said that his intention was "to enliven morality with wit, and to temper wit with morality." His graceful essays, gently ridiculing social and political follies, made him the foremost social humorist of the English Augustan Age.

Addison is best remembered for the 274 papers he wrote for the *Spectator,* a periodical published daily except Sunday from March 1, 1711, to December 6, 1712. The *Spectator* was revived briefly by Addison in 1714. In the original series Steele introduced, and Addison more fully developed, the character of Sir Roger de Coverley, an amiable country squire. Addison announced that his ambition in the *Spectator* was to bring "philosophy out of closets and libraries, schools, and colleges, to dwell in clubs and assemblies, at tea-tables, and in coffeehouses."

Ewing Galloway
Joseph Addison

Addison was more than a social reformer and commentator on the contemporary scene. He spurred new literary tastes, and some of his charming tales and allegories were forerunners of the short story. His critical essays on *Paradise Lost* stimulated interest in Milton. Richardson's epistolary novels probably were influenced by Addison's use of the letter as a literary form. Addison perfected the character sketch, as exemplified by Sir Roger de Coverley. His hymn, "The Spacious Firmament on High," long survived him.

Poet and Politician

Joseph Addison was born in Wiltshire, the son of a clergyman. A fellow student at the Charterhouse was Richard Steele. At 15 Addison entered Oxford University, where he wrote Latin verse. His first attempt at English verse was a poem addressed to John Dryden. Dryden then included Addison's rhymed "Account of the Greatest English Poets" in his fourth annual miscellany (1694). In his "Account" Addison ignored Shakespeare, chided Spenser, and hailed Cowley as a "mighty genius."

In 1699 Charles Montagu, a friend who later became Lord Halifax, obtained for Addison an annual pension of £300, to be spent in travel while preparing for a career in civil service. After he had spent four pleasant years on the Continent, mainly in France and Italy, the death of William III and the fall of the Whigs brought an end to his pension and forced his return to London. He joined the Kit-Cat Club there, and made a habit of spending his evenings talking and listening in coffeehouses. *The Campaign* (1704), a patriotic poem in heroic couplets written to celebrate Marlborough's victory at Blenheim, brought about Addison's appointment as under-secretary of state in 1706. It was the first of several government positions he held.

Addison wrote pro-Whig articles and pamphlets. The success of *Cato* (1713), a blank-verse tragedy, was believed to be due more to a general impression that it was a veiled defense of the Whigs than to its artistic merit. Addison was a member of Parliament from 1708 until his death.

Addison and Steele

Addison helped Richard Steele with a play, *The Tender Husband* (1706), for which he provided a prologue, and this association led to Addison's writing for Steele's magazine the *Tatler,* 1709-11. He continued his contributions when Steele abandoned the *Tatler* for the *Spectator.* The *Spectator* became more closely identified with Addison than with Steele. After the revived *Spectator* was discontinued in 1714, Addison wrote for the *Guardian* and the *Englishman,* short-lived periodicals edited by Steele.

Addison's praise of Thomas Tickell's translation of the first book of the *Iliad* (1715) led Alexander Pope to believe that Addison was trying to eclipse Pope's own translation. Pope retaliated with a poem in which he satirized Addison as "Atticus." This poem later appeared in *Epistle to Dr. Arbuthnot* (1735).

In 1716 Addison married the Countess of Warwick, a wealthy widow whose influence led to his appointment as secretary of state in 1717. He resigned the next year. A political quarrel with Steele, begun in 1719, was not settled when Addison died. He was buried in Westminster Abbey.

See also STEELE, Sir RICHARD.

Addison, Thomas (1793-1860), a British physician. In 1855 he described the disease of the adrenal glands now known as Addison's disease. Pernicious anemia is sometimes called Addison's anemia because of his investigations into that condition. Addison was born near Newcastle, England. He received his medical degree from the University of Edinburgh, 1815, and established a practice in London.

Addison's Disease. See ADRENAL GLANDS, subtitle *Diseases of the Adrenal Glands*.

Addition. See ARITHMETIC, subtitles *Computation with Whole Numbers* and *Rational Numbers:* Operations with Rational Numbers, and illustration *The Fundamental Operations:* Addition.

Additive, ăd′ĭ-tĭv, a chemical substance added to a material — usually in small amounts—to impart or enhance desirable properties or to lessen or suppress undesirable properties. Among the most familiar products in which additives are used are gasoline, lubricating oils, rubber, and foods.

For example, dye is added to gasoline to give it color, which is necessary for identification purposes. Other gasoline additives prevent or reduce carburetor icing, gum formation, and spark-plug fouling. Additives in lubricating oils provide the proper viscosity. The use of additives in vulcanized rubber greatly retards its oxidation. There are hundreds of additives used in foods to improve their nutritive value, retard spoilage, or enhance their flavor.

See also FOOD ADDITIVE; GASOLINE, subtitle *Gasoline Production:* Additives; RUBBER.

Address, Forms of. Besides the common forms of address, such as Mr. and Mrs., various special forms are used which depend on the profession, office, or position of the person addressed. The list that follows applies to written correspondence and includes some of the forms used most frequently in the United States. There is often more than one acceptable way of beginning the

letter and addressing the envelope; the forms given in this list are those generally preferred for formal correspondence. In writing to a woman, "Madam" should be substituted for "Sir" or "Mr.", except in the case of a congresswoman, who is addressed as "Miss", "Mrs.", or "Ms."

Air Force, Army, and Marine Corps Personnel
Lieutenant Colonel John Doe, U.S.A.F. (or U.S.A. or U.S.M.C.)
Sir:
Note: This form applies for all ranks, officers as well as enlisted men. In less formal usage, the letter may begin "My Dear Colonel Doe." Traditionally second lieutenants and warrant officers are addressed as "Mr." (or "Miss"). It is correct also to use "Mr." instead of the actual rank of enlisted men—"My dear Mr. Doe" or "My dear Corporal Doe." (When the rank is used it should be remembered that a lieutenant general, major general, or brigadier general is called "general" in the salutation; a lieutenant colonel is called "colonel"; a first or second lieutenant, "lieutenant"; a sergeant, regardless of grade, "sergeant"; an airman, regardless of grade, "airman"; a lance corporal, "corporal"; and a private first class, "private.")

Ambassador (Foreign)
His Excellency, The Ambassador of (country)
Washington, D.C.
Dear Mr. Ambassador:

Ambassador (United States)
The Honorable John Doe
The Ambassador of the United States
(city, country)
Dear Mr. Ambassador:

Archbishop (Roman Catholic)
The Most Reverend John Doe
Archbishop of (archdiocese)
Your Excellency:

Associate Justice of the U.S. Supreme Court
The Honorable John Doe
Justice of the United States Supreme Court
My dear Mr. Justice:

Bishop (Methodist)
The Very Reverend John Doe
Dear Sir:

Bishop (Protestant Episcopal)
The Right Reverend John Doe
Bishop of (diocese)
Dear Bishop Doe:

Bishop (Roman Catholic)
The Most Reverend John Doe
Bishop of (diocese)
Your Excellency:

Cabinet Member
The Honorable John Doe
The Secretary of State (or other appropriate title of head of department)
Sir:

Cardinal
His Eminence John Cardinal Doe
Your Eminence:

Chief Justice of the United States
The Chief Justice
The Supreme Court
Washington, D.C.
Sir:

Clergyman (Protestant)
    The Reverend John Doe
    Dear Mr. Doe:
Congressman
    The Honorable John Doe
    House of Representatives
    Dear Mr. Doe:
Governor
    The Honorable John Doe
    Governor of (state)
    Dear Governor Doe:
    Note: The following alternative form is required
only in Massachusetts, New Hampshire, and North
Carolina; it may as a courtesy be used for the
governor of any state, especially if the writer is from
another state:
    His Excellency The Governor of (state)
    Dear Governor Doe:
Judge
    The Honorable John Doe
    Judge of the United States District Court
    My dear Judge Doe:
Mayor
    The Honorable John Doe
    Mayor of (city)
    Dear Mayor Doe:
Monsignor
    The Right Reverend Monsignor John Doe
    Right Reverend and dear Monsignor:
Naval Personnel
    In general, these forms are the same as those for
Air Force and Army personnel. For petty officers,
the rank is written after the name: "John Doe,
Yeoman 2." If the less formal salutation is used,
commissioned officers below the rank of commander
are called "Mr."
Pope
    His Holiness, The Pope
    Your Holiness:
President of the United States
    The President
    The White House
    Dear Mr. President:
Priest (Roman Catholic)
    The Reverend John Doe, (initials of order, if
        any)
    Dear Father Doe:
Rabbi
    Rabbi John Doe
    Dear Rabbi Doe:
Senator
    The Honorable John Doe
    The United States Senate
    Dear Senator Doe:
State Legislator
    The forms for state legislators are the same as for
United States senators and congressmen, with appro-
priate change of address. (Some state legislators have
different titles, such as, for example, assemblyman.)
Vice President
    The Vice President
    The United States Senate
    Mr. Vice President:

Ade, ād, **George** (1866-1944), a United
States humorist and playwright. *Fables in
Slang* (1900) is a collection of sketches written in a breezy, colloquial style. The appended morals usually have a satirical twist.

The Torrens River in Adelaide

Artie (1896), *Pink Marsh* (1897), and *Doc
Horne* (1899) contain gently humorous
sketches of odd Chicago characters. *The
Sultan of Sulu* (1902) was the first of several
successful musical comedies. *The College
Widow* (1904), a comedy, reappeared in a
musical version, *Leave It to Jane* (1917),
with songs by Jerome Kern.

Ade was born in Kentland, Indiana. He
graduated from Purdue University in 1887.
In 1890 he joined the staff of the Chicago
Record, where much of his work first appeared.

The America of George Ade (Putnam, 1960), edited by Jean Shepherd, is a collection of Ade's works.

Adelaide, ăd″l-ād, Australia, the capital
of the state of South Australia. The city lies
on the Torrens River between the Mount
Lofty Ranges to the east and the Gulf of St.
Vincent, an inlet of the Great Australian
Bight, seven miles (11 km) to the west.

The city is completely surrounded by
1,700 acres (688 hectares) of parkland
known as the "green belt," consisting of
parks, gardens, and playgrounds and sports
fields. A dam on the Torrens River im-
pounds narrow, winding Torrens Lake,
which divides the city into northern and
southern sections. South Adelaide is the
business section; North Adelaide is primarily
residential. Bridges across the lake link the
two parts of the city.

Adelaide is the commercial and industrial
center of South Australia. Products include
agricultural machinery, chemicals, plastics,
textiles, automobile bodies, and engineering
and electronic equipment. The city is an
important trade center for the surrounding
region, which produces wheat, wool, hides,

wine, and fruit. There are coal, iron ore, and copper mines nearby. Adelaide's docks are at Port Adelaide on the Gulf of St. Vincent. The city's mild climate and its location, near the sea and the mountains, make it a popular resort.

In the city are the University of Adelaide, several small colleges, a conservatory of music, and a school of arts. A museum of natural history, an art gallery, and botanical and zoological gardens are here.

Adelaide was founded in 1837 as the site of a British colony. The city was named after the wife of King William IV. It was the first Australian community to be incorporated as a city (1840).

Population (urban Adelaide): 900,431.

Adelphi University. See UNIVERSITIES AND COLLEGES (table).

Aden, ä'd'n; ā'd'n; ăd''n, the capital and largest city of Yemen (Aden). Lying on the Gulf of Aden near the entrance to the Red Sea, it is a major port, a petroleum refining center, and a refueling station, especially for ships using the Suez Canal route. Aden was a centuries-old Arab port when taken by the British in 1837. It was administered as part of India until 1937, when it became a separate British colony. Aden became the national capital of Southern Yemen, now Yemen (Aden), in 1967.

Population: 264,326.

Aden, Gulf of, a western arm of the Arabian Sea between Africa and the Arabian Peninsula. The gulf is bordered by Yemen (Aden) on the north, Djibouti on the west, and Somalia on the south. It is about 600 miles (950 km) long and up to 250 miles (400 km) wide, with a maximum depth of nearly 9,000 feet (2,700 m). The gulf is part of the Suez shipping route between the Mediterranean Sea and the Indian Ocean. Aden is the gulf's principal port.

Adenauer, ä'd'n-ou'ēr, **Konrad** (1876-1967), a German statesman. He was the first chancellor of the Federal Republic of Germany (West Germany). He had the leading role in the revival and rearmament of West Germany after World War II and led his country into close alliance with Western Europe and the United States against the threat of Soviet Russia. He supported the European Defense Community and brought Germany into NATO.

Adenauer was born in Cologne. He became a lawyer, engaged in politics, and was

chief burgomaster (mayor) of Cologne and a member of the Prussian legislature, 1917-33. When the Nazis came into power he lost his offices. In 1934 and again in 1944 he was imprisoned briefly.

In 1945 Adenauer helped found the Christian Democratic Union and soon became president of the party. When the West German government was set up in 1949 he was elected to the *Bundestag* (lower house of parliament) and later that year was elected chancellor. He was reelected in 1953, 1957, and 1961. He was also foreign minister during 1951-55. Holding an office of great powers, Adenauer exercised his authority to the limit. Critics dubbed his government a *Demokratur*—implying "democratic dictatorship." To admirers he was *Der Alte*—"the old man."

Under pressure because of his extreme age and his inflexible policies, Adenauer retired unwillingly in October, 1963, in favor of Ludwig Erhard.

Adenauer wrote *Memoirs, 1946-1953* (1965; English translation, 1966).

Adenoids, ăd'ĕ-noidz, the name applied to the pharyngeal tonsil when it is abnormally enlarged. The pharyngeal tonsil is a mass of tissue on the upper rear wall of the pharynx (the passage leading from the mouth and nasal cavities to the esophagus and larynx). The tissue that makes up the pharyngeal tonsil is called *adenoid tissue*. (The pharyngeal tonsil is not the same as what is commonly called "the tonsils"; these are the two masses of tissue found near the base of the tongue [see diagram].)

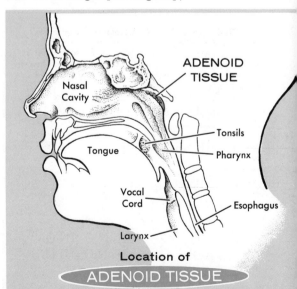

Location of **ADENOID TISSUE**

Adenoid tissue functions much like a lymph node, filtering bacteria and other particles from the lymph that passes through it. The amount of adenoid tissue in babies is small, but it increases in children until they are about six years old. After this age, adenoid tissue normally withers away slowly.

Occasionally the adenoid tissue increases in size (usually as a result of repeated infection) and is then called adenoids. Adenoids may become large enough to block the nasal passages and prevent breathing through the nose. A person with adenoids is susceptible to frequent colds. He may develop hearing difficulty and dental problems because he constantly breathes through his mouth. Adenoids can be easily removed in a simple surgical procedure. Often adenoids and tonsils are removed at the same time.

Adenosine Diphosphate (ADP). See ADENOSINE TRIPHOSPHATE (ATP).

Adenosine Triphosphate (ATP), á-děn'ŏ-sēn trī-fŏs'fāt, an energy-bearing molecule found in all living cells. Formation of nucleic acids, transmission of nerve impulses, muscle contraction, and many other energy-consuming reactions of metabolism are made possible by the energy in ATP molecules. The energy in ATP is obtained from the breakdown of foods.

An ATP molecule is composed of carbon, hydrogen, nitrogen, oxygen, and phosphorus atoms. There are three phosphorus atoms in the molecule. Each of these phosphorus atoms is at the center of an atomic group called a *phosphate*. The phosphate groups

are linked to one another by chemical bonds called *phosphate bonds*. (See diagram.) The energy of ATP is locked in these bonds.

The energy in ATP can be released as heat or can be used in the cell as a power source to drive various types of chemical and mechanical activities. For example, when the terminal phosphate group of the ATP molecule is removed by hydrolysis (a decomposition process that occurs when a substance reacts with water), energy in the form of heat is released and *adenosine diphosphate* (ADP) and inorganic phosphate (P_i) are formed.

The hydrolysis of ATP is accelerated by an enzyme called adenosine triphosphatase, or ATP-ase. The reaction can be written as:

$$ATP \xrightarrow{\text{ATP-ase}} ADP + P_i + energy$$

The regeneration of ATP from ADP requires energy, which is obtained in the process of oxidation. (See OXIDATION.) The energy released in the oxidation of carbohydrates and fats initiates a complex series of chemical reactions that ultimately regenerate ATP molecules from ADP molecules. The complete oxidation of a typical molecule of fat results in the formation of about 150 molecules of ATP.

ATP was discovered in muscle tissue by scientists in Germany and the United States in 1929. Its role in the storage and supply of energy was first explained in 1941 by the German-American biochemist Fritz A. Lipmann. For this achievement, he shared the 1953 Nobel Prize in physiology or medicine.

See also METABOLISM; PHOTOSYNTHESIS.

Adhesion. See COHESION.

Adhesives. See GLUES AND ADHESIVES.

Adige River, ä'dĕ-jå, a river in northeastern Italy, 225 miles long. From its source in the Rhaetian Alps of northern Italy, near the Austrian border, it flows generally southeastward through the provinces of Trentino-Alto Adige and Venetia. It empties into the Adriatic Sea about eight miles north of the Po River delta. The Isarco, a tributary of the Adige, extends generally north from Bolzano. It has long served as part of a trans-Alpine route from Italy to northern Europe via the Brenner Pass. It also is used for irrigation and for hydroelectric power. Major cities on the Adige include Merana, Bolzano, Verona, and Trent. The river is used for power and irrigation.

A-64

Simplified diagram of ATP molecule. The molecule is composed of adenosine, A, and three phosphate groups, Ⓟ . ATP is changed to ADP when the terminal phosphate group is removed from the molecule. The phosphate bonds that bear ATP energy are indicated by wavy lines.

Adenosine Triphosphate (ATP)

A – Ⓟ ～ Ⓟ ～ Ⓟ

Adenosine Diphosphate (ADP)

Adenosine: $C_{10}H_{13}N_5O_4$
ATP: $C_{10}H_{13}N_5O_4(HPO_3)_3$
ADP: $C_{10}H_{13}N_5O_4(HPO_3)_2$

ADJUTANT STORK

Adirondack Mountains, ăd'ĭ-rŏn'dăk, mountains in northeastern New York. They lie just south of the Canadian border, between the St. Lawrence and Mohawk valleys and the lowlands containing Lakes Champlain and George. The mountains cover some 8,000 square miles (21,000 km²).

The Adirondacks are usually considered as part of the Appalachians, although geologically they are an extension of the vast Canadian Shield. They are among the oldest mountains in the United States and consequently have an aged and worn appearance. Slopes are long and gentle; virtually nowhere is the terrain rugged. The loftiest part lies just west of Lake Champlain where Mount Marcy, the highest peak in New York, rises 5,344 feet (1,629 m) above sea level. Elsewhere, especially in the south and the west, elevations are considerably lower.

Lakes abound in the Adirondacks, mostly small, clear ones created by glaciers during the last Ice Age. Among the many rivers that drain the region are the Hudson, Ausable, Raquette, Oswegatchie, and Black. The Adirondacks are densely forested, chiefly with spruces, firs, beeches, birches, and maples. Much of this wilderness land—some 3,800 square miles (9,800 km²)—is within the state-owned Adirondack Forest Preserve.

Because of their scenic beauty, the Adirondacks have become a popular resort and recreation area. They offer a wide variety of facilities and activities throughout the year. The chief attraction in fall is the brilliantly colored foliage; in winter it is primarily skiing. Most prominent among the resort towns are Lake Placid, site of the 1932 and 1980 Winter Olympics; Saranac Lake; and Tupper Lake. There are no large cities in the Adirondacks.

Adjective. See GRAMMAR, subtitle *Parts of Speech.*

Adjutant, ăj'ŏŏ-tănt, a military officer whose duty is to take care of the internal details, correspondence, reports, and records of an army unit. He receives and issues orders on behalf of the commanding officer and superintends the administration of the unit and the keeping of books and records, including personnel records. The adjutant of a unit commanded by a general is called *adjutant general.* The adjutant general of a division ordinarily holds the rank of lieutenant colonel. The adjutant general of the

New York Zoological Park
Greater Adjutant Stork

United States Army is in charge of official correspondence, reports, and records for the entire army. He ordinarily has the rank of major general.

Adjutant Stork, a bird of Asia and Africa. The name adjutant comes from the stiff, erect walk of these storks, which resembles that of a military officer. Two species live in India and southeastern Asia, the other in tropical Africa. The African adjutant is also called *marabou stork.* Its long, thin undertail feathers, also called marabou, are used for trimming garments.

The two larger species, the African adjutant and the greater adjutant of Asia, are about 5 feet long and have a wingspan of from 6 to 8½ feet. All adjutant storks have

A-65

long, thin legs; dark-gray backs; and white undersides. An adjutant's head and neck are pinkish in color, and either naked or covered with sparse down. From the neck hangs a naked sac that is part of the respiratory system. The bill is thick and about 12 inches long. Adjutant storks eat carrion (dead flesh) and small animals.

Adjutants nest in colonies in groups of trees or on cliff ledges. They build shallow nests of sticks in which they lay two or three rough-shelled white eggs. The young stay in the nest about eight weeks.

Adjutant storks form the genus *Leptoptilus* of the stork family, Ciconiidae. The greater adjutant is *L. dubius;* the lesser adjutant, *L. javanicus;* the African adjutant, or marabou stork, *L. crumeniferus.*

Adler, Alfred (1870-1937), an Austrian psychologist, founder of the school of individual psychology. Adler believed that man spends his entire life in pursuit of the goal of power (superiority), in an attempt to

compensate for strong feelings of inferiority developed in childhood. Most persons are able to compensate satisfactorily; those who are unsuccessful develop *neuroses.* Adler explained his theories in *The Theory*

Austrian Information Service
Alfred Adler

and Practice of Individual Psychology (1918), *Understanding Human Nature* (1927), and *Pattern of Life* (1930).

Adler was born in Vienna. He received a degree in medicine from the University of Vienna in 1895. In 1902 Adler became associated with Sigmund Freud, founder of psychoanalysis. Rejecting Freud's emphasis upon sex as the motive behind all human behavior, he broke with him in 1911. Adler spent much of his time after 1925 lecturing in the United States.

Adler, Cyrus (1863-1940), a United States Jewish educator and leader. He was born in Van Buren, Arkansas, and was graduated from the University of Pennsylvania and the Johns Hopkins University. Dr. Adler taught Semitic languages at Johns Hopkins and was librarian at the Smithsonian Institution, Washington, D.C., 1892-1905. He was the first president of Dropsie College for Hebrew and Cognate Learning, Philadelphia, 1908-40. From 1916 until his death,

he was the head of the Jewish Theological Seminary of America. Adler helped found many Jewish organizations and publications and wrote and edited a number of works on Jewish culture and leaders.

Adler, Dankmar (1844-1900), a United States architect. The acoustics in his Central Music Hall, Chicago (1879, demolished 1900), brought him wide recognition. With his partner Louis H. Sullivan, Adler designed the Auditorium Building (1889, now occupied by Roosevelt University), Chicago, and the Guaranty (now Prudential) Building (1895), Buffalo, New York. Adler was born in Germany and came to the United States in 1854. He became a draftsman in Chicago in 1861 and began to practice architecture there in 1869. Louis Sullivan became his partner in 1881. In this partnership, which lasted until 1895, Adler specialized in engineering, Sullivan in design.

Adler, Felix (1851-1933), a United States educator and founder of the Ethical Culture movement. (See ETHICAL CULTURE.) Adler was born in Germany, the son of a rabbi, and was brought to the United States as a youth. He was graduated from Columbia University and from Heidelberg University. Adler was professor of social and political ethics at Columbia, 1902-33, and was a leader in many fields of social welfare.

His books include: *Creed and Deed* (1877); *An Ethical Philosophy of Life* (1918); *Reconstruction of the Spiritual Ideal* (1923).

Adler, Mortimer J. (Jerome) (1902-   ), a United States educator, writer, and philosopher. Adler became principally known for his belief that a liberal education can be obtained from reading works by the world's major thinkers. In connection with this theory, he organized, along with Robert M. Hutchins, an adult discussion-group program centered on great books of the past. Adler and Hutchins edited *Great Books of the Western World* (54 volumes, 1952). Adler was also noted as a leading Neo-Scholastic philosopher, who believed that Aristotelian logic and late medieval Catholic theology were valid as an intellectual framework for modern times.

Mortimer J. Adler
Proctor Jones

Adler was born in New York City and received a Ph.D. from Columbia University in 1928. He taught philosophy of law at the University of Chicago, 1930-52, and then founded and became director of the Institute for Philosophical Research. He was also director of planning for *Encyclopaedia Britannica* (15th edition, 1974).

Other works include: *The Revolution in Education* (with Milton Mayer, 1958); *The New Capitalists* (1961); *The Conditions of Philosophy* (1965); *The Difference of Man and the Difference It Makes* (1967); *How to Read a Book* (with Charles Van Doren, revised edition 1972); *Philosopher at Large: an Intellectual Autobiography* (1977).

Adler Planetarium. See PLANETARIUM.

Admetus. See ALCESTIS.

Administration. See PUBLIC ADMINISTRATION; STAFF.

Administrative Law. See LAW, subtitle *Kinds of Law:* Administrative Law.

Administrator. See EXECUTOR.

Admiral, ăd′mĭ-răl, a naval officer of the highest rank. The word comes from the Arabic *amir-al-bahr* (commander of the sea). In the U.S. Navy there are five grades of admiral. The highest ranking is admiral of the fleet, which corresponds to general of the army. An admiral of the fleet wears five stars. The other ranks are: admiral (four stars); vice admiral (three stars); rear admiral (two stars); and commodore admiral (one star). All admirals are called *flag officers,* and when aboard ship display a flag with the appropriate number of stars.

In the 19th century and in World War II U.S. Navy officers in the one-star pay grade bore the rank of commodore. In the postwar years, until 1980, the grade existed only for pay purposes; the rank of rear admiral had two pay grades, the lower being that of a commodore. The commodore rank was reactivated in 1980 and its name changed to commodore admiral.

David G. Farragut was the first United States naval officer to become a rear admiral (1862), vice admiral (1864), and admiral (1866). In 1899 Congress gave George Dewey the special rank admiral of the navy, the highest rank ever held by a United States naval officer. The five-star rank was created in 1944. William Leahy, Chester Nimitz, and Ernest J. King were the first to hold it.

See also RANK, MILITARY OR NAVAL. For insignia, see NAVY, UNITED STATES.

Admiralty Islands, ăd′-mĭ-răl-tĭ, a group of about 18 islands forming part of the

Bismarck Archipelago in the southwest Pacific Ocean. They are part of the country of Papua New Guinea. The islands are about 200 miles (320 km) off the northern coast of New Guinea and have a total area of about 850 square miles (2,200 km²). Manus, the largest island, is 65 miles (105 km) long and up to 17 miles (27 km) wide. It has an area of 633 square miles (1,639 km²).

Most of the islands are coral formations, and a few, including Manus, are of volcanic origin. The highest peak, on Manus, is 2,136 feet (651 m) above sea level. The islands, lying just south of the Equator, have a hot, humid tropical climate with an average yearly temperature of 80° F. (27° C.). Rainfall is between 130 and 250 inches (3,300-6,350 mm) annually. Growing coconuts and diving for pearl shell are the leading economic activities. The people are primitive Papuans of Melanesian origin with a well-established tribal civilization. Lorengau, on Manus, is the main port and administrative center for the islands.

The islands were discovered in 1616 by William Schouten, a Dutch navigator. They were annexed by Germany in 1884, and after World War I were governed by Australia under a League of Nations mandate. During World War II the Japanese occupied the islands. After the war they became a United Nations trusteeship administered by Australia. During 1949-75 they were administratively a part of the Trust Territory of New Guinea, which became part of independent Papua New Guinea in 1975.

Population: 33,300.

Admiralty Law. See LAW, subtitle *Kinds of Law:* Admiralty Law.

Adobe, à-dō′bĭ, a building material of sun-baked clay, usually mixed with straw or

Molding Adobe Bricks in Mexico
Burton Holmes from Ewing Galloway

an asphalt solution as a binder. It may be molded into bricks or formed directly into thick walls. Adobe (from a Spanish word meaning "to plaster") also means structures of this material, especially those in Latin America and the southwestern United States.

Adobe buildings have long been used by Indians in hot, relatively arid regions. They remain fairly cool and, if well cared for, last indefinitely. Adobe using straw as a binder must be protected from moisture to prevent it from disintegrating; after a rain any cracks that develop must be repaired at once. Modern adobe, which uses an asphalt solution as the binder, does not have this problem.

Adobe houses in the southwestern United States are left the natural off-white color of the dried clay. Pueblo Indians who live in adobe homes plaster the walls with fresh clay once a year. In Mexico and Central America, however, colored surfaces are preferred. Tinted plaster, a color wash on stucco, and glazed tiles are used to face the adobe.

Many early peoples who lived in regions where timber and stone were scarce used sun-dried clay as a building material. It was common in the Near East, the Mediterranean area, and the New World. In rainy regions a mud-brick house dissolved in about 15 years.

At the time of the Spanish conquest, the Spaniards, who knew adobe from Africa, found it being used also in the New World. They taught the Indians to mold the clay into large bricks. Adobe-brick construction proved so satisfactory that it was widely used for colonial buildings, many of which are still standing.

For pictures of adobe structures, see MISSIONS, CHRISTIAN (San Esteban Rey Mission); PUEBLO INDIANS.

Adolescence, ăd'ŏ-lĕs'ĕns, the period of life between childhood and adulthood. It starts during puberty, the physical beginning of womanhood and manhood, at an average age of about 13 for girls and 14 for boys, and extends to maturity, about 18 to 21. There are no exact limits to the period of adolescence, however; every child grows at his own rate. For example, some normal boys and girls reach puberty as much as five years before other boys and girls.

During the two to four years of puberty the sex organs begin to function and the child's body gradually takes on the shape of the adult's body with the development of the secondary sex characteristics. (The secondary sex characteristics are physical features, other than sex organs, that distinguish the male body from the female body. They are called "secondary" because, unlike the sex organs, they are not related directly to reproduction.)

Physical Changes

Both boys and girls grow rapidly in height just before and during the early period of adolescence. The arm and leg bones lengthen, and the chin and jaws develop so that the face takes on a more mature look. The girl's body becomes more rounded and soft, the boy's more firm and angular. The boy's voice deepens, his chest develops, hair develops on the body and face, and his feet and hands increase in size. The girl's hips broaden and her breasts develop. Sex glands mature and sex differences increase as boy and girl reach manhood and womanhood.

A normal boy or girl seems to be always hungry doing the first years of adolescence because rapid physical growth requires added nourishment. Some parts of the body grow more rapidly than others, creating a lack of balance and stability that often leads to awkwardness. Rapid physical growth may cause low energy, often accompanied by anemia. Disturbance and change in the glands may cause embarrassing acne and pimples. The increase in muscular strength is reflected in boys, and to a lesser degree in girls, by greater interest in athletics, particularly in competitive games.

Emotional and Social Changes

Adolescent boys and girls often disturb and baffle parents with behavior that seems strange and unreasonable. Some of these behavior problems have a cultural rather than biological origin. Friction between the age groups is typical of the United States and other Western cultures, where adolescence is a rather prolonged preparation for adulthood. The friction is slight or nonexistent, however, in cultures where there are fewer social pressures and where the completion of puberty rites marks the end of childhood and clearly entitles the adolescent to recognition as a young adult.

Adolescence is a no-man's land in the sense that the adolescent is neither a child nor an adult. He does not wish to give up the pleasures and protection he knew in child-

Tasks of Adolescence

As they develop from the dependence of childhood into the independence of adulthood, adolescents face a number of tasks that must be accomplished. Each adolescent must learn to:

1. Accept his or her body and appearance and masculine or feminine role.
2. Develop ways of getting along with others of the same age of both sexes.
3. Achieve emotional independence of parents and other adults.
4. Accept his or her responsibilities to the community and society.
5. Select and prepare for an occupation.
6. Prepare for marriage and family life.
7. Build moral and religious values.

Accomplishing these major developmental tasks is important if the tasks that arise in adulthood are to be carried out successfully.

Parents and teachers can help by understanding each task with which an adolescent is struggling at any particular time, and by providing guidance.

stage in the adolescent's progress toward emotional stability.

Books about Adolescence

Bottel, Helen. *Parents' Survival Kit: a Reassuring Guide to Living Through Your Child's Teenage Years* (Doubleday, 1979).

Dorr, L. C. *How to Enjoy Life Between Twelve and Twenty* (Corwin, 1978).

Eagen, A. B. *Why Am I So Miserable If These Are the Best Years of My Life?* (Lippincott, 1976).

Fine, L. L. *"After All We've Done for Them": Understanding Adolescent Behavior* (Prentice-Hall, 1977).

Gallagher, J. R., and H. I. Harris. *Emotional Problems of Adolescents* (Oxford, 1976).

Hurlock, E. B. *Adolescent Development*, 4th edition (McGraw-Hill, 1973).

Kett, J. F. *Rites of Passage: Adolescence in America, 1790 to the Present* (Basic Books, 1977).

McCandless, B. R., and R. H. Coop. *Adolescents: Behavior and Development*, 2nd edition (Holt, Rinehart & Winston, 1979).

Schowalter, J. E., and W. R. Anyan. *The Family Handbook of Adolescence* (Knopf, 1979).

hood, but rebels against the authority he obeyed then. He also is attracted by the pleasures of adulthood, but is usually unwilling to accept the responsibilities that go with such added privileges.

One of the strongest urges of the adolescent is to identify himself with his own age group. The right to choose his own companions often brings him into conflict with his parents, who are not yet accustomed to thinking of him as a person capable of making decisions for himself.

Parents' uncertainty as to whether they should treat the adolescent as a child or as an adult confuses the adolescent. His insecurity may be expressed in violent revolt against the rules set up by his parents and by adult society in general. Outlandish clothing and hair styles, slangy and profane speech, gang fights, and hot-rod races are some of the indications of such rebellion. The adolescent often chafes under the discipline of school, looking upon it as a form of bondage.

It is common for an adolescent to hero-worship a teacher or a motion-picture, television, or athletic star. The object of this worship may serve as a kind of substitute for the parent who seems to lack understanding. Interest in the opposite sex grows, ordinarily beginning in a casual way. Later, interest focuses more seriously on one individual. "Puppy love" and "crushes" may seem humorous to adults, but they are a necessary

Adonais. See SHELLEY, PERCY BYSSHE.

Adonis, *á*-dō'nĭs or *á*-dŏn'ĭs, in Greek mythology, a handsome young shepherd loved by Aphrodite, the goddess of love. Adonis was born from a tree into which his mother had been transformed. One day Aphrodite, playing with some of the love-inducing arrows of Eros (Cupid), accidentally cut her bosom. She saw Adonis nearby and the spell of the arrow made her fall madly in love with him. When Adonis was killed by a wild boar, Zeus responded to her plea that he be restored to life. Zeus decreed that Adonis should spend half the year with the dead in Hades and half with Aphrodite in the upper world.

Aphrodite caused the red buttercup called pheasant's-eye to spring from the blood of the dying Adonis. Because of his birth from a tree and his annual descent into Hades and subsequent arising to the upper world, Adonis became a vegetation god symbolizing the death and resurrection cycle of plants. Annual festivals called the Adonia were held in his honor.

Adonis, a genus of annual and perennial flowers of the buttercup family, native to temperate regions of Europe and Asia. Adonises have a single flower of 5 to 16 petals and finely divided (almost fernlike) leaves. Three species commonly grown in the United States are *Adonis vernalis,* a yellow, 9-inch-high perennial; *A. amurensis,* a golden-yellow, 12-inch-high perennial; and *A. annua* (pheasant's-eye), a red, 18-inch-high annual. According to legend, the pheasant's-eye sprang from the blood of Adonis, a character in Greek mythology.

The 20 species of adonis belong to the buttercup family, Ranunculaceae.

Adoption, in law, the act of taking a child of other parents into one's family as a son or daughter. Adoption is a legal process, and permission of a court is necessary. Consent of the natural parents or the child's legal guardian is required, and if the child is of a certain age his consent also is required. The adopted child acquires the same rights and duties as he would have if born in the family. Adoption was common in ancient Rome but was not recognized in English common law. Massachusetts passed the first adoption law in the United States in 1851.

Adrenal Glands, ăd-rē′năl, or **Suprarenal Glands,** sū′prá-rē′năl, a pair of endocrine (ductless) glands located above the kidneys. These glands secrete vital hormones into the bloodstream. Each adrenal gland forms a yellow cap two inches high and one inch wide over the upper end of a kidney. Each gland is divided into two main areas: the inner area, or *adrenal medulla,* and the outer area, or *adrenal cortex.*

Functions of the Adrenal Glands

The adrenal medulla produces two main hormones: epinephrine (also called *adrenalin*) and *norepinephrine.* Both of these hormones help the body to respond to stressful situations. (See ADRENALIN.) The adrenal medulla and its secretions are controlled by the sympathetic nervous system, a division of the autonomic nervous system.

The adrenal cortex produces several steroid hormones. The most important are:

Aldosterone, which partially regulates the amount of water in the body and the metabolism of sodium, potassium, and chlorine.

Hydrocortisone, or Cortisol, which influences the body's storage and use of carbohydrates, proteins, and fats; the inflammation reactions of tissues; the amount of water in the body; and the pigmentation of the skin.

Androstenedione, which affects the rates of sexual maturation and growth.

Synthetic hormones similar in structure and effect to these natural hormones are used as drugs. (See CORTISONE.)

The health of the adrenal cortex is maintained by *adrenocorticotropic hormone,* or *ACTH,* one of the hormones secreted by the pituitary gland. ACTH also controls the

A-70

rate of secretion of most of the hormones produced by the adrenal cortex. (See ACTH.)

Diseases of the Adrenal Glands

Disorders of the adrenal glands are of two main types: tumors, which usually cause the glands to overproduce; and afflictions that cause them to stop producing hormones. Adrenal tumors can often be removed by surgery. *Addison's disease* is a serious illness that occurs when the adrenal cortex does not function because of an infection (such as tuberculosis or a fungus infection) or because of the breakdown of the glandular tissue. A disease similar in effect to Addison's disease results from a disorder that causes the pituitary gland to stop producing ACTH. The main treatment for these diseases is to replace the missing hormones.

For location of adrenal glands, see ANATOMY (Plate D, number 40); GLAND (illustration).

Adrenalin, ăd-rĕn′ăl-ĭn, a common name for a hormone secreted by the medulla (inner layer) of the adrenal glands. The medical name for the hormone is *epinephrine.* (Adrenalin is actually a trade name.) Epinephrine causes the blood pressure to increase, the heart to beat faster, and the body to use more oxygen and to produce more energy. Its secretion is stimulated by the sympathetic nervous system when the body needs to meet an emergency. Epinephrine is also used as a drug to stimulate the heart, to constrict the blood vessels, and to counteract allergic reactions.

The adrenal medulla secretes another hormone, *norepinephrine,* which has an effect similar to that of epinephrine on the blood pressure. Both hormones were synthesized in 1904, but norepinephrine was not shown to be an adrenal hormone until 1949.

The chemical formula of epinephrine is $C_9H_{13}O_3N$; that of norepinephrine, $C_8H_{11}O_3N$.

Adrenocorticotropic Hormone. See ACTH.

Adrian, ā′drĭ-ăn, or **Hadrian,** hā′drĭ-ăn, the name of six popes of the Roman Catholic Church.

Adrian I (?-795), pope 772-95. He asked Charlemagne, king of the Franks, to protect him from the Lombards. The Lombards were crushed, and the pope was able to strengthen his temporal (political) power over Rome and central Italy. (See PAPAL STATES.) Adrian co-operated in calling the Second

Council of Nicaea. (See ECUMENICAL COUNCIL; NICAEA.)

Adrian II (792?-872), pope 867-72.

Adrian III, Saint (?-885), pope 884-85. His feast day is July 8.

Adrian IV (Nicholas Breakspear; 1115?-1159), pope 1154-59. He was the only English pope. He served as legate to Scandinavia with much success before he was chosen pope. Adrian's reign was marked by conflict with Frederick I (Barbarossa), emperor of the Holy Roman Empire, on the question of papal authority over the emperor.

Adrian V (Ottobuono Fieschi; ?-1276), pope 1276.

Adrian VI (Adrian Florisze Boeyens; 1459-1523), pope 1522-23. He was the only Dutch pope and the last non-Italian pope until the election of John Paul II in 1978. As a priest he taught theology at Louvain and was vice chancellor of the university. He was a tutor of the future Charles V and was regent of Spain. He was pope early in the Reformation and in response to critics of the Church he tried to eliminate abuses. The church hierarchy, however, prevented Adrian from achieving any reforms.

Adrian, Roman emperor. See HADRIAN.

Adrian, Edgar Douglas Adrian, First **Baron** (1889-1977), a British physiologist. For researches on the neuron and its functions, he shared the 1932 Nobel Prize in physiology or medicine with Sir Charles Sherrington. He developed methods of using electricity to study sense organs. Adrian graduated from Cambridge University. He was professor of physiology there, 1937-51, served as master of Trinity College, 1951-65, and was chancellor of the university, 1968-75. Adrian was created a baron in 1955.

Adrian, Michigan, the seat of Lenawee County. It is on the Raisin River, about 60 miles (97 km) southwest of Detroit. Products include automobile parts, aluminum goods, and laboratory equipment. The city is a processing and trading center for the surrounding agricultural area. Siena Heights College and Adrian College are here. Adrian was settled in 1825 and incorporated in 1853.

Population: 21,276.

Adrian College. See UNIVERSITIES AND COLLEGES (table).

Adrianople. See EDIRNE.

Adrianople, Battle of, August 9, 378 A.D., a crushing defeat of the Roman imperi-

al army under Emperor Valens by hordes of Visigoths led by Fritigern, aided by Ostrogoths and members of other barbarian tribes. Valens and two-thirds of his army, about 40,000 men, were killed when trapped in a double envelopment. The Battle of Adrianople was the first barbarian victory over the Romans within the empire. It was a turning point in the history of warfare, establishing a dominance of cavalry that was to last 1,000 years.

Adrianople, Treaty of, 1829, a pact that ended war between Russia and Turkey and set Greece free from Turkish rule. A Greek rebellion had started in 1821. In 1827 Great Britain, France, and Russia intervened, and destroyed a Turkish-Egyptian fleet in the Battle of Navarino. Russia declared war on Turkey in 1828, invaded Bulgaria, and seized Adrianople, where Turkey was forced to sign peace terms.

See also GREECE, subtitle *History of Modern Greece:* Independence; RUSSO-TURKISH WARS.

Adriatic Sea, ā'drĭ-ăt'ĭk, an arm of the Mediterranean Sea. The name comes from the city of Adria in northeast Italy. (It was once a port but now is 13 miles inland due to silt deposition at the mouths of the Po River.) The Adriatic lies between Italy on the west and north and Yugoslavia and Albania on the east. The only entrance to the sea is by the Strait of Otranto, which lies in the south between Italy and Albania and connects the Adriatic with the Ionian Sea.

The Adriatic Sea is about 500 miles long (northwest-southeast) and up to 140 miles wide. It has an area of approximately 51,000 square miles, slightly less than that of Lakes Superior and Michigan combined. The Adriatic is one of the shallowest parts of the Mediterranean, with an average depth of about 800 feet. The deepest spot (4,110 feet) is about midway between Dubrovnik, Yugoslavia, and the Italian coast.

In contrast to the northern part of Italy's Adriatic coast, where marshes and lagoons abound, the central and southern portions consist of sandy lowlands and beaches in many places backed by foothills of the Apennines. In Yugoslavia, where the Dinaric Alps descend abruptly to the sea, the coast is mountainous and studded with islands. Especially scenic is the Dalmatian region, which has many resorts.

The Adriatic's balmy climate and excellent seaside and island resorts attract many tourists. Fishing and sponge diving are also important. Major cities and ports on the sea include Trieste, Venice, and Bari in Italy; Rijeka and Split in Yugoslavia; and Durrës, the port city of Tiranë, capital of Albania.

Adsorption, ăd-sôrp′shŭn, the process by which a substance attracts and holds solid, liquid, or gaseous particles of another substance on its surface. The adsorbed particles can be molecules or atoms contained in a gas or in a liquid solution, and the adsorbing surface can be either a solid or a liquid.

Adsorption is important both in nature and industrially. Proteins, found in all animal and plant cells, adsorb water, which is essential for their activity. Clays in the earth adsorb organic matter from ground water, and thus help to purify the water.

Both solids and liquids adsorb most effectively when they are in a form that presents a large amount of surface area. Finely divided or porous solids, such as powdered metals, charcoal, clay, and activated carbon (a powdered, granular, or pelleted form of carbon), are therefore widely used as industrial adsorbents. Fine liquid droplets, such as those that occur in aerosols and sprays, are also effective adsorbents.

Charcoal will adsorb phosgene and other toxic gases, and is commonly used as a filter-

ing material in gas masks. Activated carbon, which will adsorb many substances in amounts nearly equal to its own weight, is the most important industrial adsorbent. It is used in air conditioner filters; to remove impurities from sugar during refining; to withdraw impurities and unwanted moisture from air and other gases; in the treatment of municipal water supplies; and in a number of other ways.

Other important industrial adsorbents include silica gel, a coarse, porous sand; activated alumina, a granular, highly porous form of aluminum oxide; and Fuller's earth, composed mainly of clay minerals.

Absorption, the internal penetration of a substance by matter or radiant energy, sometimes occurs simultaneously with adsorption. (See ABSORPTION.)

Adult Education. See EDUCATION, ADULT.

Adult Education Association of the U.S.A. See EDUCATION, ADULT, subtitle *History of Adult Education.*

Adulteration, à-dŭl′tẽr-ā′shŭn, the lowering of the quality of products, especially foods and drugs. Adulteration is accomplished by (1) using harmful, tainted, unsafe, impure, or inferior ingredients; or (2) altering or deceptively treating the products in order to give a false appearance or hide defects. There are federal and state laws, as well as municipal ordinances, that forbid or restrict the shipment and sale of adulterated products. Federal law regulates the safety of food additives.

The adding of water to milk is an example of lowering quality by using a cheaper ingredient that in itself is not harmful. The use of safrole as a flavoring ingredient in soft drinks was prohibited by regulation after safrole was found to be harmful. Some food preservatives, such as sodium benzoate, are safe in small amounts, but can be injurious to health if excessive amounts are added to food preparations. Many additives that are intended to prevent spoilage of foods, or improve their taste and appearance, are considered adulterants if used in amounts greater than those specified by law or regulation.

Drugs are considered adulterated if there is a deficiency of any of the active ingredients listed on the label, if the potency of the drug is greater than that specified on the label, or if there are impurities in the drug. In order to control adulteration, the federal Food and Drug Administration inspects drug manufacturing plants at regular intervals and makes frequent tests on samples from drug shipments. Furthermore, drug manufacturers are required by law to indicate on the container the contents of each product.

See also PURE FOOD AND DRUG LAWS.

Advent, in the Christian church, the holy season before Christmas. The word is from the Latin for "coming" and refers to the coming of Christ. Advent is a time of special preparation. Christians prepare for the celebration of Christ's birth—Christmas —and also for his second coming. The church year begins with Advent Sunday. For most churches Advent begins on the Sunday nearest St. Andrew's Day (November 30) and includes four Sundays. In the Eastern Orthodox Church Advent begins in November and is six weeks long. Observance of Advent apparently started in the sixth century.

Advent is a penitential season, although not observed as strictly as Lent. Fasting is generally not required, but weddings seldom take place and festivities are discouraged. Purple, the color of penance, may be used for church vestments.

Adventists, ăd'věn-tĭstz, the general name of several Protestant groups that stress the early second coming of Christ. They believe that the second coming, or advent, will open the Biblical millenium, the time when they will live and reign "with Christ a thousand years" (Revelation 20:4).

The Seventh-day Adventists, the largest group, observe Saturday instead of Sunday as the Sabbath. (See SEVENTH-DAY ADVENTIST CHURCH.) Other Adventist bodies are the Advent Christian Church, the Church of God General Conference (Abrahamic Faith), and the Primitive Advent Christian Church.

The adventist movement sprang up in both Europe and America in the early 1800's. William Miller (1782-1849), a New York farmer, began preaching in 1831 that the second coming would be in 1843-44 and would bring the end of the world. He gained thousands of followers, but many fell away when 1844 passed. One group formed the Seventh-day Adventists. In 1845 Miller organized his remaining followers into an association, out of which various churches were formed.

Adverb. See GRAMMAR, subtitle *Parts of Speech;* INFLECTION, subtitle *Comparison.*

SHOP EARLY · MAIL EARLY

USE ZIP CODE

U.S. Postal Service
Noncommercial Ad urges use of the ZIP code.

Advertising, any way of attracting favorable attention to products, property, and services for sale or for rent. Advertising may also be applied to ideas or projects to win support for them. Advertising is a large and important industry in the United States, Western Europe, and Japan.

Most advertising is prepared professionally by men and women who work for an advertising agency (company) or in the advertising department of a business concern. Those who plan the advertising often have training in business management and economics. They must decide not only how much money to spend and where to spend it, but what features of their product (or service or project) have the greatest appeal, and how best to make the public aware of it. Their decisions are thus based in part on information supplied by market-research specialists— men and women who study and analyze the likes and dislikes of prospective customers.

Salesmen working for the advertising *media*—the means by which advertising messages are delivered to the public, such as radio and television, publications, and billboards—sell the time or space for advertisements. The services of writers, illustrators, photographers, models, typographers, layout artists, actors, and announcers are required to create advertisements. These people may work on a full-time or free-lance basis.

Uses of Advertising

Most advertising is intended to sell specific products or services. Advertising is also

A-73

widely used, however, for noncommercial purposes. An advertisement may solicit votes for a political candidate, urge people not to litter the streets, or explain a company's position in a labor-management dispute. The federal government directs many messages to the public through advertisements.

As a selling aid, advertising is designed to create a desire to buy. Advertising can also be an aid to the customer by helping him decide whether the merchandise or service offered is a good value and whether it meets his desires.

Product advertising is used at all three stages of selling—by the producer, by the wholesaler, and by the dealer.

The producer—a manufacturing or processing company—advertises its products to the general public in order to create a demand for them. It seeks to create a demand both for a certain product, such as an air conditioner, and for the company's brand in particular. A large company tries to win public confidence so that customers will choose its products on the basis of the company or brand name. Many companies have some advertisements that mention no product at all, but are designed only to create good will. The manufacturer also advertises to the wholesale and retail merchants who deal in his products.

Electric Spectacular. This huge animated electric sign is designed to put over a brief message—a brand name and listing of four products.
Outdoor Advertising Association of America, Inc.

The wholesaler, or middleman—the person or firm that buys merchandise from the manufacturer and sells it to stores or other retail dealers—does not advertise to the general public. His need is to let retailers know what merchandise he stocks. His usual form of advertising, therefore, is a catalog.

The dealer advertises in order to bring customers into his place of business. He stresses not only the goods he offers, but also his own reliability, convenience of location, and customer service. Generally he prefers to deal in merchandise that is nationally advertised. Often a manufacturer provides local advertising in which his dealers may participate on a co-operative basis.

Media—the Kinds of Advertising

The largest share of national advertising expenditures is for advertisements appearing in newspapers and magazines. Almost as large a share goes to television and radio. Other widely used media are outdoor advertising, and printed matter sent through the mails or used at the point of purchase (the place where the merchandise is sold).

In choosing his media, an advertiser considers his market—the people who are likely to buy the product or service. A product may appeal primarily to persons of certain ages, habits, and tastes; it may be available nationally or only in certain parts of the country. The advertiser also considers comparative costs. The price of an advertisement ranges from a few dollars in a rural newspaper or on local radio to thousands of dollars in a national magazine or on network television.

Publications. Newspapers carry two kinds of advertisements. *Display advertising* uses devices such as borders, headlines, and illustrations to attract attention. Display advertisements appear throughout a newspaper. The space is sold usually by the column-inch (a space one column wide and one inch in depth). *Classified advertising,* sold by the line, is grouped by subject, in its own section of the paper. The advertisements are largely solid lines of small type, and appear under such headings as "Help Wanted" and "Apartments for Rent." Public announcements such as lost-and-found notices are also included in the classified section.

Some newspapers have special combinations of display and classified advertising; for example, display advertisements of automobile dealers in the classified section.

Creating a Printed Advertisement

A printed advertisement is developed out of a basic idea — in this case, to show the many kinds of youngsters who eat a certain cereal for breakfast.

Copywriter's Rough Layout

The copywriter at the advertising agency interprets the idea with a group of rhymes describing "kids." He types up a rough draft of the rhymes and shows in a rough layout how he thinks they may be used, combined with pictures of children.

Rough Copy

The art director develops the idea in a layout featuring two large illustrations and a small one. The writer edits and revises the copy to fit this layout, which is approved by the cereal company.

Art Director's Layout

Finished Copy

In translating the layout illustrations into photographs, further refinements are made. The pictures finally selected are pasted up on a sheet together with the copy, which has been set in type. This sheet is called a "mechanical comprehensive." From it will be made the plates that print the advertisement in the magazine.

Mechanical Comprehensive

Ad in Magazine

Leo Burnett Company, Inc., Chicago, for Kellogg's

Pasting up a Billboard. The poster, printed on many sheets, is assembled on the billboard.

Newspapers carry advertisements also in their Sunday supplements, in special magazine sections, and sometimes in the comics sections.

Most magazines carry display advertising, selling the space by the page or fraction of a page. Some also carry classified advertising. The classified telephone directory (the "yellow pages") also carries display advertising. Other publications in which advertising space is sold include programs for entertainments and yearbooks.

See also AUDIT BUREAU OF CIRCULATIONS; NEWSPAPER, subtitle *Publishing a Newspaper:* Advertising; and PERIODICAL, subtitle *Makeup of Periodicals:* Advertisements.

Radio and Television. Broadcast advertisements are called commercials. In the United States most broadcast time is sold to advertisers, called sponsors, who pay also for the programs produced in their time periods.

Painting an Outdoor Display. A large advertisement is painted in sections in the studio and fitted together at the display site.

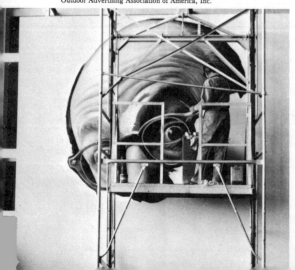

They are permitted to use part of the broadcast period for commercials. An advertiser may also buy all or part of the time between programs, during station breaks, and during programs presented by the station or network, such as movies. These messages are called spot commercials, or spot announcements.

Broadcast time is sold by the hour or portion of an hour for sponsored programs, and by the minute or portion of a minute for spot commercials. Spot commercials are sold in "packages," a certain number broadcast during a specified period of time. The rates for broadcasting time vary according to the size of the audience at various times of day. The most expensive period, called prime time, is the evening. Several companies specialize in providing the television industry with audience ratings—the percentage of the total audience tuned to each program on the air during a particular time period.

See also RADIO, section "Uses and Regulation of Radio," subtitle *Broadcasting;* TELEVISION, section "Television Broadcasting," subtitle *Types of Television.*

Outdoor Advertising. *Posters* make up the greater part of outdoor advertising. They are pasted, or posted, on *billboards*—flat panels erected on framework or attached to buildings. There are two standard sizes of outdoor posters. The large-size poster is displayed beside a road or street to be seen from vehicles. The smaller is usually mounted on a building wall where it will be seen by pedestrians. The company that owns the billboards sells the use of them to the advertiser. *Painted displays* are painted on metal panels called bulletins, or on walls.

Electric spectaculars are animated electric signs created for congested metropolitan areas where the heavy traffic justifies the great expense. *Electric semispectaculars* are painted displays with neon tubing or other special lighting effects. Other forms of outdoor advertising include all manner of painted and electric signs, three-dimensional figures, and such devices as giant clocks and thermometers.

See also POSTER.

Direct Mail. A vast amount of advertising matter is mailed to the public. Some of it advertises goods and services that may be purchased by mail. Sometimes samples are included, or coupons entitling the consumer to a special price on the advertised products.

PRODUCING A TELEVISION COMMERCIAL

The filming of a television commercial by an advertising agency is the result of much planning and preliminary work. In the commercial shown here, for a soup company, the basic idea is a jingle telling of the loving care given children.

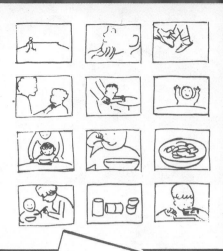

Rough Storyboard. The main action in each scene that will illustrate the jingle and the announcer's remarks is sketched in rough form in the order in which it will appear. The complete set of pictures is called a storyboard.

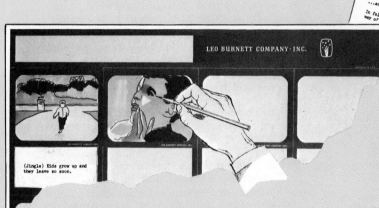

Copy. This is the copy that the action will illustrate. It includes the words of the jingle and of the announcer. The score for the musical theme is not shown, but the music will be one of the most important parts of this commercial.

Finished Storyboard. The agency's art director makes finished drawings with the copy beneath them to serve as a guide to the film director. Actors will follow the storyboard closely.

Televising the Commercial. This is a still photograph from the filmed commercial as it appears on television. It is the scene shown in the second picture on the storyboard.

Leo Burnett Company, Inc., Chicago, for Campbell Soup Co.

"HIS MASTER'S VOICE"

Registered Trademark of Radio Corporation of America in United States

TIME TO RE-TIRE ®

U. S. Rubber Tire Co.

Trade Mark, Slogan, and Trade Character. *Top,* "His Master's Voice" was first used in 1900 to identify the new Victor Talking Machine. *Center,* the punning slogan "Time to Re-Tire" was adopted about 1908 by Fisk. *Below,* these "Campbell Kids" trotted over soup cans during World War I.

Campbell Soup Company

Mailing lists for direct-mail advertising are compiled from such sources as telephone directories, voter registration rolls, and motor vehicle registration lists. Advertisers may compile their own or obtain them from brokers specializing in the renting, bartering, and selling of mailing lists. In addition, most publications and mail-order companies market, either directly or through brokers, names of their subscribers or customers.

Point-of-purchase Advertising. There are numerous ways of advertising merchandise at the place where it is sold. The simplest method is by displaying a sign, the merchandise, or both in the window or in the store. From this has developed the special display, most frequently a brightly colored cardboard construction that serves as a receptacle, backing card, or embellishment for the product. Sometimes a demonstrator will show how a product is used, or hand out samples or leaflets. In some stores a public-address system is used to advertise special values.

Other Kinds of Advertising. A product's *label* and *package* may also serve as advertising. They are usually designed not only to identify the merchandise, but to attract attention. Messages may be printed on the package, or on an enclosed leaflet.

See also LABEL; PACKAGING.

Transit advertising consists mainly of printed placards, called *car cards,* that are displayed inside buses and rapid-transit cars. It includes also signs on vehicles, and in and on rapid-transit stations.

Advertising films may be either motion pictures, or a sequence of still pictures, called slide films or film strips, accompanied by transcribed or live narration. Films with a direct advertising message are used at sales meetings, dealers' conventions, and sometimes in theaters. Others, designed for the general public and shown at exhibitions or loaned to organizations, present information or entertainment and advertise a product or company in only an indirect manner.

Samples, besides being sent through the mails, may be given out in a store or distributed house to house.

Advertising specialties are inexpensive items such as match books, calendars, and ball-point pens that an advertiser inscribes with his name and perhaps a brief message and passes out to prospects and customers.

Stunt advertising includes skywriting with smoke, streamers towed by aircraft, and other novel means of displaying a commercial message.

Principles of Advertising

Winning Attention. To reach a prospect with a message, the advertiser must first capture his attention. This is done visually with an eye-catching headline or design.

In television commercials, the announcer is sometimes presented in a closeup for visual impact. An exclamatory phrase or a strident tone of voice may be employed as well. This strident approach, known as the "hard-sell" style of advertising, has been used so extensively that many advertisers feel that it has lost its effectiveness, and that it tends to antagonize some persons. Hard-sell advertising, however, is still extensively used with effectiveness for certain products, such as patent medicines. Advocates of this approach point out that it does not matter that persons may dislike a commercial if it succeeds in capturing their attention and selling the product.

Many advertisers use a "soft-sell" approach that depends on uniqueness rather than more obvious methods of gaining attention. An advertisement that is amusing, appealing, or unusually clever is often noticed and remembered by many persons. A danger of "soft-sell" advertising is that the advertiser's message is sometimes obscured and ineffectively conveyed by an excessively cute or clever commercial.

Using Repetition. Advertisers recognize that the public is exposed constantly to advertising messages, and that many persons have learned to ignore them. To overcome this, a radio or television commercial often gives the name of the product repeatedly and sometimes repeats the main advertising message word for word several times. An advertisement, either printed or broadcast, is normally used many times so that persons seeing it or hearing it will gradually absorb the message.

Establishing Identity. The first object of an advertiser's message is to make his product, brand name, company, or cause familiar to the public. An identifying design called a trade-mark is one means of doing this. Other ways of accomplishing that purpose include using a slogan (a short, distinctive phrase); a jingle (a brief song with a catchy tune); or a trade character (a fictional character creater by an artist or played by an actor) who always appers in the advertisement.

See also TRADEMARK.

Persuading the Prospect. To persuade the prospect to act—generally, to buy—an appeal may be made to, among other things, reason; pride; desire for admiration, enjoyment, or comfort; a man's need to feel masculine or a woman's desire to feel feminine. Much advertising appeals to a person's eagerness for a bargain, and in the case of noncommercial advertisements, a person's social consciousness or sense of civic duty.

The Advertising Agency

Many business concerns have an advertising department or employ an advertising agency, and many companies that have an advertising department also employ an agency. A department may handle all of the company's advertising. When an agency is used also, the advertising department represents management in planning and approving the advertising program, and possibly executes some portions of it.

An advertising agency by tradition receives its income from commissions. The media in which the agency's client advertises allow the agency a certain percentage of the charges, or *billing,* paid by the client. The usual commission is 15 per cent. In some cases a service fee is charged the client for agency work not covered by commissions, such as consumer surveys or product-testing.

There are in the United States about 4,000 advertising agencies, not including a number of one-man operations. The largest have annual billings in the hundreds of millions of dollars. Top-billing foreign agencies are located in Japan, West Germany, and Great Britain. Many United States advertising agencies maintain branches in other countries.

Agency Organization. The plan of organization given here is typical of larger agencies. The client for whom an agency handles the advertising is called an *account.* The *account executive* is in charge of the account for the agency. Working with the client and creative director or member of the copy (writing), art, and broadcasting departments, he helps plan the advertising program. Determination of the product's market and the choice of media, style of approach, and type of appeal will be based in part on the findings of the *research department* or an outside research consultant.

After the client and agency personnel have decided on an advertising program, *space buyers* contract for space in publications,

Cigar Store Indian. Symbols were used to advertise wares when few persons were able to read. From about 1730 a wooden Indian meant tobacco. This carved wooden figure stood in front of a Boston shop in the early 19th century.
American Tobacco Company

sponsored television show also is usually produced by a special company.

Regulation of Advertising

False and misleading advertising for anything sold across state lines is prohibited by law; the law is enforced by the Federal Trade Commission. Other federal agencies with authority to regulate various aspects of advertising are the Federal Communications Commission, the Food and Drug Administration, the Securities and Exchange Commission, the U.S. Postal Service, and the Alcohol and Tobacco Tax Division of the Internal Revenue Service.

See also FEDERAL COMMUNICATIONS COMMISSION; FEDERAL TRADE COMMISSION; FOOD AND DRUG ADMINISTRATION; PURE FOOD AND DRUG LAWS; SECURITIES AND EXCHANGE COMMISSION.

History of Advertising

From ancient times merchants cried, or shouted, their wares in the street. In England in the 17th and 18th centuries each kind of tradesman had his special street cry, and the custom was brought to the American colonies. In the United States a few street vendors still advertise this way.

When merchants moved into shops, they adopted symbols to show what goods or services they sold, such as a goat for a dairy shop, a grinding mill for a bakery. The practice continued until modern times. Then, as more people learned to read, written signs began to replace symbols. But even today one may see a watch in front of a jewelry shop or a slipper on a shoe-store sign.

In ancient times notices were sometimes written on papyrus and posted in public places. During the Middle Ages, when parchment was the only writing material in Europe and most people were illiterate, written notices were rare. With the introduction of paper and the expansion of learning, tack-up signs became common.

Printed Advertisements. Printing, introduced in the 15th century, revolutionized advertising. Tack-up signs led to handbills, called tradesmen's cards, which a merchant

and *time buyers* schedule broadcasting time. The *copy writers* write the message, or *copy,* for the advertisements.

For print media, the *art department* provides illustrations by staff or free-lance artists or from an art studio or photographer, and prepares a *layout* (arrangement) of the advertisement. When the client has approved everything in rough form, the *print production department,* working with typesetters, printers, engravers, and lithographers, prepares the advertisement for publication. The completed advertisement is then sent to the publications in which it will appear.

Radio commercials, if they are to be broadcast by a station announcer, are delivered to the station in manuscript form. For recorded commercials, the *broadcast production department* hires announcers and has tape recordings made. It also hires actors for television commercials, most of which are filmed at studios specializing in television productions. The entertainment part of a

A Busy Billboard. A lot of reading matter was posted in this display of theater advertising in 1896—but in horse-and-buggy days there was no lack of time to take in the message.
Outdoor Advertising Association of America, Inc.

A-80

could have printed and distributed by the hundreds. Advertisements in newspapers became common in the 17th century. The first successful newspaper in the American colonies, the Boston *News-Letter,* carried three advertisements in May, 1704. Benjamin Franklin made newspaper advertising an important source of revenue with his *Pennsylvania Gazette,* acquired in 1729.

Magazines were considered too dignified for any advertising other than notices of new books and a few scholarly announcements. In 1866, however, *The Atlantic Monthly* began carrying advertisements of all kinds. By the end of the century magazines were a major advertising medium.

Beginning of Advertising Agencies. The persons responsible for the rapid growth of advertising in the United States were the advertising agents. In the 1840's newspaper-advertising solicitors began representing groups of newspapers. In 1865 George P. Rowell introduced a system of buying newspaper space and dividing and selling it to advertisers at a higher price. J. Walter Thompson Company, founded in 1864, adapted the system to magazines. These pioneer agencies were in the beginning merely agents for the publications, selling their space for them.

N. W. Ayer & Son, which began operation in 1869, in 1875 set up the commission system based on the actual cost of publication space. The first agency to consider that it represented the advertiser rather than the publication, Ayer soon began writing copy for its clients. In Chicago Lord & Thomas, founded in 1892, developed the principles and techniques of writing advertising copy that would not only direct attention to merchandise, but would actually sell it.

Early Trade Card. In 1470 a hatter in Paris advertised the variety of his merchandise.

Irresponsible Advertising. Reputable manufacturers rarely made untruthful statements in their advertising, but claims for many products, especially patent medicines, were often fraudulent and even dangerous. Toward the end of the century responsible publications began demanding reform. The Pure Food and Drug Act of 1906 prohibited misleading statements on labels. The act was broadened in 1912, 1913, 1923, and 1938.

False Claims and Bad Taste. Nineteenth-century advertisers were often unscrupulous. *Left,* a patent medicine maker's advertisement boldly states that his product "will cure rheumatism." *Right,* an 1878 advertiser puts words in the mouths of the President and First Lady, endorsing his product.

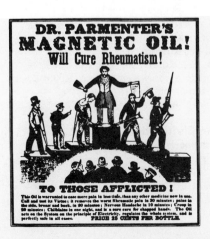

The Advertising Federation of America (founded in 1905 as the Associated Advertising Clubs of America) in 1911 drew up a code of ethical practices. With prodding from the federation, most states enacted laws forbidding fraudulent advertising. Publications established standards of their own, and the worst practices were largely eliminated.

The prosperity of the 1920's led to flamboyant advertising, and again claims often exceeded facts. During the sobering years of the Great Depression, 1929-40, advertising was subjected to strenuous criticism and scrutiny. Organizations for the evaluation of consumer products published their findings. The Wheeler-Lea Act of 1938 brought interstate advertising under the control of the Federal Trade Commission.

Radio and Television. In 1922 radio station WEAF in New York City began selling program time to advertisers. Fearing public disapproval, the station named the sponsors but did not permit them even to give an advertising message. But experimentation soon showed that the public was not offended by commercials, and that broadcasting was a powerful advertising medium. The use of television for advertising purposes began shortly before the end of World War II, and grew rapidly in the postwar period.

The American Advertising Federation has as members national associations of advertisers; publishers, broadcasters, and other media firms; advertising agencies; advertising trade associations; local advertising clubs; and suppliers, such as engravers and printers. Its headquarters are at 1225 Connecticut Avenue, Washington, D.C. 20036.

The national organization of advertising agencies is the American Association of Advertising Agencies, founded in 1917, with headquarters at 200 Park Avenue, New York, N.Y. 10017.

The Advertising Research Foundation, 3 East 54th Street, New York, N.Y. 10022, was founded in 1936 to promote the use of research in the industry. Its regular members are advertising agencies, advertisers, and media; colleges and universities are associate academic members.

The major advertising periodical is *Advertising Age,* 740 North Rush Street, Chicago, Illinois 60611.

See also ADVERTISING COUNCIL; ART, COMMERCIAL; PROPAGANDA; PUBLIC RELATIONS.

Books about Advertising

Advertising Age (periodical). *How It Was in Advertising, 1776-1976* (Crain Books, 1976).
Barnouw, Erik. *The Sponsor: Notes on a Modern Potentate* (Oxford University, 1978).

Book, A. C., and N. D. Cary. *The Radio and Television Commercial* (Crain Books, 1978).
Dirksen, C. J., and Arthur Kroeger. *Advertising Principles and Problems,* 5th edition (Irwin, 1977).
Kleppner, Otto, and Norman Govoni. *Advertising Procedure* (Prentice-Hall, 1979).
Lewis, H. G. *All You Ever Wanted to Know about Advertising* (Nelson-Hall, 1979).
Lois, George. *The Art of Advertising* (Abrams, 1977).
Nelson, R. P. *The Design of Advertising,* 3rd edition (Brown, 1977).
Roman, Kenneth, and Jane Maas. *How to Advertise* (St. Martin's Press, 1977).
Solomon, Marc, and Norman Wiener. *Marketing and Advertising Careers* (Watts, 1977).
Ulanoff, S. M. *Advertising in America: an Introduction to Persuasive Communication* (Hastings House, 1977).
Winters, K. G. *Your Career in Advertising* (Arco, 1979).

Advertising Council, a private, nonprofit organization that conducts public service advertising. All its advertising programs are prepared and presented free of cost, for

Council's Emblem

use in newspapers and magazines, on posters, and on radio and television. These media publish the advertising without charge. Projects and causes helped by the council include the Red Cross, Forest Fire Prevention, Religion in American Life, Rehabilitation of Handicapped People, United Negro College Fund, and U.S. Savings Bonds.

Funds for administrative expenses come from the national advertising organizations and from donations by business firms. The council was founded in 1942 to aid the war effort. Headquarters are in New York City.

Advocate. See ATTORNEY.

AE. See RUSSELL, GEORGE W.

AEC. See ATOMIC ENERGY COMMISSION, UNITED STATES.

Aedes. See MOSQUITO.

Aedile. See ROME AND THE ROMAN EMPIRE, subtitle *Government:* The Republic (table of Roman officials).

AEF. See AMERICAN EXPEDITIONARY FORCES.

Aegean Civilization, ē-jē'ăn, the civilization of the people living around the Aegean Sea before the emergence of ancient Greece about the ninth century B.C. There were two major cultures—the Minoan, which flour-

...ished from about 2500 to the 1400's B.C., and the Mycenaean, from about 1600 to 1100 B.C.

The Minoans were a seafaring people from Crete and Thera (modern Greek: Thíra). Their early form of script writing, Linear A, has been tentatively identified as Phoenician. This identification raises the possibility that the earliest Aegean civilization may have been Phoenician. The Mycenaeans were a Greek-speaking people who had come from the north and settled on the Greek mainland.

It is not known if the Minoans and the Mycenaeans were on friendly or hostile terms. Cretan cities were severely damaged about 1700 B.C. by earthquake or enemy attack. In the 1400's B.C. the island was devastated by the effects of a volcanic eruption on Thera (which may have been legendary Atlantis). Later it was partially rebuilt under the Mycenaeans, who learned seafaring from the Minoans and adopted their arts and crafts. The intermingling of the two cultures produced the great civilization described by Homer in his account of the Trojan War.

See also GREECE, ANCIENT, subtitle *The Making of Ancient Greece;* MINOAN CULTURE; MYCENAEAN CIVILIZATION; THERA.

Aegean Sea, an arm of the Mediterranean Sea. It lies between Greece on the west and the north and Turkey on the east. In the south, where Crete, Kárpathos, Rhodes, and other Greek islands lie, the Aegean merges with the Mediterranean. Numerous gulfs, bays, and inlets create a highly indented coast. The greatest distances are about 400 miles north-south and 275 miles east-west. The Aegean's area is roughly 69,000 square miles.

The basin of the Aegean is an old submerged land block; higher parts remain exposed as islands. Like other geologically unstable areas, the basin undergoes periodic volcanic eruptions and earthquakes. An especially violent one about 1450 B.C. nearly destroyed the island of Thera, which may have been legendary Atlantis. Depths of the Aegean range from broad shallows to more than 8,000 feet below sea level. The deepest point, 8,298 feet, is off the northeast coast of Crete.

The Sea of Crete, between Crete and the Cyclades, forms the southernmost part of the Aegean. In the northeast the Dardanelles leads into the Sea of Marmara, which in

Location of the Aegean Sea

turn is connected to the Black Sea by the Bosporus. West of Athens the Corinth Canal provides a narrow water route westward to the Ionian Sea. The origin of the name Aegean is uncertain. It has been said to derive from Aegea, a city of Évvoia; Aegeus, father of Theseus; and Aegea, an Amazon queen.

The Aegean Islands

Hundreds of islands, almost all of them belonging to Greece, lie scattered throughout the Aegean. In size they range from such large ones as Crete, Évvoia, Rhodes, Lésvos, Límnos, Khíos, and Thásos to rocky, uninhabited islets. Most of the islands lie within loosely defined groups: the Northern Sporades; the Cyclades; and the Sporades, or Southern Sporades, including the Dodecanese Islands.

Island landscapes range from rugged mountains, extinct volcanoes, and craggy coastal cliffs to fertile green valleys and gentle slopes. As throughout the Mediterranean region, the climate is mild, much like that of southern California. Vegetation is everywhere scant. Dotting the islands are small villages and towns.

Although it provides only a bare subsistence, agriculture is the basis of the economy. Olives, grapes, vegetables, and a few grains (particularly wheat) are the principal crops; goats make up most of the livestock. Fishing, shipping, and the gathering of sponges provide additional income. Tourism is of increasing significance, for the islands are an idyllic land where highly advanced civilizations once flourished.

See also AEGEAN CIVILIZATION; AEGINA; CRETE; CYCLADES; DODECANESE ISLANDS; EUBOEA; GREECE, ANCIENT; MINOAN CULTURE; MYCENAEAN CIVILIZATION.

Aegeus. See THESEUS.

Aegina (modern Greek: Aíyina), an island off the coast of Greece in the Saronic Gulf about 20 miles southwest of Athens. It is triangular in shape and about 32 square miles in area. Aegina has ruins of several temples from the early fifth century B.C. The sculptures from one of them, known as the Aeginetan marbles, are in Munich. Aegina is visited by many tourists.

Aegina, already settled in the Minoan and Mycenaean eras, was conquered by the Dorians in the 11th century B.C. It was an important commercial center by the sixth century B.C., and had the first official coinage on the west side of the Aegean Sea. As Athens rose to prominence, it became a commercial rival of Aegina, and in 457 B.C. Athens conquered the island. In 431, at the start of the Peloponnesian War, the Aeginetans were expelled from the island by the Athenians. In 1828-29, during the last part of the Greek war for independence from Turkish rule, the town of Aegina served as capital of the revolutionary government.

Population of the island: 9,584.

Aegis, ē'jĭs, in Greek mythology, a goatskin shield, breastplate, or cloak worn by Zeus and his daughter Athene. When shaken, the aegis caused a thunderstorm. It also had the power to protect friends and frighten enemies. The aegis of Zeus was made for him by Hephaestus. It was supposed to be indestructible, being impervious even to lightning bolts.

In art the aegis usually is depicted as a cloak worn by Athene over her shoulders or as a shield over her left arm. It is fringed with snakes, and the center bears the head of Medusa (the sight of which turned mortals to stone), which was presented to Athene by Perseus. The word *aegis* is used figuratively to mean any protective power or influence.

Aegisthus. See CLYTEMNESTRA.

Aegospotami, Battle of. See PELOPONNESIAN WAR.

Aegyptus. See DANAÏDES.

A-84

Aelfric, ăl'frĭk (955?-1020?), an English writer and churchman called Grammaticus, grä-măt'ĭ-kŭs (The Grammarian). His rhythmical, alliterative prose in *Lives of Saints* (about 997) and *Catholic Sermons* (990-98) often is cited as the finest Anglo-Saxon writing of the period. He also translated religious works from Latin into Anglo-Saxon, adapted a Latin grammar, and compiled an Anglo-Saxon-Latin dictionary. Aelfric was trained in the monastery of Winchester. He left in 987 to go to the Cernel Monastery in Dorsetshire, where he became abbot. He later became abbot of Eynsham in Oxfordshire.

Aeneas, ê-nē'ăs, in Greek and Roman legend, a Trojan hero in the war with the Greeks. The Romans claimed him as founder of their nation. He is an important character in Homer's *Iliad,* the story of the Trojan War, and is the hero of Virgil's *Aeneid,* an account of his adventures after the fall of Troy.

According to Homer, Aeneas was the son of the goddess Aphrodite (known as Venus to the Romans) and Anchises, the king of Dardania, a Trojan city. Aeneas did not join Troy when the Greeks first besieged it, but when his lands were attacked he became second only to Hector among the Trojan leaders. Although brave, Aeneas would not have survived but for divine help. His life was saved by the gods so that, according to prophecy, he might establish a new home for the Trojans.

After the war Aeneas, with his son, Ascanius, and a band of Trojan survivors, set out on a voyage that, according to Virgil, lasted seven years. After landing in the kingdom of Latium in Italy, according to the Roman historian Livy, the Trojans intermarried with the Latins and so became ancestors of the Romans.

There appears to be no historical basis for such ancestry. The Romans adopted many of the gods and legends of the Greeks and sought to give themselves equally impressive origins by claiming descent from heroes.

See also AENEID; ASCANIUS.

Aeneid, ê-nē'ĭd, a Latin epic poem in 12 books by Virgil. Begun at the request of the emperor Augustus, the *Aeneid* was unfinished when Virgil died in 19 B.C. Varius and Tucca are said to have completed it.

The *Aeneid* is the first and foremost of the great European literary epics. (The earlier

Iliad and *Odyssey* are folk, rather than literary, epics.) Dante and many other poets from various countries owe it an immense debt. It has been called the most influential book ever written in the Latin tongue. The *Aeneid* is the supreme achievement of the Augustan Age, when there was a general flowering of literature. Its style is polished, and literary and historical allusions are numerous. Virgil searches for the meaning of suffering and death, voicing a deep pity for mankind's woes.

The author's dramatic skill, philosophical acumen, and descriptive powers transcend the primary purpose of the work: to glorify Augustus and the Roman nation and to trace the ancestry of the Romans to the Trojans who settled with Aeneas in Italy. The lineage of the Julian gens (clan) is traced from Ascanius (Iulus), son of Aeneas, down to Julius Caesar and Augustus himself.

The first six books, modeled on the *Odyssey,* record the wanderings of Aeneas and his followers after the fall of Troy. They are looking for a promised land, and mistakenly try several places before the ancestral gods (penates) who had accompanied Aeneas reveal to him that the destined home is in Italy. When the Trojans are almost there, their ships are driven by a storm to Carthage, North Africa. There Queen Dido welcomes them, and falls in love with Aeneas. She commits suicide when Aeneas and the Trojans depart. At length they reach Italy.

The final six books, patterned on the *Iliad,* tell of Aeneas' experiences in Italy. He settles in Latium at the mouth of the Tiber, and woos Lavinia, daughter of King Latinus. However, she is betrothed to King Turnus of the Rutulians. Enlisting the aid of the Etruscans and neighboring King Evander, Aeneas defeats the forces of Turnus in battle. The *Aeneid* ends with Aeneas killing Turnus in hand-to-hand combat.

The *Aeneid* was written in dactylic hexameter. It has been translated into English a number of times. The translation of Gavin Douglas (1512-13) is rhymed. John Drydens' verse translation (1697) was popular. Other verse translations are those of James Rhoades (1907), Rolf Humphries (1950), C. Day Lewis (1952), and L. R. Lind (1963). Prose translations include those of J. W. Mackail (1885), H. Rushton Fairclough (1916), and Jackson Knight (1956).

See also AENEAS; DIDO.

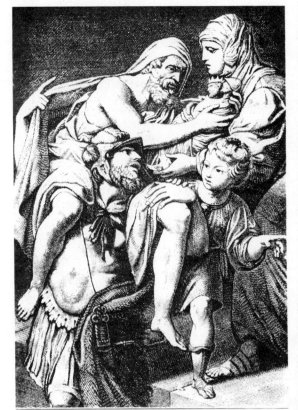

NEW STANDARD Collection

Aeneas Escaping from Troy with his family. He is carrying his father, Anchises. Neither wife nor father survived to reach Italy, but Aeneas' son, Ascanius, was the legendary ancestor of Julius Caesar.

Aeolian Harp, ē-ō′lĭ-ăn, a stringed instrument sounded by the wind. It is named for Aeolus, guardian of the winds. The aeolian harp consists of six or more catgut strings stretched over two bridges in a long, narrow sound box. The strings are tuned in unison but have different thicknesses. When the instrument is placed in an open window, the wind blows across the strings, causing them to vibrate and produce a variety of harmonics. Wind pressure and the strings' vary-

Aeolian Harp. This instrument, made to be played upon by the wind, is about three feet long.

Museum of Fine Arts, Boston

ing thicknesses cause the sound to vary, creating a distant, elusive effect. The aeolian harp was known to the ancient Chinese. It was especially popular in Europe during the 19th-century Romantic period.

Aeolian Islands. See LIPARI ISLANDS.

Aeolians, ē-ō′lĭ-ănz, a branch of the ancient Greeks. Aeolian was one of the Greek dialects spoken by the Achaeans, who settled in Greece between 2000 and 1700 B.C. The Aeolians lived in Thessaly and central Greece, which was invaded by the Dorians about 1100 B.C. The Aeolians retreated eastward into Attica, onto the northern Aegean islands, and to the west coast of Asia Minor. The island of Lesbos and the coastal area adjacent to it became known as Aeolis, or Aeolia, where the Aeolian dialect was spoken until the fifth or fourth century B.C.

The cities of mainland Aeolis were small, and of little influence in Greek life. Lesbos, however, was a center of commercial activity and of culture. In the early seventh century B.C. the Aeolians of Lesbos occupied the Troad (the area around ancient Troy) and founded cities on the Hellespont. At the end of the century Lesbos produced two of the great poets of ancient Greece—Sappho and Alcaeus. (See also ALCAEUS; SAPPHO.)

See also LESBOS.

Aeolus, ē′ō-lŭs, in Greek and Roman mythology and legend, the guardian of the winds. According to the Greek epic *The Odyssey*, Aeolus was a human king of the island of Aeolia. Ulysses stopped at Aeolia on his way home, and Aeolus gave him a favorable wind for his voyage. He also gave him a bag containing unfavorable winds, which Ulysses' companions opened after continuing the voyage. The winds drove Ulysses' ship back to Aeolia but Aeolus angrily refused to let it land. In Roman myths, Aeolus is god of the winds, keeping them in a cave on one of the Aeolian (Lipari) Islands.

Later Roman classical writers confused the guardian of the winds with Aeolus, a king of Thessaly. This Aeolus is the legendary ancestor of the Aeolian branch of ancient Greeks.

Aepyornis, ē′pĭ-ôr′nĭs, a genus of gigantic flightless birds of the extinct elephant bird order. These birds resembled large, bulky ostriches. The largest were about 10 feet tall and weighed nearly 1,000 pounds. While the extinct New Zealand moas were

taller, aepyornises are the heaviest known birds. They laid the largest bird eggs ever discovered. One egg measured 13½ inches by 9½ inches and had a volume of two gallons. The egg cell it contained is the largest known animal cell. Fossils of the largest aepyornises are found on the island of Madagascar off the east coast of Africa. The birds are believed to have become extinct 500 to 700 years ago. The aepyornis probably gave rise to stories about the roc, a gigantic bird of Arabic legend.

The largest elephant bird was *Aepyornis maximus*. It belongs to the single family in the elephant bird order, Aepyornithiformes.

See also ROC.

Aerial. See ANTENNA.

Aerial Navigation. See NAVIGATION, subtitle *Kinds of Navigation:* Air Navigation.

Aerial Perspective. See PERSPECTIVE.

Aerial Photography. See MAP, subtitle *Gathering Information for Maps;* PHOTOGRAPHY, subtitle *Kinds of Photography:* Aerial Photography.

Aerial Surveying. See MAP, subtitle *Gathering Information for Maps.*

Aerial Warfare. See AIR FORCE.

Aerobic Bacteria. See BACTERIA, subtitle *Life and Growth of Bacteria.*

Aerodynamics, âr′ō-dī-năm′ĭcs, the branch of physics that deals with the motion of air and with the relative motion between air and objects in the air. The bodies in the air can be moving (for example, aircraft, missiles, birds, and automobiles), or they can be stationary structures (for example, bridges and buildings) acted upon by moving air. Aerodynamicists are concerned mainly with the design of airplanes. The flight of birds demonstrates many of the principles of aerodynamics.

See also AIR; AIRPLANE, section "Why an Airplane Flies"; BIRD, subtitle *Flight and Diving;* WIND TUNNEL.

Aeroembolism. See CAISSON DISEASE.

Aeronautics, âr′ō-nô′tĭks, the science and practice of aircraft flight. (An *aircraft* is a vehicle that is supported in flight by its own buoyancy or by the action of air on its surfaces.) The term "aeronautics" takes in all phases of the design, construction, and operation of aircraft. Both lighter-than-air craft (airships and balloons) and heavier-than-air craft (such as airplanes, helicopters, convertiplanes, autogiros, gliders, and kites) are included. The term "aviation" is usually restricted to powered, heavier-than-air craft.

See also AVIATION and cross references; BALLOON; BLIMP; DIRIGIBLE.

Aeronautics and Space Administration. See NATIONAL AERONAUTICS AND SPACE ADMINISTRATION.

Aerosol, âr′ṓ-sŏl′, a dispersion of liquid or solid particles in air or in some other gas. These particles, which can be either natural or man-made, are usually too small to be seen individually with the unaided eye. Fog, clouds, smoke, mist, smog, and volcanic ash are aerosols that commonly occur in the atmosphere. Aerosols belong to the class of dispersions called colloids. (See COLLOID.)

Commercial aerosols come in small pressurized containers, usually made of metal. They were first devised in the early 1940's to dispense insecticides. The typical aerosol container holds the product to be dispensed and a *propellant* gas which provides the necessary pressure. Some of the propellant mixes with the product to form a solution, the rest remains in vapor form. When a valve is released, the pressure of the propellant forces the solution out of the container and into the air, where it breaks into a fine spray.

The most common propellant gases are hydrocarbons and carbon dioxide. *Chlorofluorocarbons,* commonly known as *fluorocarbons,* were used extensively until the late 1970's, when the United States government banned them from general use as propellants. (The ban was based on evidence that they might accumulate in the upper atmosphere and chemically decompose ozone, thus depleting the ozone layer, which absorbs harmful solar ultraviolet radiation. [See OZONE.])

Insecticides are highly effective in aerosol form because the insecticide particles remain in the air for a relatively long time. Hundreds of other types of products are also available in aerosol form, including such diverse items as hair sprays, paints, deodorants, starches, and foods.

Because their contents are under pressure, aerosol containers can explode if punctured or exposed to high heat, even if the container is nearly empty. Some aerosol products, such as paints and solvents, are toxic and should be used only in well-ventilated areas. Whatever the product, the inhaling of concentrated aerosol vapors should be avoided, since some propellants can cause serious illness and even death.

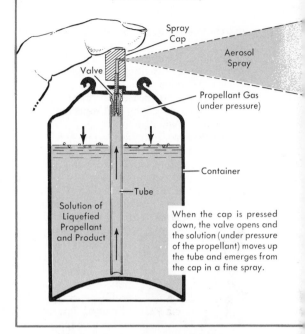

AEROSOL CONTAINER
(cross section)

Spray Cap

Aerosol Spray

Valve

Propellant Gas (under pressure)

Container

Tube

Solution of Liquefied Propellant and Product

When the cap is pressed down, the valve opens and the solution (under pressure of the propellant) moves up the tube and emerges from the cap in a fine spray.

Aerospace, âr′ṓ-spās′, the earth's atmosphere and the space beyond it. For many years, the term "aeronautics" has been used to refer to manned flight through the atmosphere. When space flight became a reality in the late 1950's, the term "aerospace" was coined to designate the entire area in which man could fly.

The *aerospace industry* includes all firms engaged in the development and production of aircraft, missiles, and spacecraft. In the United States, this industry is one of the leading employers.

See also AIRPLANE, section "How Airplanes Are Manufactured"; SPACE EXPLORATION.

Aerospace Medicine. See AVIATION AND SPACE MEDICINE.

Aeschines, ĕs′kĭ-nēz (389-314? B.C.), an orator of ancient Greece. His oratory is overshadowed by that of his relentless rival Demosthenes, but shows considerable force and wit. Aeschines' three surviving orations are in opposition to Demosthenes and other members of the anti-Macedonian political party.

Aeschines and Demosthenes were part of an embassy to Macedonia in 346 B.C. After their return to Athens, Demosthenes accused Aeschines of accepting bribes from Philip II of Macedonia. Aeschines defended himself successfully with the orations "Against Timarchus" (345 B.C.) and "On the False Embassy" (343 B.C.). In "Against Ctesiphon" (330 B.C.) Aeschines indicted a friend of Demosthenes for illegal actions. Demosthenes defended Ctesiphon in a brilliant speech and won the case. As a result, Aeschines lost his civic rights and went into voluntary exile in Asia Minor.

Aeschylus, ĕs'kĭ-lŭs (525?-456? B.C.), the earliest of the three great Greek tragic dramatists. (The others are Sophocles and Euripides.) Aeschylus frequently is called the "father of tragic drama."

His plays are marked by a strong moral sense, demonstrating that suffering is the in-

Art Institute of Chicago
Aeschylus

evitable consequence of sin until the wrongdoing has been expiated. Thus man is punished by the inexorable workings of a universal law of *justice* rather than by the whimsical or capricious intervention of the gods. This concept established an implicit law for tragedy later observed by Shakespeare and many others. Aeschylus' plays, written in verse, are noted for lofty eloquence and magnificent descriptions.

Aeschylus enriched the drama with his technical innovations. He introduced a second actor where only one and a chorus had been used previously. This made possible the conflict of wills and ideas that is so essential to dramatic development. By changing masks and costumes, each of the two actors could take several parts successively. This innovation also enabled the playwright to introduce a plot through which he could strongly express human emotions. Aeschylus reduced the size and importance of the chorus, although he still retained it as a major element. He introduced elaborate costumes, and is credited with inventing the *cothurni,* a high-soled boot that added to the actor's stature.

His Plays

Aeschylus is believed to have written 90 or more plays, but only seven have survived. The *Oresteia* trilogy (458 B.C.), consisting of *Agamemnon, Choephoroe,* and *Eumenides,* is generally regarded as his most ambitious work. The trilogy is based on the story of Orestes, and its central theme is the blood guilt and the purification of the house of

Atreus. The prevailing emphasis is upon the inevitability of retribution.

Agamemnon, son of Atreus, has returned victorious from the Trojan War to his palace in Argos, but not to happiness. Strong-willed Clytemnestra, his wife, hates him for his willingness to sacrifice their daughter Iphigenia to the gods in return for a favorable voyage, even though Artemis had spared Iphigenia. Clytemnestra, encouraged by her lover Aegisthus, murders Agamemnon. Cassandra, a captive Trojan princess, prophesies the fall of the house of Atreus as well as her own murder by Clytemnestra.

In *Choephoroe (The Libation Bearers)* Agamemnon's son Orestes arrives in disguise to avenge his father's murder. His sister Electra recognizes him and they plot successfully to murder Clytemnestra and Aegisthus. Though the chorus assures Orestes that the murders were justifiable, he is tormented by guilt. The Furies appear with bloody eyes and snaky locks, and remorse-stricken Orestes flees Argos.

In *Eumenides* the Delphian oracle sends Orestes to Athens, where he is tried in the temple of Athena by a court of judges convened for the occasion. Athena presides, and casts the deciding vote that exonerates Orestes and frees him from his curse. The trial marks the beginning of a new system of justice—judgment by reason and law rather than by blood vengeance. The Furies are placated, become benevolent, and are renamed the Eumenides (Kindly Ones).

The Persians (472 B.C.) is probably the earliest of Aeschylus' plays. It is the earliest surviving Greek drama about contemporary history, its background being the battle of Salamis.

Seven Against Thebes (467 B.C.) is concerned mainly with the legendary struggle between Eteocles and Polynices, sons of Oedipus, for the throne of Thebes.

The Suppliants (463? B.C.) tells the legend of the 50 daughters of Danaüs, king of Argos, and their flight from their 50 Egyptian suitors. It was once thought to be Aeschylus' earliest known play.

Prometheus Bound (date uncertain), is concerned with the myth of Prometheus, one of the Titans. Zeus orders him chained to a rock as punishment for giving fire to man. Prometheus prophesies that Zeus will be killed by one of his own sons, yet unborn, but refuses to reveal which one unless he is unchained. Zeus hurls Prometheus into Hades with a thunderbolt. Prometheus figures as the champion of mankind against tyranny, of knowledge and the arts against barbarism.

His Life

Aeschylus was born in an aristocratic family of Eleusis. He served in the Athenian army in the war against Persia, and may have fought at Marathon and Salamis. He entered the annual Athenian competition for the tragedy prize 20 times or more between 499 and 458 B.C. In 484 B.C. Aeschylus won the first of his 13 first prizes for tragedy; the last was given in 458 B.C. for the *Oresteia* trilogy. He lost to Sophocles in 468 and then left Athens to settle in Gela, Sicily.

A familiar story about the death of Aeschylus in Sicily is that a high-soaring eagle mistook his bald head for a rock and dropped a tortoise on it to break the shell. According to the epitaph that tradition says he wrote for himself, he considered his military service to have been more important than his dramatic triumphs. It reads:

Beneath this stone lies Aeschylus, son of Euphorian, the Athenian, who perished in the wheat-bearing land of Gela, of his noble prowess the grave of Marathon can speak, or the long-haired Persian who knows it well.

Books about Aeschylus

Gagarin, Michael. *Aeschylean Drama* (University of California, 1976).
McCall, M. H., editor. *Aeschylus: a Collection of Critical Essays* (Prentice-Hall, 1972).
Taplin, O. P. *The Stagecraft of Aeschylus: the Dramatic Use of Exits and Entrances in Greek Tragedy* (Oxford University, 1978).

Aesculapius. See ASCLEPIUS.

Aeson. See JASON.

Aesop's Fables, ē'sŏpz, a collection of brief tales traditionally ascribed to Aesop, a Greek slave of the sixth century B.C. Most of the tales are about animals with human traits, but in some there are human characters. The stories are simple, short, and direct. Their purpose always is to illustrate some human folly, frailty, vice, or virtue. This intent is made plain by an appended moral. The moral, though obvious, never gets in the way of the story. Among the more familiar fables are "The Fox and the Grapes," "The Dog in the Manger," and "The Goose that Lays the Golden Eggs." One of Aesop's fables is told in the caption for the accompanying illustration. For another, see FABLE.

Boris Artzybasheff's *Aesop's Fables*, Viking Press

The Bat, the Birds, and the Beasts. During a war between birds and beasts, the bat, at first believing the birds would win, claimed to be a bird. When the battle favored the beasts, he went over to their side. But the birds, led by the eagle, won, and the bat fled. Since then the bat skulks in caves and hollow trees by day to avoid the beasts, and flies only after dark, when the birds have gone to roost. Moral: He that is neither one thing nor the other has no friends.

A number of the fables can be traced to much earlier Mesopotamian and Egyptian sources. About a fourth of them can be identified as coming directly from India. Most of the stories are believed to have been folk fables current in ancient Greece at the time Aesop is supposed to have lived. It is possible, though not probable, that someone named Aesop did collect, adapt, and pass on the fables credited to him. There is general doubt, however, that any such person as Aesop ever lived.

No written collection of Aesop's fables seems to have appeared during his traditional lifetime. Plato knew the work attributed to Aesop, and Socrates is reported to have spent his last days in prison making verse adaptations of some of the fables. Aristophanes mentioned Aesop as having told his stories at banquets.

About 300 B.C., Demetrius Phalereus, a Roman scribe, compiled 10 books, but they were lost. Phaedrus, during the reign of Augustus in the first century A.D., told some of the fables in Latin iambic verse. Another early version was that of Valerius Babrius, a Roman writer of the second century A.D. It was written in Greek verse.

Herodotus identifies Aesop as a slave on the island of Samos. Apparently freed by his master, he was sent by King Croesus of Lydia on a mission to Delphi. There Aesop is reported to have met a violent death at the hands of priests who, enraged at his irreverent remarks about the gods, hurled him over a cliff. Maximus Planudes, a 14th-century Greek monk, prefaced his collection of the Aesopic fables with a brief biography that contains most of the legends about Aesop.

Aesop's fables have been translated into many languages and have supplied subjects for countless poems, stories, and pictures. The adaptations of Jean de La Fontaine (1668) are especially noteworthy.

Aesthetics. See ESTHETICS.

Aestivation, or **Estivation.** See HIBERNATION, subtitle *Dormancy and Estivation.*

Aeta. See PYGMIES, subtitle *Asiatic Pygmies.*

Aethelbert. See ETHELBERT.

Aethelred II. See ETHELRED II.

Aethelstan. See ATHELSTAN.

Aëtius, â-ē′shĭ-ŭs, **Flavius** (396?-454), a Roman general who protected Gaul against repeated barbarian attacks. He repulsed the Visigoths, threw back the Franks, and in 451 won his most famous victory—over Attila's Huns at the battle of Châlons. By intrigue and murder Aëtius made himself actual ruler of the Roman Empire during the reign of Valentinian III. He was finally stabbed to death by the emperor.

See also FIFTEEN DECISIVE BATTLES OF THE WORLD (6. Châlons).

Aetna, Mount. See ETNA.

Aetolian League and Achaean League, ē-tō′lĭ-ăn; à-kē′ăn, two rival federations of cities in ancient Greece. In structure they were forerunners of modern federal governments. By their jealousy, political maneuvering, and recourse to war the federations sacrificed their country's independence to their own interests.

The Aetolian League began as a small confederation at the end of the fourth century B.C., when Greece was part of the kingdom of Macedonia. After the Celtic invasion of 279 B.C., Macedonia held only Corinth and Piraeus. The Greek towns and villages north of the Gulf of Corinth, anxious to retain their freedom, joined the league, which by mid-century covered most of north-central

Greece. Meetings were held at Thermum (modern Thérmon), Aetolia. Member communities had authority over their own local affairs, and elected a council to manage the armed forces and affairs of the league.

The Achaean League was begun immediately after the Celtic invasion as a confederation of towns in Achaea, on the south shore of the Gulf of Corinth. It grew to encompass all of the Peloponnesus except Sparta, which was independent, and Elis, which belonged to the Aetolian League. Its organization was similar to that of the older league. In 247 B.C. the Achaean League freed Corinth and Piraeus from Macedonian rule. However, when Sparta began a war in 227, the league turned to Macedonia, which helped it defeat the Spartans.

The Aetolian League, fearing Achaean dominance, formed an alliance with Sparta and started a civil war that lasted until 217 B.C. When Macedonia encroached on Roman territory, the Aetolians supported Rome in the First Macedonian War (214-05). Rome and the league then persuaded independent Athens to make war on Macedonia, an act that led to the Second Macedonian War (200-197). Victorious Rome declared all Greece to be free, expecting peace to follow. In 195, however, the Achaean League incited the Romans to go to war against Sparta, bringing to an end Spartan military power.

The Aetolian League then turned against Rome and requested aid from the Seleucid kingdom of Syria, which held Asia Minor. Seleucid forces marched into Greece in 191 B.C., but were defeated by the Romans at Thermopylae. The Aetolian League was forced to pay an indemnity and give up territory. Its power ended, it was dissolved in 167 B.C.

In the Third Macedonian War (171-168 B.C.) the Greek cities remained neutral. It was discovered afterward, however, that the Achaean League had worked secretly against Rome. In punishment the league was forced to send 1,000 hostages, the historian Polybius among them, to Rome in 167. When a frontier dispute with Sparta developed in 147, the Achaean League refused to accept Rome's settlement of it and again went to war. The next spring the Roman legions marched into Greece. At Corinth, then the leading city in the league, the Romans killed the men, sold the women and children into slavery, and burned the city. The league was abolished, and its remaining leaders put to death.

Afars and Issas. See DJIBOUTI.

Affenpinscher. See DOG, subtitle *Breeds of Dogs:* Toy Breeds (and picture).

Afferent Neuron. See NERVOUS SYSTEM, subtitle *Cells and Organs.*

Affidavit, ăf′ĭ-dā′vĭt, in law, a sworn statement in writing. An affidavit must follow a formalized pattern and must be sworn to and signed before a notary public or other officer entitled to administer oaths. Affidavits are commonly used to show that certain legal formalities have been properly performed.

Affinity. See ATTRACTION.

Affirmation. See OATH.

Affirmative Action, a name given to various programs designed to compensate for the effects of past discrimination in employment and education. Under such programs, special consideration is given to certain groups whose members have traditionally been victims of discrimination, especially blacks and Hispanics (persons of Latin-American ancestry) and—in the cases of employment opportunities and professional education—women of all races and ethnic backgrounds.

Educational institutions and business corporations have developed affirmative-action programs to comply with various federal laws and regulations. In education, affirmative-action programs usually call for colleges and universities to give consideration to an individual's race and economic status in their admissions procedures so that their student-body composition will better reflect the pluralistic nature of American society. In employment, such programs involve giving special consideration in hiring and promotion to members of groups previously discriminated against. Sometimes employers, usually under pressure from the government, establish quotas for minorities and women.

Affirmative action has been controversial since its inception. Supporters say such programs are necessary to raise the economic level of groups subjected to long-standing patterns of discrimination. Critics claim that preferential treatment, especially when it involves the use of quotas, leads to discrimination (often called "reverse bias") against white males.

Affirmative-action programs originated as a means to comply with a directive, issued by the Kennedy administration in 1961, requiring firms holding federal contracts to

increase the employment of minorities. The number and scope of such programs increased following passage of the Civil Rights Act of 1964 and the Equal Employment Opportunity Act of 1972. Opposition grew as the programs spread, and in the 1970's there were numerous court challenges by opponents. The U.S. Supreme Court gave approval to affirmative action in two significant rulings:

Regents of the University of California v. *Bakke* (1978). The Court held that race could be a factor in selecting applicants for admission to universities, but indicated that rigid quotas were unacceptable.

Kaiser Aluminum & Chemical Corporation v. *Weber* (1979). The Court ruled that federal law does not prohibit private employers from adopting quotas to remedy past discrimination.

Afghan Hound. See DOG, subtitle *Breeds of Dogs:* Hounds (and picture).

Afghanistan, ăf-găn′ĭ-stän, a country in south-central Asia. It is bounded on the north by the Soviet Union, on the northeast by a tip of China and Kashmir, on the east and south by Pakistan, and on the west by Iran. Afghanistan's area is not known exactly; it is estimated at about 250,000 square miles—

Bamian, site of an ancient Buddhist setttlement in the Hindu Kush mountains of northern Afghanistan. A figure of Buddha is carved into the cliff.

slightly less than that of Texas. Maximum dimensions are roughly 550 miles north-south and 600 miles east-west.

Physical Geography

Land. Afghanistan is a dry, landlocked country, consisting mainly of rugged mountains, barren plateaus, and wind-swept steppes and deserts. Its most prominent feature is the Hindu Kush, a towering mountain range trending northeast-southwest from Kashmir to central Afghanistan. Within the country the range's loftiest peaks attain heights of more than 20,000 feet; just beyond the Pakistan border, more than 25,000 feet. Plateaus and fingerlike mountain spurs, such as the Koh-i-Baba and Paropamisus ranges, make up most of central Afghanistan.

South of this central plateau and mountain belt, the land changes to steppes and deserts, chief of which are Registan and Dasht-i-Margo. In northern Afghanistan, beyond the Hindu Kush, lie mountain foothills and intervening valleys, both of which merge into steppelike plains along the Russian border.

Water. Nearly all of Afghanistan's rivers rise in the mountains, yet most carry limited amounts of water. Only those fed by the high Hindu Kush, especially its glaciers, have relatively steady flows. Many streams are *intermittent* (seasonally carry water and then dry up). Among the principal rivers are the Amu Darya (Oxus) in the north, the Kabul in the east, the Helmand in the south,

and the Hari in the west. Except for the Kabul, its tributaries, and a few headstreams in the east, Afghanistan's rivers never reach the sea. They drain internally and end in steppes, deserts, salt lakes, and alkali flats.

Climate. Dryness and great ranges in temperature are the chief marks of the climate. Both are due mainly to the mountainous terrain of south central Asia and to the country's distance from the sea.

In the north, winters are cold, for the region lies in the path of frigid winds from Siberia. During the coldest periods, temperatures drop well below 0° F. Summers on the northern steppes are hot, with daytime temperatures often rising above 100° F. Southern Afghanistan has less severe winters and hotter summers. Climate on the high plateaus and in the mountains becomes more temperate with increasing elevation, especially during the summer.

Precipitation varies from less than 2 inches to about 10 inches a year, depending on location. Everywhere but in the south, part of it falls as snow. The period from late fall to early spring brings most of the precipitation, for the country lies too far inland to receive much moisture from the southwest (summer) monsoon. Prolonged and sometimes violent winds, accompanied by dense clouds of dust, are among the country's worst storms.

The Economy

Agriculture. Afghanistan is predominantly an agricultural country, yet only about 12

Shearing Karakul Sheep. Wool and pelts, including Broadtail and Persian lamb, are of major importance in the economy of Afghanistan.

AFGHANISTAN

per cent of the land is farmed. Most of it consists of irrigated steppes and river valleys north of the Hindu Kush. Some farming is also carried on in the more humid river valleys and on the steppes through the use of dry-farming methods. Of particular importance is the Helmand River Valley, where a large irrigation project is being developed.

Products include both cash and subsistence crops: chiefly wheat, rice, fruits, nuts, cotton, sugar beets, sugar cane, and some vegetables. For most Afghans, the basic food is unleavened bread made from wheat flour. Most of the farms are individually owned small plots; farming methods nearly everywhere are primitive and centuries old. There is little use of fertilizer or modern machinery.

Livestock raising employs probably a third of the people, many of whom are nomads wandering with their flocks. Sheep and goats are by far the most numerous animals. Their meat, wool, hides, and skins make up the biggest single source of the national income. Karakul skins (Persian lamb) are Afghanistan's most important single export.

Manufacturing. Most of the personal and household goods required by the people are still made at home and in small village shops. Textile weaving and, particularly, the making of rugs are among the oldest and most important handicrafts.

Modern industry, though developing, is hampered by lack of technical knowledge and capital. Much that has been accomplished is due to assistance from the United States, the Soviet Union, and West Germany. Among their chief contributions have been hydroelectric plants and factories to make textiles (cotton, wool, and rayon), cement, porcelain, footwear, carpets, glass, sugar, and soap.

Mining and Lumbering. Afghanistan's mineral resources are largely unknown. Coal and salt have the largest commercial produc-

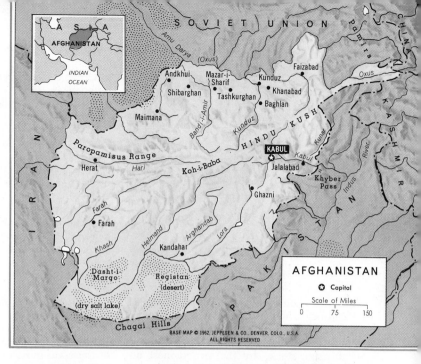

tion; sulfur, beryl, slate, talc, and lapis lazuli are also produced. In addition, there are known deposits of iron, chrome, lead, zinc, silver, copper, mica, and petroleum.

Forests once covered much of Afghanistan, but centuries of overcutting have greatly depleted them. Only in northern and eastern mountain districts do sizable stands of timber remain. Lack of transportation has been the chief reason for their limited exploitation.

Transportation. Not only is Afghanistan located in one of the least accessible parts of the world, but transportation is poorly developed within the country. There are no railways and no navigable waterways, and roads are largely unsurfaced. The chief roads, however—those linking Kabul, the capital, with major provincial cities—are being improved, primarily with foreign help. There are few motor vehicles; camels and donkeys continue to provide much of the transportation. Two of Afghanistan's six airports, one at Kabul and the other at Kandahar, serve foreign carriers as well as Ariana-Afghan Airlines, the national airline.

The People

All citizens of the country are called Afghans, but there are numerous ethnic groups. Pashtuns (the name is also written Pushtun, Pakhtun, Pukhtun, and Pathan) make up roughly 60 per cent of the people. They are of Caucasian stock and have lived in Afghanistan for at least 1,300 years. Usually

Afghan Embassy
Village Street Scene in Afghanistan

1932, and the University of Nangarhar, founded in 1962, are the country's main institutions of higher learning. Many of those who teach at secondary and higher levels come from Western countries.

Due to lack of funds, wide scattering of villages and tribes, and a tradition that has opposed education for women, only a small proportion of the people are literate.

Religion. Islam is the predominant religion of Afghanistan. It is the most important unifying influence on the people. Almost 99 per cent of the people are Moslems. About 80 per cent belong to the Sunnite sect; the others are Shiites. Non-Moslems, totaling about 1 per cent of the population, are mainly Hindus, Sikhs, and Jews.

Culture. Afghanistan bears the traces of many civilizations, including Greek, Buddhist, and Mogul. Afghan art, architecture, literature, and music reveal the interaction of these various cultures over the centuries. However, Islam, from its introduction in the seventh century A.D. to the present, has been the predominant influence. The gracefully sculptured minarets (towers of the mosques) are considered the best surviving examples of Moslem architectural and artistic effort.

Since modern Afghanistan is still principally a rural and agricultural society, most cultural activity centers around the capital city of Kabul. Here are the Kabul Museum, the Afghan Academy of Science, and the Kabul Art School.

they are considered the "true Afghans." Pashtuns, who are divided into many tribes and sub-tribes, follow an ancient code of conduct called Pashtunwali. Tajiks, also of Caucasian stock, are the second most numerous group. People of Mongolian descent include Turkomans, Uzbeks, Kirghiz, and Hazaras.

Population. According to the 1979 census, Afghanistan had a population of 15,540,000. The density was 62 persons per square mile (24 per km²). Only about 10 per cent of the people live in cities; the rest are villagers, farmers, and nomadic herders.

Afghanistan's Largest Cities

Kabul, the capital	 749,000	Herat 157,000
Kandahar	 209,000	Kunduz 108,000

Language and Education. The official languages of Afghanistan are Pashto (also known as Pushtu) and Persian. Both belong to the Indo-European language family. Pashto is spoken in the east and south and is sometimes called Afghan. Persian dialects are spoken in northeastern, western, and central Afghanistan. Persian is the language of government, business, and literature. Some 30 other languages are spoken by various groups throughout Afghanistan.

Education is free at the primary and secondary levels and is compulsory from ages 7 to 13. Where the six-year primary course is not available, village schools provide a rudimentary three-year program. The central government maintains a small number of teacher-training and vocational schools. There are some private schools, mainly those conducted by the Moslems. The University of Kabul, established in

Government

Under the constitution of 1977, Afghanistan is a republic with a president and an elected legislature. However, following a coup in 1978, the constitution was suspended. Under the new leadership, a premier rules by decree. He is advised on policy matters by the Revolutionary Council, which is composed primarily of members of the People's Democratic Party and military officers.

History

The independent existence of Afghanistan dates only from the mid-18th century, but archeologists believe that the area was inhabited as early as the Old Stone Age.

Invasions. Because of Afghanistan's strategic location, the country was invaded repeatedly. About 2000 B.C., Indo-European nomads moved into what is now Afghanistan, displacing the early settlers. Centuries later, Ariana, as it was known, was invaded by Alexander the Great, who introduced Hellenistic civilization, 330-326 B.C. Buddhism spread to Afghanistan in the third century B.C. During the same period, Greeks from Bactria established an independent kingdom, which included part of Afghanistan and northern India.

For centuries Afghanistan remained divided, a battleground in the struggle for domination of central Asia. The Moslems began their conquest in 652 A.D. Following the invasion by the hordes of Genghis Khan, 1219-27, Afghanistan was controlled by Mongols for some 100 years. In the 14th century, forces led by Tamerlane took possession of the region. In the early 1500's Baber invaded Afghanistan and then India, founding the great Mogul Empire in 1526. Until the 18th century, both India and Persia held parts of Afghanistan.

Independence. Nadir Shah succeeded in conquering all of Afghanistan and unifying it under a Persian regime in 1738. After Nadir's death in 1747, Ahmad Shah founded the independent kingdom of Afghanistan. Dost Mohammed became emir (ruler) in 1835, establishing the Barakzai Dynasty, which ruled for almost a hundred years.

During the 19th century, the little country was involved in the power struggle between Great Britain and Russia. Two wars were fought for control of Afghanistan, the First (1839-42) and Second (1878-79) Afghan Wars. In 1880 the British persuaded Abder-Rahman Khan, the emir, to accept an annual subsidy in return for control of the Khyber Pass. Although the country remained independent, Britain directed its foreign policy and guaranteed its boundaries. Friction between Russia and Britain over Afghanistan continued until the early 20th century.

In 1919, Amanullah Khan became emir and invaded India. Although the invasion was unsuccessful, the resulting peace treaty with Great Britain recognized the complete independence of Afghanistan. Amanullah attempted to introduce modern reforms into his backward country, but the conservative tribal groups revolted, and he was forced to abdicate in 1929. Mohammed Nadir Shah, his successor, was proclaimed king and followed a policy of ruling in consultation with the tribes. He was assassinated in 1933, and his son, Mohammed Zahir Shah, ascended to the throne.

After World War II. The country was neutral in World War II and pursued a policy of nonalignment in the cold war. Both the United States and Russia provided extensive economic aid and built airports and many roads. During 1953-63, under Premier Mohammed Daoud, a cousin of the king, modern industries were established, education was expanded, and women for the first time were permitted to obtain an education, to work, and to wear Western dress.

In 1964 Afghanistan became a constitutional monarchy with an elected parliament. Parliamentary rule proved ineffectual, however, and in 1973, Mohammed Daoud overthrew the government and the monarchy and returned to rule as virtual dictator. He, in turn, was overthrown in 1978 by Marxist officers in the armed forces.

The new regime established close ties with the Soviet Union and attempted to impose Communism on the country. The strongly religious and tradition-bound Afghans rebelled against the government and civil war broke out. The inability of the government to defeat the rebels led to a coup by rival Communists in September, 1979. They, in turn, were overthrown in December in a coup engineered by the Soviet Union, which installed a puppet leader and brought in an estimated 80,000 troops to help put down the rebellion. Hundreds of thousands of Afghans fled the country but the fighting continued.

For further information, see:

Geography
AMU DARYA	KABUL
HERAT	KANDAHAR
HINDU KUSH	

Miscellaneous
FLAG (color page)
MONEY (table)
PATHANS

Books about Afghanistan

Dupree, Louis. *Afghanistan* (Princeton University, 1973).
Hanifi, M. J. *Historical and Cultural Dictionary of Afghanistan* (Scarecrow Press, 1976).

For Younger Readers:
Caldwell, J. C. *Let's Visit Afghanistan,* revised edition (Day, 1970).
Clifford, M. L. *The Land and People of Afghanistan,* revised edition (Lippincott, 1973).

AFL-CIO. See AMERICAN FEDERATION OF LABOR AND CONGRESS OF INDUSTRIAL ORGANIZATIONS.

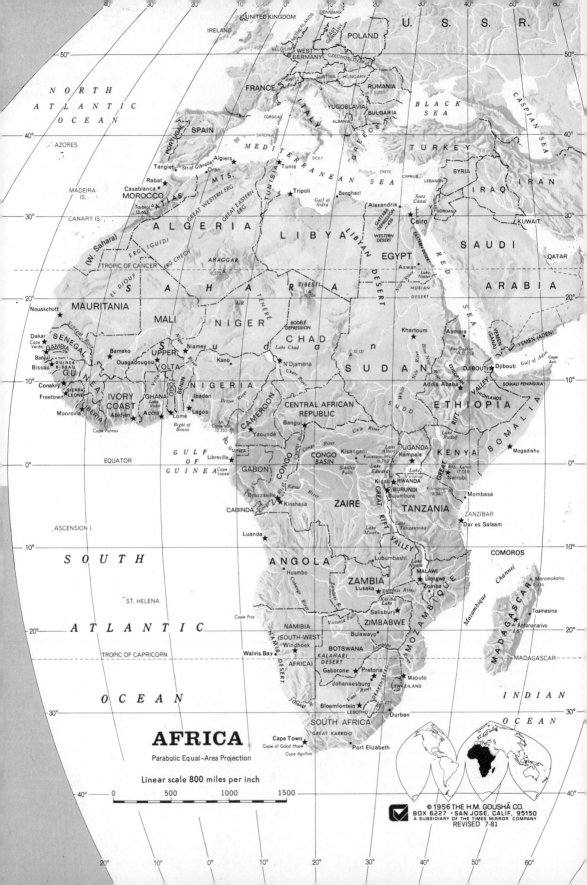

AFRICA

Parabolic Equal–Area Projection

Linear scale 800 miles per inch

0   500   1000   1500

© 1956 THE H.M. GOUSHA CO.
BOX 6227 · SAN JOSE, CALIF. 95150
A SUBSIDIARY OF THE TIMES MIRROR COMPANY
REVISED 7-81

Africa, ăf′rĭ-ká, a continent, second in size only to Asia. For centuries it was known as the "Dark Continent," since except for its coastal regions little was known of the land. Penetration of the interior was long hampered by Africa's vast deserts, dense tropical forests, and rivers that are difficult to navigate near the coast.

Not until the latter half of the 19th century did foreign explorers reach deeply into the interior. About the same time, Africa was being carved into colonies by various European powers, notably Belgium, Germany, Great Britain, France, Italy, Portugal, and Spain.

Though national control and boundaries of colonies changed from time to time, the continent remained under colonial rule until roughly the middle of the 20th century. Many new African nations then emerged.

With independence came many internal problems. One of these is how to achieve governments and economies that are stable, productive, and efficient. A second problem is that of handling racial, tribal, or socioeconomic differences. A third is how to raise health and education standards. In many parts of the continent development has proceeded slowly; in others, with unexpected speed. Independence in many countries has been marked by strife and overthrow of constitutional government.

Physical Geography

Africa is an enormous landmass that connects with Asia at the Isthmus of Suez and almost joins Europe at Gibraltar. Major bodies of water that bound the continent are the Mediterranean Sea on the north, the Red Sea on the northeast, the Indian Ocean on the southeast, and the Atlantic Ocean on the west. Arms of the oceans include the Gulf of Aden, the Mozambique Channel, and the Gulf of Guinea.

Lying on the Equator (0° latitude) and the Prime Meridian (0° longitude), Africa is the only continent occupying part of all four hemispheres. It is also unique in that there are no deep indentations and few well-defined peninsulas. The coast line, which measures some 18,900 miles, is nearly everywhere regular. There are few islands. Madagascar is by far the largest island; the Canaries are the largest group.

Land. Despite its great size, Africa does not have a great variety of physical features. Nearly the entire continent consist of vast

plateaus, or tablelands, the surfaces of which lie at varying elevations and are generally rolling to flat. Rarely are the plateau surfaces rough. The plateaus' edges, however, especially the eastern and the southern ones, are marked by sharp *escarpments* (mountainous walls) that descend to narrow plains along the coast. There are few broad coastal plains comparable to those of most other continents. Underlying the continent, and in many areas exposed, is an ancient block of stable crystalline rock, sometimes called *Gondwanaland.*

Most of the wide northern part of Africa is covered by the vast stretches of gravel, rock, shifting sand, and dunes of the Sahara—the largest arid region on earth. Included in the Sahara are such smaller deserts as the Libyan and Nubian deserts in the east and the Great Eastern Erg, Great Western Erg, and Erg Iguidi in the west. Wind-scoured highlands jut above the surrounding surface in several areas. The most prominent are Tibesti (maximum, about 11,200 feet) and Ahaggar (almost 9,600 feet), in

---

Facts about Africa

Origin of Name—Believed to have derived from a Phoenician word referring to ancient Carthage or possibly to a northern African tribe. The Romans applied the name to their province in northern Africa, and it gradually came to include the entire continent.

Size—Including Madagascar and several smaller islands, 11,706,000 square miles (30,319,000 km²). Only Asia is larger. Africa is three times as large as the United States and has about one-fifth of the earth's total land area.

Length—From the northern coast of Tunisia to Cape Agulhas, almost 5,000 miles (8,000 km).

Width—From Cape Verde to the eastern tip of Somalia, about 4,700 miles (7,600 km).

Population—Estimated at 484,000,000 in 1981, 10.7 per cent of the world total.

Highest Mountains—Kilimanjaro, 19,340 feet (5,895 m); Mount Kenya, 17,058 feet (5,199 m).

Lowest Elevation—Lake Assal in Djibouti, 512 feet (156 m) below sea level—nearly twice as deep as Death Valley in North America.

Longest Rivers—Nile, 4,100 miles (6,600 km), longest in the world; Congo, 2,900 miles (4,700 km).

Largest Natural Lakes—Victoria, 26,800 square miles (69,400 km²), second largest freshwater lake in the world; Tanganyika, 12,700 square miles (32,900 km²).

Tropical Rain Forest. Only a small part of Africa has a hot, humid climate capable of producing such dense vegetation. Most extensive are the rain forests of the Congo River basin and along the Gulf of Guinea.
A. C. Twomey from Shostal

the central part of the Sahara. The land is also marked by widely separated depressions, deepest of which is Lake Assal's basin— 512 feet below sea level.

Along the southern margin of the Sahara are three immense basins: Djouf, through which runs part of the Niger River; Chad, containing Lake Chad; and Sudan, centered on the junction of the Blue and the White Nile rivers. Flanking all three basins are tablelands. Those inland from the Gulf of Guinea coast, such as the Fouta Djallon in Guinea and the Jos Plateau in Nigeria, have deeply eroded seaward slopes.

The Congo Basin, in central Africa, is almost surrounded by plateaus, the highest being the East African Plateau. The basin contains most of the broad Congo River Valley, which narrows abruptly in the Crystal Mountains near the Atlantic coast.

East and south of the Sudan and the Congo basins are the highest plateaus on the continent. There are considerable expanses of almost level tableland in the interior, especially in Tanzania, Zambia, and South Africa. The interior's only large basin, the Kalahari, is in the southwest. Through the eastern part of the plateau region, from northern Ethiopia into Mozambique, runs the Great Rift Valley, a series of deep trenches caused by faulting, or fracturing, of the earth's surface. In several areas, steep sides of the valley appear as mountains, among which are the Ruwenzori Mountains

Desert. Hot, sandy dunes make up part of the Sahara, which stretches 3,300 miles across northern Africa, covering nearly one-third of the total area of the continent.
Publix from ZFA

A-98

Mountains. Most of the mountains of Africa are at the east and south edges of its vast plateaus. Highest in the continent is Tanzania's Kilimanjaro, whose two peaks are viewed here from the Kenya border.

Ace Williams from Shostal

in central Africa. Associated with the faulted valleys are numerous volcanoes, including Africa's two highest peaks—Kilimanjaro in Tanzania (19,340 feet) and Mount Kenya in Kenya (17,058 feet).

Along the east and southeast coast, high plateau edges form a series of escarpments. The loftiest of these is South Africa's 10,000-foot-high Drakensberg. In the southwest, along part of the coast, lies the Namib Desert.

Water. Rivers cut through all parts of the continent except the Sahara, where rains are extremely infrequent. Only the Nile—longest river in the world—survives the desert path to the sea. The well-watered equatorial regions are drained mainly by the Congo

River, which carries more water than any but the Amazon of South America. Chief river of west Africa is the Niger; the Orange, Zambezi, and Limpopo systems drain most of the south.

Many of the rivers are interrupted by falls and cascades that limit navigation but provide great hydroelectric potential. Most important are 350-foot-high Victoria Falls, on the Zambezi River, and Stanley Falls, a series of cataracts on the Lualaba branch of the Congo River.

The principal lake region is in the Great Rift Valley, where several large, narrow lakes lie between steep valley walls. These include Lakes Albert, Tanganyika, and Nyasa, or Malawi. Lake Victoria, on the

Savanna. This area of thorn bushes and knee-high grass has rain during only two to four months in the year. A few drought-resistant trees grow in the savannas.

Publix from ZFA

A-99

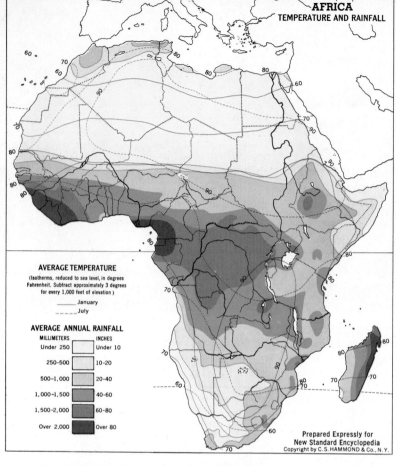

AFRICA
TEMPERATURE AND RAINFALL

AVERAGE TEMPERATURE
(Isotherms, reduced to sea level, in degrees Fahrenheit. Subtract approximately 3 degrees for every 1,000 feet of elevation)

——— January
- - - - - July

AVERAGE ANNUAL RAINFALL

MILLIMETERS	INCHES
Under 250	Under 10
250-500	10-20
500-1,000	20-40
1,000-1,500	40-60
1,500-2,000	60-80
Over 2,000	Over 80

Prepared Expressly for
New Standard Encyclopedia
Copyright by C. S. HAMMOND & Co., N. Y.

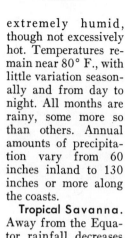

extremely humid, though not excessively hot. Temperatures remain near 80° F., with little variation seasonally and from day to night. All months are rainy, some more so than others. Annual amounts of precipitation vary from 60 inches inland to 130 inches or more along the coasts.

Tropical Savanna. Away from the Equator rainfall decreases and a distinct dry season develops during the cooler parts of the year—the period when the sun is on the opposite side of the Equator. Lasting as long as six months, the dry period is this climate's most distinguishing feature. Rainfall totals 20 to 60 inches a year. There is a slightly greater seasonal range in temperature here than in the tropical rainy regions, the warmest month averaging in the 80's and the coolest in the 70's. Much of eastern and southern Africa has a modified savanna climate, with slightly lower temperatures because of increased elevation. This kind of climate is typical of regions with savanna-type vegetation.

Tropical Steppe. Bordering the tropical savanna is the tropical steppe climate. It is more seasonally extreme in both temperature and rainfall than is the savanna. The warmest month averages in the high 80's, the coolest in the 60's. Average annual rainfall varies from 10 to 20 inches.

Tropical Desert. A relatively large part of Africa has a tropical desert type of climate. In such a climate, temperature ranges are greatest, for the bare to sparsely covered land heats and cools rapidly under cloudless skies. Daytime temperatures during the hotter months often exceed 100° F.; occasionally they rise above 130°. The coolest month averages 50° to 60° during the day, though freezing weather may occur at night. Aver-

broad plateau between branches of the Great Rift Valley, is Africa's largest lake and the chief source of the White Nile. The only large natural lake outside eastern Africa is Lake Chad, on the southern edge of the Sahara. Its size varies, depending on seasonal rainfall.

Climate

Since annual temperatures are high nearly everywhere in Africa, division of the continent into climatic regions is based chiefly on amount and seasonal distribution of rainfall. Seven main types of climate affect the continent. Four are tropical, ranging from arid to extremely wet; they cover at least three-fourths of Africa. The other three are subtropical to temperate.

Tropical Rainy. The tropical rainy climate covers only a comparatively small part of Africa. It occurs in a 700-mile-wide band along the Equator, ending at the highlands of east-central Africa. There are also narrower belts along the Gulf of Guinea, which has strong monsoonal influences, and along the east Madagascar coast. These areas are age yearly rainfall does not exceed 10 inches anywhere; some areas go without rain for years.

Mediterranean. Mild yearly temperatures, dry summers, and moderately rainy winters are the chief marks of the Mediterranean climate. It occurs along part of the northern and southern coasts, where climatic influences from the middle latitudes are felt. During the warmest month temperatures average in the low 70's near the coast and in the low 80's inland. Temperatures for the coolest month are roughly 20 degrees less. The annual rainfall is about 20 to 30 inches.

Humid Subtropical. Part of the southeastern coast has a humid subtropical climate, which in temperature is similar to the Mediterranean type. Yearly rainfall, however, reaches 40 to 60 inches and is concentrated in the summer rather than the winter months.

Highland. In the highland regions, especially the loftiest sections of eastern Africa, temperatures are much lower than in areas of comparable latitude at lower elevations. This is particularly true in the Ethiopian Highlands and in some of the Rift Valley mountains. In areas of sharp relief lying in the path of moisture-bearing winds, rainfall is heavy.

Natural Vegetation

There are still extensive areas in Africa where few people live and where man and his crops and domestic animals have not crowded out natural vegetation and wild animals. In some parts of the continent large forest preserves have been established.

Tropical Rain Forests. Most of Africa's forests are tropical rain forests, or *selvas*. They cover less than a tenth of the continent and occur where rainfall is heavy through-

A-101

out most of the year. Such a forest is made up of several layers of vegetation. The top layer consists of the crowns of trees rising 125 to 250 feet in height; the lower layers are made up of the tops of shorter trees, shrubs, and vines. Most of the trees are broad-leaved evergreens, though some are conifers. They yield pulp, timber, and such cabinet woods as mahogany, ebony, and teak. Oil palms, rubber-producing trees and vines, orchids, and lilies are among the numerous kinds of plants found in these forests.

Tropical Savannas. Savannas, which cover probably a third of the continent, consist of areas where the ground cover is mainly grass. They are, however, dotted by woodlands, scattered trees, or shrubs, depending on the length of dry season. Those bordering the tropical rain forests have coarse grasses up to 12 feet high and large woodlands of deciduous trees. Trees of these savannas also include many evergreens found in tropical rain forests, such as oil palms, rubber trees,

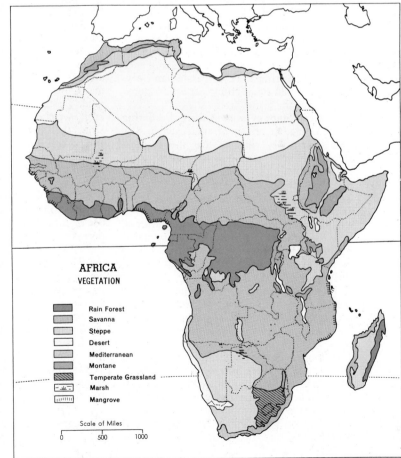

AFRICA
VEGETATION

- Rain Forest
- Savanna
- Steppe
- Desert
- Mediterranean
- Montane
- Temperate Grassland
- Marsh
- Mangrove

Scale of Miles

0   500   1000

Publix: D. Forbert
Victoria Falls on Zambezi River

and African ebony trees. There are also shea trees (which yield an edible fat), baobabs, flat-topped acacias, kapok, and many trees that bear edible fruit.

Where the dry season becomes more pronounced, grass is shorter than in the more humid savannas; seldom is it more than five feet high. Palms, baobabs, acacias, and such brightly flowering trees as cassias and erythrinas grow in small clumps or are scattered singly over the grassy areas.

Tropical Steppes and Deserts. Bordering the savannas in areas of increased aridity and longer dry seasons are the tropical steppes. These are regions where short grasses prevail and trees are scarce. Among the trees found here are thorny acacias, euphorbias, dwarf palms, and jujube trees. In steppes bordering on deserts—often called subdesert steppes—there are almost no trees, and the grasses grow in widely scattered bunches. After rains a thin carpet of various grasses and flowering plants springs up and thrives for several weeks.

True deserts, such as the Sahara and the Namib, have virtually no vegetation except at oases (places watered by springs or wells). Vegetation at oases includes date palms, fig trees, willows, poplars, and tamarisks.

Mediterranean vegetation occurs along parts of the northern and southern coasts. It consists of many kinds of shrubs and small trees, both deciduous and evergreen. Many of the plants have waxy, leathery leaves and long taproots, which enable them to with-

stand long, dry summers. Some are scrubby and thorny, especially the deciduous varieties. Characteristic in the north are cork oak, olive trees, cedars, and pines; in the south, laurels, cedars, and ironwood. Grasses and low flowering plants grow only during the rainy months.

Others. In some parts of Africa, vegetation results from highly localized conditions. Probably the most varied is the montane vegetation of highlands, particularly in Ethiopia and the mountains of the Great Rift Valley. The kind of vegetation that grows there depends on elevation, latitude, and direction of the winds.

Often the slopes are mantled by luxuriant forests, which are predominantly evergreen. Montane forests yield valuable timber and cabinet woods. Bamboo and wild varieties of coffee and banana also grow here. Giant lobelias and tree-groundsels characterize some of the montane forests of eastern Africa. At higher elevations, grasses and colorful, low-growing plants are typical. The High Veld of southern Africa is a temperate grassland between 3,500 and 11,000 feet above sea level.

Mangrove forests occur along many parts of the African coast, but are most extensive along the Gulf of Guinea. These contain mangrove and other trees adapted to life in muddy estuaries and tidal flats. Relatively large areas of swamp and marsh also occur along the larger rivers and lakes of western and central Africa. Papyrus, tall grasses, and lotus are the most common plants. The Sudd region of the White Nile River is one of the largest marshes in the world.

Wild Animals

Africa is rich in animal life, but the number of large game animals has been rapidly decreasing for many years. In some parts of the continent, few such animals can be found outside game parks. Some of these parks cover thousands of square miles. Game parks have been established mainly in eastern and southern Africa.

Many kinds of animals are native only to Africa. Among them are such mammals as gorillas, chimpanzees, zebras, giraffes, hippopotamuses, African elephants, aardvarks, and several species of antelopes. Among large native birds are crested cranes, secretary birds, guinea fowl, and numerous species of storks, ibises, herons, and eagles. Madagascar has several kinds of animals

AFRICA

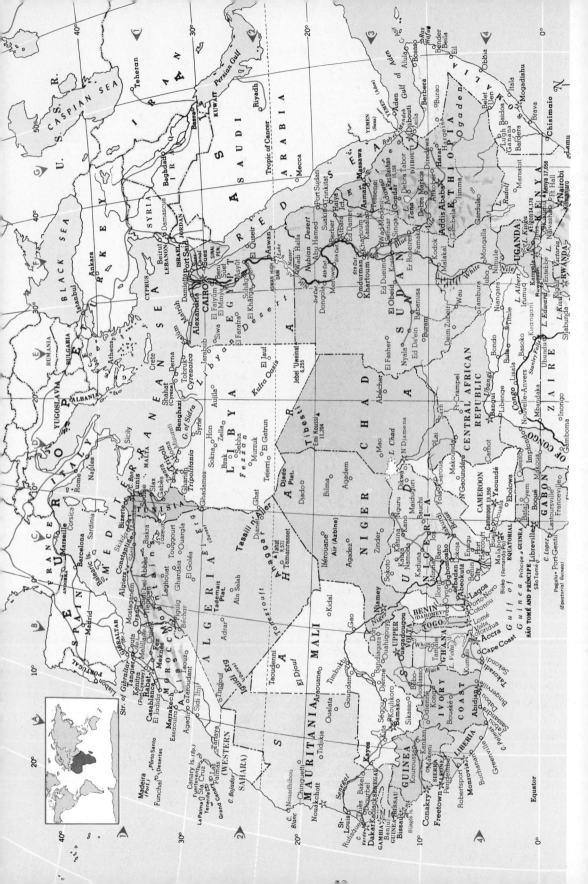

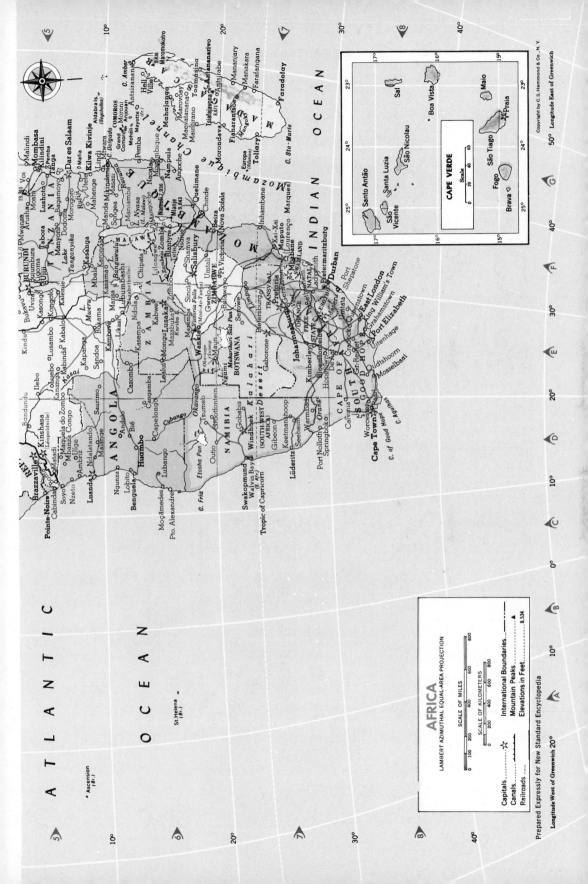

AFRICA (Continued)

Lilongwe (capital), Malawi ... F 6
Limpopo (river) ... E 7
Lindi, Tanzania ... G 5
Lisala, Zaire ... E 4
Livingstone (Maramba), Zambia ... E 6
Lobito, Angola ... D 6
Lomé (capital), Togo ... C 4
Lopez (cape), Gabon ... C 5
Lourenço Marques (Maputo) (cap.), Mozambique ... F 7
Luanda (cap.), Angola ... D 5
Lubango, Angola ... D 6
Lubumbashi, Zaire ... E 6
Lüderitz, Namibia ... D 7
Luebo, Zaire ... E 5
Lugh, Somalia ... G 4
Lusaka (cap.), Zambia ... E 6
Lusambo, Zaire ... E 5
Lushoto, Tanzania ... F 5
Madagascar ... G 6
Madeira (isls.), Portugal ... A 1
Maevatanana, Madagascar ... G 6
Mafia (isl.), Tanzania ... G 5
Mahajanga, Madagascar ... G 6
Maintirano, Madagascar ... G 6
Maio (isl.) C. Verde ... H 9
Makarikari (salt pan), Botswana ... E 7
Makoua, Rep. of Congo ... D 4
Malabo (cap.), Equat. Guinea ... C 4
Malakal, Sudan ... F 4
Malanje, Angola ... D 5
Malawi ... F 6
Malawi (Nyasa) (lake) ... F 6
Mali ... B 3
Malindi, Kenya ... G 5
Manakara, Madagascar ... G 7
Mananjary, Madagascar ... G 7
Mangoche, Malawi ... F 6
Mangoky (riv.), Madagascar ... G 7
Maniamba, Mozambique ... F 6
Manyoni, Tanzania ... F 5
Mao, Chad ... D 3
Maputo (cap.), Mozambique ... F 7
Maramba, Zambia ... E 6
Maromokotro (mt.), Madagascar ... G 6
Marovoay, Madagascar ... G 6
Marrakech, Mor. ... A 1
Maseru (capital), Lesotho ... E 8
Massawa, Ethiopia ... G 3
Matadi, Zaire ... D 5
Mauritania ... A 3
Mayotte (isl.) ... G 6
Mbabane (capital), Swaziland ... F 7
Mbandaka, Zaire ... D 4
Mbanza Congo Angola ... D 5
Meknès, Morocco ... B 1
Melilla, Spain ... B 1
Merowe, Sudan ... F 3
Misurata, Libya ... D 1
Mlanje (mt.) ... F 6
Moçambique, Mozambique ... G 6
Moçâmedes, Angola ... D 6
Mogadishu (Mogadiscio) (cap.), Somalia ... G 4
Mohéli (isl.), Comoros ... G 6
Mombasa, Kenya ... G 5
Monrovia (cap.), Liberia ... A 4
Morocco ... B 1
Morogoro, Tanzania ... F 5
Morondava, Madagascar ... G 7
Moroni (cap.), Comoros ... G 6
Moshi, Tanzania ... F 5
Mosselbaai, Cape of Good Hope ... E 8
Mostaganem, Algeria ... B 1
Mozambique ... F 6
Mozambique (channel) ... G 6
Mtwara-Mikindani, Tanzania ... G 5
Murzuk, Libya ... D 2
Mwanza, Tanzania ... F 5
Mweru (lake) ... E 5
Nacala, Mozambique ... F 6
Nairobi (capital), Kenya ... F 5
Namibia (S.W. Africa) ... D 7
Nampula, Mozambique ... G 6
Namuli (mt.), Mozambique ... F 6
Nasser (lake) ... F 2
Natal (prov.), South Africa ... F 7
N'Djamena (capital), Chad ... D 3
Ndola, Zambia ... E 6
Ngami (lake) Botswana ... E 7
N'Gaoundéré, Cam. ... D 4
Ngunza, Angola ... D 6
Nguru, Nigeria ... D 3
Niamey (cap.), Niger ... C 3
Niangara, Zaire ... E 4
Niger ... C, D 3
Niger (river) ... C 3
Nigeria ... C 4
Nile (river) ... F 2
Nouadhibou, Mauritania ... A 2
Nouakchott (cap.), Mauritania ... A 3
Nouvelle-Anvers, Zaire ... D 4
Novo Sofala, Moz. ... F 7
Nsanje, Malawi ... F 6
Nubian (desert), Sudan ... F 2
Nyala, Sudan ... E 3
Nyasa (lake) ... F 6
Nzeto, Angola ... D 5
Obbia, Somalia ... G 4
Odienné, Ivory Coast ... B 4
Ogaden (region), Eth. ... G 4
Ogbomosho, Nigeria ... C 4
Okavango (Cubango) (river) ... D 6
Okavango (swamp), Botswana ... E 6
Omdurman, Sudan ... F 3
Oran, Algeria ... B 1
Orange (river) ... D 7
Orange Free State (prov.), South Africa ... E 7
Ouagadougou (cap.), Upper Volta ... B 3
Ouahigouya, Upper Volta ... B 3
Oualata, Mauritania ... B 3
Ouargla, Algeria ... C 1
Oudtshoorn, Cape of Good Hope ... E 8
Ouesso, Republic of Congo ... D 4
Oujda, Morocco ... B 1
Outjo, Namibia ... D 6
Oyem, Gabon ... D 4
Oyo, Nigeria ... C 4
Paarl, Cape of Good Hope ... D 8
Pagalu (isl.), Equat. Guinea ... C 5
Palma, La (island), Canary Is., Spain ... A 2
Palmas (cape) ... B 4
Pemba, Mozambique ... G 6
Pemba (island), Tanzania ... G 5
Pietermarizburg (capital), Natal ... F 7
Pietersburg, Transvaal ... E 7
Pointe-Noire, Republic of Congo ... D 5
Port Elizabeth, Cape of Good Hope ... E 8
Port-Gentil, Gabon ... C 5
Port Harcourt, Nigeria ... C 4
Port-Lyautey (Kénitra), Morocco ... B 1
Port Nolloth, Cape of Good Hope ... D 7
Port Said, Egypt ... F 1
Port Shepstone, Natal ... F 8
Port Sudan, Sudan ... F 3
Pôrto Alexandre, Angola ... D 6
Porto-Novo (cap.), Benin ... C 4
Pôrto Santo (isl.), Portugal ... A 1
Praia (capital), Cape Verde ... G 8
Pretoria (capital), South Africa ... E 7
Qena, Egypt ... F 2
Queenstown, Cape of Good Hope ... E 8
Quelimane, Mozambique ... F 6
Rabat (capital), Morocco ... B 1
Red (sea) ... F 2
Rhodesia (Zimbabwe) ... E 6
Río Muni (reg.), Equat. Guinea ... C 4
Rudolf (lake), Kenya ... F 4
Rufiji (river), Tanzania ... F 5
Rufisque, Senegal ... A 3
Ruvuma (river) ... F 6
Ruwenzori (mts.) ... E 4
Rwanda ... F 5
Sahara (desert) ... C 2
Saint Helena (isl.) ... B 6
Saint-Louis, Senegal ... A 3
Sainte Marie (cape), Madagascar ... G 7
Sal (island), Cape Verde ... G 8
Salisbury (cap.), Zimbabwe ... F 6
Salûm, Egypt ... E 1
Sandoa, Zaire ... E 5
Santa Cruz, Canary Is., Spain ... A 2
Santa Luzia (isl.), Cape Verde ... F 8
Santo Antão (isl.), Cape Verde ... F 8
São Nicolau (isl.), Cape Verde ... G 8
São Tiago (isl.), Cape Verde ... G 9
São Tomé and Príncipe ... C 4
São Vicente (isl.), Cape Verde ... F 8
Sarh, Chad ... E 4
Sassandra, Ivory Coast ... B 4
Saurimo, Angola ... E 5
Sebha, Libya ... D 2
Ségou, Mali ... B 3
Sekondi, Ghana ... B 4
Senegal ... A 3
Senegal (river) ... A 3
Sennar, Sudan ... F 3
Serowe, Botswana ... E 7
Sétif, Algeria ... C 1
Sfax, Tunisia ... D 1
Shabunda, Zaire ... E 5
Shahat, Libya ... E 1
Shamva, Zimbabwe ... F 6
Sidi-bel-Abbès, Algeria ... C 1
Sidi Ifni, Morocco ... B 2
Sidra (gulf), Libya ... D 1
Sierra Leone ... A 4
Sikasso, Mali ... B 3
Sinai (pen.), Egypt ... F 2
Singa, Sudan ... F 3
Sinoia, Zimbabwe ... E 6
Sixth Cataract, Sudan ... F 3
Skikda, Algeria ... C 1
Sohâg, Egypt ... F 2
Sokna, Libya ... D 2
Sokoto, Nigeria ... C 3
Somalia ... G 4
Songea, Tanzania ... F 6
Sousse, Tunisia ... D 1
South Africa ... E 7
South-West Africa (Namibia) ... D 7
Soyo, Angola ... D 5
Springbok, Cape of Good Hope ... D 7
Stanley (falls), Zaire ... E 4
Suakin, Sudan ... F 3
Sudan ... E 3
Suez, Egypt ... F 2
Suez (canal), Egypt ... F 1
Swakopmund, Namibia ... D 7
Swaziland ... F 7
Syrte, Libya ... D 1
Tabora, Tanzania ... F 5
Tabou, Ivory Coast ... B 4
Tademait (plat.) ... C 2
Takoradi, Ghana ... B 4
Tamale, Ghana ... B 4
Tamanrasset, Algeria ... C 2
Tana (lake), Ethiopia ... F 3
Tanezrouft (desert) ... C 2
Tanga, Tanzania ... F 5
Tanganyika (lake) ... F 5
Tangier, Morocco ... B 1
Tanzania ... F 5
Tarfaya, Morocco ... A 2
Taroudant, Morocco ... B 1
Tenerife (isl.), Canary Is., Spain ... A 2
Tete, Mozambique ... F 6
Thiès, Senegal ... A 3
Third Cataract, Sudan ... E 3
Tibesti (mts.) ... D 2
Tidjikja, Mauritania ... A 3
Timbuktu, Mali ... B 3
Tindouf, Algeria ... B 2
Titule, Zaire ... E 4
Tlemcen, Algeria ... B 1
Toamasina, Madagascar ... G 6
Tobruk, Libya ... E 1
Togo ... C 4
Toliary, Madagascar ... G 7
Touggourt, Algeria ... C 1
Tozeur, Tunisia ... C 1
Transvaal (prov.), South Africa ... E 7
Tripoli (capital), Libya ... D 1
Tripolitania (region), Libya ... D 1
Tsiafajavona (mt.), Madagascar ... G 6
Tsumeb, Namibia ... D 6
Tunis (cap.), Tunisia ... D 1
Tunisia ... C 1
Ubangi (river) ... E 3
Ubundu, Zaire ... E 5
Uganda ... F 4
Uitenhage, Cape of Good Hope ... E 8
Ujiji, Tanzania ... F 5
Umtali, Zimbabwe ... F 6
Umtata, Transkei ... E 8
Upper Volta ... B 3
Utete, Tanzania ... F 5
Uvira, Zaire ... E 5
'Uweinat (mt.) ... E 2
Vaal (river), South Africa ... E 7
Verde (cape), Senegal ... A 3
Victoria (falls) ... E 6
Victoria (lake) ... F 5
Volta (lake) ... B 4
Volta (river) ... C 4
Wad Medani, Sudan ... F 3
Wadi Halfa, Sudan ... F 2
Walvis Bay, Cape of Good Hope ... D 7
Wankie, Zimbabwe ... E 6
Warmbad, Namibia ... D 7
Wau, Sudan ... E 4
White Nile (river) ... F 4
White Volta (river) ... B 4
Windhoek (cap.), Namibia ... D 7
Worcester, Cape of Good Hope ... D 8
Xai Xai, Mozambique ... F 7
Yaoundé (cap.), Cameroon ... D 4
Zaire ... E 5
Zambezi (river) ... E 6
Zambia ... E 6
Zanzibar (isl.), Tanzania ... G 5
Zella, Libya ... D 2
Zimbabwe ... E 7
Zinder, Niger ... C 3
Zomba, Malawi ... F 6
Zwara, Libya ... D 1

that are not found elsewhere, including aye-ayes and indris. Lemurs are found only on Madagascar and the nearby Comoro Islands. Among animals of the continent that are not found on Madagascar are elephants, lions, giraffes, and poisonous snakes.

Widely Distributed Animals. Some animals are adapted to life in more than one of Africa's climatic regions. Elephants, buffaloes, and various species of monkeys and antelopes are among mammals that are able to live in all regions but deserts. Birds that are represented by different species in two or more climatic regions include bulbuls, hornbills, francolins, and sunbirds. Some species —such as the fish eagle—are adapted to several regions.

Jackals and hyenas range throughout all regions except the tropical rain forests. Leopards live in forests and savannas. Lions and cheetahs live in various types of grasslands. The hippopotamus is found in lake and river areas in many parts of Africa. The Nile crocodile and the Nile monitor lizard also have a wide range. The rock python, Africa's largest snake, is found throughout most of Africa south of the Sahara except in desert regions.

Numerous kinds of fish are widely distributed off Africa's coasts and in its inland waters. Among commercially important marine life in coastal waters are barracuda, tuna, mackerel, tarpon, eel, marlin, octopus, shark, sole, sailfish, swordfish, sardines, shrimp, and clams. Edible fish found in most rivers and lakes include catfish, perch, barbel, and tilapia.

Among the hundreds of thousands of species of insects found in Africa, the mosquito is perhaps the most widely distributed. It is a major health hazard, especially in tropical Africa. The tsetse fly, which transmits dis-

Wildlife. Africa is the home of many kinds of wild animals. *Above left,* lions, found in many parts of the continent. *Above right,* rhinoceroses, among the largest and fiercest of mammals. Pictures were taken in Ngorongoro Crater, Tanzania. *Below,* giraffes, zebras, and topis (barely visible at left) are among the animals found in Nairobi Park in Kenya.

ease to domestic animals and man, is found in bush country and swamps everywhere except in very arid regions.

Animals of Certain Regions. Mammals found only in forests include chimpanzees, gorillas, okapis, pygmy hippopotamuses, and some species of wild pigs and wild cats. The forests are especially rich in reptiles, amphibians, and insects, with a number of species not found in other climatic regions. Congo peacocks and the brilliantly colored trogons are forest birds. Several colorful species of turacos (or plantain-eaters) are found only in forests.

Savannas and other grasslands are the home of baboons, zebras, giraffes, wart hogs, aardvarks, rhinoceroses, and such antelopes as the eland, gnu, kob, Grant's gazelle, and

The Countries and Territories of Africa

NAME	AREA (Sq. Miles)	(Sq. Km.)	POPULATION (1981 est.)	CAPITAL
MAINLAND COUNTRIES AND TERRITORIES				
Algeria	919,595	2,381,741	19,590,000	Algiers
Angola	481,354	1,246,700	7,262,000	Luanda
Benin	43,484	112,622	3,520,000	Porto-Novo
Botswana	231,805	600,372	937,000	Gaborone
Burundi	10,747	27,834	4,348,000	Bujumbura
Cameroon	183,569	475,442	8,650,000	Yaoundé
Central African Republic	240,535	622,984	2,349,000	Bangui
Ceuta *(Enclave in Morocco)*	7	19	70,000	. . . . .
Chad	496,000	1,284,000	4,547,000	N'Djamena
Congo	132,000	342,000	1,578,000	Brazzaville
Djibouti	8,494	22,000	323,000	Djibouti
Egypt	386,662*	1,001,449	43,465,000	Cairo
Equatorial Guinea	10,831	28,051	372,000	Malabo
Ethiopia	471,780	1,221,900	32,158,000	Addis Ababa
Gabon	103,347	267,667	555,000	Libreville
Gambia	4,361	11,295	619,000	Banjul
Ghana	92,100	238,537	12,063,000	Accra
Guinea	94,926	245,857	5,147,000	Conakry
Guinea-Bissau	13,948	36,125	810,000	Bissau
Ivory Coast	124,504	322,463	8,298,000	Abidjan
Kenya	224,960	582,646	17,348,000	Nairobi
Lesotho	11,720	30,355	1,374,000	Maseru
Liberia	43,000	111,369	2,038,000	Monrovia
Libya	679,362	1,759,540	3,096,000	Tripoli
Malawi	45,747	118,484	6,123,000	Lilongwe
Mali	479,000	1,240,000	7,160,000	Bamako
Mauritania	398,000	1,030,700	1,681,000	Nouakchott
Melilla *(Enclave in Morocco)*	5	12	60,000	. . . . .
Morocco	275,000	712,550	20,646,000	Rabat
Mozambique	302,330	783,030	10,757,000	Maputo
Namibia	317,827	823,168	1,001,000	Windhoek
Niger	489,200	1,267,000	5,479,000	Niamey
Nigeria	356,669	923,768	79,680,000	Lagos
Rwanda	10,169	26,338	5,109,000	Kigali

Thompson's gazelle. Among the many birds of the open country are kites, cattle egrets, and most of Africa's species of weaverbirds. The brackish lakes of the plains of eastern and central Africa are frequented by flamingoes.

Ostriches and sand grouse are among birds found in the drier grasslands and steppe regions. Deserts are inhabited by hares, jerboas, foxes, wild asses, and gazelles. Several species of insects and reptiles are found only in desert regions and steppes bordering on deserts.

Economic Activities

Agriculture has long been the mainstay of Africa's economy, subsistence farming being the prevailing type. It was not until the colonial period that commercial farming and mining were introduced. Under European control, Africa became a source of agricultural and mineral raw materials. In many parts of Africa, colonialism led to economic development that generally advanced European objectives, which were not necessarily suited to the needs of Africa itself.

Some diversification came with the decline of colonialism in the 20th century. Nevertheless, many countries remain dependent on the export of one or two commodities; for example, Ghana on cacao, Zambia on copper, and Gambia on peanuts. The economies of such countries are strongly

NAME	AREA		POPULATION	CAPITAL
	(Sq. Miles)	(Sq. Km.)		
Senegal	75,750	196,192	5,811,000	Dakar
Sierra Leone.	27,699	71,740	3,571,000	Freetown
Somalia	246,200	637,657	4,895,000	Mogadishu
South Africa	471,445	1,221,037	30,131,000	Pretoria and Cape Town
South-West Africa. See Namibia.				
Sudan	967,500	2,505,813	18,901,000	Khartoum
Swaziland.	6,704	17,363	566,000	Mbabane
Tanzania.	364,900	945,087	18,510,000	Dar es Salaam
Togo.	21,600	56,000	2,705,000	Lomé
Tunisia.	63,170	163,610	6,513,000	Tunis
Uganda	91,134	236,036	13,620,000	Kampala
Upper Volta	105,869	274,200	7,094,000	Ouagadougou
Zaire	905,568	2,345,409	29,450,000	Kinshasa
Zambia.	290,586	752,614	5,961,000	Lusaka
Zimbabwe	150,804	390,580	7,600,000	Harare

ISLAND COUNTRIES AND TERRITORIES

NAME	AREA		POPULATION	CAPITAL
Canary Islands	2,808	7,273	1,450,000	Las Palmas; Santa Cruz de Tenerife
Cape Verde.	1,557	4,033	329,000	Praia
Comoros.	838	2,171	369,000	Moroni
Madagascar	226,658	587,041	8,955,000	Antananarivo
Madeira Islands	308	798	258,000	Funchal
Mauritius.	790	2,045	971,000	Port Louis
Réunion	970	2,510	503,000	Saint-Denis
Saint Helena and Dependencies	162	419	6,000	Jamestown
São Tomé and Príncipe.	372	964	86,000	São Tomé
Seychelles	108	280	66,000	Victoria

All places listed are independent except for Ceuta, Melilla, and the Canary Islands (under the control of Spain); Namibia (South Africa); the Madeira Islands (Portugal); Réunion (France); and St. Helena (Great Britain).
*Includes the Sinai Peninsula, which is part of Asia.

affected by fluctuations in the prices of their products in the world market.

Throughout much of the continent, numerous factors hinder economic development. Among them are the pervasiveness of subsistence farming and accompanying poverty, lack of capital to invest, a shortage of skilled workers and managers, poorly developed transportation systems, and, in some areas, political instability.

Agriculture. Though predominantly agricultural, Africa, in comparison to its large size, has little productive farmland. Much of the land consists of deserts, steppes, and rain forests, where unfavorable climate, poor soil, or dense vegetation make cultivation difficult or impossible. Where farming is practiced, much of the land, over time, has become less productive or badly eroded through overuse and poor farming methods. In some areas, the introduction of modern methods and equipment has increased production; however, much of this improvement has been in the growing of commercial crops for export, rather than food crops. Throughout Africa, population growth has outstripped increases in output. As a result, most Africans have barely enough food to sustain themselves and many suffer from severe malnutrition.

Most farmers work small plots of land. They use primitive tools, little fertilizer, and almost no animal power. Crop yields are low and quality is generally poor. Cassava, sweet potatoes, yams, rice, and plantains are among staple food crops. Cash crops include peanuts, cacao, palm nuts, cotton, coffee, and sisal. Some of these crops are also produced on African- and foreign-owned plantations. Many Africans practice a shifting type of agriculture. One plot of land is used until its fertility is exhausted; then the process is repeated on another.

Farming in northern Africa is slightly more advanced than in sub-Saharan Africa, mainly because of European and Arabic influences. Especially in Morocco, Algeria, and Egypt, there is a greater use of machinery, animal power, and tools. Wheat and barley, citrus fruits, grapes, olives, and many kinds of vegetables are grown in much of this region. In some areas irrigation is important—the classic example is the Nile Valley, where cotton and grains are predominant crops.

In parts of southern and eastern Africa, especially South Africa, Zimbabwe, and Kenya, are Africa's most productive farms. Using modern methods and machinery, some farmers produce a great variety of crops, both for local markets and for export. However, even in these countries subsistence farming is the main type.

Livestock is raised in every African country; however, this activity is not prevalent in equatorial regions, partly due to the pres-

ence of disease-bearing insects such as the tsetse fly. For the continent as a whole, there are large, and nearly equal, numbers of sheep, cattle, and goats, but few pigs and horses.

Livestock raising varies from nomadic herding on steppes and deserts to commercial ranching on grasslands in southern and eastern Africa. In some savannas, herding is combined with cultivation. Livestock production varies greatly from country to country. Where commercial ranching predominates, large amounts of meat, dairy products, wool, and hides are produced. Among the tribes for whom herding is a major activity, livestock is often considered a measure of wealth and is not used commercially.

Mining. The discovery of diamonds in southern Africa in the late 19th century signaled Africa's rise as a major mineral producer. The continent now supplies almost all of the world's diamonds and probably half its gold, as well as large quantities of copper, chromite, cobalt, manganese, antimony, phosphate rock, asbestos, and platinum. Bauxite, tin, iron ore, uranium, tungsten, lead, zinc, silver, vanadium, and coal are also mined.

In most African countries, the utilization of mineral resources has proceeded more rapidly than has any other economic activity. But mining on a large scale requires complex machinery, skilled technicians, and heavy financial investment, and few countries can afford to exploit their resources fully. The bulk of Africa's minerals, excluding fuels, is produced by four countries— South Africa, Zaire, Zimbabwe, and Zambia. From these countries come diamonds, gold, copper, cobalt, and a variety of other minerals.

Other mining areas have grown in the last few decades. Western Africa, once important only for gold, now yields most of Africa's bauxite and major portions of its tin, tungsten, and iron ore. Nigeria and Libya have become major producers of petroleum. Morocco supplies most of the continent's phosphate rock.

Besides its direct benefits, mining has had important secondary effects. It has introduced wage labor; encouraged road and railway building; and stimulated the development of processing industries and hydroelectric power.

A-110

Pineapple Plantation in Ivory Coast. Plantation-grown crops in Africa include pineapples, cacao, cotton, and coffee.
Marc & Evelyne Bernheim from Rapho-Guillumette

Farmers' Market. In African countries much farm produce is sold or traded in marketplaces such as this one in Nabeul, Tunisia. Here, farmers and merchants bargain over piles of red peppers.

Manufacturing and Processing. Industrially, Africa is the least developed of all the continents except uninhabited Antarctica. This situation is slowly changing, however, as many countries obtain financial and technical aid and establish industries. In some areas, development of hydroelectric power has been one of the chief steps toward industrialization. Among the principal power projects are the Cabora Bassa Dam in Mozambique, the Inga Dam in Zaire, the Aswan High Dam in Egypt, the Akosombo Dam in Ghana, and the Kariba Dam in Zimbabwe.

Except in areas where there is heavy foreign investment, African industry is characterized by small workshops that produce relatively simple products. However, such industries as the processing of foods and minerals and the making of textiles are developing in many parts of the continent. Traditional handicrafts such as leatherworking and weaving have long been major activities in northern Africa, and their importance is slowly growing elsewhere. The growth of urban areas has stimulated production of cement, bricks, and other construction materials.

Only in South Africa is manufacturing highly developed. Here a wide variety of goods—from processed foods to complex industrial machinery—are produced. Several other countries are in an intermediate stage of development, producing light industrial products mainly for consumer markets. These include Morocco, Algeria, and Egypt in the north; Nigeria in western Africa; and Zaire and Zimbabwe in central Africa.

Fishing. Africa's potential fish catch is enormous; however, most nations lack modern fleets and equipment, and the overall catch is small. Traditional fishing methods predominate in most parts of the continent. South Africa, Nigeria, Namibia, and Senegal land the largest catches by tonnage.

Transportation. Modern transport is poorly developed throughout most of the continent. In tropical regions, large amounts of goods are still moved by porters, canoes, and small barges. Camels and other pack animals are used in the north.

The continent has few railways. Most of them link coastal areas and ports with inland sources of mineral and agricultural raw materials; few extend far inland. Only in southern Africa are there sizable interconnecting networks. By far the most developed system is in South Africa. Railways that serve the copper-producing districts of south-central Africa provide the only transcontinental route.

Roads are far more extensive than railroads, but of less use. The greater part of them are dirt trails, and even the better roads are often unusable during the rainy months. Paved all-weather roads are located almost entirely in and around large cities.

Water routes have long been used. River transport is of local importance, but in many areas is hampered by rapids. Along the coasts, goods and passengers are often transported in small vessels, such as the *dhows* (Arab sailing boats) of the eastern coast. There are few good natural harbors; nevertheless, numerous ports have developed along parts of the coast. With few excep-

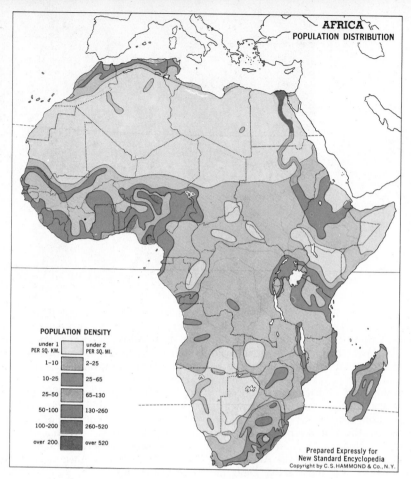

AFRICA
POPULATION DISTRIBUTION

POPULATION DENSITY

under 1 PER SQ. KM.		under 2 PER SQ. MI.
1–10		2–25
10–25		25–65
25–50		65–130
50–100		130–260
100–200		260–520
over 200		over 520

Prepared Expressly for
New Standard Encyclopedia
Copyright by C.S. HAMMOND & Co., N.Y.

tions, the principal ports lie along the Mediterranean Sea, the Gulf of Guinea, and the coasts of South Africa and Mozambique. The Suez Canal carries international traffic between the Mediterranean and Red seas.

Almost every nation has at least one local airline, but many of these lines are too small to operate efficiently. Most of the principal cities are served by major international carriers.

The People

Race. In northern and northeastern Africa the people are predominantly of the Caucasoid race. South of the Sahara they are predominantly Negroid. Most of the inhabitants of Madagascar are in part Mongoloid, some of their ancestors having migrated from Indonesia as long ago as the third century B.C. In eastern, central, and southern Africa there are large numbers of Caucasoid peoples whose ancestors came from Europe, Arabia, and India during the last 300 years.

Some African peoples have not been precisely classified according to race. Many

A-112

of these people live in the southern Sahara and in eastern Africa. They have certain Caucasoid facial characteristics and Negroid skin color and hair structure. An almost extinct group are the Bushmen of the Kalahari desert. Most ethnologists classify them as Negroid, but others consider them a separate race. The Pygmies of the Congo forest are usually classified as Negroid.

See BUSHMEN; PYGMIES; RACES OF MAN, subtitle *Classification of Races.*

Language. There are more than 800 African tongues and several Asian and European languages spoken in Africa. African languages are divided into 12 large groups. The groups spoken by the greatest number of people are *Semito-Hamitic, Niger-Congo, Central Saharan, Macro-Sudanic,* and *Click.*

Semito-Hamitic, or Afro-Asiatic, Languages are spoken mainly in North Africa, but extend into eastern Africa. They include the Hamitic languages, such as Berber, Coptic, and Cushitic; Chad; and the Semitic languages, such as Arabic, Hebrew, and Amharic.

Niger-Congo Languages, spoken by most of the Negroid peoples of Africa, are divided into about eight subgroups. The largest subgroup is the Benue-Cross, which includes the widely spoken Bantu languages.

Central Saharan Languages are spoken in a large area north of Lake Chad.

Macro-Sudanic Languages include the Nilotic subgroups spoken by the Suk, Shilluk, and Masai—among others—of eastern Africa.

The Click Languages employ a clicking sound in addition to the common consonant and vowel sounds. They are spoken by the Bushmen and one or two other Negroid peoples, and the clicking sound has been incorporated into certain Bantu languages.

Hausa, a Chad language of western Africa, and *Kiswahili* (or *Swahili*), a Bantu language of eastern Africa, have become *lingua francas* (languages spoken widely outside their original culture groups). Both Hausa and Kiswahili have been strongly influenced by Arabic. *Afrikaans* is a language spoken by South Africans of Dutch descent. A Malayo-Polynesian language is spoken on Madagascar. English and French, the languages of the major former colonial powers, are widely used in business and government and are taught in many African countries.

Religion. Islam and the traditional religions of Negroid peoples are the dominant religions of Africa. Christianity was introduced into North Africa early in the Christian Era, but the Coptic Church of Egypt and Ethiopia is the only large sect that remains of this early influence. Later missionary efforts—especially after the 18th century—made many Christian converts in Africa south of the Sahara. Judaism is represented mainly in urban areas. The Falasha of Ethiopia comprise a sect of Judaism that dates from the first century B.C.

Islam was introduced into North Africa in the seventh century, and its influence began to extend south of the Sahara desert by the 13th century. It is the leading religion of northern and much of eastern Africa.

There is considerable variation in the traditional beliefs of the Negroid peoples of Africa. Generally speaking, religion is a vital part of everyday as well as ceremonial life. A supreme being, the creator of all things, is central to most traditional African religions. He is the ultimate source of all good, but punishes antisocial acts. He can be approached through the mediation of lesser supernatural beings by the use of prayer, sacrifice, and other rituals.

The individual personality is believed to consist of several parts, and death is not

A-113

Screen Traveler, from Gendreau

Feluccas (cargo sail boats) at Cairo

thought to be the end of the total personality. Ancestor worship, common to most African religions, is based on the belief that the ancestors of a group—such as family, clan, or tribe—continue after their death to play an important part in the lives of their descendants.

Totemism—the belief in a mystical relationship between a group and a particular

Copper Miners in Zaire

Ewing Galloway

United Nations
Teacher-training College in Yaba, Nigeria

animal or plant—influences the social structure of some groups. Magic, including witchcraft, plays a large part in traditional African beliefs.

See MAGIC; TOTEM; WITCHCRAFT.

Education. Educational opportunities vary greatly from one African country to another as a result of social and geographical influences. For example, education is hampered in Sudan because the country is large and sparsely settled, and the nomadic people speak 30 different languages. In some countries, children are kept out of school because they are needed to help support the family. School attendance is irregular in some areas because children suffer from chronic ill-health caused primarily by malnutrition, malaria, and parasitic infestation. Many African peoples are traditionally opposed to formal education for girls. A few tribal

A Schoolroom in Mali
Agence Nationale Information Mali

groups resist all education that is foreign to their own cultures.

Political differences are also important. Until after World War II, most of Africa was under European rule, and each colonial region reflected the educational policies of the nation that governed it. The effects of these policies have continued after the countries have become independent. In South Africa education is racially segregated.

Most African nations emphasize education, with increasing portions of their national budgets being set aside for educational purposes. They have continued many programs begun by colonial powers and missionary groups, and initiated others. Universal, free, compulsory education at the primary level has been made a goal in virtually all the countries. The number of teacher-training, technical, vocational, and agricultural schools and colleges is continually being increased. Adult education programs stressing literacy and hygiene are expanding at a rapid rate.

Financial and technical aid from America, Europe, and Asia has played an important part in African educational progress. In many countries, mission schools provide much of the elementary and high school education. At the university level in most of the countries, foreign instructors are common. The Peace Corps (United States) and the Volunteer Services Organization (United Kingdom) also supply primary and secondary school teachers to various African countries.

Almost every African country has a national university. The countries with the most extensive systems of higher education, each with more than 20 universities and colleges, are Egypt, Nigeria, and South Africa. Most African nations send large numbers of secondary-school, college, and graduate students abroad for their education.

Literature and the Arts. For centuries the art, music, and literature of North Africa have been an important part of world culture. For a discussion of these, see ISLAMIC CULTURE.

There was little recognition of the arts of Negroid Africans south of the Sahara until early in the 20th century. At that time the Fauve group of French painters became interested in West African sculpture and were consciously influenced by it. However, since the beginning of the 17th century, Af-

Leopard. This 15½-inch-high bronze, cast in Benin in the late 16th or early 17th century, is typical of the fine metalwork for which this Nigerian kingdom is famous.

The Museum of Primitive Art

AFRICAN ART

Terra Cotta Head of the ancient Nok culture dating back to about 900 B.C.

Federal Dept. of
Antiquites, Nigeria

Dance Mask, a rare study of wood, monkey fur, and white pigment made by members of the Guro tribe, Ivory Coast—19th century.

The Art Institute of Chicago

Headdress, Baga tribe, Guinea—19th century. Carved of wood, this 47-inch-high mask was worn by dancers in fertility ceremonies.

The Art Institute of Chicago

The Great Bieri, the largest known wood and metal reliquary head (18¼ inches) of the Fang tribe in Gabon—19th century. The rhythmic design of Fang sculpture influenced many 20th-century artists.

The Museum of Primitive Art

Market in Ivory Coast Village

rican folklore, music, and dance—introduced by slaves—have had an increasing effect upon culture in the Americas.

By the middle of the 20th century, the importance and the uniqueness of the African plastic arts (sculpture, pottery, and the like) were widely recognized. African writers, musicians, dancers, and actors were gaining acceptance in other parts of the world. African intellectual and political leaders were interested in preserving African art objects in African museums, and in developing creative expression in schools and other cultural centers.

Traditionally, African literature (mainly in the form of songs, stories, and proverbs), music, and art are interrelated and play a part in almost every phase of life. Special music and dances are used for weddings, initiations, preparation for battle and the hunt, and healing the sick. There are songs for various kinds of work. Stories and proverbs are used to instruct the young. The various literary and art forms are also used purely for entertainment. The use of drums is widespread, although unknown to a few peoples. Other traditional instruments include the lyre, the xylophone, and several kinds of harps and wind instruments.

West African sculpture is considered to be the most important of the African plastic arts. The human body is the usual subject, but the style is seldom representational. Figures are often distorted to give them religious or emotional meaning. In modern times, most sculpture has been of wood, and the most common forms are masks used in various ceremonies. There is some metal-casting and jewelry-making. In the past, there was a considerable amount of fine work in gold, bronze, and ivory.

Among the oldest existing works of art in Africa are the rock paintings and engravings that are found in arid and highland regions from the Sahara to the Kalahari. Some of this rock art dates back to about 13,000 B.C. Terra cotta figurines from as early as 900 B.C. have been found in archeological remains of the Nok civilization in Nigeria. Also from Nigeria are the terra cotta and bronze sculptures of Ife (12th to 14th centuries A.D.) and the bronze sculptures of Benin (16th and 17th centuries).

Ways of Life. Most educated and well-to-do Africans live in towns and cities and have adopted a European style of life in regard to housing, dress, recreation, and—to some extent—food. Even country people have come into contact with Western customs and products, and their traditional habits have been modified. However, Africans have not lost their own traditions and philosophies, and are beginning to show a new regard for them.

The great majority of Africans live in rural areas. A few groups—such as the Pygmies and Bushmen—live by hunting and gathering wild plants, but most Africans are farmers. Many men who work in towns spend part of their time in farming communities where their families live, and eventually return to their farm homes to stay.

Traditional African homes are built of locally available materials. Herdsmen of North Africa live in tents of cloth or skins of goats or sheep, with skins or woven rugs on the sandy floor. In the tropics and subtropics, herdsmen usually live in round huts made of wooden poles, osier (pliable twigs), and hides. Farming people tend to build square, thatched huts of wattle (wooden framework) and clay, or of sun-dried bricks. Floors may be of tamped-down earth, and may be covered with grass mats. A family dwelling usually consists of one or more one-roomed huts and several small granaries. Some African peoples live in villages, others live in isolated family dwellings.

The family is of great importance in African life. It is usually extended to include near relatives such as grandparents, aunts and uncles, and cousins. With the exception of the Berber-speaking peoples, the Pygmies, and a few other groups, most African peoples accept *polygyny* (more than one wife for each husband) as the ideal form of marriage. However, most Africans are monogamous for economic reasons and because the

Downtown Buildings in Dakar, Senegal
Philip Gendreau, New York

South African Tourist Corp.: Sabena
Lower Court in Session at Kitega, Burundi

numbers of men and women are approximately equal. Christian Africans are monogamous for religious reasons. *Bridewealth,* a gift by the groom to the bride's family, is generally a required part of an African marriage.

At a certain age, often corresponding to puberty, the young people of most tribes undergo elaborate initiation rites, which admit them to adult status. All the young men in a community who are initiated at the same time form an *age set* that lasts through life and whose members have mutual rights and obligations. Young women may have corresponding age sets. In some parts of Africa there may also be initiation into one of the men's or women's secret societies that perform certain traditional functions to keep order in the tribal community.

Governments in Africa

Various forms of government can be found in Africa. Morocco is a monarchy. Virtually all other African countries are republics, at least in name. Their constitutions usually provide for the forms of parliamen-

tary democracy, but most of them are virtual dictatorships. Many of these governments are based on military power; others are one-party regimes that prohibit political opposition. A few areas are still under foreign control.

The reasons for the often undemocratic nature and, even more frequently, unstable character of African governments are many. There is a high rate of illiteracy. Trained leaders are scarce. Many African countries have not been independent long enough to have gained sufficient experience in self-government. There is little unity within the countries.

When the European powers carved out their colonial empires, they drew arbitrary boundaries, often crossing tribal lines. When the colonies became independent, they inherited those boundaries, so that many African countries have populations consisting of members of a number of tribes, with different languages and cultural heritages. And agitation for tribal unity, which would require the redrawing of national boundaries, is a source of unrest.

Another problem is economic. According to 19th-century economic theory, the purpose of colonies was to provide raw materials for the industries of the colonial power. As a result, little was done to develop industry in the colonies themselves. In addition, many African countries are poor in natural resources. Both these countries and those whose resources are underdeveloped must rely on economic aid from other countries. This dependence on aid is one reason why African countries usually take a neutral position in international politics. (See AFRO-ASIAN BLOC; COLD WAR.)

History of Africa

Archeological discoveries indicate that the earliest forms of man and manlike creatures originated in Africa. Scientists working in Ethiopia, Kenya, and Tanzania during the 1960's and 1970's found skeletal remains of prehistoric men dating back about 3,750,000 years and of prehistoric manlike creatures called *Australopithecines* dating back 5,-500,000 to 1,000,000 years.

The earliest African people about whom anything is definitely known inhabited the Sahara region during an era of rainfall and luxuriant vegetation some 10,000 years ago.

They left many cave paintings as a record of their culture. These early people lived mainly by fishing. When the climate became dry and the desert began to develop, perhaps around 5000 B.C., the Saharan people apparently were dispersed and their culture destroyed.

Bushmen, Negroes, and possibly Pygmies are considered to be racial types native to Africa; they developed in the regions south of the Sahara desert. The first Caucasoid Africans, who spoke Semito-Hamitic languages, probably came across the Isthmus of

Suez from southwestern Asia sometime before 6000 B.C. Their descendants spread out from the Lower Nile Valley southward along the river and westward along the Mediterranean coast. Agriculture was introduced into Egypt in the 4000's. It had appeared south of the Sahara by 2000.

North Africa to 1500

Ancient Egypt. About 4000 B.C. the Egyptians moved from sandy hill country down to the fertile plain of the Nile. There followed a surge in population and the growth of a brilliant civilization. Intellectually, culturally, and militarily, Egypt flourished from about 3000 to 1000 B.C. The area along the Nile to the south, a source of gold, ivory, and slaves, was annexed. Sea trade was carried on with Arabia, Mesopotamia, Phoenicia, and the islands of the Aegean.

Green and prosperous Egypt attracted the Libyans (later called Berbers), nomads from the west. In an invasion in the 13th century B.C. they were defeated, but succeeded in the 10th and ruled Egypt for more than 100 years. The Libyan rulers were followed by a dynasty from Cush, a kingdom south of Egypt. The Assyrians invaded Egypt in the seventh century B.C., and the country became subject successively to the Persians, Greeks, Romans, and Byzantines.

Phoenician, Greek, and Roman Colonies. The Phoenicians, the first great seafaring people of the Mediterranean, began colonizing the Tunisian coast in the ninth century B.C. Utica was settled first, then Carthage, which became the center of an empire stretching west to Morocco and across the Mediterranean to Spain and Sicily.

In the seventh century B.C. the Greeks founded Cyrene, on the coast directly opposite Greece, as the nucleus of a colony. However, the Carthaginian language, *Punic* (from the Latin for "Phoenician"), became the common trade tongue of North Africa, even for the Greeks. Cyrenaica allied itself with the Persian masters of Egypt about 500 B.C., and passed with Egypt into the empire of Alexander the Great (332 B.C.) and the later Ptolemaic kingdom (323 B.C.).

By the third century B.C. Rome had grown strong enough to challenge Carthage for the control of the Mediterranean. The Punic Wars started in 264 and ended in 146 B.C. with the complete destruction of Carthage. The Carthaginian region became a province named "Africa." Rome gradually extended

Authenticated News International
Prehistoric Cave Painting of giraffe and hunter of about 5000 B.C. was found in the Libyan Desert.

its North African holdings both east and west. It annexed Cyrenaica in 96 B.C., Numidia (roughly the coastal area of modern Algeria) in 46 B.C., Egypt in 30 B.C., and Mauretania (Morocco) in 42 A.D. Some of the Berbers were converted to a settled agricultural life.

The Romans in Africa west of Egypt were concentrated along the western portion of the Mediterranean coast, where rainfall was sufficient to grow crops. Cyrene fell into ruin before the Christian Era began. The major cities were Leptis Magna (near modern Tripoli), Carthage (rebuilt by Julius Caesar and Augustus), Hippo Regius (Bône), Cirta (Constantine), Caesarea (Cherchel), and Tingis (Tangiers). The Berbers living be-

Roman Ruin. Arch and columns of a theater at Sabratha, ancient Roman city near Tripoli.
Standard Oil Co. (N. J.)

The Brooklyn Museum
Unidentified Ptolemaic Ruler. Black basalt sculpture of about the third century B.C.

return for religious freedom. In 642 the Byzantines were forced from the country, and Egypt became part of the Islamic world.

The Arabs moved on westward to the borders of Tunisia in 647, but withdrew upon receiving tribute. In 670, however, they returned to seize most of the area (which they called Ifriqiya) and to found the city of Kairouan. A march to the Atlantic in 681-83 aroused resistance that briefly halted Arab expansion. The fall of Carthage in 698 and the conversion of the Berbers to Islam brought all of the Maghrib (northwest Africa) under Arab control. Spain, where the North Africans were known as Moors, was conquered in 711-13. Sicily, where they were known as Saracens, fell in the next century.

Internal Wars and Invasions. A change in Islamic rulership in 750 was followed by bitter factional differences among the Moslems. In North Africa many Berbers joined the fanatical Kharijite sect and slaughtered orthodox Moslems. New African Moslem dynasties arose—among others, the Idrisids and the Aghlabids in the 9th century; the Fatimids in the 10th; the Almoravids in the 11th; the Almohads in the 12th; and the Hafsids and Marinids in the 13th. The Almoravids and other western dynasties were Berber rather than Arab. In Egypt the Fatimids were succeeded by the Ayyubids, who, in turn, were succeeded by the Mamelukes.

Savage fighting accompanied the constant struggle for power. In addition to internal conflict, there were invasions by various outsiders. At the beginning of the 11th century hordes of Arabian nomads known as Bedouins surged into Egypt. Sent on westward by the Fatimids to help subdue insubordinate areas, the Bedouins sacked and pillaged their way across North Africa, absorbing all but the urbanized coastal fringe.

In the 12th century the Normans, who had expelled the Saracens from Sicily, annexed the coastal area of Tunisia and held it for two decades. The Crusaders, fighting against the Moslems in the Holy Land, also attacked them in North Africa. There were invasions of Egypt in the Fifth Crusade (1218-21) and the Seventh (1248-54), and of Tunisia in the Eighth (1270-72). A Christian victory at Las Navas de Tolosa, Spain, in 1212 was followed by the expulsion of the Moors from the Iberian Peninsula.

yond the area of cultivation came to resent Roman rule and in the latter part of the fourth century began raiding the settled areas.

Vandal Invasion and Byzantine Reconquest. In 429 the barbarian Vandals crossed the Strait of Gibraltar to Mauretania. Their landing was unopposed by the Romans and the Berbers. The Vandal leader, Genseric, and his horde moved eastward along the coast, leaving slaughter and destruction behind them. Numidia was quickly occupied, and Carthage fell to the barbarians in 439. In 455 Genseric raided lower Italy and Rome. Back in Africa, he easily repulsed a Roman attack in 468.

Genseric's heirs, however, grew indolent. By the end of the fifth century they were unable to check the raids of the desert Berbers. In 533 the Eastern Roman (Byzantine) Emperor Justinian sent his general Belisarius to Africa, and by the following year Vandal power had been utterly destroyed. The Berbers, however, continued in revolt, and European influence receded toward the coast. In the early 600's the Persians seized Egypt, but were driven out by the Byzantine Emperor Heraclius.

Islamic Conquest. In 639 the Moslems, followers of the Arab prophet Mohammed and his religion of Islam, swept into Egypt. Members of the Coptic (Egyptian) Church, who had split away from the Byzantine Church, agreed to support the invaders in

Culture and Trade. In spite of their political and religious dissension, the Islamic peoples developed a rich culture. From Persia, which had been overrun in the first Arabic conquest, a highly developed art, literature, and science were spread westward. Mingling with elements of Syrian, Egyptian, Greek, and Roman civilization, Islamic culture was carried across North Africa. (See also ISLAMIC ART; ISLAMIC CULTURE.)

In the early centuries of Moslem rule, North Africa was completely cut off from Europe. Gradually small-scale trading was established, mainly by Jewish merchants who transported furs and swords from Europe and carried back precious spices and drugs.

At the time of the Crusades, Venetian and Genoese sailors discovered that their trade was welcome at North African ports. Soon business was flourishing in iron and lumber from Europe and gold, ivory, and spices from Africa. The spices, whether from eastern Africa or the East Indies, were brought to Egypt to be traded. So little was known of Africa and Asia that one European who visited Egypt reported that cinnamon, ginger, wood of aloe, and rhubarb came from the Nile and were harvested with nets.

In the 13th century the Franciscan and Dominican orders of the Roman Catholic Church were permitted to establish missions in Morocco. In the 15th century the Portuguese, who had already explored the Canary Islands, visited Madeira and attempted to set up trading centers on the coast of Barbary, as Europe called the Maghrib. (The inhabitants were non-Christian, therefore barbarian.) Several ports were taken by Portugal, but Moorish resistance was fierce. The Portuguese determined to by-pass the Moors and trade directly, by sea, with the African gold merchants and the Indies.

Sub-Saharan Africa to 1500

Early records of Africa south of the Sahara desert, often referred to as Black Africa, are extremely scanty. Archeological research in much of the region had scarcely begun by the mid-20th century. It is known, however, that as early as 900 B.C. an advanced agricultural civilization called the Nok culture arose in northern Nigeria.

Another civilization had emerged about 1800 B.C. south of Egypt in a region later known as Nubia, which the Egyptians valued for its gold. From time to time Egypt invaded Nubia, and finally about 1500 B.C. conquered it and made it a province.

Kingdom of Kush. Sometime after 1000 B.C., a Nubian people called the Kushites broke away from Egyptian rule and established an independent kingdom of their own. The Kushites became so powerful that they were able to conquer Egypt in the eighth century B.C. A century later, invading Assyrians drove the Kushites back into their homeland in northern Nubia. Later Kush was centered in central Nubia around the city of Meroe. The original Kushites were Caucasian. However, Meroe was in a region of dark-skinned peoples, and the Kushites soon intermarried with this population.

Kush became one of the most powerful kingdoms south of the Sahara. The Kushites are believed to be the first people of sub-Saharan Africa to make practical use of iron, having possibly learned ironworking from the Assyrians. The region was rich in iron ore, and iron became important to the kingdom's prosperity. Many historians believe that knowledge of ironworking was carried by the Kushites to central and west Africa. During the third century A.D., powerful nomadic peoples began migrating into Kush, gravely weakening the kingdom.

Meanwhile, about 100 A.D., there had arisen to the southeast of Nubia in what is now Ethiopia a kingdom called Axum. It was founded by Semites from southern Arabia, who intermarried with the native Ethiopians to form a new civilization. Axum flourished as a result of trade that passed through the kingdom and soon surpassed Kush as a power. In the fourth century A.D., an Axumite invasion destroyed the declining Kushite kingdom.

The Christian Kingdoms. Kush was succeeded by three less advanced kingdoms—Nobatia in northern Nubia, Makuria in central Nubia, and Alwa in southern Nubia. In the sixth century, missionaries converted the kingdoms to Christianity. In the seventh century, Makuria absorbed Nobatia. Makuria was also known as Dongola, after its capital.

The growth of Islam in the eighth century left the Christian kingdoms surrounded by hostile Moslem powers. Makuria managed to maintain its Christian identity until the 14th century, and Alwa survived until the early 16th century when it was destroyed and replaced by the Moslem Sennar kingdom.

Meanwhile, Axum had adopted Christianity in the fourth century. Moslem pressure after the eighth century forced the Axumites to fall back into the Ethiopian highlands. From there, the Ethiopian empire later emerged and expanded in the 13th century.

In the later Middle Ages, European contact with Ethiopia began. Hearing of the isolated Christian country from Ethiopian pilgrims in the Holy Land, the Dominicans sent representatives to Ethiopia in the early 14th century. Strong military and diplomatic ties with Portugal were established in the 15th and 16th centuries.

Central and West Sudanic Kingdoms. From ancient times, the western part of the Sudan (the grassland belt south of the Sahara) engaged in trade with North Africa. The central Sudan also had contact with the north and, in addition, traded with Egypt and Nubia. At first goods were transported by donkey or horse, but after the camel was introduced into the Sahara from Egypt early in the Christian era, the camel caravan became the means of transport.

Ivory Sculpture from Benin. This 16th-century ceremonial bell was used in rituals to designate prisoners for sacrifice. The face of the bell shows the king of Benin and attendants.
The Brooklyn Museum

The principal trade commodities were salt from North Africa and gold from the western Sudan. Much of the gold came from coastal areas farther south and was accumulated in Sudanese cities before its shipment across the desert. Later, ivory and slaves from the western and central Sudan were traded for metal tools, cotton goods, and horses.

Strong and extensive kingdoms grew up around the great sub-Saharan trading centers. The populations of these kingdoms were predominantly black, with some Caucasian mixture. Most of the urban people were, or later became, Moslems. Many of the country people remained animistic in religious belief. Most of the kingdoms were urban in character, with complex political organization. They had well-trained cavalry units, which in time of war were supplemented by mass armies of conscripts.

Among the earliest of the western kingdoms was Ghana, lying between the Senegal and Niger rivers. Ghana was founded in the fifth or sixth century A.D. Of slightly later development was Kanem, which grew up around Lake Chad in the central Sudan. Of about the same age as Kanem were the Hausa city-states, such as Kano, Gobir, and Katsina, west and south of Kanem in what is now northern Nigeria.

The Berbers of the Sahara, who controlled the Saharan trade routes, gradually penetrated the sub-Saharan grasslands. In the 11th century, a group of Berbers (the Almoravid Moslems) conquered Ghana. Although Ghana recovered its independence, it never regained commercial dominance and had broken up into a number of petty states by the early 13th century.

With the fall of Ghana, the Mali kingdom emerged as the leading power in the western Sudan. Its inhabitants, the Mandingo people, were converted to Islam in the 14th century. The empire encompassed a vast area from the Atlantic coast east to Timbuktu, a Berber trading city on the Niger that became a center of Moslem scholarship. At times Mali had possession of Gao, a trading city of the Songhai people east of Timbuktu.

Mali went into decline in the late 14th century. In 1375 the Songhai threw off Mali domination, and began pressuring the empire from the east. From the north the Tuareg (a Berber people) seized cities, including Timbuktu, and from the south the Mossi people made raids on Mali. The empire was gradually reduced to a small state, and Gao became the center of a rapidly growing Songhai empire that by 1500 controlled the western Sudan. (See also SONGHAI.)

Meanwhile, in the central Sudan during the 14th century, Kanem emerged as a powerful state, the Kanem-Bornu empire. It became noted for its large standing army—cavalry and infantry uniformed in quilted armor and chain mail. Kanem-Bornu grew prosperous from the export of slaves to the north and east. The empire continued to expand after 1500. (See SUDAN [region].)

In the 15th century, the Portuguese began exploration of the Atlantic coast. They colonized the Cape Verde Islands in the 1460's and established trading contacts with the western Sudanic kingdoms.

Guinea. About the beginning of the Christian era Asiatic food plants, including the banana and the yam, were introduced into Africa. Suitable for tropical culture, they became the basis of a forest civilization. As the population of the Sudan swelled, tribes at the southern edge moved down the rivers toward the coast, taking with them Sudanic political and social patterns.

Since the Arabs who traded with the Sudanic kingdoms did not travel as far as Guinea, records for this area are extremely scarce. It appears that some of the early kingdoms, such as Bono and Banda along the Volta River and Yoruba and Benin along the lower Niger, were probably founded about the 13th century and were located first at the northern edge of the forest. By some 200 years later they were within the forest.

Active trade was carried on with the Sudan, kingdoms west of the Volta dealing mainly with Ghana and Mali and those to the east with the Hausa states and Kanem-Bornu. Guinea's major exports were gold, kola nuts, and ivory. Imports were salt, copper, horses, and cattle. Cloth and beads, in common use throughout Guinea, were both imported and exported. There is no record of a Guinea slave trade before the Europeans came to the coast, although the Sudan had then been supplying slaves to North Africa for several centuries. The forest kingdoms became more powerful after the beginning of the European slave trade, for which the native rulers provided slaves.

The Portuguese reached the Senegal River

Temple Ruins are among the remains of Zimbabwe, capital of a succession of Bantu states. The city was established in the 11th century and abandoned by the early 19th century.

in 1445 and the island of Fernando Po in 1472. Their trading station of Elmina, on the Gold Coast, was founded in 1482. A port for Benin in the west delta of the Niger was opened in 1486.

The Bantu States. Only fragmentary knowledge exists of the early history of the Bantu-speaking peoples, who occupy most of Africa south of a line from Cameroon to southern Ethiopia. On linguistic evidence it appears that they originated in the area of modern Cameroon and migrated eastward and southward. Apparently a great population expansion and dispersal occurred around the beginning of the Christian era.

The great Kongo kingdom at the mouth of the Congo River came to power about 1400. The Portuguese discovered this river and made coastal explorations in 1482-86. In 1491 Portuguese missionaries and craftsmen arrived in Kongo and began creating a Christian kingdom, based on the capital of San Salvador. It declined during the late 17th and 18th centuries.

Northwest of Lake Victoria, Bantu-speaking peoples established a strong kingdom called Bunyoro (or Kitara) during the 14th century. It ruled what is now Uganda. In the 16th century the kingdom of Buganda began to vie with Bunyoro for control of the region, and by the early 19th century it was the dominant power. Further south there were a number of smaller kingdoms—Ankole, Burundi, and Rwanda.

Centered in the upper Zambezi Valley was the Shona (or Rozwi) confederation. In the 11th century the Shona built a city called Zimbabwe to serve as their capital. During the 15th and 16th centuries, Zimbabwe was the capital of the Mutapa Empire (named

Historical Pictures Service, Chicago
Slave Market. In the 19th century, Europeans bought slaves at African ports. Most slaves had been captured in raids into Africa's interior.

after the Shona leader, Mutapa), which covered all of the present-day countries of Zimbabwe and Mozambique. Its prosperity was based on the export of gold to the east. The empire went into decline in the 16th century and eventually Zimbabwe was abandoned.

The Eastern Coast. From very early times Arab sailors visited the upper east coast of Africa to trade iron implements for ivory. From Africa came also palm oil, rhinoceros horn, and frankincense. The Arabs transported this merchandise to the Mediterranean countries by way of the Red Sea and to Arabia, Persia, and India across the Indian Ocean. The Chinese were also involved in this early trade. (Axum, an Ethiopian kingdom built on this trade, was discussed earlier in this section, under the subtitle *Sub-Saharan Africa to 1500:* Kingdom of Kush.)

There is no mention of Negro inhabitants or of slave trade in the early records of the east coast. As the Bantu population expanded eastward, however, black slaves became an item of trade throughout the Indian Ocean area. Indonesians, who had colonized Madagascar, dominated the trade routes from the 8th century to the 12th.

In about the eighth century, Moslems began to found settlements along the coast. Some of these were communities of Arabian refugees from religious conflicts within the Islamic world. Others were trade settlements established by Persian and Arab merchants. Malindi, Mombasa, Kilwa, Mozambique, and Sofala—the major gold port for Zimbabwe—were among important coastal cities. In the 13th century Arab seafarers gained control of the Indian Ocean, and east Africa was absorbed into the Islamic world.

Beginning of Foreign Exploitation

The Portuguese. When Bartholomeu Dias rounded the southern tip of Africa in 1488, Portugal had achieved its direct water route to the East Indies. It had also, on the way south, established itself on Africa's Gold Coast and at the mouth of the Congo. In 1493 Pope Alexander VI drew the Line of Demarcation, which gave Portugal exclusive rights to explore and trade in Africa.

Before the turn of the century the Portuguese had discovered the gold and the rich trade of the east coast. They seized Kilwa and Mozambique in 1502 and Zanzibar in 1503. Under Francisco de Almeida the rest of the coastal cities were brought to submission by 1510. Fortified trading stations were built on both coasts.

Other European Nations. For a century no European nation had the sea power to challenge Portugal in Africa. Then in 1598 the Netherlands founded two posts on the Gold Coast. During the 17th century the English settled at the mouth of the Gambia River; the French at the mouth of the Senegal River; the English and Danes along the Gold Coast. The Dutch established themselves also at the Cape of Good Hope. The Portuguese were largely driven from Africa, retaining only their settlements south of the Gambia (Portuguese Guinea), south of the Congo (Angola), and around the Zambezi (Mozambique).

At first the coastal trade was mainly in ivory and gold, although Portugal also supplied slaves to the Latin American colonies. As the sugar plantations of the West Indies were developed, the demand for slave labor grew enormously, and ship captains learned that the most profitable cargo was slaves. The Dutch became dominant in the slave trade when Portuguese power declined, but by the end of the 18th century British ships were carrying more than half the slaves to America.

Inland raids by the coastal tribes to provide slaves for the traders brought perpetual warfare. Meanwhile Morocco seized the gold trade of the western Sudan. The Songhai empire disintegrated, and chaos prevailed. There were tribal migrations, and new kingdoms arose.

Moslem Africa. Ottoman Turks occupied Egypt in 1517. Turkish corsairs (sea raiders) quickly gained control of the Red Sea and of the North African coast as far west as Morocco, with the exception of Oran, which was seized and held by Spain. Tripoli, Tunis, and Algiers became administrative centers in the Ottoman Empire, but under the bold rule of the corsairs they were virtually autonomous. Trade connections with the Sudan were established from the Maghrib, and with the southern Nile Valley from Egypt. Ethiopia, with aid from Portugal, successfully defended itself against the Turks. Morocco also repelled Turkish attacks, as well as those of Spain, although the Spanish won control of a few ports.

On the east coast the previously Arab ports north of Cape Delgado were taken back from Portugal by the Arabs of Oman during the latter half of the 17th century. African slaves were transported by the Arabs throughout the Indian Ocean area and by the Turks and the corsairs throughout the Mediterranean area. The Barbary corsairs also harassed shipping in the Mediterranean. (See also BARBARY.)

Exploration and Colonization

Exploration. By the end of the 18th century a strong antislavery feeling was developing among Western nations. Establishment of Christian mission stations in Africa, beginning in 1792, was an expression of this growing moral concern. During the 19th century the western slave trade was gradually abolished, although the Arab trade in the east lingered on into the 20th century. Early exploration of the interior of the continent was undertaken for humanitarian and scientific as well as for political reasons.

Mungo Park led an expedition into the western Sudan in 1795-97 for a British association (later called the Royal Geographical Society). His second journey in 1805-06 was sponsored by the British government. The government also sent the Denham-Clapperton-Oudney expedition from Tripoli across the Sahara in 1823-25; Richard and John Lander to the Niger River in 1830-31; and Heinrich Barth across the Sahara to the Sudan in 1850-55. A Frenchman, René Caillié, in 1827-29 was the first European to visit Timbuktu and return. The German missionaries Johann Krapf and Johannes Rebmann discovered Mount Kilimanjaro in 1848. Between 1862 and 1869 Gerhardt Rohlfs crossed North Africa from Agadir to Cairo.

Outstanding among the explorers was the Scottish missionary David Livingstone, who

British Information Services

"Dr. Livingstone, I Presume?" is what H. M. Stanley (center, left) is reputed to have said when he located Livingstone at Lake Tanganyika in 1871.

during his residence in Africa, 1841-73, traveled extensively in the southern area. Henry M. Stanley gained fame by locating Livingstone in the interior in 1871, and went on to make important explorations of his own. In the meantime John Hanning Speke discovered Lake Victoria in 1858 and in 1862 proved it to be the source of the Nile.

Colonization. Except for the Dutch colony at Cape Town, for more than two centuries the Europeans had no territorial ambitions in Africa. Two native states were founded on the west coast by antislavery groups— Sierra Leone by the British in 1788 and Liberia by Americans in 1821. The Cape Colony passed to Britain in 1814.

The first move toward building a colonial empire in Africa was the French occupation of Algeria in 1830. The Danes and the Dutch, having given up the slave trade, relinquished their Guinea stations to the British in mid-century, and in 1874 Britain declared the Gold Coast a colony. France established a protectorate over Tunisia in 1881, and Britain began occupying Egypt in 1882, while Belgium took control of the Congo basin.

The rivalry among European powers for possession of African territory became so intense that the Berlin Conference (1884-85) was called to settle the claims. Free trade was established in the Congo basin, but most of the rest of the continent was divided into European spheres of influence.

The Germans established themselves in Togoland, the Cameroons, South-West Africa, and what is now Tanganyika (Tanzania). North Africa was gradually occupied by the French. The Spanish held the coast southwest of Morocco, and the Italians were in Somaliland and Eritrea.

Historical Pictures Service, Chicago

Boer War. Contemporary drawing shows British troops cheering surrender of General Piet Arnoldus Cronje after the Battle of Paardeberg in 1900.

Under the urging of Cecil Rhodes, Great Britain annexed Bechuanaland, and Rhodes himself took over Zambezia. Great Britain increased its African holdings further by crushing the Dutch colonists of South Africa in the Boer War of 1899-1902 and annexing the Transvaal and the Orange Free State. In 1910 these two states became part of the Union of South Africa. Two years earlier Belgium had taken possession of the Congo Free State.

The Turkish-Italian War of 1911-12 resulted in victorious Italy acquiring Tripoli

Ethiopian War. Ras Nasibu, Ethiopian general, center, inspects a captured Italian tank in 1935.
United Press International

and Cyrenaica and forming them into Libya. At the start of World War I in 1914, only Liberia and Ethiopia remained independent. After the war the German colonies were mandated to France, Great Britain, Belgium, and Portugal. Ethiopia was seized by Italy in 1935.

For further details of the colonial era, see the articles on the various African nations.

Independence Movement

North Africa. The Africans of the Mediterranean region, with access to education and exposure to modern attitudes, began working for independence in the 1920's. The movement in Tunisia had such success before World War II that its leader, Habib Bourguiba, was jailed by the French. The war broadened North Africa's contacts and created greater restlessness. Formation in 1945 of the Arab League encouraged the Moslem countries in their desire for national sovereignty.

Libya, lost by Italy in the war, became independent in 1951, and Eritrea joined Ethiopia in a federation in 1952. Guerrilla warfare started in Tunisia in 1952, the Algerian war began in 1954, and a revolt broke out in Morocco in 1955. Tunisia and Morocco were granted independence by France in 1956, and Algeria achieved nationhood in 1962.

Sub-Saharan Africa. The general practice of colonial governments in central and southern Africa was to maintain nonwhites in a menial position, deny them virtually all voice in government, and make little or no effort to improve their way of life. The fact that colonialism was no longer commercially profitable was very apparent during the world-wide depression of the 1930's. The demand for minerals, rubber, and other products in World War II revived the economy. Not only did Africa provide valuable resources, but it was recognized as a promising new market. The European colonial powers found it advantageous after the war to concern themselves with the education and social welfare of their African subjects.

A nationalistic fervor developed rapidly among the Africans, and demands for independence began to be voiced. The Mau Mau uprisings in Kenya in the early 1950's were one of the most violent expressions of discontent. Great Britain gave independence to Sudan in 1956 and Ghana in 1957, and in 1958 France made Guinea a nation. Seventeen independent nations were created in

Independence of African Nations

DATE	NAME	COLONIAL POWER
1910	South Africa*	Great Britain
1922	Egypt†	Great Britain
1941	Ethiopia‡	Italy
1951	Libya	Italy
1956	Morocco	France
	Sudan	Great Britain
	Tunisia	France
1957	Ghana	Great Britain
1958	Guinea	France
1960	Benin	France
	Cameroon§	France
	Central African Republic	France
	Chad	France
	Congo	France
	Gabon	France
	Ivory Coast	France
	Madagascar	France
	Mali	France
	Mauritania	France
	Niger	France
	Nigeria§	Great Britain
	Senegal	France
	Somalia	Italy and Great Britain
	Togo	France
	Upper Volta	France
	Zaire	Belgium
1961	Sierra Leone	Great Britain
	Tanganyika**	Great Britain
1962	Algeria	France
	Burundi	Belgium
	Rwanda	Belgium
	Uganda	Great Britain
1963	Kenya	Great Britain
	Zanzibar**	Great Britain
1964	Malawi	Great Britain
	Zambia	Great Britain
1965	Gambia	Great Britain
1966	Botswana	Great Britain
	Lesotho	Great Britain
1968	Swaziland	Great Britain
	Equatorial Guinea	Spain
1974	Guinea-Bissau	Portugal
1975	Mozambique	Portugal
	São Tomé and Príncipe	Portugal
	Cape Verde	Portugal
	Angola	Portugal
1976	Comoros	France
1977	Djibouti	France
1980	Zimbabwe††	Great Britain

*Became a dominion of the British Empire under the name Union of South Africa. Upon becoming a republic in 1961, it withdrew from the Commonwealth.
†British troops were not withdrawn until 1936.
‡Had been independent until 1935.
§Acquired part of British Cameroons in 1961.
**Tanganyika and Zanzibar joined together in 1964 to become Tanzania.
††Zimbabwe had been independent as Rhodesia, 1965-79.

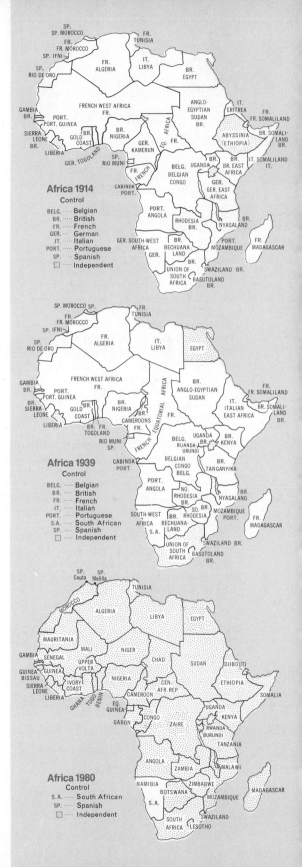

A-127

British Information Services
Independence Day in Ghana, one of Africa's first independent nations (1957). Kwame Nkrumah, then prime minister, opens the national parliament.

sub-Saharan Africa in 1960, and more followed. The new African nations tended to collaborate with the newly independent Asian countries in international politics, especially in the United Nations. (See also AFRO-ASIAN BLOC.)

The African Nations

Within a few years after independence, most of the democratically established African governments had been upset in coups and replaced by dictatorships or military rule. Political instability was primarily the result of weak economies and tribal loyalties that prevented national unity. In Nigeria, tribal conflict led to a devastating civil war (1967-70). During the 1970's, continuing drought in the sub-Saharan countries caused famine and unrest.

Trade and economic development in Africa was promoted by a number of regional organizations. The largest was the Economic Community of West African States (ECOWAS), formed in 1975.

In southern Africa, black liberation movements arose in the 1960's against white-dominated governments. They achieved significant success in 1975 when Mozambique and Angola won independence and in 1980 when Rhodesia became independent as Zimbabwe. Only South Africa and South-West Africa remained under white minority rule.

For further information, see:

Land

AGULHAS, CAPE	LIBYAN DESERT
ATLAS MOUNTAINS	QATTARA DEPRESSION
CAPE OF GOOD HOPE	RUWENZORI
KALAHARI DESERT	SAHARA
KENYA, MOUNT	SINAI PENINSULA
KILIMANJARO, MOUNT	TANEZROUFT

A-128

TÉNÉRÉ	TIBESTI

Water

ALBERT, LAKE	RUDOLF, LAKE
CHAD, LAKE	SENEGAL RIVER
CONGO RIVER	SUEZ CANAL
EDWARD, LAKE	TANA, LAKE
LIMPOPO RIVER	TANGANYIKA, LAKE
MOZAMBIQUE CHANNEL	UBANGI RIVER
NIGER RIVER	VICTORIA, LAKE
NILE RIVER	VICTORIA FALLS
NYASA, LAKE	ZAMBEZI RIVER
ORANGE RIVER	

History

AFRICAN SLAVE TRADE	HENRY THE
ALEXANDER THE	NAVIGATOR
GREAT	LIVINGSTONE, DAVID
ARAB LEAGUE	MOORS
ARIANISM	NUBIA
ATHANASIUS, Saint	NUMIDIA
AUGUSTINE, Saint	PARK, MUNGO
BARBARY	PRESTER JOHN
BURTON, Sir RICHARD	PTOLEMIES
FRANCIS	RHODESIA AND
CARTHAGE	NYASALAND,
DIAS, BARTHOLOMEU	FEDERATION OF
DIDO	RUANDA-URUNDI
DONATISM	SCHWEITZER, ALBERT
EGYPT, ANCIENT	SPEKE, JOHN
FRENCH EQUATORIAL	HANNING
AFRICA	STANLEY, Sir HENRY
FRENCH WEST AFRICA	MORTON
GAMA, VASCO DA	UTICA
HAMILCAR BARCA	VANDALS
HANNIBAL	

Miscellaneous

ASWAN DAM	ORGANIZATION OF
LITERATURE,	AFRICAN UNITY
AFRICAN	SIROCCO

Books about Africa

Davidson, Basil. *Africa: History of a Continent,* revised edition (Macmillan, 1972).
The Encyclopedia of Africa (Watts, 1976).
Fage, J. D. *A History of Africa* (Knopf, 1978).
Hiernaux, Jean. *The People of Africa* (Scribner's, 1975).
Jefferson, Margo, and E. P. Skinner. *Roots of Time: a Portrait of African Life and Culture* (Doubleday, 1974).
July, R. W. *A History of the African People,* 3rd edition (Scribner's, 1980).
Legum, Colin, and others. *Africa in the 1980's: a Continent in Crisis* (McGraw-Hill, 1979).
McEvedy, Colin. *Atlas of African History* (Facts on File, 1980).
Martin, P. M., and Patrick O'Meara, editors. *Africa* (Indiana University, 1978).
Sagay, J. O., and D. A. Wilson. *Africa: a Modern History, 1800-1975* (Holmes & Meier, 1979).

For Younger Readers:

Couffer, Jack and Mike. *African Summer,* revised edition (Putnam's, 1976).
Jenness, Aylette. *Along the Niger River: an African Way of Life* (Lippincott & Crowell, 1974).
Murphy, E. J. *Understanding Africa,* revised edition (Lippincott & Crowell, 1978).
Wellman, Alice. *Africa's Animals: Creatures of a Struggling Land* (Putnam's, 1974).

African Elephant. See ELEPHANT, subtitle *Types of Elephants*.

African Goose. See GOOSE, subtitle *Domestic Geese*.

African Methodist Episcopal Church. See METHODISTS, subtitle *Organization: Other Methodist Bodies*.

African Slave Trade, the gathering, transport, and sale of blacks from tropical Africa to other lands. The sale of blacks into slavery at commercial centers in North Africa and the Middle East lasted for thousands of years. The sale of blacks from western Africa to the New World took place from the 16th through the 19th century. Unrivaled in volume, this Atlantic slave trade transported millions of men, women, and children to the Americas to meet labor needs there. The traffic brought misery to its victims, but African slave labor also played an important part in the settlement of the New World and the growing prosperity of Europe.

The Atlantic Slave Trade

The origins of the Atlantic slave trade lay in the pioneering Portuguese voyages of the 15th century that made known the west coast of Africa. In 1444, Portuguese sailors captured some coastal Africans and brought them back to Lisbon. A thriving slave trade soon developed in Portugal.

Shipment of African slaves to America began by 1517. Spanish officials had discovered that Caribbean natives were dying off because they were unsuited for heavy labor. Africans were found to be hardier and more capable of doing heavy work. Perhaps 900,000 Africans reached America in the 16th century.

During the 17th century a large European market developed for such cash crops as sugar, cotton, coffee, and tobacco, which were grown in Brazil, the West Indies, and the English colonies of southeastern North America. As demand for plantation labor increased, the traffic in slaves swelled. The Portuguese, who were the first slavers (carriers in the slave traffic), were supplanted by the Dutch, who were in turn replaced by the English and French.

It is estimated that about 2,750,000 slaves were brought to the Americas during the 17th century and 7,000,000 during the 18th century.

The Operation in Africa. European slavers did not themselves capture the Africans they transported, but bought them from native slave traders. Since ancient times, war captives, criminals, and debtors in Africa had been sold into slavery among their own people. For several centuries the western Sudanese kingdoms had been supplying slaves to Moslem North Africa on a commercial basis. When European traders first came to the Guinea coast, African masters sold them their own slaves. As the demand increased, the coastal tribes began making slave raids against peoples farther inland, aided by firearms supplied by the traders. Soon blacks belonging to a variety of tribes from Senegal south to Angola were being enslaved in great numbers.

Captured slaves were marched to the sea in single file, shackled and watched by armed African guards. Fatalities were high on the grim journey. The slaves were placed in compounds at points along the coast, where European traders arriving by ship would examine them and reject the old and infirm. The remaining captives were branded and taken on board. Payment for slaves was in goods such as textiles, firearms, knives and other hardware, and liquor.

African Slave Trade. Slaves crowded on deck of a small sailing vessel seized for violation of importation law and brought into Key West in 1860.

Library of Congress

African kingdoms such as Ashanti and Dahomey grew in power through the slave trade, because of the European goods they received. However, western Africa as a whole suffered from slave wars and the depopulation of wide areas through slave raids. Also, the Africans did not learn new productive skills from their contact with Europeans; rather, their own production of articles declined with the bringing in of European goods.

The Middle Passage. For sea captains engaged in the slave trade, the voyage across the Atlantic was the "middle passage" in a triangular trade route. An English trader, for example, would typically sail from Liverpool with goods that Africans would accept in payment for slaves. After collecting the slaves, he would transport them to the West Indies or the North American mainland and barter them for supplies such as molasses or tobacco, which he would then take back to England for sale. A successful voyage brought extremely high profits.

The middle passage was a dreadful ordeal for the slaves. They spent most of the voyage below deck, manacled and tightly packed in cramped positions. They were allowed on deck only for short periods of exercise. About one of every six died on the ocean voyage. Between the time of their capture and delivery in America, probably one slave died for each one who arrived in the New World.

At the end of the middle passage the slaves were sold to slave dealers or individual owners. American ports had slave markets where Africans were auctioned off. Until the 18th century, almost all the markets were in Brazil or the West Indies. The English mainland colonies usually bought their slaves from West Indian owners. After 1700, Charleston, South Carolina, became a busy port of call for slave ships from Africa, the largest on the mainland.

Suppression of the Trade. By about 1785, more than half the slaves sent across the Atlantic were being shipped by British sea captains. Protests by British humanitarians such as William Wilberforce grew, however, until Britain abolished the slave trade in 1807. Gradually, British diplomatic pressure forced other nations to ban the traffic officially. Foreign governments were reluctant to enforce the ban, however, and made little effort to do so.

A-130

In the United States, Congress forbade the importation of slaves after 1808, but the ban was not effectively enforced. Indeed, a thriving illegal trade developed as cotton plantations became the economic foundation of the South. The Atlantic slave trade was only truly stamped out after the American Civil War. From 1800 until the effective suppression of the trade, an estimated 4,000,000 slaves entered the Americas.

During the 350 years of the Atlantic slave trade, about 15,000,000 Africans were transported to the Americas. The West Indies became predominantly populated by blacks, while Brazil, Central America, and the southern United States acquired a substantial black population.

East African Slave Trade

Slave shipments across the Indian Ocean began before the Christian Era. As a wealthy Moslem civilization developed during the eighth century A.D., Arab traders began to send a steady stream of slaves from East African ports to the markets of Turkey, Arabia, India, and Persia. The Arab traders were more brutal than Europeans and knew far less about how to keep the slaves from dying of disease. For every five blacks captured in the African interior, perhaps only one reached the Middle East markets.

In the 19th century, the island of Zanzibar and the port of Kilwa on the mainland slightly to the south became the largest African shipping points for the trade. Arab slavers began to penetrate farther and farther inland, as far as Uganda and the Congo, in search of slaves.

British pressure finally forced Zanzibar's ruler, in 1873, to close his slave markets and forbid the export of slaves from his dominions. However, enforcement was not easy, until an agreement was made by the great powers in 1890 to police the coast effectively. As late as the 1970's, the United Nations was receiving complaints of a thriving trade in black slaves in East Africa.

African Violet, or **Saintpaulia,** a flowering perennial plant native to tropical Africa. It is not a true violet, but is related to gloxinia. It is named Saintpaulia for its discoverer, Baron Walter von Saint Paul. The African violet is popular as a potted house plant in the United States. Hundreds of varieties have been developed.

The hairy, often stemless plant reaches about five inches (12.5 cm) in height. Its oval or heart-shaped leaves grow on long stalks and have scalloped, toothed, or nearly smooth margins. The unscented flowers are about one inch (2.5 cm) wide. They grow on single or branching stalks, which may reach four inches (10 cm) in height and bear up to six flowers each. The petals are violet in the wild form, but in potted varieties range in color from purple to pink and white.

African violets grow best in fertile, well-drained soil. They may be injured by direct light, over-watering, or excessive cold. New plants are started from seeds, leaf cuttings, side shoots, or divisions of old plants.

The 11 species of Saintpaulia belong to the family Gesneriaceae. The common African violet is *Saintpaulia ionantha*.

Tinari Greenhouses

African Violet

Afrika Korps (Africa Corps), a World War II German army organization that fought in North Africa, 1941-42. Its principal units were the 15th and 21st Panzer (armored) divisions and the 90th Light Division. Attached were seven Italian divisions, including one armored division. Under the able generalship of Field Marshal General Erwin Rommel this small striking force won many victories, notably the capture of Tobruk on June 21, 1942.

The Afrika Korps was halted at the end of June by the British 8th Army under General Claude Auchinleck, and was turned back by the same army under General Bernard Montgomery, at the Battle of El Alamein, October 23-November 3, 1942. After the Allied invasion of western North Africa the Axis forces were reorganized as Army Group Africa. In March, 1943, Rommel was succeeded by Jürgen von Arnim, who surrendered on May 12, 1943.

See also EL ALAMEIN, BATTLE OF; ROMMEL, ERWIN; WORLD WAR II, section "Other Fronts, 1940-41," subtitle *North African Campaigns, 1940-41,* and section "The War with Germany and Italy, 1942-45," subtitles *North African Campaign, 1942* and *African Invasion, 1942-43.*

Afrikaners. See BOERS.

Afro-Americans. See BLACK AMERICANS.

Afro-Asian Bloc, in international politics, a number of African and Asian nations that consult informally on matters of mutual concern. These nations, most of which did not achieve their independence until after World War II, are generally underdeveloped and nonaligned in the rivalry between the Western democracies and the Communist nations. By coordinating their policies when in agreement, they can exert much influence on world affairs.

The collaboration of the Afro-Asian countries is most evident in the United Nations. In the General Assembly, where each country has one vote, nations from Africa and Asia make up a majority of the membership and form the largest voting bloc.

The first formal consultation of independent Asian and African nations took place at Bandung, Indonesia, in 1955. Since that first meeting Afro-Asian states have conferred frequently, both informally and formally.

Some African and Asian countries are also members of regional organizations, such as the League of Arab States (founded in 1945) and the Organization of African Unity (1963), which attempt to further common goals.

See also ARAB LEAGUE; COLD WAR, subtitle *History:* Peaceful Coexistence, 1955-60; NEUTRALISM.

AFS International/Intercultural Programs, an organization that provides students 16 to 18 years of age with scholarships for study in foreign countries. Each year more than 3,000 students from 80 foreign countries attend high school while living with American host families. American students live abroad during the summer.

AFS was organized in 1914 as a volunteer ambulance unit in France and was called American Field Service. It was reactivated during World War II, serving the French and British forces. In 1947, the organization began its scholarship program, and in 1978 adopted its present name. Headquarters are in New York City.

Afterburner. See JET PROPULSION, subtitle *Types of Jet Engines:* The Ramjet.

Afterdamp. See DAMP.

Afterimage. See COLOR, subtitle *Complementary Colors.*

Aga Khan, ä′gȧ kän′, the title of the imam, or spiritual leader, of the Ismaili sect of Islam. These hereditary rulers claim descent from Mohammed through his daughter Fatima and son-in-law Ali.

Aga Khan I (Hasan Ali Shah; 1800-1881). A native of Persia (Iran), he received his title from the shah. While serving as governor of a province he led an unsuccessful revolt. He fled to India, where many of his followers lived.

Aga Khan II (Ali Shah; ?-1885), imam 1881-85. He succeeded his father, and was succeeded by his son.

Aga Khan III (Sultan Sir Mohammed Shah; 1877-1957), imam 1885-1957. An international sportsman, he lived mostly in Europe. Although known outside the Moslem world mainly for his immense wealth and for his horse breeding and racing, he was an effective leader of his people. Concerned that the Moslem minority would be subject to persecution in an independent India, he supported British rule. He was a founder of the All-India Moslem League. He headed India's delegation to the League of Nations (1932; 1934-37) and was president of the League's Assembly in 1937.

Aga Khan IV (Karim Al Hassaini Shah; 1937-   ), imam 1957-   . The son of Prince Aly Khan, he was nominated to the imamate by his grandfather, Aga Khan III. He was born in Switzerland and graduated from Harvard University after becoming imam. He is a British subject.

Agade. See AKKADIANS.

Agamemnon, ăg′à-měm′nŏn, in Greek legendary history, a king of Mycenae and commander in chief of the Greek forces in the Trojan War. He was the son of Atreus, and a brother of King Menelaus of Sparta. Iphigenia and Electra were his daughters; Orestes was his son. Paris, son of King Priam of Troy, carried away Menelaus' wife, Helen. Agamemnon was leader of the army that assembled to avenge his sister-in-law's abduction.

When Agamemnon deprived Achilles, the Greek hero, of a beautiful female captive named Briseis, Achilles wrathfully withdrew from the fight and sulked in his tent.

Louis Agassiz
Harvard
University

The quarrel between Agamemnon and Achilles provides the central theme for the opening of Homer's *Iliad.*

After the sack of Troy, Agamemnon returned to Mycenae. According to Aeschylus, he was murdered there by his wife, Clytemnestra, at the urging of her lover, Aegisthus. Homer, however, names Aegisthus as the murderer.

In the latter half of the 19th century, the German archeologist Heinrich Schliemann uncovered the ruins of both Troy and Mycenae. Schliemann believed that he had discovered the tomb of Agamemnon. Actually, the tombs that he excavated were several centuries older than the era of the Trojan War. His findings and those of later archeologists indicate, however, that Agamemnon and other Homeric heroes may have been historical characters.

See also AESCHYLUS, subtitle *His Plays;* CLYTEMNESTRA; ILIAD, THE, AND THE ODYSSEY, subtitle *The Iliad;* IPHIGENIA; MYCENAE; MYCENAEAN CIVILIZATION; ORESTES; TROJAN WAR.

Agar, or **Agar-agar.** See ALGAE, subtitle *Economic Importance.*

Agassiz, ăg′à-sē, the family name of two scientists, father and son.

(Jean) **Louis** (Rodolphe) **Agassiz** (1807-1873), the father, was a Swiss-American naturalist and educator. He was an authority on ichthyology (the study of fish) and geology. Agassiz was the first to set forth the theory, based on his observations of the movement of glaciers, of the earlier existence of a great Ice Age, during which an ice sheet covered much of the Northern Hemisphere. An influential teacher and lecturer, he gave impetus to the study of natural history in the United States. Lake Agassiz was named in his honor.

Louis Agassiz was born in Môtier-en-Vuly, Switzerland. He received a degree in medicine from the University of Munich in 1830, but his major interest was zoology.

His first published work was *Fishes of Brazil* (1829). In 1832 Agassiz became professor of natural history at Neuchatel. He gained renown for his *Researches on Fossil Fishes* (5 volumes, 1833-44) and *Fresh Water Fishes of Central Europe* (1839-42). He studied the glaciers of the Alps with the geographer Arnold Henry Guyot and published his theories in *Études sur les Glaciers* (2 volumes, 1840).

In 1846 Agassiz came to the United States to lecture at the Lowell Institute in Boston. He accepted the chair of natural history at Harvard in 1848, a post he held until his death. He also taught for brief periods at a medical school in Charleston, South Carolina, and at Cornell University. In 1858 Agassiz established the Museum of Comparative Zoology at Harvard. A minister's son, he was the leading opponent in the United States of Darwin's theory of evolution. He became a United States citizen in 1861. Combining research with teaching, Agassiz made a series of geological and zoological expeditions, 1865-71.

His other books include *Système Glaciaire* (1846) and *Contributions to the Natural History of the United States* (4 volumes, 1857-62).

Alexander Agassiz (1835-1910), the son, was a United States naturalist. After amassing a fortune in copper mining, Agassiz devoted his time and his wealth to zoological research. From 1875 to 1904 he conducted a series of zoological explorations in Caribbean and Pacific waters. These expeditions produced valuable marine animal collections, improved techniques of deep-sea research, and knowl-

Chicago Historical Society
Alexander Agassiz

edge of the formation of coral reefs and the configuration of ocean beds and continental shelves.

Alexander Agassiz was born in Neuchatel, Switzerland. He came to the United States in 1849. After being graduated from Harvard in 1855, he did further study in engineering and chemistry. In 1867 Agassiz became superintendent of the Calumet and Hecla copper mines at Lake Superior. He developed these deposits into the most valuable copper mines in the world. From 1872 to 1876 Agassiz helped arrange the collec-

A-133

tions made during the oceanographic expedition of the British ship *Challenger*. In 1874 he was appointed curator of the Museum of Comparative Zoology at Harvard, which his father founded and which he endowed.

His writings include: *Seaside Studies in Natural History* (1865), with Elizabeth Cabot Agassiz, his stepmother; *A Revision of the Echini* (2 volumes, 1872-74); *North American Starfishes* (1877).

Agassiz, Lake, a prehistoric glacial lake of North America. It existed temporarily near the end of the Pleistocene Epoch, or Ice Age. (See GLACIAL PERIOD.) Lake Agassiz centered around what is now Lake Winnipeg and covered parts of present-day Manitoba, Ontario, Saskatchewan, North Dakota, and Minnesota. At its greatest extent, the lake was about 650 miles long (north-south) and up to 400 miles wide. Total area was roughly 100,000 square miles, larger than that of the Great Lakes combined.

Lake Agassiz was formed when numerous northerly flowing rivers, including the Red River of the North, were blocked by the southern end of a continental ice sheet. For a thousand or more years the temporary ice dam impounded their water as well as water that was melted from the glacier. At that time the lake discharged southward into the Mississippi River by way of the Minnesota

Location of Lake Agassiz

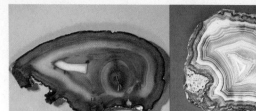

Banded Agate   **Fortification Agate**   **Moss Agate**

River Valley. Eventually the ice sheet re-treated far enough north to permit Lake Agassiz to drain into Hudson Bay. Remnants of this once giant body of water include Lakes Winnipeg, Winnipegosis, and Mani-toba, and Lake of the Woods. Its former bed is a belt of rich farmlands. It was named in 1879 for Louis Agassiz.

Agate, ăg′ĭt; ăg′ăt, a semiprecious variety of quartz valued both for its beauty and for its hardness. Pieces of agate range in size from that of a pea to more than two feet in diameter. Most forms of agate are *banded,* having numerous curved or irregular bands of varying widths and different colors. *For-tification agate* has angular bands that re-semble the plan of a fort. A variety of quartz called *onyx* is similar to banded agate, except that in onyx the bands are straight and paral-lel. (See ONYX.)

A form called *moss agate* contains dark, mosslike patterns on a milky or nearly trans-parent background. These patterns are caused by the presence of manganese oxide or other impurities. Some forms of agate have colored patterns that resemble familiar natural scenes and many have their colors arranged in irregular patterns.

All forms of agate take a high polish. Most of the agate used for ornamental pur-poses is artificially colored. Banded agate can be readily dyed in a variety of colors. Because the adjacent bands differ in their permeability to dye solutions, the dye pene-trates unevenly, giving rise to marked dif-ferences in appearance between bands.

Because of its hardness (6.5-7 on the Mohs scale), agate is used for such things as instrument bearings and grinding mortars. Because of its beauty agate is used in jewelry, bookends, paperweights, and other orna-ments.

A district in southern Brazil and northern Uruguay is a major source of agate; another is the area near Oldenburg in West Ger-many. In the United States, agate is obtained from the Pacific Coast and Rocky Mountain states, and from Texas.

A-134

Agate Fossil Beds National Monu-ment. See NATIONAL PARKS, section "United States."

Agave, á-gā′vê, in Greek mythology, the mother, by Echion, of King Pentheus of Thebes. She was the daughter of Cadmus and Harmonia. Pentheus opposed and for-bade the orgiastic rites practiced by the bac-chantes, female worshipers of Bacchus. Vengeful Bacchus caused Agave to join his cult. When she caught Pentheus spying on secret dances of the bacchantes, she led the other women in tearing him to pieces. She sometimes is represented as having mistaken Pentheus for a wild beast. The story of Aga-ve is told in *Bacchae,* a play by Euripides.

See also BACCHUS.

Agave, á-gā′vê, a genus of cactuslike plants belonging to the amaryllis family. There are more than 300 species. Agaves are native to the frost-free arid and semiarid areas of North and Central America. Some species are cultivated in other dry tropical areas. They are raised for ornament and for the fibers and beverages that can be made from their leaves.

The agave plant has either a short trunk —less than 10 feet tall—or no trunk at all. The spiny, swordlike leaves are gray or green. They grow in a cluster at the top of the trunk or in a rosette close to the ground. In larger species, the leaves are up to nine feet long; in the smallest species, about one foot.

The small, tubular agave flowers are greenish yellow. They often have an unpleas-ant odor. In most species, the flowers grow on a stalk up to 30 feet tall. They occur in loose clusters on branches of the stalk or in a continuous cluster along the stalk. Agaves reproduce by seeds, by sending out suckers (shoots that develop roots), or by producing bulbils (bulblike structures). They grow in well-drained, sandy soil.

Among the agaves used for ornament, the century plant, or American aloe, is popular. Its leaves form a low rosette and grow to be five to six feet long and about six inches wide. It produces a 20- to 30-foot-tall, branching flower stalk after it is about 15 years old. After flowering the century plant dies. (The origin of its name is the mistaken idea that it blossoms once in a century.)

The sisal and henequen agaves are the source of sisal and henequen fibers. Other fibers, such as istle, letona, and cantala, come from several agave species. The fibers are the veins of the leaves.

The sap and the leaves of some agaves are used in making alcoholic beverages— pulque, mescal, and tequila. The name *maguey* is given to several Mexican agaves used to make these beverages and fiber.

The agaves form one genus in the amaryllis family, Amaryllidaceae. The century plant is *Agave americana*.

See also PULQUE; SISAL; TEQUILA.

Agazzi, ȧ-gȧt′zē, Count **Angelo** (1936-), an Italian-American artist known primarily for his special technique of reverse painting on glass. This technique is based on methods used in the 13th century to create mosaics on the reverse side of Venetian glass.

Agazzi was born in Venice and studied fine arts in Paris and Venice. He came to the United States in 1965, becoming a citizen in 1969.

Age, a term for (1) periods of time, as in the history of man or of the earth, and (2) the length of time an organism has lived or normally lives, or the length of time an object or material has existed.

The Stone Age, Bronze Age, and Iron Age are broad stages in the development of civilization, named for the materials from which man made his tools. In the history of a country, an entire era is sometimes known by the name of a prominent person. Examples are the Age of Pericles in ancient Greece and the Elizabethan Age in 16th-century England. Periods in the history of Western thought are also sometimes called ages—the Age of Belief and the Age of Reason, for example. (See also GOLDEN AGE.)

Some periods of time in the history of the earth have been given the name *age*—for example, the Age of Reptiles. Geologists use the term *age* to mean a subdivision of an epoch. (See GEOLOGY, subtitle *Geologic Time: Time-Rock Units.*)

For methods used by archeologists, geologists, and other scientists to determine the age of an object or material, see ARCHEOLOGY, subtitle *The Archeologist's Work:* Classifying and Dating; GEOLOGY, subtitle *Historical Geology.*

Longevity and Aging

The *longevity* of an organism is its length of life, or life span. Longevity depends mainly on the organism's species. Large trees are the longest-lived organisms. Bristlecone pines and giant sequoias live thousands of years. Tortoises are probably the longest-lived animals, and man is the longest-lived mammal. When life spans differ for male and female (as they do in man), the female is usually the longer-lived.

Many species have a characteristic longevity—a fixed age at which most individuals would die through loss of vigor or completion of a genetically determined life cycle. *Aging,* gradual loss of vigor marked by increasing probability of death, sets an upper limit to longevity in warm-blooded animals (birds and mammals). Man's characteristic longevity is probably between 70 and 80 years, although some individuals live to be more than 100. Many species of cold-blooded animals (fishes, reptiles, amphibians, and invertebrates) and most plants also have a characteristic longevity. However, aging is either imperceptible or absent.

The average longevity of a group is the age most individuals in the group actually reach, as shown by mortality (death) rates. It may be sharply fixed, as for plants and animals that normally die soon after reproduction. Or it may vary greatly with conditions, as for organisms that are normally killed by predators or disease at an early age.

Average longevity in humans is often expressed as *life expectancy*—the number of years a person can expect to live under current conditions. A baby born in the United States today can expect to live about 70 years. Its life expectancy is 30 years longer than that of a baby born in India and more than twice the average life span of the ancient Greeks and Romans. See also GERIATRICS; MORTALITY; POPULATION, subtitle *Population Growth.*

For information about human age levels, see ADOLESCENCE; BABY; CHILD DEVELOPMENT; MINOR.

Age of Reason. See REASON, AGE OF.

Agee, ā′jē, **James** (1909-1955), a United States novelist, film critic, and poet. *A Death in the Family* (1957) is a novel about the accidental death of a Knoxville, Tennessee, father in the early 1900's and its tragic effects upon various members of his family. It was awarded the Pulitzer Prize for fiction in 1958. (*All the Way Home,* a dramatization by Tad Mosel, was awarded the 1961 Pulitzer Prize for drama.)

Agee was born in Knoxville, Tennessee. After his graduation from Harvard in 1932, he joined the editorial staff of *Fortune.* He then was film critic for *Time* and later for *The Nation.* After 1948, he worked mostly in Hollywood as a scriptwriter.

Permit Me Voyage (1934), a collection of poems, was included in the Yale Series of Younger Poets. *Let Us Now Praise Famous Men* (1941), with photographs by Walker Evans, is a study of Alabama sharecroppers. *The Morning Watch* (1954), Agee's first novel, records the events in one day of a Tennessee boy's life. *Agee on Film* (2 volumes, 1958-60) contains reviews, articles, and motion-picture scripts. In *James Agee's Letters to Father Flye* (1962) he reveals much about his life and views.

Agency for International Development (AID), a unit in the U.S. Department of State. It carries out nonmilitary foreign assistance programs. AID operates chiefly through loans and grants to less developed friendly countries to promote social and economic development. Countries receiving aid must do long-range planning, establish community self-help programs, and strive toward economic self-sufficiency.

President John F. Kennedy established the agency by executive order in November, 1961. Foreign assistance was administered previously by a number of agencies: the International Cooperation Administration (1955-61), the Foreign Operations Administration (1953-55), the Mutual Security Agency (1951-53), and the Economic Cooperation Administration (1948-51).

See also FOREIGN AID, subtitle *History.*

Agency Shop. See OPEN SHOP AND CLOSED SHOP.

Agenor, in Greek legend, the father of Cadmus. See CADMUS.

Agent, in law, a person who is authorized to transact or manage some business for another person or for a company, called a *principal.* The relation of agent and principal is called *agency.* The agent's authority to act for the principal is often based on a document called a *power of attorney,* but authority may be granted orally.

The agent's acts, within the scope of his express or implied authority, are legally binding on his principal and, under certain circumstances, the principal may be bound even by unauthorized acts. The principal may also ratify an unauthorized act and thus become bound. The principal may, under certain circumstances, be liable for torts committed by the agent in the course of conducting the principal's business. (A tort is a civil wrong for which the wronged person may collect damages.)

For rendering service an agent is generally entitled to wages, salary, commission, or other compensation. The law imposes upon an agent the duty of loyalty to his principal and upon the principal the duty to protect his agent against loss or damage incurred while carrying out authorized acts.

The word *agent* is a general term and includes many classes, such as attorneys, brokers, clerks, consignees, and masters of ships. A *general agent* is authorized to represent his principal in all matters, or in all matters of a certain class. A *special agent* is authorized to act on one occasion or in one transaction. A person who represents or substitutes for another in performing one action is sometimes called a *proxy,* a term also used to describe the document in which his authority to act is set forth. A *trustee* is an agent who keeps or administers some property or other interest for another person.

Ageratum, ăj′ĕr-ā′tŭm; ȧ-jĕr′ȧ-tŭm; an annual garden plant of the composite family. It is native to the warmer parts of North and South America. It grows 5 to 18 inches (13 to 46 cm) high. The tiny blue, white, or pink flowers form sticky, tassellike clusters. The hairy leaves are heart-shaped. Dwarf ageratums, about 3 inches (7.5 cm) high, are used to border gardens.

The ageratums form the genus *Ageratum* of the composite family, Compositae. There are some 30 species. The common garden ageratum is *A. houstonianum.*

Ageratum

Agglutinative Languages. See LANGUAGE, subtitle *Types of Language:* Agglutinative.

Agincourt, Battle of, ăj'ĭn-kōrt, October 25, 1415, an English victory over France in the Hundred Years' War. It was fought near the village of Agincourt, 33 miles west of Arras in northern France. Henry V of England, reasserting his claim to the French throne held by Charles VI, invaded France and took Harfleur. By marching toward Calais, Henry provoked an attack by the much larger French army under the Constable Charles d'Albret. The French depended on armored knights, and at this period plate armor had become very heavy. Bogged down in mud, the knights were slaughtered by English archers, armed with the longbow.

Agnes, Saint (about 291-304), according to tradition, a Christian maiden of Rome, martyred after rejecting an influential suitor. She is the Roman Catholic patron saint of young girls. A once popular belief was that a girl who went to bed without supper and in silence on St. Agnes' Eve (January 20, the night before her feast day) would dream of her destined husband. John Keats used this legend in his poem *The Eve of St. Agnes* (1819). In religious art Saint Agnes is usually shown with a lamb.

Agnes Scott College. See UNIVERSITIES AND COLLEGES (table).

Agnew, ăg'nū, **Spiro Theodore** (1918-), the 39th Vice President of the United States. A Republican, he was elected to the Vice Presidency in 1968 as the running mate of Richard M. Nixon and was reelected in 1972. In 1973 he was forced to resign when evidence indicated that he had received payoffs for political favors while holding office in Maryland and as Vice President. He was convicted of income-tax evasion, fined, and given a suspended sentence.

Spiro T. Agnew

During his tenure in the Vice Presidency, Agnew had been one of the most controversial figures to hold that post in recent times. Serving as a major spokesman for the Nixon administration, he toured the country, seeking to rouse support for Presidential policies and denouncing critics. His outspoken oratory and his conservative views on issues such as the Vietnamese War, civil rights, and dissent and protest won Agnew high praise from some but strong condemnation from others. He came to be regarded by many as a champion of white, conservative, middle-class America, the so-called silent majority.

Agnew was born in Baltimore, Maryland, the son of a Greek immigrant surnamed Anagnostopoulos (shortened to Agnew). He attended Johns Hopkins University, where he studied chemistry. During World War II, he served in the U.S. Army, commanding an armored company in Europe. In 1947 Agnew received a law degree from the University of Baltimore and began to practice law in Baltimore. He was elected Baltimore County executive in 1962 and in 1966 was chosen governor of Maryland, serving 1967-69.

Frankly Speaking (1970) is a collection of Agnew's speeches.

Agnon, Shmuel Yosef. See NOBEL PRIZES (Literature, 1966).

Agnosticism, ăg-nŏs'tĭ-sĭz'm, the doctrine that God, or any first cause, is unknown and probably unknowable. The term is from a Greek word that means "unknown." Agnosticism is a form of skepticism, the view that knowledge is limited. Agnosticism differs from *atheism,* the doctrine that there is no God or other deity. The agnostic insists he does not know about God; the atheist insists he does know about God: there is none.

The term *agnosticism* was coined in 1869 by Thomas Huxley to describe his own theological position. Other prominent agnostics were Robert G. Ingersoll and Herbert Spencer. In the 20th century the term *agnosticism* has lost ground to the older and more general word *skepticism.*

See also ATHEISM.

Agnus Dei, ăg'nŭs dē'ī, in Christian churches, a term used in liturgy and symbolism. The words are Latin and mean "Lamb of God," a name for Jesus Christ used in John 1:29, 36. In the Roman Catholic Mass the Agnus Dei is an invocation that comes between the Lord's Prayer and the communion. The Agnus Dei sounds the themes of sacrifice and adoration. Several other churches, including the Lutheran and Anglican (Episcopal), retain the Agnus Dei in the communion service.

In symbolism the Agnus Dei is an image

New York Zoological Society
Central American Female Agouti and Young

of a lamb, usually with a halo and bearing a cross. In the Roman Catholic Church a wax medallion with the image of a lamb, also called Agnus Dei, is used as an object of devotion. These medallions are blessed by the pope in the first and in every seventh year of his pontificate.

Agora, ăg'ō-rá, in ancient Greece, the square where the business and political life of a city was centered, similar to the Roman forum. The name in Greek means "market place." It was an open area with statues, altars, trees, and fountains, surrounded by markets, public buildings, and temples. Extensive archeological work has been done in the Agora in Athens, a six-acre (2.4-hectare) square north of the Acropolis.

Agouti, á-gōō'tĭ, a rodent found in South and Central America, the West Indies, and southern Mexico. The agouti is approximately the size of a large rabbit. Its habitat varies from damp lowland forests to dry, elevated hillsides and cultivated areas.

The agouti has short ears, and either a short tail or none at all. Its body is long and its feet are slender. It has three claws on each hind foot and five claws, one of which is inconspicuous and underdeveloped, on each forefoot. The agouti is covered with coarse, glossy fur ranging from pale orange and shades of brown to black. Some species have a rump of contrasting color, while others have lightly striped fur. The underparts are generally light colored.

The agouti feeds on fruit, vegetables, and other plant matter. It lives in burrows dug along riverbanks or between boulders and roots. A litter contains two to four young.

A-138

Agouti flesh is edible, and is frequently eaten by South American Indians. The agouti is easily tamed, and can live up to 20 years in captivity.

Agoutis make up the genera *Dasyprocta* and *Myoprocta* of the family Dasyproctidae.

Agra, ä'grá, ä'grä, India, a city in the state of Uttar Pradesh. Agra is on the Jumna River, a tributary of the Ganges River, about 115 miles (185 km) south-southeast of New Delhi. Products include handicraft items and cotton and silk textiles. Agra is the commercial and transportation center for the surrounding region. Agra University is here.

The city is the site of several buildings of the Hindu-Islamic style of architecture erected during the Mogul period of Indian history (1527-1707). The Taj Mahal, the tomb built in the 17th century by Shah Jahan in honor of his wife, is one of the outstanding buildings in the world. (See TAJ MAHAL.) The huge, crescent-shaped Fort of Agra was built in the 16th century by Akbar. Within its walls are the palace of Akbar; the Pearl Mosque (1646), built by Shah Jahan; and Itimad-ud-Daulah's tomb (1626), built by Shah Jahangir's wife.

Agra, an ancient city, has an obscure early history. In the mid-15th century the Lodi king Sikander made it his capital. The city became important after 1483 as the residence of the Mogul rulers of India. In 1639 Shah Jahan made Delhi his capital, and Agra declined in importance. It was the capital of the British North-Western Province (modern Uttar Pradesh) from 1835 to 1862.

Population: 591,917.

Agrarian Reform. See LAND REFORM.

Agrarians, or **Fugitives,** a group of Southern writers in the United States, centered in Nashville, Tennessee, at Vanderbilt University. They contributed to *The Fugitive,* a poetry magazine published from 1922 to 1925. Their purpose, stated in *I'll Take My Stand: the South and the Agrarian Tradition by Twelve Southerners* (1930), was to foster a non-industrial, agrarian economy and establish a regional culture modeled on that of the South before the Civil War. Most of the members eventually drifted away from this position, but their ideas influenced other writers in their conceptions of American history and tradition.

Prominent members were John Crowe Ransom, Allen Tate, Donald Davidson,

Herbert Agar, Robert Penn Warren, and John Gould Fletcher.

Agricola, á-grĭk′ŏ-lá, **Georgius** (1490-1555), a German physician and scientist, called "the father of mineralogy." He used the Latin form of his name, Georg Bauer. Agricola was educated in Leipzig and in Italy. He was city physician in the mining center of Joachimsthal (Jachymov), Bohemia, and later practiced medicine in Chemnitz, Germany. His *De natura fossilium* (1546) became the first mineralogy textbook. His *De re metallica* (1556) was first translated into English in 1912 by Herbert Hoover (who was a mining engineer before becoming President of the United States) and his wife, Lou Henry Hoover.

Agricola, Gnaeus Julius, nē*ŭs* (37?-93 A.D.), a Roman general and statesman. He conquered most of Britain and did much to Romanize the island. A biography of Agricola was written by the historian Tacitus, his son-in-law.

Agricola saw military service in many parts of the Roman Empire. In 78 he was appointed governor of Roman Britain. Agricola conquered northern Wales and southern Scotland as far as the Highlands. He later defeated the Scottish Caledonians in battle but did not entirely subdue them. Agricola sent his fleet around Britain to prove it was an island. In his effort to establish Roman culture he built roads, temples, baths, and other public works.

Agricola was recalled in 84 and spent his later years in retirement. Tacitus portrays him as a man of the highest Roman virtues, and writes that he was removed because Emperor Domitian was jealous.

Agricultural Adjustment Acts. See PRICE SUPPORTS (introduction).

Agricultural Adjustment Administration. See NEW DEAL, table titled *Important New Deal Agencies.*

Agricultural Clubs. See FOUR-H (4-H) CLUBS; FUTURE FARMERS OF AMERICA.

Agricultural Credit. See FARM CREDIT ADMINISTRATION.

Agricultural Education, vocational education in the production of crops, livestock, and poultry and in related operations. It includes training in such areas as farm-business management, soil management, processing and marketing of farm products, supply of farm goods and services, and farm equipment repair. In the United States, agricultural education is available through high schools, colleges and universities, youth groups such as the Future Farmers of America and 4-H Clubs, and a variety of programs for working farmers.

The federal government supports agricultural and other vocational education below the bachelor's degree level through the Smith-Hughes Act of 1917 and later laws. Full-time students in rural high schools can combine agricultural subjects with academic subjects in their programs of study. The vocational agriculture programs, supervised by graduates of agricultural colleges, include both classroom instruction and farming projects outside of school. Many community colleges also offer vocational agriculture programs.

Each state has at least one land-grant college or university—an institution that teaches agriculture and engineering and also other subjects. These schools are maintained through state and federal funds. They were established through the Land-Grant College Act of 1862, called the Morrill Act after its sponsor, Justin S. Morrill.

Agricultural education is also offered in many non-land-grant colleges and universities, both public and private.

The Hatch Act of 1887 provided federal funds to establish agricultural experiment stations in each state. The Smith-Lever Agricultural Extension Act of 1914 provided on a national basis an educational program for farmers. Under the act, an extension service disseminates agricultural information through *county extension agents.* The service is operated jointly by the U.S. Department of Agriculture, land-grant colleges and universities, and county governments. (See also AGRICULTURE, U.S. DEPARTMENT OF, subtitle *Divisions:* Science and Education.)

For further information, see:
EXPERIMENT STATION
FOUR-H (4-H) CLUBS
FUTURE FARMERS OF AMERICA
LAND-GRANT COLLEGES AND UNIVERSITIES
MORRILL, JUSTIN SMITH

Agricultural Experiment Station. See EXPERIMENT STATION.

Agricultural Fair. See FAIR, subtitle *Agricultural Fairs.*

Agricultural Parity. See PRICE SUPPORTS, subtitle *Parity in Agriculture.*

Agricultural Subsidies. See PRICE SUPPORTS.

Agriculture, ăg′rĭ-kŭl′tûr, the growing of plants or raising of animals for human use and enjoyment. The word agriculture comes from the Latin *ager,* meaning "field," and *cultura,* "care."

Agriculture consists of two kinds of activities: improving the environment of the plants grown and the animals raised, and improving the usefulness of the plants and animals themselves. Among ways of improving the environment are the preparation of soil for planting, the use of fertilizers, the killing of injurious insects and other pests, and the sheltering and feeding of the animals. The usefulness of the plants and animals is improved primarily through *selective breeding.* Seeds from the most productive plants of the previous harvest are chosen for planting. Unwanted animals are *culled,* or removed, from herds and flocks, so that only the healthiest and most useful will breed.

The practice or business of agriculture is usually called *farming.* A person engaged in

A-140

farming is a *farmer;* the place where he works is called a *farm. Agribusiness* is a term used to describe farming and its related activities—the manufacturing and distribution of farm equipment and supplies and the processing, storing, shipping, and marketing of agricultural products.

See also FARM.

Importance of Agriculture

Economic. Agriculture is man's most important source of food. Hunting and gathering—that is, obtaining food by killing wild animals and collecting wild grains, fruits, nuts, and edible roots—are of no importance except in the technologically most backward areas of the earth. Only fishing, among nonagricultural activities, provides an important—though not a major —share of the world's food supply. Agriculture also provides important raw materials for various industries, and many drugs.

See also FARM, box titled *Farm Products.*

Growth of cities and increased use of

machines are steadily reducing the farm populations of many parts of the world. Before the Industrial Revolution began in the mid-18th century, more than 90 per cent of the world's workers were agricultural. By the late 1930's this percentage was down to 60; today it is below 45. Nevertheless agriculture is still man's most widespread single occupation.

Synthetic products have lessened the usefulness of many nonfood agricultural products. Nylon, for example, has largely replaced silk. New uses, however, have been found for farm products in the chemical industry and other industries. For example, hundreds of products—from cosmetics to plastics—are made from peanuts and corn.

See also CARVER, GEORGE WASHINGTON; CHEMURGY; DRUG, subtitle *Sources of Drugs;* FIBER, subtitle *Types of Fibers;* LEATHER; PLASTICS, subtitle *History of Plastics;* QUININE; RUBBER; TEXTILE.

Agriculture is one of the most important *sectors* (parts) in the economies of most nations. It contributes its share of the total economic output of a nation through the sale value of its products. Also, agriculture uses great quantities of equipment, fertilizers, and other products—thus creating a market for goods and services of other sectors such as manufacturing and trade.

Historical and Social. Agriculture, by providing man with an adequate, stationary, and renewable food supply, changed his way of life from a wandering one of hunting and gathering to a settled one of cultivation. Man's society changed from that of the independent small family group to that of the interdependent community of families. Urban life, commerce, increasing population —all of the major characteristics of modern life—stem from the drastic change in man's way of life brought about by agriculture.

See also section "History of Agriculture," in this article; CIVILIZATION; FOOD AND NUTRITION, subtitle *Food and Civilization;* POPULATION, subtitle *Population Growth:* Growth to the 17th Century.

Customs and religions have historically had close ties to agriculture. Soil, crop, and livestock fertility is the basis of many religious rites in primitive societies. The rituals of many ancient religions were based on agricultural themes. Harvest celebrations, practiced since the dawn of civilization, are carried on today, although their agricultural origin and their meaning have, in many cases, been forgotten.

See also DANCE, THE, subtitles *Folk Dancing:* In Other Countries, *Ritual Dances,* and *History of the Dance:* Medieval Dances; FAIR, subtitle *Fairs in Early Times;* MAY DAY; MYSTERY; MYTHS AND LEGENDS, subtitle *Types of Myths:* Ritual Myth; THANKSGIVING DAY.

Politics and law in all parts of the world are closely involved with agriculture. One reason for this is that productive land and livestock have traditionally been the most widely recognized forms of wealth and property. Throughout history battles for the control of agricultural wealth have been fought in courts, in political contests, and on battlefields.

See also section "History of Agriculture," in this article; LAND REFORM and cross references; LAND TENURE and cross references; POLITICAL PARTIES, subtitle *History:* Minor Parties in the United States, and cross references.

A Topic Guide to Agriculture

This outline shows the six major sections of this article and their division into topics by subtitles.

I. Introductory section
   A. Importance of Agriculture
II. Types of Agriculture
   A. Economic Types
   B. Product Types
   C. Types of Farming Methods
III. Agricultural Regions
IV. Agriculture in the United States
   A. The Farm Problem
   B. The Farm Program
   C. Agricultural Management
   D. Agricultural Technology
   E. Agricultural Marketing
   F. Agricultural Trade
V. Agriculture in Other Nations
   A. The Advanced Non-Communist Nations
   B. Agriculture in Communist Nations
   C. Agriculture in the Underdeveloped Nations
VI. History of Agriculture
   A. Agriculture in the Ancient World (9000 B.C. to 500 A.D.)
   B. Medieval Agriculture (500 to 1500)
   C. Agriculture in the Age of Discovery (1500 to 1700)
   D. Modern Agriculture (1700 to World War II)
   E. Agriculture after World War II

Note: For farming practices, see FARM and cross references. Farming practices used for specific kinds of crops or livestock are discussed in articles on those subjects. For farming practices that are employed in specific geographic areas, see the section on agriculture in articles on those areas.

Types of Agriculture

There are many ways of classifying agriculture. Three of the most commonly used are: (1) economic classification; (2) classification by product; and (3) classification by farming methods.

Economic Types

Farms and other agricultural enterprises are usually classified as either *commercial* or *subsistence,* and as either *diversified* or *specialized.*

Commercial farms produce items primarily for sale to others, rather than for the farmer's own use.

Subsistence farms produce items primarily for the use of the farmer, rather than for sale to others.

Diversified farms produce a variety of crops and livestock. Diversification may allow the farmer to space his periods of heavy work around the year. Such a farm may be commercial or subsistence.

For commercial farmers, diversification lessens danger of financial ruin when one crop or animal product suffers a loss in value. Whether a commercial farm is classed as diversified is based not on how many different crops and kinds of livestock products are produced, but on how many are sold. A Midwestern farmer who produces and sells wheat, soybeans, poultry, eggs, milk, and hogs, for example, is a diversified farmer. However, if he grows grain for hog feed only, raises vegetables and poultry for his own use, and sells only the hogs, he is a specialized farmer.

Specialized farms are commercial or subsistence farms that produce only one major product or group of products. This economic classification may be applied to a farm (wheat farm, cattle ranch, etc.) or to a region (milk shed or truck farming area).

Product Types

There are two major classifications of agriculture by product—crop production agriculture and animal husbandry—and many more specific classifications.

Crop Production Agriculture. In the list that follows, the products of a specific type are often also products of a broader type. The products of *floriculture,* for example— flowers—are usually products of *horticulture.*

Agronomy refers to the production of *field crops* —crops, such as wheat and oats, raised in large-scale farming—and to soil management. See AGRONOMY.

Fruit Culture includes all fruit production from trees, shrubs, and vines. See FRUIT and cross references (except Dry Fruits).

Horticulture deals with the cultivation of fruits, vegetables, flowers, herbs, and ornamental trees and shrubs. See FLOWER, subtitle *Garden Flowers;* FRUIT; GARDENING AND LANDSCAPING; VEGETABLE.

Truck Farming refers to the production of commercial vegetable crops on relatively large farms. (Small commercial vegetable farms that are near their markets are often called *market gardens.*) See VEGETABLE.

Other Types of crop production agriculture include the cultivation of fruit, vegetables, flowers, herbs. and other useful plants on small plots near the cultivator's home. The collective term for these activities is *gardening.* (It is difficult to set a distinct dividing line between gardening and horticulture.) See GARDENING AND LANDSCAPING.

There are several specialized gardening, or horticultural, activities. *Arboriculture* (from the Latin for "tree" and "care") is the cultivation of trees and shrubs for decorative, shade, or ornamental

AGRICULTURAL REGIONS

Irrigation Agriculture: Kansas Corn Field
Kansas Department of Economic Development

Oriental Rice Agriculture: Rice in Japan
Publix: Ira Spring

Shostal

Publix: George Hunter

purposes. *Floriculture* (from the Latin for "flower" and "care") is the cultivation of flowering plants for ornamental purposes. (See FLORICULTURE.) *Nursery farming* is intensive cultivation of young plants, principally trees and shrubs, for later sale to the final user. (See NURSERY.)

Animal Husbandry refers to all types of farming concerned with raising animals.

Dairy Farming in North America and northern Europe refers to the production of milk, cream, and related products (such as cheese) using domesticated cattle as a source. In various other areas of the world buffalo, yaks, and goats are sources of milk and milk products. See DAIRYING.

Fur Farming is the raising of fur-bearing animals for their pelts. See FUR, subtitle *Sources of Fur: Fur Farms.*

Poultry Farming is the raising of birds for meat and eggs. See POULTRY and cross references.

Ranching originally meant raising cattle on the open plain. Today cattle, sheep, and other forms of livestock are raised on fenced pasture as well as open range. Thus ranching today is any form of large-scale agriculture involving livestock raised for meat, hides and skins, and hair products (wool). See RANCH and cross references.

Other Types. *Apiculture* (from the Latin for "bee" and "care") is the keeping of bees for the production of honey and wax. (See BEE, subtitle *The Honeybee:* Beekeeping.) *Aviculture* (from the Latin for "bird" and "care") is the raising of birds for ornamental, recreational, or scientific purposes. (See CANARY; COCKFIGHTING; LOVEBIRD; PARAKEET; PIGEON, subtitle *Domestic Pigeons.*) *Seri-*

culture (from the Latin for "silk" and "care") is the raising of silkworms for their silk. (See SILK.) See also ANIMAL HUSBANDRY.

For a complete list of articles on agricultural products, see FARM, box titled *Farm Products.*

Types of Farming Methods

Following is a list of some special types of agriculture classified by the general techniques used.

Dry Farming is practiced where rainfall is slight and irrigation is impractical. It involves the use of soil-moisture conservation and drought-resistant crops. See DRY FARMING.

Greenhouse Culture is used to grow plants throughout the year. Greenhouses produce vegetables out of season, give plants an early start in the spring, and grow tropical flowers, trees, and plants in all climates. See GREENHOUSE and cross references.

Hydroponics, or **Tank Farming,** is the growing of plants without soil. A solution of chemical nutrients in water is used instead, and plant roots draw nourishment from this solution. See HYDROPONICS.

Irrigation Agriculture is used to produce crops in areas where there is not enough natural rainfall to support crops and in areas where rainfall is adequate but irregular. See IRRIGATION.

Organic Gardening is the raising of foods without the use of chemical fertilizers or pesticides. See ORGANIC GARDENING.

Plantation Agriculture is the world's major source of crops from tropical and subtropical regions. See PLANTATION.

Agricultural Regions

Farming varies greatly from one part of the world to another. Four factors influence the kind of farming found in any given area:

1. Natural conditions such as soil, climate, and amount of water determine what crops can be grown and what animals can be raised. Man can alter natural conditions to a certain extent through such techniques as irrigation.

2. The number and the cultural and technological state of the people in any given area affect the agricultural activities of that area.

3. Economic conditions are important, for they determine how much the farmer will receive for his products and how easily he can market them.

4. In most technologically advanced nations, government activities have a decided effect on agriculture.

Though different combinations of the four factors described produce different types of farming, almost all of the world's agricultural areas can be included in the following list of 10 types of farming regions. These

A-143

Publix: Richard Hufnagle

AGRICULTURAL REGIONS
Mediterranean: Orange Grove in Israel

Publix: George Hunter

Diversified Commercial: Strip Farming in Quebec

types are based on general similarity of products and practices.

For information on agricultural regions of the United States, see UNITED STATES, section "The Economy of the United States," subtitle *Agriculture*.

Irrigation Agriculture. This type of farming is scattered throughout the world, with most of the areas in Asia. Without irrigated farmlands, China, India, the western United States, Mexico, the Middle East, and many other areas would have only a fraction of their present agricultural productivity. Rice, vegetables, fruit, cotton, alfalfa, and sugar beets are commonly raised in irrigated areas.

Oriental Rice Agriculture. Though the cultivation of rice in eastern Asia and the Indian subcontinent is the most widespread form of agriculture known, production is barely enough to feed huge and growing populations. Only in Formosa and on the Indochinese Peninsula, the "rice bowl" region of Southeast Asia, is there usually a sizable surplus. In Communist China and India, the two greatest producers, crops sometimes fail to meet even domestic needs.

Tropical Subsistence Agriculture. In scattered parts of central and western Africa and in north-central South America, this type of agriculture provides diversified crops and a small amount of animal food to the farm population. Plots are generally small, only a few acres. Where soil is poor, the land is cleared and used only for one to three years. On better soils cultivation is more permanent.

Commercial Tropical Agriculture. Most of the world's tropical agricultural products—rubber, sugar cane, coffee, cacao, and many others—are raised on highly specialized farms. These may be huge plantations, managed more like factories than farms; or they may be small farms worked by the owner and his family. Such highly specialized farms depend on stable world-wide market and political conditions for profitable operation. The West Indies, Central and South America, Africa, Southeast Asia, and the East Indies are principal sites.

Mediterranean Agriculture. Practiced wherever the climate is similar to that found around the shores of the Mediterranean, this type of agriculture is the world's principal source of citrus crops, grapes, dates and figs, and olives. Irrigation is important in all areas of Mediterranean agriculture.

In Europe, Africa, and the Middle East much of this type of agriculture is on a subsistence basis. Farms are usually small. The major products are supplemented by grains, legumes, tobacco, sheep, and goats. Exportable surpluses are mostly of olive oil, citrus fruit, tobacco, grapes, and winter vegetables.

In the southwestern United States (California), Mediterranean agriculture is almost totally commercial. Major products are fruits, nuts, and vegetables. Smaller areas of Mediterranean agriculture are found in the Murray River Basin of Australia and in central Chile.

Diversified Commercial Agriculture. This type of agriculture is found in the eastern part of the

AGRICULTURAL REGIONS
Commercial Feed Grain and Livestock: Indiana
J. C. Allen & Son

Dairying: Holstein Cows near Yakima, Washington
Union Pacific Railroad

AGRICULTURAL REGIONS

Commercial Wheat: Fields in Saskatchewan

Grazing: Hereford Cattle in Australia

United States and Canada; eastern Scandinavia; the Amur lowlands in northeastern Asia; and in a broad belt that runs from northern Spain through the middle of Europe into Russia. A great variety of crops are grown, including grains, fruits, and vegetables. Many small, specialized farming areas are found within this region. Livestock is important, especially cattle.

Commercial Feed Grain and Livestock Agriculture. The Corn Belt of the Midwestern United States is the outstanding example of this type of agriculture. Here corn, which occupies nearly 50 per cent of the cropland, is raised as a feed grain for hogs, cattle, and poultry. Soybeans are an important cash crop.

Other feed grain and livestock regions are found in southeastern Europe; in southeastern South America; and between the Black Sea and Caspian Sea. None of these regions is as productive as the Corn Belt.

Dairying. The principal areas of concentrated commercial dairying are the northeastern United States from Minnesota to the Atlantic Ocean and the north coast of Europe from the Low Countries to East Germany. Local dairy industries are found on the outskirts of many cities throughout middle-latitude regions.

Commercial Wheat Farming. Two great expanses of former prairie land dominate world wheat production. The first stretches north from the Texas Panhandle well into Canada's Prairie Provinces—

Alberta, Saskatchewan, and Manitoba. The second extends from south-central Europe through the Ukraine eastward into the heart of central Asia, in Kazakhstan. Smaller areas of high productivity are in northern Argentina and southeastern Australia.

Commercial wheat agriculture is the most notable example of large-scale, highly mechanized agriculture. On the flat, vast plains, great combines harvest crops rapidly and efficiently. Varieties of wheat are created to fit regional differences in climate and soil conditions and to resist plant disease and insect infestation.

Other grains grown in wheat regions are barley, rye, grain sorghums, and oats.

Commercial Grazing. The prairies and plains of the western United States and northern Mexico, the Argentine Pampas and neighboring areas in Uruguay and southern Brazil, and Australia support great numbers of cattle, sheep, and goats. Though many beef cattle are *finished* (prepared for market by being fattened) in areas similar to the Corn Belt, a large proportion are bred and partially raised in short-grass regions. Sheep and goats are raised mostly on drier natural grazing areas, except in Great Britain and New Zealand.

Material in this section has been adapted, with permission of the publisher, from *Geography of Commodity Production*, second edition, by Richard M. Highsmith, Jr., and J. Granville Jensen (Philadelphia: J. B. Lippincott Company). The material was critically reviewed by Dr. Highsmith.

Agriculture in the United States

There are many ways of viewing agriculture in the United States. To the farmer it is a business. To the economist it is one of the major sectors of the nation's economy. To many persons, both farmers and nonfarmers, agriculture has a moral and spiritual value as a way of life and an important part of the nation's heritage.

The agriculture industry of the United States leads the world in production. With its surpluses it helps feed millions of persons around the world who would otherwise go hungry or starve. But agriculture in the United States faces serious problems, many

of them common to agriculture in other parts of the world.

The Farm Problem

Since the end of World War I the prices farmers must pay for goods and services they buy have increased at a much faster rate than the prices farmers receive for products they sell. During this period farm income has fluctuated widely. In prosperous times farm income has not risen as high as nonfarm income, however, and during the depression of the 1930's it fell much farther. As a result of these trends, which continued in the decades after World War II, a much greater

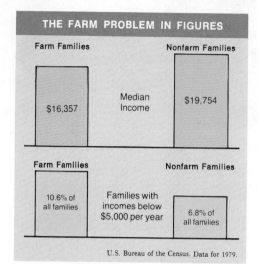

THE FARM PROBLEM IN FIGURES

Farm Families — Median Income — Nonfarm Families
$16,357 — $19,754

Farm Families — Families with incomes below $5,000 per year — Nonfarm Families
10.6% of all families — 6.8% of all families

U.S. Bureau of the Census. Data for 1979.

proportion of farm families than of nonfarm families suffer from below-standard living conditions. (See chart titled *The Farm Problem in Figures*.)

Farm poverty, combined with the need for farmers to purchase and maintain expensive equipment, has led to a population movement away from the farm. (This movement creates a kind of vicious circle: as the number of farms decreases, the more successful farmers—or, frequently, large corporations in the agricultural business—buy up the abandoned land; the resulting larger farms are more efficient, making it even more difficult for owners or tenants of small farms to compete.) Many of those leaving the farm have little formal education or training in nonfarm occupations. They make up a large part of the nonfarm unskilled labor force, and often experience unemployment and poverty.

The cause or causes of these problems of the farm population, often collectively called "the farm problem," are the subject of controversy. Most economists agree on one basic point: the number of farmers is so great that the farming industry is unable to control the supply of farm products that goes to market. This fact, they say, lies at the heart of the farmer's inability to get high enough prices for his products to make profits comparable to those of other businesses. If all the nation's farmers could cooperate so as to adjust farm production to consumer demand, prices would be higher and fluctuate less.

But the acceptance of this theory (and many do not accept it) does not solve the problem. Solutions have been offered, but on the basis of these two opposing points of view:

1. Agriculture is different from other forms of industry and therefore requires special treatment by government. The goals of government programs should be to aid the farmer while protecting the consumer from excessively high prices. Though this point of view has been held by the government since the 1930's, the proper way of reaching the goals is still the subject of continual debate in Congress and among economists. (Some of the methods in use are discussed in the remainder of this section.)

2. Agriculture is not different from other industries. To subsidize agriculture is to keep in production inefficient farms that would otherwise disappear. The efficient producers should be permitted to drive out the inefficient, thus eliminating overproduction. With fewer and larger producers, output would adjust to consumer demand and prices would be higher and more stable. Displaced farmers, like displaced workers from other industries, would eventually be absorbed into the labor force in other kinds of jobs.

This theory has not been official government policy since the farm problem became acute in the 1930's, though many changes it sought to make have been taking place—shrinking farm population, consolidation of small farms into larger units, and others.

The Farm Program

The federal government began a large-scale program of aid to agriculture during the depression of the 1930's. Federal aid attempts to do three things, principally: (1) keep prices paid for farm products at a level comparable to that of prices farmers pay for goods and services they buy; (2) stabilize prices received for farm products from year to year; and (3) help the farmer achieve more efficient production. The term for all government aid is "the farm program."

The *price support* program is the major government activity designed to achieve the first two goals. It operates chiefly in two ways—guaranteeing certain prices to farmers for their products, and establishing limitations on production.

See also PRICE SUPPORTS.

The third goal of federal farm aid is the objective of a number of government programs. Some of these are soil, crop, and livestock improvement research; the extension of easy credit to farmers; aid to agricultural education; and marketing aid.

In addition to the federal programs, all states promote farm improvement. One of the major factors in introducing improved techniques has been the efforts of manufacturers to bring better machinery and chemical aids to the farmer.

Agricultural Management

The Farming Business. The farmer's goal is to use his resources to obtain a high, sustained income from the sale of his products. His resources include climate and weather; soil and water; *topography,* or land contours; crops and livestock; machinery and equipment; buildings; mechanical and electrical power; fertilizers, pesticides, and other agricultural aids; and the aid of government and farm organizations.

Combining these resources in the most profitable manner calls for skillful management. Crops and animals must be chosen to suit the climate, weather, soil, and water conditions of the farm. Soil must be tested so that the farmer can choose the most suitable crops and discover what chemicals are needed to improve its fertility. Crop rotation helps to maintain the fertility of the soil. The topography of the land must be considered. Contour plowing on rolling land helps to prevent erosion. Land too hilly and uneven for crop cultivation can be left in grass and used as pasture.

See also ROTATION OF CROPS; SOIL.

The farm must have proper buildings, machinery, and equipment if it is to be efficient. To purchase them the farmer must have funds or, more likely, credit.

See also FARM; FARM CREDIT ADMINISTRATION.

Farm Labor. Most United States farms are family farms. Their owner-operators provide most of the labor. Farmers often hire farmhands to help the family with farm work. Some hired labor is specialized, such as wheat harvesters who bring their own combines to one farm after another during harvest time. Large corporation farms often hire hundreds of workers. California, Florida, Arizona, and southern Texas are the major centers for hired farm workers. Some farm laborers are unionized and negotiate their wages and working conditions through collective bargaining. Families of migrant workers travel from state to state, following the harvests.

See also MIGRANT LABOR; TENANT FARMING.

Government Farm Activity. Most of the farm program—including the price support program, crop damage insurance, and research activities—is administered by the U.S. Department of Agriculture. The Farm Credit Administration provides long- and short-term loans to farmers. The National Weather Service, through its weather forecasts, provides useful information to farmers.

See also AGRICULTURE, U.S. DEPARTMENT OF; FARM CREDIT ADMINISTRATION; FEDERAL CROP INSURANCE CORPORATION; PRICE SUPPORTS; WEATHER SERVICE, NATIONAL.

Farmers' Organizations. Through many organizations, clubs, and other groups farmers obtain financial and business aid, information, and education. These groups also act as political spokesmen for their members.

See also AMERICAN FARM BUREAU FEDERATION; COOPERATIVE; FARMERS EDUCATIONAL AND CO-OPERATIVE UNION OF AMERICA; FOUR-H (4-H) CLUBS; FUTURE FARMERS OF AMERICA; FUTURE HOMEMAKERS OF AMERICA; GRANGE, NATIONAL; NATIONAL FARMERS ORGANIZATION.

Agricultural Management. Contour plowing is an important technique on hilly land.

U. S. Department of Agriculture

Central Soya: Neuman

Marketing. The first step is often processing. Here soybeans are brought to a processing plant.

Agricultural Technology

Perhaps the outstanding feature of the agriculture industry in the United States is its use of technology. Irrigation is in use throughout the nation. *Reclamation*—land improvement by irrigation or drainage—in the Columbia River Basin and the Central Valley of California has increased arable land. The Tennessee Valley Authority, created in 1933, developed the Tennessee River Basin. The amount of land under irrigation in the United States is increasing at the rate of 3 per cent per year. Large-scale programs to control soil and water use have resulted in reduction of flood damage and control of erosion.

The health of crops and livestock is protected by a variety of pesticides, animal feed supplements and plant nutrients, and drugs and vaccinations.

Most of the electric power required for farm operation is supplied by central power stations. Tractors provide motive power for harvesters, planters, mowers, and other machinery. Structures needed include barns, silos, poultry houses, and tool sheds. Fencing, cordage, special containers, and other items are necessary to efficient operation.

See also BARN; CONSERVATION; ELECTRIFICATION, subtitle *Rural Electrification;* FARM; FENCE; FERTILIZER; RECLAMATION; SILO; TENNESSEE VALLEY AUTHORITY; TRACTOR; WEED, subtitle *Weed Control.*

Research. While the farmer improves his farm's productive capacity, researchers, mainly at state agricultural schools and U.S. Department of Agriculture facilities, find new uses for his products. The soybean, for example, introduced as a source of animal feed, margarine, flour, and plastics, became one of the nation's leading crops. Research in plant and animal breeding led to improved strains—healthier, more produc-

tive, more resistant to disease and to adverse weather and soil conditions.

Private industry, as well as government, engages in agricultural research. Industry's participation in developing new pesticides and plant varieties is a major factor in the American farmer's production success.

See also CATTLE, subtitle *Breeds of Beef Cattle;* CORN, subtitle *Hybrid Corn;* SOYBEAN, subtitle *Uses of Soybeans.*

Education and Engineering. Formal education in agriculture usually begins in high school. Agricultural colleges train young people for scientific farming and related vocations. Extension services provide education to practicing farmers. Agricultural engineering involves the improvement of technology, including development of machines and equipment, conservation aids, and structures.

See also AGRICULTURAL EDUCATION.

Agricultural Marketing

Marketing is the term for all activities that bring a product from manufacturer to consumer. Agricultural marketing includes all processing that transforms a farm product into a usable commodity. Wheat, for instance, is processed into flour, baked goods, and cereal. Storage is significant in marketing since farm production is seasonal and products must be stored until used. Refrigerated warehouses have lessened the storage problem for fresh fruits and vegetables, meat and poultry, and eggs.

Rail, water, air, and highway carriers transport farm goods from the farmer to intermediate handlers and processors and on to the retail market. Transportation of bulky, perishable food products, such as milk and fresh fruit and vegetables, accounts for a large part of their marketing costs.

Farm commodities are inspected by federal food inspectors at various stages during the marketing process to assure sanitary handling. Some products are graded according to size and quality, and some are dated, so the consumer can tell how fresh they are.

Middlemen. A middleman is a link in a chain of people who may handle farm products between their sale by the farmer and their purchase by the consumer. He may be a country grain elevator operator, who buys grain from farmers. He in turn sells to a commission merchant, who may store the grain in terminal elevators until it is sold to a processor or to an exporter.

AGRICULTURE

Another type of middleman is the traveling buyer. He is employed by a large retail grocery chain or by a trucking company to follow the harvest and buy farm products. Some farmers, instead of dealing with a traveling buyer, deliver their products to a wholesale middleman in a central location. Livestock markets called stockyards developed in this way. Now, because of the increasing number of frozen food lockers and direct purchases by large retail chains, stockyards are becoming obsolete. Large wholesale fruit and vegetable markets, as in Boston, and poultry and egg markets, as in New York City, often have branches in outlying areas to supply retailers.

Commodity Exchanges. These financial institutions are located in large cities, principally New York City and Chicago. They are centers that arrange immediate and future delivery of certain farm commodities. A firm or individual may buy wheat that has already been harvested and is awaiting shipment, wheat that has been stored, or wheat still in the field. The contract assures the buyer that he will receive the wheat at a specific time, place, and price.

Marketing Cost. Farmers receive approximately one-third of the money spent by American consumers for domestic food products. Marketing costs—including transportation, packaging, wages, and profits of middlemen and retailers—make up the balance. (See chart titled *Where the Food Dollar Goes.*) Similarly, marketing costs make up the major part of the price of nonfood agricultural products.

Government Activities. The federal government has become increasingly involved in agricultural marketing. The Meat Inspection Act of 1906 began federal inspection and grading of meat, while the Food Production Act of 1917 authorized grading of fresh fruit and vegetables. The Federal Farm Board, created in 1929, helped stabilize farm prices by government purchases of surplus wheat and cotton. The Agricultural Adjustment Act of 1933 initiated crop production controls. Under various agricultural acts passed by Congress since 1935, the federal government can purchase surplus perishable farm commodities, such as eggs, turkeys, potatoes, and milk. By thus removing the surpluses from the marketplace, it assures that the farmer will receive higher prices for his remaining production

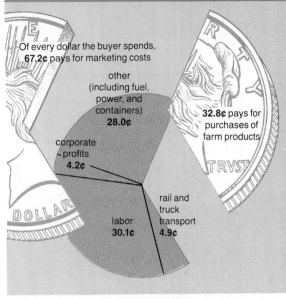

Of every dollar the buyer spends, 67.2¢ pays for marketing costs

other (including fuel, power, and containers) 28.0¢

32.8¢ pays for purchases of farm products

corporate profits 4.2¢

rail and truck transport 4.9¢

labor 30.1¢

Source: Economic Research Service, USDA. Data for 1979.

The government-bought goods are distributed to school districts (as part of the school lunch program), to needy persons, and to other nations. Products are also sold to processors for diversion to other uses.

Orderly Marketing. The government sometimes helps the farmer market his goods through *marketing agreement and order programs.* The secretary of agriculture may issue marketing orders to regulate the sale of specific products. These orders help stabilize prices and assure an adequate supply to the consumer. An order is put into operation only after a public hearing and approval by affected farmers.

Marketing Cooperatives. Many farmers find it profitable to sell in cooperation with nearby producers. The Cooperative Marketing Act of 1926 provided government assistance to marketing cooperatives through the U.S. Department of Agriculture. Cooperatives also perform such related services as trucking, storage, and processing.

Coordinated Farming. The close association of a farmer and a processor is termed coordinated farming. There are two major types.

Contract farming is a type of coordinated farming in which the farmer shares risks and profits with others—farmers, cooperatives, processors, or middlemen. The farmer agrees to grow crops or raise livestock or poultry according to the buyer's terms, while the buyer agrees to purchase them at a stated price. The buyer may also supply credit and other services.

A *corporation farm* usually is a farm owned and operated by a processor, such as a canning company. (It may, however, be a legally incorporated family farm.)

See also AGRICULTURE, U.S. DEPARTMENT OF; COMMODITY EXCHANGE; COOPERATIVE, subtitle *Producer Cooperatives;* MEAT PACKING, subtitle *The Stockyards.*

Agricultural Trade

The United States exports surplus wheat, cotton, tobacco, soybeans, and other agricultural goods. Imported farm products include coffee, tea, rubber, and jute.

See also UNITED STATES, section "The Economy," subtitle *Trade:* Foreign Trade.

Reciprocal trade agreements between the United States and other nations, begun in 1934, control the tariffs (import taxes) levied by these nations. Since World War II these agreements have generally favored lower tariffs to encourage trade. Of particular importance to the agricultural trade of the United States are trade relations with the European Common Market, a major consumer of United States agricultural exports. A major buyer of United States wheat is the Soviet Union.

See also EUROPEAN COMMUNITY; TARIFF, subtitle *United States Tariff History:* Reciprocal Trade Policy.

United States agriculture is also discussed in UNITED STATES, section "The Economy of the United States," subtitle *Agriculture;* FARM; and in articles on the states under the subtitle *Agriculture* or *Economy.*

Agriculture in Other Nations

French Tourist Office
Farmland between hedgerows in France. Beasts of burden are still used in areas where plots are too small or too scattered to make efficient use of tractors and other farm machines.

The Advanced Non-Communist Nations

Canada. Farming conditions in Canada are much like those in the United States. Wheat is the main crop, produced on large, highly mechanized farms. The Canadian Department of Agriculture supplies farmers with information on research and world trade.

Australia. Australia and the United States have the highest average agricultural production per worker in the world. The main crop, wheat, is raised on large, highly mechanized farms. Australia is the world's leading sheep-farming nation, with more than half of its total area in pasture land.

Japan, New Zealand, and South Africa. These nations, though comparatively small, have developed outstandingly productive agriculture industries. Japan's productivity per acre is among the highest in the world. New Zealand is one of the world's leading exporters of dairy products and wool. South Africa is a major producer of citrus fruits and wool.

Western Europe. British agriculture is highly mechanized. The farms, while large by European standards, are small by North American standards; the average size is about 100 acres (40 hectares).

Western European governments encourage mechanization by helping farmers purchase machines. Many farms are too small for efficient use of machines, however. Also, many farm holdings are on separated plots of land. Programs to consolidate small farms have met with little success.

Farms are diversified, providing a variety of food products for use within each nation. The Common Market is a branch of the European Community. Common Market goals include free trade in farm products among member nations and a common agricultural policy. Countries in western Europe import more than one-fourth of their food needs.

Southern Europe. Farms are small, usually two or three acres, and are intensively cultivated. Cereal grains and grapes are among leading crops. Cattle, sheep, goats, and poultry are raised. Farmers are usually employed on large estates and own small private plots.

Agriculture in Communist Nations

Communist governments have replaced peasant farmers with a farm *proletariat,* or working class, who live and work on state and collective farms. These large farms are becoming mechanized. The farmers are trained by specialists and production organizers.

Soviet Russia. There are three types of farms in Russia—collective, state, and private. The *collective farm* is a state-owned enterprise operated by farmers who are paid a share of the total output. Several villages may be included in a collective farm. Peasants were forced to join and contribute their lands to the collectives when Russia began to industrialize in 1928. A *state farm* is publicly owned and operated. It is worked by employees paid by the state.

Each worker on a collective farm is given a small *private plot* on which he may grow crops and raise livestock. The total area of these private plots is about 4 per cent of the total collective farm cropland.

Under the seven-year plan for 1959-65, agriculture was almost totally mechanized by the mid-1960's.

Communist China. Collective farms, and later communes, were substituted for private farms between 1955 and 1960. Each commune is operated by production teams. Farmers are paid according to the "work points" they accumulate. Crops are shared with the government. In the 1960's, Chinese peasants were given larger private plots and permitted to raise their own food and sell on the free market.

Other Communist Nations. The Soviet agricultural system was adopted by European Communist countries after World War II. As in Russia, production and efficiency were poor. Poland later changed its farm policy, reverting to privately owned farms. Yugoslavia, a Communist nation often at odds with Russia, disbanded collective farms in 1953.

United Nations

Helicopter Sprays Weeds in Israel

Agriculture in Underdeveloped Nations

Asia. Rice is the main food crop, produced by primitive methods on small farm plots. Most of the people live by agriculture. There is a great need for fertilizer, better seed, and better marketing facilities.

Latin America. The export crops of Latin America—mainly coffee, bananas, and sugar, with some grain and meat from Argentina and Uruguay—are grown on well-managed, well-financed farms of the plantation type. Food crops for local consumption are grown in small fields still cultivated largely with a hoe. Most of Latin America suffers from a deficiency of food due to lack of improvement in productivity and a rapidly increasing population.

Africa. Colonial rule by European powers, which extended throughout Africa until

Lunchtime on a Collective Farm
USSR Magazine from Sovfoto

after World War II, led to efficient development of export crop production on plantations but did little to improve the native farmer's output of food and other products. The northern edge and southern tip of the continent have a Mediterranean climate and were developed by European colonists, using African labor, for the production of citrus and other fruits, wine grapes, and vegetables.

Central Africa produces coffee on the eastern highlands and peanuts, cacao, and palm nuts (for oil) in the western bulge. Nigeria and Senegal, leading peanut producers, have entered world trade through marketing cooperatives.

See also *Agriculture* subtitle in articles on individual continents, regions, and countries; EUROPEAN COMMUNITY; PLANTATION.

History of Agriculture

Early man obtained food by hunting and gathering—that is, by killing wild animals and collecting wild cereals (grain from seed-bearing grasses), fruits, nuts, and edible roots. By 9000 B.C. some primitive people of southwestern Asia were herding sheep to assure a steady supply of meat. At the same time or a little later they began planting and harvesting cereal seed in locations convenient to their pastures.

These early food producers learned before 7000 B.C. that roasting seed killed the germ so that surplus grain could be stored during the rainy season without sprouting, thus allowing an all-year food supply. They gave up their nomadic way of life for a settled existence as farmers. Sites of their villages have been found in the grassy highlands of eastern Turkey, northern Iran and Iraq, and Afghanistan. By 6000 B.C. these early farmers had learned to irrigate their fields with river water. This enabled them to grow abundant crops in the fertile flood plains of the Tigris and Euphrates rivers.

See also IRRIGATION, subtitle *History of Irrigation.*

The practice of agriculture apparently spread from the Middle East into Europe. It seems to have started independently in other areas, such as Southeast Asia (where peas and root plants were cultivated in the 9000's B.C.), Mexico and Central America, and possibly the Far East and West Africa.

Agriculture in the Ancient World (9000 B.C. to 500 A.D.)

From settled village life, made possible principally by agriculture, came the social, economic, and political developments that are regarded as characteristics of civilization. Religion grew with agriculture as people sought to gain favor with the seemingly mysterious forces that destroyed their crops or made them grow. Among the earliest agricultural civilizations were those of the Fertile Crescent (up the Tigris-Euphrates Valley and down along the Mediterranean Sea), the Indus and Nile valleys, the flood plain of the Hwang Ho (Yellow River), the northern and western shores of the Black Sea, the Danube Basin, and, in the Western Hemisphere, southern Mexico.

Crops and Livestock. In the Middle East barley and wheat were the first grains cultivated. They became basic foods of a vast area of western Asia, southern Europe, and northern Africa. Peas and lentils were early legume crops. Rice had its origin in eastern Asia and became the staple cereal there. Rye and oats, suitable to cooler climates, apparently were domesticated by northern peoples long after the beginnings of agriculture and were never known to older civilizations. In the Sudan, the earliest cereals grown were sorghum and millet. The equatorial forest region of Africa lacked a food crop until yams and bananas were introduced from southeastern Asia early in the Christian Era.

Corn, a grain native to the New World, was cultivated in Mexico by about 5000 B.C. Pumpkins, squash, chili peppers, and avocados were probably cultivated very early also. Other native crops included white and sweet potatoes, five kinds of beans, peanuts, tomatoes, and chocolate.

Olives, for oil, and grapes, for wine, were major crops in ancient Greece. They were introduced into the Middle East by Alexander the Great. Under the Romans, Egypt supplied grain for much of the empire, while Italy raised mainly livestock. Olive groves were planted in North Africa, grape orchards were introduced into Gaul (France); wheat was grown in Britain.

Goats were domesticated in the Middle East about 6500 B.C., perhaps for their milk, which was used for making yogurt and

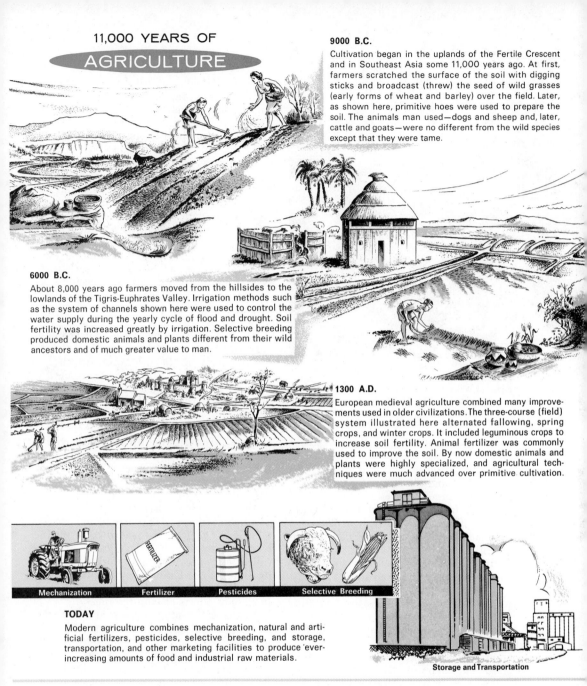

11,000 YEARS OF AGRICULTURE

9000 B.C.

Cultivation began in the uplands of the Fertile Crescent and in Southeast Asia some 11,000 years ago. At first, farmers scratched the surface of the soil with digging sticks and broadcast (threw) the seed of wild grasses (early forms of wheat and barley) over the field. Later, as shown here, primitive hoes were used to prepare the soil. The animals man used—dogs and sheep and, later, cattle and goats—were no different from the wild species except that they were tame.

6000 B.C.

About 8,000 years ago farmers moved from the hillsides to the lowlands of the Tigris-Euphrates Valley. Irrigation methods such as the system of channels shown here were used to control the water supply during the yearly cycle of flood and drought. Soil fertility was increased greatly by irrigation. Selective breeding produced domestic animals and plants different from their wild ancestors and of much greater value to man.

1300 A.D.

European medieval agriculture combined many improvements used in older civilizations. The three-course (field) system illustrated here alternated fallowing, spring crops, and winter crops. It included leguminous crops to increase soil fertility. Animal fertilizer was commonly used to improve the soil. By now domestic animals and plants were highly specialized, and agricultural techniques were much advanced over primitive cultivation.

Mechanization   Fertilizer   Pesticides   Selective Breeding

TODAY

Modern agriculture combines mechanization, natural and artificial fertilizers, pesticides, selective breeding, and storage, transportation, and other marketing facilities to produce ever-increasing amounts of food and industrial raw materials.

Storage and Transportation

cheese as well as for drinking. Pigs, probably introduced from southeastern Asia, were used for meat, but cattle, including zebus, yaks, and water buffaloes, were tamed and bred mainly for milk and hides and as beasts of burden.

None of the familiar farm-animal species was native to the Americas except the turkey. The peccary, an American wild hog, was never domesticated. In the era before Co-lumbus there were no draft animals in the Western Hemisphere.

Tools and Techniques. The first agricultural tool may have been a sickle, used to reap wild grains before farming began. The first implement for cultivation was a digging stick. With the addition of a crossbar it became a spade; with the addition of a blade of stone or shell, a hoe. Very heavy hoes pulled by draft animals were probably the

Culver Pictures, Inc.

Death of Wat, the Tyler. The leader of the peasants' rebellion of 1381, while conferring with young King Richard II of England (right foreground) was stabbed by the Lord Mayor of London. The peasants, unable to subsist by farming, wanted the right to take other work.

forerunners of plows. With the discovery of metal, blades and plow points were made of bronze and later of iron.

Ancient farmers invented many devices for easing their labor. As early as 2800 B.C. the Chinese were using a wheelbarrow seeding drill (sowing machine). By about 2000 B.C. the Babylonians had a sowing plow, which combined a plow and sower.

See also PLOW, subtitle *History;* REAPING AND THRESHING, subtitles *Hand Reaping* and *Hand Threshing.*

The earliest farmers planted a field continuously until the yield declined, then moved to a new field. Such usage is called *natural husbandry.* Later, land was rested for a year, then planted again. In time, fertilizers such as ashes, manure, and composts were used to enrich the soil. The Greeks and Romans also treated the soil with lime to make it less acid.

During the Roman era, *fallowing,* a system of soil restoration that had been used by the Chinese as early as 2000 B.C., became common practice. Each year some part of the land was left unplanted. The stubble and weeds were plowed under, adding vegetable

matter to the soil as well as destroying weeds, and also permitting moisture to accumulate. Roman fields, square in shape, were plowed first one way and then crossways.

The Romans next adopted crop rotation. They planted a field to legumes, which add nitrogen to the soil, one year and grain the next, and left it fallow the third year. Sometimes fallow was omitted from the rotation.

Land Ownership. Ancient man used the land freely, with no thought of ownership. After permanent villages were established, the land worked by the villagers was considered to belong to them. Sometimes it was held in common and parceled out each year to the families of the village. Sometimes a family owned the fields it cultivated. Pasture and woodland belonged to the village, to be used by all.

An ancient king, having established his authority by force of arms, usually claimed ownership to all the land over which he ruled. His subjects paid taxes or tribute to him for the use of it, tenant farmers paying in produce and, often, services. In ancient Greece, however, the city-states were autonomous, and most of the land was privately owned, except in the region conquered by Sparta. There the government owned the land and held the conquered people who lived on it (the Helots) in bondage, or serfdom.

See also FEUDALISM; HELOTS.

Roman farmers in the early period owned their land. As Rome expanded there was a tendency toward building great estates, called *latifundia,* that were worked entirely by slave labor. Gradually even the public lands were appropriated by wealthy citizens, in spite of efforts at land reform.

By the third century A.D. war and barbarian invasion had created a desperate economic crisis. The free peasants were forced to become tenant farmers, and many abandoned their rented fields. To stop this flight from farms so the great landowners could collect taxes, the emperors Diocletian and Constantine passed laws that reduced peasants to serfdom, making it unlawful for them to leave their farms.

See also LAND REFORM and cross references.

Medieval Agriculture
(500 to 1500)

The civilizations of the Roman and Byzantine empires and the Middle East were largely destroyed in the early Middle Ages by the migrations of primitive peoples into settled regions. In Europe commerce and communication were disrupted. Many agricultural improvements were abandoned and inventions lost to memory.

Peasants led a miserable existence that showed no improvement from one century to the next. In the 14th century Europe suffered a financial depression. This brought on peasant uprisings in many countries—Denmark in 1340, Majorca in 1351, France in 1358, and England (Wat Tyler's rebellion) in 1381. In no case did the revolt immediately improve the peasants' lot. The leaders were usually put to death, and in the case of the Jacquerie, as the French uprising was known, thousands of persons were slaughtered.

See also WAT, THE TYLER.

Crops and Livestock. Regional crops were often changed by the movement of peoples. The Germanic tribes that overran western Europe brought with them rye as their principal grain, and wheat flour became a luxury in areas where it had been a common food. In the Middle East and North Africa pig breeding was abolished after the Moslem conquest, because Islam forbids the eating of pork. Cotton was introduced into Europe in the eighth century when the Moors conquered Spain. Sugar cane, native to India, was being grown in Syria when the Crusaders arrived there in 1097. By the 13th century it was grown in Sicily.

The era of the Crusades was a period of expansion and population growth, during which the grain crop had to be constantly increased. In the 14th century came the Black Death, which reduced Europe's population by a third. Vacant fields were turned to commercial crops—flax for linen, rapeseed for oil, hops for ale, and dye plants such as madder (red), woad (blue), and weld (yellow). With land available for forage crops, cattle-raising was expanded. By the late 15th century, population growth made it necessary to discontinue commercial crops and resume the growing of food grain.

Tools and Techniques. A heavy, wheeled plow with a moldboard to turn over the soil was in general use in western Europe by about the seventh century. Two to four oxen were required to pull it. Horses could not pull a heavy load with a yoke harness. Not until a wooden head-collar came into use about the 10th century could they be used

for plowing. In the 15th century a lightweight plow was introduced from Flanders into adjacent countries. It could be drawn by one or two horses and operated by one man.

Sowing and reaping machines were completely forgotten. Seed was broadcast by hand, and raked into the soil with a horse-drawn harrow. Grain was cut with a sickle, later with a scythe. By age-old tradition, after a field was reaped it was gleaned—that is, poor people were permitted to go through it to gather any remaining stalks of grain for their own use. (For a picture, see MILLET, JEAN FRANCOIS.)

Two systems of land use were prominent during the Middle Ages. With the two-course system, one-half the arable land was left fallow and the other half planted. The three-course system rotated fallow, a winter grain, and a spring grain. For hundreds of years livestock was grazed in permanent pastures apart from arable land. Eventually the fallow field was turned to pasture and became enriched by manure. In the latter Middle Ages the advantage of replacing fallow with a crop of legume was rediscovered.

Country Life in the 15th Century, from a breviary of Cardinal Domenico Grimani of Venice
Culver Pictures, Inc.

Land Ownership. A type of proprietorship known as the manorial system developed during the Middle Ages. It was an aspect of feudalism, in which a nobleman owned, protected, and politically controlled a large estate. The feudal lord's estate was known as a manor. The peasants were sometimes tenants and sometimes serfs or villeins.

See also FEUDALISM, for details of the manorial system; LAND TENURE.

The manorial system provided safety and sustenance in regions subject to frequent warfare. The system ended quickly when commercial towns and trade grew up, as in Italy. It never existed in the Scandinavian countries, or along the coast of northern Europe where sheep were raised for the export of wool and grain was imported. In Germany colonization of the eastern frontier created a class of free peasants there.

In the 14th century the Black Death, which made farm labor scarce and valuable, brought an end to serfdom in much of western Europe. In England freehold (landowning) farmers, known as yeomen, became numerous in the 15th century. In France, however, the tenant farmer was often reduced to a condition fully as miserable as serfdom. This was especially true of sharecroppers, who owed up to half of their small harvests to their landlords. As landed estates were built up in central Europe, the free peasants were gradually deprived of their independence and became serfs.

See also YEOMAN.

Agriculture in the Age of Discovery
(1500 to 1700)

The discovery of America in 1492 and of the route to India in 1497-98 opened an era of far-ranging trade and communication. Plants and animals, people and ideas were exchanged between countries and continents. The spirit of adventure pervaded all areas of life, including agriculture, where experimentation and improvement came after generations of virtual stagnation.

In the 16th century many American plants, including potatoes, corn, tobacco, and cacao, were introduced into Europe. In return, livestock and draft animals, as well as the plow, were brought to the Americas. Coffee was brought from Arabia through Turkey to Europe, and was carried by the Dutch to Java in the late 17th century.

In Europe efforts were turned toward mechanizing agriculture. Seed drills were invented in Italy in the 16th century and in England and Austria in the 17th century. Improvements were made in other farm devices, including churns and gristmills. In England and the Low Countries fallow was abandoned completely, and field grasses were included in improved systems of crop rotation. Intensive farming requiring great quantities of manure and a large labor force was fully developed in Flanders by 1700. The land there was used for raising livestock, market gardening, and growing commercial crops.

See also BUTTER, subtitle *History;* FLOUR, subtitle *History;* WINDMILLS.

In England the arable land surrounding a village consisted of open fields divided into strips. Each farmer, either freehold or tenant, had strips here and there in the fields, instead of adjacent to each other. This open-field system was inconvenient for the individual farmer.

In the 16th century, when wool was in demand, there was a movement among landlords to turn their land to sheep-raising. Dispossessing tenants, they enclosed the fields with hedges and used them for pasture. Farmers who were able to consolidate their strips into unified farms joined the enclosure movement.

At first the government tended to protect the open-field system. By the mid-17th century, however, the official attitude had changed, and enclosure was encouraged. Landlords began also enclosing the village pasture and woodlands. Inefficient farmers were forced off the land. Those who remained adopted the new methods of soil enrichment, selective livestock breeding, and other features of this English agricultural revolution.

Modern Agriculture
(1700 to World War II)

In Europe. Several British farmers led the agricultural revolution. Jethro Tull (1674-1741) invented a seed drill, used manure for fertilizer, and practiced pulverizing the soil. He spread his ideas through his writings. Charles Townshend (1674-1738) promoted the cultivation of turnips and clover as soil restoratives and practiced crop rotation. Robert Bakewell (1725-1795) was a pioneer in animal breeding and care of livestock. Arthur Young (1741-1820) popularized better farming methods through his writings. The new practices spread from

Diderot's Encyclopédie

Threshing in the 18th Century. Sheaves, spread on floor, were beaten with flails. Grains were shoveled into basket and winnowed.

Great Britain to continental Europe and North America.

A milestone in agricultural technology was the publication of *Chemistry in Its Application to Agriculture and Physiology* (1840) by the German scientist Justus von Liebig. This book marked the beginning of the development of artificial fertilizers, which, with the tractor and harvester, led directly to the great increases in crop productivity of the 19th and 20th centuries.

See also LIEBIG, BARON JUSTUS VON.

By 1870 the competition of cheap grain from the United States caused a crisis in European agriculture. In Great Britain many farmers were ruined, and moved to cities. Arable land was turned to pasture. Denmark shifted its agriculture from crops to livestock. Most other European countries abandoned free trade in agricultural goods and extended tariff protection to farm products. Under tariff protection many features of the old farming systems were retained: many small farms, a large percentage of people in agriculture, and older farming methods. By keeping to free trade and adjusting to competition, Great Britain and Denmark developed progressive agricultural industries.

European agriculture was hard hit by World War I and by the economic depression of the 1930's. Farmers had suffered greatly during the war, and in the 1920's had benefited little from the general prosperity. After the depression struck in the 1930's, government control of agriculture became firmly established. Great Britain abandoned free trade. All countries, even Denmark, established controls over farm production and marketing. Governments encouraged and assisted farmers in adopting mechanization and in the use of fertilizers.

In the United States. The first English colonists brought English farming methods to North America, but soon developed their own practices. Since land was plentiful and labor scarce, there was a tendency to revert to natural husbandry. Land was farmed year after year to the same crop until the soil was worn out. Then the farmers moved on to new land. A distinctively American pattern was the scattering of farms instead of the establishing of agricultural villages.

Corn and tobacco soon took the place of European plants as principal crops.

In the Southern colonies, subsistence farming gave way to commercial farming. Tobacco became the first cash crop. Large plantations developed with the use of Negro slave labor. Cotton, rice, and indigo were other important cash crops. After Samuel Slater built the first American cotton mill in 1790 and Eli Whitney invented the cotton gin in 1793, cotton became the predominant crop in the South. The sway of King Cotton was not shaken until the 1920's when the boll weevil destroyed crops, forcing a turn to diversification.

After the Revolutionary War there was a great westward expansion of population and agriculture. Since land was cheap and seem-

Threshing in the 19th Century. Steam engine drove thresher on a Dakota Territory farm in 1878.

ingly unlimited, most farmers wore their land out quickly by continually growing the same crop. Farming during this pioneering period was mainly on a subsistence level. Farmers hoped for cash income from the sale of their lands, as land prices rose continuously.

The wasteful agricultural practices of this period were of concern to George Washington and Thomas Jefferson, among others. Washington corresponded with British farm leaders, made plans for crop rotation, and secured better seed, livestock, and implements from them. Another progressive American agriculturist was Edmund Ruffin (1794-1865). He advocated the use of fertilizers, better plowing techniques, and crop rotation.

After 1800 agriculture began making rapid advances from the hand tool stage, led by United States discoveries. In 1819 Jethro Wood patented a cast-iron plow with interchangeable parts. Reapers were invented by Obed Hussey in 1833 and Cyrus McCormick in 1834. John Deere's steel moldboard plow made it possible to farm the heavy prairie soil. Improvements and other inventions followed quickly: the two-row corn planter (1847); disk plow (1850); portable steam engine for farm use (1863); wagon-

type manure spreader (1883); and gasoline tractor (1901).

Other developments included the first large-scale use of irrigation (by the Mormons in Utah, beginning in 1847). The Homestead Act of 1862 made it possible for farmers to obtain quarter sections (160 acres) of land free. In the same year the Morrill Land-Grant College Act encouraged agricultural education.

During the mid-19th century the growth of cities gave farmers huge markets. The building of railways about 1850 stimulated commercial agriculture. After the Civil War there was a great expansion in wheat farming in the Midwest and in ranching in the West. The invention of barbed wire, patented by Joseph F. Glidden in 1874, made possible the private ownership of grazing lands on the treeless plains. About 1900 the federal government began to encourage irrigation by its reclamation policies.

The period from 1900 through World War I was the brightest period for United States agriculture. Never since then have farmers been so close to the rest of the population in general prosperity. The tremendous wartime markets of the farmers collapsed completely during the early 1920's as European agriculture regained productivity and nations adopted high tariffs. The depression of the 1930's further hurt agriculture.

Beginning with the Agricultural Adjustment Act of 1933 the federal government intervened drastically in farm production and marketing to raise farm prices and income. This government intervention continued during World War II and in the postwar period.

Agriculture after World War II

Though the period before World War II was one of depression for world agriculture, discoveries and advances continued. During the war these advances—such as improved artificial fertilizers, self-propelled combines, and one-man balers—helped United States agriculture reach new peaks of productivity. The destruction of millions of farms, the disruption of transportation, and most of all the death and injury of millions of persons in Europe and Asia ruined agriculture in those areas. Nations whose lands were unharmed by the war, principally in the Americas and Australia and New Zealand, helped feed and clothe the people of war-torn countries.

Several World War II developments spurred agricultural production. These included DDT, the most effective insecticide found until that time; and mechanical improvements such as self-propelled mechanical cotton pickers and corn pickers, specially designed aircraft for spraying, and special agricultural machines for crops never before handled mechanically, such as tree fruits.

After 1950 agriculture in Europe began to regain prewar productivity. Farmers, afraid of another postwar depression, called for government protection. As a result, there was no return to more freely competitive economic policies as there had been after World War I. The Korean Conflict temporarily brought a war boom to United States agriculture, but afterwards the same old problems returned.

The growth of Communism brought a new pattern of land ownership to eastern Europe and China, as Communist governments forced free peasants to turn their lands over to the state. In nations dependent on plantation crops such as coffee and cacao, there was economic instability as these crops fluctuated in price on the world market. The Common Market, formed to unite the economies of France, West Germany, Belgium, the Netherlands, Luxembourg, and Italy, had a significant and continuing effect on the agricultural policies of these nations.

During the early and mid-1960's agricultural productivity and efficiency increased in nations that were already agriculturally and economically advanced. These were principally countries of North America and northwestern Europe, and Australia, New Zealand, Japan, and a few others. In general, the Communist nations made slow advances marked by many setbacks. Each year saw a new agricultural reform or policy designed to increase production. This was especially true in Russia and China. The underdeveloped nations, with few exceptions, struggled to feed their people while concentrating on industrialization.

Agriculture and Population. It is in the underdeveloped nations that the greatest need for improvement in agricultural methods exists. These nations experienced a sudden rise in population growth after World War II, largely through the reduction of death rates by public health measures. This "population explosion" has outrun the ability of agriculture in these countries to feed

Threshing in Early 20th Century. Horses were still used, but a tractor replaced the steam engine.
Culver Pictures, Inc.

their growing populations. Since World War II many underdeveloped nations, notably India and Egypt, have depended on loans and gifts of food to feed their populations. The United States and Canada have been the principal sources of food for underdeveloped nations.

In the decades after World War II, world food production grew at roughly the same rate as world population. However, the greatest rises in production were in nations with the lowest rates of population increase—such as the United States, Canada, the countries of northwestern Europe, Australia and New Zealand, and Japan. In Russia and eastern Europe the yearly average production of food per capita (per person) rose during the first few years of this period, then fell, then rose again. In the Far East, Africa, and Latin America, food production per capita made few gains in this period. These three areas are the sites of the world's swiftest rise in population.

Increased agricultural production—of food, especially—is one of mankind's most pressing needs today. Production is increased through use of fertilizers, pesticides, and machinery; improved seed and livestock and poultry breeds; better livestock management; and expanded irrigation and soil conservation. Crop yields in underdeveloped nations are so low that an increase to only one-half that of advanced nations would allow self-sufficiency with no increase in acreage farmed. But accomplishing such increases calls for great effort, planning, and large sums of money. The nations that most need improvements are least able to pay for them. According to some economists and agricultural experts, many underdeveloped nations could afford to improve their agriculture by reducing industrial investment.

Production may also be increased by bringing more acreage under cultivation. Some agronomists estimate that the world's 3,500,000,000 acres of cropland could be doubled by the use of reclamation techniques. The development of new lands, however, is expensive when transportation and living facilities must be established, and very expensive where it is necessary to develop irrigation systems.

Soilless agriculture is another source of food, although it is still too expensive for widespread use. The cultivation of fish in small bodies of water and the cultivation of

seaweed (for human food and animal feed) are becoming increasingly important in the Far East and are being tried elsewhere as a means of increasing the food supply.

See also POPULATION, subtitle *Population Growth:* After World War II. The history of specific crops, livestock animals, machines and equipment, and methods are discussed in the articles on these subjects.

Books about Agriculture

Archer, Jules. *Hunger on Planet Earth* (Crowell, 1977).

Bender, Barbara. *Farming in Prehistory from Hunter-Gatherer to Food-Producer* (St. Martin's Press, 1975).

Bennett, G. W., and others. *Food and Fiber for a Changing World* (Interstate, 1976).

Borgstrom, Georg. *Harvesting the Earth* (Abelard-Schuman, 1973).

Campbell, J. R., and J. F. Lasley. *The Science of Animals That Serve Mankind,* 2nd edition (McGraw-Hill, 1975).

Campbell, K. O. *Food for the Future: How Agriculture Can Meet the Challenge* (University of Nebraska, 1979).

Conrat, Maisie and Richard. *The American Farm: a Photographic History* (Houghton Mifflin, 1977).

Cox, G. W., and M. D. Atkins. *Agricultural Ecology: an Analysis of World Food Production Systems* (Freeman, 1979).

Gurney, Gene and Clare. *Agriculture Careers* (Watts, 1978).

Lapedes, D. N., editor. *McGraw-Hill Encyclopedia of Food, Agriculture, and Nutrition* (McGraw-Hill, 1977).

Martin, J. H., and others. *Principles of Field Crop Production* (Macmillan, 1976).

Roy, E. P. *Exploring Agribusiness,* 2nd edition (Interstate, 1975).

Schapsmeier, F. H. and E. L. *Encyclopedia of American Agricultural History* (Greenwood Press, 1975).

Schlebecker, J. T. *Whereby We Thrive: a History of American Farming, 1607-1972* (Iowa State University, 1975).

Schwenke, Karl. *Living on the Land: Successful Small-Scale Farming* (Garden Way, 1979).

Seim, R. K. *The American Farmer* (Rand McNally, 1974).

Smith, H. P., and L. H. Wilkes. *Farm Machinery and Equipment* (McGraw-Hill, 1976).

Symons, Leslie. *Agricultural Geography* (Westview Press, 1979).

U.S. Department of Agriculture. *Yearbook of Agriculture* (Government Printing Office, annual).

For Younger Readers:

Buehr, Walter. *Food from Farm to Home* (Morrow, 1970).

Hellman, Hal. *Feeding the World of the Future* (Evans, 1972).

Roth, C. E., and R. J. Froehlich. *The Farm Book* (Harper & Row, 1977).

Shuttlesworth, D. E. and G. J. *Farms for Today and Tomorrow: the Wonders of Food Production* (Doubleday, 1979).

Department of Agriculture Buildings, Washington, D.C. The administration building is at left; at the right is the South Building.

Agriculture, U.S. Department of (USDA), an executive department of the United States government. It is headed by the secretary of agriculture, who is a member of the President's cabinet. Although a primary objective of the department is service to United States farmers and ranchers, many of its activities benefit all American consumers. The USDA promotes farming efficiency and improvement of the quality of food and fiber, helps improve the distribution of farm products, protects the income of farmers, and promotes conservation and wise use of land, water, and timber resources.

Work of the USDA includes research, education, soil conservation, marketing regulation, agricultural adjustment (price support and production control), surplus disposal, and rural development. It conducts both basic and applied research and makes the results available to farmers and others through its publications and extension service. It provides crop reports, commodity standards, meat and poultry inspection, and other inspection, grading, and marketing services. It seeks to eradicate or control plant and animal diseases and pests. The USDA administers the national forests, promotes soil and water conservation, sponsors the national school lunch program, and provides loans to farmers and farmer cooperatives.

The USDA operates several hundred research installations and experimental farms. It publishes hundreds of books and booklets each year. Research and experiments deal with soils and land use, higher-yielding crops, improved livestock and poultry, better fertilizers, animal nutrition, farm engineering, control of animal and plant diseases and pests, marketing of farm products, farm statistics, human nutrition, home economics, and forestry.

The Department of Agriculture was created by Congress in 1862, and was at first headed by a commissioner of agriculture. In 1889 Congress made the USDA an executive department headed by a secretary of agriculture.

Divisions

The department's activities are organized into various divisions, each headed by an assistant secretary or a director.

Small Community and Rural Development. This division provides a variety of technical and financial services to people living in rural areas. Its units are the following.

Farmers Home Administration provides loans and grants for such purposes as ownership and improvement of family-size farms, community facilities, and disaster relief.

Federal Crop Insurance Corporation provides insurance against crop loss from natural disasters.

Rural Electrification Administration makes loans to bring electric power and telephone service to people in rural areas. See RURAL ELECTRIFICATION ADMINISTRATION.

Marketing and Inspection Services. This division administers inspection, marketing, transportation, and regulatory programs to aid producers and handlers of agricultural commodities. Its units are the following.

Agricultural Cooperative Service provides technical assistance to cooperatives and conducts research on topics of importance to them. The service also collects and publishes statistics on the activities of cooperatives in the United States.

Agricultural Marketing Service provides market news and inspects and sets standards for grades and classes of many farm products.

Animal and Plant Health Inspection Service is responsible for programs designed to control and eradicate pests and diseases in plants and livestock.

Federal Grain Inspection Service administers a nationwide system of grain inspection. The service also works to assure honest weighing and proper handling of grain in its shipment.

The Science and Education Administration seeks ways to increase yields and to control disease. Here technicians prepare to inject an experimental chemical into a tree trunk in an attempt to immunize the tree against disease.
USDA

The Soil Conservation Service offers advice on methods of preventing erosion not only on farms but also on projects such as this road fill.
USDA—Soil Conservation Service

Food Safety and Inspection Service inspects and grades meat and poultry, eggs, and dairy products. The service also monitors livestock slaughter to ensure that it is humane.

Office of Transportation performs a number of functions designed to facilitate the transportation of agricultural goods.

Food and Consumer Services. This division handles federal food welfare programs. Its principal units are the following.

Food and Nutrition Service administers programs to combat hunger and malnutrition. It provides food for needy persons through the food stamp program, and it administers the national school lunch program. See SCHOOL LUNCH PROGRAM.

Human Nutrition Information Service conducts research in nutrition and collects and disseminates information on nutrition.

International Affairs and Commodity Programs. This division works toward price, market, and farm income stabilization. Its principal units are the following.

Agricultural Stabilization and Conservation Service is responsible for programs in production adjustment, conservation assistance, and price and market stabilization.

Commodity Credit Corporation administers loan, purchase, and payment programs to help stabilize and protect farm income and prices and maintain adequate and balanced supplies of agricultural products. It also operates a grain storage program.

Foreign Agricultural Service develops foreign markets for United States farm products.

Science and Education. The work of this division is carried out by the following units.

Agricultural Research Service conducts research on how to improve agricultural output.

Cooperative State Research Service administers federal grant funds for agricultural research and also assists in planning and coordinating various research programs. Funds are available to state agricultural experiment stations, land-grant colleges, and other designated institutions. (See EXPERIMENT STATION.)

Extension Service is the educational arm of the USDA. There are Extension offices in nearly every county in the nation. The federal government, the states through their land-grant colleges and universities, and county governments share in financing, planning, and carrying out Extension educational programs and together form the Cooperative Extension Service.

Through *county extension agents* (usually called simply county agents), the Cooperative Extension Service advises farmers and ranchers on production and management methods and demonstrates new scientific and technological developments relating to agriculture. Through *home economics agents,* the service provides farm families with information and advice on nutrition, child care, and household management.

The Cooperative Extension Service also helps to teach boys and girls farming and homemaking in association with the Four-H Clubs. See FOUR-H (4-H) CLUBS.

National Agriculture Library, Beltsville, Maryland, is the largest agricultural library in the United States.

Natural Resources and Environment. Its units are the following.

Soil Conservation Service carries out a national soil and water conservation program through several thousand local conservation districts.

United States Forest Service is responsible for the management of federal forest reserves. See FOREST SERVICE, UNITED STATES.

Economics. Its important units include the following.

Economic Research Service provides research reports on commodities and national and international economics.

Statistical Reporting Service issues statistical reports on crop and livestock production estimates.

World Food and Agricultural Outlook Board oversees and reviews all reports prepared by the USDA on food production.

See also articles in this encyclopedia on the following secretaries of agriculture: MORTON, J. STERLING; WILSON, JAMES; WALLACE, HENRY A.

Agrimony, ăg′rĭ-mō′nĭ, a genus of hardy perennial herbs of the rose family. These herbs are native to the north temperate zone, and are considered wild flowers, although they are sometimes cultivated. The flowers, which are yellow, are not showy. The leaves are aromatic. The fruit of the agrimony has hooked bristles, and can cling to clothing and fur. Agrimonies grow to a height of about four feet (120 cm).

The most common North American species abounds from Nova Scotia south to North Carolina, and west to Michigan. This species is also found in New Mexico. The most common European species has been used to make a mild astringent tea. The flowers of several other species yield a pale yellow dye.

The common North American species is *Agrimonia gryposepala.* The most common European species is *A. eupatoria.* Agrimonies belong to the family Rosaceae.

Agrippa, Herod. See HEROD.

Agrippa, ă-grĭp′ă, **Marcus Vipsanius** (63-12 B.C.), a Roman general and statesman. He was of humble birth but became the leading general, chief adviser, and son-in-law of Octavian, who became the emperor Augustus. Agrippa won the decisive battle of Actium (31), between Octavian and Mark Antony, for Octavian. During the rest of his life he acted as deputy to the emperor. An able organizer and engineer, Agrippa built aqueducts and the original Pantheon. He prepared a map of the world. His third wife was Octavian's daughter Julia.

Brookhaven National Laboratory

Agronomists seek to improve the quality and yield of field crops. Here research biologists examine a tobacco plant crossbred by fusion of ordinary cells rather than by the normal reproductive process.

Agronomy, ă-grŏn′ŏ-mĭ, the branch of agriculture that deals with field crop production and soil studies. Crop scientists study plant species and varieties for the purpose of developing plants best adapted to various soil and climatic conditions. Such scientists employ the principles of genetics, chemistry, physics, and biology to plants and soils in order to develop more efficient methods of crop production.

Plant Breeding

Because the supply of agricultural land is steadily decreasing and the population is increasing, it is necessary to use the available land to greatest advantage. By breeding higher-yielding plant varieties, agronomists aid in increasing agricultural productivity. Annual crop production is increased through the development of plant varieties that are resistant to disease, drought, heat, cold, wind, and various insects. Plant breeding has also aided in improving crop quality, giving crops, among other things, better flavor and higher vitamin content.

Soil Studies

Agronomists study the soil extensively. They determine the mineral content of the soil and use this as a basis on which to recommend the proper fertilizer. The composition of fertilizers is of interest to agronomists because virtually every type of soil requires a different fertilizer. Physical and chemical properties of soils are also studied to determine the suitability of a particular soil for a given crop.

Soil conservation is an important aspect of agronomy. Much soil is carried away every year by erosion. (See EROSION.) Agronomists help curtail erosion by devising means to keep the soil in place, including planting grass and shrubs, using contour plowing and other cultivation methods, or planting windbreaks (rows of trees or shrubs, or both) in dry areas. Agronomists also recommend proper irrigation methods to help maintain soil conditions that are beneficial to crops.

See also FERTILIZER; IRRIGATION; PLANT, subtitle *Plant Improvement;* SOIL.

Books about Agronomy

Roberts, W. O., and Henry Landford. *The Climate Mandate* (Freeman, 1979).
Stoskopf, N. C. *Understanding Crop Production* (Reston, 1981).

Aguascalientes, ä′gwäs-kä-lyän′tås, Mexico, the capital of Aguascalientes state. It is 265 miles (425 km) northwest of Mexico City. Products include leather goods, furniture, paint, textiles, pottery, and serapes. Large railway repair shops are here. Aguascalientes is a health resort with hot springs (the name is Spanish for "hot waters") and is situated at an altitude of 6,225 feet (1,897 m) above sea level. Under the city is a large network of tunnels built by ancient Indians of unknown origin.

Aguascalientes was founded in 1575 as a Spanish outpost against hostile Indians. Nearby silver mines influenced the city's early growth but later declined. The establishment of railway shops helped in the growth of the modern city.

Population: 247,764.

Aguinaldo, ä′gê-näl′dȯ, **Emilio** (1869-1964), a Filipino patriot. In 1896 he led a revolt against Spain; he won many notable victories but when faced with enemy reinforcements had to retreat into the mountains. In January, 1898, he agreed to go into exile on the promise of a large subsidy. When the Spanish-American War broke out a few months later, Aguinaldo returned home and helped lead Filipino guerrillas against the Spanish.

Aguinaldo soon turned against the United States because his homeland was not granted immediate independence, and proclaimed

Emilio Aguinaldo
Manila *Chronicle*

an independent Philippine republic. He conducted a skillful guerrilla campaign until he was captured by Colonel Frederick Funston in 1901. He then took an oath of allegiance to the United States.

Aguinaldo was born near Manila and was educated there in the University of Santo Tomás. As a young man he became mayor of Cavite Viejo. After the failure of his insurrection he lived mostly in retirement from public life, but advocated good relations with the United States. In 1935 he ran for the presidency of the newly established Commonwealth of the Philippines, but lost to Manuel Quezon. During World War II as a private citizen Aguinaldo made radio broadcasts in support of the Japanese occupation government. He was arrested in 1945 but was later released. In *A Second Look at America* (1957) he states that he was under compulsion when he cooperated with the Japanese.

Agulhas, Cape, ȧ-gŭl′ȧs, South Africa, the southernmost point of the continent. It lies where the Atlantic and Indian oceans meet, 100 miles (160 km) southeast of Cape of Good Hope. The name *Agulhas* (Portuguese for "needles") refers to the jagged reefs and sunken rocks around the cape, on which many ships have been lost.

Agulhas Current, a warm surface current of the Indian Ocean. It is a branch of the South Equatorial Current. North of southern Madagascar it is known as the Mozambique Current. The Agulhas Current flows southwestward along the southeastern and southern coast of Africa. It is deflected eastward and southeastward at Cape Agulhas by the cold Benguela Current. The Agulhas is one of the world's strongest currents, with a speed of up to 4 miles per hour (6.4 km/h).

Ahab, ā′hăb, or **Achab,** ā′kăb, a king of Israel (reigned 875?-853? B.C.). He was an able ruler, and under him Israel reached the peak of its power and prosperity. The kingdom of Judah was a subordinate ally. When Ahab's wife, Jezebel, a daughter of the king of Sidon, introduced the worship of Baal, the prophet Elijah denounced Ahab.

Ahab joined other rulers to check temporarily the advance of the Assyrian Empire. He was killed in a battle with the Syrians. His story is told in I Kings 16-22.

See also JEZEBEL.

Ahasuerus. See ESTHER.

Ahaz, ā'hăz, or **Achaz,** ā'kăz, a king of Judah (reigned 735?-720? B.C.). He refused to join the kings of Israel and Syria in a revolt against Assyria. Instead, he allied himself with Assyria, disregarding the advice of the prophet Isaiah. After the revolt was put down Ahaz became a vassal of the Assyrian king, paid tribute, and adopted Assyrian gods. His story is told in II Kings 16.

Ahmadabad, ä'mȧd-ȧ-băd', or **Ahmedabad,** ä'mȧd-ä-bäd', India, the capital of Ahmadabad district and of Gujarat state. The city is on the Sabarmati River, 285 miles (460 km) north of Bombay. Ahmadabad is a center of cotton and silk textile milling. It also manufactures a great variety of light consumer goods. Several technical schools and Gujarat University are here. Ahmadabad is a sacred city of the Jain religion, and has many 15th- to 17th-century mosques and tombs. Jami Masjid, a mosque completed in 1424, is noted for its sanctuary with 260 carved pillars supporting 15 stone domes.

Ahmadabad was founded in 1421 by Ahmed Shah as the capital of the Gujarat kingdom.

Population: 1,585,544.

Ahriman, in the Zend-Avesta, the source of all evil. See ZOROASTER, subtitle *Zoroastrianism.*

Ahura Mazda, or **Ormazd,** in the Zend-Avesta, the source of all good. See ZOROASTER, subtitle *Zoroastrianism.*

Ahvaz. See AHWAZ.

Ahvenanmaa. See ÅLAND ISLANDS.

Ahwaz, ä-wäz', or **Ahvaz,** ä-väz', Iran, the capital of Khuzistan province. It is on the Karun River about 70 miles (113 km) north-northeast of Abadan. Ahwaz lies in the midst of Iran's richest oil fields and has numerous related industries. The city is a river port as well as a hub of southern Iran's highway, railway, and petroleum pipeline systems. As early as the 12th century Ahwaz flourished as an agricultural trade center. It became prominent after 1908 when oil was discovered.

Population: 329,006.

Ai, the three-toed sloth. See SLOTH.

Aïda, ä-ē'dȧ, an opera in four acts by Giuseppe Verdi. The Italian libretto by Antonio Ghislanzoni is based on a French version by Camille du Locle. *Aïda* was commissioned in 1869 to celebrate the opening of the khedive's new theater in Cairo, Egypt, and of the Suez Canal. It was first produced in Cairo in 1871. One of Verdi's most popular operas, *Aïda* combines rich pageantry with an outpouring of emotionally intense music. Two of its most famous arias are "Celeste Aïda" and "O terra, addio," the final love duet. The "Grand March," or "Triumphal March," and ballet music are popular concert pieces.

The story takes place in ancient Egypt. Aïda, a prisoner of the Egyptians and slave to Amneris, daughter of the king of Egypt, is in love with Radamès, captain of the Egyptian army. Aïda's father, King Amonasro of Ethiopia, attempts to rescue her, but his army is defeated by Radamès' men. Amonasro forces Aïda to get secret information from Radamès about the Egyptian army. When Radamès realizes that he has unwittingly betrayed his country, he gives himself up. Amneris, in love with him and jealous of Aïda, promises freedom to Radamès if he will forget Aïda. He refuses and is condemned to be buried alive. In the tomb he finds Aïda, who has hidden there to share his fate. The lovers die together.

Aide, ād, or **Aide-de-camp,** ād'dĕ-kămp', an officer who assists a general,

A Scene from the First Act of *Aïda*
Metropolitan Opera Assn.

admiral, or chief of state as member of a personal staff. Duties are not prescribed, but in general are those of a personal secretary in taking care of time-consuming details. The rank of an aide ranges from lieutenant or ensign to colonel or naval captain, depending on the rank of the officer being served.

Before development of general staffs in the late 19th century generals and admirals depended on aides for many services now prescribed for staff officers.

AIDS (in full: **Acquired Immune Deficiency Syndrome**), a severe, often fatal, disorder characterized by increased susceptibility to various acute infections. It is spread through sexual or other intimate contact, through blood transfusions, or by the use of contaminated hypodermic needles. The infectious agent is believed to be carried in the blood, semen, saliva, sweat, and mucus. AIDS occurs most frequently in males, particularly homosexuals, intravenous drug users, and hemophiliacs. Women and children can contract it through contact with an infected male.

The cause of AIDS is uncertain, but it has been linked to the *human T-cell leukemia virus*. This virus inhibits the production of and suppresses the activity of specific white blood cells called T lymphocytes. T lymphocytes are produced in the thymus gland and help the body fight bacterial and fungal infections. The virus, by suppressing the activity of the T lymphocytes, makes the body susceptible to infections and diseases.

Symptoms of AIDS include swollen

Ailanthus, with Leaves, Bark, and Seeds
NEW STANDARD photos by Emil Zunker

lymph glands, fever, weight loss, diarrhea, and persistent viral infections such as influenza, shingles, and oral thrush. AIDS victims are prone to two rare diseases that often lead to death: a form of pneumonia caused by a microorganism called *Pneumocystis carinii* and a form of skin cancer called *Kaposi's sarcoma*. The pneumonia causes acute infection in the lungs and respiratory tract. In Kaposi's sarcoma, purplish-brown lesions form on the toes and legs and in the gastrointestinal tract.

No specific treatment has been found and there is no known cure for AIDS. Drugs are often prescribed to kill infections and stimulate the production of antibodies.

Aigrette. See EGRET.

Aiken, ā'kĕn, **Conrad** (Potter) (1889-1973), a United States author. His poems, novels, and short stories reflect his interest in philosophy and psychoanalysis. This interest is especially evident in his novel *Blue Voyage* (1927) and in his short story "Silent Snow, Secret Snow." He experimented with the adaptation of musical forms and elements to poetry in such works as *The Jig of Forslin* (1916) and his various "Preludes." Aiken received a Pulitzer Prize in 1930 for *Selected Poems,* and a National Book Award in 1954 for *Collected Poems.* In 1969 he received the National Medal for Literature.

Aiken was born in Savannah, Georgia, but was reared in Massachusetts. He graduated from Harvard in 1912. Aiken lived in England much of the time until the late 1940's; after that he divided his time between his homes in Savannah and Brewster, Massachusetts. He was poetry consultant at the Library of Congress from 1950 to 1952.

His many books include: Poetry—*Earth Triumphant* (1914); *The Charnel Rose* (1918); *John Deth* (1930); *Brownstone Eclogues* (1942); *Sheepfold Hill* (1957); *Thee* (1968). Novels—*King Coffin* (1935); *The Conversation* (1939). His collected essays of literary criticism were published in 1958; his collected short stories, in 1960; and a collection of his letters, in 1978. *Ushant: an Essay* (1952) is autobiographical.

Aikido. See MARTIAL ARTS.

Ailanthus, ă-lăn'thŭs, a genus of trees native to central and southern Asia and northern Australia. These trees grow rapidly up to 100 feet (30 m), attaining most of their height within 10 or 12 years. The leaves and branches give off a disagreeable odor when cut or broken. The Chinese species are used for street and landscape planting because they grow in almost all types of soil, resist smoke and dust, and are not attacked by insects or disease.

In the United States, the most common ailanthus is the *tree of heaven,* native to China. It grows up to 60 feet (18 m) high, with the trunk 2 to 3 feet (60 to 90 cm) in diameter. Its crown is loose and spreading, and its small flowers are green.

Propagation of the ailanthus is by seeds and root cuttings. The fluid extract of the bark of one species is used medicinally as a purgative and a tonic, and for destroying intestinal worms. The ailanthus silkworm of eastern Asia feeds mainly on ailanthus leaves.

The tree of heaven is *Ailanthus altissima.* The bark of *A. glandulosa* is used medicinally. All species belong to the family Simarubaceae.

Aileron. See AIRPLANE, section "Parts of an Airplane," subtitle *Wings.*

Aime, ām, **Valcour** (1798-1867), a United States sugar planter. He was born in Louisiana of French ancestry. Aime developed a large sugar plantation in St. James Parish near New Orleans. The first sugar refining in the United States was done on his plantation. He engaged in agricultural experimentation, introduced improvements on his plantation and in his refineries, and promoted crop diversification. Aime made liberal donations to churches and schools.

Ainu, ī′nōō, or **Aino,** ī′nō, the earliest known inhabitants of Japan. They are of special interest to anthropologists because their physical characteristics and traditional customs differ markedly from those of the Japanese and other Oriental people.

The Ainu are a short, sturdily built people with light skin, round eyes, and wavy black hair. Their body hair is as heavy as, or heavier than, that of any other people. Some anthropologists believe that the Ainu are descended from a Caucasoid group. Others believe that they developed from a Siberian Mongoloid group or migrated from an island in the South Pacific. Their language is not related to Japanese or to any known group of languages. It has several dialects.

Originally living throughout Japan, the Ainu were pushed to the northern islands during centuries of warfare with the Yamato clan. There they established coastal and mountain villages and lived as hunters, fishermen, and food gatherers. Each village was headed by a hereditary chieftain. Villagers lived in thatched one-room huts. They wore

JAL; Japan Tourist Assn.

Ainus. *Top,* a weaver at work. *Bottom,* a religious ceremony.

animal furs and elaborately decorated clothes woven from bark fibers. Men grew long beards, women were tattooed with false mustaches. The Ainu believed that all things living and nonliving have a spirit dwelling in them. They honored the spirits of bears in a sacred ceremony that included the sacrifice of a bear and prayer, dancing, and feasting.

After the Japanese began to settle northern Japan in the 1860's, the Ainu gradually adopted their language and customs. By the 1950's, the Ainu way of life was preserved in only a few villages, mainly as a tourist attraction. Most Ainu live in Japanese communities or in Ainu villages that look like those of the Japanese. They farm, fish, work in towns, or make traditional handicraft articles. Only about 12,000 Ainu remain, all on Hokkaido Island; few are full-blooded.

See also RACES OF MAN (picture).

Air, the mixture of gases that surrounds the earth and forms the earth's atmosphere. Air is invisible and tasteless, and pure air has no odor. Air has weight, can be expanded or compressed, and at extremely low temperatures, can be changed into a liquid or solid. Air in motion, called *wind,* has enough force to turn windmills, to move ships, and, in hurricanes and tornadoes, uproot trees and wreck buildings.

Composition of Air

Air is a somewhat variable mixture, consisting chiefly of nitrogen (about 78 per cent by volume) and oxygen (about 21 per cent by volume). All land animals and many plants take in oxygen from the air—without it, they would die. Air also contains carbon dioxide, water vapor, hydrogen, methane, ozone, the noble gases (helium, neon, argon, krypton, xenon, and radon), nitrous oxide, nitrogen dioxide, and various solid and gaseous impurities.

The carbon dioxide contained in air is essential to the life of all green plants that live on land. These plants take in carbon dioxide from the air and, in the process of photosynthesis, use it to manufacture the carbohydrates required for their growth. The carbon dioxide in the air—which accounts for only about 0.03 per cent of the air by volume—is produced from the burning and decaying of organic matter and from the respiration of animals and plants.

The water-vapor content of the air is referred to as *humidity.* (See HUMIDITY.) The humidity constantly changes, varying with the temperature of the air and with conditions on the earth's surface.

The air also contains fine volcanic dust, pollen, spores of molds and algae, bacteria, soot, and finely pulverized earth. After a nuclear explosion, the air may contain billions of dangerous particles of radioactive matter. The wind often carries these particles for hundreds and even thousands of miles before they settle to the earth. The radioactive matter that is produced by a nuclear explosion and falls to earth afterward is called *fallout.* (See NUCLEAR WEAPONS, subtitle *Effects of Nuclear Explosions:* Fallout Radiation.)

Dust particles in the air can be seen in a beam of sunlight that penetrates into a darkened room. On a larger scale, the action of sunlight on dust and other particles in the air causes beautiful sunsets. The scattering of sunlight by the molecules of the gases

making up the air causes the blueness of the sky.

Man-made impurities in the air, which come primarily from furnaces and motor vehicles, have created serious problems over some cities and industrial areas. (See AIR POLLUTION.)

Air Density and Pressure

Air is densest (heaviest) at or below sea level. At sea level, air exerts an average pressure of 14.7 pounds per square inch in all directions and weighs 0.08 pounds (1.28 ounces) per cubic foot. A pressure of 14.7 pounds per square inch is called *one atmosphere.* At an altitude of 20,000 feet, the pressure is 6.76 pounds per square inch; the weight, 0.04 pounds per cubic foot. Air pressure is measured by an instrument called a *barometer.* (See BAROMETER.)

A balloon will rise when it is filled with helium or any other gas that is lighter (less dense) than the surrounding air. Birds and airplanes, which are heavier than air, fly through the air by creating a lifting force (called *lift*) that is greater than the force of gravity. Lift is created when the air pressure on the top surface of a wing is less than the air pressure on the bottom surface. (See AIRPLANE, section "Why an Airplane Flies"; BALLOON; BIRD, subtitle *Flight and Diving.*)

Special Forms of Air

Compressed Air. When air is compressed —that is, forced into a smaller space than it normally occupies—it has a tremendous expansive pressure. This pressure, which can reach thousands of pounds per square inch, is used to drive such piston-operated machines as rivet guns and rock drills. It also is used to operate hoists, jacks, hammers, mining locomotives, and molding machines.

In sandblasting, compressed air is used to hurl jets of sand against a hard material, such as stone or glass. The *air cushion vehicle,* a device developed in the late 1950's, rides on a layer of compressed air. (See AIR CUSHION VEHICLE.)

See also AIR COMPRESSOR; PNEUMATIC APPLIANCES.

Liquid Air. Liquid air is an intensely cold, clear, pale-blue substance. Its density is about nine-tenths that of water. Liquid air is obtained by compressing air until its pressure is about 2,000 pounds per square inch and then cooling this air to a temperature below −200° F.

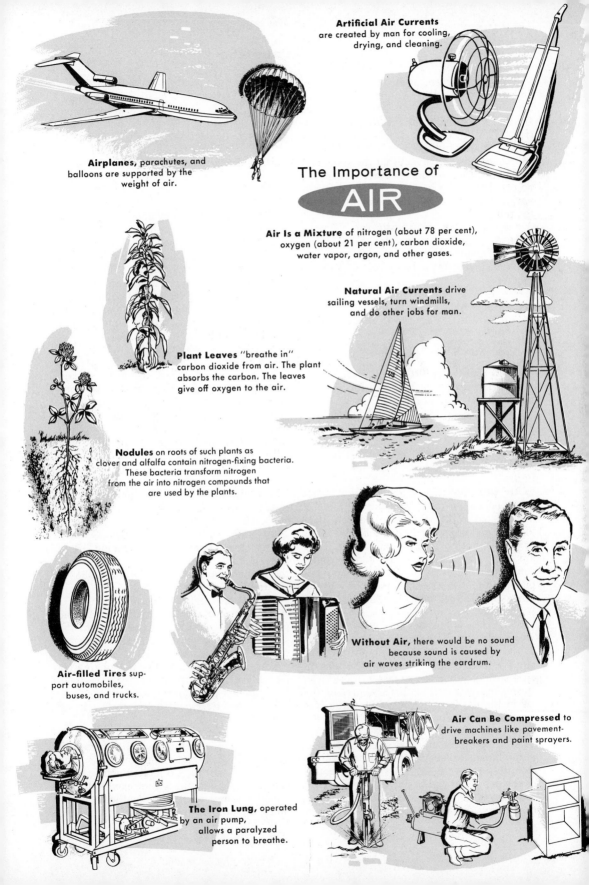

Artificial Air Currents are created by man for cooling, drying, and cleaning.

Airplanes, parachutes, and balloons are supported by the weight of air.

The Importance of

AIR

Air Is a Mixture of nitrogen (about 78 per cent), oxygen (about 21 per cent), carbon dioxide, water vapor, argon, and other gases.

Natural Air Currents drive sailing vessels, turn windmills, and do other jobs for man.

Plant Leaves "breathe in" carbon dioxide from air. The plant absorbs the carbon. The leaves give off oxygen to the air.

Nodules on roots of such plants as clover and alfalfa contain nitrogen-fixing bacteria. These bacteria transform nitrogen from the air into nitrogen compounds that are used by the plants.

Without Air, there would be no sound because sound is caused by air waves striking the eardrum.

Air-filled Tires support automobiles, buses, and trucks.

Air Can Be Compressed to drive machines like pavement-breakers and paint sprayers.

The Iron Lung, operated by an air pump, allows a paralyzed person to breathe.

Nitrogen, oxygen, argon, neon, krypton, and xenon are produced commercially by the fractional distillation of liquid air. (See DISTILLATION, subtitle *Fractional Distillation*.) This process, which was developed by the German physicist Carl von Linde in 1895, depends on the fact that the gases that make up the air have different boiling points. Liquid air is also used as a refrigerant, and in low-temperature scientific investigations.

See also AIR CONDITIONING; ATMOSPHERE; CARBON, illustration *The Carbon Cycle;* CARBON DIOXIDE; GAS; NITROGEN; NOBLE GASES; OXYGEN; OZONE; WEATHER; WIND.

Books about Air

Turber, W. A., and others. *The Atmosphere* (Allyn and Bacon, 1976).
For Younger Readers:
Berger, Melvin. *The New Air Book* (Lippincott & Crowell, 1974).
Simon, Seymour. *Projects with Air* (Watts, 1975).

Air, Liquid. See AIR, subtitle *Special Forms of Air:* Liquid Air.

Air Academy. See UNITED STATES SERVICE ACADEMIES, subtitle *The Air Force Academy.*

Air Almanac. See NAVIGATION, subtitle *Methods of Navigating:* Celestial Navigation.

Air and Gas Guns, devices that shoot BB's, pellets, or darts by using the force of compressed air or compressed carbon dioxide. Air and gas guns usually look like rifles or pistols, but are smaller and lighter. They are used for target practice and to shoot small animals. The range of air and gas pistols is 25 feet (8 m) or more, while the range of shoulder guns is 150 to 200 feet (45-60 m).

How Air and Gas Guns Work

Air guns are of either the *spring-powered* or the *pump-up* type. A spring-powered air gun is cocked with a lever that puts tension on a spring. When the trigger is pulled, the spring moves a piston that compresses the air inside the barrel, forcing the projectile out the muzzle. The toy *popgun* works on the same principle.

A pump-up air gun has a hand-operated pump handle or lever that moves a piston to compress and store air. The speed and range of the projectile can be increased by giving the gun extra pumps, because each pump compresses the air further.

A gas gun is often called a *CO_2 gun* because disposable cylinders of liquefied carbon dioxide (CO_2) gas furnish the propulsive force. With CO_2 guns no cocking or pumping is necessary; each pull of the trigger releases a small amount of liquid carbon dioxide, which changes almost instantaneously to a gas and expands. One CO_2 cylinder can furnish power for 20 to 100 shots.

The projectile fired by an air or gas gun is usually either a *BB* (a spherical, solid object made of steel) or a *pellet* (a hollow object made of lead and most commonly shaped like a cylinder or an hourglass). The projectiles can be inserted one at a time, loaded in a magazine, or (in the case of some pistols) placed in a revolving chamber like that of a six-shooter. The magazines of some BB guns can hold 850 BB's.

Air Rifles

An air rifle is a pellet-firing shoulder gun with grooves, or *rifling,* inside the barrel. (The term "air rifle," however, is also commonly applied to shoulder guns with smoothbore barrels.) The grooves increase accuracy by causing the pellet to spin in flight. Many air and gas pistols also have rifled barrels. All BB guns have smoothbore barrels.

History

The air gun was invented and developed in Germany. Hans Lobsinger of Nuremberg made the first one, a shoulder gun, about 1560. In the United States, the Daisy Manufacturing Company began producing BB air guns in 1886. A CO_2 gun was patented by the French engineer Paul Giffard in 1889.

Air Bladder. See BLADDER.

Air Brake. See BRAKE.

Air Compressor, any device that compresses air; that is, forces air into a smaller space than it normally occupies. Air is a mixture of gases, and, like all gases, it can be compressed so that its pressure is increased. At sea level, air exerts an average pressure of 14.7 pounds per square inch (101,300 pascals, or newtons per square meter) in all directions.

Devices that are used to compress air range from electric fans, which increase air pressure by less than one pound per square inch (6,895 pascals), to large machines that can compress air to such an extent that its pressure is hundreds or even thousands of times the normal atmospheric pressure. At

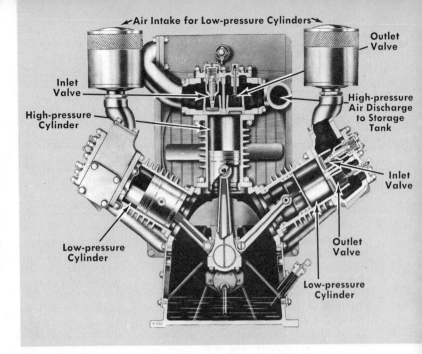

Air Intake for Low-pressure Cylinders

Inlet Valve

High-pressure Cylinder

Outlet Valve

High-pressure Air Discharge to Storage Tank

Inlet Valve

Low-pressure Cylinder

Outlet Valve

Low-pressure Cylinder

Air Compressor. Shown is a two-stage reciprocating compressor, which uses the same principles as the simple air pump. First, air is compressed in the two large cylinders. Then it is passed on to the small cylinder, where it is compressed further. Finally, the air is discharged into a storage tank (not shown).

Worthington Corp.

such pressures, the air is squeezed to a tiny fraction of its normal volume.

Uses of Air Compressors

Compressed air is used to inflate automobile tires; to drive pneumatic tools, such as dentists' drills, artists' airbrushes, and rivet guns; in blast furnaces; in ventilating systems; to operate air brakes; to enable divers to breathe under water; and for many other purposes.

Compressors can also be used to compress other gases. Reciprocating compressors, for example, are often used in air conditioners and refrigerators to compress the Freon or other gas used as a refrigerant. An air compressor can function as a *vacuum pump* if it draws air from a closed container.

Capacities and Types of Compressors

Air compressors are rated by the pressure of air they can furnish and also by their capacity; that is, the amount of air they can compress in a given time. Capacities of various types of compressors range from 1 cubic foot (28 dm³) per minute to 1,000,000 cubic feet (28,000 m³) per minute. In general, the larger the capacity, the smaller the pressure furnished. Fans and blowers, for example, handle a large volume of air but compress it only slightly.

Air compressors can be classified as reciprocating, rotary, jet, centrifugal, or axial-flow types, depending on the mechanical methods used to produce the compression. The reciprocating compressor is described in

this article. For other types of compressors, see BLOWING MACHINE; PUMP.

Reciprocating Compressors

In a reciprocating compressor, air is compressed by a piston that reciprocates (moves alternately backward and forward) in a cylinder. During each suction stroke an intake valve opens, admitting air into the cylinder. At the end of the suction stroke the inlet valve closes, the piston reverses direction, and the air is compressed and expelled through an outlet valve during the discharge stroke. To develop higher pressures there are several stages of compression, each represented by a separate piston and cylinder. In each stage the compressed air from the previous stage is drawn in and compressed further.

A tire pump is a single-stage reciprocating compressor that is operated by hand. Other types are commonly driven by an internal combustion engine or electric motor. Pressures produced by multi-stage reciprocating compressors range up to 35,000 pounds per square inch (240 megapascals) or more; capacities range up to 100,000 cubic feet (2,800 m³) per minute.

When air is highly compressed, it becomes hot. Therefore, to avoid mechanical breakdown, the air discharged from a cylinder in a multi-stage reciprocating compressor often must be cooled, by air or by flowing water, before it enters the next cylinder.

See also SUPERCHARGER.

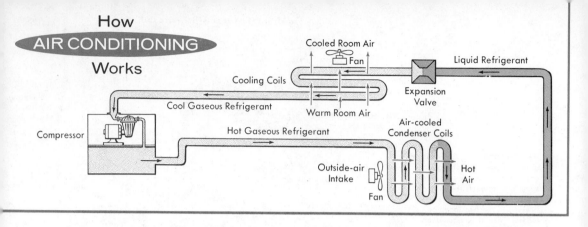

Cooled Room Air
Fan

Cooling Coils

Liquid Refrigerant

Expansion Valve

Cool Gaseous Refrigerant

Warm Room Air

Compressor

Hot Gaseous Refrigerant

Air-cooled Condenser Coils

Outside-air Intake

Hot Air

Fan

Air Conditioning, the process of controlling the quality and movement of air within a room or other enclosed space. The object of air conditioning is to ensure that the air is comfortable and wholesome for people or is suited for certain industrial operations. A complete air-conditioning system operates both summer and winter, controlling the temperature, humidity (moisture content), cleanliness, and circulation of the air being treated.

Popularly, however, the term "air conditioning" refers to *summer air conditioning.* This process, designed primarily for warm-weather use, cleans, cools, dehumidifies, and circulates the air. This article deals mainly with summer air conditioning.

Benefits and Limitations

When properly used, air conditioning increases personal comfort and improves efficiency, since high temperatures tend to increase fatigue. It is especially beneficial to people with heart disease and to older people whose general health is poor or who suffer from ailments that are aggravated by excessive heat. The filtered air is a comfort to victims of hay fever and asthma.

In virtually the entire United States (excepting Alaska), air conditioning has become almost a necessity for most stores, hotels, theaters, and restaurants. Without it, they would lose business during hot weather. Air conditioning is also common in automobiles, buses, airplanes, and railway cars.

Air conditioning is used in hundreds of industries. It is especially important in textile mills; in factories where precision instruments are made; and in pharmaceutical and printing plants and other plants where the moisture content, purity, and temperature of the air affect the material being handled.

Air conditioning is comfortable to most people when regulated at about 75° F. A person entering an air-conditioned room that is too cold will feel chilly and uncomfortable. When a person leaves an air-conditioned

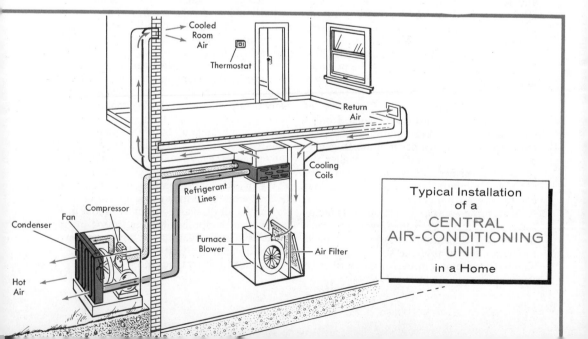

Cooled Room Air

Thermostat

Return Air

Cooling Coils

Refrigerant Lines

Compressor

Condenser

Fan

Furnace Blower

Air Filter

Hot Air

Typical Installation of a
CENTRAL AIR-CONDITIONING UNIT
in a Home

room and goes outdoors on a hot day, the sudden change in temperature will usually produce discomfort.

Types of Air Conditioners

Air conditioning in buildings is provided by *room air conditioners, packaged units,* or *built-up systems.*

Room Air Conditioners. These compact units are usually designed to fit in a window or through a hole cut in an outside wall. They are capable of conditioning the air in one or two rooms, and are widely used in homes and small offices and shops. Most room air conditioners are designed for summer use only, although some can be used for heating as well as cooling.

Packaged Units. Packaged units may be in one or more containers, and are generally larger and more powerful than room air conditioners. They can be mounted on the floor, on the roof, or in any other convenient location. They can provide cooling only, or both cooling and heating with either gas or electricity. Singly or in groups, such units can be used in factories, offices, stores, or homes.

An example of a two-piece packaged unit is the typical *central residential system.* This is composed of (1) a cooling coil, mounted atop a conventional furnace; and (2) a condensing unit placed outside the house so that outdoor air can remove heat picked up within the house. The condensing unit delivers liquid refrigerant to the cooling coil, and the furnace fan forces cool air through ductwork to the rooms.

Built-up Systems. A built-up air-conditioning system is made up of several components that are assembled on the site. It is used to air-condition all or part of a large building. The equipment, which weighs several tons in large systems, is installed at any convenient place in the building. As in a central residential system, the basic cooling operation takes place in a central location. The air itself, however, does not necessarily come into direct contact with the central equipment, but can be conditioned locally through a system that circulates cooling fluids throughout the building.

Cooling Capacity

The cooling capacity of an air conditioner is measured in British thermal units (Btu's) removed per hour. The term "refrigeration ton" is used for convenience in large systems where Btu figures would become unwieldy. One refrigeration ton is equal to 12,000 Btu's

Hot Air from Condenser Coils — Cooling-air Fan — Condenser Fan

Compressor

Outside Air

Cooled Room Air

Controls

Warm Room Air

Grille — Air Filter

Cooling Coils

Hot Air from Condenser Coils

Air-cooled Condenser Coils

ROOM AIR CONDITIONER

Carrier Corporation

per hour, and is the amount of cooling produced by the melting of one ton of ice in 24 hours.

The cooling capacity of room air conditioners ranges from about 4,000 Btu's for the smallest unit to about 30,000 Btu's for large units. Refrigerating machines used in built-up systems are available up to 4,500 tons, or 54 million Btu's.

The required cooling capacity of an air conditioner depends on the following factors:

1. Size of the enclosed space that it must cool.
2. Outdoor temperatures that normally occur in the area during the summer.
3. Amount of heat generated in the enclosed space by cooking stoves and other appliances, lights, machines, and other heat-producing devices.
4. Thickness of the walls of the enclosed space, and effectiveness of insulation.
5. Size and number of windows in the enclosed space, and their location with respect to the sun.
6. Number of persons normally present in the enclosed space.

How Air Conditioning Works

A complete all-year air-conditioning system consists of an air-filtering unit; a refrigeration unit with its accompanying cooling and dehumidifying apparatus; a heating unit, which may also be equipped with a humidifier; fans, ducts, and vents to distribute the air; and a thermostat.

Cleaning. A fan draws air through one or more screens or filters. Throw-away air filters are usually made of loosely packed, wool-like glass or plastic fibers. Permanent, cleanable filters are made of foam plastic or of thin, interwoven strips of aluminum or other metal. Air filters are often coated with a sticky substance so that they can more effectively trap tiny particles in the air. Dust, pollen, dirt, and other impurities will collect on the filters. In an electrostatic filtering system, particles in the air are charged electrically and collected on plates that are oppositely charged.

Summer Cooling. Most air conditioners use a *mechanical* refrigeration system, in which the cooling equipment is similar to that of an ordinary refrigerator. The equipment, shown in the illustration *How Air Conditioning Works,* consists of a motor-driven compressor, cooling coils (or *evaporator*) and a condenser, all connected with tubing through which a *refrigerant* (an easily liquefied gas) flows.

The compressor draws the gaseous refrigerant at low pressure from the cooling coils, compresses it (thereby increasing its temperature) with pistons or high-speed rotors, and sends it at high pressure to the condenser. There the refrigerant is cooled and liquefied by air passing over the coils of tubing that constitute the condenser. As shown in the illustration, this air is drawn in from the outside. (In some large air conditioners, the condenser coils are cooled by flowing water, or by a combination of air and water.)

The liquid refrigerant then passes through an expansion valve, where the pressure is greatly reduced, to the cooling coils. When the pressure drops, the cooled liquid refrigerant evaporates to a gas. This evaporation absorbs heat. A similar cycle takes place in a mechanical refrigerator. (See REFRIGERATION, subtitle *Mechanical Refrigeration.*)

Most compressors operate automatically and shut off when cooling is not needed.

In central residential systems, liquid refrigerant is piped to a coil atop the furnace. The furnace fan draws air from the house, forces it over the coil for cooling and dehumidification, and sends it back into the house.

In built-up systems, the refrigerant may chill water instead of air. The cold water, in turn, cools and dehumidifies the air. The refrigerating machine can be powered by electricity, gas, or steam. In another type of refrigerating unit, called an *absorption* machine, heat, as from a gas flame, is the direct energy source, and no compressor is required. (See REFRIGERATION, subtitle *Absorption-cycle Refrigeration.*)

Some mechanical refrigeration systems, called *heat pumps,* can be used to heat as well as cool. (See HEAT PUMP.)

Winter Heating. In winter, the cooling equipment is shut off and the air is heated

by passing it over the heat exchanger of a hot-air furnace or, in the case of some packaged and room units, over electric heating elements. Buildings using steam, hot-water, or radiant (electric-resistance) heating usually cannot be air-conditioned during the summer unless special ductwork or packaged units are installed.

Humidity Control. When warm, humid air passes over the evaporator coils, it is cooled to such an extent that it reaches the *dew point* — the temperature at which excess moisture leaves the air and collects on nearby cool objects. (See DEW POINT.) This moisture is deposited on the cooling coils. In room air conditioners, the moisture is eventually forced outdoors, where it evaporates. In larger units, it is usually drained or pumped away.

In winter, when the incoming air usually has a low humidity, the problem is not to remove moisture, but to add it. This is usually done by allowing water to evaporate into the moving air. (See HUMIDITY.)

Circulation. A fan forces the conditioned air into the room, either directly or through ducts. When one unit serves several rooms or an entire building, the air is usually carried by ducts to outlets in the various rooms. Stale air is returned to the unit through another network of ducts. Grilles or adjustable louvers control distribution of the air in such a way that drafts can be avoided.

In some built-up systems for large buildings, chilled water from the refrigerating machine is piped to a number of air-conditioning units placed throughout the building. In winter, hot water is circulated through the same units for heating. This method reduces the amount of ductwork and provides for more individual control of temperature.

Evaporative Coolers

An evaporative cooler, or air cooler, consists basically of a fan that blows air through a water-saturated pad. It has a reservoir that occasionally must be filled with water, and a pump that circulates the water in order to keep the pad wet. Under favorable conditions of humidity and temperature, such as those found in the southwestern United States, evaporation of water from the pad can lower the air temperature by 10 degrees or more.

Evaporative coolers range in size from small portable units to units weighing well over 100 pounds. They are not nearly as

Air Cushion Vehicle
SFO Helicopter
Airlines Inc.

effective as air conditioners in controlling the quality of the air because (among other reasons) they humidify the air instead of dehumidifying it.

Air Purifiers

An air purifier is a portable device consisting of a fan and one or more air filters. The effectiveness of an air purifier depends both on the amount of air its fan circulates and on the quality of its filters; it is most effective in comparatively small, closed rooms.

History

The first system that would cool, dehumidify, and circulate air was designed by the United States engineer Willis H. Carrier in 1902. It used an ammonia refrigerating machine and well water for cooling. It was installed in a lithographing and publishing firm in Brooklyn, New York.

For the next 20 years air conditioning was used almost exclusively to aid industrial processing. Air conditioning for human comfort was successfully demonstrated in 1922, when the first practical system was installed in Grauman's Metropolitan Theater in Los Angeles. Until then it had been customary for many theaters to close during hot weather.

The commercial success of theater air conditioning, together with the development of safe, nontoxic refrigerants in 1921, led to the installation of air conditioning in restaurants, stores, hotels, and office buildings throughout the United States. Railway passenger cars were first air-conditioned in 1936.

After World War II, air conditioning became a major industry in the United States. Virtually all large office buildings constructed in the United States since World War II are either completely or partially air-conditioned. Most large apartment buildings constructed since the late 1950's are air-conditioned. Air conditioning for automo-

biles, pioneered in the 1940's, became increasingly popular after World War II. Residential air conditioning expanded rapidly in the 1950's, and air conditioning of schools and libraries was begun in the early 1960's.

Books about Air Conditioning

Air Conditioning and Refrigeration Institute. *Refrigeration and Air Conditioning* (Prentice-Hall, 1979).
Lang, P. V. *Basics of Air Conditioning,* 3rd edition (Van Nostrand Reinhold, 1979).
Stoecker, W. F., and J. W. Jones. *Refrigeration and Air Conditioning* (McGraw-Hill, 1982).

Air Cooler. See AIR CONDITIONING, subtitle *Evaporative Coolers.*

Air Cushion Vehicle, a vehicle that is supported by a cushion of air provided by one or more fans. The fans draw in air through openings at the top or sides of the vehicle and blow the air downward. Air cushion vehicles, also called *ground effect machines* or *hovercraft,* can travel over solid ground, mud, swamps, snow, ice, the ocean, and inland waters. Some of these vehicles can land on, take off from, and hover over both water and land surfaces.

In thickness the air cushion can range from one inch (2.5 cm) to three feet (90 cm) or more, depending on the size and design of the vehicle. Some air cushion vehicles have aircraft-type propellers for forward and reverse movement and aircraft-type rudders for steering. Other models are propelled by ejecting, in the direction opposite to the direction of travel, some of the air taken in by the fan.

Air cushion vehicles have both commercial and military uses. They have been developed for such purposes as Arctic and Antarctic exploration, cargo carrying, passenger service, military landing operations, and patrol missions on rivers, marshes, and coastal waters.

Because the air cushion vehicle can rise no higher than the thickness of the air cushion beneath it, early models were restricted to travel over calm water or smooth terrain. This problem was largely overcome by the addition of a flexible skirt around the lower edge of the vehicle. The skirt is strong enough to contain the air cushion and force it downward—thus lifting the vehicle higher off the surface—but is flexible enough to give way when the vehicle passes over waves or obstacles.

Although the principle of the air cushion vehicle has long been known, serious development did not begin until the 1950's. Sir Christopher Cockerell, a British engineer, built the first working model in 1956. In 1959, a British air cushion vehicle crossed the English Channel at an average speed of about 9 knots. Later vehicles have achieved speeds close to 90 knots. The largest air cushion vehicles can carry several hundred passengers, plus cargo, and are used as ferries and on coastal routes.

Air Defense. See DEFENSE, AIR.

Air Filter. See AIR CONDITIONING, subtitle *How Air Conditioning Works:* Cleaning.

Air Force, the air arm of a nation's military forces, usually separately organized as coequal with the army and the navy. The striking power of an air force is based on airplanes and missiles. Armies and navies may also employ airplanes and missiles for specific purposes.

Air forces have four principal missions:

Strategic—to destroy an enemy's means of making war, and his will to fight, by attacks on industrial, communications, and government centers; transportation systems; supply sources; and armed forces, particularly strategic forces.

Defensive—to protect against aerial attack.

Tactical—to support ground or sea forces by attacking enemy troop concentrations, artillery, and prepared defenses that are an immediate threat; and by interdicting (cutting off) communications and supply routes to the front lines.

Logistical—to transport troops, weapons, equipment, and supplies.

The Concept of Air Power

The concept of an air force's missions as described above developed as technological progress increased the scope of the airplane. During the rapid development of aviation after World War I, such men as General Giulio Douhet of Italy and General William Mitchell of the United States foresaw the increasing importance of strategic air power. They envisioned that aerial bombardment

would be so decisive a factor in warfare that armies and navies would be obsolete—that they would not even have time to mobilize once war began.

The destruction caused by aerial bombs in World War II was widespread, yet bombing was not as decisive as Douhet and Mitchell had predicted. Cities were largely destroyed by bombs, but nations continued to fight. Armies and navies still played a major role in warfare. Nevertheless, air power became increasingly important as military leaders realized that strategic bombing could severely reduce a nation's capacity to make war.

With the growth of strategic air power came a corresponding growth in defensive air power. The greater the potential of aerial attack, the more important it became to prevent enemy bombers from reaching their targets. Superiority in the air came to be an accepted military doctrine.

The German invasion of Poland at the beginning of World War II demonstrated the effectiveness of tactical air support for ground forces. Carrier-based aircraft played an important part in supporting American troop landings in the World War II Pacific campaigns.

The capture of Crete by German paratroops in 1941 was a striking example of the effectiveness of logistical employment of air power. Throughout World War II, airplanes were used to bring men, arms, and supplies quickly to areas where they were needed.

The concept of air power underwent a radical change in 1945 with the development of the atomic bomb. Two such bombs were dropped on Japan by American bombers, and within days Japan surrendered. The strategic bomber, armed with nuclear weapons, seemingly possessed the power to win wars singlehandedly.

Another development—the long-range bombardment missile, pioneered by Germany during the war—soon promised to provide an even more effective method of delivering nuclear weapons to their targets. "Push-button warfare," making not only armies and navies, but also air forces obsolete, seemed possible.

The awesome destructive capability of the nuclear weapons accumulated by Russia and the United States, however, thus far has served to prevent their use. When the United States in 1962 demanded the removal of Russian missiles from Cuba, Russia dismantled its missile bases on that island rather than risk nuclear war. While both sides in the cold war have refrained from using nuclear weapons, there have been numerous "limited wars" in which conventional air power has been employed.

Thus, air forces must be prepared for a twofold role—to fight "limited wars" with conventional weapons and to be capable of immediately delivering the immensely more destructive nuclear weapons to their targets in the event of all-out war.

Weapons and Equipment

Intercontinental and intermediate-range nuclear missiles are currently the ultimate weapons to be used in strategic air war of major proportions. But many short-range missiles that may be used in "limited wars" have also been developed. The various kinds of missiles are described in the article MIS-SILES AND ROCKETS, section "Military Missiles."

The aircraft an air force uses in carrying out its missions, classified according to function, include fighters, bombers (tactical and strategic), transports, trainers, and reconnaissance craft. Carrier-based planes, though usually assigned to the control of the navy rather than the air force, are also considered part of a nation's air power. Details of weapons systems and special equipment for various types of airplanes are given in the article AIRPLANE, section "Types of Airplanes," subtitle *Classification by Use:* Military Airplanes.

Maintenance and support of the fighting arm of an air force requires an administrative and supply organization immensely larger than the fighting arm itself. Programs for research and development and for training are essential. Landing fields are needed, and there must be facilities for the fueling and repair of fighting planes. For organizational details of one air force, see AIR FORCE, UNITED STATES.

Major Air Forces of the World

About 100 nations have air forces, and they employ planes of some 400 different designs. But many of the smaller nations have only a few planes, and most of those are of obsolete designs.

Large air forces are maintained by the United States, Russia, Great Britain, and France. These nations, together with Sweden, Canada, and Italy, also produce most of the world's airplanes.

AIR FORCE EMBLEMS

Australia

Canada

China (Communist)

China (Nationalist)

France

Germany (West)

Great Britain

Italy

Mexico

Russia

Sweden

United States

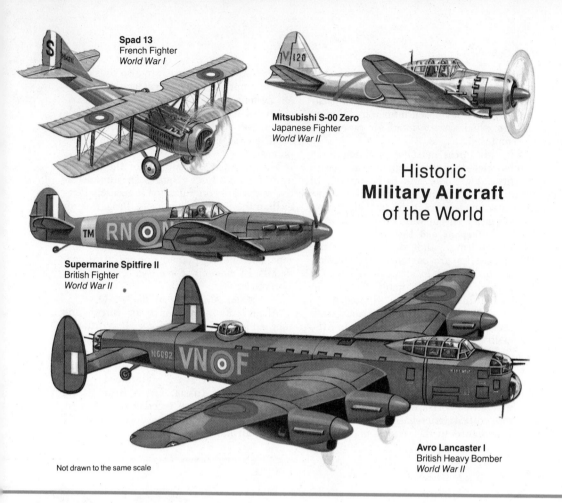

Spad 13
French Fighter
World War I

Mitsubishi S-00 Zero
Japanese Fighter
World War II

Historic
Military Aircraft
of the World

Supermarine Spitfire II
British Fighter
World War II

Avro Lancaster I
British Heavy Bomber
World War II

Not drawn to the same scale

Not all nations have separate air forces, and those that do may assign some types of tactical and defense planes and missiles, as well as planes used for transport and supply, to army or navy control.

The United States has the largest air force. It has about 560,000 persons on active duty and includes not only bomber and fighter units, but also the country's land-based strategic missile force. (See AIR FORCE, UNITED STATES.)

Russia has more than 470,000 officers and enlisted personnel in its air force. It has few long-range bombers but a very strong force of medium bombers. The air force is not responsible for Russia's strategic missile force, which is under the command of a separate branch, but it does have tens of thousands of tactical missiles.

Great Britain's Royal Air Force has about 87,000 officers and enlisted personnel. Most of its strength consists of bomber and fighter aircraft based in Great Britain, but it also

has units in West Germany, Hong Kong, and a few other locations.

The French air force numbers about 100,000 persons. It has a strategic nuclear-armed bomber fleet as well as conventionally armed fighters. West Germany's air force of 105,000 is assigned to NATO. Its principal weapons are fighter-bombers and fighters, but it is also heavily armed with tactical missiles.

China has an air force of 490,000 persons. Most of its aircraft are of obsolete Russian design.

History of Air Warfare

The first air reconnaissance in battle was made in 1794 at Fleurus, a French victory over Austria in the wars of the French Revolution. It occurred only 11 years after the first successful balloon was built by Joseph and Jacques Montgolfier. Napoleon made some use of observation balloons in his campaigns, and in the American Civil War both sides used balloons. Balloons were a

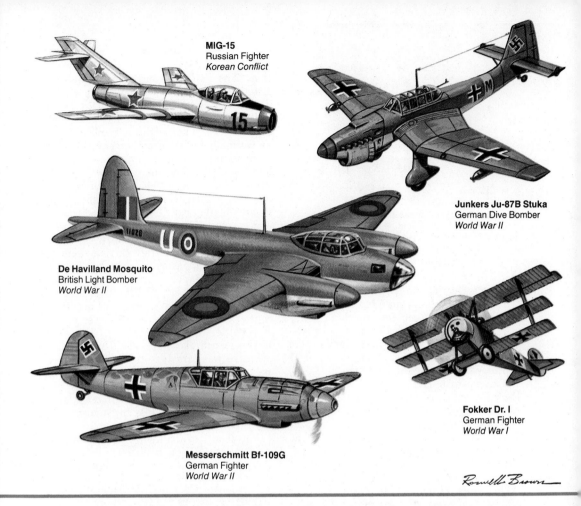

MIG-15
Russian Fighter
Korean Conflict

Junkers Ju-87B Stuka
German Dive Bomber
World War II

De Havilland Mosquito
British Light Bomber
World War II

Fokker Dr. I
German Fighter
World War I

Messerschmitt Bf-109G
German Fighter
World War II

Roswell Brown

means of communication in 1871 during the siege of Paris in the Franco-Prussian War. Captive balloons performed important observation missions in the Spanish-American War (1898) and in World War I.

Count von Zeppelin began successful experiments with dirigibles in 1900, and Germany used fleets of dirigibles (called *Zeppelins*) to bomb London and other targets during World War I. A number of large military dirigibles were built after the war, but a series of disasters discouraged further development after 1937.

Invention of the airplane in 1903 was followed by much experimenting by the armed forces of Europe and the United States. Airplanes were used from the beginning of World War I in 1914. At first they were unarmed and were used only for observation.

An important development was invention of a device to synchronize the fire of a machine gun with the revolution of the

blades of a propeller. It was first used in the German Fokker monoplane in 1915. Up to this time most of the fighting had been "dogfights" between individual planes. The Allies then adopted formation flying to protect observation planes from machine-gun attacks. The Germans, notably Baron Manfred von Richthofen's "Flying Circus," took the lead in perfecting formation maneuver.

Bombing also started as individual effort, but by 1916 day bombardment squadrons and night bombardment squadrons were attacking railway yards and airports. The largest bomber offensive of the war, September 12 to 15, 1918, supported the St. Mihiel offensive with 1,481 aircraft under command of Colonel William Mitchell of the United States. (See WORLD WAR I, section "Aerial and Colonial Warfare, 1914-18," subtitle *Aerial Warfare*.)

The first separate air force was the Royal Air Force of Great Britain, which was created from the Royal Flying Corps, April 1,

United Press International
Russian "Backfire" Bomber is one of the most advanced aircraft of its kind. The photo was made over the Baltic Sea by a Swedish plane.

1918. After Hitler came to power in Germany the *Luftwaffe* under the leadership of Hermann Goering, one of the aces of World War I, became the world's largest air force.

The period between the world wars was one of great technical advances. Airplane engines of World War I, for example, were of about 200 horsepower; many of those of World War II exceeded 2,000 hp.

The Spanish civil war (1936-39) gave Nazi Germany, aiding Franco's Nationalists, an opportunity to test the *Luftwaffe's* equipment and tactics. At the beginning of World War II, in September, 1939, the *Luftwaffe* demonstrated its power by destroying the Polish air force in four days. Within a month Poland was defeated.

Blitzkrieg (literally "lightning war," a combination of air and ground power, with parachute troops and tanks spearheading the advance) was applied in larger scale in the 1940 campaign that knocked France out of the war. German saturation bombing of Rotterdam, Netherlands, on May 13, 1940, was a rehearsal for the strategic warfare that was turned loose against Great Britain after the fall of France. (See WORLD WAR II, sec-

Great Britain's Hawker P-1127. This tactical attack-reconnaissance plane takes off vertically.
Wide World

tion "The Fall of France and the Battle of Britain," subtitle *The Battle of Britain, July, 1940-June, 1941.*)

British retaliatory bombing was small-scale at first. The weight of bombs dropped on Germany by Allied air forces in 1944 was more than 40 times that dropped in 1940 and nearly 15 times that dropped in 1941. Strategic bombing (1944-45) deprived Germany of needed coal and oil. In the closing months of the war Germany introduced the V-2 rocket bomb and jet-powered planes, but both came too late to avert defeat.

In the Pacific, aircraft carriers were the most important factor in early stages of the war against Japan. Japan's carrier attack on Pearl Harbor crippled the U.S. fleet and made possible Japan's seizure of a vast perimeter of island defenses. A series of carrier battles—notably Midway, June 4-6, 1942—turned the tide. The United States offensive was largely a campaign for bases ever closer to Japan. Long-range bombing offensives and an air-sea blockade crippled the Japanese war industry before the dropping of two atomic bombs in August, 1945, led Japan to surrender.

For details of the fighting see the following sections in WORLD WAR II:

"Outbreak of World War II," subtitle *The Campaign in Poland, 1939;*
"The Fall of France and the Battle of Britain," subtitles *The Defeat of France, May-June, 1940:* Aerial Warfare, and *The Battle of Britain, July, 1940-June, 1941;*
"Other Fronts, 1940-41," subtitle *Balkan Campaign, 1941:* Crete;
"The War with Germany and Italy, 1942-45," subtitle *Air Warfare Against Germany, 1942-45;*
"The War with Japan, 1941-45," subtitles *The Atomic Bomb* and *The Air and Submarine War Against Japan:* Air War.

As World War II ended, most of the weapons of air warfare were obsolete. Not only had the atomic bomb changed the entire concept of strategic bombing, but developments in jet power soon made all existing aircraft obsolescent, and the German V-1 and V-2 experiments pointed the way toward new missile weapons. (See MISSILES AND ROCKETS; NUCLEAR WEAPONS.)

In the years since World War II giant strides have been made in weapons and aviation technology. Airplanes have become ever larger and faster, and capable of flying at ever higher altitudes. Missiles have become almost a standard part of a fighter's armament. Major air forces are concerned not

Training Flight. A pair of U.S. Air Force jet trainers prepare to land.

only with superiority in the air, but also with superiority in space.

For further information, see:

Books about Air Forces

Hewish, Mark, and others. *Air Forces of the World* (Simon & Schuster, 1979).

Jackson, Robert. *World Military Aircraft Since 1945* (Scribner's, 1979).

Krivinyi, Nikolaus. *World Military Aviation: Aircraft, Airforces, Weaponry, and Insignia* (Arco, 1977).

Taylor, J. W., and Gordon Swanborough. *Military Aircraft of the World* (Scribner's, 1978).

For Younger Readers:

Cooke, D. C. *Planes They Flew in World War I* (Dodd, Mead, 1969).

Cooke, D. C. *Planes the Allies Flew in World War II* (Dodd, Mead, 1969).

Air Force, Department of the. See AIR FORCE, UNITED STATES.

Air Force, United States, the branch of the armed forces of the United States that is concerned with aerospace warfare and defense. The Department of the Air Force is coequal with the Departments of the Army and the Navy within the Department of Defense (which is headed by the secretary of defense, a member of the President's cabinet).

The Air Force is organized primarily for prompt and sustained offensive and defensive aerospace operations. It includes combat equipment and personnel, as well as the support forces, such as ground crews and administrative personnel, necessary to conduct combat operations. Not all aerospace weapons, equipment, and personnel, however, are assigned to the Air Force; both the Army and the Navy have aviation components.

Organization

The Air Force is administered by the secretary of the air force, who is not a cabinet member. He is assisted by an under secretary, several assistant secretaries, and various other civilian officials.

The chief of staff, U.S. Air Force, a four-star general, is the military head. Members of his staff are responsible for such matters as intelligence, personnel, plans, budget, research and development, and logistics. The air staff also includes the heads of specialized services. They include the surgeon general, inspector general, judge advocate general, chief of chaplains, and comptroller.

Field Organization. Below the Department of Air Force staff are the operating forces. They are organized into a number of major commands and a number of operating agencies, which together make up the *field organization* of the Air Force. The commands are organized by function in the United States and by area overseas.

Aerospace Defense Command (ADC) is concerned with air defense of the United States and is the U.S. Air Force component of the joint Canada-U.S. North American Aerospace Defense Command (NORAD). Because the Army and Navy also supply personnel and equipment to the ADC, it is not strictly an Air Force command but comes under the authority of the Joint Chiefs of Staff. Basic functions of ADC are aircraft and missile detection, identification, interception, and destruction.

Air Force Communications Command (AFCC) provides communications, air traffic control, and similar services.

Air Force Logistics Command (AFLC) procures, stores, and delivers supplies necessary to Air Force operations throughout the world.

Air Force Systems Command (AFSC) is responsible for the development, testing, and procurement of new weapons systems. (A weapons system is a weapon together with the equipment needed to operate it, such as a missile and its launching apparatus.)

Air Training Command (ATC) is responsible for recruiting and for training of officers and enlisted personnel. This includes basic training and indoctrination, flight training, and technical and special training. (See also AIR UNIVERSITY.)

Electronic Security Command (ESC) provides to other commands personnel and equipment involving electronic communications. The command also monitors all Air Force communications to ensure compliance with security practices and procedures.

Military Airlift Command (MAC) provides transportation for personnel and cargo for all the military services. It is organized as an Air Force command, but also includes naval personnel. MAC also furnishes weather, rescue, medical evacuation, and photographing and charting services.

Strategic Air Command (SAC) maintains a worldwide force prepared to destroy an enemy's war-making capacity. SAC includes bombardment, missile, and reconnaissance units. SAC also provides personnel to the Aerospace Defense Command for space surveillance, tracking, and warning.

Tactical Air Command (TAC) organizes, trains, and equips forces for tactical air operations. The com-

Air Force Battle Staff Position. Display area at NORAD headquarters allows observers to see positions of airborne objects thousands of miles away.

NORAD

mand includes fighter, air defense, and reconnaissance units. Its units also support the Army and the Navy.

Each of the three area commands is responsible for Air Force functions in its area of operation; it also assists air forces of other countries. The commands and their headquarters are:

Alaskan Air Command, Elmendorf Air Force Base (AFB), Alaska.

Pacific Air Forces, Hickam AFB, Hawaii.

U.S. Air Forces in Europe, Ramstein Air Base, West Germany.

The operating agencies are concerned with such matters as finance, public affairs, safety, testing, personnel, intelligence gathering, reserves, and internal security.

United States Air Force Academy. Cadets are educated and trained at the academy for careers as officers in the Air Force. (See UNITED STATES SERVICE ACADEMIES, subtitle *The Air Force Academy*.)

Units. The basic administrative unit is the *squadron,* comparable to an Army company. A *wing* includes up to four squadrons, and two or more wings with auxiliary units make up an *air division*.

An aircraft squadron has 15 to 24 planes assigned to it. It is subdivided into *flights* of three or more aircraft each. The strength of ballistic missile squadrons and wings depends on the type of missile. A wing of Minuteman missiles usually consists of three or four squadrons of 50 missiles each. Titan II wings consist of two squadrons, and each squadron has 9 missiles. Some squadrons, such as maintenance squadrons, have no aircraft or missiles.

Strength. Air Force personnel on active duty total about 560,000. Reserve forces number about 155,000. Airplanes number about 6,900 with another 500 in the Air Force Reserve and 1,500 in the Air National Guard. In addition, the Air Force has about 1,000 intercontinental ballistic missiles.

Aircraft

The U.S. Air Force's combat planes are classified as bombers (B) and fighters (F). (Letters in parentheses are type designations. The Stratofortress bomber, for example, is the B-52.) Bombers include strategic bombers and tactical bombers. Bombers attack enemy defensive and offensive forces, industrial centers, supply bases, and transportation and communication systems. Fighters are classified as fighter interceptors

A-183

U.S. Air Force

Rescue Team removes the pilot from a burning aircraft during a fire-fighting demonstration.

U.S. Air Force

Maintenance Work occupies a large number of Air Force personnel. This sergeant is checking electronic equipment in a missile.

Navigator of an Air Force transport plane plots a course. Navigators, like pilots, are officers.

U.S. Air Force

U.S. Air Force
F-15 Eagle. This single-seat attack fighter can exceed 1,700 miles per hour (2,736 km/h). Its armament normally consists of missiles and a 20-mm cannon, but the plane can be converted into a tactical bomber and carry up to 17,300 pounds (7,800 kg) in bombs.

and tactical fighters. Their main purpose is to destroy enemy aircraft. Tactical bombers and tactical fighters are normally used in support of ground forces.

Cargo and transport planes (C) may be equipped as troop carriers or as freighters, or as a combination of both. Aircraft used for special purposes include tankers (KC), weather reconnaissance bombers (WB), reconnaissance fighters (RF), helicopters (H), and trainers (T). (For detailed descriptions of these types see AIRPLANE, section "Types of Airplanes," subtitle *Classification by Use:* Military Airplanes.)

Personnel

Duties. Almost 40 per cent of the male officers in the Air Force are on flying duty as pilots, navigators, or electronic warfare officers. Officers of both sexes can serve in about 250 specialties in more than 50 other officer occupation and career fields.

Enlisted personnel, including women, are called *airmen.* They may be mechanics, cooks, clerks, weathermen, radar operators, or air crewmen, or may choose from some 240 other specialties. Ninety-five per cent of these jobs are on the ground. Enlisted

women serve in all but four of the specialties.

Training. Officers are commissioned from officer training schools, college ROTC programs, or the Air Force Academy. Men and women with special qualifications, such as physicians and nurses, may be commissioned directly from civilian life.

Pilots and navigators are trained at several bases. The courses take about a year for pilots and about eight months for navigators. There are special courses for navigator-bombardiers and electronic warfare officers.

Enlisted men and women are given six weeks of basic training, which includes military courtesy and discipline, care and handling of weapons and equipment, and other general military subjects. After basic training, recruits go to specialized schools to prepare for specific jobs.

History

Beginnings. The balloon was the first practicable air vehicle. Both Union and Confederate armies made some use of balloons for observations during the Civil War. James Allen of the First Rhode Island Regiment made the first army balloon ascent at Washington, D.C., June 9, 1861. T. S. C. Lowe, a civilian aeronaut, organized a balloon group for the Union's Army of the Potomac. Observations were reported by telegraph from a balloon at Falls Church and Arlington, Virginia, June 22-24, 1861, and artillery fire was directed from a balloon over Fort Corcoran, Washington, D.C., September 24. The balloons had no official military status and were discontinued in 1863.

In 1892 a balloon section was attached to Army Signal Corps telegraph units. In the Spanish-American War (1898) the presence of the Spanish fleet in Santiago Harbor was

Boeing B-52 Stratofortress. This strategic bomber has a range of 12,000 miles (19,000 km). It is powered by eight turbojet engines and can exceed 650 mph (1,046 km/h). B-52's can carry nuclear weapons, conventional weapons, and cruise missiles.

The Boeing Company

U.S. AIR FORCE
INSIGNIA OF RANK

ENLISTED PERSONNEL

No Insigne				
Airman Basic (E-1)	Airman (E-2)	Airman First Class (E-3)	Senior Airman (E-4)	Sergeant (E-4)

Staff Sergeant (E-5)	Technical Sergeant (E-6)	Master Sergeant (E-7)	Senior Master Sergeant (E-8)	Chief Master Sergeant (E-9)

OFFICERS

Second Lieutenant	First Lieutenant	Captain	Major	Lieutenant Colonel	Colonel

Brigadier General	Major General	Lieutenant General	General	General of the Air Force

reported by balloon, and a balloon was used for observation in the Battle of San Juan Hill.

Congress in 1898 gave Samuel P. Langley an appropriation to aid in developing a heavier-than-air flying machine for the Army. He was unsuccessful, but the Wright brothers made the first powered flight in 1903.

In 1907 the Aeronautical Division (one officer and two enlisted men) was established in the Office of the Chief Signal Officer and negotiations were started for a Wright airplane. Lieutenant T. E. Selfridge was killed in one of the tests in 1908, becoming the first military air casualty. The first plane was accepted in 1909. It had a top speed of 42.5 miles per hour (68.4 km/h) and made a sustained flight of one hour, 12 minutes over a 10-mile (16-km) course. By 1912 the Aeronautical Division had 12 planes, 12 officers, and 38 enlisted men.

The First Aero Squadron was organized in 1913. In 1916 it took part in General Pershing's Punitive Expedition into Mexico. The squadron's eight airplanes were worn out in carrying mail and dispatches and in scouting; six were abandoned or destroyed, and two were condemned at the close of the campaign.

Refueling in the Air. An F-105 fighter is refueled by flying boom from a KC-135 tanker.

Minuteman in Silo. Airman technicians standing in a special lift perform technical work on a missile in its underground silo at the Air Force Missile Test Center, Cape Canaveral, Florida.

World War I. The Aviation Section of the Signal Corps, created in 1914, had only 55 training planes when the United States declared war on Germany, April 6, 1917. A huge manufacturing program was started. An important contribution was the 320-horsepower Liberty engine, most powerful of its day. Even at the close of the war, however, only about one-fourth of the United States pilots were flying planes made in the United States.

Single-plane combats, called "dogfights," were common before formation flying was developed. A flyer who downed five enemy aircraft was rated as an "ace." Leading United States aces were Captain Eddie Rickenbacker, with 26 victories (including 4 balloons), and Lieutenant Frank J. Luke, who downed 14 balloons and 4 planes.

The first bombing raid by United States forces was made near Metz, Germany, on June 12, 1918. Colonel William Mitchell commanded the biggest bomber offensive of the war, September 12-15, 1918, when 1,481 aircraft attacked German lines in the Battle of St. Mihiel.

Between World Wars. A separate Air Service within the Army was set up in 1918. Mitchell, then a brigadier general and director of military aeronautics, encouraged many experiments in the use and development of air power. One of these experiments, in 1921, proved that airplanes could sink warships. In one test the captured German battleship *Ostfriesland,* regarded as unsinkable, was sunk by bombing. In a period when military preparedness was much neglected, Mitchell stressed the need for air power. His criticism of his superiors resulted in his court-martial and suspension. He resigned.

In 1926 the Air Service was renamed the Army Air Corps. The period between wars was one of great technical progress, and records for speed, distance, and endurance were frequently broken. The first all-metal bomber and fighter planes were produced in 1931. The B-17 Flying Fortress, developed during 1935-37, was designed to carry out high-altitude precision bombing—a key concept in American military thinking.

When war started in Europe in 1939, President Franklin D. Roosevelt called for 6,000 planes for the Air Corps; in 1940 he asked for 50,000 a year. The Army Air Forces were set up on June 20, 1941, under

Curtiss JN-4 Jenny
Trainer
World War I

Republic P-47D Thunderbolt
Fighter
World War II

North American P-51D Mustang
(Later designated F-51D)
Fighter
World War II and Korean Conflict

Boeing B-17G Flying Fortress
Heavy Bomber
World War II

North American B-25H Mitchell
Medium Bomber and Fighter Bomber
(Fighter-bomber version is shown)
World War II

Historic
U.S. Military Aircraft

Boeing B-29A Superfortress
Heavy Bomber
World War II and Korean Conflict

Lockheed F-80A Shooting Star
Fighter; First operational U.S. jet
After World War II

North American F-86F Sabre
Fighter
Korean Conflict

Boeing B-47E Stratojet
Strategic Bomber
After World War II

Not drawn to same scale.

Roswell Brown

General H. H. Arnold, who commanded them throughout the war.

World War II. The Air Forces grew from 300,000 men and 12,000 planes in 1941 to a peak strength of 2,400,000 men and 80,000 planes in 1944. They lost about 22,900 planes, half of them on combat missions, and destroyed more than 40,000 enemy aircraft.

The 8th Air Force, set up in Great Britain in early 1942, advocated a policy of daylight precision bombing. After a successful raid on the German-occupied port of Rouen, August 17, the policy was accepted, with the British Royal Air Force (RAF) taking over night strategic bombing. On D-Day, June 6, 1944, more than 8,000 sorties were flown. (A sortie is one mission or attack by one plane.) The 8th and 9th Air Forces attacked the Channel coast of France, while the 12th and 15th Air Forces, based in the Mediterranean, hit southern France.

The strategic air campaign waged by the Army Air Forces and RAF destroyed or severely damaged many German cities, but, because the factories were decentralized, had little effect on war production. The campaign in 1944-45 against Germany's fuel supplies, however, succeeded in eliminating effective resistance of the Luftwaffe (German air force) by cutting off its fuels and lubricants.

Japanese air strikes at Pearl Harbor and in the Philippines, December, 1941, had destroyed half the United States air strength in those areas. By April 18, 1942, however, the Army was able to stage its first air raid against Japan, a daring, small-scale attack led by Lieutenant Colonel Jimmy Doolittle. The B-25's took off from the Navy's aircraft carrier *Hornet* and landed in China.

Heavy bombers of the 13th Air Force aided the counteroffensive in the Solomon Islands in late 1942. The 5th Air Force was assigned to the Southwest Pacific. These two were combined as the Far Eastern Air Force under General George C. Kenney in 1944 for the final assault on the Philippines.

The 7th Air Force was assigned to the Central Pacific. The extent of its field of operations is shown by the fact that actions in 1944 reduced the distance of its forward bases to Tokyo from 3,467 to 1,267 nautical miles. Late in the war the 20th Air Force was organized for the strategic bombing (with B-29's) of Japan.

In China the 14th Air Force was commanded by Major General Claire L. Chen-

nault, who had organized the volunteer "Flying Tigers" for China before the United States entered the war. The 10th Air Force in Burma was credited with two unusual achievements. The First Air Commando Group, led by Colonel Philip G. Cochran, moved by transport and glider 150 miles behind Japanese lines to build an airstrip and base. Merrill's Marauders, commanded by Brigadier General Frank D. Merrill, captured Myitkyina behind Japanese lines and held it as an air base.

In the final months of the war, long-range bombing attacks were made on major Japanese industrial centers. In the meantime, an air-sea blockade had almost completely cut off Japan from its supply sources in Asia. The bombing raids and the blockade caused the collapse of the Japanese war industry. Transportation and communications systems also were destroyed. Japan surrendered after atomic bombs were dropped on Hiroshima and Nagasaki in August, 1945.

For details of the fighting, see WORLD WAR II, section "The War with Germany and Italy, 1942-45," subtitle *Air Warfare against Germany, 1942-45:* Strategic Bombing; and section "The War with Japan, 1941-45," subtitle *The Air and Submarine War Against Japan:* Air War.

Separate Air Force. Although the Army Air Forces operated virtually as a separate body through the war, a complete reorganization was postponed until the war was over. In 1947 the U.S. Air Force was set up, co-equal with the Army and Navy in the National Military Establishment, which was renamed the Department of Defense in 1949. First secretary of the Air Force was W. Stuart Symington. General Carl Spaatz became first chief of staff of the U. S. Air Force. He had succeeded General H. H. Arnold as commanding general of the Army Air Forces the year before.

In 1948 the Russians clamped a land blockade on Berlin. The U. S. Air Force, assisted by Navy transports and British planes, supplied the city entirely by air for more than 10 months. The Berlin airlift was the first important peacetime use of air power as an instrument of national policy.

In the Korean Conflict the Air Force supported ground action and bombed supply lines, oil refineries, and factories. It was challenged by Russian-built MIG-15 fighters, and the first jet plane aerial combat took

B-17 Flying Fortresses, above, dropping bombs on German installations. The B-17 was the principal U.S. heavy bomber in Europe.

U.S. Army Air Force in
WORLD WAR II

P-38 Lightning, right, a long-range fighter, was often used to escort bombers.

P-40, below P-38, saw action in Asia and Africa early in the war.

Japanese Plane, above, being shot down over the Pacific. A gun camera on a U.S. fighter took the photo.

B-24 Liberator, a heavy, long-range bomber used in Europe and the Pacific.

place on November 10, 1950. By the war's end in 1953 the U.S. F-86 Sabrejets had shot down 14 MIG's for every Sabre lost.

The Air Force Academy was authorized in 1954 and graduated its first class in 1959 at Colorado Springs, Colorado. Until then, a large number of West Point and Annapolis graduates entered the Air Force each year.

As early as 1946 the Air Force started experiments leading to development of the intercontinental ballistic missile (ICBM). It was not until 1959 that the Atlas, the first United States ICBM, became operational. The Air Force was given exclusive responsibility for land-based strategic guided missiles in 1950. In 1957 the first strategic missile wing was organized.

During the Vietnam War, U.S. Air Force planes supported United States combat troops and bombed military targets in North and South Vietnam and supply routes in neighboring Laos.

For further information, see:

Books about the U.S. Air Force

Apple, Nick, and Gene Gurney. *The Air Force Museum,* revised edition (Crown, 1978).

Kinney, A. H. *Air Force Officer's Guide,* 24th edition (Stackpole Books, 1976).

MacClosky, Munro. *Your Future in the Air Force* (Richards Rosen Press, 1972).

Mason, H. M., Jr. *The United States Air Force: a Turbulent History, 1907-1975* (Mason/Charter, 1976).

For Younger Readers:

Mohr, Peter. *The Thunderbirds* (Childrens Press, 1980).

Air Force Academy. See UNITED STATES SERVICE ACADEMIES, subtitle *The Air Force Academy.*

Air Force Association, an organization that promotes aerospace power for the United States. Through its affiliate, Aerospace Education Foundation, Inc., the organization promotes education on all developments in aerospace power. Membership is open to all United States citizens. The official publication is *Air Force Magazine.* The association was organized in 1946. Membership is about 150,000. Headquarters are in Washington, D.C.

Air Force Cross. See DECORATIONS AND MEDALS, subtitle *United States Awards:* Decorations, and color page.

Air Force Institute of Technology. See AIR UNIVERSITY.

Air Force Reserve. See RESERVES.

Air Gun. See AIR AND GAS GUNS.

Air Hammer. See PNEUMATIC APPLIANCES, subtitle *Piston-action Pneumatic Tools.*

Air Line. See AIRLINE.

Air Mail. See POST OFFICE, subtitles *Kinds of Mail:* International Mail; and *History of Postal Service:* 20th Century.

Air Mass. See WEATHER, subtitle *Air Masses.*

Air Medal. See DECORATIONS AND MEDALS, subtitle *United States Awards:* Decorations.

Air Museum. See SMITHSONIAN INSTITUTION (National Air and Space Museum).

Air National Guard. See NATIONAL GUARD.

Air Navigation. See NAVIGATION, subtitle *Kinds of Navigation.*

Air Piracy. See HIJACKING.

Air Plant. See EPIPHYTE.

Air Police, the group that exercises police functions among personnel of the U.S. Air Force. The Air Force Air Police was organized in 1948, shortly after the Air Force was separated from the Army, to perform law enforcement and security duties.

Air Pollution, the contamination of the atmosphere by the addition of impurities called pollutants. Pollutants can be of natural or man-made origin. Natural pollutants include dust, pollen, and smoke from forest fires. Most man-made pollution is directly or indirectly caused by burning, particularly of coal and other fuels for the production of heat and power.

The most serious consequence of air pollution is its impact on human health. The high concentration of pollutants in industrial regions and urban areas can contribute to respiratory diseases such as chronic bronchitis, asthma, emphysema, and lung cancer. Air pollution also harms or destroys plant and animal life, and damages property.

Types of Air Pollutants

The most significant man-made pollutants include oxides of carbon, sulfur, and nitrogen; hydrocarbons; particulate matter; and various photochemical substances that are among the principal ingredients in the irritating mixture known as smog. (See SMOG.)

Oxides of carbon make up the largest single group of pollutants. Carbon monoxide, a colorless and odorless poison, is a gas produced when fuel is incompletely burned in engines and furnaces. Automobiles and other vehicles are probably the largest source of this pollutant. Another gas, carbon dioxide, is a product of all normal combustion (burning), and is also formed by the breakdown of carbon monoxide. Although carbon dioxide is not a serious pollutant in itself, some scientists believe that a long-term buildup of this gas in the atmosphere could cause what they call a "greenhouse effect" by reducing the flow of heat from the earth back into space, thus causing a dangerous warming of the earth.

Oxides of sulfur—notably sulfur dioxide—are among the most dangerous and irritating of all air pollutants. Factories and electric power plants are the main producers of sulfur oxides, since their fuels often are sulfur-containing coal or oil. In the air, some sulfur dioxide is converted to sulfuric acid and other corrosive compounds. *Nitrogen oxides* are products of automobile engines and other sources where combustion takes place at high temperatures. When exposed to sunlight, these oxides are among the chief contributors to smog.

Hydrocarbon pollutants are products of unburned fuel, and are largely emitted by gasoline-powered vehicles. Like nitrogen oxides, hydrocarbons contribute to smog.

Particulate matter refers to tiny liquid or solid particles in the air. These include smoke, dust, soot, and toxic substances such as lead and fluorides. Steel mills and oil refineries are major producers of particulate matter.

Photochemical substances—one of which is ozone—are formed when certain other pollutants go through complex chemical reactions upon exposure to the ultraviolet portion of sunlight. These substances, together with fog and smoke, form smog.

Reducing Air Pollution

Although most of the world's cities and industrial regions have been plagued with air pollution for centuries, there was little organized effort to combat the problem until the mid-20th century. In the United States, many cities and all of the states began to set legal standards regarding the amount and types of pollutants that were permitted. The federal government in 1970 established the Environmental Protection Agency (EPA), which among its other duties administers the Clean Air Act. This act provides for financial assistance to state pollution-control agencies and sets strict standards for automotive emissions. The EPA also sets general standards for air quality and operates an air monitoring network.

Many devices and systems have been developed to reduce or prevent industrial air pollution. *Electrostatic precipitators,* for example, remove pollutant particles by ionizing them (charging them electrically) and collecting them on electrodes that are oppositely charged. *Cyclone separators* rotate impure air with a force that hurls particles against the side walls of the separator. In *scrubbers,* air is passed through water sprays that remove impurities.

Federal regulations for restricting automotive air pollution require the installation of various antipollution devices on automobiles and trucks at the time of manufacture. The most common of these is the *catalytic converter.* (See AUTOMOBILE, section "How an Automobile Runs," subtitle *Power Plant: Emission Controls.*)

See also DUST; ENVIRONMENTAL PROTECTION AGENCY; OZONE; SMOG; SMOKE; SULFUR DIOXIDE.

Books about Air Pollution

Lynn, D. A. *Air Pollution: Threat and Response* (Addison-Wesley, 1976).

Meetham, A. R., and others. *Atmospheric Pollution: Its History, Origins, and Prevention,* 4th edition (Pergamon Press, 1980).

Stewart, C. T. *Air Pollution, Human Health, and Public Policy* (Lexington Books, 1979).

Air Power. See AIR FORCE, subtitle *The Concept of Air Power.*

NEW STANDARD Photo by Ralph Miller
Air Rights were obtained from the Chicago Union Station to build the Gateway Center Building (background). The station owns the land and its tracks run under the building. A second building was later built over the platform in the foreground.

Air Pressure. See AIR, subtitle *Air Density and Pressure.*

Air Pump. See AIR COMPRESSOR; PUMP.

Air Raid Shelter. See CIVIL DEFENSE, subtitle *Fallout Shelters.*

Air Rifle. See AIR AND GAS GUNS, subtitle *Air Rifles.*

Air Rights, in law, the right of a land owner to use the air space over his property. The right is not absolute; an owner cannot, for example, prevent an airplane from flying over his land at a proper altitude or erect a building into his air space if its height violates zoning restrictions. If the owner does not use his air space, he may lease it to another.

In international law under the principle of national sovereignty, any country may prohibit foreign aircraft from flying over its territory. International civil aviation is made possible by agreements in which aircraft of each country are given certain rights in the air space of the other countries.

The beginning of the space age in 1957 brought up questions about national sov-

ereignty over outer space (the space outside the earth's atmosphere). No country ever made an issue out of these questions; by the principle of usage and practice international law seems to have established "freedom of the skies" in outer space.

Air Traffic Control. See AVIATION, subtitle *Aviation Regulation.*

Air Training Command. See AIR FORCE, UNITED STATES, subtitle *Organization: Field Organization.*

Air Transport Association of America (ATA), the national trade and service organization of the regularly scheduled United States airlines. The ATA works with the airlines to make air transportation safer, more efficient, and more convenient for the public. Its chief publication is *Facts and Figures about Air Transportation,* an annual. The ATA was organized in 1936. Headquarters are in Washington, D.C.

Air Travel. See AIRLINE; AVIATION.

Air University, the center for the professional education of officers and senior non-commissioned officers of the United States Air Force. It operates colleges, schools, institutes, and supporting agencies. Headquarters and most of the command's major activities are at Maxwell Air Force Base, Montgomery, Alabama.

At the core of the Air University system are its four professional schools: Air Force Senior NCO Academy, for chief and senior master sergeants; Squadron Officer School, for junior officers; Air Command and Staff College, for captains and majors; and Air War College, for senior officers.

The Air University also includes the Academic Instructor and Foreign Officer School, which trains teachers and prepares foreign officers for entry into other schools, and the Leadership and Management Development Center, which includes schools for comptrollers, chaplains, historians, and judges advocate.

The Air Force Institute of Technology, at Wright-Patterson Air Force Base, Dayton, Ohio, includes a graduate-level school of engineering and other schools specializing in aerospace engineering and related Air Force subjects. The Extension Course Institute, at Gunter Air Force Base, near Montgomery, Alabama, offers correspondence courses to all Air Force personnel.

The Air Force Reserve Officers Training Corps is administered from Maxwell Air

Force Base but is conducted by detachments in various universities and colleges.

Air Warfare. See AIR FORCE.

Airborne Troops. See PARATROOPS.

Airbrush. See PNEUMATIC APPLIANCES, subtitle *Airbrushes.*

Aircraft. See AIRPLANE; BALLOON; BLIMP; DIRIGIBLE; HELICOPTER.

Aircraft Carrier, a naval vessel that uses airplanes and helicopters as its principal weapons. The carrier is a floating air base that can go great distances to launch air attacks against enemy land or naval forces. It can be used for hit-and-run raids, sustained air offensives, antisubmarine warfare, and amphibious operations, and to provide aerial support for troops ashore.

Carriers are the principal surface ships in the navies of the United States, Great Britain, France, and Australia. Russia has several carriers designed for helicopters and STOL (short takeoff and landing) planes. Some naval experts believe that nuclear-powered submarines carrying nuclear missiles may make carriers unnecessary in a major war. Some question the wisdom of building such large ships when they have become increasingly vulnerable as nations have armed their navies and air forces with guided missiles. However, the carrier is still valued for limited wars and peacekeeping missions.

Description

An aircraft carrier is readily recognized by its *flight deck*—the flat top deck from which planes are launched and on which they land. (The characteristic shape of carriers gave rise to the nickname "flattops.") A large carrier usually has an angled, or *canted,* deck—a projection that juts out at an angle from the *axial* (fore-and-aft) flight deck. The canted deck is the landing area; the axial flight deck is used for launching and parking planes. Planes can be launched from a carrier with a canted deck at the same time that other planes are being landed.

Heavy airplanes with high takeoff speeds are launched by steam-operated catapults

Fixed-wing Aircraft Carrier. Shown is the nuclear-powered USS *Nimitz* (CVN-68). The canted deck is at the right, the island at the left.

U.S. Navy

Launching Plane by Catapult. Crewman hooks a bridle to plane as another signals for takeoff.

that accelerate the planes to high speeds in seconds. Slower planes may be launched under their own power by short runs down the deck, the method used in World War II.

Special techniques are needed to land a plane on a carrier. Not only is the landing area small, but it is also moving and, often, pitching as well. Relatively slow planes can be guided by an officer standing on deck using hand-held flags or lights as signals.

Jet planes are usually landed with the aid of a mirror system, in which a beam of light travels from the plane to a mirror on the carrier and back. The pilot guides his plane according to the location of the reflected beam. At the same time, a computer on the carrier determines the proper landing speed, and radio signals control the plane's throttle accordingly. As the plane touches down, a hook projecting from its tail catches on one of several cables, or *arresting wires*, stretched across the deck, bringing the plane to a quick stop.

A carrier's *island* is a mass of superstructure at one side of the flight deck. It houses the bridge and flight-control center and is topped by radar and radio masts. Some carriers have been built without superstruc-

Helicopter Carrier. The USS *Okinawa* (LPH-3) is an amphibious assault ship. The circles mark landing areas for its helicopters.

ture, notably the flush-deck carriers used by Japan in World War II.

Below the flight deck is a hangar deck for stowage of planes. Elevators transfer planes between the hangar deck and the flight deck. Repair shops are also on the hangar deck.

Carriers have antiaircraft guns and missile launchers. The large flight deck, however, limits the number and placement of these weapons to such an extent that the carrier cannot adequately protect itself. For this reason carriers are generally used in striking forces (formerly called task forces), which include cruisers, destroyers, radar picket ships, and submarines.

Types of Carriers

Fixed-wing Aircraft Carriers. These carriers (formerly called attack carriers) are primarily used in striking forces with other vessels to project a nation's offensive power. Only the United States, France, and Australia have purely fixed-wing aircraft carriers. The Soviet Union has carriers carrying both fixed-wing STOL (short takeoff and landing) aircraft and helicopters, but they are considered mainly antisubmarine vessels with limited offensive capabilities.

The U.S. Navy designates its conventionally powered fixed-wing carriers as CV, and nuclear-powered carriers as CVN. United States carriers are in five classes, corresponding to size. The largest carriers in the world are in the Nimitz class—the *Nimitz* (completed in 1975), *Eisenhower* (1977), and *Vinson* (1982). Each is about 1,100 feet (335 m) long and displaces about 95,000 tons (loaded). Each carries about 95 planes, 300 officers, and 5,400 enlisted men.

VTOL Aircraft Carriers. These carriers, used in the British navy, are equipped with VTOL (vertical takeoff and landing) planes. The British use the VTOL carriers for antisubmarine warfare and in striking forces.

Helicopter Carriers. In the navies of Great Britain, France, and the Soviet Union, the helicopter carrier is used in antisubmarine warfare. In the United States Navy, the helicopter carrier is used to deliver Marines into combat in amphibious assaults. The U.S. Navy's designation for the helicopter carrier is LPH.

Carrier Planes

Carrier planes must have relatively low landing speeds and be capable of performing varied missions. Most types have folding wings to save space on the hangar deck.

AIRCRAFT CARRIER

Attack Planes seek out and destroy enemy targets both on land and at sea. These planes carry rockets, guided missiles, torpedoes, mines, and conventional or nuclear bombs. Attack planes have replaced the torpedo planes and dive bombers used by carriers in World War II.

Fighter Planes are generally lighter, faster, and more maneuverable than attack planes. Fighters intercept enemy planes, defend surface forces, escort attack planes, and may support ground troops. They are armed with fixed weapons, usually one or two pairs of 20-mm guns, and may carry missiles and other weapons.

Helicopters are the primary aircraft used on the smaller carriers assigned to antisubmarine warfare and amphibious assault missions. Helicopters also are used on minesweeping missions and for general utility purposes, including rescue, transport, and reconnaissance duties. Large carriers may carry one or two helicopters.

Reconnaissance Planes, equipped with radar, infrared sensors, and cameras, are used for seeking out enemy vessels and planes. The reconnaissance planes also have ECM (electronic countermeasures) equipment to confuse enemy radar and targeting devices.

History

The first shipboard takeoff was made in 1910 by Eugene Ely, a civilian, in a Curtiss plane from the cruiser USS *Birmingham.* In 1911 Ely made a landing on an improvised flight deck on the battleship USS *Pennsylvania.* A catapult using compressed air for thrust successfully launched a seaplane from a barge in a 1913 test.

In 1913 the British navy built a launching platform for seaplanes on the cruiser *Hermes.* The *Hermes* was torpedoed and sunk in the early months of World War I. The British packet *Engadine,* equipped with a seaplane hangar, sent up an observation plane that spotted early German actions in the Battle of Jutland, 1916.

The *Argus,* converted by Britain from an Italian liner in 1917, is considered the first true aircraft carrier—previous British carriers could handle only seaplanes. A second *Hermes,* completed in 1924, was the first ship designed from the keel up as a carrier.

The U.S. Navy's first carrier was the flush-deck *Langley,* converted from a collier (coal supply ship) in 1922. Two battle cruis-

U.S. Navy

Russian Carrier. Helicopters equipped for antisubmarine warfare use the flight deck aft of the ship's superstructure. Rocket launchers are on the forward deck.

ers laid down during World War I were completed in 1928 as the carriers *Saratoga* and *Lexington.* The *Ranger,* completed in 1934, was the first U.S. Navy ship originally planned as a carrier.

Japan was another pioneer in the use of carriers. Its first, the *Hosho,* was completed in 1922. At the beginning of World War II Japan had nine aircraft carriers—two more than the United States.

Six carriers formed the Japanese main striking force in the attack on Pearl Harbor, December 7, 1941. With its battleship fleet badly crippled by this attack, the U.S. Navy had to depend on carriers and submarines to fight the Japanese. The first carrier battle was the Battle of the Coral Sea, May 4-8, 1942, in which each side lost one carrier. In the decisive Battle of Midway, June 4-6, 1942, the Japanese lost four carriers, the U.S. Navy one.

U.S. Navy carriers spearheaded drives in the Central and South Pacific. Japanese losses of planes and pilots were so severe that Japan withdrew its remaining carriers from the area. Early in 1943 new attack carriers began joining the American fleet; they were

First Shipboard Landing. Eugene Ely in 1911 landed a Curtiss plane on an improvised deck on the battleship USS *Pennsylvania.*

Navy Department-National Archives

soon supplemented by large numbers of escort carriers.

Japan committed its naval air power again in the Battle of the Philippine Sea, June 19-21, 1944; almost all its carrier planes were shot down. In the Battle of Leyte Gulf, October 23-26, 1944, the Japanese fleet was eliminated as an effective fighting force. Four of its carriers were destroyed.

In the Korean Conflict (1950-53) British and American attack carriers were used, and escort carriers took part in many actions. Carrier strikes supported the Inchon landing and the evacuation of Hungnam.

During the Vietnamese War, the United States used carriers as bases for air strikes against the North Vietnamese, 1964-73.

See also AIRPLANE, section "Types of Airplanes," subtitle *Classification by Use:* Military; CATAPULT; NAVY, subtitle *How a Navy Fights:* Striking Forces; NAVY, UNITED STATES, subtitles *Organization: Operating Forces,* and *Ships and Aircraft:* Combatant Ships; WORLD WAR II, section "The War with Japan, 1941-45."

Aircraft Instruments. See AIRPLANE, section "Parts of an Airplane," subtitle *Instruments.*

Aircraft Model. See AIRPLANE, MODEL.

Aircraft Owners and Pilots Association (AOPA), an organization of civil airplane pilots and owners. The objectives are "to promote, protect, and represent the interests of aeronautics and the pursuit of flying." The chief publication is *The AOPA Pilot,* a monthly. The AOPA was organized in 1939. Headquarters are in Frederick, Maryland.

Airedale. See DOG, subtitle *Breeds of Dogs:* Terriers, and picture.

Airfoil. See AIRPLANE, section "Why an Airplane Flies," subtitle *Gravity and Lift.*

Airline, an organization that owns and operates a fleet of aircraft for transporting passengers, cargo, or both. Airlines are a major means of transporting people and goods, and in some parts of the world they are the only fast and reliable means of public transportation. The airlines of most nations are government-owned, but those of the United States are privately owned.

In the United States a federal agency, the Civil Aeronautics Board (CAB), grants airlines licenses for operation. The CAB must approve certain rates and fares, as well as any proposed mergers. The Federal Aviation Administration (FAA) sets and enforces safety standards. Groups that regulate international airlines are the International Air Transport Association and the International Civil Aviation Organization. The Air Transport Association of America is a trade association of United States airlines but has no regulatory powers.

Types of Airlines

The CAB has several classifications of commercial air carriers (airlines):

International Lines, which are assigned air routes between major cities throughout the world. Some of

Opposite, top: Computer terminals used in handling flight reservations. *Opposite, bottom:* Ground crew member refuels a jet. *Right, top:* Workers with automated equipment direct luggage to and from the docking area. *Right, middle:* Jet airliner cockpit, with its array of switches and instruments. *Right, bottom:* Dining in the first-class section of a jumbo jet.

Delta Air Lines (opposite, top); New Standard Encyclopedia (opposite, bottom); American Airlines (all others)

the most prominent are Pan American, Aeroflot (Russia), British Airways Group (Great Britain), KLM (Netherlands), Lufthansa (West Germany), Air France, and SAS (Scandinavia).

Domestic Trunk Lines, which have permanent operating rights within the United States and are assigned air routes between major cities. The largest trunk lines, such as American, Eastern, Trans World (TWA), and United, also offer international service.

Local Service Lines, usually called "feeder" lines, which operate between smaller United States cities and usually have passenger service to the major airports. They include such lines as Frontier, Ozark, Piedmont, and Republic.

All-cargo Lines, which do not carry passengers. Some of the largest all-cargo lines are Flying Tiger, Airlift International, and Wright.

Supplemental Air Carriers, which conduct passenger and cargo charter services. They are usually unscheduled, but may operate on a limited schedule basis.

Commuter Lines, which are not subject to CAB regulations. Their main purpose is to transport passengers from small airports to airports served by the larger airlines. There are more than 180 such lines in the nation.

Airline Operations

International lines use jet aircraft almost exclusively, as do most domestic trunk lines. Some smaller foreign lines rely mainly on propeller (piston-engine) craft. Local service lines are equipped with both jet and propeller aircraft. Cargo lines mainly use propeller craft. Commuter lines use small turboprop or propeller craft that seat up to 20 passengers.

The crew of a passenger airliner is headed by a pilot, who is assisted by one or more copilots and a flight engineer. They all must meet rigorous professional qualifications for licensing and employment. The crew also includes one or more flight attendants (stewardesses or stewards).

In addition to flight crews, airlines employ ground personnel to assist the crews on board the aircraft and to take care of the many duties involved in the operation of an airline. Ground personnel include mechanics, flight superintendents, cargo handlers, meteorolo-

Loading Cargo Aboard a DC-8F Jet Freighter

gists, chefs, and clerks and reservations agents.

History of Airlines

Commercial aviation began in Europe shortly after World War I. KLM (Royal Dutch Airlines) was one of the pioneers. In the United States, regularly scheduled commercial passenger flights did not begin until 1927. Such flights were an outgrowth of the Kelly Act of 1925, which directed the U.S. Post Office to give airmail contracts to private operators. This encouraged the growth of airlines at a time when freight and passenger revenue was too small to support their existence. The first airline stewardesses were employed in 1930.

The first scheduled transcontinental passenger flight was made, by a predecessor of TWA, in 1930. The plane was a Ford trimotor "Tin Goose." It took 39 hours to reach Los Angeles from New York City.

As the speed, size, and convenience of airplanes grew, passenger traffic increased, more than tripling in the United States between 1935 and 1940. A landmark during this period was introduction in 1936 of the Douglas DC-3, a model so suited to airline use that it is still in service today. The first regularly scheduled transatlantic flight was made in 1939 with a Pan American Boeing Clipper flying boat.

After World War II the growth in air traffic continued, but competition was intense, particularly in the international field. The mass changeover to jets in the late 1950's was a heavy financial burden for the airlines, but it enabled them to attract even more customers. Modern airports were soon under construction to provide for the increased volume of air traffic. By 1960 air travel had replaced rail travel as the primary mode of commercial transportation.

During the 1960's, however, the airlines encountered a number of serious problems.

The tremendous increase in air traffic caused congestion and delay at many airports. A new phenomenon, the hijacking of airliners, became a source of concern to airline officials. And airlines were criticized, especially by urban dwellers, for the loud, irritating noises and air-polluting exhaust fumes produced by their jetliners. Despite these problems, the passenger volume continued to rise. In the 1970's "jumbo jets," each with a capacity of more than 300 persons, were in use and supersonic transports (SST's) that could exceed 1,500 miles per hour (2,400 km/h) were developed in Russia, France, and Britain.

For further information, see:

Airliner. See AIRLINE, subtitle *Airline Operations:* Equipment; AIRPLANE, section "Types of Airplanes," subtitle *Classification by Use:* Commercial Airplanes.

Airlock. See CAISSON.

Airmail. See POST OFFICE, subtitles *Kinds of Mail:* International Mail; and *History of Postal Service:* 20th Century.

Airman. See RANK, MILITARY OR NAVAL (table); for pictures of insignia, see AIR FORCE, UNITED STATES.

Airman's Medal. See DECORATIONS AND MEDALS, subtitle *United States Awards:* Decorations.

Airplane, a powered, fixed-wing, heavier-than-air aircraft; it is called an *aeroplane* in Great Britain. Airplanes (commonly termed "planes") have been successfully powered by piston engines, jet engines, and rocket engines. An airplane is held in flight by the action of the air through which it moves. "Airplane" does not include balloons and dirigibles, which are lighter than air; helicopters and autogiros, which have rotary wings; ornithopters, which have flapping wings; or gliders, which are not powered.

The importance of the airplane is discussed in the article AVIATION.

Why an Airplane Flies

The scientific principles that explain why an airplane flies are included under the branch of physics known as *aerodynamics.* To understand airplane flight, it is necessary first to understand the nature of air and a few simple principles of aerodynamics.

Air is a mixture of gases that surrounds the earth. Although the gaseous particles that make up the air are too small to be seen with the unaided eye, they have weight and can exert pressure. At sea level, the layer of air around the earth exerts a force, during normal weather conditions, of 14.7 pounds on each square inch of surface. This pressure is exerted not only downward, but in all other directions as well. At higher altitudes, the air pressure is less because the air is lighter (less dense) than at sea level; that is, there are fewer particles of air at higher altitudes. Variations in air pressure over the surface of an airplane as it moves through the air enable the plane to fly.

Gravity and Lift

The force of gravity attracts (pulls) an airborne object toward the earth's surface. The magnitude of this attractive force is defined as the object's *weight.* To achieve flight a lifting force opposing the pull of gravity must be obtained. This force is called *lift.*

Lift in an airplane is created by the wing moving through the stream of air caused by the plane's forward motion. The wing's cross section (called the *wing profile,* or *airfoil*) is shaped in such a way that the motion of the wing through the air lowers the air pressure on the upper surface of the wing and raises it on the lower. Thus, the wing is partially "pulled" and partially "pushed" upward.

The combined effect of the wing's shape and its *angle of attack* causes the air flowing over the wing's upper surface to travel farther and faster than the air flowing under the wing. Angle of attack is defined as the angle between the wing and the direction of the airstream as it meets the wing. According to *Bernoulli's Principle,* a relation discovered by the 18th-century Swiss scientist and mathematician Daniel Bernoulli, the

A-199

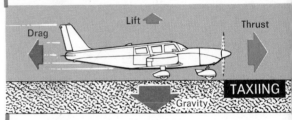

The Forces That Affect Flight. *Lift* holds the plane in the air by overcoming the downward pull of *gravity.* Lift is developed by the movement of the plane through the air. *Thrust* is the force that overcomes *drag* and gives the plane its forward movement. Thrust is developed by the plane's engine.

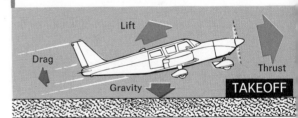

Taxiing. The forward movement of a plane on the ground is called *taxiing.* It takes place when thrust becomes greater than drag.

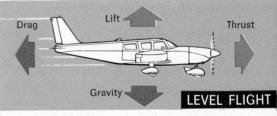

Takeoff. Lift increases as the plane picks up speed. Finally, lift becomes greater than gravity and the plane rises in the air.

In Level Flight at constant speed, lift equals gravity and thrust equals drag.

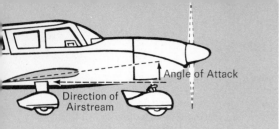

Angle of Attack. The angle of attack is the angle at which the wing meets the airstream. (The airstream, which is caused by the plane's forward motion, is always directly opposite in direction to the plane's course.)

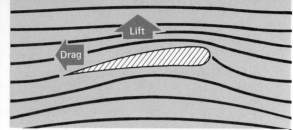

How Lift Is Produced. Because of the shape of the wing, the air passing over its top moves faster than the air passing along its underside. According to Bernoulli's Principle, the faster the motion of the air, the less pressure it exerts. This means that less pressure is exerted on the upper side of the wing than on the underside. The fact that the wing meets the airstream at a slight angle (the angle of attack) increases the pressure difference. The net upward force that results is called *lift*.

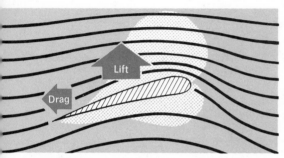

When the Angle of Attack Is Increased, two things happen: (1) The pressure under the wing is increased slightly, and (2) air moves faster across the top of the wing, reducing the pressure above the wing. The result is an increase in lift.

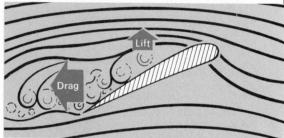

If the Angle of Attack Is Too Large, the air does not flow smoothly over the top of the wing. Instead it breaks away from the surface, and turbulent masses of air form. Lift is decreased, and the wing is said to stall.

faster a fluid moves, the lower is the pressure that it exerts. As the wing displaces the air (which acts in this case as a fluid), the pressure above it is decreased. At the same time, the speed of the air below the wing is decreased somewhat, causing the pressure there to become greater. This difference in pressure creates an upward force that maintains the plane in flight.

Lift varies with the density of the air and with the speed of the plane or airstream. The denser the air, the greater the lift produced; and the greater the speed of the plane or of the airstream, the greater the lift.

Lift also varies with the angle of attack. The angle of attack changes as the plane's nose is pointed upward or downward. Usually, lift increases as the angle of attack increases. This is because the increased tilt of the wing results in an increase in the speed of the airflow over the upper side of the wing, thus reducing the pressure there.

This increase in lift, however, occurs only up to a certain point. If the angle of attack is larger than about 20° (which might be the case if the pilot points the plane's nose too high in climbing), the air no longer flows smoothly over the wings. Instead, turbulent masses of air form, decreasing the lift, and the airplane stalls (loses so much lift that it becomes uncontrollable).

Thrust and Drag

Besides gravity and lift, there are two other forces that must be considered in the flight of an airplane—thrust and drag. *Thrust* is the forward force of propulsion. It can be furnished by the action of an engine-driven propeller or by a jet or rocket engine.

Drag is a force opposing the thrust. Drag occurs because the particles of air resist the advance of the airplane. As the speed of the airplane increases, so does the drag. Drag can be reduced by *streamlining* the airplane;

that is, by shaping the airplane so that the airstream will flow more smoothly around it. (See STREAMLINING.)

A plane will be in level flight at constant speed if lift is equal to the weight of the plane and if thrust is equal to drag. When thrust is greater than drag the plane will climb or its speed will increase. The problem of overcoming drag is exceedingly important in the design of high-speed aircraft.

Supersonic Flight

At 70° F. (the average temperature at sea level), sound travels through air at about 740 miles per hour. The speed of sound in air decreases with increasing altitude because the air temperature decreases with altitude and sound travels more slowly in colder air. When a plane flies faster than the speed of sound, it has entered *supersonic* flight. *Transonic* flight occurs when a plane passes from slower-than-sound to faster-than-sound speeds. When a plane reaches five times the speed of sound, it is in *hypersonic* flight.

When a plane flies at *subsonic* speeds (speeds lower than the speed of sound), the air-pressure waves it creates by its motion spread with the speed of sound in all directions. These waves prepare the air ahead of the plane to flow smoothly over the plane's surfaces. In supersonic flight the waves cannot precede the plane because its speed exceeds the speed of sound. Consequently the air receives no advance "warning" and is pushed out of the way abruptly by *shock waves* (strong disturbances characterized by a rapid increase in density and pressure) created by the nose of the plane and the leading (front) edge of the wing. When the shock wave reaches the ground it makes itself felt as a small explosion. The loud noise caused by this explosion is called a *sonic boom.*

To keep the strength of the shock wave at a minimum, a supersonic airplane usually

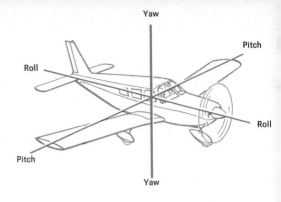

Axes of Rotation. When an airplane is in flight, there are three fixed lines, called axes, about which it can rotate. Each of these lines is perpendicular to the other two, and all pass through the plane's center of gravity. They are called the *axis of pitch* (lateral, or transverse, axis), the *axis of roll* (longitudinal axis), and the *axis of yaw* (vertical axis). Movement about the axis of pitch can be controlled by the elevators in the tail assembly and the amount of thrust. Movement about the axis of roll can be controlled by the ailerons; movement about the axis of yaw, by the rudder.

has a sharp nose and sharp leading edges on its wings and tail surfaces. Also, the wings and tail surfaces are often swept back to form a V. In airplanes with variable-sweep wings, such as the United States' F-111 jet fighter, the wings are extended for low-speed flight and swept back for supersonic flight.

In transonic flight, air travels past some parts of the plane at supersonic speeds, and past other parts at subsonic speeds. This uneven flow creates shock waves that may rapidly change in location and strength, making it difficult to control the plane. Because of this difficulty the transonic range of flight speed has been called the *sound barrier.*

High speeds are often stated in *Mach* (mäk) *numbers.* Mach 1 is the speed of sound at the altitude at which the plane is flying, Mach 2 is twice that speed, Mach 0.5 is half that speed, etc. This system is named for Ernst Mach (1838-1916), an Austrian physicist and philosopher.

Parts of an Airplane

Fuselage

The fuselage, or body of the airplane, contains the pilot's cockpit, crew or passenger quarters, and cargo space. The framework of the fuselage is generally a lightweight alloy. In planes designed for subsonic flight, the cover of the fuselage usually consists of a sheet of aluminum alloy. Because aluminum cannot withstand the high temperatures produced by air friction at speeds above

Mach 2, the entire outer surface of a supersonic plane is covered with stainless steel, titanium alloy, or some other material with a high melting point.

Wings

Airplane wings have been designed in a number of different shapes, such as rectangular, tapered, and triangular. Several structural units called *spars* extend from the fuselage frame to the wing tip. *Ribs,* running

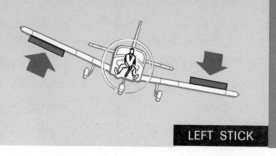

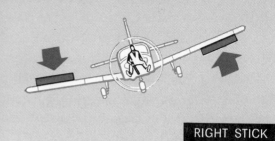

LEFT STICK

RIGHT STICK

Ailerons. One way to make an airplane turn sideways is to move the *ailerons* (hinged flaps at the back, or trailing edge, of each wing). The *control stick* in the cockpit will move them up or down. When the control stick is moved to the left, the aileron on the left wing moves up and the one on the right wing moves down. Lowering the aileron increases the lift of the wing; raising the aileron decreases lift. The left wing therefore drops and the right wing rises, causing the plane to *bank,* so that it turns to the left. When the control stick is moved to the right, the aileron on the left wing moves up and the one on the right wing moves down. Then the difference in lift of the two wings causes the right wing to drop and the left one to rise, and the plane starts banking to the right.

fore and aft, are attached to the spars. The spars and ribs are usually made of aluminum, although other materials, including wood, have been used. The wing is covered with a skin of aluminum alloy or some other suitable material. The top of the wing is usually cambered (convex in shape). The bottom surface is usually flatter.

In most planes, the wings house the fuel tanks. In most multi-engine planes, they also support streamlined enclosures, called *nacelles* (or pods), that contain the engines. To melt ice that may form during flight, hot air can, in many planes, be passed along

Rudder. The other way to cause an airplane to turn sideways is to move the *rudder.* The rudder is in the tail of the airplane. Pedals control the rudder. When the left pedal is pushed, the rudder moves to the left. Lift is produced on the right side of the rudder, causing the tail to move to the right and the nose of the airplane to the left. Likewise, when the right pedal is pushed, the nose turns to the right. Since the rudder alone will cause a flat or "skidding" turn, it is always used together with the ailerons in the same direction to start a more comfortable banked turn.

the leading edge of the wing. This air is heated by electric heaters or by the engine exhaust. In some planes, the leading edge of the wing is covered with a rubber sleeve that can be inflated to crack the ice; the airstream then blows it away.

At the wing's trailing (rear) edge near the tips there are narrow, hinged portions called *ailerons.* These can be deflected up or down by the pilot. To bank (tilt) the plane to the left, the pilot raises the aileron on the left wing and lowers the one on the right, causing the right wing to rise and the left one to drop.

Between each aileron and the fuselage is another hinged strip, called a *flap.* When the flaps are extended downward they increase the lift of the wings. They are used during takeoff and landing when the flight speed is too low to support the plane with the wings alone. They can also be used to increase drag during landing, thus reducing the plane's speed.

Tail Assembly

At the rear of the plane is the *tail assembly,* or *empennage.* It consists of horizontal and vertical *stabilizers* that help keep the plane in level flight; a *rudder;* and *elevators.* The rudder is a movable control surface attached to the trailing edge of the vertical stabilizer. *Elevators* are movable control surfaces attached to the rear of the horizontal stabilizer. When the elevators are swung down, the plane noses down. When they are raised, the plane's nose rises. High-speed planes often have movable, one-piece horizontal stabilizers instead of separate elevators and stabilizers.

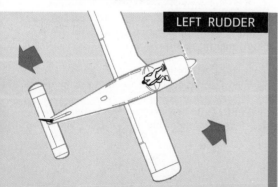

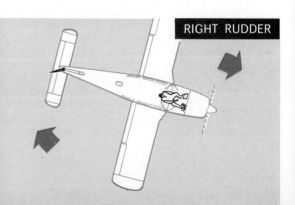

LEFT RUDDER

RIGHT RUDDER

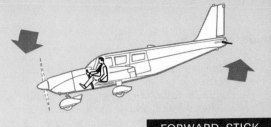

FORWARD STICK   **BACKWARD STICK**

Controls

The flight controls are located in the cockpit. They consist of the control stick (or wheel) and rudder pedals. The stick or wheel controls the ailerons and elevators. Moving it to the side causes the plane to bank. Pushing it forward causes the plane to nose down, and pulling it back makes the plane climb. The rudder pedals control the rudder, which can make the airplane's nose move to the right or left.

Another way to make a plane go up is to increase the thrust, since lift increases with speed. The amount of thrust is controlled by a throttle that regulates the power being delivered by the engine.

Propeller

In an airplane powered by a piston or turboprop engine, a propeller is used to convert the rotational power of the engine drive shaft into thrust. An airplane propeller is made of laminated wood, phenolic plastic, a lightweight metal or alloy, or steel, and has two or more blades. The blades are designed to bite into the air with enough force to propel the airplane. They are mounted on a hub at the end of the engine drive shaft. The plane perpendicular to the drive shaft is called the *plane of rotation*. Each propeller blade is twisted, so that its leading edge

Elevator. One way to make the plane go up or down is to move the *elevator*. The elevator is a hinged flap, crosswise in the tail of the plane. It is controlled by the same stick that operates the ailerons. When the stick is pushed forward, the elevator is moved down, and the lift of the tail surface is increased. The tail of the airplane therefore rises, the nose is pointed down, and the plane goes downward. When the control stick is pulled back, the elevator is raised. Lift is decreased, the tail drops, and the airplane begins to climb.

strikes the airstream at a certain angle relative to the plane of rotation. This angle is called the *pitch*.

The simplest kind of propeller is the two-blade, fixed-pitch type, which is used on small, low-speed airplanes. On most high-speed airplanes, the pitch of the propellers can be adjusted—either on the ground or in flight—to suit various flying conditions. This is done by rotating the blades in the hub.

Adjustable-pitch propellers are of three basic types:

1. **Two-position Propeller.** This propeller has two pitch settings—one for takeoff and the other for cruising flight.

2. **Variable-pitch Propeller.** The pitch of this propeller can be adjusted to any desired setting.

3. **Constant-speed Propeller.** The pitch of this propeller is changed automatically to maintain constant engine speed under varying flight conditions.

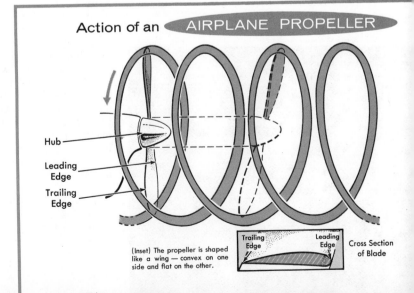

A Propeller works like a revolving wing. Moving through the air, it pulls the airplane along by its lifting force, which provides the thrust.

Action of an AIRPLANE PROPELLER

Hub

Leading Edge

Trailing Edge

(Inset) The propeller is shaped like a wing — convex on one side and flat on the other.

Trailing Edge   Leading Edge   Cross Section of Blade

As a safety measure, the blades of a variable-pitch or constant-speed propeller can be *feathered*—rotated to a pitch angle of about 90 degrees so that the propeller will not rotate in case of engine failure. The blades can also be *reversed*—set so that the direction of the thrust is reversed, causing the propeller to slow the plane upon landing.

Engine

An airplane engine provides the power needed to get the plane into the air and keep it there. It does this by creating enough force to cause the airplane to move in relation to the air and thus set up an airflow over its wings. An airplane may have one or more engines. Piston, turbojet, turbofan, turboprop, ramjet, and rocket engines have been successfully used to power airplanes. All of these except the rocket engine are classified as *air-breathing* engines because they require the oxygen in air to operate.

Piston Engines. The gasoline-burning piston engine was the first type of engine to be successfully used in airplanes. It is still widely used, particularly in small, nonmilitary airplanes. The pistons of this engine are connected to a drive shaft, at the end of which the propeller is located. The engine can be either water-cooled (like most automobile engines) or air-cooled. Devices known as *superchargers* are often used with these engines to provide sufficient oxygen for combustion at high altitudes, where the air density is low. (See also GASOLINE ENGINE; SUPERCHARGER.)

Jet Engines. The thrust of a jet engine is created by expelling a stream, or *jet,* of high-pressure gases from the engine exhaust. The *turbojet* engine, used in most military combat planes and in many commercial and private planes, is the most widely used type of jet engine. A turbojet engine equipped with a propellerlike fan, which provides a larger but lower-speed stream of exhaust gases, is called a *turbofan* engine. Turbofan engines are widely used in planes designed for subsonic flight, but at supersonic speeds turbojet engines perform better.

A *turboprop,* or *propjet,* engine provides both exhaust thrust and propeller thrust. The *ramjet* engine is effective only at supersonic speeds, and its use has been limited mainly to experimental airplanes.

For additional information on jet engines, including diagrams, see JET PROPULSION.

Rocket Engines. The thrust of a rocket engine, like that of a jet engine, is created by expelling gases under pressure. The gases are produced by a chemical reaction between a fuel and an oxidizer, both of which are carried in the airplane. Since rocket engines do not require air for their operation, they can be used in the airless space beyond the earth's atmosphere.

From the late 1940's to the 1960's, experimental rocket-powered planes played a vital role in high-altitude and high-speed flight research. Knowledge from this research went into the planning of the United States' Space Shuttle, a manned, reusable earth-orbiting craft designed to be launched and orbited like a spacecraft but flown and landed like a plane on its return to earth.

See also MISSILES AND ROCKETS, section "Missile Engines."

Instruments

In his cockpit the pilot faces an instrument panel on which various gauges and dials indicate the plane's *attitude* (position with regard to level flight), its direction, its altitude, and its speed in the air. Other indicators tell how the engine is performing. In a large plane, there are two identical instrument panels, one each for the pilot and the copilot.

On long flights there is a navigator who uses his instruments to keep track of the plane's position and plots its course, in a manner somewhat similar to that used in navigating a ship. Because a plane travels many times faster than a ship, however, quicker and more frequent findings are required.

The development of specialized instruments has made it possible for the pilot to fly *blind;* that is, fly with the aid of instru-

Instrument Panel of Douglas DC-8 Jetliner
Sperry Gyroscope Company

AIRPLANE INSTRUMENTS

(Instruments for a light plane are shown)

SIX BASIC INSTRUMENTS

Airspeed Indicator

Altimeter

Magnetic Compass

Horizon Indicator

Fuel Gauge

Tachometer

Engine
Oil-pressure Gauge

Turn-and-bank Indicator

Rate-of-climb Indicator

ments when he cannot see the ground or other objects outside the plane because of darkness or bad weather.

Every airplane that flies in the United States is required by the Federal Aviation Administration (FAA) to have the following instruments:

Airspeed Indicator, which shows what is called the "indicated airspeed" of the airplane, in miles per hour or in knots. Indicated airspeed is the difference between the pressure of the airstream and the atmospheric pressure; it represents the speed of the air that is providing lift for the wings. The airspeed indicator does not compensate for the effects of temperature and altitude on air pressure; to calculate *true airspeed,* the pilot must make allowances for these effects. Indicated airspeed is important to the pilot in controlling the plane in flight; true airspeed is important to him for navigation.

When there is no wind, true airspeed is equal to ground speed (the speed of the plane relative to the ground). A tail wind increases ground speed, a head wind reduces it.

A *Machmeter* is a special type of airspeed indicator carried by a supersonic airplane; it gives the airspeed of the plane relative to the speed of sound.

Altimeter, which shows the plane's height in feet or meters. A *pressure* altimeter, which is basically a sensitive aneroid barometer, shows the plane's altitude above sea level. A *radio* altimeter indicates the plane's distance above the ground; it operates by measuring the time required for a radio signal to travel to and from the ground. A *laser* altimeter uses a narrow beam of light instead of a radio signal.

Magnetic Compass, which indicates the direction in which the plane is traveling. To prevent the large errors introduced when it tilts, an airplane's magnetic compass is usually stabilized by a gyroscope. In addition to the magnetic compass, many airplanes contain a *gyrocompass,* a north-seeking instrument whose basic mechanism is a gyroscope. (See COMPASS, subtitle *Non-Magnetic Compasses: The Gyrocompass.*)

Fuel Gauge, which indicates the quantity of fuel in the fuel tanks.

Engine Oil-pressure Gauge, which, as in automobiles, indicates the state of the oil pressure in the engine. Dropping oil pressure is a sign that engine failure is about to occur.

Tachometer, which measures engine speed. (See TACHOMETER.)

In addition, most planes in the United States must be equipped with an *emergency locator transmitter* (ELT). The ELT is a small radio transmitter that automatically begins sending out a special signal if the plane crashes. For planes with retractable landing gear, the FAA requires an indicator to show when the landing gear is up.

Other common instruments and equipment include the following:

Radio, which is used not only for voice communication with the ground but also as a navigation aid. (See NAVIGATION, subtitle *Methods of Navigation: Piloting.*)

Automatic Pilot, which is a gyroscope-operated system for steering the plane automatically. (See AUTOMATIC PILOT.)

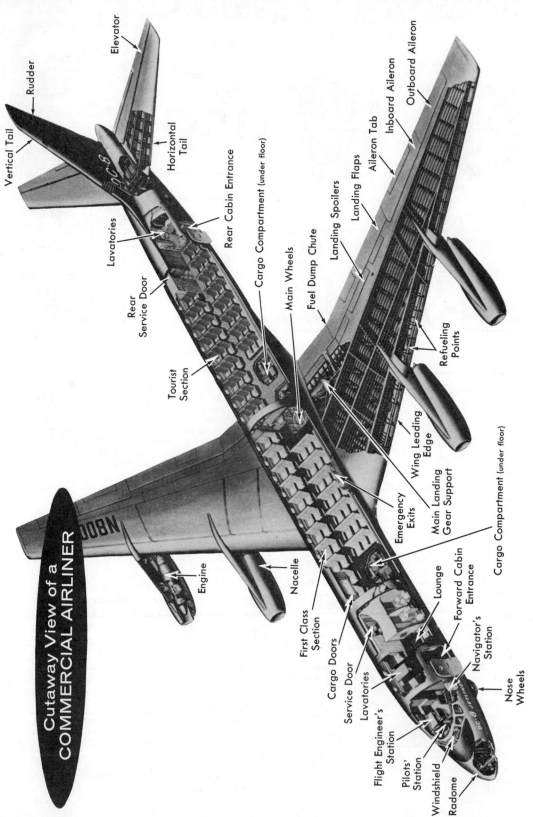

Cutaway View of a
COMMERCIAL AIRLINER

Elevator

Rudder

Vertical Tail

Horizontal Tail

Inboard Aileron

Outboard Aileron

Douglas Aircraft Company

Lavatories

Rear Cabin Entrance

Cargo Compartment (under floor)

Landing Spoilers

Landing Flaps

Aileron Tab

Rear Service Door

Main Wheels

Fuel Dump Chute

Tourist Section

Refueling Points

Wing Leading Edge

Main Landing Gear Support

Emergency Exits

Cargo Compartment (under floor)

Engine

Nacelle

First Class Section

Cargo Doors

Service Door

Lavatories

Lounge

Forward Cabin Entrance

Flight Engineer's Station

Pilots' Station

Windshield

Radome

Navigator's Station

Nose Wheels

Horizon Indicator, which makes use of a gyroscope to show the attitude of the plane relative to the horizon. It indicates whether the plane is flying level, banking, climbing, or descending.

Flight Recorder, which is a device that provides a record of indicated airspeed, altitude, vertical acceleration, and magnetic heading at any given time. It is extremely valuable in the investigation of crashes.

Turn-and-bank Indicator, which shows the rate and direction of the plane's turning. It is actually two separate instruments: a turn indicator, which

has a pointer operated by a small gyroscope; and a bank indicator, which is essentially a spirit level consisting of a ball that rolls in a curved, liquid-filled glass tube.

Rate-of-climb Indicator, or Vertical-speed Indicator, which shows (usually in feet per minute) the plane's rate of climb or descent. The pointer responds to changes in atmospheric pressure as the plane changes altitude.

Radar Equipment, which locates weather disturbances and assists in navigation. (See RADAR.)

Types of Airplanes

All airplanes have certain characteristics in common, but the size and design of planes may differ radically. There are many ways of classifying and identifying the various types of planes. The most common ways are by use, landing gear, wing structure, type of propulsion, or number of engines.

Classification by Use

Commercial Airplanes. These planes, which usually have two, three, or four engines, are built for service on commercial airlines. Most of them are powered by turboprop, turbojet, or turbofan engines, although piston-engine models are still used in some regions for short runs.

Commercial passenger airliners are used in local, transcontinental, and transoceanic travel. The largest United States airliners can carry up to 490 passengers, have kitchen equipment for preparing meals, and can carry large amounts of luggage, freight, and mail. Almost all types of passenger planes can be adapted to haul freight.

Military Airplanes. Some military planes are propeller-driven, but most combat types are jet-propelled. Propeller-driven planes are still useful in some combat situations, however, such as counter-insurgency (antiguerrilla) operations. Most types of combat planes can carry nuclear weapons. The following classification system is based on that of the U.S. Department of Defense (with some simplification).

Antisubmarine Aircraft are designed to search out, attack, and destroy enemy submarines. Such planes can operate from aircraft carriers and, since they fly at relatively low speeds, are propeller-driven. They carry depth charges and other antisubmarine weapons.

Attack Aircraft are designed to search out, attack, and destroy enemy land or sea targets, using machine-gun or cannon fire, rockets, high-explosive bombs, or nuclear weapons. They are also used to disrupt enemy communications (by bombing bridges, for example) and to support ground

troops. American attack planes are mainly naval aircraft capable of operating from carriers. Attack aircraft have replaced the torpedo bombers and dive bombers of World War II.

Bombers are designed to attack enemy targets with high-explosive or nuclear bombs. They can be classed as tactical or strategic.

Tactical bombers are relatively small, generally twin-engine planes with missions similar to those of attack aircraft. COIN (counter-insurgency) aircraft are especially equipped to operate in areas with primitive airfield facilities.

Strategic bombers can carry large bomb loads long distances to attack enemy cities, industries, transportation centers, and other targets far from the battle lines. For long-distance missions, strategic bombers are refueled in flight from flying tankers.

World War II bombers bristled with defensive weapons, including .50 caliber machine guns and 20 mm. cannon. Modern bombers are generally armed lightly, relying mainly on speed and altitude to evade enemy aircraft. Various kinds of decoy equipment may be used to confuse enemy radar and antiaircraft missiles. Bombs are aimed electronically or optically, depending on the plane and target.

Cargo/Transport Planes carry cargo, passengers, or both. Some are similar to commercial airliners,

Military Airplane. A U.S. Navy attack aircraft, an A-7E Corsair II, comes in for a landing on an aircraft carrier.

U.S. Navy

Cessna Aircraft Company
Private Plane. The Cessna 150 is used for pleasure flying and as a trainer. Tricycle landing gear simplifies takeoffs and landings.

while others are specially designed for military use. Some are used mainly for ground-to-ground missions—carrying men or supplies from one airfield to another—while others are used to drop paratroopers and parachute-borne supplies. Cargo/transport planes are generally unarmed.

Fighters are designed primarily to intercept and destroy enemy aircraft and missiles, but also have a variety of other missions. *Fighter-bombers* serve as attack planes or tactical bombers. *Tactical fighters* support ground troops by attacking enemy troop concentrations, tanks, guns, and other targets; their targets are often selected by ground observers. *Fighter-escorts* guard bombers and attack planes against enemy fighters.

Fighters are armed with a wide variety of weapons. These include multi-barreled cannon, air-to-air or air-to-ground rockets, high-explosive bombs, and nuclear weapons. Most modern fighters can be refueled in flight.

Helicopters are used to carry troops and supplies, to rescue downed aviators, and to carry wounded to medical aid stations. Some are armed with cannon and machine guns for ground-support work. Helicopters are also used for reconnaissance and for gunfire spotting. See HELICOPTER.

Observation, Patrol, and Reconnaissance Aircraft gather information on enemy activities.

Observation planes, generally light, single-engine craft capable of operating from crude airfields, are used to observe enemy movements in and near the combat area. They are often used to direct artillery or naval gunfire. These planes are unarmed.

Patrol planes are generally naval aircraft. They are long-range, all-weather airplanes designed to detect enemy submarines or shipping, to lay mines, and to search for survivors of plane wrecks and ship sinkings. These are large airplanes, heavily laden with radar and other search equipment. They carry little or no defensive armament.

For Business Travel. The Twin Comanche B has retractable landing gear, automatic pilot, and many of the navigation instruments of larger planes.
Piper Aircraft Corporation

Reconnaissance planes, like patrol planes, have long ranges and can operate in all kinds of weather. Their main mission is to study enemy territory, either through photography or electronic devices, to assist intelligence experts in gathering data. These planes also gather weather information. The United States armed forces ordinarily do not class reconnaissance aircraft as a separate type because these planes are usually modified bombers or fighters. Perhaps the most famous of all reconnaissance aircraft—the Lockheed U-2—is classified as a "utility" plane.

Tankers carry aviation fuel for supplying bombers and fighters in flight. A boom, supported by short wings, is extended from the tail to link up with the plane being fueled. Tankers are generally similar in design to transport planes.

Trainers are used for training pilots and aircrews. *Primary trainers* are used to teach flying. They are light, single-engine, propeller-driven planes, usually with two sets of controls. *Basic trainers* have higher performance than primary trainers and are used to teach novice pilots military skills. *Advanced trainers* are modified or obsolete combat aircraft. *Crew trainers* are used for navigators, electronics specialists, and other flight-crew personnel. They are often modified transport planes.

Utility Aircraft are used for miscellaneous missions such as towing targets or carrying light passenger or cargo loads.

Private Airplanes. The private plane is used by individuals or companies for transportation, work, or sport. It is usually a light, single-engine plane. Multi-engine planes, commercial-type airliners, or converted bombers are sometimes used, especially by large corporations. Although airplanes are rather expensive to operate and maintain, these expenses are often offset by savings in time.

Personal airplanes are used by businessmen, hunters, and others as a quick means of transportation. For persons in out-of-the-way places, an airplane can be almost a necessity. Many amateur flying enthusiasts use planes for recreation. Most airports have facilities for storing and servicing personal airplanes.

Business airplanes are used for fast transportation of personnel or materials over long distances, when the scheduled commercial flights either do not serve the areas involved or do not run often enough. Ranchers and farmers use light planes for transportation and for such work as seed planting and crop dusting. Forest rangers use them to detect fires, and to drop fire fighters by parachute.

Classification by Landing Gear
Landplane. The landplane is designed to take off and land on the ground or on aircraft carriers. It usually has three wheels or

Airliner. The Boeing 747 "jumbo jet" can carry up to 490 persons at speeds exceeding 600 miles per hour. The distinctive "humpnose" design allows for an upper-deck passenger lounge. This plane has five doors on each side and two aisles. It is powered by four turbofan engines.

Boeing

sets of wheels. Two sets ease the shock of landing and are placed under the center of gravity of the plane. In large planes, the third set is usually placed under the nose of the plane, an arrangement called a *tricycle landing gear*. In smaller planes, the center of gravity may be too far forward for a leading wheel, so the third wheel is located under the tail assembly.

Some military planes have a *tandem* landing gear system—two sets of main wheels are mounted on the bottom of the fuselage, one behind the other. Small wheels extending down from the wings prevent the plane from tilting.

On most planes, the landing gear is drawn, or *retracted,* into the wings, engine housing, or fuselage during flight to reduce drag. Some light private planes and military trainers have fixed wheel-struts that cannot be retracted.

In Arctic regions, planes are frequently fitted with skis in place of, or in addition to, wheels. Where a plane is required to land on rough or soft ground, crawler-tractor devices may replace the wheels.

Seaplane. The seaplane is designed to take off and land on water. Instead of wheels, it rests on one or two buoyant pontoons, or *floats.* A single-float plane is provided with smaller outrigger floats, called *sponsons,* under the wing tips to balance it on the water.

The *hydro-ski* seaplane does not use floats. It rests on the fuselage, and has one or more skis that can be extended for taking off and landing on water and retracted when the plane is in flight.

Flying Boat. Flying boats, like seaplanes, take off and land on water. They do not rest on floats, however. Instead, the plane fuselage is a hull, similar in design to the hull of a ship. Flying boats are usually large, having passenger and cargo space for long flights. The hull is streamlined and can withstand fairly rough seas. The wings, mounted at the top of the hull, are usually fitted with

A-209

sponsons. Because of their relatively low speed, flying boats are no longer in commercial service. A few are still used as naval patrol craft.

Amphibian. Planes of this type can take off and land on either land or water. The amphibian has retractable wheels as well as a hull or floats. It is used for naval patrol work and by surveyors and hunters.

Classification by Wings

Number of Wings. By far the most common type of plane since the mid-1930's has been the *monoplane*—a plane with a single fixed wing extending from each side of the fuselage.

Airplanes having two wings, one above the other, are called *biplanes.* They were widely used in the early days of aviation because two wings produce almost twice the lift of a single wing with the same span. Biplanes have more drag than monoplanes, however, and eventually dropped from favor. The few still in service are used mainly as trainers, crop-dusters, and stunt planes.

Before World War I, experimental planes with as many as four wings were built. These proved very inefficient, chiefly because of the drag. Planes with three wings were used with some success, however. Such *triplanes* included German fighters that were among the best combat planes of World War I.

Shape of Wings. Some types of planes can be identified by the shape of their wings. When seen from below, *swept-back* wings

Russian AN-22 Turboprop. Like other Russian commercial planes, it has a glassed-in "greenhouse" in the nose, similar to that of bombers. The double propellers rotate in opposite directions.

APN: Polikashin

Sud Aviation

Concorde, a supersonic transport (SST) designed and built jointly by Great Britain and France. It travels at twice the speed of the fastest conventional airliner and was expected to revolutionize air travel when it entered service in 1976. However, steadily rising fuel costs made the airplane unprofitable to operate, and its manufacture was discontinued in 1979.

form a V and *delta wings* a triangle. *Variable-angle wings* can be pivoted during flight to vary the amount of sweep; on takeoff the wings are at nearly right angles to the fuselage, while at high speeds they are adjusted to form a V or triangle. Such wings, by increasing lift when extended, make it possible for supersonic planes to use relatively short runways.

Other Classifications and Types

Airplanes are sometimes classified by the type of propulsion (for example, turbojet, turboprop, piston-engine) or number of engines used. A *pusher* plane has its propellers in the rear; a *tractor* has them in front.

Special types of planes have been designed to take off and land in small areas.

These are called VTOL (vertical takeoff and landing) and STOL (short takeoff and landing) planes. Helicopters, of course, specialize in such flight, but their speed, range, altitude, and load are limited.

One kind of jet-powered VTOL plane has adjustable engine outlets on the underside of its fuselage, enabling the plane to lift straight up at takeoff and then begin normal forward flight when clear of surrounding obstacles. Short-takeoff planes are specially designed to gain increased lift and, in many cases, thrust. A common method of gaining extra lift is by the use of special flaps at the wings' leading edges and extra-large flaps at the trailing edges.

See also AUTOGIRO; HELICOPTER.

How Airplanes Are Manufactured

Airplane manufacture is dominated by four countries—the United States, the Soviet Union, Great Britain, and France. Most of the military and commercial aircraft in service today were either designed or built in one of these four countries. Only a handful of other countries produce aircraft in signifi-

cant amounts. These include Sweden, Canada, West Germany, Italy, Spain, Brazil, and Czechoslovakia.

Research and Design

It usually takes several years of research, development, and testing before a new airplane can be put into production. Some research aircraft do not reach the flight stage for 10 years or more.

The first step in making a new airplane is to find ways of meeting the necessary specifications regarding speed, weight, size, power, and safety. Preliminary designs based on this research are drawn up and used to make small models. Each model is usually tested in a *wind tunnel,* a duct in which flight conditions are simulated by blowing streams of air over the model. (See WIND TUNNEL.) These and other tests help in formulating the final design.

Next, a full-scale version of the plane, called the *prototype,* is made and test-flown. Corrections are made until the plane per-

Engine Assembly. Technicians carry out the final steps in the manufacture of a large jet engine.
Rolls Royce

forms satisfactorily. Finally, manufacturing methods are developed, production lines are planned, and actual manufacturing begins. Further corrections and modifications are made whenever necessary.

Manufacturing

A modern jet airliner has more than 500-000 parts, compared to about 15,000 for a typical automobile. It is not practical for any one company to attempt to make all these parts. The company that undertakes to produce an airplane, the *prime contractor,* may use hundreds or even thousands of other companies, called *subcontractors,* to make parts for the airplane.

Designs are modified so frequently that parts manufacturers cannot afford to build new tools for each new design or to stop production to install new tools. Instead, they use machines equipped with *jigs,* special tools that are easily removed and replaced. When designs are changed, new jigs are installed in the basic machines.

Assembling

The various parts are assembled at the home manufacturing plant. Small parts are first combined, on moving production lines, into larger units called *sub-assemblies.* The

Douglas Aircraft Company, Inc.

Plane Assembly. Joining nose to fuselage of 187-foot-long Super 61 DC-8, a 251-passenger liner.

sub-assembly lines meet the main production line at the place where they are needed, and the sub-assemblies are added to the airframe as it moves along the line. The various parts are fitted, riveted, and welded together almost entirely by hand, although automatic methods are used where possible. For example, tape-controlled automatic riveting machines make various sub-assemblies.

History of the Airplane

Man's Earliest Attempts to Fly

Ancient drawings and legends show early man's interest in flight. A Greek legend tells of Daedalus making wings of feathers and wax for himself and his son Icarus to escape imprisonment in the labyrinth of Crete. Daedalus' flight succeeded but Icarus plunged to his death when he flew too high and the sun melted the wax in his wings.

Although most early attempts to fly were made in imitation of the flight of birds, it is believed that the Chinese and other Orientals constructed man-carrying kites. Unsuccessful attempts to fly with flapping-wing apparatus were made repeatedly during the Middle Ages.

Systematic investigation awaited the genius of Leonardo da Vinci in the late 15th and early 16th centuries. From his observations of birds in flight and their physical structure, da Vinci made a number of sketches to illustrate how he believed man could apply his muscular strength to raise himself into the air. Da Vinci's drawings also included designs of an airscrew, a para-

chute, and a helicopter. (See also HELICOPTER, subtitle *History of Helicopters.*)

Seeking Mastery of the Air

As the search for a way of achieving human flight progressed, experiments took two directions. One group of experimenters worked on lighter-than-air craft, which would be kept aloft by their own buoyancy. (See BALLOON, subtitle *History of Balloons;* DIRIGIBLE, subtitle *History of Dirigibles.*) The second group proposed to use heavier-than-air craft, which require movement—and hence a power source for propulsion—to stay aloft. Lighter-than-air flight came first, but aviation pioneers who were interested in more dynamic flight preferred to experiment with heavier-than-air machines.

Early Flying Machines. In the early 1800's Sir George Cayley in Great Britain designed several forms of aircraft, including gliders and helicopters. His first successful glider, 1804, was a modified kite, about 4 feet long. In 1852 he made a man-carrying glider. His observations on heavier-than-air flight laid the foundation for later work. Cayley

First Airplane in Flight near Kitty Hawk, North Carolina, in 1903. Orville Wright was at controls, with Wilbur alongside.

determined that a craft with fixed wings and mechanical power would be the most desirable vehicle for sustained directed flight. The need for mechanical power ruled out the glider, which uses gravity and air currents as its source of power.

Cayley's work was carried further by William Henson and John Stringfellow. In 1842 Henson designed an aircraft powered by a small steam engine. Improving upon Henson's design, Stringfellow in 1848 constructed a steam-driven model plane that could lift part of its weight.

In the second half of the 19th century, experimentation with gliders continued in several countries. The most important contributions were made by Otto Lilienthal, a German, who constructed and flew his first glider in 1891. He made more than 2,000 successful glider flights before his death in a crash in 1896. Lilienthal demonstrated the importance of the lifting power of curved

First to Cross the English Channel was Louis Blériot of France. His was the first monoplane, and also the first plane to have the propeller in front. He flew from Calais to Dover in 1909, covering 23½ miles in about 37 minutes.

surfaces and developed some measure of balance and control in the air.

Other early glider pilots included Percy S. Pilcher of Great Britain and John J. Montgomery (the first successful American in the field) and Octave Chanute of the United States. Many brave pioneers lost their lives attempting to fly. (See also GLIDER, subtitle *History*.)

Attempts with Powered Airplanes. During this period of the late 1800's a number of efforts were made to develop a man-carrying powered airplane. Experimenters included Clement Ader in France, Wilhelm Kress in Austria, Sir Hiram S. Maxim of Great Britain, and Professor Samuel P. Langley of the Smithsonian Institution, Washington, D. C.

Maxim built a steam-powered plane in 1894, but it was wrecked during a test. Langley, who had begun to experiment with unmanned small airplanes in 1886, constructed a tandem-winged monoplane model with a one-horsepower steam engine and two propellers. It flew more than half a mile in 1896. His gasoline-engined unmanned model of 1901-03 was the first heavier-than-air craft to use successfully this form of power. Subsequent failures, however, with his full-scale gasoline-engined monoplane caused him to abandon his efforts in 1903.

First Successful Airplanes

On December 17, 1903, near Kitty Hawk, North Carolina, the first controlled, powered flight of a heavier-than-air machine carrying a man was accomplished by the Wright brothers.

Orville and Wilbur Wright, proprietors of a bicycle shop in Dayton, Ohio, had been fascinated with flying since childhood. In the 1890's, reports of the experiments of

A-212

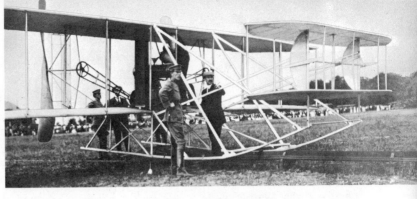

First Army Airplane, at Fort Myer, Virginia, July 27, 1909. Left to right: Lieutenant B. D. Foulois, later chief of Air Corps; Wilbur Wright; Lieutenant Frank P. Lahm; and Orville Wright.

United Press International

Chanute, Lilienthal, and Langley activated this interest. Working methodically, the Wright brothers gathered all available data on flying. Their early experiments with kites and gliders, however, showed that much of the information they had obtained was unreliable. They were thus forced to solve the basic problems of control and power by themselves.

The brothers designed and constructed a wind tunnel to test various wing shapes. They also studied birds in flight to determine how to achieve stability. They designed and built a lightweight gasoline engine, propellers, and flight controls—a vertical rudder, a horizontal stabilizer and elevator, and warped wings for lateral stability, warping being a forerunner of the aileron action later adopted.

Eventually, the Wrights had accumulated enough data to construct an effective flying machine. It was a wooden-frame biplane covered with muslin and powered by a 12-horsepower gasoline engine driving two propellers. It was equipped with instruments for measuring duration of flight, revolutions of the engine, and air velocity.

On a cold, windy December morning in 1903, the plane was readied for flight near the base of Kill Devil Hill, about 4 miles from Kitty Hawk. With Orville at the controls and Wilbur running alongside balancing the wings, the plane was released. It moved along the horizontal rail on its rollers, lifted about 8 or 9 feet off the ground, and flew a distance of some 120 feet in 12 seconds. The longest of the four flights that day was the final one, made by Wilbur Wright, which lasted 59 seconds and covered 852 feet. (For further details, see WRIGHT, WILBUR and ORVILLE, subtitle *The First Flight.*)

Other Pioneering Flights. The first officially witnessed airplane flight in Europe was made in 1906 by the Brazilian Alberto Santos-Dumont, who flew about 720 feet in 21 seconds. In 1908 Wilbur Wright made an uninterrupted flight of 77 miles near Le Mans, France. In 1909 Louis Blériot became the first man to cross the English Channel, flying his monoplane from Calais, France, to Dover, England, in about 37 minutes. Soon aviation meets were inaugurated in the United States, Europe, and Canada.

World War I. The Italians used observation planes during the Italo-Turkish War, 1911-12, but aviation did not become significant in military operations until World War I. The beginning of that war in 1914 hastened advances in both airplane design and the art of flying. Observation planes, fighters, and (toward the end of the war) bombers were used in large numbers. (See also WORLD WAR I, section "Aerial and Colonial Warfare," subtitle *Aerial Warfare.*)

The Age of Aviation

The decade after World War I was a period of record-setting exploits, reckless stunts, and serious exploration of the airplane's potential. The war's end left a surplus of pilots and planes. Many of these flyers barnstormed in Europe and the United States, introducing the airplane to thousands

Coast-to-coast Airmail. Loading a plane at Mineola, N. Y., airport in 1920 for start of first transcontinental service. The schedule called for arrival in San Francisco in three days.

Underwood & Underwood

Nonstop Flight, Coast-to-coast. In 1923 this Fokker monoplane flew from Mineola, N. Y., to San Diego in 26 hours, 51 minutes. Pilots were Army Lieutenants J. A. McCready and O. G. Kelly.

of people. In May, 1919, a U. S. Navy flying boat, the NC-4 under Lieutenant Commander Albert C. Read, made the first transatlantic flight—from New York to Lisbon, by way of Newfoundland and the Azores, and on to Plymouth, England.

The first round-the-world flight was completed by two U. S. Army biplanes in 1924. The flight took 175 days, of which 351 hours (about 15 days) was actual flying time. In 1926 Commander Richard E. Byrd and Floyd Bennett flew a three-engine Fokker over the North Pole. (See also AVIATION, chart *Flights That Made Aviation History*.)

Commercial Uses of Airplanes. During the 1920's, the commercial possibilities of the airplane became apparent. Manufacturers strove to produce safer, more comfortable, and more powerful aircraft. In the United States, cross-country trips by airplane were not unusual by the mid-1920's. Airmail service began on a continuously scheduled public service basis in 1918. However, it was the nonstop, solo transatlantic flight of Charles A. Lindbergh in 1927 that did most

U. S. Navy's Helldiver. This type of Curtiss biplane of 1930, with a supercharged engine, was important in developing dive-bombing techniques.

to dramatize the airplane's potential and stimulate commercial aviation.

In the 1930's, international air routes were established. Passengers, mail, and cargo were carried by a number of newly formed airlines. Large, multi-engine planes were developed, and aircraft instruments were improved. In 1939 the first turbojet airplane was flown in Germany.

World War II. With the beginning of World War II, in 1939, emphasis shifted from the airplane's commercial role to its use as a weapon of warfare. The warring nations mass-produced hundreds of thousands of fighters, bombers, transports, and other aircraft. Air power played a decisive role in the early German and Japanese victories—and in the ultimate defeat of these countries. Heavy bombers inflicted devastating damage on military targets and cities. Large transports were used extensively for carrying men and equipment. Although most World War II planes were propeller-driven, research into other forms of propulsion was stimulated by the war. As a result, jet- and rocket-powered planes were developed. (See also WORLD WAR II, sections "The War with Germany and Italy, 1942-45," subtitle *Air Warfare Against Germany, 1942-45*, and "The War with Japan, 1941-45," subtitle *The Air and Submarine War Against Japan*.)

Postwar Developments. The demand for air transportation, both public and private, accelerated. In 1947 a rocket-powered research plane, the Bell X-1, became the first airplane to break the sound barrier. Within six years, jet planes were traveling at supersonic speeds. During the Korean Conflict, 1950-53, helicopters and jet-propelled planes demonstrated their value in combat.

In 1952 the first regularly scheduled jet airliner began service in Great Britain. New structural materials influenced airplane construction and design in the 1950's. Bigger, faster, and safer commercial planes were put into service. The expansion of commercial aviation made even the remotest areas of the world quickly accessible.

By the 1970's, virtually all major airlines were using only jet-powered planes, with propeller-driven models largely restricted to some small foreign airlines and charter service in remote areas. The need for larger and more efficient passenger planes brought on a trend to the *jumbo jet,* or wide-body plane. The first of these was the Boeing 747, with a capacity of nearly 500 passengers.

Scheduled flights of a new type of commercial transport, the SST (supersonic transport) began in the mid-1970's. Its average speed is more than twice that of ordinary jet transports. SST's were placed in service by airlines of Great Britain, France, and Russia. The United States had earlier dropped its SST plans because of rising costs and public protest over noise and possibly serious air pollution problems.

In business flying, many large corporations began using *executive transport* planes that accommodate from 8 to 20 passengers. Usually powered by turbofan or turboprop engines, these planes cruise at 400 miles per hour or more and are ideal for businessmen and others who must travel long distances on short notice. Short-takeoff-and-landing (STOL) planes were introduced by several aircraft firms. These planes, especially the larger models adaptable for passenger service, were expected to be used for intercity travel to reduce congestion at major airports.

In the 1970's, military planes flying at two to three times the speed of sound were commonplace. Technological advancements in military aircraft included the variable-angle wing design and automatic radar control.

In 1977 the first successful flight by a man-powered airplane was achieved by Bryan Allen in the *Gossamer Condor.* The plane was designed by Paul MacCready.

United Press International
Record Breaker. Major James H. Doolittle, later an Air Force general, set many records, including a speed record in 1932 in this Gee Bee "Flying Motor" of 800 hp in annual Thompson Trophy race.

Curtiss, G. H.	Loening, Grover
De Havilland, Sir Geoffrey	Mach, Ernst
	Martin, Glenn L.
De Seversky, A. P.	Maxim (Sir Hiram S.)
Doolittle, James H.	Mitchell, William
Earhart, Amelia	Nobile, Umberto
Fairchild, Sherman M.	Odom, William P.
	Post, Wiley
Farman, Henri	Rickenbacker, E. V.
Fokker, A. H. G.	Santos-Dumont, Alberto
Hughes, Howard	
Langley, S. P.	Sikorsky, I. I.
LeMay, Curtis E.	Vinci, Leonardo da
Lilienthal, Otto	Wilkins, Sir Hubert
Lindbergh, C. A.	Wright, Wilbur and Orville
Link, Edwin A.	

Manufacturers

Boeing Company	General Dynamics Corporation
Curtiss-Wright Corporation	Lockheed Corporation

Miscellaneous

Air Force	Jet Propulsion
Aircraft Carrier	National Aeronautic Association of the U.S.A.
Airline	
Airport	
Automatic Pilot	Navigation
Aviation	Parachute
Aviation and Space Medicine	Supercharger
	Tanker
G (in physics)	Wind Tunnel

Books about Airplanes

Ellis, J. E. *Buying and Owning Your Own Airplane* (Iowa State University, 1980).

Green, William. *The Observer's Book of Aircraft,* revised edition (Scribner's, 1979).

Mondey, David, editor. *The Complete Illustrated Encyclopedia of the World's Aircraft* (A & W, 1979).

Taylor, J. W. and M. J., editors. *Encyclopedia of Aircraft* (Putnam's, 1978).

For Younger Readers:

Bendick, Jeanne. *The First Book of Airplanes,* revised edition (Watts, 1976).

Dwiggins, Don. *Why Airplanes Fly* (Childrens Press, 1976).

Navarra, John. *Superplanes* (Doubleday, 1979).

Tunney, Christopher. *Aircraft* (Lerner, 1979).

Williams, Brian. *Aircraft* (Watts, 1976).

For further information, see:

Other Aircraft

Autogiro	Dirigible	Missiles and Rockets
Balloon	Glider	
Blimp	Helicopter	

Biography

Amundsen, Roald	Blériot, Louis
Arnold, H. H.	Byrd, R. E.
Balchen, Bernt	Cayley, Sir George

Airplane, Model, a miniature airplane. Model airplanes are built for educational, recreational, industrial, and military purposes. In the aircraft industry, models are used for testing the flight performance of new types of airplanes. Model airplanes are used in motion pictures for such scenes as crashes and dogfights. Large radio-controlled model airplanes called *drones* are used as targets in military gunnery practice.

Recreational model airplanes are usually built from materials packaged in kits. Prefabricated kits have all the parts shaped, ready to be assembled. Models of every type of aircraft, including helicopters, seaplanes, and ornithopters (wing-flapping vehicles), are available in kit form.

Nonflying Models

Nonflying model airplanes are usually scale models of full-sized airplanes. These models are made of wood, plastic, metal, or other material. They are used for educational purposes (such as teaching airplane identification), as toys and decorative objects, and for wind-tunnel testing. (See WIND TUNNEL.)

Flying Models

Flying model airplanes can be either miniatures of existing aircraft or original designs. The framework is usually made of balsa wood and covered with balsa wood, paper,

Model Airplane. A free-flight model is shown the instant after launching.
Academy of Model Aeronautics

plastic film, silk, or nylon. Gliders fly without a source of power. Other models are powered by "gas" or jet engines or by rubber strands. So-called "gas" engines are usually small one-cylinder engines with piston displacements of less than one cubic inch (16 cc); they use an alcohol-oil mixture. Jets use an ether-kerosene mixture. In rubber-powered models, twisted rubber strands turn the propeller when they unwind.

Flying models are classified as free-flight, control-line, and radio-controlled.

Free-flight models fly without restraining lines or other means of control from the ground. Free-flight models may be gliders or may be powered by an engine or a rubber-band motor. Indoor free-flight models are rubber-powered and bear little resemblance to full-size airplanes. Outdoor powered models may be miniatures of actual aircraft or may have elongated wings and enlarged tail structures to allow them to soar after the power has cut off.

Control-line models fly in a circular path. The control line consists of a single wire or pair of wires attached to a lever in the model that controls the movement of the elevators; the other end of the control line is held by the operator. Control-line models are engine-powered and can attain speeds of 175 miles per hour (280 km/h) or more. Many are highly accurate scale models, while others are modified for stunt flying.

Radio-controlled models are operated by remote control. They may be gliders or engine-powered craft, and they fly without restraining lines. A transmitter on the ground sends radio signals to a receiver in the model that regulates the throttle (in the case of a powered model), rudder, elevators, and other controls.

The Academy of Model Aeronautics, Reston, Virginia, founded in 1936, is the governing body of model aviation in the United States. It sanctions 1,700 local model contests across the country each year, and the annual national championships.

Books about Model Airplanes

Winter, W. J. *The World of Model Airplanes* (Scribner's, 1983).
For Younger Readers:
Curry, Barbara. *Model Aircraft* (Watts, 1979).
Linsley, Leslie, and Jon Aron. *Air Crafts: Playthings to Make and Fly* (Lodestar Books, 1982).

Airplane Carrier. See AIRCRAFT CARRIER.

Airplane Records. See AVIATION.

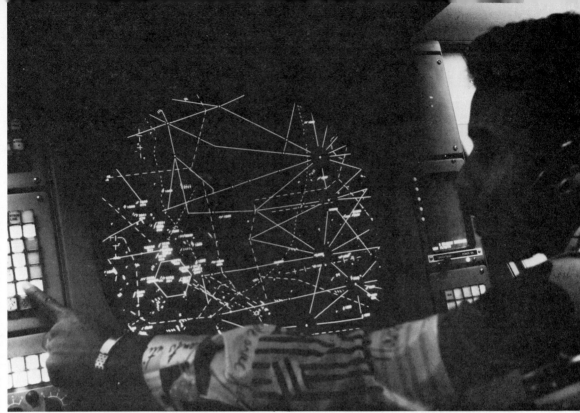

Air Traffic Controller at a major airport monitors incoming and outgoing traffic. The computerized radarscope shows the route, identity, and location of each aircraft within range of the airport.

Airport, a place where airplanes take off and land. Most airports accommodate airplanes on land. An airport that provides facilities for planes that take off and land on water is called a *seaplane base.* An airport that serves helicopters is called a *heliport.* In Great Britain, airports are often called *aerodromes.* An *airstrip* is a crude airport without facilities for servicing airplanes and handling passengers or cargo.

There are three kinds of airports in the United States: commercial, private, and military. Commercial and private airports are subject to the regulation of the Federal Aviation Administration (FAA), which includes among its powers the authority to set standards and specifications for the design, construction, and operating procedures for civil airports. Other nations have similar agencies and regulations. The International Civil Aviation Organization, a specialized agency of the United Nations, sets standards and regulations for airports serving international air commerce.

In the United States, more than 11,000 airports are registered with the FAA. About half of these are open to the general public and can supply attendants and fuel. Only a small number are lighted and paved.

The FAA classifies commercial airports into two kinds: general aviation and air-carrier airports. Air-carrier airports are larger in size and have more facilities. They are in turn classified into local, trunk, continental, and intercontinental airports, depending on the length of flights they serve normally.

Most important commercial airports are owned by a county or municipality. Because of the need for cheap land and open space far from obstructing buildings, and the necessity of reducing noise discomfort for residents, airports are usually located well outside city limits.

The remainder of this article is concerned with large commercial airports. Permanent military airports are similar, but lack terminals and have barracks, ammunition dumps, and other military facilities.

The Field

Large international airports need fields with a radius of at least 13,000 feet (2½

Federal Aviation Administration
An Airport Control Tower

miles) from the center point. An airport field consists of grass, except for the runways and taxiways.

Runways. Runways are strips of concrete, asphalt, or macadam, on which airplanes take off and land. They must be of sufficient length, width, smoothness, and strength to allow safe takeoffs and landings for many types of aircraft under varying weather conditions. Large airports have a number of runways, laid out at angles designed to avoid crosswinds; they frequently intersect each other.

The length of a runway is determined not only by the takeoff and landing speed of airplanes accommodated, but also by ground temperature, winds, elevation, weight of the planes, and other factors. To accommodate large jets, a runway typically must be at least 11,000 feet long.

To guide airplanes landing at night, high-intensity runway white lights are placed on the edge of the runway at 200-foot intervals. For the last 2,000 feet the lights are yellow, to inform the pilot that he is coming to the end. Center lights are imbedded in the center of the runway through its entire length. Pilots are also aided by a standard marking pattern painted on every runway.

Taxiways. Taxiways are paved strips on which airplanes taxi (move, under their own power, on the ground) between runways and the terminal area or hangars. Holding aprons, often referred to as "run-up" or "warm-up" pads, are areas at the ends of taxiways for aircraft to make final checks or

wait for clearance prior to takeoff, without obstructing traffic.

Apron. The apron, or ramp, is the area adjacent to the terminal building where airplanes are fueled and passengers and cargo taken on and off. Because of space limitations, maneuvering from the apron to the taxiway can be difficult, and large jets are sometimes towed out to the taxiway.

The Control Tower

The control tower, equipped with radio, radar, and other electronic devices, is the center from which landings and takeoffs are directed. The tower is situated in such a way that the entire field is visible from it.

Arriving and departing aircraft are kept separate by being assigned different altitudes or courses to avoid the possibility of collisions. When traffic is heavy, airplanes are "stacked up"—separated vertically in 1,000-foot intervals before being directed, in order, to land. Computers now play a large role in gathering information—such as the direction and speed of incoming aircraft—and translating this information into instructions for routine control-tower operations.

In the United States, air-route traffic-control centers direct traffic along the nation's airways. Once an airplane is within 15 miles of an airport, the airport's own traffic controllers take over from the air-route centers and guide the plane's movements. These operations are directed from the control tower.

Terminal Building

Most large airports have one terminal building where all passengers, baggage, and cargo from the various airlines are handled. Where the traffic volume is very high, each large airline may have its own separate terminal building, as at Kennedy International Airport.

Major airports customarily have two levels in the terminal building. The lower level is for baggage, which is transferred to and from airplanes by means of baggage carts or pods, and by a conveyor-belt system within the building. The upper level, for passengers, is sometimes subdivided into two different areas for domestic and international flights.

The terminal building provides space for ticket and reservations counters; baggage claims; handling and processing of mail, express, and light cargo; and governmental functions such as customs inspection. For the convenience of passengers, there are a central lobby, toilet facilities, public telephones, storage lockers, a first-aid room, and a nursery. Concessions such as restaurants, newsstands, and barber shops also serve the public.

Getting passengers from the terminal building into an airplane is not an easy operation. Because of the large number of aircraft leaving and arriving at a major airport, passengers generally must walk through a long pierlike corridor from the terminal building to the apron area, or to smaller buildings on the apron. At some airports, however, such as Dulles International Airport (Washington, D. C.) and the London and Frankfurt am Main airports, passengers are transported to the plane from the terminal building by bus.

At smaller airports, passengers usually board outdoors by means of a ramp on wheels. At larger ones, airlines have installed enclosed, telescoping gangplanks that protect passengers from bad weather by leading directly into the plane from the pier or subsidiary building.

Other Facilities

If the airport handles a large volume of cargo, there may be a separate building for cargo handling, with space for aircraft alongside. Other facilities include maintenance hangars and shops to repair and store aircraft. Firefighting and other emergency equipment is kept ready for use at all times.

History

In the early days of aviation, landing fields were simply level plots of meadow, without regular attendants or maintenance facilities. Conditions improved after World War I, and by the 1930's cities such as New York, Paris, and London were served by airports equipped to handle relatively large and heavy passenger planes such as the Boeing 247 and Douglas DC-3.

The heavy increase in commercial air traffic after World War II resulted in the construction of more and larger airports. Increases in size again became necessary in the late 1950's, when the introduction of passenger jets caused many airports to become obsolete due to inadequate runways. The introduction in the 1970's of "jumbo jets," such as the Boeing 747, made it necessary for major airports to enlarge and expand their terminal facilities.

By 1970 airport congestion had become a critical problem in many major cities. Other problems were air pollution and noise from aircraft engines and an overburdened air-control system.

The crime of skyjacking, or air piracy, had become such a serious menace that security measures were taken at many airports. In the United States a screening of passengers and any articles to be carried on board the plane became mandatory in 1972.

Airship. See DIRIGIBLE.

Airsickness. See MOTION SICKNESS.

Airspeed Indicator. See AIRPLANE, section "Parts of an Airplane," subtitle *Instruments.*

Airstrip. See AIRPORT.

Airy, Sir **George Biddell** (1801-1892), a British astronomer. Airy was astronomer royal from 1835 to 1881. He modernized the Royal Observatory at Greenwich, equipping it with new instruments of his own design. He developed a rapid means of calculation that made possible the systematizing of all lunar and planetary data gathered at the observatory from 1750 to 1830. Airy uncovered a new inequality (deviation) in the motions of Venus and the earth. He developed eyeglass lenses to correct astigmatism in vision.

Airy was graduated from Trinity College, Cambridge, in 1823. He taught mathematics and then astronomy there until 1835.

Aix-la-Chapelle. See AACHEN.

Aix-la-Chapelle, Congress of (1818), a meeting of the members of the Quadruple Alliance—Great Britain, Austria, Prussia, and Russia. The congress agreed to remove the occupation armies that had been kept in France since the defeat of Napoleon in 1815. France was then admitted to the group to form an informal Quintuple Alliance. Alexander I of Russia, sponsor of the Holy Alliance, tried unsuccessfully to turn this alliance into a police force to put down all democratic and liberal movements in Europe. The five countries did form the so-called Concert of Europe; they agreed to meet at intervals to preserve peace and to consider common problems.

See also HOLY ALLIANCE; QUADRUPLE ALLIANCE.

Aix-la-Chapelle, Treaties of, historic treaties signed in 1668 and 1748. The 1668 Treaty of Aix-la-Chapelle ended the War of Devolution between France and Spain. France fought the war to win the Spanish Netherlands (now Belgium) and Franche-Comté. By the treaty Louis XIV of France

Museum of Fine Arts, Boston

Achilles and Ajax Playing a Game, a common subject of early Greek vases such as this one by Andokides. The incident is not mentioned in the *Iliad* or in other known literature.

gained several cities in the Spanish Netherlands but gave up Franche-Comté, which his army had occupied.

The 1748 Treaty of Aix-la-Chapelle ended the War of the Austrian Succession. Great Britain and France took opposite sides in this war, and their hostilities extended to America (King George's War) and to India. By the peace treaty nearly all the conquests on both sides were returned, but Frederick the Great of Prussia was permitted to keep Silesia, which he had taken from Maria Theresa of Austria.

See also DEVOLUTION, WAR OF; FREDERICK, subtitle *Prussia:* Frederick II; KING GEORGE'S WAR; MARIA THERESA; SUCCES-

SION WARS, subtitle *War of the Austrian Succession.*

Ajax, ā'jăks, in Greek legend, the name of two heroes of the Trojan War.

Ajax the Greater was the son of Telamon, king of Salamis, and often is called the Telamonian Ajax. He was second only to Achilles in bravery and fighting ability. Ajax defeated Hector several times in single combat, and was greatly feared by the Trojans. When Achilles was killed by Paris, Ajax carried away his body while Odysseus (Ulysses) held back the Trojans. Thetis, mother of Achilles, then directed that Achilles' armor be given to the one who deserved it the most. It was decided that the armor should go to Odysseus.

Ajax went mad from humiliation and disappointment and sought Odysseus, intending to kill him. In his disordered mind he saw a flock of sheep as human enemies, and he killed them. Sophocles, in his earliest surviving play, represents Ajax as coming to his senses after killing the sheep only to commit suicide in shame and remorse.

Ajax the Lesser was so called because he was inferior to the Telamonian Ajax both in stature and in military prowess. He was a son of Oileus, king of the Locrians. Ajax led the Locrian forces in the Trojan War. When the city fell and was being sacked, he broke into the temple of Athene and dragged Cassandra from the altar. Enraged at this sacrilege, Athene persuaded Poseidon to send winds to wreck Ajax's ship on the return journey. Ajax managed to swim ashore, and afterwards boasted that he had saved himself despite the wrath of Poseidon. Poseidon then caused the rock he was standing on to fall into the sea, and Ajax was drowned. Another story is that Ajax was killed by a lightning bolt.

Ajmer, ŭj-mēr'; ŭj-mär', India, a city and administrative center in Rajasthan state. It lies in a hot, semiarid hilly region about 220 miles (355 km) southwest of New Delhi, the nation's capital. Ajmer is served by several railways and roads and has long been a locally important trade and transportation center. Products include cotton textiles, salt, and wooden handicraft items. Among notable buildings and institutions are Mayo Rajkumar College and the marble mausoleum of Mu'in al-Din Chishti, a Moslem religious leader. Ajmer was settled early in the 12th century. From the 16th to the

18th century it was a military stronghold and a favorite retreat of Mogul emperors.

Population: 262,851.

Akbar, ăk'băr (1542-1605), called Akbar the Great, third ruler of the Mogul Empire in India; reigned 1556-1605. Akbar is considered the greatest of the Mogul emperors. He restored and consolidated the power of the Mogul Empire and initiated many administrative and religious reforms. Akbar was the grandson of Baber, founder of the Mogul dynasty. He succeeded to the throne at the age of 13 after the death of his father, Humayun, and ruled under a regent until 1560.

As emperor, Akbar gradually subdued all of Hindustan north of the Deccan. He ruled with wisdom and tolerance, winning the cooperation of the Hindus. He strengthened the central government, encouraged religious tolerance, reformed the tax system, promoted trade, and established a civil service. Akbar's son, Prince Selim, rebelled against his father, 1601-04, but was returned to favor and succeeded him as Emperor Jahangir.

Akeley, Carl Ethan (1864-1926), a United States taxidermist, inventor, explorer, and sculptor. Akeley raised taxidermy from a trade to a fine art by his realistic mounting of *habitat groups* (animals mounted in natural settings). The use of habitat groups was adopted by museums throughout the world.

Akeley's most famous works are the Virginia deer groups and "The Fighting Bulls" in the Field Museum of Natural History, Chicago, and "The Alarm" and "Gorilla Group" in the American Museum of Natural History, New York. Animals for his groups were collected on African expeditions made when Akeley was with the Field Museum, 1895-1909, and the American Museum, 1909-26. He invented a spray gun for applying cement to vertical surfaces and an improved motion-picture camera for naturalists, and did a number of sculptures of African subjects.

Akeley was born in Clarendon, New York, and was trained in taxidermy at Ward's Natural Science Establishment in Rochester, New York. He wrote *In Brightest Africa* (1923).

Akhmatova, äκ'mȧ-tō'vȧ, **Anna,** the pen name of Anna Andreyevna Gorenko (1888-1966), a Russian poet. Her poetry is characterized by its precision of language,

lyricism, and concise imagery. *The Rosary* (1914) and *Requiem: a Cycle of Poems* (1964), two of her most popular works, are noted for their sensitivity to the suffering of the Russian people under Stalin. Most of Akhmatova's early poetry, such as *Evening* (1912), deals with the theme of love.

Akhmatova was born near Odessa, Russia, and attended colleges in Leningrad and Kiev. Her poetry was denied publication during 1922-40 and 1946-52 for political reasons.

Her other poems include: *The White Flock* (1917); *Anno Domini* (1923); *Poem Without a Hero* (1960); *Race of Time* (1965).

Akhnaton, äk-nä't'n, or **Ikhnaton,** ĭk-nä't'n, a pharaoh of the 18th Dynasty of Egypt, reigning from about 1379 to 1362 B.C. He was one of the first men in history to advocate the worship of a single god. Akhnaton believed that Aton was the only true god, creator and father of all life. After coming to the throne as Amenhotep IV, he changed his name to Akhnaton ("Aton is satisfied") and abolished the worship of other Egyptian gods. Because Thebes was associated with the old religion, he built a new capital city, Akhetaton ("the horizon of Aton"). Later the site was called Tell el' Amarna, giving the name "Amarna Age" to Akhnaton's reign.

Akhnaton and his wife, Nefertiti, devoted themselves to the worship of Aton and to the support of the arts. They encouraged a departure from the traditional stiff art forms, inspiring a brief period of realistic sculpture and greater use of natural poses and situations. (For example, see NEFERTITI, picture.) Akhnaton neglected foreign affairs and lost part of his empire. His religious and artistic reforms died with him. Akhetaton was abandoned.

See also ATON.

Akiba ben Joseph, à-kĭ'vä běn jō'zěf (50?-132 A.D.), a Jewish teacher and martyr. He assembled and edited the oral teachings of Jewish scholars and laid the foundations for the *Mishnah* (the first part of the Talmud). There are many traditions about Akiba. He is said to have been an illiterate shepherd until he was 40, when his wife inspired him to study. He supported the disastrous revolt of Simon Bar Cocheba (Kokba) against Rome. The Romans put Akiba to death by torture.

See also MISHNAH.

Akihito, ä-kĕ-hĭ-tŏ (1933-   ), crown prince of Japan, the eldest son of Emperor Hirohito. He was proclaimed heir to the Japanese throne in 1952. Departing from imperial tradition, Akihito married a commoner, Michiko Shoda, in 1959. He made frequent goodwill tours of foreign countries.

Akins, ā′kĭnz, **Zoë** (1886-1958), a United States playwright. Her dramatization of Edith Wharton's novelette *The Old Maid* won the Pulitzer Prize for drama in 1935. *Déclassée* (1919), her first successful play, starred Ethel Barrymore. *A Royal Fandango* (1923) and *The Greeks Had a Word for It* (1930) are typical of her romantic comedies. The screenplay (1926) for Edna Ferber's *Showboat* is among several she wrote. She also wrote novels, short stories and verse. She was born in Humansville, Missouri.

Akkadians, ă-kā′dĭ-ănz, an ancient people who inhabited a region of lower Mesopotamia known as Akkad, so called from their capital city (Accad in the Bible; Agade in inscriptions). The Akkadians were Semitic nomads from Arabia who appeared in Akkad around 3000 B.C. About 2340 B.C., Sargon, an Akkadian king, conquered the Sumerian city-states to the south and part of Assyria to the north, establishing the Akkadian Empire. The empire gradually declined until it was overthrown some two centuries later by the Guti, a tribe of northern barbarians. Akkad itself was conquered by the Amorites around 2000 B.C. and became part of the Old Babylonian Empire.

See also BABYLONIA.

Akko. See ACRE.

Akron, ăk′rŭn, Ohio, the seat of Summit County. It lies on the Cuyahoga River, about 30 miles (48 km) south-southeast of Cleveland. Akron's name comes from the Greek word *akros,* meaning "highest"—the city is 1,081 feet (329 m) above sea level, the highest elevation on the old Ohio and Erie Canal.

Economy

Akron's chief industry is the manufacturing of rubber and rubber products. Since 1870, when Benjamin Goodrich established a rubber-hose factory in Akron, the rubber industry has grown to dominate all others. Firestone, General, Goodrich, and Goodyear are among rubber companies with headquarters in Akron. Other industries are the making or preparation of cereals, salt, ceramics, automobile parts, industrial ma-

chinery, plastics, fishing tackle, batteries, paint, matches, and books and toys for children. Akron is a major trucking center and is sometimes called "the birthplace of the trucking industry." Akron-Canton Airport is about 12 miles (19 km) southeast of downtown Akron.

Points of Interest

The municipally controlled University of Akron is the city's leading institution of higher learning. Akron Art Museum has a notable collection of 19th- and 20th-century American and European paintings, sculptures, and prints. John Brown Home, occupied by the noted abolitionist in the 1840's, and the Akron Museum of Natural History and Children's Zoo attract many visitors. Stan Hywet Hall, a 65-room English Tudor mansion built 1911-15 for Frank A. Seiberling, exhibits paintings and antiques of the 17th century.

Within the city are some of the original locks of the Ohio and Erie Canal. Annually in August, Akron is host for the All-American Soap Box Derby at Derby Downs. South of the city is the Portage Chain of Lakes, used for fishing, boating, and swimming.

History and Government

Akron was first settled in 1825. Two years later the Ohio and Erie Canal was opened. It was the invention of the automobile late in the 19th century and the subsequent demand for tires and other rubber products that caused Akron to become a major industrial center. Akron was incorporated as a city in 1865. It has the mayor-council form of government.

Population: 237,177.

Akron, University of. See UNIVERSITIES AND COLLEGES (table).

Aksakov, ŭ-ksá′kôf, **Sergei Timofeevich** (1791-1859), a Russian author. His reminiscences of early years on the steppes led critics to rank him as a prose writer with Pushkin, Turgenev, and Lermontov. Aksakov mixed fiction with personal recollections in *The Family Chronicle* (1856), *Reminiscences* (1856), and *Years of Childhood* (1858). These were written at the urging of Nikolai Gogol, a close friend. Aksakov was born in Ufa. After graduation from the University of Kazan he entered government service in Moscow.

Al Kuwait. See KUWAIT.

Al Riyad. See RIYADH.

Alabama

Symbol of the New South: Steel Mill at Birmingham

Origin of Name: Derived from a Choctaw Indian word meaning "thicket clearers" or "vegetation gatherers"; it was the name of a Muskhogean tribe that once occupied the area.
Nickname: The Heart of Dixie
Total Area: 51,705 square miles (133,915 km²); rank—29th
Capital: Montgomery
Largest City: Birmingham
Statehood: December 14, 1819 (order—22nd)

Alabama's Capitol at Montgomery

Alabama, one of the southeastern states of the United States. Productive farms, modern factories, and an abundant supply of water, minerals, and forests have made it one of the South's most economically progressive states. Alabama's scenic attractions include pine-forested Appalachian slopes; large, clear reservoirs; and sandy Gulf Coast beaches. A long history of settlement is evidenced by Indian burial mounds, French and Spanish forts, and restored pre-Civil War mansions.

Physical Geography

Land. Alabama occupies parts of three major physiographic regions of the United States: the Gulf Coastal Plain, the Appalachian Highlands, and the Central Lowlands.

The Gulf Coastal Plain, the largest of the three, covers most of western and southern Alabama. It begins as a narrow neck of flat terrain near the coast and rises gradually in a

Pulpwood, a leading Alabama product, is carried from Scottsboro by barge on the Tennessee River.

series of almost parallel terraces, cuestas (escarpment-like ridges), and hills toward the north. The Black Belt region, named for its rich soil, stretches across the central section of the state and is the most extensive level part.

The Appalachian Highlands, in the northeast, extend diagonally from Georgia and Tennessee into the central part of the state. This southern tip of the Appalachians includes the broad, hilly Cumberland Plateau; the low, parallel ridges and intervening valleys of the so-called Ridge and Valley region; and the eroded Piedmont Plateau. Marking the southern limit of the highlands is the *fall line,* a belt of sloping land leading down to the Gulf Coastal Plain. The highest point in the state is Cheaha Mountain, 2,407 feet (734 m) above sea level.

The Central Lowlands section of Alabama is a narrow belt of land in the northwest along the Tennessee border. Structurally, it is part of a low, rolling plateau that forms the southern rim of the Nashville Basin in Tennessee.

Water. Alabama lies in one of the rainiest parts of the continent, and is drained by numerous rivers. The Alabama River system, including the Coosa and Tallapoosa rivers in east-central Alabama, flows diagonally across the state to join the Mobile River near the coast. The Black Warrior-Tombigbee system of the west also empties into the Mobile, which continues on to Mobile Bay, an arm of the Gulf of Mexico. These systems, along with that of the Tennessee, which loops across the north, drain most of the state. The southeast is drained by the Pea, Conecuh, and Chattahoochee rivers.

There are few natural lakes in Alabama. Most of the large inland bodies of water are man-made reservoirs, created by damming rivers. The largest of these are Wheeler and Wilson lakes, in the Muscle Shoals area of the Tennessee River; Guntersville and Pickwick lakes, also on the Tennessee; Martin Lake, on the Tallapoosa; Weiss Lake, on the Coosa; and Walter F. George Reservoir, on the Chattahoochee.

Climate. Alabama has a *humid subtropical* climate that becomes more temperate with distance from the coast and with increased elevation in the Appalachians. Chief distinguishing marks are long, hot, and humid summers, relatively mild winters, and abundant rainfall. Average July temperatures range from about 81° F. (27° C.) near the coast to 78° F. (26° C.) in the northeast. Winters, though seldom cold, are made variable by alternating cool air masses from the continental interior and warm, moist air masses from the Gulf of Mexico. Average January temperatures vary from 54° F. (12° C.) near the coast to 42° F. (6° C.) in the highlands.

Precipitation, mostly rain, is moderately heavy and well distributed throughout the year. The greatest amount, 64 inches (1,625 mm) annually, occurs near the coast. Elsewhere it varies from 48 to 55 inches (1,220 to 1,400 mm). An average of three inches (76 mm) of snow falls in the highlands; in other areas snow is almost unknown. Among the severe storms that occasionally strike Alabama are tornadoes, between November and May, and hurricanes, between July and November.

Economy

Until the early 20th century, the economy of Alabama was dependent almost solely on agriculture. In the first decades of the 1900's, the development of the iron and steel industry in Birmingham helped lead the state into the industrial age. Today, the largest portion of the work force is employed in manufacturing, and a great variety of goods are produced. Services and commerce employ a growing portion of the work force. Although Alabama's economy has greatly diversified, agriculture continues to contribute a large share of the state's wealth.

Manufacturing. The chief manufacturing activities ranked by employment are the making of apparel, textiles, and primary and fabricated metal products. The making of textiles and apparel is concentrated in the Tennessee River valley. The iron and steel industry centers in and around Birmingham. Paper, lumber, and furniture are also among the state's chief products. Other well-established industries are the making of chemicals, plastic and rubber goods, machinery, and electronic and transportation equipment. Food processing has long been a primary activity. Birmingham, Huntsville, and Mobile are the largest manufacturing centers. Huntsville, the home of the George C. Marshall Space Flight Center, is especially noted for aerospace and electronics industries. Shipbuilding and ship repairing are important in Mobile.

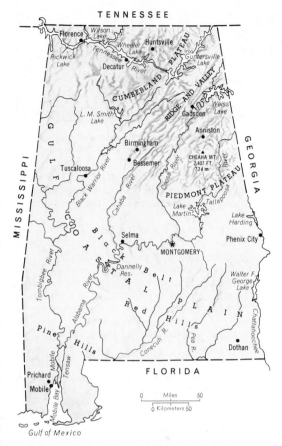

Physical Features Summary

AREA: land, 50,767 square miles (131,486 km²); inland water, 938 square miles (2,429 km²)
GREATEST DIMENSIONS: length, 325 miles (525 km); width, 200 miles (320 km)
ELEVATIONS: highest, Cheaha Mountain, 2,407 feet (734 m); lowest, sea level (Gulf of Mexico); mean, 500 feet (152 m)

Agriculture. Farming in Alabama has undergone great change since the 1940's. The number of farms has decreased greatly while the average farm size has doubled. However, farms in Alabama are still relatively small, averaging roughly 200 acres (80 hectares)—about half the national average. The use of modern equipment and methods has brought a substantial increase in the quantity and variety of farm products.

Farms occupy about 35 per cent of the state's land area. The Black Belt region, in south-central Alabama, is the richest agricultural part of the state. For many decades

TVA
Wheeler Dam and Its Power Plant. This dam, on the Tennessee River, is part of the TVA system.

it produced primarily cotton, but now the raising of livestock and the growing of a number of other crops are the chief activities.

By value, the leading farm products are broiler chickens, of which Alabama is a leading national producer; cattle; eggs; and soybeans. In general, livestock and livestock products account for about 60 per cent of farm income. The main crops, in addition to soybeans, are corn, cotton, and peanuts. A variety of fruits and vegetables, including melons, peaches, beans, and sweet corn, are also grown.

Mining. Alabama is one of the few states to produce bauxite and ranks high among states in the production of mica and asphalt. Moderate amounts of coal are also produced. Local sources of iron ore, coking coal, and limestone, which once met most of the needs of the state's iron and steel industry, are now depleted.

Petroleum and natural gas, although produced in relatively small amounts, are Alabama's most valuable mineral resources after coal. Stone, sand and gravel, and clay

Rocket Research. A booster engine for a space vehicle undergoes a test at the George C. Marshall Space Flight Center at Huntsville.
NASA

are produced in many parts of the state. Decorative Alabama marble is used nationwide.

Forestry and Fishing. Forests of commercial quality, including stands of timber on farms, occupy about two-thirds of the state's land area. Alabama is one of the South's leading producers of saw timber. Pine is the chief commercial variety, but oak and a number of other hardwoods are also harvested.

Fishing is an important activity along the Gulf coast; however, Alabama's fish catch is the lowest in quantity and value of all Gulf coast states. Croaker, menhaden, mullet, oysters, red snapper, and shrimp make up most of the catch.

Transportation. The state has an efficient transportation system, including not only highways and railways but waterways as well. Four Interstate highways serve the state. Birmingham is the main center of the highway system, followed by Montgomery. These two cities are also the main railway centers. Most major cities are served by scheduled airlines. Birmingham has the busiest airport.

A large amount of traffic is carried on Alabama's navigable waterways. The busiest route is the canalized Black Warrior-Tombigbee-Mobile system, between Birmingham and Mobile. Mobile, the only seaport, is one of the nation's busiest. It is also served by the Intracoastal Waterway.

People

The population of Alabama in 1980 was 3,893,978—an increase of 449,624, or 13.1 per cent, over the 1970 total. The population density was 76.7 persons per square mile (29.6 per km²), about one-fifth greater than that of the United States as a whole. Whites made up slightly less than 74 per cent of the population, blacks more than 25 per cent. There were about 7,500 Indians living in the state.

Alabama's Largest Cities

Birmingham	284,413	Decatur	42,002
Mobile	200,452	Prichard	39,541
Montgomery, the capital	177,857	Florence	37,029
		Bessemer	31,729
Huntsville	142,513	Anniston	29,185
Tuscaloosa	75,211	Auburn	28,471
Dothan	48,750	Phenix City	26,928
Gadsden	47,565	Selma	26,684

An article on each of these cities appears in this encyclopedia.

Education

Alabama's superintendent of education is appointed by the state board of education,

ALABAMA

COUNTIES

Autauga 32,259 .... E5
Baldwin 78,556 .... C9
Barbour 24,756 .... H7
Bibb 15,723 .... D5
Blount 36,459 .... E2
Bullock 10,596 .... G6
Butler 21,680 .... E7
Calhoun 119,761 .... G3
Chambers 39,191 .... H5
Cherokee 18,760 .... G2
Chilton 30,612 .... E5
Choctaw 16,839 .... B6
Clarke 27,702 .... C7
Clay 13,703 .... G4
Cleburne 12,595 .... G3
Coffee 38,533 .... G8
Colbert 54,519 .... C1
Conecuh 15,884 .... E8
Coosa 11,377 .... F5
Covington 36,850 .... F8
Crenshaw 14,110 .... F7
Cullman 61,642 .... E2
Dale 47,821 .... G8
Dallas 53,981 .... D6
De Kalb 53,658 .... G2
Elmore 43,390 .... F5
Escambia 38,440 .... D8
Etowah 103,057 .... F2
Fayette 18,809 .... C3
Franklin 28,350 .... C2
Geneva 24,253 .... G8
Greene 11,021 .... C5
Hale 15,604 .... C5
Henry 15,302 .... H7
Houston 74,632 .... H8
Jackson 51,407 .... F1
Jefferson 671,324 .... E3
Lamar 16,453 .... B3
Lauderdale 80,546 .... C1
Lawrence 30,170 .... D1
Lee 76,283 .... H5
Limestone 46,005 .... E1
Lowndes 13,253 .... E6
Macon 26,829 .... G6
Madison 196,966 .... E1
Marengo 25,047 .... C6
Marion 30,041 .... C2
Marshall 65,622 .... F2
Mobile 364,980 .... B9
Monroe 22,651 .... D7
Montgomery 197,038 .... F6
Morgan 90,231 .... E2
Perry 15,012 .... D5
Pickens 21,481 .... B4
Pike 28,050 .... G7
Randolph 20,075 .... H4
Russell 47,356 .... H6
Saint Clair 41,205 .... F3
Shelby 66,298 .... E4
Sumter 16,908 .... B5
Talladega 73,826 .... F4
Tallapoosa 38,766 .... G5
Tuscaloosa 137,541 .... C4
Walker 68,660 .... D3
Washington 16,821 .... B8
Wilcox 14,755 .... D7
Winston 21,953 .... D2

CITIES and TOWNS

Abbeville⊙ 3,155 .... H7
Abernant 405 .... D4
Ackerville 200 .... D6
Adamsville 2,498 .... D3
Addison 746 .... D2
Adger 400 .... D4
Akron 604 .... C5
Alabaster 7,079 .... E4
Alberta 100 .... D6
Albertville 12,039 .... F2
Aldrich 500 .... E4
Alexander City 13,807 .... G5
Alexandria 600 .... G3
Aliceville 3,207 .... B4
Allen 149 .... C7
Allgood 387 .... F3
Allsboro 300 .... B1
Alma 500 .... C8
Alpine 150 .... F4
Alton 150 .... E3
Altoona 928 .... F2
Andalusia⊙ 10,415 .... E8
Anderson 405 .... D1
Annemanie 100 .... D6
Anniston⊙ 29,185 .... G3
Arab 5,967 .... E2
Ardmore 1,096 .... E1
Argo 600 .... E3
Ariton 844 .... G7
Arkadelphia 150 .... E3
Arley 276 .... D2
Arlington 200 .... C6
Ashby 500 .... E4
Ashford 2,165 .... H8
Ashland⊙ 2,052 .... G4
Ashville⊙ 1,489 .... F3
Athens⊙ 14,558 .... E1
Atmore 8,789 .... C8
Attalla 7,737 .... F2
Auburn 28,471 .... H5
Autaugaville 843 .... E6
Avon 433 .... H8
Axis 500 .... B9
Babbie 553 .... F8
Baileyton 396 .... E2
Baker Hill 300 .... H7
Banks 160 .... G7
Bankston 125 .... C3
Barlow Bend 300 .... C8
Barnwell 700 .... C10
Barton 150 .... C1
Bashi 225 .... C7
Batesville 100 .... H6
Battles Wharf 300 .... C10
Bay Minette⊙ 7,455 .... C9
Bayou La Batre 2,005 .... B10
Bear Creek 353 .... C2
Beatrice 558 .... D7
Beaverton 360 .... B3
Belgreen 500 .... C2
Belk 308 .... C3
Bellamy 700 .... B6
Belle Mina 675 .... E1
Bellview 200 .... D7
Bellwood 400 .... G8
Beloit 100 .... D6
Bermuda 120 .... D8
Berry 916 .... C3
Bessemer 31,729 .... D4
Beulah 500 .... H5
Billingsley 106 .... E5
Birmingham⊙ 284,413 .... D3
Black 156 .... G8
Blacksher 200 .... C8
Bladon Springs 125 .... B7
Blanton 100 .... H5
Bleecker 250 .... H5
Blountsville 1,509 .... E2
Blue Mountain 284 .... G3
Blue Springs 112 .... G7
Boaz 7,151 .... F2
Boligee 164 .... C5
Bolinger 175 .... B7
Bolling 100 .... E7
Bon Air 118 .... F4
Bon Secour 850 .... C10
Booth 200 .... E6
Boyd 100 .... B5
Braggs 180 .... E6
Branchville 365 .... F3
Brantley 1,151 .... F7
Bremen 125 .... E3
Brent 2,862 .... D5
Brewton⊙ 6,680 .... D8
Bridgeport 2,974 .... G1
Brierfield 250 .... E4
Brighton 5,308 .... D4
Brilliant 871 .... C2
Brooklyn 300 .... E8
Brookside 1,409 .... E3
Brooksville 120 .... F2
Brookwood 492 .... D4
Browns 375 .... D6
Brownsboro 150 .... F1
Brownville 2,386 .... C4
Brundidge 3,213 .... G7
Bryant 300 .... G1
Bucks 201 .... B8
Buhl 100 .... C4
Burkville 250 .... E6
Burnsville 100 .... E6
Butler⊙ 1,882 .... B6
Cahaba 75 .... D6
Calcis 200 .... F4
Calera 2,035 .... E4
Calhoun 950 .... F6
Calvert 600 .... B8
Camden⊙ 2,406 .... D7
Campbell 200 .... C7
Camp Hill 1,628 .... G5
Canoe 560 .... D8
Canton Bend 300 .... D6
Carbon Hill 2,452 .... D3
Cardiff 140 .... E3
Carlowville 100 .... D6
Carlton 275 .... C8
Carolina 203 .... E8
Carrollton⊙ 1,104 .... B4
Carrville 820 .... G5
Carson 400 .... C8
Castleberry 847 .... D8
Catherine 250 .... D6
Cedar Bluff 1,129 .... G2
Cedar Cove 100 .... D4
Central 300 .... F5
Centre⊙ 2,351 .... G2
Centreville⊙ 2,504 .... D5
Chancellor 200 .... G8
Chandler Springs 100 .... F4
Chapman 300 .... E7
Chase 175 .... E1
Chastang 200 .... B8
Chatom⊙ 1,122 .... B8
Chelsea 600 .... E4
Cherokee 1,589 .... C1
Chestnut 125 .... D7
Chickasaw 7,402 .... B9
Childersburg 5,084 .... F4
Choccolocco 500 .... G3
Choctaw 600 .... B6
Chrysler 400 .... C8
Chunchula 700 .... B9
Citronelle 2,841 .... B8
Claiborne 125 .... D7
Clanton⊙ 5,832 .... E5
Clayhatchee 560 .... G8
Clayton⊙ 1,589 .... G7
Cleveland 487 .... E3
Clinton 150 .... C5
Clio 1,224 .... G7
Cloverdale 100 .... C1
Coaling 400 .... D4
Coden 600 .... B10
Coffee Springs 339 .... G8
Coffeeville 448 .... B7
Coker 800 .... C4
Collinsville 1,383 .... G2
Collirene 100 .... E6
Columbia 881 .... H8
Columbiana⊙ 2,655 .... E4
Cooper 250 .... E5
Coosada 980 .... F5
Copeland 160 .... B7
Cordova 3,123 .... D3
Corona 300 .... C3
Cottondale 500 .... D4
Cottonton 324 .... H6
Cottonwood 1,352 .... H8
County Line 199 .... E3
County Line 124 .... F8
Courtland 456 .... D1
Cowarts 418 .... H8
Coy 950 .... D7
Crane Hill 355 .... D2
Creola 1,652 .... B9
Cromwell 650 .... B6
Crossville 1,222 .... G2
Cuba 486 .... B6
Cullman⊙ 13,084 .... E2
Cullomburg 325 .... B7
Cusseta 650 .... H5
Cypress 300 .... C5
Dadeville⊙ 3,263 .... G5
Daleville 4,250 .... G8
Dancy 116 .... B4
Danville 300 .... D2
Daphne 3,406 .... C9
Darlington 150 .... D7
Dauphin Island 950 .... B10
Daviston 334 .... G4
Dayton 113 .... C6
De Armanville 350 .... G3
Deatsville 200 .... F5
Decatur⊙ 42,002 .... D1
Deer Park 300 .... B8
Delmar 200 .... C2
Demopolis 7,678 .... C6
Detroit 326 .... B2
Dickinson 250 .... C7
Dixons Mills 100 .... C6
Dixonville 125 .... E8
Dora 2,327 .... D3
Dothan⊙ 48,750 .... H8
Double Springs⊙ 1,057 .... D2
Douglas 116 .... F2
Dozier 494 .... F7
Duke 250 .... G3
Duncanville 150 .... D4
Dutton 276 .... G1
Dyas 250 .... C9
Eastaboga 300 .... F3
East Brewton 3,012 .... E8
Echo 200 .... G8
Echola 300 .... C4
Eclectic 1,124 .... F5
Edwardsville 207 .... H3
Edwin 296 .... H7
Elamville 180 .... G7
Elba⊙ 4,355 .... F8
Elberta 491 .... C10
Eldridge 230 .... C3
Eliska 200 .... C8
Elkmont 429 .... E1
Elmore 600 .... F5
Elon 125 .... F1
Elrod 746 .... C4
Emelle 150 .... B5
Empire 600 .... D3
Enterprise 18,033 .... G8
Epes 399 .... B5
Equality 125 .... F5
Estillfork 200 .... F1
Eufaula 12,097 .... H7
Eunola 169 .... G8
Eutaw⊙ 2,444 .... C5
Eva 185 .... E2
Evergreen⊙ 4,171 .... E8
Excel 385 .... D8
Fabius 150 .... G1
Fackler 250 .... G1
Fairfax 3,776 .... H5
Fairfield 13,242 .... E4
Fairford 200 .... B8
Fairhope 7,286 .... C10
Fairview 450 .... E2
Falkville 1,310 .... E2
Farmersville 200 .... E6
Faunsdale 174 .... C6
Fayette⊙ 5,287 .... C3
Fayetteville 200 .... F4
Finchburg 150 .... D7
Fitzpatrick 108 .... G6
Five Points 197 .... H4
Flat Rock 750 .... G1
Flatwood 300 .... C6
Flint City 673 .... D1
Flomaton 1,882 .... D8
Florala 2,165 .... F8
Florence⊙ 37,029 .... C1
Foley 4,003 .... C10
Forestdale 10,814 .... E3
Forkland 429 .... C5
Forney 100 .... H2
Fort Davis 500 .... G6
Fort Deposit 1,519 .... E7
Fort Mitchell 900 .... H6
Fort Payne⊙ 11,485 .... G2
Fosters 400 .... C4
Fostoria 200 .... E6
Frankfort 125 .... C1
Franklin 133 .... G6
Frankville 200 .... B7
Fredonia 300 .... H5
Freemanville 200 .... D8
Frisco City 1,424 .... D8
Fruitdale 500 .... B8
Fruithurst 239 .... G3
Fulton 606 .... C7
Fultondale 6,217 .... E3
Furman 200 .... E6
Fyffe 1,305 .... G2
Gadsden⊙ 47,565 .... G2
Gainestown 300 .... C8
Gainesville 207 .... B5
Gallant 475 .... F2
Gallion 239 .... C6
Gantt 314 .... E8
Garden City 655 .... E2
Gardendale 7,928 .... E3
Garland 155 .... E7
Gasque 100 .... C10
Gateswood 200 .... C9
Gaylesville 192 .... G2
Geiger 200 .... B5
Geneva⊙ 4,866 .... G8
Georgiana 1,993 .... E7
Geraldine 911 .... G2
Gilbertown 218 .... B7
Glen Allen 312 .... C3
Glencoe 4,648 .... G3
Glenwood 341 .... F7
Good Hope 1,442 .... E2
Goodsprings 360 .... D3
Goodwater 1,895 .... F4
Goodway 200 .... D8
Gordo 2,112 .... C4
Gordon 362 .... H8
Gordonsville 100 .... E6
Gorgas 500 .... D3
Goshen 365 .... F7
Gosport 500 .... C7
Graham 100 .... H4
Grand Bay 3,185 .... B10
Grant 632 .... F1
Graysville 2,642 .... D3
Greenbrier 100 .... E1
Green Pond 750 .... D4
Greensboro⊙ 3,248 .... C5
Greenville⊙ 7,807 .... E7
Grimes 298 .... H8
Grove Hill⊙ 1,912 .... C7
Guin 2,418 .... C3
Gulf Crest 1,349 .... B8
Gulf Shores 1,349 .... C10
Guntersville⊙ 7,041 .... F2
Gurley 735 .... F1
Gu-Win 266 .... C3
Hackleburg 883 .... C2
Haleburg 106 .... H8
Haleyville 5,306 .... C2
Halsell 250 .... B6
Hamilton⊙ 5,093 .... C2
Hammondville 369 .... G1
Hanceville 2,220 .... E2
Hardaway 600 .... G6
Harpersville 934 .... F4
Hartford 2,647 .... G8
Hartselle 8,858 .... E2
Harvest 200 .... E1
Hatchechubbee 840 .... H6
Hatton 950 .... D1
Havana 150 .... C5
Hayden 268 .... E3
Hayneville⊙ 592 .... E6
Hazel Green 1,503 .... E1
Headland 3,327 .... H8
Healing Springs 100 .... B7
Heath 354 .... F8
Heflin⊙ 3,014 .... G3
Heiberger 310 .... D5
Helena 2,130 .... E4
Henagar 1,188 .... G1
Higdon 925 .... G1
Highland Home 150 .... F7
Highland Lake 210 .... F3
Hillsboro 278 .... D1
Hissop 250 .... F5
Hobbs Island 100 .... F1
Hobson City 1,268 .... G3
Hodges 250 .... C2
Hokes Bluff 3,216 .... G3
Hollins 500 .... F4
Holly Pond 493 .... E2
Hollywood 1,110 .... G1
Holtville 150 .... F5
Holy Trinity 400 .... H6
Homewood 21,412 .... E4
Honoraville 200 .... F7
Hoover 19,792 .... E4
Hope Hull 975 .... F6
Horn Hill 186 .... F8
Horton 100 .... F2
Houston 100 .... D2
Hueytown 13,469 .... D4
Hulaco 225 .... E2
Huntsville⊙ 142,513 .... E1
Hurricane 300 .... C9
Hurtsboro 752 .... H6
Huxford 141 .... D8
Hybart 200 .... D7
Hytop 350 .... F1
Ider 698 .... G1
Irondale 6,510 .... E3
Irvington 150 .... B9
Isbell 250 .... C2
Isney 145 .... B7
Jachin 150 .... B6
Jack 100 .... F7
Jackson 6,073 .... C8
Jacksons Gap 800 .... G5
Jacksonville 9,735 .... G3
Jamestown 147 .... G2
Jasper⊙ 11,894 .... D3
Jeff 150 .... E1
Jefferson 300 .... C6
Jemison 1,828 .... E5
Jenifer 300 .... G3
Jones 135 .... E5
Joppa 200 .... E2
Josephine 200 .... C10
Kansas 267 .... C3
Keener 125 .... G2
Kellerman 100 .... D4
Kellyton 375 .... F5
Kennedy 604 .... B3
Kent 180 .... G5
Key 400 .... G2
Killen 747 .... D1
Kimberly 1,043 .... E3
Kimbrough 150 .... C6
Kinsey 1,239 .... H8
Kinston 604 .... F8
Knoxville 200 .... C4
Laceys Spring 400 .... E1
Lafayette⊙ 3,647 .... H5
Lakeview 441 .... G2
Lamison 200 .... C6
Landersville 150 .... D2
Lanett 6,897 .... H5
Langdale 2,034 .... H5
Langston 300 .... G1
Lapine 300 .... F7
Larkinsville 425 .... F1

⊙County seat.

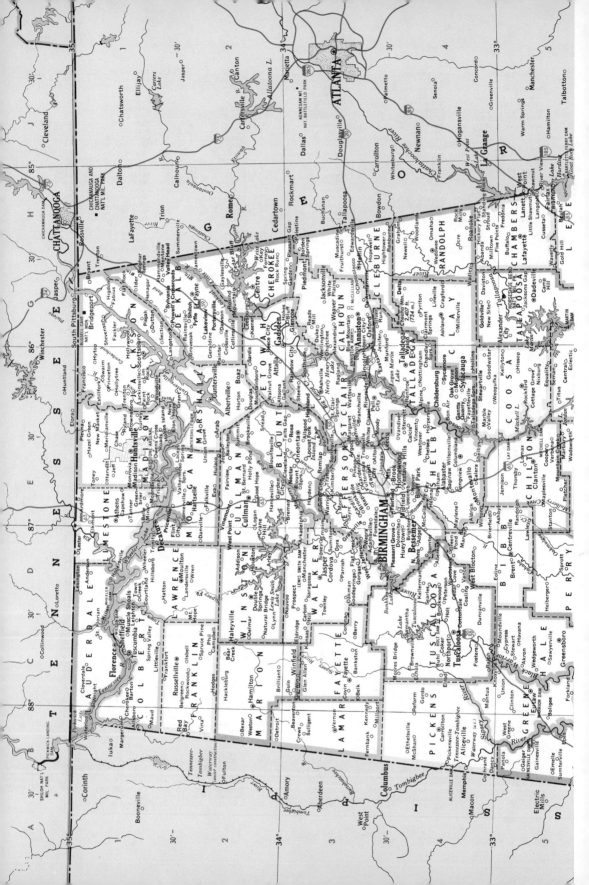

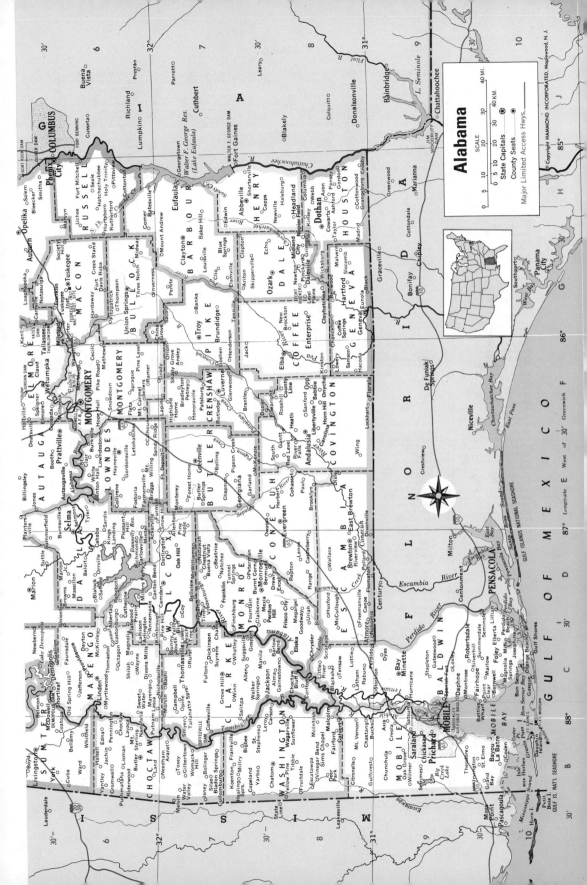

Alabama

SCALE

0 10 20 30 40 MI.

0 5 10 20 30 40 KM.

⊛ State Capitals

◉ County Seats

Major Limited Access Hwys.

GULF OF MEXICO

Copyright HAMMOND INCORPORATED, Maplewood, N.J.

ALABAMA

Latham 133 C8
Lavaca 500 B6
Lawley 125 E5
Leeds 8,638 E3
Leesburg 116 G2
Leighton 1,218 D1
Lenox 150 D8
Leroy 699 B8
Lester 117 D1
Letohatchee 250 E6
Level Plains 867 G8
Lexington 884 D1
Libertyville 141 F8
Lillian 350 D10
Lincoln 2,081 F3
Linden⊙ 2,773 C6
Lineville 2,257 G4
Lipscomb 3,741 E4
Lisman 638 B6
Little River 400 C8
Little Shawmut 2,793 H5
Littleville 1,262 C1
Livingston⊙ 3,187 B5
Loachapoka 335 G5
Lockhart 547 F8
Locust Fork 488 E3
Logan 300 E2
Lomax 300 E5
Longview 475 E4
Lottie 150 C8
Louisville 791 G7
Lower Peach Tree 926 C7
Lowery 100 F8
Lowndesboro 207 E6
Loxley 804 C9
Luverne⊙ 2,639 F7
Lynn 554 C2
Madison 4,057 E1
Madrid 172 H8
Magnolia 100 C6
Magnolia Springs 800 C10
Malcolm 300 B8
Malvern 558 G8
Manchester 400 D3
Manila 100 C7
Maplesville 754 E5
Marbury 300 E5
Margaret 757 F3
Margerum 250 B1
Marion⊙ 4,467 D5
Marion Junction 400 D6
Marvel 100 D4
Marvyn 300 H6
Maud 150 B1
Maylene 500 E4
McCalla 657 E4
McCullough 500 D8
McIntosh 319 B8
McKenzie 605 E7
McKinley 100 C6
McShan 150 B4
McWilliams 305 D7
Megargel 240 D8
Melvin 300 B7
Mentone 476 G1
Meridianville 1,403 F1
Mexia 200 D8
Midfield 6,203 E4
Midland City 1,903 H8
Midway 593 H6
Miflin 150 C10
Mignon 2,054 F4
Millbrook 3,101 F6
Millers Ferry 300 D6
Millerville 345 G4
Millport 1,287 B3
Millry 956 B7
Milltown 125 H4
Milstead 150 G6
Minter 450 D6
Mobile⊙ 200,452 B9
Monroeville⊙ 5,674 D7
Monrovia 500 E1
Montevallo 3,965 E4
Montgomery (cap.)⊙ 178,857 F6
Montrose 750 C9
Moody 1,840 F3
Morris 623 E3
Morvin 355 C7
Moulton⊙ 3,197 D2
Moundville 1,310 C5
Mountainboro 266 F2
Mountain Brook 19,718 E4
Mountain Creek 300 E5
Mount Carmel 300 F6
Mount Hope 125 D2
Mount Meigs 150 F6
Mount Sterling 175 B6
Mount Vernon 1,038 B8
Mount Willing 300 E6
Munford 700 F3

Muscadine 105 H3
Muscle Shoals 8,911 C1
Myrtlewood 252 C6
Nanafalia 500 B6
Napier Field 493 H8
Natchez 135 D7
Natural Bridge 125 C2
Nauvoo 259 D3
Nectar 367 E3
Needham 125 B7
Newbern 307 C5
New Brockton 1,392 G8
New Hope 1,546 F1
New Market 680 F1
New Site 430 G4
Newton 1,540 G8
Newville 814 H8
Nicholsville 200 C6
Nixburg 150 F5
Nokomis 125 D8
North Johns 243 D4
Northport 14,291 C4
Notasulga 876 G5
Nottingham 175 F4
Oak Grove 200 B9
Oak Grove 638 F4
Oakman 770 D3
Ocre 180 H4
Octagon 150 C6
Odenville 724 F3
Ohatchee 860 G3
Oneonta⊙ 4,824 E3
Onycha 147 F8
Opelika⊙ 21,896 H5
Opine 101 C7
Opp 7,204 F8
Orange Beach 600 C10
Orrville 349 D6
Owassa 130 E8
Owens Cross Roads 804 E1
Oxford 8,939 G3
Ozark⊙ 13,188 G8
Painter 265 F2
Paint Rock 221 F1
Panola 200 B5
Pansey 300 H8
Parrish 1,583 D3
Pelham 6,759 E4
Pell City⊙ 6,616 F3
Pennington 355 B6
Perdido 500 C8
Perdido Beach 250 C10
Perdue Hill 225 C8
Peterman 600 D7
Phenix City⊙ 26,928 H6
Phil Campbell 1,549 C2
Pickensville 132 B4
Piedmont 5,544 G3
Pigeon Creek 100 E7
Pike Road 150 F6
Pinckard 771 G8
Pine Apple 298 E7
Pine Hill 510 C7
Pine Level 200 F6
Pisgah 699 G1
Pittsview 300 H6
Plantersville 650 E5
Pleasant Grove 7,102 D4
Point Clear 1,812 C10
Pollard 144 D8
Portersville 100 G2
Powell's Crossroads 636 G1
Prairie 100 D6
Prattville⊙ 18,647 E6
Priceville 966 E1
Prichard 39,541 B9
Princeton 300 F1
Providence 363 C6
Pushmataha 200 B6
Putnam 276 B6
Rabun 300 C8
Ragland 1,860 F3
Rainbow City 6,299 F3
Rainsville 3,907 G2
Ramer 680 F6
Ranburne 417 H3
Randolph 100 E5
Range 275 D8
Reads Mill 150 G3
Red Bay 3,232 B2
Red Level 504 E8
Reece City 718 G2
Reform 2,245 C4
Rehoboth 200 D6
Remlap 800 E3
Renfroe 400 F4
Repton 313 D8
Republic 500 E3
Richmond 100 D6
River Falls 669 E8
Riverside 849 F3

River View 1,314 H5
Riverview 132 D8
Roanoke 5,896 H4
Robertsdale 2,306 C9
Rockford⊙ 494 F5
Rock Mills 600 H4
Rockwood 145 C2
Rogersville 1,224 D1
Roosevelt City 3,352 E4
Rosa 204 E3
Rosehill 132 F8
Russellville⊙ 8,195 C2
Rutherford 232 H6
Rutledge 496 F7
Safford 150 D6
Saginaw 475 E4
Saint Clair 120 E6
Saint Clair Springs 300 F3
Saint Elmo 700 B10
Saint Florian 305 C1
Saint Stephens 700 B7
Salem 350 H5
Salitpa 550 C7
Samantha 400 C4
Samson 2,402 F8
Sandy Ridge 300 E6
Sanford 250 F8
Saragossa 200 D3
Saraland 9,833 B9
Sardis 300 E6
Sardis 883 F2
Satsuma 3,822 B9
Sawyerville 175 C5
Sayre 700 E3
Scottsboro⊙ 14,758 F1
Scranage 150 C8
Scyrene 200 C7
Seale 350 H6
Section 821 G1
Sellers 200 F6
Selma⊙ 26,684 E6
Selmont-West Selmont 5,255 E6
Seminole 275 D10
Semmes 200 B9
Shawmut 2,284 H5
Sheffield 11,903 C1
Shelby 500 E4
Shiloh 297 G2
Shorter 200 G6
Shorterville 400 H7
Shortleaf 253 C6
Silas 343 B7
Silverhill 624 C9
Silver Run 250 G3
Sims Chapel 232 B8
Sipsey 678 D3
Skipperville 100 G7
Slocomb 2,153 G8
Smiths 950 H5
Snead 667 F2
Snowdoun 250 F6
Society Hill 150 H6
Somerville 140 E2
Southside 5,141 F3
Spanish Fort 3,415 C9
Speigner 150 F5
Sprague 140 F6
Spring Garden 100 G3
Spring Valley 600 C1
Springville 1,476 E3
Spruce Pine 300 C2
Standing Rock 300 H4
Stanton 250 E5
Stapleton 975 C9
Steele 795 F3
Sterrett 350 F4
Stevenson 2,568 G1
Stewart 450 C5
Stewartville 250 F4
Stockton 500 C9
Stroud 100 H4
Suggsville 400 C7
Sulligent 2,130 B3
Sulphur Springs 150 G1
Sumiton 2,815 D3
Summerdale 546 C10
Summerfield 100 E5
Summit 120 F2
Sumter 150 D4
Sumterville 175 B5
Sunny South 350 C7
Swaim 125 F1
Sweet Water 253 C6
Sycamore 800 F4
Sylacauga 12,708 F4
Sylvania 1,156 G1
Taits Gap 150 F3
Talladega⊙ 19,128 F4
Talladega Springs 196 F4
Tallahatta Springs 161 C7
Tallassee 4,763 G5

Tanner 600 E1
Tarrant City 8,148 E3
Taylor 1,003 H8
Tensaw 200 C8
Theodore 6,392 B9
Thomaston 679 C6
Thomasville 4,387 C7
Thorsby 1,422 E5
Tibbie 675 B8
Titus 125 F5
Toney 200 E1
Town Creek 1,201 D1
Townley 500 D3
Toxey 265 B7
Trafford 673 E3
Trenton 200 F1
Triana 285 E1
Trinity 1,328 D1
Troy⊙ 12,945 G7
Trussville 3,507 E3
Tunnel Springs 200 D7
Tuscaloosa⊙ 75,211 C4
Tuscumbia⊙ 9,137 C1
Tuskegee⊙ 13,327 G6
Tyler 200 E6
Union 358 C5
Union Grove 127 E2
Union Springs⊙ 4,431 G6
Uniontown 2,112 D6
Uriah 450 D8
Valhermoso Springs 500 E2
Valley Head 609 G1
Vance 254 D4
Vandiver 700 F4
Verbena 500 E5
Vernon⊙ 2,609 B3
Vestavia Hills 15,722 E4
Vina 346 B2
Vincent 1,652 F4
Vinegar Bend 200 B8
Vredenburgh 433 D7
Wadley 532 G4
Wadsworth 500 E5
Wagarville 550 B8
Waldo 231 F4
Walker Springs 500 C7
Wallace 150 D8
Walnut Grove 510 F2
Ward 100 B6
Warrior 3,260 E3
Waterloo 260 B1
Wattsville 550 F3
Waugh 150 F6
Waverly 228 G5
Weaver 2,765 G3
Webb 448 H8
Wedgeworth 100 C5
Wedowee⊙ 908 H4
Wellington 180 G3
Weogufka 500 F4
West Blocton 1,147 D4
West End-Cobb Town 5,189 G3
West Jefferson 357 D4
Weston 350 B2
Westover 500 E4
West Point 248 D2
Wetumpka⊙ 4,341 F5
Whatley 800 C7
Wheeler 100 D1
White Hall 195 E6
White Plains 350 G3
Whites Chapel 336 F3
Whitfield 175 B6
Wicksburg 400 G8
Wilmer 581 B9
Wilsonville 914 E4
Wilton 642 E4
Winfield 3,781 C3
Wing 100 E8
Woodland 192 H4
Woodstock 340 D4
Woodville 609 F1
Wren 200 D2
Wright 180 C1
Yantley 500 B6
Yarbo 150 B7
Yellow Bluff 200 C7
Yellow Pine 350 B8
York 3,392 B6

OTHER FEATURES

Alabama (riv.) C8
Aliceville (dam) B4
Anniston Army Depot F3
Bankhead (lake) D4
Bartletts Ferry (dam) H5
Big Canoe (creek) F3
Big Creek (lake) B9
Black Warrior (riv.) C5
Bon Secour (bay) C10

Brookley Air Force Base B9
Buttahatchee (riv.) B3
Cahaba (riv.) D5
Cedar (pt.) B10
Chattahoochee (riv.) H8
Chattooga (riv.) H2
Cheaha (mt.) G4
Choctawhatchee (riv.) H8
Coffeeville (dam) B7
Conecuh (riv.) D8
Coosa (riv.) F4
Cowikee, North Fork (creek) H6
Cumberland (plat.) F1
Dannelly (res.) D6
Demopolis (dam) C5
Demopolis (lake) C5
Elk (riv.) D1
Escambia (creek) D8
Escambia (riv.) D8
Escatawpa (riv.) B9
Eufaula (Walter F. George Res.) (lake) H7
Fort Gaines B10
Fort McClellan Mil. Res. 7,605 G3
Fort Morgan C10
Fort Rucker 8,932 G8
Gainesville (dam) B5
Goat Rock (dam) H5
Goat Rock (lake) H5
Grants Pass (chan.) B10
Gunter Air Force Base F6
Guntersville (dam) F2
Guntersville (lake) F2
Harding (lake) H5
Herbes (isl.) B10
Holt (dam) D4
Horseshoe Bend Nat'l Mil. Park G5
Inland (lake) E3
Jordan (dam) F5
Jordan (lake) F5
Lay (dam) E5
Lay (lake) F4
Lewis Smith (dam) D3
Lewis Smith (lake) D2
Little (riv.) C8
Little (riv.) G2
Locust Fork (riv.) E3
Logan Martin (lake) F4
Lookout (mt.) G2
Martin (dam) G5
Martin (lake) G5
Maxwell Air Force Base F6
Mexico (gulf) E10
Mississippi (sound) B10
Mitchell (dam) E5
Mitchell (lake) F5
Mobile (bay) B10
Mobile (pt.) B10
Mobile (riv.) C9
Mulberry (creek) E5
Mulberry Fork (riv.) E3
Neely Henry (lake) F3
Oakmulgee (creek) D5
Oliver (dam) J5
Paint Rock (riv.) F1
Patsaliga (creek) F7
Pea (riv.) F8
Perdido (bay) D10
Perdido (riv.) C9
Pickwick (lake) B1
Pigeon (creek) E7
Redstone Arsenal 5,728 E1
Russell Cave Nat'l Mon. G1
Sand (mt.) G1
Sandy (creek) H7
Sepulga (riv.) E7
Sipsey (riv.) B4
Sipsey Fork (riv.) D2
Tallapoosa (riv.) G4
Tennessee (riv.) C1
Tennessee-Tombigbee Waterway B4
Tensaw (riv.) C9
Thurlow (dam) G6
Tombigbee (riv.) B7
Town (creek) C1
Tuscaloosa (lake) D4
Tuskegee Institute Nat'l Hist. Park G6
Walter F. George (dam) H7
Walter F. George (res.) H7
Warrior (dam) C5
Weiss (lake) G2
West Point (lake) H4
Wheeler (dam) D1
Wheeler (lake) D1
Wilson (dam) C1
Yates (dam) G5

⊙County seat.

Interesting Places in Alabama

Alabama Publicity and Information Bureau
Cathedral Caverns at Grant

Alabama Space and Rocket Center, at Huntsville. Exhibits on missile development and space travel are open to the public. Bus trips through Marshall Space Flight Center are also available.

Army Aviation Museum, at Fort Rucker near Ozark, houses a large collection of early Army aircraft and other aviation memorabilia.

Bayou La Batre, on the Gulf of Mexico. Visitors can observe the annual blessing of the shrimp fleet in late July or early August.

Birmingham, central Alabama. The "Pittsburgh of the South" is host to the annual Alabama State Fair in the fall. Other attractions include the Museum of Art, the Botanical Gardens, and the Zoo. Atop nearby Red Mountain is a 55-foot (17-m) iron statue of Vulcan, Roman god of the forge. The steelmaking process can be viewed at steel works outside the city. See BIRMINGHAM.

Cathedral Caverns, at Grant, contain a pink stone formation known as the Frozen Waterfall and many other interesting geologic features, including immense stalagmites and deep chasms.

Cullman, north-central Alabama. Ave Maria Grotto on the campus of St. Bernard College features more than 100 miniature replicas of famous religious shrines and churches. Nearby is Hurricane Creek Park, site of unusual rock formations.

Florence, northwestern Alabama. The restored home of composer W. C. Handy is here. To the east is Joe Wheeler State Park, with facilities for fishing, boating, and swimming.

Gulf Shores, on the Gulf of Mexico, is a resort area with beautiful white sand beaches and freshwater lakes. Nearby is Fort Morgan State Park, the site of a massive five-pointed brick fortification dating from 1819.

Horseshoe Bend National Military Park, near Alexander City, commemorates the decisive victory of General Andrew Jackson's troops over the Creek Indians in 1814.

Mobile, near the Gulf of Mexico, is Alabama's only seaport. Attractions include the antebellum mansion Oakleigh, the battleship USS *Alabama,* and the Phoenix Museum of fire-fighting memorabilia. Dog racing is held at Mobile Greyhound Park. Annual events include the Mardi Gras and the Azalea Trail Festival in the spring. Nearby are Bellingrath Gardens.

Montgomery, on the Alabama River, is the capital of the state. It also was the first capital of the Confederacy. Landmarks from the Civil War period include the Capitol Building, the White House of the Confederacy, Teague House, Chantilly plantation, and St. John's Episcopal Church. See MONTGOMERY.

Mound State Monument, near Tuscaloosa, largest group of Indian ceremonial mounds in Alabama. There are also a reconstructed Indian village and a museum.

Natchez Trace National Parkway, northwestern Alabama, follows the historic old trail known as the Natchez Trace which goes between Nashville, Tennessee, and Natchez, Mississippi.

Russell Cave National Monument, near Bridgeport. The archeological remains of an 8,000-year-old Indian culture are exhibited.

Tuscaloosa, southwest of Birmingham, is the site of the University of Alabama. Other attractions include Lake Tuscaloosa and the North River Historical Area.

Tuscumbia, northwestern Alabama, is the site of "Ivy Green," Helen Keller's birthplace. The play *The Miracle Worker,* depicting her struggle to overcome the handicaps of deafness and blindness, is performed there each summer.

Tuskegee, near Montgomery. The Carver Museum at Tuskegee Institute features exhibits of the scientific work of George Washington Carver; a collection of African art; and a display depicting Negro contributions to western civilization.

See also NATIONAL PARKS, section "United States" (Index by States).

Further tourist information is available from : Alabama Travel Department, 532 South Perry Street, Montgomery, AL 36130.

State Seal: The outline map of the state shows its rivers and boundaries. It was the official emblem from 1819 to 1868 and was readopted in 1939.

State Motto: *Audemus jura nostra defendere* ("We dare defend our rights").

State Song: "Alabama," music by Edna Goeckel Gussen, words by Julia S. Tutwiler.

State Flag: A red Saint Andrew's cross on a white field, emphasizing Alabama's role in the Civil War. (See *Flag*, color plate.)

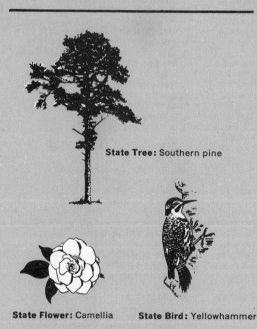

State Tree: Southern pine

State Flower: Camellia   **State Bird:** Yellowhammer

State Fish: Tarpon

whose members are elected. The superintendent is in charge of the state department of education.

Alabama's public school system was established in 1854. The first compulsory school attendance law was enacted in 1915. The present law requires attendance from age 7 to 16.

The University of Alabama was chartered in 1820 and opened in 1831 at Tuscaloosa. Only four buildings survived the Civil War. The university now includes the original campus at University, adjoining Tuscaloosa, and branches at Birmingham and Huntsville.

Auburn University is a land-grant school founded as East Alabama Male College in 1836 and renamed Alabama Agricultural and Mechanical College when taken over by the state in 1872. The name was changed to Alabama Polytechnic Institute in 1899, and to its present form in 1960. The main campus is at Auburn; there is a branch at Montgomery.

For other institutions, and for data, see UNIVERSITIES AND COLLEGES (table).

Government

Alabama is governed under its 1901 constitution, the sixth in its history. The constitution, with its more than 300 amendments and some 100,000 words, is one of the longest state constitutions.

The legislature consists of a Senate of 35 members and a House of Representatives of 105, all elected for four years. It meets annually.

Elected state officials include the governor, lieutenant governor, secretary of state, attorney general, auditor, treasurer, and commissioner of agriculture and industries. All are elected to serve four-year terms. The heads of most other state agencies are appointed by the governor.

The judiciary is headed by a Supreme Court of nine justices elected for six years. There are also courts of appeals, circuit courts, and various local courts.

Alabama is divided into 67 counties. It sends two senators and seven representatives to Congress.

History

Archeological findings indicate that Indians inhabited parts of Alabama as early as 6000 B.C. Mound-building Indians began to appear some 2,000 years ago. They were displaced by the ancestors of the Cherokees,

A-232

Creeks, Choctaws, and Chickasaws—the principal tribes in Alabama when Europeans arrived in the 16th century.

European Exploration and Settlement. The first Europeans to explore the territory were Spaniards under the command of Alonso de Piñeda in 1519. In 1540 Hernando de Soto claimed Alabama for Spain while leading an expedition in search of gold and silver. On October 18, in a bloody battle near the Tombigbee and Alabama rivers, De Soto defeated the Choctaws under Tuscaloosa. Although Spain nominally held possession of the area for more than 150 years, few Spaniards entered Alabama. A colony founded by Tristán de Luna near Mobile Bay in 1559 was abandoned three years later.

France claimed Alabama as part of French Louisiana after the Sieur de La Salle's exploration of the Mississippi, 1681-82. In 1702 a settlement was founded by the Sieur de Bienville at Fort Louis on the Mobile River and designated the capital of Louisiana. In 1711 the colony was moved to the present site of Mobile. Trade was carried on with the Indians. However, the French,

like the Spanish before them, found little in Alabama to reward their efforts.

Great Britain gained possession of the area in 1763 as a result of its victory in the French and Indian War. British settlers came to the territory in increasing numbers. Twenty years later, the greater part of present-day Alabama was ceded to the United States by the Treaty of Paris, which ended the Revolutionary War. The coastal region, however, was ceded to Spain as part of West Florida.

Statehood. Most of Alabama was included in Mississippi Territory, organized in 1798. A dispute between Georgia and South Carolina over a section of northern Alabama was resolved in 1804, when the land was added to Mississippi Territory.

Since much of Alabama remained in the hands of the Indians, white settlements centered around Mobile in West Florida. The United States claimed this area in 1803 as part of the Louisiana Purchase, but not until the War of 1812 were American forces able to capture Mobile (1813). The Creek Indians, who had allied themselves with the

Fort Mims Massacre. Creek Indians attacked the fort, located near Mobile, in August, 1813, and massacred its inhabitants. This incident began the Creek War, which was ended by General Andrew Jackson's victory at Horseshoe Bend in March, 1814.

Library of Congress

Mobile Area Chamber of Commerce
Fort Gaines, star-shaped fort on Dauphin Island, defended Mobile during the Civil War.

British, were decisively defeated by Andrew Jackson's troops at the battle of Horseshoe Bend in 1814. They were forced to give up all but a small part of their land.

In 1817 Mississippi Territory was divided into the state of Mississippi and the Territory of Alabama. On December 14, 1819, Alabama became a state, with its capital at Cahaba. The capital was later moved to Tuscaloosa and finally to Montgomery (1846).

From 1800 to 1830, population increased from about 1,250 to nearly 310,000. This surge of people to Alabama had several causes—the end of the War of 1812, the defeat of the Indians, and a substantial rise in the British demand for cotton. Cotton culture was thriving in the bottomlands and the Black Belt. The first cotton gin in the state had been built in 1802; by the 1830's,

Two Governors. Prohibited by the state constitution from serving two consecutive terms as governor, George C. Wallace helped to elect his wife, Lurleen B. Wallace, to that office in 1966. The constitution was later amended, and Wallace was elected governor three more times.
Wide World

cotton mills were being constructed. During the 1830's, the Indian tribes of Alabama were removed by the federal government to the Indian Territory (now Oklahoma).

Alabama developed economic, social, and political structures based on the plantation system and slavery. It strongly favored the expansion of slavery and supported the Mexican War (1846-48) in the hope that more slave territory would be gained. As the conflict between North and South intensified in the 1850's, Alabama moved toward secession.

Civil War and Reconstruction. In January, 1861, Alabama seceded from the Union and declared itself an independent republic. In February, Alabama joined the Confederacy; Montgomery became the first Confederate capital. During the Civil War, Union forces penetrated the Tennessee Valley in 1862. At Mobile Bay in 1864, Admiral David G. Farragut destroyed the Confederate fleet and seized the forts around Mobile. The state was occupied by Union troops in 1865.

The Reconstruction period following the Civil War was a decade of continued upheaval. Alabama was ruled first by the military and then by a Republican coalition that included blacks, recently arrived Northerners (derisively called carpetbaggers), and local whites who supported Reconstruction (called scalawags). (See CARPETBAGGERS.) Inflation and inefficiency and corruption in government brought bankruptcy to the state's war-ravaged economy. However, some beneficial social services were effected, particularly in education. In the election of 1874, conservative Democrats, running on a platform of economy and honesty in government and white supremacy, were restored to power, and Reconstruction in Alabama came to an end.

The political aftermath of Reconstruction was one-party rule by the Democratic party and determined efforts to maintain white supremacy. Alabama's industrialization began in the late 19th century with the opening of some steel and cotton mills and the expansion of coal and iron mining. The state, however, remained predominantly agricultural. Cotton continued to be the predominant crop, and Alabama's prosperity depended on the demand for that commodity.

20th Century. Agitation by white farmers in the 1890's for improved economic and

A-234

social conditions eventually led to a number of reforms and gained them a degree of political power. In 1901 a new constitution was adopted. Among its provisions was the virtual disenfranchisement of blacks, whose voting power was viewed by whites as a threat to their control of the state.

Early in the century, diversified farming began. This change was brought about by soil depletion, the ravages of the boll weevil, and the demand for food crops during World War I. Rapid industrialization began in the late 1930's and early 1940's, when expansion was spurred by hydroelectric power from the Tennessee Valley Authority and by World War II production demands. After the war, industrial growth continued. In 1949 a rocket and missile research center was erected at Huntsville.

Racial tension was high after the U.S. Supreme Court's 1954 decision on public school desegregation. During 1955-56, the modern civil rights movement began in Montgomery, when blacks led by Martin Luther King, Jr., ended segregated seating on municipal buses. In the 1950's and 1960's, Alabama was the scene of widespread civil rights demonstrations and determined resistance by segregationists. In 1965 Selma was the site of a violent confrontation between demonstrators led by King, who were protesting racial discrimination in voter registration, and the police. This incident led to the passage of the federal Voting Rights Act of 1965.

For more than two decades beginning in the 1960's, George C. Wallace dominated Alabama politics. He was first elected governor in 1962. He gained national prominence as a staunch advocate of segregation and was four times a Presidential candidate. Later in his career, Wallace called himself a champion of the "little man" and gained support from both whites and blacks. He won reelection as governor in 1970 and 1974 and was again elected in 1982.

For further information, see:
Cities. For list, see subtitle *People.*
Physical Features

ALABAMA RIVER	MUSCLE SHOALS
CHATTAHOOCHEE RIVER	TENNESSEE RIVER
MOBILE RIVER	TOMBIGBEE RIVER

History

BIENVILLE, SIEUR DE	KING, MARTIN
CARPETBAGGERS	LUTHER, JR.
CHEROKEE	KU KLUX KLAN
CHICKASAW	LA SALLE, SIEUR DE
CHOCTAWS	MOBILE BAY,
CIVIL RIGHTS MOVE-	BATTLE OF
MENT, subtitle	RECONSTRUCTION
History	TENNESSEE VALLEY
CREEKS	AUTHORITY
DE SOTO, HERNANDO	TUSCALOOSA
FARRAGUT, DAVID G.	

Selected Biography

BLACK, HUGO L.	UNDERWOOD, O. W.
CARVER, GEORGE W.	WALLACE, GEORGE C.
CURRY, JABEZ L. M.	WASHINGTON,
KING, WILLIAM R.	BOOKER T.
MORGAN, JOHN T.	YANCEY, WILLIAM L.

Alabama. See ALABAMA CLAIMS.

Alabama, University of. See ALABAMA, subtitle *Education;* UNIVERSITIES AND COLLEGES (table).

Alabama A & M University. See UNIVERSITIES AND COLLEGES (table).

Alabama Claims, claims entered against Great Britain by the United States for destruction of shipping by Confederate cruisers built or armed in Britain during the Civil War. Early in the war, the Confederacy contracted to have warships built by British shipyards. The United States minister to Britain, Charles Francis Adams, protested these arrangements as violations of Britain's neutral status. Before the British government intervened, 11 vessels had been built or armed.

The *Alabama,* by whose name the claims negotiations are known, was the most famous of the Confederate raiders. During two years at sea, 1862-64, under Captain Raphael Semmes, she destroyed or captured more than 60 United States vessels. In a battle off the coast of France in 1864, the *Alabama* was sunk by the USS *Kearsarge.*

After the war, the United States insisted upon compensation of $19,021,000 from the British government for damages caused by the 11 Confederate ships. Negotiations supervised by Secretary of State William Seward continued for some time, but without success. Then in 1869 the Johnson-

Books about Alabama

Hamilton, V. V. *Alabama: a Bicentennial History* (Norton, 1977).
Liddell, V. G. *With Southern Accent* (University of Alabama, 1983).
Walker, A. B., and Harry Hansen, editors. *Alabama: a Guide to the Deep South* (Hastings House, 1975).
For Younger Readers:
Carpenter, Allan. *Alabama* (Childrens Press, 1978).
Fradin, Dennis. *Alabama in Words and Pictures* (Childrens Press, 1980).

Library of Congress
The Confederate Cruiser *Alabama*

Clarendon Convention was signed, providing for arbitration of Civil War claims and all other controversies dating from 1853. However, the agreement was rejected by the U.S. Senate. Opponents, led by Charles Sumner, objected to the lack of an apology from Britain and the failure to consider "indirect damages" resulting from Britain's alleged partiality to the Confederacy.

Informal negotiations with Britain were conducted for two years by Secretary of State Hamilton Fish. The result was the signing of the Treaty of Washington in 1871. It expressed Britain's regrets, called for international arbitration of the *Alabama* claims, and arranged for the settlement of all other controversies between the two countries.

An arbitration tribunal at Geneva, Switzerland, in 1872 awarded the United States

$15,500,000 in damages. It held Britain responsible only for the destruction committed by the *Alabama, Florida,* and *Shenandoah*. The sum was promptly paid, and more cordial relations were restored.

Alabama River, a river in southern Alabama, about 315 miles (507 km) long. It is formed by the junction of the Coosa and Tallapoosa rivers near Montgomery and flows generally westward to Selma. It then veers south-southwestward to join the Tombigbee River near Calvert. Together they form the Mobile River, which empties into Mobile Bay. Several dams along the Coosa and Alabama rivers are used for power and flood control.

Alabama State University. See UNIVERSITIES AND COLLEGES (table).

Alabaster, ăl′á-bàs′tēr. True alabaster is a soft, fine-grained form of gypsum (calcium sulfate) that is easily carved. It is slightly translucent and its color usually ranges from white to pink, although other colors sometimes occur. Alabaster is used to make statues, vases, lamp bases, jewel boxes, and other ornamental objects. These objects can be made as hard as marble by being subjected to intense heat. The ancient Assyrians used alabaster to make statues and to decorate temple interiors. Alabaster quarries are found in many parts of Europe. The alabaster mined near Florence, Italy, is especially pure and fine-grained. Italian alabaster is sometimes called *Florentine marble*.

When "alabaster" is used as an adjective, it refers to something (not necessarily alabaster) with a nearly white color and a light-diffusing surface, as in the words from the hymn "America, the Beautiful": "Thine alabaster cities gleam . . ."

Oriental Alabaster

The term "alabaster" is also used to designate a substance that resembles true alabaster but is actually a fine-grained form of calcite. Calcite alabaster, often called *oriental alabaster* or *onyx marble,* is a calcium carbonate found in the stalagmites and stalactites of caves. It is a translucent, milky-white or yellow substance, and (like onyx) is sometimes streaked with light and dark bands. Quarries are found in Egypt, Algeria, Iran, Mexico, and the United States.

Oriental alabaster has long been used for ornamental purposes. The ancient Greeks and Romans made vases, statues, ointment boxes, and even columns out of this sub-

Alabaster Burial Jars from Ancient Egypt, used in expensive burials. Before the body was mummified, internal organs were removed to the jars, which were entombed with the mummy.
The St. Louis Art Museum

stance, and many examples are preserved in art museums. Egypt was famous for its oriental alabaster, and the tombs of wealthy Egyptians were often made of this material. The alabaster mentioned in several places in the New Testament (for example, see Matthew 26:7) is oriental alabaster.

Aladdin, *à-lăd'ĭn,* the hero of "Aladdin or the Wonderful Lamp," one of the *Arabian Nights* stories. The lazy, mischievous boy is the son of a poor Chinese tailor. An African magician gives him a magic ring and sends him into a cave to bring out a magic lamp. Aladdin refuses to give up the lamp, and the angry magician shuts him up in the cave. When Aladdin accidentally rubs the lamp, a genie appears and offers to grant any wish. Aladdin wishes himself out of the cave and into riches and a magnificent palace, and marries a princess. Unaware of the lamp's value, she is persuaded by the magician to trade it for a new one. He then transports her and the palace to Africa. Aladdin, aided by the magic ring, recovers lamp, wife, and palace, and kills the magician.

The idea of a wish-granting lamp occurs often in Asiatic and European folklore. The *Arabian Nights* version of the story for some time was thought to have been written by Antoine Galland (1646-1715), French translator of the Arabic manuscripts. Discovery of an Arabic manuscript in the 1890's, however, seemed to indicate that the story was authentically Arabic.

Alameda, *ăl'à-mē'dà,* California, a city in Alameda County. It occupies an island and a tip of a peninsula, called Bay Farm, in San Francisco Bay. The city lies immediately south of Oakland; to the west, across the bay, is San Francisco. Five bridges and an underwater tunnel link Alameda with Oakland. Industrial activities include shipbuilding, aircraft repair, and steel fabricating. Most of the industrialization has occurred since the early 1940's. Alameda Naval Air Station is here. The city has a number of sandy beaches, sports grounds, parks, and yacht clubs.

Alameda was first settled in 1850 and incorporated as a town in 1872. A city charter was granted in 1883.

Population: 63,852.

Alamein, El. See EL ALAMEIN, BATTLE OF.

Alamo, The, a mission building in San Antonio, Texas. It is the only structure that

Texas Highway Dept.
The Alamo

remains on the site of the most famous battle in the Texas war for independence from Mexico, 1835-36. The building is preserved by the state as "the cradle of Texas liberty." The Alamo was built in 1744 by Franciscan friars as the chapel of the Mission San Antonio de Valero (founded in 1718). The original chapel collapsed due to faulty construction. The present building was erected in the 1750's. Abandoned in 1793, the mission was later used as a military barracks and renamed *El Alamo* (after the town of Alamo de Parras in Mexico).

Texans captured the fortress in December, 1835. Although ordered by General Sam Houston to abandon it, some 150 Texans garrisoned the Alamo. They were commanded by William Barret Travis and James Bowie, and included Davy Crockett of Tennessee. Also in the fortress were about 30 women and children.

On February 23, 1836, the troops of General Antonio Lopez de Santa Anna (ultimately numbering about 3,000) began the 13-day siege of the Alamo. The Texans were hopelessly outnumbered. A few volunteers crept through the Mexican lines to bring their number to an estimated 187 men. On March 6, the Mexicans stormed the Alamo. Bloody hand-to-hand fighting followed, and all of the defenders were killed. The women and children were spared. Mexican casualties were estimated between 600 and 1,600. Reports of the slaughter at the Alamo rallied Texans to the cause of independence. "Remember the Alamo!" became their battle cry.

Alamogordo, ăl'*à*-mŏ-gôr'dō, New Mexico, the seat of Otero County. It is about 160 miles (260 km) south-southeast of Albuquerque, in the foothills of the Sacramento Mountains. Lumber from nearby forests is processed in Alamogordo, which also serves as a trading center for the cattle ranchers of the surrounding area. Holloman Air Force Base, White Sands National Monument, and Lincoln National Monument are nearby. Alamogordo was founded in 1898 and incorporated in 1910. It has the mayor-council form of government.

Population: 24,024.

Alanbrooke, Viscount. See BROOKE, Sir ALAN FRANCIS.

Åland Islands, ō'lànd' (*Finnish:* **Ahvenanmaa,** àκ'vĭ-nàn-mä'), a group of about 6,500 rocky islands and islets making up a province of Finland. They lie at the entrance to the Gulf of Bothnia, between Sweden on the west and the Turku Archipelago of Finland on the east. Their area is about 570 square miles (1,476 km²), about half of which is accounted for by the island of Åland. Mariehamn, on Åland, is the capital and chief port of the province. Shipping, farming, lumbering, tourist trade, and fishing are leading industries. Only about 80 of the islands are inhabited, almost entirely by Swedish-speaking people.

The Ålands were first settled by the Swedes in the 12th century. They continued to be Sweden's until 1809, when, along with Finland, they were ceded to Russia. With Russia's collapse and Finland's independence near the end of World War I, the Ålands were claimed by both Sweden and Finland. In 1921 the League of Nations awarded the islands to Finland. Under the terms of the award, the Ålands are largely self-governing, with representation in Finland's parliament.

Population: 22,542.

Al-Anon. See ALCOHOLICS ANONYMOUS.

Alarcón, ä'lär-kôn', **Hernando de** (1500?-?), a Spanish explorer. He and Coronado were sent out in 1540 to discover the fabled Seven Cities of Cibola. Alarcón com-

manded a naval expedition while Coronado conducted an overland search. Alarcón discovered the mouth of the Colorado River and proceeded by boat up the river to search for the Seven Cities and to make contact with Coronado, but he failed to find either. On the return voyage he explored the Gulf of California.

Alarcón, ä'lär-kôn', **Pedro Antonio de** (1833-1891), a Spanish novelist. The wit and romantic irony found in his novels are well exemplified in *El Sombrero de Tres Picos* (*The Three-Cornered Hat,* 1874), the comic retelling of an old folk ballad. Alarcón was born in Andalusia. He studied law and theology, and was successively a journalist, a soldier, a member of the Cortes (legislature), a state councilor, and a diplomat.

Alaric, ăl'à-rĭk (370?-410), a king of the Visigoths who led his barbarian hordes against the Roman Empire at the beginning of the fifth century. Alaric belonged to a princely family of Visigoths (western Goths) from the Danubian provinces of the Roman Empire. An able and ambitious leader, in 394 he commanded a Gothic army employed by Emperor Theodosius I in putting down a rebellion in northern Italy.

After Theodosius' death in 395, Alaric was elected king of the Visigoths and led his tribe in revolt. The Visigoths wanted land and the payment that was overdue for their military service. During 395-96, Alaric ravaged the Greek peninsula. He was stopped at the Peloponnesus in 396 by Stilicho, a Vandal general in the service of Honorius, emperor in the West. To pacify the Visigoths, Arcadius, the Eastern emperor, offered Epirus on the Balkan Peninsula to Alaric.

After a short period, discontent again broke out, and in 400 Alaric invaded northern Italy. He was resoundingly defeated by Stilicho at Pollentia in 402 and forced to withdraw. Alaric returned to Italy after hearing of Stilicho's death and besieged Rome in 408 and 409. In 410 he captured the city and pillaged it for three days. Moving his warriors south toward Sicily, Alaric menaced the entire Western empire. His death from fever in southern Italy ended the immediate threat to the empire's survival.

Alarm Clock. See CLOCK, subtitle *Special Kinds of Clocks:* Alarm Clocks.

Alarm Devices. See BURGLAR ALARM; FIRE ALARM; SMOKE DETECTOR.

Alaska

Steve McCutcheon, Anchorage
Matanuska Glacier

Origin of Name: Derived from an Aleut word meaning "great land."
Nickname: The Last Frontier
Total Area: 591,004 square miles (1,530,693 km²); rank—1st
Capital: Juneau
Largest City: Anchorage
Statehood: January 3, 1959 (order—49th)

J. M. Kauffmann/National Park Svc.
Mount McKinley, North America's Highest Peak

Alaska, à-lăs′kà, one of the Pacific Coast states of the United States. Like Hawaii, it is geographically separated from the rest of the country. Alaska is by far the largest state (more than twice the size of Texas). Its 591,004 square miles (1,530,693 km²) account for almost one-sixth of the nation's area. The general coastline—more than 6,600 miles (10,600 km)—is longer than the coastlines of all the other states combined. Alaska has few inhabitants, however—fewer than any other state.

Alaska is mainly a wilderness of great natural beauty, one largely unchanged by man. In the north lies a barren arctic plain, like other polar regions a "land of the midnight sun." Here may best be seen the colorful aurora borealis, or northern lights. Equally impressive are Alaska's majestic mountains, capped by ice and snow and cut by enormous glaciers.

Despite its northern latitude and remote location, Alaska is a frontier land of increasing opportunity. Its vast resources of forests, minerals, and fish provide the basis for an expanding economy.

Physical Geography

Land. Alaska's large size is matched by its great variety of surface features. Extending east-west across the state in rough bands are four regions: the North, or Arctic, Slope; the Brooks Range; the Central Uplands and Plains; and the Pacific Mountains.

The North Slope begins at the Arctic Ocean as an almost featureless plain. It is marked by shallow river valleys, sparse tundra vegetation, and numerous ponds, swamps, and marshes. Toward the south it becomes more rolling, especially at the edge of the Brooks Range.

The Brooks Range, a continuation of the Rocky Mountains, rises abruptly above the

North Slope as a wall of peaks reaching elevations of 4,000 to 9,000 feet (1,200-2,700 m). This mountainous region includes several smaller ranges, notably the De Long, Baird, Endicott, and Philip Smith mountains. The northern limit of tree growth follows a zigzag pattern through the Brooks Range.

The Central Uplands and Plains region lies between the Brooks Range and the Pacific Mountains along the Gulf of Alaska. It is a vast expanse of alluvial lowlands and eroded, mountainous plateaus. The heavily eroded Seward, Koyukuk, Yukon, and Kuskokwim uplands overlook the broad, flat plains of the Yukon River system. Valleys are wooded but many of the uplands are barren. There are also areas that resemble the frost-scarred North Slope. In the Bering Sea lie two of the state's largest islands—Nunivak and St. Lawrence.

The Pacific Mountains consist of several major ranges that extend in a wide arc from the Aleutian Islands through the Panhandle, the narrow strip of Alaska between Canada and the ocean. These mountains are marked by jagged ridges, glaciers, deep valleys, and fjords. Snow-covered peaks jut out high above the lower, forested slopes.

The Aleutian Range, dotted by several active volcanoes, runs the length of the Alaska Peninsula. It merges on the northeast with the massive Alaska Range, site of 20,320-foot (6,194-m) Mount McKinley, the loftiest peak in North America. Rugged, towering peaks also mark the Chugach, Wrangell, and St. Elias mountains. Mount St. Elias, for example, soars to 18,008 feet (5,489 m) on the Alaskan-Canadian border. Glaciers flank many of the peaks; some, such as Bering, Guyot, Malaspina, and Muir glaciers, descend all the way to the sea.

In several areas the ranges of the Pacific Mountains are separated by lowlands, part of a series of troughs extending as far south as Washington and Oregon. These lowlands reach their greatest size in the basins around Anchorage. Islands and island groups include the Aleutians, the Alexander Archipelago, and Kodiak.

Water. Hundreds of streams and rivers drain the state, but there are few large lakes. The chief river system is the Yukon, which flows into the Bering Sea. With its main tributaries, the Tanana and Koyukuk rivers, the Yukon drains most of central Alaska.

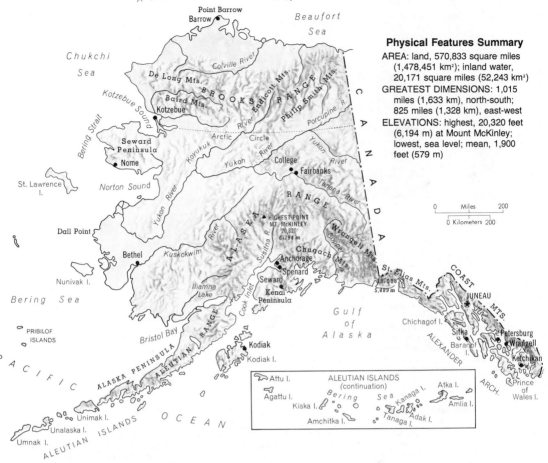

ARCTIC OCEAN

Point Barrow
Barrow

Beaufort
Sea

Chukchi
Sea

Colville River

De Long Mts.

BROOKS RANGE

Endicott Mts.

Philip Smith Mts.

Porcupine R.

Kotzebue Sound

Baird Mts.

Kotzebue

Bering Strait

Seward
Peninsula

Nome

Arctic   Circle

Koyukuk   River

Yukon   River

Yukon River

College
Fairbanks

Tanana River

St. Lawrence
I.

Norton Sound

R A N G E

A L A S K A

HIGHEST POINT
MT. McKINLEY
20,320'
6,194 m

Wrangell Mts.

Cooper R.

Dall Point

Kuskokwim   River

Bethel

Susitna R.

Chugach Mts.

Anchorage
Spenard

St. Elias Mts.

18,008
5,489 m

COAST

JUNEAU

Nunivak I.

Iliamna
Lake

Cook Inlet

Seward

Kenai
Peninsula

Bering   Sea

PRIBILOF
ISLANDS

Bristol Bay

ALASKA PENINSULA

ALEUTIAN   RANGE

Gulf
of
Alaska

Chichagof I.

Sitka

Baranof
I.

Petersburg

Wrangell

MTS.

ALEXANDER

Ketchikan

Prince
of
Wales I.

ARCH.

P A C I F I C

Unimak I.

Unalaska I.

Umnak I.

ALEUTIAN   ISLANDS

O C E A N

Kodiak

Kodiak I.

Physical Features Summary

AREA: land, 570,833 square miles
(1,478,451 km²); inland water,
20,171 square miles (52,243 km²)

GREATEST DIMENSIONS: 1,015
miles (1,633 km), north-south;
825 miles (1,328 km), east-west

ELEVATIONS: highest, 20,320 feet
(6,194 m) at Mount McKinley;
lowest, sea level; mean, 1,900
feet (579 m)

0   Miles   200

0   Kilometers   200

CANADA

ALEUTIAN ISLANDS
(continuation)

Attu I.

Agattu I.

Kiska I.

Amchitka I.

Bering   Sea

Kanaga I.

Tanaga I.

Adak I.

Atka I.

Amlia I.

The Kuskokwim River system, which flows through the southwest, also drains into the Bering Sea. In the north are the Colville and Noatak rivers; in the south, the Copper and Susitna rivers.

Largest lakes are Iliamna and Becharof, in the southwest, and Teshekpuk, on the North Slope. Small, deep lakes occur in mountainous areas, particularly in the southwest. Other small, but shallow, lakes are found in the alluvial lowlands along the Arctic and Bering Sea coasts.

Climate. Chief influences on the climate are Alaska's northerly latitude, its large land mass, and its coastal waters. Except along the southeast coast, winters are long and bitterly cold. Summers throughout the state are short and cool. Precipitation, both rain and snow, varies from large amounts in the Panhandle to negligible amounts along the Arctic shore.

The Panhandle has a relatively mild climate because of the moderating effects of offshore ocean currents and winds. Average temperatures at Juneau, for example, vary from about 25° F. (−4° C.) in January to about 55° F. (13° C.) in July. Sitka's average January temperature is slightly above freezing. Precipitation for the year is close to 90 inches (2,290 mm) in most areas, but some receive as little as 25 inches (635 mm) and others more than 150 inches (3,810 mm). Snowfall amounts to about 100 inches (2,540 mm) a year.

The western coast, from the Aleutians to the Seward Peninsula, is cooler and drier than the Gulf of Alaska coast. At Nome, temperatures average about 4° F. (−16° C.) in January and 49° F. (9° C.) in July. Average yearly precipitation is about 20 inches (510 mm), including as much as 80 inches (2,030 mm) of snow. Cold, moist winds, frequent fog, and sudden storms often make this region unpleasant.

Temperature ranges increase and precipitation decreases away from the coasts. Janu-

Interesting Places in Alaska

Totem Poles at Klawock, a Haida Indian village on Prince of Wales Island, offshore from the southern extreme of the Alaskan Panhandle
J. Malcolm Greany, U.S. Forest Service

Alaska Marine Highway, a string of bays, sounds, and channels stretching along the southeastern Alaska coast and making up the Alaskan portion of the Inside Passage, the coastal water route from Seattle, Washington, to Skagway, Alaska. Ferries cruise these waters the year round, making stops at various ports.

Anchorage, on Cook Inlet, is the state's financial and commercial center. Attractions include the Mount Alyeska ski area and the Anchorage Historical and Fine Arts Museum. The Fur Rendezvous, a winter carnival, is held each February.

Denali National Park, southeast of Fairbanks. Within the park are mountains, including Mount McKinley, the highest peak in North America; glaciers; streams; and a variety of wildlife.

Fairbanks, central Alaska, is the state's second largest city. At the nearby University of Alaska is the University Museum, featuring Eskimo and Indian arts and crafts. Alaskaland, a recreational and historical park, is also nearby. In July the World Eskimo/Indian/Aleut Olympics are held, as is Golden Days, commemorating the discovery of gold in 1902.

Glacier Bay National Park, northwest of Juneau, contains one of the world's most impressive icefields. More than 20 mammoth glaciers are in the area.

Juneau, southeastern Alaska, is the state capital. The Capitol Building, the Governor's Mansion, and the Alaska State Museum, which houses Eskimo, Indian, Russian, and gold rush memorabilia, are here. Nearby is Mendenhall Glacier, a spectacular river of ice.

Katmai National Park, near the base of the Alaska Peninsula, is the location of the Valley of the Ten Thousand Smokes, site of a violent volcanic eruption in 1912.

Ketchikan, on the southern tip of the Alaskan Panhandle, is called the "Gateway to Alaska." Visitors may tour Totem Bight State Park; Saxman Indian Village; the Cultural Heritage Center; the Centennial Museum Library, which displays Indian arts and crafts; and the Ketchikan Indian Museum. Sport fishing for salmon in the waters around the city is a popular tourist activity.

Klondike Gold Rush National Historical Park, Skagway, preserves historical structures associated with the 1898 gold rush in Skagway, Chilkoot Trail, and White Pass Trail.

Kodiak Island, off the southwest coast, attracts hunters and fishermen. It is the home of the Kodiak bear, and king crab are found in the nearby waters.

Kotzebue, north of the Arctic Circle, is an Eskimo village. Visitors can observe Eskimos in their daily activities. Other attractions include the Living Museum of the Arctic and dog-sled rides.

Nome, northwestern Alaska, was a gold rush camp during the boom days of 1893. Several landmarks from that period can be viewed. Nome is also the home of the King Island Eskimos, famous for their ivory carving and other handicrafts.

Sitka, southeastern Alaska, was the capital of Russian America. Points of interest include the Sheldon Jackson Museum, the reconstructed 19th-century Russian Orthodox Cathedral of St. Michael, and Sitka National Historical Park, which commemorates an 1804 battle between Indians and Russians.

See also NATIONAL PARKS, section "United States" (Index by States).

Further tourist information is available from: Alaska State Division of Tourism, Pouch E, Juneau, AK 99811.

ary temperatures average well below 0° F. (−18° C.). July temperatures generally are 60° to 70° F. (16° to 21° C.), though readings of 90° F. (32° C.) or more occasionally occur. Yearly precipitation is less than 15 inches (380 mm), including an average snowfall of 40 to 60 inches (1,020-1,520 mm).

On the North Slope, winters are severe, summers are cool, and freezes may come in the warmest months. Arctic waters have a slight modifying effect. Barrow averages −16° F. (−27° C.) in January and 40° F. (4° C.) in July. Precipitation is less than elsewhere in Alaska, seldom exceeding 8 inches (200 mm) a year. Snowfall averages about 28 inches (710 mm) annually.

ALASKA

Natural Vegetation. Forests cover about one-third of the state. They vary from tall, dense coniferous (evergreen) forests in the south and southeast to the woodlands of mixed coniferous and deciduous trees in the interior. The southern and southeastern forests are dominated by Sitka spruce and western hemlock, occasionally mixed with red cedar, Alaska cedar, and some red alder and cottonwood. These forests rapidly diminish north of the Alaska Range. The interior woodlands are variously composed of white and black spruce, Alaska birch, cottonwood, balsam, and aspen. Farther north the trees become increasingly sparse and stunted.

Much of the remaining land, especially in the interior and on the North Slope, is carpeted with low-growing tundra vegetation—grasses, mosses, and lichens—during the brief warm months. Most of the tundra region is underlaid by permanently frozen subsoil, called *permafrost.*

Economy

The utilization of its natural resources—especially fish, forests, and minerals—has long been Alaska's chief economic activity. Since World War II, however, and especially since statehood was achieved in 1959, a more diversified economy has developed. More of the resources are extracted and processed, and new industries have arisen.

Admission to statehood was followed by a sizable influx of people. This in turn brought increased housing and other construction, greater wholesale and retail trade, and improved transportation and communications. The tourist industry also grew considerably. The federal government is the largest single employer in the state, mainly through military installations and defense projects. More than 98 per cent of Alaska—mostly wilderness—is owned by the federal government.

Manufacturing, other than the relatively simple processing of resources, is little developed. Most of the consumer goods and virtually all industrial equipment are imported. Manufacturing, however, has considerable potential because of the state's wealth of resources and possibilities for hydroelectric power. Probably the chief hindrance to industrialization has been the smallness of the population.

Fishing. By value of the catch, Alaska is the leading fishing state, and the fishing

Fishing is a major industry in Alaska. Shown are fishermen unloading salmon.

Farm in the Matanuska Valley, one of the few areas in Alaska suitable for crops

Prudhoe Bay, on Alaska's northern coast, is the center of one of the largest oil fields ever discovered in North America.

ALASKA

Alaska Travel Division
Automobile and Passenger Ferry. Ships of the Alaska State Ferry System operate year-round in the sheltered waters of the Inside Passage and in the coastal waters around Anchorage.

industry is an important segment of its economy. Fishing fleets and canneries are major sources of income and employment in coastal cities of the south. Kodiak and Dutch Harbor-Unalaska are the chief fishing ports.

Salmon is the most valuable fish; the catch consists primarily of sockeye (red) and pink salmon. The crab catch, made up mainly of king and snow crabs, is also extremely valuable. Halibut and shrimp are also a significant part of the catch.

Mineral Production. By value, petroleum is the state's leading product. It was first discovered on the Kenai Peninsula in 1957; major deposits have since been found in Cook Inlet and in the Prudhoe Bay area on the North Slope. The Prudhoe Bay strike, made in 1968, is one of the largest ever made in North America. A pipeline, completed in 1977, carries oil 789 miles (1,270 km) from the Prudhoe Bay field to the ice-free port of Valdez for export. Natural gas is produced in the Kenai and Cook Inlet fields. The reserves are enormous but production is limited by the lack of adequate transportation facilities.

Forestry. Lumber and pulp wood are also among Alaska's principal products. The most important sources of timber are in the Tongass and Chugach national forests.

Their coastal location in the south makes water transportation of logs and wood products possible. Ketchikan and Sitka are among the cities with mills. Most of the forest products are exported, mainly to Japan. Interior forests of commercial quality are kept from full economic development by lack of transportation.

Agriculture. Alaska produces very little of the food needed in the state, for agriculture is limited in both area and production. Only a tiny part of the land is devoted to crops; the pastured area is somewhat larger. Most of the farming is carried on in the Matanuska Valley, northeast of Anchorage; the Tanana Valley, near Fairbanks; on the Kenai Peninsula; and on the island of Kodiak. Dairy products (mainly milk), hay, and potatoes are the chief products.

An extremely short growing season, frequent early and late frosts, and poor, thin soils hinder agricultural expansion. Much remains to be done in land utilization research.

Fur Industry. Fur seals on the Pribilof Islands provide much of the value of Alaska's fur output. The seal herd is protected by federal law, and the annual kill is under strict government supervision. Trapping of wild animals such as beaver, fox, marten, muskrat, and mink is carried on by residents of many small outlying communities.

Transportation. Almost all of the state's roads are in southern Alaska. The Alaska Highway, leading southeastward from Fairbanks, is the only road link with the lower 48 states. Also in the south is all of the trackage of the state's two railways. One is the federally owned Alaska Railroad (between Seward and Fairbanks). The other is the privately owned White Pass and Yukon Railway (between Skagway and Whitehorse in Yukon Territory, Canada).

A passenger and automobile ferry service operates in the sheltered waters of the Inside Passage, between Skagway and Prince Rupert, British Columbia. There is also service to Seattle, Washington. In addition, ferry service is available between Anchorage, Kodiak Island, and Seward, and on Prince William Sound.

Air travel has been a major factor in opening Alaska's interior and north and west coasts to development. Airports at Anchorage, Fairbanks, and Juneau handle most commercial flights.

The People

The population of Alaska in 1980 was 401,851—an increase of 99,268, or 32.8 per cent, over the 1970 total. Despite its growth rate—one of the highest in the nation—it continued to rank 50th among the states in population and remained one of the earth's most sparsely populated regions. The population density in 1980 was 0.7 persons per square mile (0.3 per km²).

Whites made up 77 per cent of the population. Of the nonwhites, most are native Indians, Eskimos, and Aleuts; blacks accounted for less than 4 per cent of the state's population.

Alaska's Largest Cities

Anchorage*...	174,431	Valdez	3,079
Fairbanks*...	22,645	Petersburg.....	2,821
Juneau*, the		Soldotna	2,320
capital	19,528	Nome*	2,301
Sitka*	7,803	Barrow	2,267
Ketchikan*...	7,198	Homer	2,209
Kodiak*.....	4,756	Wrangell......	2,184
Kenai	4,324	Palmer	2,141
Bethel	3,576	Kotzebue......	2,054

*An article on each of these cities appears in this encyclopedia.

Indians. The principal Indian groups in Alaska are the Tsimshian, Haida, and Tlingit tribes and seven small tribes belonging to the Athapascan language family.

Mountainous, heavily forested southeastern Alaska is the home of the Tsimshians, Haidas, and Tlingits, whose ancestors migrated from Canada in the 18th and 19th centuries. Most of the Tsimshian Indians live along the Nass and Skeena rivers. The Haidas, located on Prince of Wales Island, and the Tlingits, settled along the coast from Ketchikan to Katalla, are distantly related. Both, particularly the Haida, are noted for their totem-pole carving. Most of the southeastern Indians are fishermen or work in fish canneries. They have generally abandoned their old tribal customs.

In the wide, flat river valleys west of Fairbanks in the Alaskan interior are various Athapascan Indians, whose forebears 700 to 800 years ago separated from the main body of related tribes now in Canada. Hunting and trapping are their main occupations.

See also HAIDA INDIANS; TLINGIT INDIANS; TSIMSHIAN INDIANS.

Eskimos. The Eskimos live along the Bering Sea and Arctic Ocean coasts and the lower Yukon River and Kuskokwim River regions. Scattered over this harsh and frigid

A-247

area, they hunt, fish, trap, and herd reindeer. More than any other native Alaskans, the Eskimos have preserved their ancient customs and language. Yet even their traditional way of life is changing as the Eskimo, with his remarkable mechanical ability, is in increasing demand for work in the skilled trades. (See also ESKIMO.)

Aleuts. Inhabiting the Aleutian Islands and the Alaska Peninsula are the Aleuts. Although closely related to the Eskimos (both are descended from Asian migrants who came to what is now Alaska some 10,000 to 15,000 years ago), these people have their own customs, tradition, and language. They engage in sealing, fishing, and farming. (For further information about the Aleuts, see ALEUTS.)

Education

A commissioner of education appointed by the state board of education supervises the state department of education. The board is appointed by the governor. Alaska enacted a compulsory school attendance law in 1929. Children must attend school from age 7 to 16.

The University of Alaska, a land-grant school, was founded in 1917 and opened in 1922 as the Alaska Agricultural College and School of Mines. The name was changed to University of Alaska in 1935. The main

Eskimo uses a primitive bow drill in carving a figurine from walrus ivory.

Economic & Tourist Development, Alaska

State Seal: Depicts the resources and industries that have contributed to Alaska's development—fur seals, fish, trees, mining, shipping, and farming.

State Motto: North to the Future.

State Song: "Alaska's Flag," words by Marie Drake, music by Elinor Dusenbury.

State Flag: Consists of eight gold stars, on a blue field. The Big Dipper (the constellation Great Bear) symbolizes strength, the North Star the fact that Alaska is the northernmost state. (See FLAG, color page.)

State Tree: Sitka spruce

State Bird: Willow ptarmigan

State Flower: Forget-me-not

State Fish: Chinook salmon

campus is in Fairbanks. There are other campuses at Anchorage and Juneau. The University of Alaska system also includes several community colleges.

For data, see UNIVERSITIES AND COLLEGES (table).

Government

Alaska's constitution was ratified in 1956 and became effective on admission to the Union in 1959. The constitution provides for a strong executive branch; the governor is given extensive powers, including supervision of all principal departments of government. The governor and lieutenant governor are elected together on the same ticket for four-year terms and may not serve more than two consecutive terms. Most other officials of the executive branch are appointed by the governor with the consent of the legislature.

The legislature consists of a Senate of 20 members elected for four-year terms and a House of Representatives of 40 members elected for two years. It meets annually beginning in January.

Alaska's constitution provides for direct legislation through the initiative and referendum, and for the recall of elected officials. (See INIATIVE AND REFERENDUM; RECALL.)

The Supreme Court consists of five justices. Superior courts are the trial courts of general jurisdiction. The governor appoints judges from nominations made by a judicial council. Judges must be approved by the voters on a nonpartisan ballot every few years.

Alaska is divided into boroughs and "census areas." The boroughs, 11 in all, are administrative districts similar to counties; the census areas, established jointly by the state and the U.S. Census Bureau, were created for statistical purposes. The cities of Juneau, Sitka, and Anchorage have the same boundaries as their boroughs.

Alaska sends two senators and one representative to Congress.

History

In prehistoric times, a land bridge joined Alaska to Asia where the Bering Strait now lies. Across this bridge, most archeologists believe, came Asiatic peoples who migrated to the North and South American continents—ancestors of the Indians. Probably 10,000 to 15,000 years ago, the ancestors of the Eskimos and the Aleuts came to Alaska. More than 100 centuries passed, however, before the first Europeans discovered Alaska.

Russian America. Russia began to expand eastward across Siberia toward the Pacific Ocean in search of furs in the late 16th century. However, not until the early 18th century was Russia able to send an expedition to determine whether Asia and America were connected. In 1724 Czar Peter the Great commissioned Vitus Bering, a Danish navigator, to make an exploratory voyage. Bering did not reach the North American coast on this voyage, which took place in 1728, but he did find that a body of water, later named the Bering Strait, separated the two areas.

On his second expedition, Bering discovered the Alaskan mainland in July, 1741. He died during the severe winter that followed, but the survivors returned to Russia with samples of the valuable furs to be found in the newly discovered land. The search for furs drew large numbers of Russian traders and hunters to Alaska.

Russian activity in Alaska aroused the interest of other countries. In 1775 Spanish explorers surveyed the coast of Alaska. Captain James Cook of Great Britain sailed along the coast in 1778, during his search for a northwest passage linking the Atlantic and Pacific. In 1786 a French expedition landed in Alaska. It was the Russians, however, who occupied Alaska. For over a hundred years after Bering's discovery, they exploited the coastal resources, nearly depleting Alaska of furs and enslaving or slaughtering the Aleuts.

The first permanent Russian settlement was founded on Kodiak Island in 1784. In 1786 Gerasim Pribilof discovered a group of islands that proved to be important breeding grounds for fur-bearing seals. A contract granting exclusive fur-trading rights in Alaska for 20 years was given to the Russian-American Company by Czar Paul in 1799.

Under the able but autocratic rule of Aleksandr Baranov, the company prospered. In 1804 a capital was established at Sitka. A trading post was built as far south as California, at Fort Ross, in 1812 (vacated in 1841). After Baranov's departure in 1818, the company's prosperity declined, and Russia was eventually forced to grant trading privileges in Alaska to the United States (1824) and Great Britain (1825).

Trade became less and less profitable for

the Russians. As early as 1857, Russia offered to sell Alaska to the United States. Negotiations were unsuccessful until after the American Civil War. On March 30, 1867, Secretary of State William H. Seward signed a treaty purchasing Alaska for $7,200,000, or about two cents an acre (about $5 per square kilometer). The purchase was generally unpopular in the United States, and Alaska was called "Seward's Folly" and "Seward's Icebox."

United States Territory. Alaska was at various times under the jurisdiction of the War, Treasury, and Navy departments, but no attention was given to its internal problems until 1884. In that year, an act of Congress established civil and judicial government in Alaska. The United States did not really become interested in Alaska until 1896, when gold was discovered in the Klondike in Canada's Yukon Territory. This event led to a gold rush across Alaska and substantial discoveries at Nome (1899) and Fairbanks (1902). The seat of administration was moved from Sitka to Juneau in 1900.

As a result of Alaska's growing importance, Canada pressed its claims to territory bordering British Columbia on the Pacific. An international commission decided in favor of the United States in 1903. Also in 1903, Congress enacted an Alaskan homestead law to encourage settlement. An international dispute over seal hunting in the Bering Sea was settled by treaty in 1911.

In 1912 Congress passed the Organic Act of Alaska, designating Alaska an organized territory. The territorial legislature met for the first time in 1913. In 1916 a statehood bill was introduced in Congress; it was the beginning of a 42-year struggle for admission.

Economic progress continued after the gold-rush period, but at a slower pace.

Alaska's Capitol at Juneau
Alaska Travel Division

A Street in Nome in 1900 during Gold Rush

Population, which had risen to about 64,000 at the peak of the gold rush, totaled about 55,000 in 1920. During the 1920's, the salmon industry was expanded, modern mining methods were developed, and transportation was improved. The Alaska Railroad, linking Alaska to British Columbia, was completed in 1923. Beginning in 1935, farmers from the "Dust Bowl" region of the Middle West began to migrate to Alaska.

Alaska's strategic military importance was not recognized until World War II. In 1942 the Japanese invaded the Aleutian Islands, for a time occupying Attu and Kiska. Military personnel and construction workers were sent in increasing numbers to bolster Alaska's defenses. After the war a substantial military force remained.

The 49th State. Alaskans voted for statehood in a territorial referendum in 1946 but bills introduced in Congress were unsuccessful. In 1956 a constitutional convention adopted a state constitution, which was ratified by the people. Statehood was finally approved by Congress in 1958. On January 3, 1959, Alaska was formally admitted to the Union.

The strongest North American earthquake ever recorded shook southern Alaska on March 27, 1964, causing widespread damage and more than 100 deaths. In 1971 the federal government made a settlement of nearly one billion dollars to resolve the land claims of Alaska's native peoples.

Huge oil deposits discovered at isolated Prudhoe Bay in 1968 were opened to development when Congress passed a bill in 1973 allowing construction of a trans-Alaska oil pipeline. The 789-mile (1,270-km) pipeline, linking Prudhoe Bay with the ice-free port of Valdez, was completed in 1977. (See also PIPELINE, subtitle *History*.)

In 1980, after a nine-year battle between environmentalists and developers, the U.S. Congress passed the Alaska Lands Act, which restricted commercial development of 104.3 million acres (42.2 million hectares) of federal lands in the state.

For further information, see:

Cities. For a list of cities, see subtitle *People.*

Land

ALASKA PENINSULA	KODIAK
ALASKA RANGE	MATANUSKA VALLEY
ALEUTIAN ISLANDS	MUIR GLACIER
ALEXANDER ARCHIPELAGO	NUNIVAK ISLAND
	PRIBILOF ISLANDS
KENAI PENINSULA	ST. ELIAS MOUNTAINS

Water

ALASKA, GULF OF	KUSKOKWIM RIVER
BERING STRAIT	TANANA RIVER
INSIDE PASSAGE	YUKON RIVER

History

BERING, VITUS	SEWARD, WILLIAM H.
GOLD RUSHES	SKAGWAY

Miscellaneous

ALASKA HIGHWAY	ESKIMO

Books about Alaska

Christy, Jim. *Rough Road to the North: Travels Along the Alaska Highway* (Doubleday, 1980).

Hunt, W. R. *Alaska: a Bicentennial History* (Norton, 1976).

Mead, R. D. *Journeys Down the Line: Building the Trans-Alaska Pipeline* (Doubleday, 1978).

Mobley, G. F. *Alaska: High Road to Adventure* (National Geographic Society, 1976).

Morgan, Lael, and others. *Alaska* (Abrams, 1979).

Naske, C. M., and H. E. Slotnick. *Alaska: a History of the Forty-Ninth State* (Eerdmans, 1979).

Remley, D. A. *The Crooked Road: a History of the Alaska Highway* (McGraw-Hill, 1976).

Sunset (periodical). *Alaska,* revised edition (Lane, 1977).

For Younger Readers:

Carpenter, Allan. *Alaska* (Childrens Press, 1979).

Cheney, Cora. *Alaska: Indians, Eskimos, Russians, and the Rest* (Dodd, Mead, 1980).

Wheeler, Keith. *The Alaskans* (Time-Life Books, 1977).

Anchorage Street after 1964 Earthquake

Alaska, Gulf of, a broad arm of the Pacific Ocean off the southern coast of Alaska. The gulf stretches in a broad arc between the Alaska Peninsula on the west and the Alexander Archipelago on the east. Anchorage and Seward are leading ports.

Alaska, University of. See ALASKA, subtitle *Education;* UNIVERSITIES AND COLLEGES (table).

Alaska Highway, a road in Alaska and Canada. It is 1,523 miles (2,451 km) long. Beginning at Dawson Creek, British Columbia, the Alaska Highway runs generally northwestward through northern British Columbia, southern Yukon Territory, and east-central Alaska to Fairbanks. The highway was built in 1942-43 by United States troops as a supply route for armed forces in Alaska. It was maintained by the United States as a military road until 1946, when the Canadian portion was turned over to Canada. The highway's all-weather surface is gravel through most of Canada and blacktop in Alaska. It was opened to the public in 1947.

Alaska Peninsula, a long, narrow tongue of land in Alaska. From Iliamna Lake the peninsula stretches generally southwestward for about 500 miles (800 km) almost to Unimak Island in the Aleutian chain. The waters of the Pacific Ocean wash the deeply indented and island-studded southern coast; the Bering Sea borders the more regular northern coast.

The Alaska Peninsula is largely a cold, barren region with few trees and shrubs. The rugged, desolate Aleutian Range runs the length of the peninsula. Numerous volcanoes dot the range. In Katmai National Park are thousands of steaming fissures, the most notable of which are in the Valley of Ten Thousand Smokes. Veniaminof Volcano, 8,225 feet (2,507 m) above sea level, is the loftiest peak.

People on the sparsely populated peninsula—mainly Aleuts—live in small coastal villages. Hunting and fishing in the region's wilderness attract tourists.

Alaska Range, a crescent-shaped mountain range in southern Alaska. It stretches some 500 miles (800 km), first northwestward and then southwestward, from Canada's Coast Mountains to the Aleutian Range on the Alaska Peninsula. The range is noted for its rugged beauty, unexplored regions, and glacier-capped peaks. Mount McKinley,

20,320 feet (6,194 m) above sea level, is the highest peak in North America.

See also MCKINLEY, MOUNT; NATIONAL PARKS, section "United States" (Denali National Park and Denali National Preserve).

Alaskan Malamute. See DOG, subtitle *Breeds of Dogs:* Working Dogs, and picture.

Alateen. See ALCOHOLICS ANONYMOUS.

Alba, Duke of. See ALVA, DUKE OF.

Albacore. See TUNA, subtitle *Kinds of Tuna:* The Albacore.

Alban, Saint. See ST. ALBANS.

Albanese, äl-bä-nä'sä, **Licia** (1913-   ), a United States operatic soprano. She became known for her interpretation of Cio-Cio-San in *Madame Butterfly,* Violetta in *La Traviata,* and other lyric roles. Licia Albanese was born in Bari, Italy. She studied in Milan and made her operatic debut at Parma in 1935 in *Madame Butterfly.* At her Metropolitan Opera debut in 1940 she sang the same role. Miss Albanese became a United States citizen in 1945.

Albania, äl-bā'nǐ-à, or **People's Republic of Albania,** the smallest nation on the Balkan Peninsula in Europe. The Albanian name of the country is *Shqipëri,* meaning "Land of Eagles." It lies on the eastern shore of the Adriatic Sea between Yugoslavia and Greece. Albania's area is 11,100 square miles (28,748 km²).

Physical Geography

Land. High mountains and eroded plateaus make up most of the land. In the extreme north are the North Albanian Alps, which in some areas are rugged and glacially scoured. They rise more than 8,800 feet (2,680 m) above sea level and extend northeast-southwest. Equally high mountains in the east and the south follow roughly a northwest-southeast trend. The highest peak rises 9,068 feet (2,764 m) above sea level in the Korab range on the Yugoslav border in the east. Small basins, deep river valleys, and gorges occur in Albania's mountainous interior.

Along the Adriatic coast lies a flat to hilly alluvial plain, up to 25 miles (40 km) wide. It is marked by silted river mouths, meandering rivers, and marshy areas. A hilly belt where the mountains and the coastal plain meet is the most densely settled part of the land.

Water. Rivers vary from raging torrents in the mountains to sluggish streams on the lowlands. Their flows also vary enormously

A-251

with the rainy and dry seasons. With few exceptions, Albania's rivers are unsuited to navigation. They are, however, important sources of hydroelectric power. Among the chief streams are the Drin, Drin-i-zi, Buenë, and Mat in the north and the Shkumbin, Seman, Devoll, Osum, and Vijosë in the south.

Lake Scutari in the northwest and Lake Ohrid in the east lie partly in Yugoslavia. Lake Prespa, which is connected by underground channel to Lake Ohrid, is shared with Yugoslavia and Greece. There are also small lakes and lagoons along the coast.

Climate. Albania's climate is of two types. *Mediterranean* conditions, much like those of southern Italy and southern California, predominate along the coast. Summers here are hot and relatively dry; winters are mild and rainy. The *continental* type, with colder winters, milder summers, and greater rainfall throughout the year, prevails in the mountainous interior. Average yearly precipitation is generally 30 to 60 inches (760-1,520 mm). Larger amounts fall on the western slopes of the high mountains.

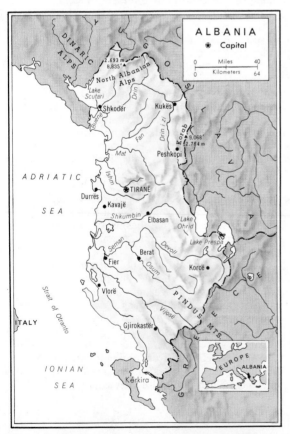

Natural Vegetation. *Maquis,* a drought-resistant kind of Mediterranean brush and shrub vegetation, grows on the coastal lowlands and hills. Many of the plants are thorny and have hairy, waxy, or thick leaves that conserve water. There are also tracts of marsh grass in the poorly drained areas.

Forests cover somewhat less than half of the land. Much of it, particularly on the low mountain slopes, is sparse woodland, brush, and shrub. Deciduous forests, mainly oak, chestnut, and beech, cover the middle slopes; pine, fir, and other conifers grow on the upper parts.

Economy

For centuries the people of Albania have had an extremely low standard of living. Before World War II its economy was based almost entirely on farming. Modern manufacturing and mining industries and motorized transportation were virtually nonexistent.

After the Communist take-over at the end of World War II, a centrally planned economy with state-owned and state-operated industries began. Development of heavy manufacturing, electric power, mining, transportation, and agriculture was stressed. Production of consumer goods and light industries received less attention. Most of the technical and financial aid given the program came first from the Soviet Union and later from Communist China. Despite considerable progress, Albania remains the poorest country in Europe.

Agriculture. Though its relative importance has declined, farming is still the mainstay of the economy. Nearly all the farmland, roughly 40 per cent of the country's area, is in collectives, much like those in the Soviet Union. Agricultural production has greatly increased in recent decades; however, crop yields are still relatively low and production insufficient to meet the needs of the country. Mechanization and new farmland, which has been put into use by reclamation projects along the coast, account for much of the increase in production.

Most of the cropland is devoted to grains, especially corn and wheat. Increased attention has been given commercial crops, such as cotton, tobacco, and sugar beets.

About half of the agricultural land is used for pasturing livestock. Sheep and goats, which are able to graze far up the mountain slopes, are the most numerous livestock.

Cattle and poultry are also raised. Pigs are few, because many Albanians are Moslems, who are forbidden by their religion to eat pork.

Mining. Albania's mineral wealth is considerable. Mining has undergone relatively rapid expansion since 1950. Chrome, nickel, petroleum, copper, and coal (including lignite), are among the chief products. Natural asphalt is also produced. In general, mining development is hampered by the lack of technicians and transportation facilities.

Manufacturing. The few manufacturing industries that existed before the rise of the Communist regime have been nationalized. New industries have been established, especially for processing mineral and agricultural goods. Among products are cement, refined petroleum, smelted copper and other primary metals, cotton and woolen textiles, and various processed foods—primarily flour, sugar, olive oil, and cheese.

Transportation. Roads form the most extensive transportation system and carry the greatest volume of traffic. However, many of the roads in rural areas are not usable by motor vehicles. Railways connect the port of Durrës with Tiranë, Elbasan, and various other towns in the interior. No line extends outside the country. Tiranë is the only city served by scheduled airlines. Seaports include Durrës and Vlorë. There is some local shipping on the three large lakes.

The People

The Albanian people are descendants of the ancient Illyrians, with a small mixture of Visigoth, Slav, and Thracian. Because of the mountainous character of much of their country, Albanians were isolated both from effective centralized rule and from the rest of the world. They developed and maintained great independence of spirit and strong loyalty to their tribes, or clans. Deadly clan feuds were common through most of Albanian history and continued into the 20th century.

Under the police state established by the Communists after World War II, traditional Albanian ways were suppressed. In spite of efforts toward modernization, many rural people still live and work under primitive conditions. Living standards in the cities remain far below those of other European nations.

Population. Albania had a population of about 2,432,000 in 1975. Its population den-

Wide World
Old Bridge in Albania's Mes Valley, near the Yugoslav border. A boy on a donkey and his father cross through bleak, stony countryside.

Wide World
Collective Farm in Albania. Women unload tomatoes from an oxcart on a farm near Tiranë.

sity, about 250 persons per square mile (85 per km²), is low for a European nation but is about four times that of the United States. There are few large cities. Approximately two-thirds of the population live in villages and on farms.

Albania's Largest Cities	
Tiranë, the capital 192,000	Vlorë 55,500
Shkodër 62,400	Elbasan 53,300
Durrës 60,000	Korçë 52,000

Language. The Albanian language is an Indo-European tongue derived from ancient Illyrian. Slavic words were introduced during the early migrations. Later, separate dialects developed in the north, where the language of the church was Latin, and in the south, where it was Greek. The Shkumbin River marks the boundary between the two

Wide World
Former Mosque. This Moslem shrine, like many other religious buildings in Communist Albania, has been put to other uses; it is now a stable.

dialect groups—the Ghegs to the north and the Tosks to the south.

During the Ottoman era a considerable amount of Turkish was absorbed into both dialects. Literary Albanian, for which a Roman alphabet was established in 1908, is based on Gheg. Greeks living in the southern tip of Albania maintain their own language. In the west the Vlachs, descendants of the Thracians, speak a Rumanian dialect.

Religion. Albania fell originally within the realm of the Byzantine, or Eastern Orthodox, branch of the Christian church. Hatred of the Orthodox Bulgarians and Serbians who conquered their country caused the northern Albanians to turn to the Roman Catholic Church. After the Turkish conquest many Albanians were converted to Islam. Prior to World War II the population was about 70 per cent Moslem, making Albania the only predominantly Moslem country in Europe. Two-thirds of the remainder, mainly in the south, belonged to the Eastern Orthodox Church; the rest, largely in the north, were Roman Catholic.

Under the postwar Communist government religion was suppressed. Uncooperative priests and Moslem leaders were imprisoned, and in 1967 all churches and mosques were closed or turned to other uses. It is impossible to estimate how many Albanians continue to profess a religion.

Education and Culture. At the time Albania gained its independence in 1912, the only educated persons were those who had attended foreign-language schools. Even after the establishment of an Albanian school system, facilities were limited. At the outbreak of World War II, 85 per cent of the population was illiterate.

After the war, with Soviet assistance, a

A-254

great effort was made to provide basic education for all children, and by the 1980's illiteracy had been reduced to about 30 per cent. Schooling is compulsory from age 7 to 15. Secondary schools are of three types: general education; technical-professional, which combine vocational training with a general education; and lower vocational, which provide training in agriculture and industry. All secondary-school graduates are required to spend a year working in a factory or on a farm. The nation's first university was established in Tiranë in 1957. There are also several teacher-training schools and a school of agriculture.

Albania has a national library and an active publishing industry. There are several national museums and a government-subsidized theater, opera, and ballet.

Government

The constitution of 1976 designates Albania as a People's Socialist Republic. The country is governed by the single-chamber People's Assembly, elected every four years. All candidates run unopposed. The chairman of the presidium (administrative committee) of the Assembly is head of state. A premier and cabinet appointed by the Assembly make up the Council of Ministers, which nominally holds executive power.

Actually, all power is held by the Communist party, which is called the Albanian Party of Labor. The party's Central Committee, elected at the party congress, names a politburo (executive committee), the first secretary of which is the real head of government.

Each of Albania's 26 districts is ruled by a council, elected for three years. Justice is administered through civil courts, except for cases of major crimes against the state, which are heard by military tribunals.

History

The Illyrians, an Indo-European people, settled the Adriatic shore (the Dalmatian coast) about the 12th century B.C. One of the Illyrian tribes was the Albani, from whom Albania takes its name. There were Greek colonies in the southern part of the country. In the fourth century B.C. the region was conquered by the Macedonians, and during the second and first centuries it was annexed by Rome. When in 395 A.D. the Roman Empire was divided, the boundary passed through southern Dalmatia, placing some of the Illyrians in the western (Roman) division and the rest in the eastern (Byzantine) division. (See ROME AND THE ROMAN EMPIRE, maps *The Roman Empire at Its Greatest Extent c. 117 A.D.* and *The Empire after Diocletian.*)

The Byzantine Era. Albania suffered repeated invasion during the centuries of barbarian migration. In 395 the Visigoths passed through. The sixth century brought destructive attacks by Huns, Avars, and Slavs. Many Illyrians of the Dalmatian coast were forced southward into the Albanian Alps. There, with the southern Illyrian tribes, they were able to repulse the invaders and preserve their own identity. Some of the people of Thrace, to the east, also found refuge in the mountains of Albania.

In the latter part of the ninth century Bulgaria annexed most of Albania. It was restored to the Byzantine Empire in 1018 by Emperor Basil II. The Venetians, however, seized several port cities, but lost them to a Byzantine prince after the Fourth Crusade (1202-04). In the 14th century Serbia conquered Albania, and Venice regained its ports.

Turkish Conquest. The Ottoman Turks entered the Balkans in 1354, reduced the Serbs to vassalage in the 1380's, and in 1403 moved against Albania. George Castriota, an Albanian chieftain's son, served the Turks as a soldier and a military governor. In 1443 Castriota—by then called Scanderbeg (a corruption of Iskander Bey, his Turkish name)—turned against the Turks and became a leader of Albanian resistance. For 24 years Scanderbeg outfought the Turks, but after his death in 1468 the country was brought under Ottoman rule. The last Venetian ports fell to the Turks in 1479.

Turkish rule was not harsh, and Albanian nobles retained their lands and feudal powers. However, the Albanians were not permitted to have schools. Culturally and intellectually Albania was the most backward country in Europe.

Nationalist Movement. Settlement of the Russo-Turkish War of 1877-78 awarded Albanian territory to Serbia, Montenegro, and Bulgaria. The League for the Defense of the Rights of the Albanian Nation was formed to protest the territorial losses and to gain autonomy for Albania. After a futile revolt against Turkey the league collapsed, but the Turks permitted Albania to open schools and to issue publications in the Al-

Wide World
Small Town Street in Albania. Cobblestones pave a narrow way in Krujë, near the capital.

banian language. The resulting surge of nationalist feeling alarmed Turkey, which restored the ban against schools and publications in 1886.

Independence. During the Italo-Turkish War of 1911-12 Albania won autonomy. In 1912, when the First Balkan War ended Turkish rule in the Balkans, independence was declared. The Conference of Ambassadors of the Great Powers made Albania a principality and established its boundaries, giving it territory in the south claimed by Greece and in the north claimed by Serbia and Montenegro. William of Wied, a German army officer, was chosen ruler. He took the throne in March, 1914. The monarchy fell six months later, at the beginning of World War I. During the war Albania was occupied by a succession of foreign armies. After the war the Albanians formed a government, and Tiranë became the capital.

Ahmed Zog, a government official, became premier in 1922 and put down all opposition by military force. In January, 1925, he had the nation declared a republic and himself elected president. The Italians gave him financial aid and gradually assumed control over his country. Zog was permitted to make himself king in 1928, but in 1939 Italy annexed Albania.

After World War II. During World War II Albanian partisans opposing Italian and

A-255

German occupation came under control of the Communists. When the country was liberated in 1944, Albania declared itself a people's republic. Enver Hoxha, first secretary of the Communist party politburo, became the first premier and soon assumed dictatorial powers. Albanian Communists grew displeased with Russia and in the 1960's the country became aligned with Communist China. Albania withdrew from the Warsaw Pact and isolated itself from all Western nations. In the 1970's Albania established friendly relations with Yugoslavia and trading ties with Greece.

See also ALARIC; EPIRUS; FLAG (color page); MONEY (table); TIRANË.

Books about Albania

Logoreci, Anton. *The Albanians: Europe's Forgotten Survivors* (Westview Press, 1978).
Marmullaku, Ramadan. *Albania and the Albanians* (Shoe String Press, 1975).
Pollo, Stefanaq, and Arben Puto. *Albania: from Its Origins to the Present Day* (Routledge & Kegan Paul, 1980).

Albania, Church of. See EASTERN ORTHODOX CHURCH, subtitle *Branches of the Church*.

Albanian Orthodox Archdiocese in America. See EASTERN ORTHODOX CHURCH, subtitle *Orthodox Branches in the United States*.

Albany, Georgia, the seat of Dougherty County. It is on the Flint River, in the southwestern part of the state. Albany is a regionally important commercial and industrial center. Among its products are cotton textiles, chemicals, farm implements, lumber, airplane parts, and paper. The surrounding agricultural area is known for peanut and pecan production. Albany State College is in Albany.

The city was settled in 1836 and incorporated in 1841. It was named after Albany, New York. Throughout 1961-63 it was the scene of numerous civil rights drives and demonstrations.

Population: 74,550.

Albany, New York, the seat of Albany County and the state capital. It lies on the west bank of the Hudson River, about 135 miles (217 km) north of New York City.

Albany is a hub of transportation and one of the nation's leading inland ports. It is the transshipment point between traffic on the New York State Barge Canal and oceangoing vessels. The city is served by railways and Interstate highways; its airport handles domestic flights. Albany's wharves, railway yards, and factories line the riverfront. Among goods produced are paper, machine tools, and textiles.

From the industrial section along the river, residential Albany reaches up slopes and across rolling terrain dominated by the capitol. Next to the capitol is the Empire State Plaza, a redevelopment project that includes several state office buildings and the New York State Museum and other cultural facilities. The Albany Institute of History and Art is noted for its Dutch colonial furnishings and European and American paintings. Schuyler Mansion (built 1762), now a museum, was the home of General Philip Schuyler, army officer and statesman. The State University of New York at Albany, the College of St. Rose, and several branches of Union University are here.

Albany is one of the nation's oldest communities. In 1624 the first permanent settlers, who were Dutch, established Fort Orange. Taken by the British in 1664, the settlement was renamed Albany after the Duke of York and Albany. In 1754 delegates from seven colonies met here for the Albany Congress. (See ALBANY CONGRESS.) The city became the state capital in 1797. The opening of the Erie Canal (1825), followed by the building of railways, caused the city's growth as an industrial and transportation center.

Population: 101,727.

Albany Congress, a conference held in Albany, New York, in 1754 to prepare a unified colonial defense against the French and their Indian allies. At this meeting, Benjamin Franklin presented a precedent-setting proposal for union of the British North American colonies; it was later known as the Albany Plan of Union. The congress had been called by the British government primarily to renew an alliance with the Iroquois Indians guaranteeing their loyalty in the event of war with the French.

The French and Indian War had begun by the time the congress met. Attending the conference were 150 Iroquois chiefs and delegations from seven colonies—Massachusetts, New York, Pennsylvania, Rhode Island, New Hampshire, Connecticut, and Maryland.

During a debate on the need for a permanent intercolonial union for defense,

Franklin introduced his plan. It provided for a union of the colonies to be governed by a president-general appointed by the king and a grand council of delegates chosen by the colonial assemblies. Representation was to be based on the amount of taxes contributed to the general treasury. The council was to pass laws, control Indian affairs, levy taxes, and raise armies, subject to the president-general's veto. It also was to have the power to declare war and make peace.

A treaty was signed with the Iroquois but it was only partly satisfactory to them. The Albany Plan was unanimously adopted by the delegates and submitted for approval to the colonies and the British Lords of Trade. The proposal was rejected. Franklin later wrote, "the assemblies . . . thought there was too much prerogative in it, and in England it was judged to have too much of the democratic." The plan, however, served as a guide for the drafters of the Articles of Confederation and, later, the federal Constitution.

Albany Convention. See ALBANY CONGRESS.

Albany Plan. See ALBANY CONGRESS.

Albany Regency, a small but powerful group of Democratic politicians who controlled the party in New York State and influenced state and national politics from about 1820 to 1850. It was one of the first successful political machines in the United States. The group was founded by Martin Van Buren and included William L. Marcy and Silas Wright. Power was maintained through strict party discipline and use of the spoils system.

Albany State College. See UNIVERSITIES AND COLLEGES (table).

Albatross, ăl'ba-trŏs, the largest sea bird. It can fly several hundred miles from land and can soar without visible effort. Albatrosses nest mainly in the Southern Hemisphere, although three species are found in the Pacific Ocean north of the Equator. There are 13 species of albatrosses.

Albatrosses range from 27 to 37 inches in length, and the larger species weigh more than 20 pounds. All have three fully webbed toes. The wings are long and pointed, and the tail is short. Albatrosses have large hooked bills. Most species are white, and have black wing feathers. The wingspread of most albatrosses ranges from six to eight feet.

The largest albatross is the *wandering albatross*. It has a wingspread of nearly 12

Karl W. Kenyon from National Audubon Society
An Albatross in Flight

feet, the longest of any living bird. The term "wandering" is not a misnomer. A wandering albatross shot in the South Pacific, west of Chile, had a small vial around its neck containing a message dated 12 days earlier in New Zealand waters, 3,150 miles away.

The fact that the albatross can glide and soar with ease has interested many students of aviation. The albatross can attain a flying speed of up to 70 miles per hour by making use of various wind patterns.

Albatrosses usually nest in colonies on small islands. After an elaborate courtship, the female lays a single, chalky-white egg. Both parents incubate the egg. It hatches after 9 or 10 weeks, and the young bird remains in the nest for as long as three months. The adults feed on common squids and other small ocean animals, and often follow ships to snatch waste food when it is dumped overboard. They feed their young by swallowing the food (in order to predigest it) and then regurgitating and depositing it into the mouth of the young bird.

Sailors often refer to albatrosses as "gooney birds" because of their disregard of danger. Sailors have long had a taboo against killing albatrosses. In his poem *The Rime of the Ancient Mariner,* Samuel Taylor Coleridge tells of the misfortunes that befell a ship after a sailor defied this tradition and killed an albatross.

Albatrosses are of the family Diomedeidae and the genus *Diomedea*. The wandering albatross is *D. exulans*. The Laysan albatross of the North Pacific is *D. immutabilis*.

Albedo, ăl-bē'dō, in astronomy, the reflecting power of a celestial body that is not self-luminous. Albedo is stated as a decimal fraction between one and zero. An albedo of almost 1 indicates a bright surface that reflects most of the light that strikes it. An object with an albedo of almost 0 would absorb most of the light that struck it; little light would be reflected. The moon, for example, with an albedo of 0.07, reflects only 7 per cent of the sunlight it receives. Albedo is determined by calculating the amount of light that strikes the body and then measuring the reflected light.

The concept of albedo is useful for attempting to determine the nature of planetary surfaces and atmospheres. For example, a planet surrounded by clouds would have a high albedo; one with no clouds and a surface composed of dark, rough rock would have a low albedo. Albedos of some of the planets are: Mercury, 0.06; Venus, 0.76; Earth, 0.34; Mars, 0.15; Jupiter, 0.41; and Saturn, 0.42.

Albee, ôl'bē, **Edward** (Franklin) (1928-), a United States playwright. *The Zoo Story* (1960), his first play, is a one-act commentary on man's alienation from the world about him and his futile attempts to communicate with his fellow man. In *The Death of Bessie Smith* (1961), which is based on an actual event, an injured black singer bleeds to death after being refused admittance to an all-white Southern hospital.

Who's Afraid of Virginia Woolf? (1962), Albee's first full-length play, deals with tensions existing among two college professors and their wives, acted out in terms of a drinking bout and bold, slashing exchanges of insults. *The Ballad of the Sad Café* (1963) is a dramatization of Carson McCullers' novel of the same name. In *Tiny Alice* (1964) the secretary of a Roman Catholic cardinal sells his soul to the world's richest woman in exchange for a large annual contribution to the church. Albee was awarded a Pulitzer prize in 1967 for *A Delicate Balance* and in 1975 for *Seascape*. *Box* (1968) and *Quotations from Chairman Mao Tse-Tung* (1968) are two one-act plays which have been staged together as "Box-Mao-Box" (1968).

Albee was born in Washington, D.C., the adopted son of wealthy parents. He attended several private schools for short periods and then worked at various odd jobs until 1958, when he decided to write plays. He used profits from his Broadway successes to run an off-Broadway experimental theater.

Albee's other plays include *The American Dream* (1961); *All Over* (1971); *Listening* (1975); *Counting the Ways* (1976); *The Lady From Dubuque* (1978).

Albemarle, Duke of. See MONK, GEORGE.

Albemarle Sound, ăl'bĕ-märl, a shallow arm of the Atlantic Ocean in northeastern North Carolina. It is separated from the open sea by a long, narrow barrier beach. The sound is about 60 miles (96 km) long, east to west, and up to 15 miles (24 km) wide. It is used for commercial and recreational fishing. Catches include clams, oysters, and shrimp. Albemarle Sound is part of the Intracoastal Waterway, a sheltered route used mainly by pleasure boats and small barges. The Chowan and Roanoke rivers empty into the sound. On the barrier beach is Wright Brothers National Memorial, commemorating the first successful airplane flight, 1903, at Kill Devil Hill.

Albéniz, äl-bā'nēth, **Isaac** (1860-1909), a Spanish composer and pianist. By using popular dance rhythms in his works, he became a leader of the Spanish nationalist school. *Iberia* (composed 1906-09), 12 piano pieces based on Spanish themes and locales, is his most famous work. Albéniz was born in Camprodón, Spain. As a child he gave piano concerts in Europe and the Americas. In 1893 he settled in Paris, where he was influenced by Vincent d'Indy and Claude Debussy.

Among his many piano works are *Córdoba, Seguidillas,* and *Tango in D.* He wrote several operas, including *Pepita Jiménez* (1896).

Albers, Joseph (1888-1976), a United States painter and teacher who greatly influenced industrial design. His geometric abstract paintings, such as the series *Homage to the Square,* are marked by precise control of color and design. Albers was born in Bottrop, Westphalia, Germany. He studied at the Bauhaus and taught there, 1923-33. Albers came to the United States in 1933 and became a citizen in 1939. While teaching at Black Mountain College, North Carolina (1933-50), and at Yale University (1950-58), Albers advanced the Bauhaus ideas of complete integration of art and industrial design.

Albert, the name of two Holy Roman emperors, one king of Belgium, and one reigning prince of Monaco.

Holy Roman Empire

Albert I (*German:* Albrecht, äl'brĕĸt) (1250?-1308), king of Germany and Holy Roman emperor, ruled 1298-1308. Albert, son of Emperor Rudolph I of Hapsburg, was duke of Austria. He was chosen emperor by the electoral princes after he helped to depose Emperor Adolph of Nassau. During his reign, Albert strengthened the Hapsburg dynasty through territorial conquest, but failed to establish a hereditary Hapsburg monarchy in Germany. After reducing the power of the princes, he subdued Meissen, Moravia, and Bohemia, 1305-06, but was unable to conquer Thuringia, 1306. Albert was assassinated by his nephew, John of Swabia.

Albert II (1397-1439), king of Germany and Holy Roman emperor, ruled 1438-1439. He became duke of Austria (as Albert V) in 1404. In 1438 Albert succeeded his father-in-law, Sigismund, as emperor and king of Germany as well as king of Hungary and of Bohemia. With his election, the Hapsburgs regained the imperial crown. They held it almost continuously from that time until the end of the Holy Roman Empire in 1806. Albert spent most of his brief reign suppressing an uprising in Bohemia and fighting the invading Turks.

Belgium

Albert I (1875-1934), king of the Belgians, ruled 1909-1934. Albert was an internationally respected diplomat, a courageous military leader, and an economic and social reformer.

Albert was born in Brussels, the son of Philip, Count of Flanders. After attending military school, he served in the Belgian Senate, 1893-98. Albert traveled extensively in Europe, the Belgian Congo, and the United States. In 1900 he married Duchess Elisabeth of Bavaria. To advance Belgium's economic development, Albert advocated new industrial methods and the establishment of technical colleges. He succeeded his uncle, Leopold II, as king in 1909.

As political tensions brought Europe to the brink of World War I, Albert made goodwill visits to neighboring countries and increased Belgium's armed forces. In 1914 he appealed to Emperor William II of Germany to respect his country's neutrality, but a few months later Germany invaded Belgium. Albert personally commanded the Belgian army until the war's end.

After the war, King Albert concentrated on the economic reconstruction of Belgium. He encouraged a coalition government of the three major political parties to strengthen the nation. He was responsible for the adoption of a new monetary system and the stabilization of currency in 1926. Albert was killed in 1934 when mountain climbing.

NEW STANDARD Collection; National Portrait Gallery
King Albert I of Belgium and **Prince Albert,** consort of Queen Victoria of England

Monaco

Albert I (1848-1922), prince of Monaco, ruled 1889-1922. Albert was noted for his scientific expeditions and contributions to oceanography. In 1910 he founded the Oceanographic Museum in Monaco, which became world-renowned for its aquarium. In 1918 Albert granted his nation a constitution that limited the power of the ruling prince by establishing legislative and executive branches of government.

Albert, Prince (1819-1861), consort of Queen Victoria of Great Britain. Throughout his marriage to Victoria, Albert was her devoted companion and constant adviser on foreign and domestic policy. Albert, the son of the Duke of Saxe-Coburg-Gotha, married his cousin Victoria in 1840. As a foreigner, he was at first viewed with suspicion by the British people. Gradually he won their respect by his interest in and understanding of Britain's problems.

Albert was also an enthusiastic supporter of science and art. At his urging, the Great (Crystal Palace) Exhibition was organized and held in London in 1851. In 1857 he was given the title prince consort by Victoria. Although gravely ill in 1861, Albert helped to avert a crisis in Anglo-American relations by persuading the government to act with moderation in the dispute with the United States over the stopping of the British ship *Trent;* among other things, he softened the wording of a British ultimatum to the United States government. (See TRENT AFFAIR.)

After Albert's death, Victoria remained in seclusion for years. She wore black the rest of her life.

See also VICTORIA (Queen), subtitle *Victoria and Albert.*

Albert, Lake, or **Albert Nyanza,** a lake in the Great Rift Valley of eastern Africa.

Ed Cooper

Pyramid Mountain in Alberta's Jasper National Park

The lake is divided between Uganda on the east and Zaire on the west. In Zaire it is called Lake Mobuto Sese Seko. The lake has an area of 2,075 square miles (5,374 km²) and a maximum depth of 170 feet (52 m). It is about 110 miles (180 km) long, northeast-southwest, and up to 30 miles (48 km) wide. The lake receives the waters of the Semliki River, which drains Lake Edward to the southwest, and the Victoria Nile, flowing from Lake Victoria to the southeast. Lake Albert discharges its waters through the Albert Nile, called the White Nile after it enters Sudan.

In 1864 Sir Samuel Baker, an English explorer, became the first European to visit the lake. He named it for Prince Albert, husband of Queen Victoria.

Albert Canal, a shipping canal in Belgium. It is about 80 miles (130 km) long and runs generally northward and then northwestward. The canal links the highly industrialized area of Liège with Antwerp, Belgium's chief port. It was completed in 1939 and named for King Albert I. In World War II the Albert Canal served as Belgium's main line of defense until crossed by German troops in 1940. It was retaken by Allied forces in 1944.

Albert Edward, Lake. See EDWARD, LAKE.

Albert the Bear. See PRUSSIA, subtitle *History of Prussia:* Brandenburg.

A-260

Alberta, ăl-bûr′tá, the westernmost of the Prairie Provinces of Canada. Its landscapes vary from lofty mountain peaks and glacial lakes of the Rockies to vast forests and fertile prairies. As in the United States, the prairies produce an abundance of wheat and other crops. Alberta is also rich in mineral resources, especially petroleum and natural gas.

Physical Geography

Land. Alberta occupies part of three great physiographic regions of North America: the Rocky Mountains, the Great Plains, and the Canadian Shield.

The Rocky Mountains in Alberta are a high range, varying from 9,000 to more than 12,000 feet (2,750 to 3,650 m) above sea level. Mount Columbia, reaching 12,294 feet (3,747 m), on the British Columbia border, is Alberta's highest point. During the last Ice Age the range was covered by glaciers, of which there are many small remnants. There are many jagged peaks and deep intermountain valleys, particularly in Banff and Jasper national parks.

The Great Plains extend northward into Alberta from the United States. Though the land is generally flat, there are broad, deep valleys, hills, and low ranges locally called mountains. The valley of the Red Deer River has typical badlands topography, with eroded saw-tooth ridges and deep ravines.

The Canadian Shield extends into the

northeast corner of Alberta. It is an area of exposed, ancient crystalline rock, part of an enormous formation that covers most of northern and eastern Canada.

Elevations in Alberta decrease from the Rockies and their foothills to an average of about 2,500 feet (760 m) on the Great Plains and 600 feet (180 m) in the Salt River Valley of the northeast.

Water. Almost all of Alberta is drained by streams that flow generally east and northeast, toward Hudson Bay and the Arctic Ocean. Rivers in the north and central parts include the Athabasca, Peace, Hay, and Slave; in the central area, the North Saskatchewan and Pembina; and in the south, the South Saskatchewan, with its tributaries, the Bow, Oldman, and Red Deer rivers. Among the province's many lakes are Athabasca (mainly in Saskatchewan), Lesser Slave, Claire, Bistcho, and Utikuma.

Climate. Alberta's climate is an extreme continental type, with great ranges between summer and winter temperatures. In the north, for example, July temperatures average 60° F. (16° C.) and January temperatures average −8° F. (−22° C.). Corresponding figures for Calgary, in the south, are 63° F. (17° C.) and 12° F. (−11° C.). The climate is also characterized by abundant sunshine.

Precipitation ranges from 10 to 25 inches (255 to 635 mm) annually, but its occurrence is highly variable. The driest area is the southeast. Snowfall is heavy throughout the province. Most of the precipitation between November and March falls as snow.

Prevailing winds are westerly the year round. An important influence is that of the *chinook*—a warm, dry, westerly wind blowing from the Rocky Mountains in winter and spring.

Vegetation and Wildlife. In the Rockies plant life is limited to hardy Alpine vegetation, while the foothills have a mixture of evergreen and broadleaf trees. The prairies of the southern Great Plains have short grasses and few, if any, trees.

A transitional zone of mixed grasses and trees marks the northern rim of the prairies. Aspen, birch, and willow become frequent. Farther north lies a great forest, composed principally of spruce, pine, larch, and fir.

In wildlife, Alberta is among Canada's richest provinces. Bear, caribou, and moose roam the northern forests. Small fur-bearing animals are abundant—beaver, mink, otter,

Physical Features Summary
AREA: land, 248,800 square miles (644,389 km²); water, 6,485 square miles (16,796 km²)
GREATEST DIMENSIONS: north-south, 760 miles (1,223 km); east-west, 405 miles (652 km)
ELEVATIONS: highest, Mount Columbia, on the Alberta-British Columbia boundary, 12,294 feet (3,747 m); lowest, 565 feet (172 m)

Facts about Alberta

Origin of Name: Named for Princess Louise Caroline Alberta, daughter of Queen Victoria

Total Area: 255,285 square miles (661,185 km²); rank—4th among provinces

Population, 1976: 1,838,037; rank—4th among provinces

Capital: Edmonton

Largest City: Calgary

Became a Province: September 1, 1905 (together with Saskatchewan)

and marten. As the boundary of settlement has moved northward, there has been a substantial decrease in the number of wild animals.

The many lakes make Alberta a haven for waterfowl. Pheasant, grouse, and partridge are found. Many other bird species pass through Alberta on their yearly migrations. Lakes and streams teem with trout, grayling, Rocky Mountain whitefish, and pike.

Economy

Until the mid-1900's, when large-scale production of petroleum began, Alberta's economy relied primarily on agriculture and the processing of agricultural products. Today, the production and processing of oil and natural gas and related activities have

Cattle, Oil, and Wheat. Three leading products of Alberta are represented in these photos. The middle picture shows oil sands in the Fort McMurray area.
Travel Alberta

made Alberta a wealthy province. Calgary and Edmonton have experienced economic booms, as centers of manufacturing, commerce, and services. Tourism, especially at Jasper and Banff national parks, is also a large source of income in the province.

Agriculture. Though declining in relative importance, agriculture is still a major activity in Alberta, with grains and livestock dominant. In volume and value hard spring wheat and barley are the chief crops. For many years wheat was the undisputed leader. Other crops, some of which are being grown in increasing amounts, include oats, hay, flax and rape (for their oilseeds), sugar beets, and potatoes. Irrigation is important in several areas, especially along major rivers in the south.

Income from livestock, mainly cattle but also hogs, exceeds income from field crops. Alberta leads all provinces in the production of beef cattle and has a large number of sheep. Dairying is a major activity in several localities, particularly around Edmonton and Calgary.

Except for the Peace River district, north of Grande Prairie, virtually all farming is done on large farms in central and southern Alberta, east of the Rocky Mountains.

Mining. Alberta produces mainly fuels. By value of production, it is Canada's chief mining province. In petroleum, natural gas, and coal production Alberta leads the nation. The petroleum industry began to boom in 1947 with the discovery of a large oil field near Edmonton, and then many others were discovered. Alberta accounts for about 85 percent of Canada's oil production and for even more of its natural gas.

In northern Alberta, particularly around Fort McMurray, are vast deposits of oil sands. Geologists estimate the sands hold a large share of the world's known crude petroleum reserves. Production began in the late 1960's.

Much of Alberta's coal is exported to Japan; the rest is used mainly within the province for generating power. A large amount of sulfur is produced, as a by-product of petroleum refining.

Manufacturing. The principal manufacturing activity is food and beverage processing —principally meat packing, processing of dairy products, flour milling, and brewing. Also important is the processing of oil and gas. Edmonton and Calgary, the major cen-

Interesting Places in Alberta

Banff National Park, west-central Alberta, is Canada's oldest national park, established in 1885. Attractions include a music and drama performance center open in the summer, chairlift tours of the Rocky Mountains, and a swimming pool filled by the park's hot sulfur springs.

Calgary, southwestern Alberta, is the province's largest city and the center of the Canadian oil industry. Calgary's zoo is the second largest in Canada, and Calgary Tower offers a sweeping view of the Rockies. The Calgary Stampede, one of North America's most famous rodeos, is held in August.

Edmonton, central Alberta, is the provincial capital. It features a large number of recreational parks, as well as Canada's Aviation Hall of Fame and the Citadel Theatre for the Performing Arts. The Queen Elizabeth Planetarium in the city offers audiovisual programs on science and astronomy.

Jasper National Park, western Alberta, is noted for its mountain scenery and numerous lakes. It includes a wildlife sanctuary with many different animals.

Lethbridge, southwestern Alberta, is the home of the Nikka Yuko Japanese Gardens, created to celebrate Canada's centennial in 1967, in Henderson Lake Park. The park includes buildings and bridges constructed in Japan, as well as five types of traditional Japanese gardens.

Medicine Hat, southeastern Alberta, features a historical museum with Indian and pioneer exhibits, as well as shops where glassmakers and potters demonstrate their crafts.

Waterton Lakes National Park, southwestern Alberta, forms the Canadian part of Waterton-Glacier International Peace Park. The park features a herd of bison, and there are boat tours through the park's many lakes.

Travel Alberta

Calgary Stampede

See also NATIONAL PARKS, section "Canada." For further tourist information write: Travel Alberta, 10065 Jasper Avenue, Box 2500, Edmonton, Alberta T5E 5V5 Canada.

---

ters, have large oil refineries, petrochemical plants, and metal and machine industries, many of which are related to petroleum. Other sizable industries include the making of cement, wood products, and paper, as well as printing and publishing.

Transportation. Alberta's central and southern prairies and, to a lesser extent, the Peace River district, are well served by rail lines and highways. Two wilderness routes, each with a road and a railway, have been opened northward. One reaches Fort McMurray; the other, Great Slave Lake in the Northwest Territories.

Airplanes are used widely and in many areas provide the only means of access. Large international airports are at Edmonton and Calgary. Edmonton is the hub of an enormous pipeline system that collects petroleum and sends it to distant markets in Canada and the United States.

The People

Alberta's population, according to the 1976 census, was 1,838,037—the largest of the Prairie Provinces. Of the total population, 78 per cent were Canadian-born; the rest came largely from Europe. About half of the population were of English, Scottish, and Irish descent. Other major groups in-

cluded those of German, Scandinavian, Ukrainian, and French-Canadian ancestry. About 2 percent were Indians.

The province's population increased 73 percent between 1951 and 1971, and about 13 per cent from 1971 to 1976. About 75 per cent of the people live in cities and towns, 25 per cent in rural areas.

Alberta's Largest Cities

City	Population	City	Population
Calgary	469,917	Red Deer	32,184
Edmonton, the capital	461,361	St. Albert	24,129
		Grande Prairie	17,626
Lethbridge	46,752	Ft. McMurray	15,424
Medicine Hat	32,811	Camrose	10,104

Religion. The largest religious denominations in Alberta are the United Church of Canada, to which about 30 per cent of the people belong, and the Roman Catholic church, with 20 per cent. Other large groups include Anglicans, Lutherans, Presbyterians, and Baptists.

Education. Schooling in Alberta is free, and attendance is compulsory from age 9 to 15. Elementary and secondary education is provided by public and Roman Catholic (called separate) schools regulated by the provincial Department of Education. In addition, there are schools for Indians maintained by the national government and a number of private schools.

Among the institutions of higher learning in Alberta are the universities of Alberta, Calgary, and Lethbridge. The largest is the University of Alberta, founded at Edmonton in 1906. It is supported by the provincial government and has affiliated colleges in Edmonton and throughout Alberta. In addition, there are institutes of technology and agricultural and vocational colleges. The Banff School of Fine Arts offers courses in the arts, music, and drama.

Government

The head of government is the premier, who is leader of the majority party in the one-house provincial legislature, the Legislative Assembly. He chooses his cabinet from members of the majority party in the assembly. The 75 members of the assembly are elected by the people. They serve five-year terms unless the assembly is dissolved before that time by the lieutenant governor. Then new elections are held.

The lieutenant governor represents the Crown and the federal government, by whom he is appointed for a five-year term. The lieutenant governor acts only on the advice of the provincial Executive Council (the premier and his ministers). He can dissolve the Legislative Assembly on advice of the premier or when the premier fails to receive a vote of confidence. The powers of the legislature are defined in the Constitution Act, 1982, which replaced the British North America Act of 1867.

Alberta has 6 members (appointed by the federal government) in the Senate and 19 elected members of the House of Commons of the national Parliament of Canada. Local government is conducted by cities, towns, villages, counties, and municipal districts (incorporated areas).

History

Early Period. Centuries before Europeans came to explore and settle what is now Alberta, Indians followed the buffalo herds, which provided them with food, clothing, and shelter. Major tribes were the Blackfeet, Blood, and Cree.

Charles II of England granted the region to the Hudson's Bay Company as part of Rupert's Land in 1670, but the first white man did not arrive until almost a century later. In 1754 Anthony Henday, a representative of the company, came to promote the fur trade among the Plains Indians.

The rival North West Company built the first trading post in the area on Lake Athabasca in 1778. In the years that immediately followed, both companies established forts in Rupert's Land and bitterly competed for the furs of the western plains. Alexander Mackenzie and David Thompson explored the area for the North West Company during this period, searching for furs and possible trade routes. In 1821 the Hudson's Bay Company absorbed the North West Company, and for the next 40-odd years it held a monopoly of the fur trade in the British-American northwest.

Canadian Possession. In 1869 Canada purchased Rupert's Land from the Hudson's Bay Company for about $1,500,000. In 1870 this region and the western Indian country became part of the Dominion of Canada as the Northwest Territories. The North West Mounted Police were sent into the Territories in 1874 to bring law and order and suppress the illegal whiskey trade. In 1882 four provisional districts were created in the southern part of the Northwest Territories. One of these districts was Alberta.

The Canadian Pacific Railway arrived in Alberta in 1883. In 1885 there was a brief uprising of the *métis* (persons of mixed French and Indian ancestry) and their Indian allies. A heavy influx of settlers began around the turn of the century; population soared from 73,022 to 374,295 during the period 1901-11.

Province. The rapid population growth led to the organization of Alberta into a province in 1905. Alberta's first legislative assembly met in 1906. The Liberal party govern-

Legislative Building at Edmonton
Alberta Government

ment concerned itself with expanding the new province's agricultural economy and providing social services.

Economic hardships followed World War I, and in 1921 brought the United Farmers of Alberta party to power. A number of economic reform measures were enacted. During the 1920's, agricultural cooperatives were formed. The depression of the 1930's led to the formation of the Social Credit party, which came to power in 1935. Conditions were slowly improving when mobilization for World War II sparked economic recovery and industrial development.

After the war, with much land still undeveloped, immigration and homesteading continued. The finding of oil in 1947 in central Alberta was the first of a series of major oil and natural gas discoveries in the province. In the 1960's and 1970's, plants were built in northeastern Alberta to extract oil from the Athabasca tar sands, one of the world's largest petroleum deposits. In 1980 construction was begun near Calgary on the Alcan pipeline, designed to bring natural gas from Alaska and Canada to the main part of the United States.

For further information, see:

Books about Alberta

MacGregor, J. G. *Alberta: a History* (Hurtig, 1972).
Simpkins, Bill. *Chinook Country: Alberta South* (Oxford University, 1979).
For Younger Readers:
Hocking, Anthony. *Alberta* (McGraw-Hill Ryerson, 1979).

Provincial Archives of Alberta, E. Brown Collection
Mechanized Farming came to Alberta in the 1890's. This steam-driven threshing machine was operated by a team that went from farm to farm.

Alberta, University of. See ALBERTA, subtitle *The People:* Education.

Alberti, äl-bĕr′tĕ, **Leon Battista** (1404-1472), an Italian architect and scholar. As he was also a painter, sculptor, musician, author, mathematician, and lawyer, Alberti exemplifies the Renaissance ideal of the universal man. Alberti's writings greatly influenced early Renaissance art. In *Della pittura* (*On Painting*, about 1435) and *Della statua* (*On Sculpture*, about 1464) he advocates a close study of nature and states his theory of perspective. He is credited with being first to formulate the laws of linear perspective. In *De re aedificatoria* (*On Architecture*, about 1452) he discusses city planning and his belief that all buildings should be functional as well as beautiful.

Alberti's own architectural works, such as the Palazzo Rucellai in Florence, are marked by decorative Classical facades. His church of San Francesco in Rimini is one of the earliest examples of Renaissance Classical style.

Alberti, Rafael (1902-   ), a Spanish poet. His versatility in many forms and themes is expressed in poetry ranging from the ironically subtle to the intimate and spiritual. *Marinero en Tierra* (*Sailor Ashore,* 1925) won the National Prize for Literature. *Sobre los Ángeles* (*Above the Angels,* 1929) is Surrealistic in tone. Alberti was born in Andalusia. He was a Cubist painter in Madrid before turning to verse. After fighting on the losing Loyalist side in the Spanish Civil War, he went into exile in Argentina.

Albertus Magnus, Saint, or Saint **Albert the Great** (about 1200-1280), a German Scholastic philosopher, theologian, and scientist. He was called the universal doctor because of the universality of his knowledge. Albertus wrote commentaries on Aristotle and tried to make Aristotelianism consistent with Christian theology. His pupil Saint Thomas Aquinas systematized Scholasticism. Albertus made scientific observations and wrote on botany and other fields of science. He described the element arsenic, and it is thought he was the first to obtain it in pure form.

Albertus was born in Swabia, southwestern Germany. He was educated in Padua, Italy, where he joined the newly formed Dominican Order. He taught chiefly in Paris and Cologne, Germany. Albertus was named bishop of Ratisbon in 1260 but resigned in 1262. He was beatified in 1622 and was made a doctor of the church and declared a saint in 1931. His feast day is November 15.

Albigenses, ăl′bĭ-jĕn′sēz, a religious sect found around Albi, southern France, in the 12th and 13th centuries. Their beliefs and practices are known only through the writings of their enemies. The Albigenses believed that the forces of good and evil are constantly fighting for control; that the soul is good, the body evil; that material things are evil. There were two classes of Albigenses: the perfect and the believers. The perfect were celibate and practiced other forms of asceticism; the believers could follow most practices of the world.

The sect flourished during the 12th century in spite of the condemnation of the Roman Catholic Church. Local feudal lords protected the Albigenses for political reasons. In 1208 Pope Innocent III ordered a military crusade against the sect. There was a terrible war of extermination until 1229. The Inquisition was then commissioned to crush the last remnants of the sect.

Albino, ăl-bī′no, an animal or plant lacking normal pigmentation. In animals, normal pigmentation is caused by melanin, a brown-black pigment present in their hair, skin, fur, and feathers. An individual lacking either melanin or tryosinase, the enzyme that converts chemicals in the body into melanin, is an albino. The condition is hereditary. Albinism may be complete, or it may affect only certain parts of the body. An extremely white patch of skin is one example of partial albinism; another is a patch of

white hair in an otherwise normally pigmented head of hair.

Some examples of albino animals are white tigers, Himalayan rabbits, and the white elephants of Thailand. Albino mice, rats, and rabbits are often used in laboratory research.

Human albinos can be of any race. An individual with complete albinism has white skin, white hair, and pink or red eyes. (The eye color is caused by lack of pigment in the iris, which makes the blood vessels visible.) Human albinos are usually cross-eyed and nearsighted. Nystagmus, a condition characterized by uncontrolled movements of the eyeballs from side to side, is common. The skin is very sensitive to sunlight and burns easily. Albinos frequently develop such skin disorders as skin cancer and actinic dermatitis, an inflammation or rash caused by exposure to ultraviolet radiation from the sun.

Albino plants have white leaves and stems because of a deficiency of chlorophyll and other leaf pigments. These plants are usually short-lived because without those pigments they cannot produce their food.

Albion, ăl′bĭ-ŭn, an ancient name for the island of Great Britain. It was used by Pliny the Elder in the first century A.D. and by Ptolemy in the second. The name may have come from the Celtic word *alp* (meaning "rock"), or it may have come from the Latin *albus* ("white"), referring to the white chalk cliffs on the Strait of Dover. Since the Renaissance Albion has often been used poetically to mean England.

Albion College. See UNIVERSITIES AND COLLEGES (table).

Albite. See MOONSTONE.

Albright College. See UNIVERSITIES AND COLLEGES (table).

Albumen. See ALBUMIN.

Albumin, ăl-bū′mĭn, a simple protein found in most animals and in some plants. Albumins dissolve in water and dilute salt solutions and coagulate (curdle or clot) in the presence of heat. Egg albumin, which is usually spelled albumen, accounts for more than half of the protein content in egg white.

Albumins are usually named according to where they are found in nature. For example, the albumin found in blood serum is called serum albumin. The blood serum of all vertebrates (animals with backbones) contains albumin. The protein value of meat and milk is partially determined by the albumin content. Albumins are contained in the seeds of certain plants, such as beans, peas, and peanuts. Albumins are also present in grains, in poppy-seed oil, and in the fleshy part of coconuts.

How Albumins Are Used

The white of an egg is sometimes a successful remedy for certain types of poisoning because, in coagulating, the albumin coats the poison and prevents it from taking effect. In some industries, such as dye-making, albumins are used as clarifying agents. As the albumins coagulate, they clarify (remove impurities from) liquids. Concentrated albumin from human blood serum is administered intravenously as a treatment for extreme shock and hemorrhage.

Blood, egg, and milk albumins are widely used in industry. Ox blood albumin, for example, is used in textile printing to hold the colors to the fabric. Egg albumin that has been beaten to a froth is often used in prepared foods to give them body. Milk albumin is used in making adhesives and varnishes.

Egg albumin is also called ovalbumin. Alternate names for milk albumin are lactalbumin and whey albumin. Albumins are compounds of carbon, hydrogen, oxygen, and (usually) sulfur. Ovalbumin contains phosphorus in addition to these elements.

Albuquerque, ăl′bŭ-kûr′kě, **Affonso de** (1453-1515), a Portuguese admiral and statesman, founder of the Portuguese Empire in the East. Albuquerque was appointed viceroy of Portugal's possessions in Asia in 1506. From 1509 to 1515, he served as governor of India, at the same time extending the empire eastward. Albuquerque seized Goa in 1510 and made it the center of Portuguese power and trade in the East. By 1515 his conquests included Hormuz in Persia (now Iran), Malabar in India, and the Sunda Isles, Ceylon (Sri Lanka), and Malacca in Southeast Asia.

Albuquerque, ăl′bŭ-kûr′kě, **New Mexico,** the state's largest city and the seat of Bernalillo County. It is on the Rio Grande, about 55 miles (90 km) southwest of Santa Fe, the state capital. Albuquerque lies in the foothills of the Sandia Mountains and is about 5,000 feet (1,520 m) above sea level.

Albuquerque is a commercial, industrial, financial,and transportation center. Among its industries are the manufacturing of wood products, machinery, electronic equipment, fabricated steel goods, wallboard, and cloth-

New Mexico State Tourist Bureau
Old Town Plaza, Albuquerque. This arcade, a relic of Albuquerque's Spanish period, which began in 1706, houses shops and restaurants.

ing. Since World War II Albuquerque has become a center of nuclear and space research and development. The federal government is one of the city's largest employers. Tourism is also a leading source of income.

Albuquerque is served by railways and Interstate highways. Albuquerque Sunport handles international and domestic air traffic.

The University of New Mexico, built in the Pueblo style of architecture, the University of Albuquerque, and the Southwestern Indian Polytechnic Institute are here. Ernie Pyle Memorial Library is in the former home of the World War II newspaper correspondent. Old Town Plaza, Albuquerque's original townsite, is a tourist attraction with its Spanish-style buildings, especially San Felipe de Neri church (built 1706). Each year the city is host to the New Mexico State Fair. A 2.7-mile (4.3-km) aerial tramway in the Sandia Mountains was opened in 1966.

Sandia Base (a federal nuclear energy installation) and Kirtland Air Force Base are on the city's outskirts. Cibola National Forest and a number of Pueblo Indian villages are nearby.

Albuquerque was founded in 1706 and named after the Duke of Alburquerque, a Spanish viceroy in Mexico City. (The first "r" was dropped.) The settlement was a trading center on the Chihuahua Trail from Mexico City. With the coming of the railway in 1880 a new town, also called Albuquerque, sprang up nearby. It was incorporated in 1890. In 1950 the older town was annexed to the newer.

Population: 332,239.

Alcaeus, ăl-sē′ŭs, a Greek lyric poet who lived during the 6th century B.C. Only fragments—mainly hymns to the gods, drinking songs, love poems, and political commentaries—remain of the 10 books of odes credited to Alcaeus. A lyrical meter called Alcaic is thought to have been invented by him. Alcaeus was born in Mytilene on the island of Lesbos. He was twice exiled for his political views.

Alcatraz, ăl′kȧ-trăz, a rocky island in San Francisco Bay, California, about one mile (1.6 km) offshore north of San Francisco. Because of its strategic location, it was occupied by a fortress during the period of early settlement and also by the first lighthouse on the West Coast. Alcatraz was the site of a maximum-security federal penitentiary, 1934-63. Because of the swift currents in the bay, escape from "The Rock," as it was called, was considered to be impossible. Among well-known prisoners who were confined there were Al Capone and Robert Stroud, the "Birdman of Alcatraz."

In 1969, a group of American Indians seized the island as a protest against loss of tribal lands and discriminatory treatment by the United States government. The occupation lasted for 19 months. The former prison was turned over to the National Park Service and opened in 1973 as a tourist attraction.

Alcalá Zamora, Niceto. See ZAMORA Y TORRES, NICETO ALCALÁ.

Alcestis, ăl-sĕs′tĭs, in Greek legend, the wife of King Admetus of Pherae in Thessaly. Admetus angered a goddess and was condemned to death, but Apollo promised him his life if someone else would die for him. No one, including his parents, would make the sacrifice except Alcestis. Hercules, however, traveled to Hades, rescued Alcestis, and returned her to Admetus. Alcestis has been the heroine of many works. Euripides' play *Alcestis* was first performed in 438 B.C. Since then there have been numerous retellings, including plays by Alfieri and Herder and operas by Handel and Gluck.

Alchemy, ăl′kĕ-mĭ, an ancient experimental science, dealing mainly with metallurgy, that was the forerunner of chemistry. In the Western world, alchemy was established as a branch of science by the Greek scholars of Alexandria, Egypt, in the early Christian Era. In the tradition of the period, which interpreted all knowledge in philosophical terms, alchemy became associated with astrology, the belief that events on earth were controlled by the planets and stars.

The alchemists invented many procedures and types of apparatus used by modern chemists. Egyptian jewelers were already highly skilled in metalworking, using alloys of base metals resembling gold and silver to produce cheap jewelry. This ability to imitate precious metals may have been the inspiration for the idea that base metals, such as iron and lead, could actually be transmuted, or transformed, into gold and silver. Many alchemists of the Middle Ages used deceit to convince customers that they had succeeded in transmuting metals.

For details of alchemical theories, see CHEMISTRY, section "The History of Chemistry," subtitle *Alchemy.*

Alcibiades, ăl′sĭ-bī′ȧ-dēz (450?-404 B.C.), an Athenian general and statesman. His unprincipled leadership helped cause the defeat of Athens in the Peloponnesian War (431-404 B.C.). He was a nephew and ward of Pericles and a favorite student of Socrates. Idolized by the young people of Athens, Alcibiades was brilliant but self-seeking, courageous but unstable in his loyalties.

After the Peace of Nicias brought a truce in the Peloponnesian War in 421, Alcibiades, who was elected one of Athens' 10 generals in 420, schemed to renew the conflict. He was opposed in the Athenian Assembly by Nicias, but succeeded in forming a Peloponnesian alliance against Sparta. Athens provided only ineffectual support, however, and the allied cities were defeated in 418. In 416 Alcibiades persuaded the Assembly to send an expedition against Syracuse, in Sicily, with himself as one of the commanders.

Accused of sacrilegious acts, Alcibiades was summoned home from Sicily for trial. Instead, he took refuge in Sparta, where he helped the Spartans against his native city. When he offended the Spartan king, Alcibiades fled to the Persians, traditional enemies of the Greeks. In 411, however, he was recalled to lead the Athenian army and navy and won several victories over the Spartans. When his navy suffered a defeat at Ephesus in 407, he was again forced to flee. Upon Sparta's final victory, won with Persian support, Alcibiades was assassinated by the Persians.

Alcindor, Lew. See ABDUL-JABBAR, KAREEM.

Alcmaeon, ălk-mē'ŏn, in Greek mythology, leader of the Epigoni, ě-pĭg'ŏ-nī. The Epigoni were seven sons of the Seven against Thebes, heroes who unsuccessfully attacked Thebes. The campaign of the Epigoni, undertaken 30 years later to avenge their fathers, succeeded. Alcmaeon blamed Eriphyle, his mother, for the death of his father, Amphiaraus the seer, in the original expedition. On his return from Thebes, Alcmaeon murdered Eriphyle. The Furies punished him by driving him mad. He made his way to Psophis, where he married Arsinoe, daughter of King Phegeus. He deserted her for Callirrhoe, daughter of a river god. When Alcmaeon returned to retrieve his mother's necklace, which he had given to Arsinoe, Phegeus had him murdered.

Alcoa. See ALUMINUM COMPANY OF AMERICA.

Alcock, Sir **John William** (1892-1919). See AVIATION, table *Flights that Made Aviation History:* 1919.

Alcohol, ăl'kō-hŏl, a chemical compound composed of carbon atoms, hydrogen atoms, and one or more *hydroxyl groups.* (A hydroxyl group consists of two atoms—one of hydrogen and one of oxygen—that act as one.) The term "alcohol" is commonly used to designate the specific alcohol (*ethyl alcohol*) that makes fermented and distilled liquors intoxicating. Ethyl alcohol is also known as *ethanol* and *grain alcohol.* When taken in excess, ethyl alcohol can become habit-forming. Damage to the brain, liver, kidneys, and other organs can result. (See ALCOHOLIC BEVERAGE; ALCOHOLISM.)

In chemistry, the term "alcohol" is applied to a large class of substances closely related to hydrocarbons. (Hydrocarbons are compounds composed of hydrogen and carbon.) There are thousands of alcohols, but only a few dozen are commercially important.

How Alcohols Are Named

There are two common systems for naming alcohols, both based on the name of the hydrocarbon to which the alcohol is most closely related. (This is the hydrocarbon having the same number and arrangement of carbon atoms as the alcohol.) In the first system, the ending of the hydrocarbon name, -*ane*, is replaced by -*yl* and followed by the word *alcohol.* For example, the alcohol most closely related to the hydrocarbon *ethane* is called *ethyl alcohol.* In the second system, the ending -*e* of the hydrocarbon name is replaced by -*ol.* In this system, the alcohol most closely related to ethane is called *ethanol.*

Some alcohols are named after the material from which the alcohol was originally isolated, such as *cinnamic* (or *cinnamyl*) alcohol, obtained from cinnamon oil.

Properties of Alcohols

The *lower* alcohols (those with molecules made up of a small number of atoms) are colorless, easily flowing liquids that will dissolve in water. Among them are ethyl alcohol, methyl alcohol (wood alcohol), and isopropyl alcohol (commonly used as rubbing alcohol). Methyl alcohol is poisonous; if taken internally it may cause blindness, coma, or even death. It can be dangerous even when inhaled as a vapor. Isopropyl alcohol is not as dangerous as methyl alcohol, but can cause severe gastric disturbances if taken as a drink.

As the size of the molecule increases, alcohols become more viscous (flow less readily) and less soluble in water. Alcohols with relatively large molecules are known as *higher* alcohols. Most of the higher alcohols with 12 or more carbon atoms per molecule are waxlike solids that will dissolve in ethyl alcohol but not in water.

How Alcohols Are Produced

Most lower alcohols are synthetic (manmade) products formed from hydrocarbons derived from petroleum, natural gas, and coal. Many higher alcohols are obtained by chemical treatment of acids that occur in natural fats and oils. For example, stearic acid (found in animal fats and vegetable oils) and lauric acid (found in vegetable oils) yield stearyl and lauryl alcohols. Some higher alcohols are derived from organic compounds called *aldehydes* and *ketones.* (See ALDEHYDE; KETONE.) A few higher alcohols occur in nature in the form of organic compounds known as *esters.* (See ESTER.)

Ethyl Alcohol, or Ethanol. The ethyl alcohol in beverages, as explained in the article ALCOHOLIC BEVERAGE, is made by fermentation. Ethyl alcohol for industrial (nonbeverage) use was formerly made by the fermentation of blackstrap molasses. It is now produced chiefly by synthetic processes, usually from the hydrocarbon *ethylene,* which is obtained from gases formed during the refining of petroleum. (See ETHYLENE.)

By use of an activating substance called a *catalyst,* a molecule of water is made to combine with a molecule of ethylene to produce a molecule of ethyl alcohol.

In an alternate method that is widely used, ethylene is treated with concentrated sulfuric acid. This produces a mixture of ethyl sulfate and ethyl hydrogen sulfate. Addition of water to this mixture yields ethyl alcohol and dilute sulfuric acid. The ethyl alcohol is then removed by distillation.

Methyl Alcohol, or Methanol. Methyl alcohol is often termed *wood alcohol* because most of it was formerly obtained by the destructive distillation of hardwood, such as beech, birch, hickory, maple, or oak. Some methyl alcohol is still obtained from wood, but since the 1920's most of it had been made synthetically from carbon monoxide and hydrogen. The chemical reaction necessary for this synthesis takes place under high pressure in the presence of a catalyst.

Denatured Alcohol

As an industrial solvent that can dissolve other substances, ethyl alcohol is second in importance only to water. Ethyl alcohol has many other industrial uses, but the high tax imposed on it often makes it impractical to use. To avoid this tax, ethyl alcohol is often made into *denatured* alcohol, a form of alcohol that is unfit for drinking.

Denatured alcohol is made by adding methyl alcohol, tert-butyl alcohol, or other chemicals to ethyl alcohol. Denatured alcohol is not a satisfactory substitute for ethyl alcohol for all industrial purposes. Some processes—the manufacture of munitions, for example—require the pure form.

Uses of Alcohols

Lower Alcohols. The importance of ethyl, methyl, isopropyl, and other lower alcohols as solvents lies in the fact that they will dissolve many substances that are not chemically affected by water, such as fats, oils, resins, enamels, and lacquers. Some lower alcohols are used as *reagents.* (A reagent is a substance that, because of its ability to undergo certain chemical reactions, is used in examining, detecting, or measuring other substances.) Many lower alcohols are used to make higher alcohols or other chemicals.

Methyl alcohol is used chiefly in the manufacture of formaldehyde and other organic chemicals. Isopropyl alcohol is used mainly for the manufacture of acetone, but is widely used as a rubbing alcohol. Ethyl alcohol is

A-270

combined with nitrated cellulose to form explosives used to fire bullets and artillery shells. Widely used in manufacturing, ethyl alcohol is important in the production of many organic chemicals and in the making of drugs, cosmetics, and dyes. Ethyl alcohol is also used as a fuel, primarily with gasoline in a mixture called gasohol. (See GASOHOL.)

Many drugs are dissolved in lower alcohols to form solutions known as *tinctures*. Tincture of iodine, an antiseptic, is an example. Lower alcohols are used as ingredients of printing inks, dyes, and brake fluids. They are also used in cleaning and polishing compounds and to preserve biological specimens. Because of their low freezing points, lower alcohols are used in thermometers, as well as in permanent and nonpermanent antifreeze mixtures for automobile and airplane engines. The chief use of ethylene glycol is in permanent antifreezes. It is chemically stable and noncorrosive. (See ANTIFREEZE.)

Higher Alcohols. Some higher alcohols are ingredients of detergents, soaps, and lubricants. Others are used in cosmetics and ointments because of the smooth, soothing effect they produce. One such alcohol is cetyl alcohol, derived from natural fats and oils. Some higher alcohols, particularly those derived from plant oils, are used in perfumes because of their pleasant scents. Geraniol, the alcohol obtained from geranium oil, imparts a geraniumlike odor to perfume.

Alcohols in Chemistry

In chemistry, an alcohol is regarded as a compound formed when one or more hydrogen atoms of a hydrocarbon are replaced by the same number of hydroxyl, or OH, groups.

Alcohols are classified according to the number of hydroxyl groups present in their molecules. Ethyl alcohol, C_2H_5OH or CH_3CH_2OH, which has only one hydroxyl group, is *monohydric*. Methyl alcohol, CH_3OH, the simplest of the alcohols, and isopropyl alcohol, C_3H_7OH, are also monohydric. Ethylene glycol, $C_2H_4(OH)_2$, and propylene glycol, $C_3H_5(OH)_2$, each have two hydroxyl groups, and are *dihydric* alcohols. Glycerol or glycerin, $C_3H_5(OH)_3$, is *trihydric*. Alcohols with two or more hydroxyl groups are also known as *polyhydric* alcohols.

Alcohols are also classified according to the arrangement of the hydroxyl groups in relation to the carbon atoms. A *primary* alcohol is one in which the hydroxyl group is attached to a carbon atom linked to one other carbon atom. A *secondary* alcohol is one in which the hydroxyl group is attached to a carbon atom linked to two other carbon atoms. An alcohol is *tertiary* if the hydroxyl group is attached to a carbon atom linked to three other carbon atoms.

See also FUSEL OIL; GLYCERIN.

Alcoholic Beverage, a drink containing ethyl alcohol. Ethyl alcohol is a *depressant,* a drug that inhibits the activity of the central nervous system and brain. In moderate amounts, it produces a pleasant, relaxing sensation. However, it can dull the senses and impair coordination, thought, judgment, and perception. Excessive amounts of alcohol in the body cause intoxication. The consumption of large amounts over a period of time can lead to alcoholism. (See INTOXICATION; ALCOHOLISM.)

Ethyl alcohol is made by *fermentation,* a process in which sugars and starches in grains (such as rye, barley, corn, and rice), fruits (such as grapes, blackberries, and peaches), potatoes, and certain other plants are converted into ethyl alcohol and carbon dioxide. (See FERMENTATION.) Some alcoholic beverages, such as beer, certain wines, and hard cider, retain the carbon dioxide, which produces their effervescence (fizz). The strongest alcoholic solution made by fermentation contains about 14 per cent ethyl alcohol by volume; when the alcohol content reaches that level, it kills the yeasts, stopping fermentation. To make *spirits—* brandy, whiskey, or other liquors that contain large amounts of ethyl alcohol—the fermented alcoholic solution is distilled. Distillation purifies and concentrates the solution. (See DISTILLATION; DISTILLING.)

The alcoholic strength of a distilled beverage is stated in terms of *proof.* In the United States, a mixture containing 50 per cent ethyl alcohol by volume is defined as having a strength of 100 proof; pure ethyl alcohol, then, would be 200 proof. Most whiskeys are 40 to 55 per cent ethyl alcohol, and thus range from 80 to 110 proof.

Alcohol in the Body

Alcohol is absorbed into the bloodstream through the walls of the stomach and small intestine. It then circulates throughout the body. Five to 10 per cent of the alcohol is eliminated from the body in urine, perspiration, and exhaled air; the rest is metabolized, or chemically broken down, in the liver, where it is converted into acetate. About 15 per cent of the acetate is used by the body to form proteins, carbohydrates, and fats; the rest is used as a source of energy and is later expelled as water and carbon dioxide. The rate of alcohol metabolism is affected by such factors as body weight, age, sex, and the presence of drugs in the body and food in the stomach. When the rate of consumption exceeds the rate of metabolism and elimination, a person begins to become intoxicated.

Alcohol is a concentrated source of calories—one-half ounce (15 ml) furnishes the body with about 100 calories. It is a poor source of nutrition and contains virtually no vitamins, trace minerals, or essential proteins. It tends to depress the appetite by inhibiting the secretion of gastric juices in the stomach. Alcohol depletes the body of B vitamins, such as niacin (B_3) and thiamin (B_1), by interfering with their absorption.

In the kidneys, alcohol acts as a diuretic, a substance that increases the production of urine. Alcohol stimulates the pancreas to produce excessive amounts of insulin, which can sometimes cause hypoglycemia, or low blood sugar.

Alcohol interacts with drugs, producing undesirable effects. Some combinations, such as alcohol and barbiturates, can be fatal. Physicians recommend that drugs should never be taken with alcohol or while there is alcohol in the body.

The consumption of alcohol can produce an aftereffect called a *hangover.* Symptoms include headache, dizziness, nausea, vomiting, extreme thirst, fatigue, and irritability. It is believed to be caused by congeners, chemicals in the alcohol that linger in the body.

See also ABSINTHE; ALE; BEER; BRANDY; CHAMPAGNE; COGNAC; GIN; PULQUE; RUM; SAKE; TEQUILA; VODKA; WHISKEY; WINE.

Alcoholics Anonymous (AA), a fellowship of men and women who share their experience, strength, and hope with each other that they may solve their common problem and help others to recover from alcoholism. The primary purpose of AA members is to stay sober and help other alcoholics to achieve sobriety.

The basic unit in AA is the local group, which may serve the whole community or only a neighborhood. At meetings members freely discuss their experiences and problems. Any member who feels that he needs help at other times may call on fellow members for support. Many persons in the medical and allied professions believe AA provides the best lasting help for the alcoholic.

The movement was started in Akron, Ohio, in 1935 by two men who were alcoholics. There are an estimated 1,000,000 members in about 40,000 local groups in the

United States, Canada, and more than 90 other countries. General headquarters are in New York City.

Al-Anon is an organization of friends and relatives of alcoholics. Its purpose is to provide mutual support for people who must face the problems of dealing with an alcoholic. It is not directly connected with AA. Al-Anon was founded in 1951. There are an estimated 450,000 members in about 16,500 local groups. Headquarters are in New York City.

Alateen is a subgroup of Al-Anon for 12-to-20-year-olds whose lives are affected by the alcoholism of a friend or family member.

Alcoholism, ăl′kŏ-hŏl-ĭz′m, compulsive habitual excessive use of alcoholic drinks. It is not the same as *drunkenness,* which may be habitual but is not compulsive. Thus an *alcoholic* is a person who is unable to control his use of alcohol. Alcoholism becomes a chronic condition; it should not be confused with acute alcoholic poisoning, which is the sudden poisoning of the body by alcohol.

Alcoholism is a serious public health problem. It afflicts millions of people, including adults and teen-agers from all types of social groups. Why people become alcoholics is not clearly understood; alcoholism can stem from emotional immaturity, insecurity, nervous tension, loneliness, or depression. Physiological causes of alcoholism, if any, have not been determined. Physicians generally consider alcoholism an addiction.

Tolerance and Withdrawal

One result of continued, excessive drinking is the development of *tolerance.* The cells of the nervous system become more tolerant of alcohol, and larger quantities must be consumed to produce intoxication. (See INTOXICATION.) When consumption is discontinued, a severe physical reaction, called *alcohol withdrawal syndrome,* may occur. Twelve to 48 hours after the last drink, the person may experience nausea, vomiting, profuse sweating, tremors, insomnia, and hallucinations. Forty-eight to 96 hours later, the person may experience delirium tremens, a disorder of the nervous system. (See DELIRIUM TREMENS.)

Effects of Chronic Drinking

Chronic drinking affects many organs and systems of the body. It irritates the lining of the stomach and pancreas, causing inflammation, tenderness, and ulcerlike lesions. Heavy consumption of alcohol inhibits the absorption of proteins, nutrients, and vitamins from the small intestine. This can cause chronic malnutrition. If untreated, it can lead to anemia, scurvy, and vitamin-

A-272

deficiency diseases such as beriberi and pellagra. A chronic deficiency of thiamin (vitamin B_1) can result in *Wernicke's encephalopathy,* a degenerative neurological disorder. Symptoms include mental confusion, impaired muscular coordination, and uncontrolled eye movement. If untreated, it can lead to brain damage. Treatment includes large doses of thiamin and other B-complex vitamins. Those who recover from Wernicke's encephalopathy are prone to *Korsakoff's psychosis,* a form of amnesia in which there is severe impairment of short-term memory.

Chronic drinking disrupts the endocrine system. In men, it increases the production of estrogen, a female hormone, while decreasing the production of testosterone, a male hormone. Some alcoholic men develop secondary female sexual traits. In women, it suppresses the menstrual cycle, often inhibiting ovulation.

Long-term drinking produces a toxic effect on the *myocardium,* or heart muscle. It often results in *cardiomyopathy,* or congestive heart failure.

The main organ damaged by chronic drinking is the liver. Damage is progressive and occurs in three stages.

1. The alcoholic develops a condition called *fatty liver.* It is characterized by the accumulation of globules of fat in the liver cells. The cells tend to retain sodium and water.

2. The second stage is characterized by the development of *alcoholic hepatitis,* an inflammation of the liver. The liver becomes enlarged and tender. Many of the liver cells die and are replaced by scar tissue.

3. The final stage is characterized by the development of *alcoholic liver cirrhosis,* a chronic degenerative disease in which there is an accumulation of scar tissue in the liver. The scar tissue blocks the flow of blood into and out of the liver. This can cause hypertension, hemorrhages in the gastrointestinal tract, kidney failure, and, eventually, coma.

Alcohol can cross the placenta and harm a developing fetus. Pregnant women are advised to abstain from alcohol during their entire pregnancy. Babies of alcoholic women are often born with a disorder called *fetal alcohol syndrome.* (See also PREGNANCY, subtitle *Prenatal and Childbirth Care:* Complications During Pregnancy.)

Treatment

The goal of most treatment programs for alcoholism is to break the dependency on alcohol. Almost all clinics and hospitals advocate total abstinence; some allow alcoholics to return to moderate, but controlled, drinking.

Alcoholism is treated as a psychological and physical disease. Therapy includes individual and group counseling, recreational and occupational therapy, psychotherapy, and drug therapy. Tranquilizers and sedatives, such as chlordiazepoxide and diazepam, respectively, are prescribed to treat anxiety, tension, nausea, insomnia, and depression that often occur during treatment. Deterrent drugs, such as Antabuse (disulfiram), are often given to induce a violent reaction. The consumption of alcohol within 12 hours after taking one of these drugs produces such unpleasant side effects as headache, vomiting, heart palpitations, double vision, and labored breathing.

Treatment centers include inpatient wards at hospitals, outpatient clinics at hospitals, community health centers, and facilities maintained by religious organizations. Alcoholics Anonymous has helped many people.

See also ALCOHOLICS ANONYMOUS.

Books about Alcoholism

Goodwin, D. W. *Alcoholism: the Facts* (Oxford University, 1981).
Kinney, Jean, and Gwen Leaton. *Loosening the Grip: a Handbook of Alcohol Information,* 2nd edition (Mosby, 1982).
Milt, Harry. *Alcoholism: Its Causes and Cure* (Scribner's, 1976).
Vaillant, G. E. *The Natural History of Alcoholism* (Harvard University, 1983).
For Younger Readers:
Claypool, Jane. *Alcohol and You* (Watts, 1981).
Hyde, M. O. *Know About Alcohol* (McGraw-Hill, 1978).

Alcorn State University. See UNIVERSITIES AND COLLEGES (table).

Alcott, ôl′kŭt, (Amos) **Bronson** (1799-1888), a United States philosopher and educator. Alcott was a leader of the Transcendentalist movement and influenced the direction of philosophic thought and educational reform in the 19th century. (See TRANSCENDENTALISM.)

Alcott was born near Wolcott, Connecticut. After a few years as a peddler and then a schoolteacher, he opened an experimental school in Boston in 1834. He taught by the conversational method, stressing self-expression for the children. Alcott also introduced gymnastics, organized play, and a children's library. His revolutionary views proved unpopular at the time, and the school closed in 1839.

In 1840 Alcott moved to Concord, Massa-chusetts, where he spent much of his time discussing philosophy with Emerson, Thoreau, and other Transcendentalists. In 1844 he founded a cooperative vegetarian community called Fruitlands; it lasted only a few months. On occasion, Alcott went on lecture tours. The family, often near poverty, was supported mainly by his wife and later by his daughter Louisa May Alcott.

Alcott was appointed superintendent of Concord schools in 1859. In 1879, with William T. Harris, he established the Concord School of Philosophy and Literature, which became a center for his mystical form of Transcendentalism. Alcott wrote few books, but kept extensive journals.

Chicago Public Library
Bronson Alcott
Chicago Historical Society
Louisa May Alcott

Alcott, Louisa May (1832-1888), a United States author. Recollections of her childhood and youth and of her three sisters gave her material for *Little Women* (2 volumes, 1868-69). It is a cheerful, wholesome account of the daily life of the March family in New England during the Civil War. The story of Meg, Jo, Beth, and Amy is considered to be one of the earliest realistic novels for older children. It retains an old-fashioned charm, despite its quaint language and constant moralizing.

Louisa May Alcott was born in Germantown (now part of Philadelphia), Pennsylvania, where Bronson Alcott, her father, conducted a school. The family soon moved to Concord, Massachusetts.

To help support the family, young Louisa May worked as a housekeeper, seamstress, and teacher before her writing brought in enough to enable the Alcotts to live comfortably. At one time her ambition was to be an actress, and she wrote several melodramas that were never produced. She had more luck with short stories and poems, selling a number to the *Atlantic Monthly*.

Flower Fables (1854), Louisa May Alcott's

first book, was a collection of fairy tales. Written when she was 16, it was not published until six years later. While an untrained nurse in a Washington, D.C., hospital for Union soldiers of the Civil War, she wrote letters for the patients. These were gathered in *Hospital Sketches* (1863). The book made her nationally known, but brought little money because she had sold all rights for $200. A fairly large sale for *Moods* (1864), a novel, enabled her to travel in Europe for her health. With the publication of *Little Women,* a prosperous period began.

In 1870-71 she was again in Europe. Back in Boston, she became an ardent crusader for temperance, woman suffrage, and other reforms.

Among her other books are *An Old-Fashioned Girl* (1870); *Little Men* (1871); *Eight Cousins* (1874); *Rose in Bloom* (1876); *Jack and Jill* (1880); *Jo's Boys* (1886). *Behind the Mask: The Unknown Thrillers of Louisa May Alcott* (1975) and *Plots and Counterplots: More Unknown Thrillers of Louisa May Alcott* (1976) contain short stories originally published under pseudonyms in various periodicals.

Alcuin, ăl′kwĭn (735-804), an English theologian, philosopher, and scholar. As adviser to the Frankish king Charlemagne on educational, cultural, and church affairs, he helped to bring about a revival of learning in Europe. Alcuin was born near York, England. He studied and taught at the cathedral school there, becoming master of the school in 778. In 782 he went to Charlemagne's court to establish a palace school for the royal family.

In 796 Alcuin was made abbot of St. Martin's Abbey at Tours, France. Under his direction, the abbey became the leading institution of learning in the early Middle Ages. Alcuin wrote treatises on grammar, rhetoric, history, theology, and a number of other subjects. His more than 300 surviving letters are a valuable source of information about life in the eighth century.

Alda, Frances (1883-1952), a United States operatic and concert soprano known for her rich, lyric voice. She was at her best in the title roles in *Manon* and *Louise* and as Gilda in *Rigoletto.* She was born in Christchurch, New Zealand. She studied in Paris and made her debut there in 1904. In 1908 she sang opposite Caruso in *Rigoletto* in her Metropolitan Opera debut. After retiring from opera in 1929, she gave concerts and taught voice. She became a United States citizen in 1939.

Aldan River, ŭl-dȧn′, a river in the Soviet Union, 1,390 miles (2,237 km) long. From its source in the Stanovoi Range some 200 miles (320 km) north of the China border, it flows in a broad curve northward through eastern Siberia. North of Yakutsk, the Aldan empties into the Lena River, which continues to the Laptev Sea, an arm of the Arctic Ocean.

Aldanov, ŭl-dȧ′nôf, **Mark,** the pen name of Mark Aleksandrovich Landau, lŭn-dou′ (1886-1957), a Russian novelist. *The Thinker,* a tetralogy about the French Revolution and the Napoleonic era, consists of *The Ninth Thermidor* (1923), *The Devil's Bridge* (1925), *The Conspiracy* (1927), and *St. Helena: Little Island* (1921). *The Fifth Seal* (1939) deals with the Spanish Civil War. Aldanov was born in Kiev. He emigrated to Paris in 1919, and in 1941 came to the United States.

Aldebaran. See TAURUS.

Aldehyde, ăl′dĕ-hīd, any chemical compound that contains an *aldehyde group* (one carbon atom, one hydrogen atom, and one oxygen atom). Aldehydes are highly reactive chemically. At room temperature, most are colorless or pale-colored liquids with noticeable odors. One of the most familiar aldehydes, *formaldehyde,* is a gas, rather than a liquid, at room temperature. Many carbohydrates that occur in natural products are aldehydes. Glucose, for example, is an aldehyde found in fruit juices and honey. (See CARBOHYDRATES.)

Aldehydes are important industrial compounds. They are used in intermediate steps in the production of paints, plastics, synthetic resins, and dyes. They are also used in the manufacture of perfumes, solvents, and flavorings.

Most of the industrially important aldehydes are produced by synthetic processes. Aldehydes can also be produced by the partial oxidation of various kinds of alcohol. (The name "aldehyde" is formed from "*alco*hol *dehyd*rogenated," which means alcohol with hydrogen removed.) With further oxidation, each aldehyde yields an acid, for which it is named. Some important industrial aldehydes, and the acids they yield, are:

Acetaldehyde—acetic acid
Benzaldehyde—benzoic acid
Formaldehyde—formic acid
Furfural (furfuraldehyde)—furoic acid
Vanillin (vanillaldehyde)—vanillic acid

The chemical symbol for the aldehyde group is

CHO. Formaldehyde, the simplest of the aldehydes, is HCHO.

See also FORMALDEHYDE; FURFURAL; VANILLA.

Alden, John (1599?-1687), one of the Pilgrims who founded Plymouth Colony. He was a cooper (maker of barrels) from Southampton, England, and came to America on the *Mayflower* in 1620. He was a signer of the Mayflower Compact. In 1623 he married Priscilla Mullens. (The poet Longfellow's account of Myles Standish as Alden's rival for Priscilla's hand is not factual.)

In 1627 Alden received a grant of land at Duxbury. By 1632 he had settled there near his friend Standish. Alden held a number of public offices, including governor's assistant in Plymouth Colony (1633-41, 1650-86), deputy from Duxbury (1641-49), and deputy governor (1664-65, 1677).

Alder, Kurt. See NOBEL PRIZES (Chemistry, 1950).

Alder, ôl'dẽr, a tree or shrub belonging to the genus *Alnus*. There are about 30 species. Alders are related to the birches and are found primarily in the Northern Hemisphere. They range in height from 4 to 100 feet (1.2 to 30 m). Six of the nine species native to North America are trees.

The majority of alders grow best in moist soils and are planted primarily for ornamental purposes. Most alders have oval leaves, about six inches (15 cm) long, with toothed edges. The leaves are shed annually without changing color. The female catkins (elongated flower clusters), which resemble those of the willow, develop into woody cones that contain the seeds. The cones are about one-half to one inch (1.3 to 2.5 cm) long. Alders can be raised from seeds or propagated from wood cuttings.

In the United States, the most important alder is the red alder, which grows along the Pacific coast from southeastern Alaska to southern California. The red alder is often mistaken for a birch because, like the birch, it has smooth, light gray or white bark. The red alder is a major source of hardwood on the Pacific coast.

The red alder is *Alnus rubra*. Alders belong to the family Betulaceae.

Alderman, ôl'dẽr-mǎn, a member of a city council. The word is from the Anglo-Saxon for "older man," and was originally applied to men of high distinction. In the United States, city councils formerly had two houses, a board of aldermen and a common council. By 1900 the one-chamber council had become almost universal, and the terms *alderman* and *councilman* are now used interchangeably. The official name, however, is usually councilman.

Alderney. See CHANNEL ISLANDS.

Alderson-Broaddus College. See UNIVERSITIES AND COLLEGES (table).

Aldine. See ALDUS MANUTIUS.

Aldington, ôl'dǐng-tǔn, **Richard** (1892-1962), an English author. He was a prominent Imagist poet, and for a while edited the Imagist magazine *The Egoist*. From 1913 to 1937 he was married to the United States Imagist poet Hilda Doolittle (H.D.). Much of his best verse is found in *Collected Poems* (1928). *Death of a Hero* (1929) is a novel reflecting his World War I military service. He wrote a biography of the Duke of Wellington (1946), *D. H. Lawrence: Portrait of a Genius, But . . .* (1950), and *Lawrence of Arabia* (1955). *Life for Life's Sake* (1941) is autobiographical.

Aldington was born in Hampshire and attended the University of London. After traveling widely, he settled in the United States in 1939.

Aldrich, Nelson Wilmarth (1841-1915), a United States legislator and financial expert. From 1881 to 1911, Aldrich was one of the most influential Republicans in the U.S. Senate and the dominant figure in Rhode Island politics. He sponsored the Gold Standard Act of 1900, Aldrich-Vreeland Currency Act (1908), and Payne-Aldrich Tariff Act (1909). His "Aldrich Plan" for banking reform was the basis for the Federal Reserve Act (1913).

Aldrich was born in Foster, Rhode Island. After making a fortune in banking, manufacturing, and utilities, he entered politics in 1869. He served in the Rhode Island legislature, 1875-77, and the U.S. House of Representatives, 1879-81. In the Senate he led the opposition to President Theodore Roosevelt's progressive policies.

Aldrich's daughter Abby was the mother of Nelson Rockefeller and his five brothers.

Aldrich, Thomas Bailey (1836-1907), a United States author and editor. *The Story of a Bad Boy* (1870), his most popular novel, is semiautobiographical. Aldrich is also noted for a collection of verse, *The Bells* (1855), and a collection of short stories, *Marjorie Daw and Other People* (1873).

Aldrich was born in Portsmouth, New Hampshire. He was a contributor to magazines and served as a war correspondent during the Civil War. He was editor of the *Atlantic Monthly,* 1881-1890, after which he retired to write.

Aldrin, Edwin E., Jr. (1930-   ), a United States astronaut. He was the second human being, after Neil Armstrong, to set foot on the moon. As members of the *Apollo 11* crew, he and Armstrong landed on the lunar surface on July 20, 1969. Aldrin had previously participated in the *Gemini 12* mission in 1966. He wrote *Return to Earth* (1973) about his experiences. Aldrin was born in Glen Ridge, New Jersey. He graduated from the U.S. Military Academy in 1951 and became an Air Force fighter pilot, serving in Korea. He received a graduate degree in astronautics from Massachusetts Institute of Technology in 1963. Aldrin retired from the Air Force as a colonel in 1972 and entered private business.

See also SPACE EXPLORATION (color picture).

Aldus Manutius, ôl'dŭs mȧ-nū'shĭ-ŭs, the Latin name of Aldo (or Teobaldo) Mannucci, män-nōōt'chĕ (1450-1515), an Italian printer and classical scholar. About 1495 he founded the Aldine Press in Venice. It produced small, inexpensive books, mostly Greek and Roman classics, that were distinguished for their typography and scholarly accuracy. The best-known Aldine edition is a five-volume set of the works of Aristotle (1498). Manutius designed italic type, which at first was called Aldine type, for an edition of Virgil (1501). After his death, the Aldine Press was managed by family members until 1597.

Ale, a fermented malt beverage flavored with hops. It is quite similar to beer, but often has a slightly higher alcoholic content and a more bitter taste. The chief difference between ale and beer is that ale is fermented at room temperature for short periods, and beer is fermented at low temperatures for long periods. Also, most ale is made with yeast that rises to the surface of the brew, while the yeast used in most beer production settles out during fermentation. Early English ales were made without hops and with more sugar than beers.

See also BEER.

Aleatory Music, ā'lĕ-ȧ-tō'rĭ, or **Chance Music,** a term used to describe music that

A-276

depends on the element of chance. It is based on the random selection and organization of musical materials, either in the process of composition or during the performance. The name comes from the Latin *alea,* meaning dice.

When composing aleatory music, a composer may flip coins, throw dice, or use other chance methods to generate patterns that can be translated into musical terms. The numbers on dice, for example, may represent pitch, duration, intensity, or some other component of music. The element of chance can also be introduced during the performance of a musical piece. The performer may be given the freedom to choose the tempo, to improvise designated sections, or to play the movements in any sequence. Aleatory music first became popular with avant-garde composers in the early 1950's. Leading composers include John Cage, Karlheinz Stockhausen, Pierre Boulez, and Luciano Berio.

Aleichem, à-lā'кĕm, **Shalom** (also **Sholom** and **Sholem**), the pen name of Solomon Rabinowitz, rä'bĭ-nô'vĭts (1859-1916), a Russian-Jewish author. (The Hebrew phrase *shalom aleichem* is a form of greeting—"peace be unto you.") In 40 volumes of short stories, novels, and plays Shalom Aleichem portrayed the Jews of the eastern European small towns of his day with a sharp but sympathetic eye and a keen sense of humor. He is best known through the musical *Fiddler on the Roof* (1964), based on a number of his tales woven around Tevye the dairyman and his family. These tales were also the basis for the play *The World of Sholom Aleichem* (1953).

Shalom Aleichem left Russia in 1905 to escape the pogroms, the periodic massacres of Jews. He settled in New York City in 1914.

The Best of Sholom Aleichem, a collection of 22 of his tales, was published in 1979.

Aleixandre, Vicente. See NOBEL PRIZES (Literature, 1977).

Alekseyev, Konstantin Sergeyevich. See STANISLAVSKY, KONSTANTIN.

Alemán Valdés, ä'lå-män' väl-däs', **Miguel** (1902-1983), a Mexican statesman. Alemán was president of Mexico from 1946 to 1952. His administration took measures to promote the economic development of Mexico.

Alemán was born in Sayula, Veracruz. He

received a law degree from the National University of Mexico in 1928 and practiced law as a labor attorney. In 1930 Alemán was appointed justice of the superior court of appeals. He was elected to the Mexican Senate later that year, serving until 1936. As governor of Veracruz, 1936-40, Alemán supported education and labor reforms. From 1940 to 1945, he was minister of government in the cabinet of President Manuel Ávila Camacho.

Alembert, Jean Le Rond d', d'á′län′-bâr′ (1717-1783), a French mathematician and philosopher. In *Treatise on Dynamics* (1743), he developed a principle of mechanics that is known as D'Alembert's principle. He also did work on gravitational theory. D'Alembert aided in the preparation of Diderot's *Encyclopédie,* writing the introduction and many biographies and mathematical articles. His other writings include *Studies of Integral Calculus* (1746-48) and works on literature, philosophy, and music.

Aleppo, á-lĕp′ō (*Arabic:* **Halab,** hă′lăb), Syria, the nation's second largest city. It is about 190 miles (306 km) north-northeast of Damascus. Aleppo is an ancient city dating from Biblical times. It was the capital of a Hittite kingdom before 1000 B.C. and was long a principal stop on the main caravan route between Persia and the Mediterranean Sea. Modern Aleppo is one of Syria's leading commercial and industrial centers, producing mainly processed foods, textiles, and clothing. The most imposing of the city's many historic structures is the Citadel, a 12th-century Moslem fortress built on the ruins of earlier Byzantine fortifications. Aleppo has a university and an archeological museum.

Population: 878,000.

Alessandri Palma, ä′lä-sän′drē päl′mä, **Arturo** (1868-1950), a Chilean statesman and president. His election marked the beginning of Chile's modern democratic revolution. From 1920 to 1924, during his first term, Alessandri proposed economic, social, and political reforms, including a new constitution adopted in 1925. During his second administration, 1932-38, he worked for stability in government and economy.

Aleutian Islands, á-lū′shăn, a chain of about 90 islands making up a district of Alaska. The Aleutians extend generally west-southwestward for about 1,100 miles (1,800 km) from the tip of the Alaska Penin-

sula. The islands, with a total area of 6,821 square miles (17,666 km²), lie between the Bering Sea on the north and the Pacific Ocean on the south. From the Alaska Peninsula west there are four main groups—the Fox, Andreanof, Rat, and Near islands. Unimak, in the Fox group, is the largest island. It is about 65 miles (105 km) long and up to 33 miles (53 km) wide.

The rocky and often rugged islands are the crests of the partially submerged Aleutian Range, an extension of the Alaska Range. There are nearly 50 active volcanoes on the Aleutians and numerous inactive cones. The highest peak, reaching 9,373 feet (2,857 m), is Shishaldin Volcano, on Unimak Island. The islands are bleak and dreary, with almost constant fog and clouded skies. They are mostly treeless and covered with grass and bushes. The climate is cool and damp; temperatures average slightly below freezing for January and nearly 50° F. (10° C.) for August. Precipitation averages above 30 inches (760 mm) a year.

Shishaldin Volcano, on Unimak Island in the Aleutians, rises above clouds hiding the island's surface.
Alaska Travel Division

The inhabitants of the Aleutian Islands are predominantly the native Aleuts. (See ALEUTS.) The population in 1980 was 7,768. The largest cities are Unalaska (population, 1,322), Sand Point (625), St. Paul (551), and King Cove (460).

The Aleutian Islands were inhabited as early as 4,000 years ago by descendants of Old Stone Age migrants from Asia. Through the centuries, these people have remained in the region, relying upon the sea for their livelihood. In 1741 the islands were discovered by Vitus Bering, leader of a Russian expedition. Trade in fur seal and sea otter pelts attracted the Russians to what they named the Catherine Islands, but which were soon called the Aleutian Islands after their native inhabitants, the Aleuts. During a century of occupation, Russian traders exploited both the land and the natives.

In 1867 the United States purchased Alaska, including the Aleutians, from Russia. The islands remained important primarily for the fur trade until World War II, when their strategic value was realized. The Japanese briefly occupied Attu and Kiska in 1942. Military bases in the Aleutians were maintained by American forces during the Korean Conflict, 1950-53. From 1965 to 1971, Amchitka Island was used as an underground nuclear test site. In 1971 the Aleuts were included in the federal government's property and financial settlement for native Alaskans.

See also ALASKA (maps); WORLD WAR II, section "War with Japan, 1941-45," subtitle *War with Japan, 1941-42:* Battle of Midway.

Aleutian Range, a mountain range in Alaska. See ALASKA PENINSULA; ALEUTIAN ISLANDS.

Aleuts, ăl'ē-ōōts, a Mongoloid people closely related to the Eskimos. They live primarily in small villages in the Aleutian Islands and along the Alaskan coast, engaging either in sheep raising or in traditional occupations such as fishing, whaling, or sealing. Many Aleuts adopted the Russian Orthodox religion and customs of the Russian traders who came to the area in the 18th century. European diseases and conflict with the Russians reduced the Aleut population from more than 20,000 in the early 1700's to less than 4,000 in 1885. In 1980 there were about 14,000 people of Aleut ancestry in the United States.

A-278

Alewife, āl'wīf', a silvery fish of the herring family, found primarily in the Atlantic Ocean. Alewives are also found in some lakes of eastern North America and in the Great Lakes. They may reach 8 to 12 inches (20-30 cm) in length. In the spring, the fish leave the sea and swim upriver to spawn. At this time they are netted by fishermen. Alewives are sold smoked, salted, or canned.

The alewife is *Alosa pseudoharengus* of the herring family, Clupeidae.

Alexander, the name of seven Roman Catholic popes and one antipope.

Alexander I, Saint (?-115?), traditionally listed as the sixth pope. He is said to have reigned 10 years and to have died a martyr. His feast day is May 3.

Alexander II (Anselm of Baggio; ?-1073), pope 1061-73. He began many church reforms; the reform movement reached its climax under his successor, Gregory VII. (See GREGORY [Gregory VII].) Alexander forced Holy Roman Emperor Henry IV to give up plans to divorce his wife.

Alexander III (Orlando Bandinelli; ?-1181), pope 1159-81. On his election he was opposed by Emperor Frederick I Barbarossa, who supported an antipope; eventually Alexander won a complete victory. The pope also forced Henry II of England to do penance for the murder of Thomas Becket, who was killed by four of Henry's knights. In 1179 Alexander called the 11th Ecumenical Council (Third Lateran Council), which decreed that popes should be elected by a two-thirds vote of the cardinals.

Alexander IV (Rinaldo Conti; ?-1261), pope 1254-61. He was elderly when he became pope, and was overwhelmed by political strife. He died in exile from Rome.

Alexander V (Petros Philargos; 1340?-1410), antipope 1409-10. He was elected by the Council of Pisa, and was one of three claimants to the papal throne. (See PISA, COUNCIL OF.)

Alexander VI (Rodrigo Borgia; 1431-1503), pope 1492-1503. He was an able politician and administrator but was notorious for his immorality and neglect of his spiritual obligations. He became pope by bribery, and used his office to advance the interests of his illegitimate children, who included Cesare and Lucrezia Borgia. (See BORGIA). Alexander ordered the reformer Savonarola put to death. (See SAVONAROLA, GIROLAMO.) After the discovery of America he drew the Line of Demarcation to divide the lands in America, Africa, and the Far East between Spain and Portugal. (See DEMARCATION, LINE OF.) Alexander VI patronized Michelangelo, Bramante, and other artists; he beautified Rome and planned the rebuilding of the city.

Alexander VII (Fabio Chigi; 1599-1667), pope 1655-67. He was deeply involved in theological disputes, and had a controversy with Louis XIV of France. Alexander VII made additions to the Vatican Library, constructed the impressive colonnade of St. Peter's Basilica, and encouraged a new style of architecture in Rome.

Alexander VIII (Pietro Ottoboni; 1610-1691), pope 1689-91.

Alexander, the name of a number of European rulers. Among the more important historically are the following.

Russia

Alexander I (*Russian:* Aleksandr Pavlovich) (1777-1825) was czar from 1801 to 1825. An absolute ruler, he used his autocratic power for what he believed to be the benefit of his subjects. However, he ruled in an age of revolutionary change, and his 18th-century view of the monarch's role soon was outdated. He was responsive to liberal ideas early in his reign, but his later advisers were conservative and the policies formed with their counsel stirred much opposition. Alexander's personality was complex and unstable. In his later years he became a religious fanatic.

Alexander was born in St. Petersburg, the eldest son of Czar Paul I. His education was supervised by his grandmother, Catherine the Great, who had a strong influence on him. Alexander assumed the throne after his father was assassinated in a palace coup (which Alexander had foreknowledge of but did nothing to stop). He then initiated social, administrative, and economic reforms—reorganizing the government's administration into ministries with defined responsibilities, fostering education and science, and freeing the serfs in the Baltic provinces.

Foreign affairs took much of Alexander's attention. At first he chose neutrality in the Napoleonic Wars, but eventually he opposed French expansion. After suffering a decisive defeat at the Battle of Friedland, 1807, Alexander signed the Treaty of Tilsit, becoming Napoleon's ally. Later, Alexander broke with Napoleon, and in 1812 Napoleon invaded Russia.

Library of Congress
Alexander II and Alexander III

In 1813 Alexander became one of the leaders of a coalition of nations opposing Napoleon. To maintain stability in Europe after Napoleon's final defeat, Alexander entered the Holy and Quadruple alliances with the other great powers, 1815. (See also HOLY ALLIANCE; QUADRUPLE ALLIANCE.) The concluding years of his reign were marked by rising discontent, as his policies became increasingly unpopular.

Alexander II (*Russian:* Aleksandr Nikolaevich) (1818-1881) was czar from 1855 to 1881, succeeding his father, Nicholas I. Although basically conservative, Alexander saw that reform was necessary in economically backward Russia. Despite bitter opposition from the landed nobility, he freed the serfs in 1861. This action made administrative and judicial reorganization necessary. Local elective assemblies and local courts were created. Alexander also reorganized the Russian army, limited the power of the secret police, and allowed greater freedom to the press and the universities.

Alexander's reforms pleased neither the nobility, who thought they went too far, nor the revolutionaries, who thought they did not go far enough. A rebellion in Russian Poland in 1863 made Alexander less disposed toward reform. Severe measures were taken to stamp out the growing revolutionary spirit in Russia. Some reforms were withdrawn, others curtailed.

During Alexander's reign, Russia expanded into the Caucasus region and Central Asia. A significant victory was won over Turkey in the Russo-Turkish War, 1877-78. Within Russia, however, tensions were increasing. Revolutionaries became as ruthless as the government. In 1881 Alexander was assassinated by a radical group called the People's Will.

Alexander III (*Russian:* Aleksandr Aleksandrovich) (1845-1894) was czar from 1881 to 1894, succeeding his father, Alexander II. Because of his father's assassination by radicals, Alexander ordered the destruction of the revolutionary movement in Russia. To strengthen autocratic rule, he set up repressive measures, much like those of his grandfather, Nicholas I.

Alexander brought back censorship, substantially reduced the power of the local governing councils, and persecuted the Jews. He began a program to impose Russian culture on the subject peoples of the empire. He encouraged industrialization and also established factory laws guaranteeing workers a minimum wage and standard working conditions, although these were widely ignored.

During Alexander's reign, Russia extended its Asiatic boundaries as far as Afghanistan without war. Alexander sought to strengthen Russia's position as the dominant power in the Balkans and formed an alliance with France, 1891-94.

Scotland

Alexander II (1198-1249) was king from 1214 to 1249, succeeding his father, William the Lion. Alexander joined the English barons opposing King John of England in 1215 and was excommunicated by the pope, who supported John. He was later reconciled with the Church, and in 1217 he established friendly relations with John's successor, Henry III, marrying Henry's eldest sister, Joan, in 1221. In 1230 Alexander turned back a Norse invasion of Scotland.

The friendship with England ended when Joan died in 1238, and Alexander then married the daughter of a French noble. In 1244 Henry massed an army to invade the Scottish kingdom and demand homage from Alexander. The dispute was settled without war by a treaty at Newcastle. In 1249 Alexander was leading an expedition to wrest control of the Hebrides Islands from Norway when he died of fever.

Alexander III (1241-1286) was king from 1249 to 1286, succeeding his father, Alexander II. He assumed the throne at the age of eight and two years later was married to Margaret, eldest daughter of King Henry III of England. During Alexander's minority, the kingdom was under the regency of English and Scottish nobles who constantly struggled with one another for power. Shortly after coming of age, he turned back an invading force led by King Haakon IV of

Norway at the battle of Largs, 1263. As a result, the contested Hebrides and the Isle of Man were ceded to Scotland, 1266.

The remaining years of Alexander's reign, a golden age in Scottish history, were marked by peace, prosperity, and independence. He died without a male heir and his dynasty ended with the brief reign of his young granddaughter, Margaret.

Yugoslavia

Alexander I (1888-1934) was king of the Serbs, Croats, and Slovenes from 1921 to 1929, and of Yugoslavia from 1929 to 1934. The son of Peter I of Serbia, Alexander was named crown prince in 1909. He led the Serbian armies in the Balkan Wars (1912-13) and in World War I. In 1918 the Kingdom of the Serbs, Croats, and Slovenes was created with Alexander as regent. He succeeded his father as king in 1921.

Continual disorder followed the formation of the kingdom because of the ethnic, religious, and language differences among its various peoples. Hoping to end the discord and promote national unity, Alexander abolished the 1921 constitution and set up a royal dictatorship in 1929. He changed the name of the country to Yugoslavia, dissolved the parliament, centralized the government, and suppressed political parties.

Although a new constitution was issued in 1931, Alexander's personal rule continued. His policies failed to end the dissension and he was assassinated by a Macedonian terrorist while on a goodwill tour to France.

Alexander of Tunis, Harold Rupert Leofric George Alexander, First **Earl** (1891-1969), a British general and statesman. Alexander directed the British evacuation from Dunkirk in 1940. In 1942 he was put in command of British forces in Burma, and later he became British commander in chief in the Middle East. As deputy Allied commander in chief in North Africa, 1943, Alexander helped plan the crucial North African campaign and commanded the ground forces in the invasions of Sicily and Italy. In 1944 he was promoted to field marshal and then served as supreme Allied commander in the Mediterranean for the remainder of the war.

Alexander was born in Northern Ireland. After graduation from the Royal Military College at Sandhurst, he served with distinction in France during World War I and later in India. After World War II, he was governor general of Canada, 1946-52. Alexander was made an earl in 1952. He served as British minister of defense, 1952-54.

Alexander, Edward Porter (1835-1910), a Confederate army officer. Alexander gained distinction as an artillery commander at the battles of Fredericksburg, Chancellorsville, Gettysburg, Spotsylvania Court House, and Cold Harbor. His *Military Memoirs of a Confederate* (1907) is an authoritative work on the Civil War, especially the operations of the Army of Northern Virginia. Alexander was born in Washington, Georgia, and graduated from West Point in 1857. After the Civil War, he taught engineering at the University of South Carolina, and later was a railroad official.

Alexander, John White (1856-1915), a United States painter. He was known especially for his decorative portraits and murals. His murals include *Evolution of the Book,* in the Library of Congress, and *The Crowning of Labor,* in the Carnegie Institute, Pittsburgh. Alexander was born in Allegheny (now part of Pittsburgh), Pennsylvania. He studied in Europe. Frank Duveneck and Whistler were among his teachers.

Alexander, William (1726-1783), an American Revolutionary War general. He was also known as Lord Stirling, a title he assumed in 1761, although his claim to the earldom of Stirling was later disapproved by the British House of Lords. In 1775 Alexander was commissioned a colonel of militia in New Jersey. In 1776 he directed the capture of a British transport off Sandy Hook, New Jersey. Promoted to brigadier general of the Continental Army in 1776 and major general in 1777, he commanded troops at the battles of Long Island, Brandywine, Germantown, and Monmouth. In 1778 he helped expose the Conway Cabal, a plot to remove George Washington as commander in chief.

Alexander Archipelago, a group of about 1,100 islands and islets of southeastern Alaska. It stretches for nearly 300 miles (480 km) along the coast of Alaska's Panhandle. The mountainous, densely forested islands have an area of roughly 13,000 square miles (33,700 km²). Prince of Wales, Chichagof, Admiralty, Baranof, Revillagigedo, and Kupreanof are the largest islands. Cities on the archipelago and the adjacent mainland include Juneau (Alaska's capital), Sitka, Ketchikan, and Skagway.

Alexander Graham Bell Association. See DEAFNESS (end of article).

Alexander Nevski, něv'skĭ; něf'skĭ (1220?-1263), a Russian national hero and saint of the Russian Orthodox Church. He gained renown as the defender of Russia when it was divided into weak principalities under Tatar suzerainty. After becoming prince of Novgorod in 1238, he defeated an invasion force of Swedes at the River Neva in 1240 and the Teutonic Knights on the ice of Lake Peipus in 1242. (He received his surname from the Neva battle.) Not militarily strong enough to expel the Tatar overlords, Alexander maintained peaceful relations with them by acting as their agent and collecting tribute. He became grand prince of Vladimir in 1250, and was recognized by the Tatars as grand prince of all Russia in 1252.

Alexander Severus, Marcus Aurelius (208-235), a Roman emperor, ruled 222-235. Alexander was the cousin and adopted son of Emperor Heliogabalus, whom he succeeded. Well-educated and a patron of the arts, he introduced social, economic, and administrative reforms. Alexander halted the invasion of Mesopotamia by Ardashir, king of Persia, 231-33. He attempted to check the advance of the Germanic tribes in Gaul, 234-35, but was forced to negotiate for peace. His troops mutinied, murdered Alexander, and proclaimed Maximinus emperor.

Alexander (III) **the Great** (356-323 B.C.), a king of Macedonia and Greece. Alexander conquered the entire Persian Empire, from the Aegean Sea to India and around the Mediterranean to Egypt. His conquests spread Greek culture over the Middle East and introduced the brilliant Hellenistic era of artistic, intellectual, and scientific accomplishment. Alexander was outstanding in personal courage, energy, and imagination. He became a legend in his own lifetime through the reports of the historian Callisthenes, who accompanied him on his great expedition. Many stories were told about Alexander's favorite steed, Bucephalus, and about exploits such as cutting the Gordian knot. (See BUCEPHALUS; GORDIAN KNOT.)

Alexander was not only a brilliant military strategist but also an able administrator. He saw the folly of the constant warfare among the Greek city-states and had a dream of uniting many peoples in a great common-

Alexander Discovering the Body of Darius after the king of Persia was slain by his kinsman Bessus; by Gustave Doré.

wealth. After his conquest of the Persian Empire, he began to organize the territory into a realm such as he envisioned. His early death brought an end to his plans.

Alexander was born in Pella, capital of Macedonia. His father was Philip II of Macedon, who had conquered Greece; his mother was Olympias, a princess from Epirus. Aristotle was Alexander's tutor, and the literature of Greece was his inspiration. The handsome youth took Achilles of Homer's *Iliad,* a reputed ancestor, as his hero. Alexander's teachers in military science were his father's generals. When he was only 16, he commanded forces in military actions against hill tribes.

Succession to Power

In 336 Philip was assassinated while preparing for a campaign against Persia. Alexander has been suspected, probably unjustly, of being party to the crime, because he had quarreled with his father when Philip divorced Olympias and remarried. Alexander was 20 when he became king of Macedonia and Greece.

The presence of a mere youngster on the throne was the signal for a general revolt of the hill tribes and insurrection in some of the Greek city-states. Alexander, however, was backed by the powerful Macedonian army. In a show of strength, he struck north to the Danube River, west to Illyria, and south to Thebes. Thebes was completely destroyed except for its temples and the home of the poet Pindar, whose odes Alexander admired. The authority of the new king was quickly acknowledged throughout Greece.

Alexander inherited a strong, well-organized army from his father. The separate units, Macedonian and Greek, had been

Alexander Before Babylon, after his victory at Gaugamela. This is a reproduction of a tapestry (now in Chateau Versailles) that was made from a painting by the French artist Charles Le Brun.
Lauros-Giraudon

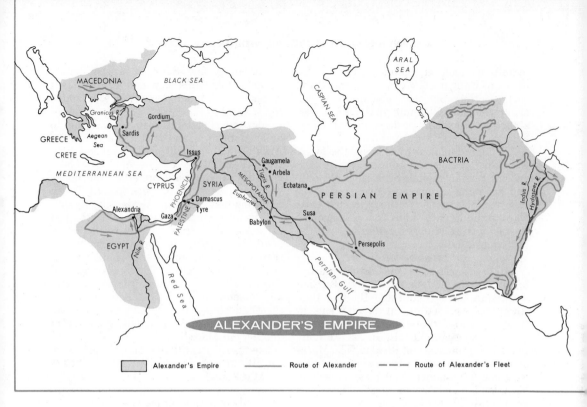

MACEDONIA   BLACK SEA   ARAL SEA

Granicus R.   Gordium   CASPIAN SEA   Oxus R.

Sardis   Aegean Sea   GREECE   Issus   Gaugamela   BACTRIA

CRETE   Arbela   Tigris R.

MEDITERRANEAN SEA   CYPRUS   SYRIA   Ecbatana   PERSIAN EMPIRE   Indus R.   Hydaspes R.

Damascus   Euphrates R.   MESOPOTAMIA

Alexandria   Tyre   Susa

Gaza   PALESTINE   Babylon

EGYPT   Persepolis

Nile R.   Persian Gulf

Red Sea

ALEXANDER'S EMPIRE

☐ Alexander's Empire   —— Route of Alexander   - - - Route of Alexander's Fleet

welded into a disciplined fighting machine, consisting of a large infantry force of some 30,000 men and smaller groups of cavalry. The *phalanx,* a narrow, deep formation of men protected by shields and armed with long spears, was the center of the line, with mobile units on the flanks. The phalanx would smash the enemy's line, and cavalry or light infantry would penetrate behind the enemy. This strategy was to be used many times after Alexander crossed the Hellespont (Dardanelles) in the spring of 334, when he began the war against Persia originally planned by Philip.

Mediterranean Conquests, 334-31

Alexander's forces met a Persian army under Memnon of Rhodes at the Granicus River on the western tip of Asia Minor and routed it in a single day. The Macedonians lost few men, while the enemy suffered heavy losses. Thousands of Greek mercenaries fighting for Persia were cut down without mercy. The western Persian headquarters at Sardis was taken, and the Greek cities on the Aegean coast were freed. His operations against these cities neutralized the Persian fleet, which needed them as bases in order to maintain its control of the Aegean. An inland campaign, centering on Gordium, completed the conquest of Asia Minor.

Macedonian governors and garrisons of soldiers were left to hold the conquered areas, while Alexander moved south toward the Phoenician coast. He defeated the forces of the Persian King Darius III at Issus in 333 B.C., and some of the Persian royal treasure, badly needed by Alexander, fell into his hands. Darius' offer to divide the empire with Alexander was refused. After a seven-month siege the Macedonians took Tyre, in southern Phoenicia, and after a two-month siege Gaza, in southern Palestine, gaining control of the coast.

Alexander moved on to Egypt, where he spent the winter of 332-31. The Egyptians accepted him as a deliverer from the Persians. Assuming the title of Pharaoh, Alexander made sacrifices to the Egyptian gods and declared himself son of the god Ammon. (All pharaohs were supposed to be half divine.) He ordered the building of a new seaport city, to be called Alexandria (as were many other towns founded by him).

Conquest of Persia, 331-30

From Egypt Alexander marched north to Damascus and crossed Mesopotamia on his way through the heart of the Persian Empire. Darius, after his defeat at Issus, had escaped to Babylon, where he assembled a great new force. Moving north to Arbela

(Erbil), he took his stand on the nearby plains of Gaugamela. Alexander routed the enemy forces, but the Persian ruler once again escaped. Claiming that Darius had abdicated, Alexander declared himself Great King of the Persian Empire.

The Macedonian army followed the Tigris River to Babylon and continued on to the ancient Persian capitals of Susa, Persepolis, and Ecbatana. From each conquered city it collected rich spoils. Darius retreated eastward until he was killed by a kinsman, Bessus, who tried unsuccessfully to halt the Macedonian advance.

Final Period

In 330-327 tribes near the Caspian Sea and in present-day Afghanistan and Russian Turkestan were conquered. By this time Alexander was setting up governments in the conquered territories under native rather than Macedonian officials. In 327 he married a Bactrian princess, Roxana. The Macedonian troops resented their king's friendly treatment of conquered peoples, as well as his adoption of Persian dress. There was growing discontent also over going farther and farther from home.

In 326 the army crossed the Indus River to the Hydaspes (Jhelum) River in northwestern India. There Alexander met and defeated the army of King Porus, who became his ally for the rest of the Indian campaign. After a few more battles, however, the army openly rebelled against continuing the campaign. Alexander was forced to turn homeward. A great fleet was built on the Indus, and the ships accompanied the army down to the Arabian Sea. From there the land forces returned through the desert to Persia, while the fleet explored the coastline all the way to the Persian Gulf.

Back at Susa in 324 Alexander took steps to merge the people under his rule into a unified empire. He ordered mass intermarriages between his Macedonian soldiers and Asiatic women, and himself took two Persian princesses as wives. Persian troops were added to his army.

At the Olympic Games of 324 a spokesman for Alexander proposed that the king should thereafter be treated as a god. In Persia the Macedonian troops were offended by what they considered their ruler's growing arrogance. When Alexander undertook to replace some of his veteran soldiers with Persians, there was another rebellion, followed in a few days by a sentimental reconciliation. In the winter of 324-323 a campaign was fought against Mesopotamian hill tribes.

Alexander had returned to Babylon to make plans for a land-sea expedition around Arabia when he fell ill with a fever and died. He was not yet 33 years old. His body, according to legend preserved in honey within a glass coffin, was placed in an imposing mausoleum in Alexandria, Egypt.

Control of the empire fell to a group of Alexander's generals, known as the *Diadochi* (Successors). In the struggle among them for supreme power, Alexander's mother and half-brother, his son by Roxana, and Roxana herself were all murdered. Eventually the empire was divided between two of the Diadochi—Seleucus in Syria and Ptolemy in Egypt—and Antigonus, grandson of another, in Macedonia.

See also FIFTEEN DECISIVE BATTLES OF THE WORLD (3. Arbela); OLYMPIAS; PHILIP OF MACEDON.

Books about Alexander the Great

Dupuy, T. N. *The Military Life of Alexander the Great of Macedon* (Watts, 1969).

Engels, D. W. *Alexander the Great and the Logistics of the Macedonian Army* (University of California, 1978).

Lane-Fox, Robin. *Alexander the Great* (Dial Press, 1974).

Plutarch. *The Age of Alexander;* translated by Ian Scott-Kilvert (Penguin Books, 1977).

Renault, Mary. *The Nature of Alexander* (Pantheon Books, 1975).

Alexanderson, Ernst Frederik Werner (1878-1975), a Swedish-American electrical engineer and inventor. He was a pioneer in radio and television. More than 320 of his inventions were patented. He developed the Alexanderson high-frequency alternator for use in transoceanic radio communication, a multiple-tuned antenna, and a color television receiver. He also worked on electric ship propulsion and equipment for railway electrification.

Alexanderson graduated from the Royal Institute of Technology, Stockholm, in 1900. He came to the United States in 1901, becoming a citizen in 1908. He joined General Electric Company as an engineer in 1902 and continued as a consulting engineer after his retirement in 1948.

Alexandra, queen consort of Edward VII of Great Britain and mother of King George V. See EDWARD.

Alexandra Fyodorovna (1872-1918), czarina of Russia, 1894-1917. A granddaughter of Queen Victoria of Great Britain, she was Princess Alix of Hesse-Darmstadt before her marriage to Czar Nicholas II in 1894. Although devoted to him, Alexandra was an obstinate and unstable woman who dominated her husband. Their resistance to reform and their autocratic policies were among the causes of the Revolution of 1917.

Alexandra came under the influence of the notorious Rasputin shortly after the birth of her only son, Alexis, heir to the throne, in 1904. She believed that Rasputin possessed mystical powers that could protect Alexis, a victim of the blood disease hemophilia. Because of this association, Rasputin played an increasingly influential role at the imperial court. When the czar was personally commanding troops during World War I, the czarina and Rasputin ran the government, 1915-16. In 1917 Alexandra, Nicholas, and their children were seized by revolutionaries. They were executed in 1918.

See also NICHOLAS (Nicholas II); RASPUTIN, GRIGORI EFIMOVICH.

Alexandria, Egypt, the nation's second largest city and chief seaport. It occupies a narrow strip of land between the Mediterranean Sea on the north and Lake Maryut on the south. The city lies near the westernmost mouth of the Nile, about 115 miles northwest of Cairo.

Modern Alexandria

Alexandria is a leading commercial and industrial center. Economic activity is concentrated around the city's port, which handles more than 80 per cent of the nation's maritime trade and passenger traffic. Industries produce textiles, clothing, cement, refined oil, sugar, tobacco goods, flour, oil from cotton seeds and olives, and pulp and paper. Barge canals connect Alexandria with the Nile. The city is also linked to the Nile Valley by railway and highway. Alexandria's airport handles international and domestic flights.

The University of Alexandria is the chief institution of higher learning. The Greco-Roman Museum has a collection of sculpture, glassware, and other historical relics. Among the few structures that remain from Alexandria's ancient past are the catacombs (built 2 A.D.). The city has many beautiful parks and gardens. It is a seaside resort, its sandy beaches lined with cabanas, and is

A-285

sometimes called "the Riviera of Egypt." El Muntazah Palace, the former home of King Farouk, lies just east of the city and is now a hotel and resort.

History

Alexandria was founded in 332 B.C. by Alexander the Great and became the capital of the kingdom established by Ptolemy I, one of Alexander's generals. The city was noted throughout the Hellenistic world for its beautiful buildings, parks, and avenues and for its modern conveniences, such as street lights and underground channels for freshwater pipes and sewers. Among its famous structures were the tomb of Alexander, the lighthouse on the adjacent island of Pharos, several great obelisks (one of which is now in New York and another in London), and numerous palaces and temples. (See CLEOPATRA'S NEEDLES; LIGHTHOUSE, subtitle *Early Lighthouses.*)

Alexandria became the commercial link between Europe and the East. Ships from Mediterranean countries crowded its fine harbor. The Nile River provided a trade route to East Africa and to Arabia by way of the Nile-Red Sea canal. The population of Alexandria, predominantly Greek and Jewish, was between 400,000 and 500,000 in 200 B.C. Many industries grew up, especially the manufacturing of glass, papyrus, and linen. The pharaohs supported an academy, known as the Museum, that had the largest library in the ancient world. Alexandrian scholars took the leadership from the Athenians in many fields of learning, particularly science and medicine.

In 48 B.C. Julius Caesar brought his army to Egypt; in 30 B.C. Rome annexed the Ptolemaic kingdom. Alexandria remained a commercial and intellectual center during the

Ramleh Mosque in Downtown Alexandria
Egyptian State Tourist Administration

Historical Pictures Service
Alexandrian Library. In this artist's conception of a hall in the library, scholars (left) are examining papyrus rolls brought to them from the storage cabinet at right.

Roman period and played an important part in the development of the Christian church. In the third century A.D. the city suffered several disasters. The Emperor Caracalla, suspecting the Egyptians of disloyalty, in 215 ordered a massacre of all male Alexandrians of military age. In 270 the city fell to Zenobia, queen of Palmyra, in a battle in which half the population died. Although retaken by Rome the next year, Alexandria had begun a long period of decline. In 642 the city was taken by the Moslems, who established a new capital at the site of what is now Cairo.

After the sea route from Europe to the Indies was discovered at the end of the 15th century, Alexandria's commerce dwindled rapidly. At the time of Napoleon's invasion in 1798, the population was no more than 10,000. Mehemet Ali, who became pasha (governor) of Egypt in 1805, undertook the restoration of the port and the city. The harbor was improved, a canal to the Nile was built to provide fresh water, and new residential areas were built up. Alexandria was connected with Cairo by railroad in 1856. The growth of traffic after the opening of the Suez Canal in 1869 restored the city to a position of importance.

Population: 2,318,655.

See also ALEXANDRIAN LIBRARY; ALEXANDRIAN SCHOOL.

A-286

Alexandria, ăl'ĕg-zăn'drĭ-à, Louisiana, the seat of Rapides Parish. It is on the Red River about 170 miles (274 km) northwest of New Orleans. The dense pine forests of central Louisiana are important to Alexandria's economy. From them comes wood for lumber, pulp, furniture, and related products. The city is a processing and trading center, serving farmlands where cotton, rice, soybeans, and sugarcane are grown. Alexandria was first settled in 1785 and incorporated in 1819. During the Civil War, in 1864, it was burned by Union troops. Population: 51,565.

Alexandria, Virginia, a city on the Potomac River opposite Washington, D.C. The city, which is independent of any county, is primarily a residential suburb. It is also a river port and industrial center. Products include electronic equipment, fabricated metals, and paper products.

Alexandria is known for its historic shrines and monuments. The home of the Revolutionary War hero "Light-Horse Harry" Lee and the boyhood home of Robert E. Lee are here. Gadsby's Tavern, an 18th-century inn, was frequented by George Washington and other notables. The George Washington Masonic National Memorial, 333 feet (101 m) tall, is patterned after the ancient lighthouse at Alexandria, Egypt. Near the city is Mount Vernon, the home and burial place of George and Martha Washington. Alexandria was settled in 1748. It was part of the District of Columbia from 1791 until 1846. In 1852 Alexandria received a city charter. Union forces occupied the city throughout the Civil War.

Population: 103,217.

Alexandria, Patriarchate of. See EASTERN ORTHODOX CHURCH, subtitle *Branches of the Church.*

Alexandrian Library, the largest and one of the most famous of the libraries of the ancient world. It was created as part of the Museum (an academy of arts and sciences dedicated to the Muses) founded in Alexandria, Egypt, about 300 B.C. Ptolemy I, the founder, summoned the foremost Greek scholars to Alexandria to study and work under his patronage. The first project of the scholars was to compile new, authoritative editions of Homer's *Iliad* and *Odyssey.*

The Museum buildings were completed in the reign of Ptolemy II (285-246 B.C.), who built up the library's collection of books (papyrus rolls) to as many as 700,000. Ptolemy III borrowed important manuscripts from Athens to be copied, then forfeited a large security deposit to keep the originals for the library. The mathematician Euclid, the physicist Archimedes, the geographer Eratosthenes, and the critic Callimachus were among the learned men who studied or worked at the library. By the end of the third century B.C., Alexandria was the intellectual capital of the Hellenistic world.

In 48 B.C. during a battle between Julius Caesar and the supporters of Ptolemy XII, a large part of the library collection was destroyed by fire. The loss was made up in the 30's when Mark Antony presented Cleopatra with the bulk of the manuscripts from the library of Pergamum (on parchment, because Egypt had refused to sell papyrus to the rival library).

As Christianity became prevalent, the Museum came to be regarded as a center of paganism. From 270 A.D. it suffered occasional destructive attacks by Christian mobs; about 390 its last surviving building and the remnants of the library were destroyed.

See also ALEXANDRIAN SCHOOL.

Alexandrian School, a name given to various groups of persons engaged in artistic and intellectual activities in Alexandria, Egypt, during the Hellenistic and Roman eras. Subject to common influences, members of each group tended to show similarity in their style, attitudes, or methods. Such groups produced work of a unique character in sculpture, literature, science, philosophy, and theology.

From about 300 B.C., when the Alexandrian Museum and its library were created, for some 600 years Alexandria was the intellectual capital of the ancient world. While its origins were Macedonian-Greek, as were its royal house (the Ptolemies) and its ruling class of citizens until the Roman conquest, the city absorbed much of the Egyptian tradition. The population, cosmopolitan in character, included Jews, Syrians, and other Middle Easterners who brought with them ideas and customs foreign to Greek and Roman culture. The blending of Western and Eastern knowledge and thought was the distinguishing feature of the schools.

See also ALEXANDRIAN LIBRARY.

The Arts

The Alexandrian school of sculpture was one of the three Hellenistic styles of the third century B.C. It was a naturalistic style, but one in which some detail was suggested rather than delineated. The individuality and human quality of the subjects were stressed, with touches of humor such as the classic Greek sculptors had never shown. Allegorical figures were an innovation, as were realistic portraits of old people and children.

Literature of the Alexandrian school was based on scholarship rather than on originality. The writers working in the Museum and library catalogued, criticized, and edited more than they wrote. When they composed poetry, it was usually in studied imitation of older forms. Callimachus introduced the epyllion, a short epic poem, and his pupil Apollonius of Rhodes revived the long epic. Theocritus, however, created an original variety of verse, the pastoral poem, for which the Alexandrian school of literature is chiefly remembered.

See also CALLIMACHUS; THEOCRITUS.

The Sciences

The mathematician Euclid came to Alexandria about the time the Museum and library were founded. His teaching and writing were the foundation for 600 years of invention and discovery in mathematics, astronomy, and physics.

Apollonius of Perga (third century B.C.) founded the study of conic sections, and Hipparchus (second century B.C.) originated plane and spherical trigonometry. In the third century A.D. Diophantus invented algebraic symbols, and Pappus laid the foundations for analytical geometry.

In the third century B.C. Eratosthenes of Cyrene used astronomy to form geographical conclusions, and Aristarchus of Samos theorized that the earth revolves about the sun. Ptolemy (second century A.D.) made major contributions to trigonometry and to astronomy but supported the theory that the sun revolves about the earth.

Ctesibius (second century B.C.) experimented with water pressure and air pressure. In the early Christian Era Hero operated devices with water, air, and steam—including a forerunner of the jet engine.

Egypt had long been a leader in medical knowledge when the Hellenistic era began. Alexandria quickly became the medical center of the Mediterranean world. Among the major physicians and their fields of discovery were Herophilus of Chalcedon, anatomy, and Erasistratus, physiology (third century

B.C.); Marinus, skull surgery (late first century A.D.); and Soranus, gynecology (second century). There were, in fact, few notable advances in surgery from the Alexandrian era to the 19th century.

See also ARISTARCHUS OF SAMOS; ERATOSTHENES; EUCLID OF ALEXANDRIA; HERO; HIPPARCHUS; PTOLEMY.

Philosophy and Theology

During the pre-Christian era, Athens retained supremacy over Alexandria as the center of philosophy. When an Alexandrian school of philosophy developed, it reflected the mysticism found throughout the Middle East. About 100 B.C. there originated in Alexandria a new philosophy, Neopythagoreanism, in which Pythagorean doctrines were given a mystical interpretation. Renunciation of worldly things and recognition of one supreme deity were emphasized.

As the Christian Era began, the Alexandrian Jew Philo, combining Jewish religious ideas with Greek philosophy, emphasized the mystical quality of man's relationship to God. Philo influenced two late-second-century Greek Fathers of the Church, Clement of Alexandria and his pupil Origen. These two in turn headed Alexandria's catechetical (Christian religious) school, where both Christian and pagan (Greek) writings were studied and where the philosophy later known as Neoplatonism evolved.

Plotinus (third century), who probably attended the school, formulated the doctrines of Neoplatonism, in which the soul was glorified and the physical senses ignored, and carried them to Rome. Although Neoplatonism was a pagan philosophy and Origen, after his death, was disowned by the Church as a heretic, much of the mysticism of the Alexandrian school of theology was absorbed into Christian thinking.

See also ARIANISM; ATHANASIUS, Saint; ORIGEN; PHILO JUDAEUS; PLOTINUS.

Alexandrite. See CHRYSOBERYL.

Alfalfa, ăl-făl′fȧ, or **Lucerne,** lů-sûrn′, a plant of the pea family grown primarily for forage, especially as hay. It is one of the most useful and widely grown hay crops in the world. In the United States, more acreage is used for alfalfa production than for any other hay crop.

Because of its high protein content, alfalfa is used as a food for almost all farm animals—as hay, as silage, or as a temporary pasture crop. Because of its nitrogen-fixing properties, it is used in crop rotation to improve soil for other crops. When planted in combination with grasses, it helps prevent soil erosion. Alfalfa is also grown commercially for seed in arid or semiarid regions. Dehydrated alfalfa is ground into meal and used in feeding poultry and livestock. Indirectly, alfalfa is a source of honey, because bees gather substantial quantities of nectar from alfalfa flowers.

Description

Alfalfa grows from one to four feet high, depending on soil conditions and water supply. Unusually long taproots (4 to 12 feet, but occasionally up to 30 feet) draw moisture and nourishment from deep in the subsoil, and enable the plant to grow in dry areas.

A thickened, woody, stemlike structure, the *crown,* develops at or near the surface of the ground. Some 15 to 30 leafy shoots grow from the crown. The leaves are small, with distinct marginal teeth at the apex. The flowers are predominantly purple and grow in short clusters. The seed pods are twisted and slightly downy, and the seeds are kidney-shaped.

Production of Alfalfa

Alfalfa is grown in almost every state of the United States and, to some extent, in all

ALFALFA

Seeds

Seed pod

Leaves and blossoms

agricultural areas of the world. Alfalfa grows best in deep, rich, well-drained soil but will adapt to almost any climate and soil. The plant requires considerable amounts of calcium, phosphorus, and potassium. Acid soils must be treated with lime to insure successful alfalfa growth.

Seeding is accomplished by sowing the seeds with a grain drill (a mechanical device that inserts the seed into the soil) or by scattering the seeds at random and then covering them. The roots of alfalfa plants have small nodules that contain nitrogen-fixing bacteria. (See NITROGEN FIXATION, subtitle *Natural Nitrogen Fixation.*) These bacteria provide nitrogen necessary for alfalfa growth, and should be added to fields where alfalfa has never been grown. The process of adding these beneficial bacteria to the soil is called *inoculation.*

A field of alfalfa requires very little cultivation, and the crop can be harvested from two to seven times a year. One acre of alfalfa can yield from two to six tons of hay and from one to five bushels of seed.

Crop Damage. Damage to alfalfa crops is sometimes caused by field mice, gophers, and ground squirrels, but these animals can be controlled by trapping or poisoning. Even greater damage is caused by diseases produced by bacteria and viruses. The most effective method, and often the only one available to combat these diseases, is to breed and plant disease-resistant varieties of alfalfa.

Damage to alfalfa crops is also caused by insects (such as caterpillars, the alfalfa aphid, and the alfalfa weevil) and by worms (such as the alfalfa webworm). These insects and worms are controlled by pesticides, by cutting the crop early, and by planting varieties of alfalfa that are resistant to them. Alfalfa is also affected by cold, drought, and humidity.

To maintain the quality of alfalfa, special attention must be paid to the harvesting methods and the weather conditions at the time of harvest. Improper harvesting can result in a loss of more than 90 per cent of the carotene (a source of vitamin A for animals) and more than 20 per cent of the protein content.

History

Alfalfa is probably native to Asia Minor and the Caucasus Mountains, and its use as a cultivated forage plant goes back into antiquity. It is known that alfalfa was grown by the Persians, Greeks, and Romans. The successful planting of alfalfa in the United States began about 1850, when seed was brought to the Pacific coast from Chile. By 1900 the cultivation of Chilean alfalfa had spread as far east as the valley of the Mississippi River. During the second half of the 19th century another variety of alfalfa was brought to Minnesota from Germany by Wendelin Grimm. Other varieties were developed from the original Chilean and Grimm strains. The Grimm varieties proved to be extremely hardy, and their use spread over the northern states.

Many other alfalfa varieties were later introduced into the United States from central Asia. In addition to the Grimm alfalfas and the Chilean varieties, Turkistan alfalfas (from Turkestan in Central Asia), Ladak alfalfas (from northern India), and variegated alfalfas (hybrids formed by breeding common alfalfa with a wild species from Siberia) are among the important varieties planted in the United States.

Most cultivated varieties of alfalfa belong to the species *Medicago sativa* (called "common" alfalfa) of the legume family, Leguminosae. The species that grows wild in Siberia is *M. falcata.*

Alfieri, äl-fyâ′rĕ, Count **Vittorio** (1749-1803), an Italian dramatist and poet. His 19 tragedies, written between 1775 and 1787, are classical in structure, adhering to the rules for tragedy outlined by French critics based on their interpretation of the writings of Aristotle. Like most of his other work, they express strong patriotism and hatred of tyranny. Alfieri's writings are credited with aiding the campaign for a united Italy. *Saul,* about the doomed king of Israel, is generally considered his best tragedy. He also wrote six verse comedies and some lyrical poetry. *L'America Libera* (1781-83), a collection of poems, celebrates the independence of the United States. His prose works include *Tyranny* (1777), *The Prince and Letters* (1778-86), and an autobiography.

Alfonso, äl-fŏn′sō, the name of a number of rulers of various Spanish kingdoms and of Portugal. Among the more important historically are the following.

Aragon

Alfonso V (1396?-1458) was king of Aragon and Sicily from 1416 to 1458. He succeeded his father, Ferdinand I. Queen Joanna II of Naples promised to make Alfonso her heir, but after a quarrel she left her kingdom to René I of Anjou. Alfonso seized Naples from René in 1442 and was acknowledged its ruler by Pope Eugenius IV. Leaving his wife and later his brother, John II, to rule Aragon, Alfonso moved his court to Naples. He did much to beautify that city and encouraged art and literature.

León and Castile

Alfonso VI (1030-1109) was king of León from 1065 to 1109, and of Castile from 1072 to 1109. He inherited León from his father, Ferdinand I, and Castile from his elder brother, Sancho II, who was assassinated in 1072. Alfonso took Galicia from his younger brother Garcia in 1073.

Alfonso's reign is notable for the impetus given the Christian campaign to reconquer Spain from the Moors. Aided by Rodrigo Díaz de Bivar (the Cid), he advanced the Christian frontier to the Tagus River by capturing Toledo in 1085. During Alfonso's reign, Roman reforms were introduced into the Catholic Church in Spain by Cluniac monks.

Alfonso X (1221-1284) was king of León and Castile from 1252 to 1284. He succeeded his father, Ferdinand III. Alfonso, known as the "learned," was a historian, poet, and patron of learning. He directed the compilation of a code of laws, *Las Siete Partidas,* and a collection of astronomical information, the Alfonsine Tables. He aided schools at Seville, Salamanca, and Murcia.

Alfonso tried to win the crown of the Holy Roman Empire but finally renounced his claim in 1275 because of papal opposition and unfavorable public opinion in Spain. After the death of his eldest son, Ferdinand, that same year, a struggle for the succession took place between Ferdinand's son and Alfonso's second son, Sancho. Sancho succeeded to the throne as Sancho IV.

Spain

Alfonso XII (1857-1885) was king of Spain from 1874 to 1885. He was the son of Queen Isabella II of the House of Bourbon. An uprising against Isabella in 1868 forced Alfonso and his mother into exile and revived the Carlist cause (a movement to place a successor of Don Carlos de Borbón, brother of Ferdinand VII, on the throne). After six years of political unrest culminating with the failure of the First Republic in 1874, General Arsenio Martínez de Campos gained the support of the army for Alfonso and proclaimed him king. Alfonso returned to Madrid in 1875 and the Carlist forces were defeated the following year.

Spain had some stability again during Alfonso's reign, largely due to the efforts of his prime minister, Antonio Cánovas del Castillo. A new constitution was adopted in 1876, providing for a legislature of two chambers, limited suffrage, and religious toleration. According to a system arranged by Cánovas, the political power alternated between two parties, both supporting the crown.

Alfonso XIII (1886-1941) was king of Spain from 1886 to 1931. Born after the death of his father, Alfonso XII, he became king as an infant. His mother, Maria Christina of Austria, was regent until he formally succeeded to the throne in 1902. During her regency Spain lost Cuba, Puerto Rico, and the Philippines in the Spanish-American War.

Alfonso's reign was marked by repeated attempts on his life, native uprisings in Spanish Morocco, and agitation for autonomy in Catalonia, a region in northeastern Spain. In 1921 a large Spanish force was de-

Alfonso XIII

feated by Rif tribesmen in Morocco. An investigation to fix responsibility for the defeat revealed corruption among high-ranking officials. Before the report of the investigation could be published, General Miguel Primo de Rivera staged a successful *coup d'état,* establishing a military dictatorship. Alfonso, who remained in Spain as king, supported the dictatorship (1923-30) and was held responsible for some of its evils.

Following an overwhelming Republican victory in the municipal elections of 1931, Alfonso left Spain and the Second Republic was established. He formally abdicated in favor of his son, Don Juan, a few weeks before his death in Rome in 1941.

Portugal

Alfonso I (Alfonso Henriques) (1112?-1185) was the first king of Portugal, reigning from 1139 to 1185. Alfonso became count of Portugal while still a child. He succeeded

his father, Henry of Burgundy, who had been given the county by Alfonso VI of León and Castile. Portugal at that time extended from the Minho River to Coimbra, covering the northern third of what is now Portugal.

Alfonso's mother, Teresa of Castile, ruled as regent until he sent her into exile in 1128. The young count began to fight both the Moors and his cousin, Alfonso VII of León and Castile, for Portuguese independence. Following victory over the Moors in the battle of Ourique in 1139, Alfonso declared himself king of Portugal. The Treaty of Zamora (1143) between Portugal and Castile recognized Portuguese independence and placed Portugal under the protection of the papacy.

Alfonso pushed Portugal's southern boundary to the Tagus River, defeating the Moors at Santarém and Lisbon. The expanded kingdom covered about half of what is now Portugal. Portugal's independence and the royal title were recognized by Pope Alexander III in 1179.

Alfred, called **Alfred the Great** (849-899), king of Wessex, the domain of the West Saxons in the south of England. He reigned 871-99.

Alfred was the most illustrious of the Anglo-Saxon kings and one of the most remarkable men of the Middle Ages. He brought to a halt the Danish conquest of England and strengthened the West Saxon monarchy, thus preparing the way for the eventual union of England under one king. Amidst the devastation wrought by years of warring against the Danes, he fostered a revival of religion, education, and literature in Anglo-Saxon England. Throughout his long reign, Alfred showed himself to be an imaginative military leader, a wise and determined ruler, and a skilled statesman.

Alfred was born at Wantage, the youngest son of King Ethelwulf and one of four brothers to become king. At the age of four he was sent to Rome for part of his early education. There he met Pope Leo IV and other churchmen and rulers from the Continent. He made a second visit to Rome in 855, but little is known of his activities over the next decade. As he grew to manhood, however, Alfred developed a marked piety and an inquiring intellect (even though he remained illiterate until he was nearly 40 years old).

Victory over the Danes

In 868 Alfred was second in command to his brother, King Ethelred, as they prepared to confront the Danes (Vikings) who had overrun northern England. By 870, the invaders were pressing into Wessex. At the battle of Ashdown in 871, Alfred routed the enemy in a surprise counterattack. In April of 871 Ethelred died, and Alfred succeeded to the throne. More Danes arrived, and the hopelessly outnumbered West Saxon army fought a series of battles that year. A tribute (later known as the danegeld) paid to the invaders brought a temporary peace.

In 876 the Danes again attacked Wessex, plundering the countryside as they advanced. Alfred was eventually forced to withdraw his soldiers to the isle of Athelney. Here he built a fort, regrouped his forces, and in the spring of 878 took the offensive. At the battle of Edington he decisively defeated the army of Guthrum, Danish ruler of East Anglia (eastern England). By an agreement signed at Wedmore (878), the Danes consented to withdraw from West Saxon lands and to accept Christianity. This victory was a turning point in early English history, for it proved that the Danes could be stopped.

In the years that followed, King Alfred strengthened Saxon defenses against future Danish penetrations. He reorganized local government in the districts ravaged by the Danes. The army was made larger and more flexible; fortification of towns throughout southern England was undertaken; and construction of a fleet of large, swift vessels was begun.

Sporadic fighting with the Danes continued during Alfred's reign. He repelled an invasion of Kent in 885 and in 886 drove the Danes from London. The treaty of Wedmore signed that year set boundaries for the Danelaw—the area in the hands of the Danes, roughly northeastern England. Alfred then combined various petty states not under Danish control into one Saxon kingdom. Gaining the loyalty of the people by his resourceful leadership, he was recognized as sovereign of an area nearly twice the size of the territory his brother had ruled.

War raged again during 892-96, when a horde of invading Vikings was joined by others from the Danelaw. After four years of withstanding their sieges Alfred drove them from Wessex. His work of bringing the whole of England into one kingdom was continued by his son, Edward the Elder, who became king in 899.

Other Achievements

During relatively peaceful times, Alfred enthusiastically devoted his attention to reviving and maintaining learning. He brought many notable scholars to Wessex, making his capital at Winchester a center of intellectual life. Among these learned men was Asser, a Welsh monk, who wrote the

first biography of Alfred and aided the king in translating literary works from Latin to English. Alfred supervised the translation of and made additions to five major works, including the *Pastoral Care* of Pope Gregory I and Bede's *Ecclesiastical History of the English People*. He also encouraged the continuation of the *Anglo-Saxon Chronicle,* an early history of England.

Alfred issued a new code of laws, in which he selected and restated the best laws of his predecessors. He established a school for young nobles in his court and restored and promoted the Christian faith.

Books about Alfred the Great

Hinton, D. A. *Alfred's Kingdom: Wessex and the South, 800-1500* (Rowman & Littlefield, 1977).
For Younger Readers:
Pelling, Jack. *King Alfred* (Cambridge University, 1977).

Alfred P. Sloan Foundation. See SLOAN, ALFRED PRITCHARD, JR.

Alfred University. See UNIVERSITIES AND COLLEGES (table).

Algae, ăl′jē (singular: **Alga,** ăl′gȧ), plants that lack true roots, stems, and leaves; that usually contain chlorophyll (the green coloring matter of plants); and whose reproductive organs are single-celled structures. Green algae and the few chlorophyll-containing bacteria are the simplest of all green plants and were probably the first capable of carrying on photosynthesis (the process of manufacturing their own food).

About 25,000 species of algae have been identified. They range in size from microscopic single-celled forms to multicellular (many-celled) forms more than 150 feet (45 m) long. They abound in both fresh and ocean water and in moist environments on land. Masses of microscopic fresh-water algae that are often seen floating on the water surface are called *pond scum*. The larger marine algae are commonly called *seaweed*. Certain species of algae contaminate reservoirs and swimming pools, giving the water a fishy taste and a foul odor.

Scientists estimate that algae may account for up to 90 per cent of the photosynthetic activity on earth. Algae are part of the first link in the sequence of organisms known as the *food chain*. Each organism of the food chain is the food for the succeeding member of the sequence. (See OCEAN, subtitle *Marine Life:* The Food Chain.) Almost all algae—even the single-celled species—can

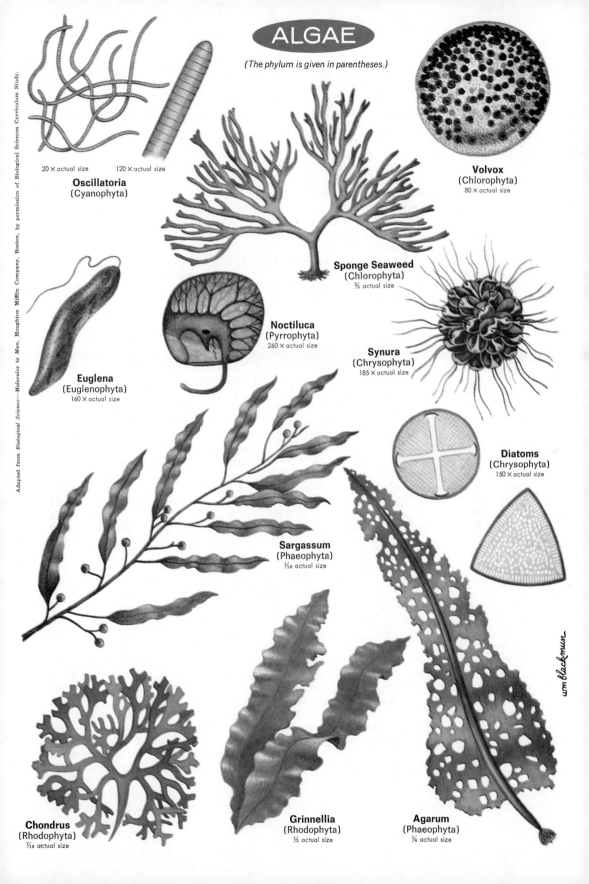

ALGAE

(The phylum is given in parentheses.)

20 × actual size   120 × actual size

Oscillatoria
(Cyanophyta)

Volvox
(Chlorophyta)
80 × actual size

Sponge Seaweed
(Chlorophyta)
⅔ actual size

Euglena
(Euglenophyta)
160 × actual size

Noctiluca
(Pyrrophyta)
260 × actual size

Synura
(Chrysophyta)
185 × actual size

Diatoms
(Chrysophyta)
150 × actual size

Sargassum
(Phaeophyta)
⅒ actual size

Chondrus
(Rhodophyta)
⁷⁄₁₀ actual size

Grinnellia
(Rhodophyta)
½ actual size

Agarum
(Phaeophyta)
¼ actual size

wm blackmun

produce their own food and carry on all life processes, such as respiration and reproduction.

Description

Structure. Algae show more variation in structure than any other plant group. The single-celled species can be round, oval, or elongate. They can exist individually or in colonies (loose groupings of similar cells). The colonies have various shapes, such as hollow spheres or slender threads. Single-celled algae called *diatoms* have cell walls covered with hydrated silica, a glasslike substance that produces a great variety of geometric patterns. (See DIATOM.) Many-celled algae usually have irregular, complex shapes, such as those seen in kelp, sea lettuce, and rockweed. (See OCEAN, color page *Ocean Life.*)

Many single-celled and colonial forms of algae move about by means of *flagella* (long, whiplike growths projecting from the main part of the cell). The larger multicellular algae usually have specialized cells for certain functions, such as reproduction.

Color. Most algae have other pigments (coloring matter), such as blue, red, and yellow, in addition to chlorophyll. These pigments often mask the chlorophyll so that the algae take on colors other than green, such as red or brown. The reddish tint sometimes seen on snow is produced by a species of single-celled alga that has a high concentration of red pigment. The red color occasionally seen on the surface of the Red Sea is also due to a species of alga.

Reproduction. Single-celled algae reproduce sexually by conjugation (fusion of gametes that are identical in appearance) or by fusion of male and female sex cells and asexually by cell division. Multicellular algae reproduce sexually by conjugation or fusion of male and female sex cells and asexually by fragmentation (formation of a new organism from a detached portion of another organism) or spore production. (A spore is a special cell that can develop directly into a new organism.) In some species of algae that reproduce sexually, alternation of generations occurs. (See REPRODUCTION OF LIVING ORGANISMS, subtitle *Alternation of Generations.*)

Distribution

Although most algae are found in bodies of fresh or ocean water, many microscopic species, which require only a thin film of

A-294

moisture, can exist on or in the soil, on damp rocks, and on trees. Some microscopic algae are found on aquatic animals and plants. A few species of algae that lack chlorophyll live in the digestive tracts of animals (including man) or inside plants.

Most many-celled algae grow on the bottom of bodies of water—usually near the shore, where sunlight can penetrate to the bottom. However, multicellular marine algae have been collected from depths as great as 600 feet. Multicellular algae also grow attached to various submerged objects, such as twigs, rocks, and even the hulls of ships. A few species of multicellular algae are free-floating; for example, those found in the Sargasso Sea—a large area in the western North Atlantic Ocean.

Most single-celled algae, including colonial forms, are free-floating or swim on or in the water, from the surface to depths of several hundred feet. Some species of single-celled algae grow attached to rocks along the shoreline, or on submerged objects. One such species, found in the Mediterranean, is the largest single-celled organism known. It can grow up to several inches in length.

Algae are found in a variety of temperature ranges. Some grow on ice and snow; others thrive in hot springs where the water temperature exceeds 180° F. Some algae are adapted to live in turbulent waters, while others live in the intertidal zone (the area between the high-tide line and the low-tide line) of seacoasts, where they are exposed to dry conditions at least a few hours each day. A few species of algae live in close association with plants called fungi, forming lichens. (See LICHEN.)

Economic Importance

In addition to being part of the first link in the food chain, algae provide bodies of water with significant amounts of oxygen, which is needed by aquatic animals for breathing. Millions of people in the Orient eat algae—mostly the larger marine species, including kelp. The large algae used commercially are gathered by hand, as well as by mechanical harvesters. Algae are excellent sources of minerals, such as iodine and potassium; and vitamins, such as vitamin C. They also contain carbohydrates and proteins. Algae are used extensively as food for livestock and as fertilizers.

Agar, or *agar-agar,* is a gelatinous substance derived from marine algae. Agar has many uses. It is used in laxatives, in materials on which dental impressions are made, in textile sizing, and in additives that thicken such foods as sherbet, cheese, soup, and bakery products. Agar is also used as a gelling agent in cooking and, in laboratory work, as a growth medium for bacteria.

Carrageenin, a jellylike substance derived from a marine alga commonly known as Irish moss, is also important in industry. Its most important use is in chocolate milk, where it holds the cocoa particles in suspension. In addition, carrigeenin is used in sauces, syrups, toothpastes, cosmetics, and cream shampoos. *Algin,* derived from giant kelp, is also widely used in industry. (See KELP.) The shells of dead diatoms make up *diatomite,* which has many commercial uses, including heat insulation and the filtration of liquids. (See DIATOMITE.) Certain species of single-celled algae have been tested for possible use in manned spacecraft as a source of oxygen and food for astronauts during flights into deep space.

Classification

Algae belong to the subkingdom Thallophyta. Many characteristics are used to determine the phylum to which a given genus of algae belongs. They include method of reproduction; pigment content; kind of food stored; nature of cell wall; and relative length, number, and arrangement of flagella. Algae have been classified by biologists into anywhere from 4 to 11 phyla. A common classification system divides them into the following seven phyla:

Cyanophyta. Blue-green algae. Single-celled and multicellular. About 1,500 species, mostly fresh-water. Some scientists classify blue-green algae and bacteria together in the phylum Schizophyta.

Chlorophyta. Green algae. Single-celled and multicellular. About 6,500 species, mostly fresh-water.

Euglenophyta. Mostly green, single-celled flagellates. About 500 species, mostly fresh-water.

Pyrrophyta. Greenish-brown to brown. About 1,000 species, mostly marine and single-celled.

Chrysophyta. Yellow-green to golden-brown. Mostly single-celled. About 10,000 species, marine and fresh-water. See DIATOM.

Phaeophyta. Mostly brown. About 1,500 species, all multicellular and marine. See KELP.

Rhodophyta. Red to purplish-black. About 3,500 species, mostly marine and multicellular. See IRISH MOSS.

Books about Algae

Bold, H. C., and M. J. Wynne. *Introduction to the Algae* (Prentice-Hall, 1978).

Chapman, V. J. and D. J. *The Algae* (St. Martin's Press, 1975).

Algardi, äl-gär′dĕ, **Alessandro** (1595?-1654), an Italian sculptor and architect. Although he lived in the Baroque age, Algardi continued the classical tradition of the Renaissance. His bronze *Innocent X* and the high relief *The Encounter of Leo I and Attila* show his skill in portraying people. (For illustration, see ATTILA.) The Villa Doria Pamphili and the facade of Sant' Ignazio in Rome are among his architectural designs. Algardi was born in Bologna, and studied with Lodovico Carracci.

Algarroba. See MESQUITE.

Algebra, ăl′jĕ-brà. The subject called algebra that is taught in high school and the first year of college (and sometimes in elementary schools) is a generalization of grade school arithmetic. In arithmetic, the student learns to perform operations (such as addition and multiplication) with rational numbers. In algebra, he learns more about the properties of numbers and about the rules that govern operations with numbers. (The different sets of numbers are explained in the box on the following page.)

To a mathematician, algebra is the study of properties of abstract mathematical systems, and there are many algebras. This article deals with what is properly called the algebra of complex numbers.

Algebra is an important part of mathematics, and an understanding of it is basic to the study of all advanced mathematics. With algebra we can solve problems that would be difficult or impossible to solve with arithmetic alone. Algebra has many practical applications in science, engineering, business, and industry. It is used, for example, to calculate life insurance rates and monthly payments on installment-plan purchases. When a service station attendant adds antifreeze to a car's radiator, he determines the needed amount from a table computed with the aid of algebra.

Algebra, as a tool for solving numerical problems, had been brought to an advanced stage of development as early as 2000 B.C. by the Babylonians. The development of a system of algebraic symbols, however, was not begun until the 15th century A.D. The development of this system—which amounts to a mathematical "shorthand"—has made possible huge advances in mathematics.

With a system of algebraic symbols, math-

Sets of Numbers

I. {natural numbers} = {1,2,3,4,...}
(The three dots indicate that the sequence of numbers is infinite, or unending, each number in this case being equal to the preceding number plus 1.)

II. {whole numbers = 0,1,2,3,...}

The set of whole numbers is composed of the natural numbers and the number zero.

III. {integers} =
{...,−3,−2,−1,0,1,2,3,...}

The set of integers is composed of the whole numbers and the negative integers.

IV. {rational numbers}

A rational number is any number that can be written as the quotient of two integers in the form $\frac{a}{b}$, where b is not zero. Every integer can be written in the form $\frac{a}{b}$, where b = 1. Every rational number can be written as either a repeating or a terminating decimal; for example, $\frac{3}{11}$ = 0.272727 ..., where the group of digits that repeats is 27, and $\frac{3}{8}$ = 0.375.

V. {irrational numbers}

An irrational number is a number that cannot be written as the quotient of two integers. Familiar examples of irrational numbers are π and $\sqrt{2}$. Irrational numbers cannot be written as repeating or terminating decimals.

VI. {real numbers}

The set of real numbers is composed of the rational numbers and the irrational numbers.

VII. {imaginary numbers}

An imaginary number is any real-number multiple of i. (i is defined as the number whose square equals −1.) Examples of imaginary numbers are $3i$ and $i\sqrt{5}$.

VIII. {complex numbers}

A complex number is represented by a numeral of the form $a + bi$, where a and b are real numbers. A typical example of a complex number is $2 + 3i$.

ematicians could think in terms of types of problems rather than individual problems. Substituting letters for specific numerals, they could make generalizations about the properties of numbers. Major contributions were made by, among others, the English mathematicians George Boole and John Venn. About 1850 Boole wrote *An Investigation of the Laws of Thought,* in which he pioneered the application of algebra to sets and logic. (The term *set* is defined later in this article.) Venn devised diagrams to illustrate operations with sets and relationships between sets.

Because of the advances that have been made in mathematics since the 15th century, especially in the last 100 years, today's high school student can cope with mathematical concepts that in ancient times were understood only by a handful of mathematicians. Consider the following problem from the eighth century A.D.:

A dog chasing a rabbit, which has a start of 150 feet, jumps 9 feet every time the rabbit jumps 7 feet. In how many jumps does the dog catch the rabbit?

Since the rabbit and the dog make the same number of leaps, the problem can be analyzed as follows:

The distance the dog covers (9 feet times the number of leaps) is equal to the distance the rabbit covers (7 feet times the number of leaps) plus the rabbit's 150-foot start.

In modern algebraic symbols, letting x equal the number of leaps, the analysis above can be written

$$9x = 7x + 150.$$

This statement can be simplified according to the rules of algebra. The answer is 75.

Sets, Elements, and Operations

Terms such as "set," "element," and "operation" have come into wide use in elementary mathematics. They are explained briefly in the following paragraphs.

A *set* is any well-defined collection of things. (The collection is "well defined" if the definition makes it possible to tell whether an object is or is not a member of the collection.) Each "thing" that belongs to the set is called a *member* or an *element* of the set. Examples of mathematical "things" include numbers; geometric figures; events that can take place in actuality or in the imagination; and logical statements.

Sets are usually designated by capital letters and defined by listing the names of their elements or giving a description of the elements. The names or descriptions are enclosed in braces. The set whose elements are 1 and 3, for example, can be designated as $A = \{1,3\}$, which is read "the set whose elements are 1 and 3," or as $A = \{$the first two odd numbers$\}$, "the set of the first two odd numbers."

The sets of algebraic numbers are shown in the accompanying table. For a more conplete discussion, see the article NUMBER.

An *operation* is an abstract process that produces mathematical objects from existing mathematical objects. For example, a number can be produced from another number or from the combination of two numbers; a set can be produced from another set or from the combination of two sets. Generation from a single object is called a *unary* operation. Examples are extracting a root (finding, for example, what number multiplied by itself equals 9) and raising a number to a power (multiplying a number by itself one or more times). Generation from two objects is called a *binary* operation. Examples are addition and multiplication.

Equation and Inequality

An equation or inequality usually takes the form of a statement that contains letters representing numerals; operation symbols (such as $+$ or $\cdot$); and a relation symbol such as $=$ (is equal to), $<$ (is less than), $>$ (is greater than), and $\neq$ (is not equal to).

The statement itself is a conditional assertion; it can be made into a true or false statement by replacing the letters with the names of elements of a specified set. In numerical problems the letters can be replaced with numerals. If the letter x in the statement $x + 3 = 8$ is replaced with the numeral 5, the resulting statement is true; if x is replaced with any other numeral, it is false.

The Rules of Algebra

The following *axioms* (statements whose truth is regarded as self-evident) are the foundation of algebra. (They may look unfamiliar; many a student has gone through high school algebra without seeing them formally stated. But every algebra student has learned them. The principle that "you can add the same thing to both sides of an equation," for example, is only another way of stating the addition axiom of equality.) In these axioms, the operations of subtraction and division are not specifically men-

Jean-claude Lejeune
Solving an Equation in Algebra

tioned. Subtraction there is regarded as included in the operation of addition, since $3 - 5 = 3 + (-5)$, and division as included in multiplication, since

$$2 \div 3 = 2 \cdot \frac{1}{3}.$$

(The dot $[\cdot]$ between the numerals indicates multiplication; it is not to be confused with the decimal point. The dot is frequently omitted between two letters or a number and a letter; for example, ab means a $\cdot$ b, and 2b means $2 \cdot$ b.) All letters in the following statements represent real numbers.

Axioms of Equality. The following five axioms govern the handling of equations:

1. Reflexive Property of Equality

$$a = a$$

Any number is equal to itself.

2. Symmetric Property of Equality

If $a = b$, then $b = a$

Example: If $n + 3 = 7$, then $7 = n + 3$

3. Transitive Property of Equality

If $a = b$ and $b = c$, then $a = c$

Example:
If $x + 4 = 7$ and $7 = y - 3$, then $x + 4 = y - 3$

4. Addition Axioms of Equality

(a) If $a = b$, then $a + c = b + c$

Example: If $y = 4$, then $y + 1 = 4 + 1$

(b) If $a + c = b + c$, then $a = b$

Example: If $x + 3 = 5 + 3$, then $x = 5$

5. Multiplication Axioms of Equality

(*Note* on the relationship between multiplication and division:

(a) any number times $0 = 0$

(b) in general, if $\frac{b}{c} = a$, then $b = ac$

$$\frac{12}{4} = 3, \text{ and } 12 = 4 \cdot 3$$

If we assume that $\frac{4}{0} = x$, then we must conclude that $4 = 0 \cdot x$. But this contradicts the statement that any number times $0 = 0$. Division by zero is therefore meaningless and is not permitted.)

    (a) If $a = b$, then $ac = bc$

    (b) If $ac = bc$, then $a = b$, $(c \neq 0)$

Note: Parenthetical stipulations such as $(c \neq 0)$ are always important. In this case, without the stipulation that the axiom holds only if c is not equal to zero, we could conclude that if $7n = 6n$, then $7 = 6$. However, $7n = 6n$ only if $n = 0$; the nonsense statement $7 = 6$ results from division by zero.

Axioms of Inequality. Unlike tne relationship of equality, the relationships $>$ and $<$ are neither reflexive nor symmetric; no number is greater than itself. If $a > b$, then $b < a$.

1. Addition Axiom of Inequality

    If $a > b$, then $a + c > b + c$

2. Multiplication Axioms of Inequality

    (a) If $a > b$, then $ac > bc$, $(c > 0)$

    (b) If $ac > bc$, then $a > b$, $(c > 0)$

Note: The stipulation $c > 0$ is important: $4 \cdot 2 > 3 \cdot 2$, but $4 \cdot (-2) < 3 \cdot (-2)$.

3. Transitive Property of Inequality

    If $a > b$ and $b > c$, then $a > c$

The Field Axioms. There are 11 of these axioms:

1. Commutative Property of Addition

$$a + b = b + a$$

Example: $2 + 5 = 5 + 2$

The result of adding two numbers is unaffected by the order in which the numbers are combined.

2. Associative Property of Addition

$$(a + b) + c = a + (b + c)$$

Example: $(2 + 3) + 4 = 2 + (3 + 4)$

The result of adding three numbers is unaffected by the way in which the numbers are grouped. (Addition is a binary operation; only two numbers can be combined at one time.)

3. Identity Element for Addition

$$a + 0 = a$$

Example: $7 + 0 = 7$

The identity element for addition is zero. Any number combined with the identity element remains unchanged.

4. Inverse Element for Addition

$$a + -a = 0 \text{ and } -a + -(-a) = 0$$

Example: $3 + -3 = 0$ and $-3 + -(-3) = 0$

Any number plus its additive inverse is equal to zero, the identity element for addition.

(*Note:* The symbol $-a$ means "the negative of a"; in practice, most people say "negative a." This

A-298

is not objectionable provided that it is not assumed that $-a$ is a negative number; $-a$ means the negative of whatever a is: if a is -7, then $-a$ is $-(-7) = +7$, which is normally written without the positive prefix as 7.)

5. Closure Property of Addition

    If $a \in S$ and $b \in S$, then $(a + b) \in S$

(*Note:* The symbol $\in$ means "is a member of." Thus, $a \in S$ is read "a is a member of set S.")

If a and b are real numbers, then their sum is a real number. If a and b are complex numbers, then their sum is a complex number. The sets of real numbers and complex numbers are said to be closed under the operation of addition because addition in these sets can never produce a number that is not a member of the set. Some subsets of the set of real numbers, however, are not:

The set of odd numbers is not closed under addition: $3 + 5 = 8$.

The set of irrational numbers is not closed under addition: $\sqrt{2} + -\sqrt{2} = 0$.

6. Commutative Property of Multiplication

$$ab = ba$$

Example: $4 \cdot 6 = 6 \cdot 4$

The result of multiplying two numbers is unaffected by the order in which they are combined.

7. Associative Property of Multiplication

$$(ab) \cdot c = a \cdot (bc)$$

Example: $(2 \cdot 3) \cdot 4 = 2 \cdot (3 \cdot 4)$

The result of multiplying three numbers is unaffected by the way in which the numbers are grouped. (Multiplication is a binary operation; only two numbers can be combined at one time.)

8. Identity Element for Multiplication

$$1 \cdot a = a$$

Example: $1 \cdot 9 = 9$

The number 1 is the identity element for multiplication. Any number combined with the identity element remains unchanged.

9. Inverse Element for Multiplication

$$\frac{1}{a} \cdot a = 1, (a \neq 0)$$

Any non-zero number times its multiplicative inverse equals 1, the identity element for multiplication. The number 0 has no multiplicative inverse.

10. Closure Property of Multiplication

    If $a \in S$ and $b \in S$, then $ab \in S$

The product of two real numbers is always a real number. The product of two complex numbers is always a complex number. These two sets are said to be closed under the operation of multiplication because multiplication in these sets can never produce a number that does not belong to the set.

The set of irrational numbers is not closed under multiplication: $\sqrt{2} \cdot \sqrt{2} = \sqrt{4} = 2$.

11. Distributive Property of Multiplication over Addition

$$a \cdot (b + c) = ab + ac$$

Example: $2 \cdot (3 + 4) = 2 \cdot 3 + 2 \cdot 4$

The distributive property links multiplication and addition. Since a combination of operations is involved, this convention has been adopted to avoid any misunderstanding as to the order in which operations are to be carried out. It can be stated thus: *All multiplications and divisions are to be done before*

additions and subtractions. This convention is important:

$$2 \cdot 3 + 4 = 6 + 4 = 10;$$

failure to observe the convention could lead to this incorrect result:

$$2 \cdot 3 + 4 = 2 \cdot 7 = 14.$$

Problem Solving

The key step in the solution of a problem is to state the numerical relationships involved in the form of an algebraic sentence that can be simplified according to the accepted rules. In textbook situations the problem is often stated directly, but in actual experience the problem solver must first recognize the problem. Textbook problems are models of the kinds of relationships that occur in real problems. They are also exercises in applying the field axioms.

A Problem and Its Solution

A six-quart mixture of alcohol and water is 75 per cent alcohol. How much alcohol must be added to the existing mixture to produce a mixture that is 80 per cent alcohol?

Analysis of situation: The amount of alcohol in the present mixture plus the amount added will equal 80 per cent of the resulting mixture. The resulting mixture will be equal to the original mixture plus the amount of alcohol added. The present mixture contains $.75 \cdot 6 = 4.5$ quarts of alcohol. Let $n =$ the number of quarts of alcohol to be added.

Statement: $4.5 + n = .8 \cdot (6 + n)$

	Steps	Reasons
Eliminating non-possible answers	$4.5 + n = .8 \cdot 6 + .8n$	Distributive property of multiplication over addition $a (b + c) = ab + ac$
	$4.5 + n = 4.8 + .8n$	Arithmetic
	$10 \cdot (4.5 + n) = 10 \cdot (4.8 + .8n)$	Multiplication axiom of equality* If $a = b$, then $ac = bc$
	$10 \cdot 4.5 + 10n = 10 \cdot 4.8 + 10 \cdot .8n$	Distributive property
	$45 + 10n = 48 + 8n$	Arithmetic
	$45 + (-45) + 10n = 48 + (-45) + 8n$	Addition axiom of equality If $a = b$, then $a + c = b + c$
	$10n = 3 + 8n$	Arithmetic
	$10n + (-8n) = 3 + 8n + (-8n)$	Addition axiom of equality
	$2n = 3$	Arithmetic
	$.5 \cdot 2n = .5 \cdot 3$	Multiplication axiom of equality
	$n = 1.5$	Arithmetic

Testing the possible answer	4.5 quarts $+$ 1.5 quarts $= 6$ quarts (alcohol in resulting mixture)
	6 quarts $+$ 1.5 quarts $= 7.5$ quarts (total of resulting mixture)
	$6 \div 7.5 = .8 = 80\%$ (percentage of alcohol in resulting mixture)

Solution: The amount of alcohol to be added is 1.5 quarts.

*This step is not necessary; it is used because the elimination of fractions makes it easier to simplify the statement.

Solving an equation is the process of finding (if any exist) all numbers, in a specified set, whose names can be used to make true statements when they are substituted for the letters in a particular sentence. The following results are possible:

1. No solution.
2. Exactly one solution.
3. More than one solution, but still a finite number of solutions.
4. An infinite number of solutions.

Case 1. The following situations provide examples of equations that have no solutions in a given set of numbers. The sequence shows how the number system was expanded from the natural numbers to the complex numbers by devising numbers that would provide answers to these equations.

$x + 1 = 1$ has no solution in the set of natural numbers. The solution, 0, is in the set of whole numbers.

$x + 2 = 1$ has no solution in the set of whole numbers. The solution, -1, is in the set of integers.

$3x = 2$ has no solution in the set of integers. The solution, $\frac{2}{3}$, is in the set of rational numbers.

$x^2 = 2$ has no solution in the set of rational numbers. The solutions, $\sqrt{2}$ and $-\sqrt{2}$, are in the set of irrational numbers.

$x^2 + 1 = 0$ has no solution in the set of real numbers. The equation was solved by the invention of the number i (the number whose square is -1). Development of the sets of imaginary numbers and complex numbers followed.

Case 2. The equation $2x + 3 = 11$ has exactly one real-number solution, 4.

Case 3. The equation $x^2 = 4x$ has two real-number solutions, 4 and 0.

Case 4. The equation $x + y = 6$ has an infinite number of solutions, which can be written in the form of ordered pairs of numbers: (1,5), (4,2), (−2,8), (6.4,−.4), etc. The first number in each pair is a value of x, the second the corresponding value of y.

The solution of an equation can be divided into two main steps: (1) eliminating all non-possible answers and (2) testing the possible answers. The accompanying sample problem shows the two main steps and illustrates how the field axioms are used in problem solving.

Books about Algebra

Asimov, Isaac. *The Realm of Algebra* (Houghton Mifflin, 1961).

Barnett, R. A. *Elementary Algebra: Structure and Use,* 2nd edition (McGraw-Hill, 1975).

Drooyan, Irving, and others. *Elementary Algebra: Structure and Skills* (Wiley, 1976).

Keedy, M. L., and M. L. Bittinger. *Intermediate Algebra: a Modern Approach,* 2nd edition (Addison-Wesley, 1975).

Satek, W. M. *Algebra: a Fundamental Approach* (Saunders, 1977).

For Younger Readers:

Weiss, M. E. *666 Jellybeans! All That? an Introduction to Algebra* (Crowell, 1976).

Algeciras Conference, ăl′jĕ-sĕr′ás, a meeting of European powers held in Algeciras, Spain, in 1906 to settle a Franco-German dispute over Morocco. Germany had been ignored in the Anglo-French Entente of 1904, an agreement giving special trade rights to the French in Morocco and the British in Egypt. Protesting that German interests were violated and hoping also to weaken French power, Germany demanded an international conference on the situation in Morocco.

The resulting Act of Algeciras opened the Moroccan trade to all nations. Although professing to reaffirm Moroccan independence, it also authorized French and Spanish control of the Moroccan police force. The conference, far from weakening the Anglo-French Entente as Germany had hoped, drove France and Britain closer together. Franco-German differences over Morocco remained, increasing world tensions and causing another crisis in 1911, when the Germans threatened the Moroccan port of Agadir. Germany then agreed to recognize French control of Morocco in exchange for sovereignty over part of the French Congo.

Alger, ăl′jĕr, **Horatio, Jr.** (1834-1899), a United States author of novels for boys. His main theme in about 130 books is that

Title Page of Book by Horatio Alger, Jr.
Harper Memorial Library, University of Chicago

Horatio Alger, Jr.

almost any poor boy, if he is hardworking and honest, can win financial and social success. Despite the moralizing and stilted plots and language, his books sold millions of copies. *Ragged Dick* (1867) was first in a series of that name. Also popular were the *Luck and Pluck* (1869) and the *Tattered Tom* (1871) series.

Alger was born in Revere, Massachusetts, the son of a Unitarian clergyman. He was graduated from the Harvard Divinity School in 1860. He was first a tutor and then pastor of a Unitarian Church in Brewster, Massachusetts. In 1866 he became chaplain of the Newsboys' Lodging House in New York City. During the 1960's, revived interest in Alger's books led to their being published in facsimile reprints and in paperback editions.

Alger, Russell A. (Alexander) (1836-1907), United States secretary of war, 1897-99. Severely criticized for the inefficiency of his department during the Spanish-Ameri-can War, he was forced to resign. He defended himself in *The Spanish-American War* (1901). Alger was born in Medina County, Ohio. During the Civil War he was colonel of a Michigan cavalry regiment. He was governor of Michigan, 1885-87, and United States senator, 1902-07.

Algeria, ăl'jẹr'ĭ-à, or **Democratic and Popular Republic of Algeria,** a country of North Africa. It is the second-largest country in Africa, smaller only than Sudan. Algeria stretches from the Mediterranean Sea deep into the Sahara. It has an area of 919,595 square miles (about 3½ times the size of Texas). Its maximum dimensions are about 1,200 miles north-south and 1,100 miles east-west.

Physical Geography

Land. The principal physical features of Algeria are the Atlas Mountains in the north and the Sahara, to the south, a vast desert that covers about nine-tenths of the country.

The Atlas Mountains are a faulted system, with steep-sided mountains and deep ravines in its more rugged parts. The region consists of three roughly parallel northeast-southwest zones. Beginning near the coast, they are (from north to south) the Tell Atlas, the High Plateaus, and the Saharan At-

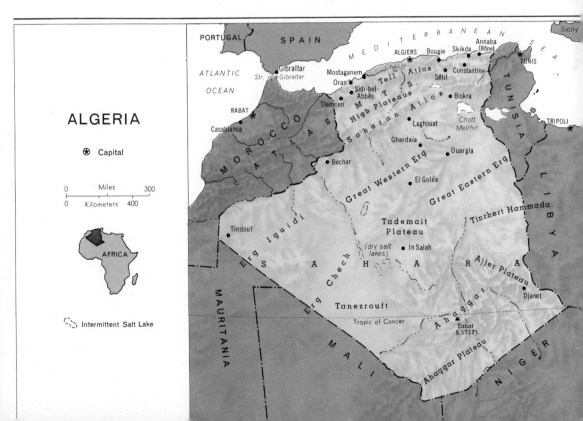

Philip Gendreau

Bridge over El Kantarra Gorge at Constantine

las. The highest ranges of the Tell Atlas rise more than 7,500 feet above sea level. Small inter-mountain plains interrupt the rough terrain, particularly along the coast.

The High Plateaus are marked by rolling hills, some steep cliffs, and flat plains, with an average elevation of 3,000 feet. Though generally low, the Saharan Atlas, which fringes the desert, rises to a height of more than 7,600 feet.

The Sahara is made up mainly of low tablelands, with occasional outcrops of high terrain, such as the Ahaggar massif in the south. Here rises 9,573-foot-high Tahat, the highest point in Algeria. Part of the Sahara consists of sand and dune areas, called *ergs,* among the largest of which are the Great Eastern Erg and the Great Western Erg. There are also areas of exposed bedrock, called *hammadas.*

Water. Because of the sparse rainfall, rivers and lakes are few. The Chéliff River, 450 miles long, is the chief river. Of the rivers that rise in the Saharan Atlas, it is the only one to reach the Mediterranean. Many water courses are dry except after winter rains. On the High Plateaus and in the Sahara are expansive salt flats and marshes, known as *chotts* or *shotts.* Many of them are covered by shallow water during winter. Chott Melrhir, in the Sahara near the Saharan Atlas, occupies a depression below sea level.

Climate. Coastal Algeria has a *Mediterranean* type of climate, with mild, rainy winters and hot, dry summers—a climate similar to that of southern California. January temperatures average about 50° F.; July temperatures, just below 80° F. Most of the area has 30 inches or more of rainfall a year. Some places receive more than 50 inches a year.

A-302

On the High Plateaus, there is a dry *steppe* climate, with cooler winters and slightly hotter summers. Rainfall averages 10 to 20 inches annually, all of it coming in winter and spring. The Atlas Mountains have a varied climate because of their elevation.

The Sahara is one of the world's most desolate areas. Summer temperatures average above 95° F. and frequently rise as high as 120° F. Temperature changes between night and day are extreme. There is little or no rain.

Natural Vegetation. In the more humid mountain areas, and occasionally along the coast, are oaks (particularly cork oaks) and coniferous trees, mainly pines, cedars, and cypresses. However, much of northern Algeria is covered with a scrubby bush-type vegetation, called *maquis.* On the High Plateaus are dry grasslands. Beyond the mountain vegetation of the Saharan Atlas begins the true desert. Here, only scattered oases have vegetation.

Economy

Since Algeria gained independence from France in 1962, virtually all industries have been nationalized. The only significant private enterprise is in the technological field, where foreign firms work in partnership with the government. The chief economic objectives are to reach self-sufficiency through rapid industrialization and to raise the standard of living. Growth of the economy was slow until the late 1960's, but accelerated thereafter. The first in a series of four-year plans (programs for economic development) was begun in 1970.

Many obstacles, however, are yet to be overcome. Among them are inadequate health and educational facilities, rapid population growth, widespread unemployment, a lack of trained personnel to run technologically complex new industries, and low agricultural production. The abrupt emigration after independence of nearly a million French Algerians, many of whom were highly skilled, was a severe setback to the nation.

Mineral Production. Most of Algeria's recent economic progress has been made possible by minerals, especially petroleum, natural gas, phosphate rock, and iron ore. Of primary importance are petroleum and natural gas. Both are produced in large amounts in the Sahara and piped to the coast for domestic use and export. Algeria's natural gas reserves are among the largest in the world and are being tapped on an increasing scale. Revenues from the two fuels have grown enormously since 1973, when world prices began rising sharply, allowing Algeria to greatly increase investment in capital improvements.

Manufacturing. Under the four-year plans, large sums have been invested in manufacturing industries and they have had considerable growth. Growth has been especially evident in the mineral-based industries, including petroleum refining, the liquefying of natural gas, and the making of petrochemicals, fertilizers, iron and steel, and cement. Other manufacturing includes truck and automobile assembly, food processing, and the making of a fairly wide variety of household and personal goods, including handicraft objects. Wine is produced in large amounts, mostly for export to France.

Agriculture. Although more than half the people are engaged in farming, agriculture contributes relatively little to the gross national product. In general, farm production has stagnated, in some cases declined, mainly because of improper management of the large commercial estates that were once predominantly French. They occupy much of Algeria's best farmland and are now operated as state farms and cooperatives. Because of low agricultural output, many basic foods must be imported.

Only about 3 per cent of Algeria's land is suitable for cultivation, and most of that is along or near the coast. Virtually all of Algeria's cash crops are produced there; they include wheat, barley, wine grapes, citrus fruit, olives, and tomatoes. In other parts of the country, crops are grown mainly for subsistence and the grazing of sheep and goats is common. Dates are the chief crop produced in the Sahara.

Transportation. Algeria's transportation facilities were built largely by the French and are now being improved and expanded. Excluding dirt tracks, there are about 37,000 miles (59,500 km) of roads, most of which are along the coast and in the Atlas Mountains. Roads have been built into the Sahara and several cross it. Railways, totaling some 2,500 miles (4,000 km), are also best developed in the north. Only one line extends into the Sahara. Algiers, Oran, and Annaba are major ports; Algiers is the main air terminal.

The People

The Algerians are of Berber stock mixed with some Arab and, in the far south, Negro. Since Arabs were the conquering invaders whose religion and language the natives adopted, it became customary for the Algerians to consider themselves Arabs. A sense of Berber identity has been preserved by some groups, however, such as the Kabyles in the mountainous section of the north between Algiers and Constantine.

Among the desert Berbers are the Tuareg, known as the "blue men." Although the Tuaregs are Moslems, the women go unveiled, but the men wear blue veils, from which their skin becomes stained. The Tuaregs have the only written Berber dialect.

Population. The population of Algeria in 1977 was about 17,910,000. An important population trend has been migration from rural to urban areas. More than half the people now live in cities.

Algeria's Largest Cities

Algiers, the capital	1,800,000	Annaba (Bône).	340,000
		Tizi-Ouzou	230,000
Oran	500,000	Blida	162,000
Constantine	430,000	Sétif	160,000

Language and Education. The constitution of 1963 made Arabic the official language, but stated that French could be used provisionally. French had been the only official language throughout the colonial era.

Most Moslems speak Arabic, a Semitic language. Dialects of Berber, a language of the Hamitic branch of the Semito-Hamitic family, are spoken by about 20 per cent of the people. These dialects are not written (except that of the Tuaregs). All Moslem Algerians dealing with European settlers

Camel Market in Algeria

Wide World

during the colonial era had to know French as a second language.

Under French rule classical Arabic, used in the Moslem religion and Islamic literature, was taught in the Moslem religious schools. It was held in high esteem, since it reflected a past era of conquest and achievement, but less than 3 per cent of the population could read classical Arabic when independence came in 1962.

The French public school system was introduced into Algeria in 1833, and schooling for the children of colonists was free and compulsory. Moslem children, although not excluded from French schools, were not encouraged to attend. A few Moslem elementary schools, in which French was taught, were established by the government. Before World War II not more than 10 per cent of the Moslem population were literate, and few Moslems of the educated class were familiar with Arabic.

When the country gained independence, a campaign was launched to provide schooling for all children and to teach adult illiterates to read and write. Available teachers were either French or French-educated Moslems; the language of instruction was French. The system has gradually become bilingual. The first two grades are taught in Arabic. In the higher grades, subjects are taught in either Arabic or French, depending on their content. It is planned to eventually make Arabic the sole language of instruction.

There is no tuition at any level, including the university level. Where facilities are available, eight years of school are compulsory. After six years of primary school, students either advance to secondary school or take a two-year postprimary course. Academic secondary schools offer a seven-year course, with three years of specialization, or a four-year general course. Other secondary schools give vocational and agricultural training.

The University of Algiers, established in 1879, is the oldest of the universities. There are also a number of specialized institutions of higher learning.

Religion and Culture. Islam is the state religion under the constitution, and most Algerians, at least nominally, are Moslems of the Sunnite branch of Islam. There are small minorities of Jews and Christians in the country.

There are in Algiers the National Library and museums of prehistory and ethnography, fine arts, antiquities and Islamic art, and Negro art. Constantine and Oran have libraries and museums. Writers who were independence fighters—Mohammed Dib, Kateb Yasin, and Mark Hadad—became active in the cultural movement. Painters and sculptors who have rejected Islam are using the human figure as a subject, a practice forbidden to Moslems.

Government

Under the constitution of 1976, Algeria is a socialist republic. The executive branch of the government is headed by a popularly elected president (chief of state), who serves a six-year term. The president also is the premier (head of government), commander-in-chief of the armed forces, and leader of the only legal party, the National Liberation Front. The president appoints a cabinet of ministers to assist him. The legislature is the National Assembly, which is popularly elected. Legislators serve five-year terms. In practice, the National Assembly is subordinate to the president and has little power to initiate laws.

The judicial system consists of a supreme court, lower courts, and special courts for crimes against the state.

The country is divided into 31 *wilayaats* (provinces) each governed by an elected assembly. Below the wilayaats are local communes, also governed by elected assemblies.

History

Cave paintings found in southern Algeria indicate that there were people living there as early as 8000 B.C. When the Phoenicians began founding settlements along the coast in the ninth century B.C., the inland area was inhabited by nomadic Berbers. By the second century B.C., when the Romans were winning control of North Africa from the Carthaginians, the Berbers nearer the coast had become settled and had organized themselves into kingdoms. Numidia was south of the coastal strip in the east, Mauretania in the west.

Sovereignty over Numidia and Mauretania changed often, being awarded by Rome to the native rulers who supported the Romans in various wars. Numidia was annexed temporarily by Rome in 46 B.C., permanently in 25 B.C. Mauretania was annexed in 42 A.D. Caesarea (Cherchel) was the major city of eastern Mauretania, Cirta (Constantine) of Numidia. Hippo Regius (Annaba, or

Bône) was seat of the Christian bishopric held by Saint Augustine (354-430), a native of the area. Northern Algeria was occupied by the Vandals in 429, and retaken by Byzantine forces for the Eastern Roman Empire in 533.

Moslem Era. In the second half of the seventh century Moslem Arabs overran western North Africa, which they called the Maghrib (Arabic for "western"). The Berbers were converted to Islam, but soon joined a fanatical sect, the Kharisites. An autonomous Kharisite state was founded at Tiaret about 776; it lasted into the 10th century.

In the 11th century the Fatimid dynasty in Egypt sent a horde of Bedouins, primitive Arab tribesmen, into the Maghrib to destroy the power of rebellious Berbers. The countryside back of the coastal strip was ravaged. However, another independent Moslem Berber dynasty arose in Tlemcen in the 13th century. It ruled much of present Algeria for 200 years.

In the early 16th century the Spanish, who had expelled the Moslems from the Iberian Peninsula in Europe, attacked the coast of Barbary, as Europeans called the Maghrib, and won control of several ports. The Ottoman Turks, however, had begun the conquest of North Africa. Turkish corsairs (sea raiders) under the Barbarossa brothers seized the port of Algiers and in 1519 organized what is now northern Algeria into a Turkish province. Theoretically tributary to the sultan, it became increasingly independent under corsair rule. Algiers was soon one of the pirate capitals of the Barbary coast.

The Spanish attacked Algiers in 1541, but failed to take it. Gradually Spain lost its garrison posts until only those on the Gulf of Oran were left. For almost 300 years efforts by the Christian nations to curb the Barbary corsairs were largely unsuccessful. (See also BARBARY; CORSAIRS.)

French Era. In the 1820's relations between the French and the Algerians grew tense. After an ineffectual naval blockade in 1829, France invaded Algiers in 1830 and won a quick victory over the coastal area. Inland, however, resistance was strong under the leadership of Abd-el-Kader, the Arab ruler of Mascara. The Algerians did not surrender until 1847. In 1848 northern Algeria was annexed to France. Although periodic insurrections continued into the 20th cen-

Philip Gendreau
Roman Ruins in Algeria. Trajan's Arch was the gate to the ancient city of Timgad in the Sahara.

tury, military posts were gradually established in the Algerian Sahara and the desert Berbers subdued.

France's efforts to colonize Algeria were only partially successful until after the Franco-Prussian War (1870-71), when a number of refugees from German-occupied Alsace moved in. Settlers came also from southern France to establish vineyards. The colonists were given the most fertile lands. The native Algerians were permitted to become French citizens only if they renounced their Moslem religion. Since few would do so, the country was run by and for the benefit of the colonists. Many Moslems, unable to find work, emigrated to France.

Independence. Resentment toward the French began building into an independence movement in the period between World Wars I and II. The French government tried at various times to improve the political status of the Moslems, who formed about 90 per cent of the population. Any change, however, was bitterly opposed by the colonists. In 1945, as World War II ended, a violent uprising of Moslems began. It was put down at once with great severity.

In 1947 France gave Algerians full citizenship, but adjusted the voting laws so the colonists would retain political control. The new status did not satisfy the Moslems, who formed a revolutionary organization, the National Liberation Front (FLN). In 1954 a rebellion began that the French were unable to put down. The Algerian crisis undermined the shaky political structure in France, and in 1958 the Fourth Republic fell. General Charles de Gaulle, premier and President of the new government, entered negotiations with the FLN, but the Algerians would accept no compromise to self-determination. At last, in 1962, a referendum was held, and Algeria became independent. Ahmed Ben Bella of the FLN was elected President in 1963.

The departure of French colonists, many skilled in government and technology, left the economy near collapse. With French governmental assistance, the nation slowly recovered. The two countries cooperated in developing oil and gas resources.

In 1965 President Ben Bella was deposed and control of the country was taken over by Houari Boumedienne, who pursued a policy of socialism. During 1970-71, most of the foreign-owned oil industry was nationalized, and during 1971-74 farmland was redistributed and organized into cooperatives. Algeria emerged as one of the leaders of the nonaligned nations in the 1970's. Boumedienne died in 1978, and socialist policies were continued by his successors.

For further information, see:

Books about Algeria

Horne, Alistair. *A Savage War of Peace: Algeria, 1954-1962* (Viking Press, 1978).

Smith, Tony. *The French Stake in Algeria, 1945-1962* (Cornell University, 1978).

For Younger Readers:

Carpenter, Allan, and Tom Balow. *Algeria* (Childrens Press, 1978).

Spencer, William. *The Land and People of Algeria* (Lippincott, 1969).

Entrance to the Casbah in Algiers
United Press International

Algiers, ăl-jērz', Algeria, the nation's capital and largest city, a seaport, and the administrative center of Algiers department. It lies in the foothills of the Tell Atlas on a small inlet of the Mediterranean Sea.

On the side of a steep hill and dominating the city is the Casbah, built as a fortress in the 16th century. Today this maze of narrow, winding streets and stairways lined with crowded houses, shops, and cafes is the center of the old Arab and Moorish section. Beyond the Casbah is the modern city.

An elevated highway supported by massive stone arches stretches across the harbor front; behind it are Western-style stores, warehouses, and office buildings. Wide boulevards and streets lead from the business section past numerous parks and gardens to residential areas in the hills above.

Algiers is the country's commercial and industrial center. Among products of its factories are trucks, machinery, electrical supplies, chemicals, and textiles. Fruits, vegetables, and grain from nearby farmlands are processed in Algiers. The city is served by several railways and many highways. Its airport handles domestic and international flights.

The University of Algiers is the chief institution of higher learning. The National Library, the National Museum of Fine Arts, and the National Museum of Antiquities with Roman, Berber, and Islamic archeological exhibits are here.

Algiers was used as a trading post by the Phoenicians as early as the ninth century B.C. and after 42 A.D. by the Romans, who called it Icosium. The Vandals destroyed much of the settlement in the fifth century. In the seventh century Arab invasions engulfed Algiers, then called al Jezair after the small island protecting its harbor. In the 16th century, under the Ottoman Turks, Algiers became a pirate stronghold and one of the chief cities of Barbary. In 1830 the French seized Algiers and put an end to piracy. The city was held by German troops for a short time during World War II. After recapture by Allied forces, it was (1943-44) the headquarters for the French provincial government.

Population: 1,800,000.

See also BARBARY.

Algin. See KELP.

Algol, ăl'gŏl, a variable star in the constellation Perseus. (A variable star is one

Algonquian wigwams, canoes, weaving, basketry, and a papoose cradle are shown in this illustration of life in the eastern woodlands. It was painted by A. A. Janson for the American Museum of Natural History under the direction of Clark Wissler.

American Museum of
Natural History

that changes in brightness.) Algol, which was observed by the ancient Greeks and named by the Arabs, is now known to be a complex system of at least four stars revolving around one another. A pair of the stars form an *eclipsing binary*—two stars that pass in front of each other in turn, causing a periodic (cyclical) dimming of their combined light. Algol dims regularly every 21 days and 21 hours.

Algonquian, or **Algonkian,** both ăl-gŏng′kĭ-ăn, a linguistic family of North American Indians. It once included 40 separate languages. The family is named for the Algonkin, or Algonquin, a tribe that formerly lived along the Ottawa River in Canada. Algonquian tribes lived along the Atlantic coast from Virginia to Newfoundland, westward through southern Canada to the Rocky Mountains, and in the Middle West east of the Mississippi River; a few groups lived on the western Plains. Between the Algonquians of the coast and those of the Middle West lived Indians of the Iroquoian linguistic family.

Most Algonquian tribes grew crops, but also did much hunting and fishing. Corn was the main crop, but beans, pumpkins, squash, and tobacco were raised and wild rice harvested. Maple trees were tapped.

Since the first Indians known to English and French settlers were Algonquians, many Algonquian words became familiar. These include wigwam, squaw, papoose, wampum, moccasin, toboggan, hominy,

succotash, persimmon, totem, chipmunk, opossum, skunk, and terrapin. Many of these words are said to have been learned from the Abnaki of the Maine coast, who were known to fishermen and traders long before permanent settlers arrived.

Tribes Important Historically

Algonquians had little government, and it is therefore difficult to define tribes and impossible to give a complete list of tribes. A chief had little authority beyond his ability to persuade and to lead. Councils of elders or chiefs of clans were the principal governing bodies. There were many confederacies and alliances, some of them temporary.

Near the English settlement at Jamestown was the Powhatan Confederacy, made up of 30 small tribes. Most of them had been conquerored by the chief Powhatan. After Powhatan's death in 1618 his brother Opechancanough fought the English, 1622-36 and 1644. During these wars the confederacy declined.

The Pilgrims of Plymouth made peace with Massasoit, chief of the Wampanoags, but his son Metacomet, or King Philip, led a confederacy in a war, 1675-76, in which he was defeated and killed. Among other Algonquian tribes of the New England coast were the Massachuset, Narraganset, Pequot, Mohegan, Mahican, Niantic, and Abnaki.

William Penn bought Pennsylvania from the Delaware, or Lenni Lenape, called a confederacy of three tribes, although only

A-307

one, the Munsee, has separate identity, and it is often considered a separate tribe. Similarly, farther west, the Miami are usually associated with the Wea and Piankashaw. The Chippewa (or Ojibway) tribe of the Lake Superior region is one of the largest, but actually is a multitude of small bands with little claim to any sort of governmental unity. The Chippewa were closely associated with the Ottawa and Potawatomi. The Illinois were a group or confederacy of several small tribes. Other Middle West tribes were the Shawnee, Kickapoo, Sac and Fox, and Menominee.

The Cree in Canada and the Blackfeet, Arapaho, and Cheyenne of the Far West were also of Algonquian stock.

See separate articles on the following tribes:

Abnaki	Kaskaskia	Niantic
Arapaho	Kickapoo	Ottawa
Blackfeet	Mahican	Pequot
Cheyenne	Menominee	Potawatomi
Chippewa	Miami	Powhatan
Cree	Mohegan	Sac
Delaware	Narraganset	Shawnee
Fox	Naskapi	Wampanoag
Illinois		

Wars of the Algonquians

Algonquian tribes seldom warred among themselves. Many of them were constantly at war with the Iroquois. Almost all of the tribes were allied with the French in the French and Indian War. An exception was the Fox tribe, which fought against the French and was badly defeated. A remnant joined the Sac, and the two tribes were thereafter united.

Pontiac, an Ottawa, was a leader in a rebellion against British rule that involved many tribes in 1763. Most Algonquians aided the British in the American Revolution. After its close several tribes joined Little Turtle, a Miami, in opposing United States expansion westward. A few years later Tecumseh, a Shawnee, sought to unite many tribes against the Americans. After the defeat of his brother, the Prophet, at Tippecanoe in 1811, Tecumseh allied his followers with the British in the War of 1812. Black Hawk, a Sac war chief, fought in Illinois and Wisconsin in 1832, but he was opposed by Keokuk in his own tribe, and got very little aid from neighboring tribes.

In the 1830's some Algonquian tribes were moved to Indian Territory, but many remained in Wisconsin. Descendants of other groups are still found scattered over much of their original territory.

———

For further information, see:

Biography

BLACK HAWK	POCAHONTAS
KEOKUK	PONTIAC
LITTLE TURTLE	TECUMSEH
MASSASOIT	

Miscellaneous

FALLEN TIMBERS,	KING PHILIP'S WAR
BATTLE OF	TIPPECANOE, BATTLE OF

Algren, äl′grĕn, **Nelson** (1909-1981), a United States novelist. His subjects usually are social outcasts and misfits. *The Man with the Golden Arm* won the first National Book Award for fiction in 1950. This naturalistic novel describes the return of soldier Frankie "Machine" Majcinek to Chicago, where he becomes a poker dealer and a narcotics addict. Algren vividly describes the fantastic horrors of the addict's world. In *Never Come Morning* (1942) Bruno Bicek, a tough hoodlum who wants to be a boxer, ends his short life in the electric chair for an accidental murder.

Algren was born in Detroit, but was brought to Chicago as a child. After he graduated in journalism from the University of Illinois in 1931, he decided against newspaper work and did odd jobs before becoming a full-time writer.

His other books include: Novels—*Somebody in Boots* (1935); *A Walk on the Wild Side* (1956). Short Stories—*The Neon Wilderness* (1947). Nonfiction—*Chicago, City on the Make* (1951); *Who Lost an American?* (1963); *Notes from a Sea Diary* (1965).

Alhambra, äl-hăm′brȧ, the medieval fortress and palace of the Moorish kings of Granada, Spain. It is on a hill overlooking the city of Granada. Lacework arches, arabesque wall carvings, and glazed tile make the Alhambra an outstanding example of Moorish art and architecture. The name, from the Arabic *al-hamra* (the red), refers to the red bricks of which the buildings are constructed.

The Alhambra consists of towers and walls of the citadel, or fortress; the palace; gardens; the ruins of a royal mosque; and other buildings. The palace was built around two oblong courts. The Court of the Pool, or Court of the Myrtles, contained a large rectangular goldfish pool surrounded by myrtles. At the north end of the court, in the Tower of Comares, is the Hall of the Ambassadors. The largest room in the palace, it was once the grand reception room. The Court of

Lions was named for a central fountain of alabaster supported by 12 marble lions. It is surrounded by an arcade resting on 124 slender white marble columns.

On one side of the Court of Lions is the Hall of the Abencerrages. According to tradition, Boabdil, the last Moorish king of Granada, put the Abencerrage chieftains to death here. Opposite is the Hall of the Two Sisters, named for the two white marble slabs that are part of the floor.

The Alhambra was built chiefly between 1248 and 1391 by the kings of the Nasrid dynasty. It was captured by the Christian forces of Ferdinand and Isabella in 1492. (After this victory the king and queen were willing to finance Columbus's expedition.) In the 16th century Charles V tore down part of the palace to make room for a palace of his own, which was never completed. This palace now houses the Alhambra Museum. During the Peninsular War (1808-14) the French blew up some of the towers of the Alhambra. Earthquakes added to the damage. Restorations were made after 1828.

Alhambra, California, a city in Los Angeles County, about seven miles (11 km) east-northeast of downtown Los Angeles. Although mainly residential, Alhambra has manufacturing, processing, and other industries. Alhambra was incorporated in 1903.

Population: 64,615.

Ali, son-in-law of the prophet Mohammed. See FATIMA; ISLAM, subtitle *Sects*.

Ali, Muhammad (Cassius Clay) (1942-   ), a United States boxer. He became known not only for his great skill as a boxer—he ranks as one of the all-time best—but also for his colorful personality. He won the heavyweight title from Sonny Liston in 1964 as Cassius Clay. (After becoming a Black Muslim he changed his name.) In 1967 he refused induction into the army on religious grounds, and the boxing authorities stripped him of his title and barred him from competition. Three years later he was allowed to resume his career. He failed to regain the title from Joe Frazier in 1971 (his first professional defeat), but succeeded against George Foreman in 1974. Ali lost the title to Leon Spinks in February, 1978, but regained it seven months later in a rematch. He retired in 1979, returned to boxing briefly in 1980, and then retired permanently.

Ali was born in Louisville, Kentucky. He

Spanish National Tourist Office
The Court of Lions in the Alhambra

won an Olympic gold medal as a light heavyweight in 1960, and then turned to a professional career.

For photo, see BOXING.

"Ali Baba and the Forty Thieves." See ARABIAN NIGHTS.

Alias, ā'lĭ-ăs, in law, a name used by a person in place of his real name. The word is from the Latin phrase *alias dictus,* which means "otherwise called." *Alias* commonly refers to a name used by a criminal to escape detection.

Alibates Flint Quarries National Monument. See NATIONAL PARKS, section "United States."

Alibi, ăl'ĭ-bī, in law, a defense made by the accused in a criminal case. The word *alibi* is Latin for "elsewhere." The defendant tries to establish that at the time the crime was committed he was at some place other than where it was committed.

Alicante, ăl'ĭ-kän'tĕ (*Spanish:* ä'lĕ-kän'tä), Spain, the capital of Alicante Province. It is a port on the Mediterranean Sea. The city is a processing and trading center and a popular resort.

Alicante was originally a Greek colony and then later the Roman city of Lucentum. In 711 it was captured by the Moors; it was retaken by Christian forces in the mid-13th century. In the early 14th century the city came under the rule of Aragon.

Population: 251,387.

Alice's Adventures in Wonderland (1865), a whimsical book for children written by Charles Lutwidge Dodgson under the pen name Lewis Carroll. It grew out of stories Dodgson wrote to amuse the three small daughters of Henry George Liddell, one of whom was the original Alice. (For a photo of this Alice, taken by Dodgson, see DODGSON, CHARLES L.)

The charm of the book is that its seeming nonsense often develops into a curious logic that conflicts with conventional ideas. The upside-down world thus created has given the book a timeless quality and an enduring appeal both to children and to adults. While children laugh at the obvious absurdity of such episodes as that of the courtroom scene in which the people change into a pack of cards, adults find keen social satire. Carroll makes odd use of some words and invents others.

Alice is a little girl who in a dream meets a fantastic assortment of people and creatures, including the Mad Hatter, the March Hare, the Cheshire Cat that fades away into a smile, and a philosophical caterpillar.

Sir John Tenniel illustrated the book and also its sequel, *Through the Looking-Glass, and What Alice Found There* (1872). Here Alice dreams that she walks through a mirror into a country divided like a chessboard and inhabited by chessmen. Humpty Dumpty and Tweedledum and Tweedledee also live there.

See also TENNIEL, Sir JOHN.

Alien, ā′lĭ-ĕn; āl′yĕn, a person living in a country of which he is not a citizen or national. The alien owes primary allegiance to another country. Under United States law an alien is a resident born outside the jurisdiction of the United States and not naturalized under its laws.

International law recognizes the right of any country to refuse to admit persons of foreign nationality or to admit them on its own terms. After they are admitted the country is obligated to protect them—in life and property—as it does its own citizens. Some countries with a high standard of living, such as the United States, attract a large number of *illegal aliens,* who immigrate secretly and illegally to find work. If discovered, they are usually deported.

An alien has both responsibilities and rights. He must obey the laws of the country in which he lives and he must pay taxes equally with citizens. Political rights—voting and office-holding—are seldom granted to aliens. As to civil rights—protection of life and property—most countries officially recognize obligations under international law. An alien, however, cannot claim greater protection than that provided for citizens; but if he suffers discrimination because he is a foreigner, he can ask his own government to intercede for him.

Enemy aliens—aliens who are citizens of a country that is at war with their country of residence—have always been subject to harsh treatment because they are considered a danger to their country of residence. They have frequently been placed under restraint —even confinement—and their property has often been seized.

In the United States aliens are given considerable economic opportunity. Some states, however, do not permit aliens to own land, and many states prohibit them from engaging in certain professions and occupations. They may not vote, although some states formerly permitted them to do so if they had declared their intention of becoming citizens. In the United States aliens are subject to conscription into the army when the draft is in effect.

During World War I the Trading with the Enemy Act of 1917 authorized the United

Alice's Adventures in Wonderland. The Mock Turtle sadly sings the "Lobster-Quadrille" to Alice as the Gryphon marks time with his forepaws.
From an illustration by John Tenniel

States government to seize the property of enemy aliens. Much property was seized, but after the war most of it was returned. The Alien Registration Act of 1940 required all aliens living in the United States to register with federal authorities and be fingerprinted and to report any change of address within 10 days. In 1942 many Japanese aliens, and United States citizens of Japanese descent, were moved from the West Coast to relocation camps. The Immigration and Nationality Act of 1952 incorporated provisions of the Alien Registration Act of 1940.

Beginning in the 1960's, illegal immigration, largely from Mexico, became a growing problem in the United States. Although thousands were deported annually, by the late 1970's it was estimated that there were at least five million illegal aliens living in the country.

See also ASYLUM, RIGHT OF; CITIZENSHIP; IMMIGRATION; NATIONALITY; NATURALIZATION.

Alien and Sedition Acts, in United States history, a series of four laws passed by Congress in 1798 during the Presidency of John Adams. At that time, war threatened between France and the United States. The acts were passed ostensibly as security measures against French agents and sympathizers in the United States. Actually, the laws were designed by the Federalist-controlled Congress to suppress criticism of the government by the opposition Republican (forerunner of the Democratic) party.

The acts were aimed particularly at a group of foreign-born (mainly French) editors and pamphleteers, sympathetic to the Republican cause, who were heaping abuse on the administration. By these measures, the Federalists hoped to weaken the political strength of the Republicans and their leader, Vice President Thomas Jefferson.

The laws, passed in rapid succession, were:

1. **The Naturalization Act,** extending the residence requirement for United States citizenship from 5 to 14 years.
2. **The Alien Act,** empowering the President to expel any alien whom he believed dangerous to the nation's security.
3. **The Alien Enemies Act,** authorizing the President to order from the country all aliens of a nation warring against the United States.
4. **The Sedition Act,** making it a crime, punishable by fine and imprisonment, to libel the President, Congress, or the government.

Although the Alien Acts were never applied, the threat of enforcement caused many French residents to leave the United States. A number of persons were prosecuted under the Sedition Act, 10 eventually being convicted in the courts. The Naturalization Act worked hardships on aliens of all nationalities.

Much resentment was aroused. Republicans assailed the acts as despotic and unconstitutional. The legislatures of Kentucky and Virginia passed resolutions denouncing the Alien and Sedition Acts and calling upon other states to nullify them. Enough indignation was stirred by these acts that Adams did not win re-election in 1800 and Jefferson and his party came to power.

The Alien Act expired in 1800 and was not renewed. In 1801 the Sedition Act also expired. All those convicted under this act were pardoned by President Jefferson, who had considered it unconstitutional. The Naturalization Act was repealed in 1802. Only the Alien Enemies Act remained on the statute books.

See also KENTUCKY AND VIRGINIA RESOLUTIONS.

Aligarh, ăl'ĭ-gär, India, a city in Uttar Pradesh state. It is about 30 miles north of Agra. Aligarh has important cotton-milling industries, but is known chiefly as the seat of a Moslem university.
Population: 254,008.

Alighieri. See DANTE ALIGHIERI.

Alimentary Canal, ăl'ĭ-měn'tá-rĭ, a tubular passage, found in almost all animals, that extends from the mouth to the anus. It is more commonly called the *digestive tract*. All animals except the protozoans (one-celled animals) and the sponges have alimentary canals. Some invertebrates (animals without backbones), such as jellyfish, corals, and tapeworms, have incomplete digestive tracts, with only one opening (the mouth) through which food is taken in and wastes are expelled.

For information about the human alimentary canal, and diagram, see DIGESTION.

Alimony, ăl'ĭ-mō'nĭ, in law, an allowance paid by a man or woman, under a court order, to his or her former marriage partner. The court determines whether or not alimony will be granted. The purpose is to provide financial support, and the amount is determined partly by the needs of the ex-partner and partly by the financial condition of the person who must pay. In most situations, the former husband pays alimony; if, however, the former wife was the principal wage earner, the court may order her to pay. The court normally orders alimony at the time it grants a divorce.

The court may at any time change the amount of alimony if a change in the financial circumstances of the former husband or former wife warrants new arrangements. Alimony is generally paid until the recipient remarries or dies. *Rehabilitative alimony* is sometimes granted to former spouses who are in good health and have no minor children. It lasts only a limited time (usually three years), during which the recipient is expected to prepare for a job by obtaining special training or schooling.

When the divorce involves minor children, the court may also order payment of child support to the former spouse. Alimony and child support are often paid together but are legally distinct.

Since payment of alimony is ordered by a court, a person who refuses to pay may be sent to jail for contempt of court.

Aliphatic Hydrocarbon. See HYDROCARBON, subtitle *Classification of Hydrocarbons:* Aliphatic Hydrocarbons.

Alizarin. See MADDER.

Alkali, ăl′kȧ-lī, an inorganic chemical compound that functions as a base (the opposite of an *acid*). Although *alkali* is sometimes used as a synonym for base, it is generally regarded as a more limited term, with several meanings. In chemistry, the term is applied to the hydroxides and carbonates of the *alkali metals* (lithium, sodium, potassium, rubidium, and cesium) and of ammonia. It is also applied to the hydroxides and oxides of the *alkaline-earth metals* (beryllium, magnesium, calcium, strontium, and barium).

In industry, the term *alkali* usually refers to soda ash (sodium carbonate), caustic soda (sodium hydroxide), or baking soda (sodium bicarbonate), but it may also refer to lime, potassium hydroxide, or other bases. In soil chemistry, soil that is basic is called *alkaline soil.* Large areas of the western United States and other parts of the world are barren because they are too alkaline.

Alkalies have chemical properties that are typical of all bases. (See BASE.) Nearly all alkalies are solids at ordinary temperatures, and are soluble in water. In concentrated form, they can cause chemical burns.

Alkalies react with fats and oils to produce soaps. The qualities of the soap depend to a large extent on the particular alkali used. For example, potassium hydroxide is used to make highly soluble liquid soaps and shampoos, while sodium hydroxide is used to make less soluble bar soaps. Pioneer women made soap by cooking beef tallow with lye, an alkaline solution that they obtained by soaking wood ashes in water.

Industrial Alkalies

Soda ash, caustic soda, and baking soda have a wide range of applications. Soda ash is used in the manufacture of glass, chemicals, soap, and cleaning solutions. Caustic soda is used in the production of chemicals, paper, aluminum, petroleum products, textiles, and soap. Baking soda is used in fire extinguishers, baking powder, remedies for stomach upset, and cleaning solutions.

Most of the soda ash commercially produced in the United States is obtained from *trona,* a flaky, chalk-white mineral that is almost pure sodium carbonate. Major deposits of trona are located in Wyoming and California.

Soda ash is also produced synthetically, primarily by a chemical process called the *Solvay process.* In this process, a saturated solution of common salt is treated with ammonia and with carbon dioxide to form crystals of sodium bicarbonate. Heating the crystals yields sodium carbonate, or soda ash. The process is named for its inventor, Ernest Solvay, a Belgian chemist.

Caustic soda is commercially produced from brine by electrolysis; that is, decomposing the brine by passing an electric current through it. The primary product of the electrolysis is chlorine, while caustic soda is formed as a by-product.

Baking soda is produced commercially by treating a saturated solution of sodium carbonate with carbon dioxide, which precipitates the less soluble sodium bicarbonate. It is also produced by purifying the bicarbonate crystals obtained through the Solvay process.

The chemical formula for sodium carbonate is Na_2CO_3; sodium hydroxide, $NaOH$; sodium bicarbonate, $NaHCO_3$.

See also BASE; LYE; LIME.

Alkaloid, ăl′kȧ-loid, a chemical substance of plant origin composed of carbon, hydrogen, nitrogen, and (usually) oxygen. The alkaloids are organic bases similar to the alkalies (inorganic bases); the name means "alkali-like." Most alkaloids have pronounced effects on the nervous system of man and other animals. Many are used as drugs. Some familiar alkaloids are caffeine, nicotine, quinine, cocaine, and morphine.

Alkaloids occur mainly in various genera of seed plants, such as the opium poppy and tobacco plant. Alkaloids can be found in almost all parts of these plants, including the leaves, roots, seeds, and bark. Each plant part usually contains several chemically related alkaloids. The function of alkaloids in plant metabolism is not known. Of the hundreds of alkaloids found in nature, only about 30 are used commercially.

Alkaloids must be extracted from plants before they can be used. After the plants have been dried and crushed, chemical reagents such as alcohol and dilute acids are used to extract the alkaloid content from the plant material. Pure alkaloid extracts are usually bitter, colorless solids. Some alkaloids, such as reserpine and morphine, are synthesized (produced artificially).

Uses of Alkaloids

Some alkaloids, such as nicotine, are used in pesticides, and others are used as chemical reagents. The primary use of alkaloids, however, is in medicine, because they can act quickly on specific areas of the nervous system. Alkaloids are the active components of many anesthetics, sedatives, stimulants, relaxants, and tranquilizers. They are taken by mouth and administered by injection. Except under a physician's supervision, use of alkaloids is dangerous, because most are habit-forming (for example, almost all narcotics are alkaloids) and large doses can be poisonous.

Strychnine, used in small doses as a stimulant and a tonic, is highly poisonous. Quinine, used in treating malaria, can cause dizziness if taken in large doses. Morphine and cocaine are among the most effective drugs known for temporarily relieving pain without causing loss of consciousness. However, these two alkaloids are habit-forming and can be harmful if their use is continued. Curare, used as a muscle-relaxing drug and in arrow poisons used by South American Indians, is a mixture of various alkaloids.

Alkaloid Substitutes

In most cases, the extraction of natural alkaloids and the synthesis of alkaloids are complicated, costly processes. Furthermore, alkaloid drugs usually produce unpleasant side effects. For these reasons, several synthetic compounds have been developed for use as alkaloid substitutes. For example, Novocaine (a trade name for procaine) is often used instead of cocaine, and Demerol (a trade name for meperidine) is often substituted for morphine. Alkaloid substitutes are usually less toxic than alkaloids, but are also generally less potent.

See also ATROPINE; CAFFEINE; COCAINE; CODEINE; CURARE; EPHEDRINE; HEROIN; MORPHINE; NARCOTIC; NICOTINE; OPIUM; QUININE; STRYCHNINE.

Alkalosis. See ACIDOSIS AND ALKALOSIS.

Alkylation. See PETROLEUM, subtitle *At the Refinery:* Conversion.

All Fools' Day. See APRIL.

All Saints' Day, a Christian festival celebrated to commemorate all saints, known and unknown. In 837 Pope Gregory IV ordered that it be observed on November 1. It is celebrated by the Roman Catholic, Anglican (Episcopal), and some Protestant churches, and also by the Eastern Orthodox Church (but on the first Sunday after Pentecost, in the spring). In England the festival was formerly called All Hallows and Hallowmas, and the night before is still called Halloween (Hallow Even [eve]).

See also HALLOWEEN.

All Souls' Day, a Roman Catholic festival celebrated on November 2 (November 3 if November 2 is on Sunday) as a day of prayer for the faithful dead. Some Anglican (Episcopal) churches also observe the day. Observance of the festival began in 998.

Allah, the name of God in the religion of the Moslems. See ISLAM, subtitle *Beliefs and Doctrine:* God.

Allahabad, ăl′ȧ-hȧ-băd′, India, a city in Uttar Pradesh state, about 350 miles southeast of New Delhi. It lies at the junction of the Ganges and Jumna, two rivers sacred to the Hindus. Each year thousands of pilgrims flock to this holy city. Even greater numbers attend Kumbh Mela festival, which occurs once every 12 years. Allahabad is a trade and transportation center. A variety of consumer goods are manufactured here. The University of Allahabad and several smaller colleges are here. The Museum of Allahabad has an archeological collection.

Allahabad, the ancient Hindu city of Prayag, came under Moslem rule in 1194. Late in the 16th century Akbar brought the city under Mogul rule. The city was ceded to the British in 1801.

Population: 490,622.

All-American Canal, an irrigation canal in southern California. Imperial Dam near Yuma, Arizona, diverts water from the Colorado River into the canal, which runs generally westward for 80 miles (130 km) through the Imperial Valley. The canal was completed in 1940 as part of the federal government's Boulder (now Hoover) Dam project. The All-American Canal and its branches irrigate more than 600,000 acres (240,000 hectares) of farmland in southern California.

Allegheny College. See UNIVERSITIES AND COLLEGES (table).

Allegheny Mountains. See ALLEGHENY PLATEAU.

Allegheny Plateau, ăl'ĕ-gā'nĭ, an upland forming part of the Appalachian Highlands in the eastern United States. The plateau occupies most of western Pennsylvania, part of eastern Ohio, more than half of West Virginia, and the western tip of Maryland. The upland area of southern New York is sometimes included.

The Allegheny Plateau is greatly eroded. Swift rivers and streams have cut deep valleys, leaving steep hills as remnants of the former surface. For the most part, elevations range from about 1,200 to 2,500 feet (370-760 m) above sea level.

The highest section is the Allegheny Mountains, also called the Alleghenies. They form the plateau's eastern edge and rise abruptly along a steep escarpment, called the Allegheny Front. In most of this area the terrain is quite rugged. Steep valleys and narrow gorges separating a series of northeast-southwest ranges are the chief characteristics. Spruce Knob, which rises to an elevation of 4,860 feet (1,481 m) in West Virginia, is the highest point.

The valleys and gentler slopes of the Alleghenies are dotted with farms on which grain is grown and dairy and beef cattle are raised. The area is rich in bituminous coal, especially in Pennsylvania, West Virginia, and Ohio. There are also deposits of petroleum and natural gas. Lumbering is an important industry, although most of the best timber has been cut. Extensive forests and numerous lakes, mountain resorts, state parks, and extensive forests provide fishing, hunting, hiking, and skiing.

The Alleghenies presented a serious barrier to the early settlement of the West. Routes across the plateau followed the valleys of several major rivers, including the Allegheny, Monongahela, Kanawha, Ohio, and Susquehanna.

Allegheny Portage Railroad National Historic Site. See NATIONAL PARKS, section "United States."

Allegheny River, a river in Pennsylvania and New York, about 325 miles (523 km) long. From its source in north-central Pennsylvania, the Allegheny flows northwestward into New York, then southwestward back into Pennsylvania, and through the northwestern part of the state. At Pittsburgh, it joins the Monongahela River, forming the Ohio River.

Allegiance, Oath of. See NATURALIZATION, box *U.S. Oath of Citizenship.*

Allegiance, Pledge of. See FLAG, box *Pledge of Allegiance to the Flag.*

Allegory, ăl'ĕ-gō'rĭ, a story or presentation that conveys a meaning in addition to the obvious, literal meaning. The term comes from a Greek expression for "one thing said for another." An allegory may be expressed by painting or sculpture, but is more common in literature. It may make use of either verse or prose. Sometimes the moral is made known by representing virtues or vices as persons. The *fable* and *parable* are related to the allegory, but are shorter and reveal their lessons in a more simple and obvious manner.

There are numerous allegories in the Bible and in the literatures of many nations. Medieval morality plays, such as *Everyman,* were often allegories. Edmund Spenser's *Faerie Queene* (1590-96) is the outstanding allegory of English poetry, and John Bunyan's *Pilgrim's Progress* (1678) has a similar rank in prose.

See also BUNYAN, JOHN, subtitle *The Pilgrim's Progress;* FABLE; MIRACLE PLAY, subtitle *Morality Plays;* PARABLE; SPENSER, EDMUND, subtitle *The Faerie Queene.*

Allegri, Antonio. See CORREGGIO.

Allele. See HEREDITY, subtitle *Principles of Heredity:* 1. Segregation and Dominance.

Allemande. See MUSIC, subtitle *Musical Form.*

Allen, Ethan (1738-1789), a military leader in the American Revolution and a Vermont patriot. His capture of strategic Fort Ticonderoga was one of the first American victories of the Revolutionary War. Allen, more than any other man, was responsible for Vermont's becoming a separate state.

Allen was born in Litchfield, Connecticut. Little is known of his early life. After serving in the French and Indian War in 1757, he invested in a farm and a smelting business. In 1769 he settled in the New Hampshire Grants (later Vermont) and was soon involved in the dispute over the territory, which was claimed by both New York and New Hampshire. To defend their claims, the Grants settlers formed a militia called the Green Mountain Boys, with Allen as its commander.

In May, 1775, Allen and 83 Green Mountain Boys, with Colonel Benedict Arnold of Connecticut, forced the surrender of British-held Fort Ticonderoga without loss of life. In September he led a handful of men in an attack on Montreal, but was captured and held prisoner by the British until exchanged in 1778.

Allen returned to Vermont, where the feud over independence was raging. (Vermont had declared itself a state in 1777, independent from both New York and New Hampshire.) Although a colonel in the Continental Army and a major general of militia, Allen confined his activities to seeking recognition of the new state by the Continental Congress. He and his brother Ira secretly attempted to make peace with Britain on behalf of Vermont, 1780-83, probably to force Congress to grant statehood. Allen was accused of treason, but the charges were never proved.

Allen wrote several works on the Vermont dispute, a narrative of his British captivity, and a controversial book on deism.

Ira Allen (1751-1814) was born in Cornwall, Connecticut. Moving to the New Hampshire Grants in 1772, he became active in the independence movement with his brothers, Ethan and Levi. Allen drafted the Vermont constitution, 1777, and was elected first treasurer of Vermont, 1778. He wrote the *Natural and Political History of the State of Vermont* (1798).

Allen, Florence Ellinwood (1884-1966), a United States judge. She was the first woman to be elected judge of a state supreme court, and the first to serve as judge, and later chief judge, of a federal court. Miss Allen was born in Salt Lake City, Utah. She received her law degree from New York University in 1913.

Fort Ticonderoga Museum
Capture of Ticonderoga, from an old painting. Colonel Ethan Allen, leading the Green Mountain Boys, routed the British commander, Captain Delaplace, from his bed, and demanded the immediate surrender of the fort, "In the name of the Great Jehovah and the Continental Congress."

Edmondson Studio
Florence E. Allen

Miss Allen served as judge in the Court of Common Pleas, Cuyahoga County, Ohio (1920-22), and in the Ohio Supreme Court (1922-34). In 1934, she was appointed to the U. S. Court of Appeals for the Sixth Circuit. She became chief judge in 1958 and retired the following year.

To Do Justly, published in 1965, contains her memoirs.

Allen, Fred (1894-1956), a United States radio comedian noted for his dry wit. He was born in Cambridge, Massachusetts. His real name was John Florence Sullivan; he took the stage name Fred Allen while a juggler in vaudeville. After appearing on Broadway in musical comedies, Allen entered radio in 1932. His weekly radio show, "Town Hall Tonight," also featured his wife, Portland Hoffa. Allen appeared in motion pictures and television, and wrote the autobiographical *Treadmill to Oblivion* (1954) and *Much Ado About Me* (1956). *Fred Allen's Letters,* edited by Joe McCarthy, was published in 1965.

Fred Allen
NBC

Allen, Frederick Lewis (1890-1954), a United States author and editor. *Only Yesterday* (1931) is an informal social history of the 1920's. *Since Yesterday* (1940) deals with the 1930's. In *The Lords of Creation* (1935) Allen traces the expansion of American capitalism since the 1890's. *The Big Change* (1952) surveys the first half of the 20th century. Allen was born in Boston. He graduated from Harvard University, where he then taught English two years. He was on the staff of *Harper's* magazine for 30 years, and was its editor in chief during 1941-53.

Allen, Henry T. (Tureman) (1859-1930), a United States army officer. As commander of the American forces in Germany after World War I, 1919-23, he was praised for fairness to the defeated enemy and for his diplomacy in handling disputes with America's allies. He was born in Sharpsburg, Kentucky, and graduated from West Point in 1882. As a second lieutenant he headed one of the most extensive explorations ever made of Alaska, covering 2,500 miles (4,000 km) and mapping the Copper, Tanana, and Koyukuk rivers.

Allen fought in the Battle of El Caney, Cuba, in the Spanish-American War. He organized the Philippine Constabulary and was its chief, 1901-07. He served in General Pershing's expedition into Mexico, 1916. In World War I Allen commanded the 90th Division in the St. Mihiel and Meuse-Argonne offensives. He retired as a major general.

Allen, Henry Watkins (1820-1866), a Confederate soldier and statesman. He is called the "greatest single administrator produced by the Confederacy." Soon after the Civil War began, he became a lieutenant colonel in the Confederate army, commanding the 4th Louisiana Regiment. Allen, a courageous and capable commander, was wounded at Shiloh and Baton Rouge in 1862 and never completely recovered. Shortly after being made a brigadier general in 1863, he was elected governor of Louisiana. Allen built up the state's economy by exporting sugar and cotton to Mexico, saving the region from chaos and starvation. In the final days of the war, Allen counseled the Confederate commander in Louisiana to surrender rather than have the state suffer the ravages of an invading army. Allen then went to Mexico, where he founded an English-language newspaper.

A-316

Allen was born in Prince Edward County, Virginia. After attending Marion College in Missouri, he taught school and then became a lawyer. Allen fought with Sam Houston in the Texas Revolution and served in the Louisiana legislature prior to the Civil War.

Allen (William) **Hervey** (1889-1949), a United States novelist and poet. His best-known work, *Anthony Adverse* (1933), is a historical romance set in the Napoleonic era. *Action at Aquila* (1937) is a novel about the American Civil War. *The City in the Dawn* (1950) is a collection of novels about frontier life in New York state. He collaborated with DuBose Heyward on *Carolina Chansons* (1922), a volume of verse. *Israfel* (1926) is a biography of Edgar Allan Poe.

Allen was born in Pittsburgh, Pennsylvania. He graduated from the University of Pittsburgh in 1915. His experiences as a soldier in World War I are described in *Toward the Flame* (1926), an autobiographical novel.

Allen, Ira. See ALLEN, ETHAN.

Allen, James Lane (1849-1925), a United States novelist. His use of authentic detail for scenes and characters in *A Kentucky Cardinal* (1894) and *The Choir Invisible* (1897) established him as a significant local colorist of the blue-grass region. He also wrote short stories, verse, and sketches. Allen was born in Lexington, Kentucky. After graduation from Kentucky University (now Transylvania University), he taught there, and later settled in New York City.

Allen Park, Michigan, a city in Wayne County. It lies on the River Rouge, about nine miles (14 km) southwest of downtown Detroit. Allen Park is mainly a residential suburb. It was incorporated as a village in 1927; a city charter was granted in 1957. Population: 34,196.

Allenby of Megiddo and Felixstowe, Edmund Henry Hynman Allenby, First **Viscount** (1861-1936), a British general in World War I. He captured Jerusalem and

Lord Allenby
Brown Brothers

ended Turkish rule in Palestine. Allenby entered the army in 1882 and served in the Boer War, 1899-1902. He became major general in 1909. In World War I he commanded a cavalry division at Mons and the Third Army at the Aisne and Arras. He went to Palestine in 1917. In his victory at Megiddo, 1918, he made extensive use of cavalry; he is called the last great cavalry commander. Allenby was promoted to field marshal and raised to the peerage in 1919. He was high commissioner to Egypt, 1919-25.

Allentown, Pennsylvania, the seat of Lehigh County. It is on the Lehigh River, about 46 miles (74 km) north-northwest of downtown Philadelphia. Allentown is one of the state's leading industrial cities. Products include fabricated metals, machinery, textiles, clothing, paper, electrical equipment, and chemicals. Nearby stone and clay quarries supply the city's cement and glass industries. Allentown is a marketing and processing center for an area in which grain and potatoes are grown and dairy cattle are raised.

Allentown is the site of Muhlenberg and Cedar Crest colleges; Allentown College of St. Francis de Sales is nearby. A replica of the Liberty Bell is in the Zion Reformed Church (built 1773), where the original bell was hidden from the British in 1777, during the Revolutionary War. In the Allentown Art Museum is a collection of Renaissance paintings and sculptures. The city maintains several parks with game preserves, beautifully landscaped gardens, and sports grounds.

Allentown was founded in 1762 by William Allen, a Pennsylvania jurist. It was known as Northampton Town and grew in importance as a trading center. It was incorporated as a borough in 1811 and renamed Allentown in 1838. A city charter was granted in 1867. Allentown has the mayor-council form of government.

Population: 103,758.

Allentown College of St. Francis de Sales. See UNIVERSITIES AND COLLEGES (table).

Allergy, ăl'ēr-jĭ, an excessive sensitivity to a substance or condition that is relatively harmless to most persons. It has been estimated that about one person in five suffers from some kind of allergy. Dogs, mice, guinea pigs, and other animals also display allergic reactions, and are often used in allergy research.

Substances that cause allergies are called *allergens*. There are hundreds of allergens, including food, dust, pollen, drugs, and bacteria. The allergic reaction can take many forms. It often produces an irritation in sensitive tissues, such as those of the eyes or nose. Skin rash, hives, cramps, headache, difficulty in breathing, or congestion in nasal passages often result.

Specific allergies are usually not hereditary, but an individual can inherit a tendency to be allergic. Race and sex have little to do with the development of allergies. Allergic reactions can begin at any age, but most persons who develop an allergy do so before they reach 40. Allergies may disappear suddenly.

Causes of Allergic Reactions

Allergens can affect the body if they are eaten, inhaled, or injected into the bloodstream, or merely come in contact with the skin. The same allergen can affect different persons in different ways. Grass pollens, for example, can cause severe asthma in one person, cause a second person to sneeze, and have no effect at all on a third.

The foods that most commonly cause allergic reactions are milk, eggs, fish, nuts, chocolate, pork, strawberries, and wheat flour. Inhaling pollen, fungi, animal dander, vapors, and strong odors can cause allergic reactions. Drugs, such as penicillin, barbiturates, and aspirin, affect some persons. Certain materials that come in contact with the skin can produce allergies. Such materials include flowers and other plant parts, dyes, rubber, metals, plastics, insecticides, furs, leather, feathers, jewelry, cosmetics, and various industrial chemicals. Some persons are allergic to heat, cold, light, or pressure. Insect bites can cause serious, or even fatal, allergic reactions.

Emotional disturbances such as anxieties sometimes trigger attacks of hay fever, asthma, or eczema, but allergic reactions are not caused by emotions alone. Many allergies are traced to air pollution; the use of synthetic materials in clothing, food, and cosmetics; and the use of antibiotics and sulfa drugs.

An allergic reaction seldom develops unless there has been an initial *sensitizing period*. Thus, a person may be exposed to pollen for several years before developing the symptoms of hay fever.

A-317

How Allergic Reactions Occur

When germs enter the body, the body produces protein substances called *antibodies* that circulate in the bloodstream. (See ANTIBODY.) These antibodies combine with the germs and attempt to render them harmless. Allergic reactions occur when the body responds to certain allergens by producing large quantities of weak antibodies called *reagins*. Reagins combine with the allergens, but instead of destroying them induce certain body cells to release chemical substances into the surrounding area. Among these substances are histamine, serotonin, acetylcholine, and heparin.

These chemicals are responsible for the two characteristic features of an allergic reaction: the contraction of smooth muscle and an outpouring of fluids by body cells. When this excess fluid is released in certain areas of the body, *wheals* (raised, sharply defined swellings) are produced.

Wheals on the skin are called *hives*. Wheals in the lining of the nasal cavities produce stuffiness by reducing the size of the air passages, and if fluids are released into the nasal cavities a runny nose results. Wheals in the throat or tongue can interfere with breathing. In bronchial asthma, there is a swelling in the lining of the bronchial tubes plus contraction of muscle. The combination constricts air passages and thus hinders normal breathing. Similar changes in the intestines can produce colic and diarrhea. Wheals can also produce a type of arthritis. Persistent wheals in the brain can cause long-lasting headaches.

In rare cases, there is a severe (and often fatal) allergic reaction, called *anaphylaxis*, that results in shock and affects the entire body. Anaphylaxis is usually evident within seconds after contact with the offending allergen. The usual cause of anaphylaxis is the injection of a drug, such as penicillin, or a foreign blood serum that is used in serum therapy. An insect sting can also cause anaphylaxis.

Diagnosis and Treatment

To identify the offending allergens, the physician studies the patient's medical history and skin tests are commonly made. These consist of the application of suspected allergens under the skin surface (scratch test) or directly on the skin (patch test) to see if there is a reaction. A list of the foods eaten over a period of several days is often made, and any allergic reactions during a given day are noted.

Special diets are sometimes helpful. These diets start out with foods that rarely produce allergies, such as rice, lamb, and butter. Each day a new food is added to the list. If an allergic reaction is observed on a certain day, then the newly added food is suspect. These diets are called *elimination diets*.

There is no sure treatment for allergies. In some cases, the treatment is simply to avoid the offending allergen. However, this is not always practical.

In treating certain patients (for example, hay-fever victims), the physician may administer a small amount of the offending allergen and—over a period of time—gradually increase the dosage so that the patient's sensitivity will be reduced. Other treatments include the use of antihistaminic drugs, which interfere with the effects of histamine. In some cases the use of hormones, such as Adrenalin and cortisone, can help. (See ADRENALIN; CORTISONE.)

The Asthma and Allergy Foundation of America furthers medical research and training in the field of allergic diseases and has a public education service. Headquarters are in New York City.

The National Institute of Allergy and Infectious Diseases carries on an extensive program of research in the field of asthma and allergic diseases. It is a component of the National Institutes of Health, which is part of the U.S. Department of Health and Human Services.

See also ANTIHISTAMINE; ASTHMA; ECZEMA; HAY FEVER; HIVES; POISON IVY.

Books about Allergy

Gerrard, J. W. *Understanding Allergies* (Thomas, 1977).
Rapp, D. J. *Allergies and Your Family,* revised edition (Sterling, 1979).

For Younger Readers:

Burns, S. L. *Allergies and You* (Messner, 1980).
Silverstein, Alvin and V. B. *Allergies* (Lippincott & Crowell, 1977).

Alliance, Ohio, a city in Stark County. It lies on the Mahoning River, about 23 miles (37 km) southeast of Akron. Alliance is a regional center of commerce and industry. Aluminum goods, machinery, electrical appliances, and plastic and rubber products are manufactured. Mount Union College is here. Early in the 1800's three small communities occupied the site of the present city. In 1854 they merged and were incorporated as Alliance. The city has the mayor-council form of government.

Population: 24,315.

Alliance, an agreement between two or more nations to support one another in case of war; also, the group of nations that make the agreement. Usually, alliances are formed through treaties, open or secret. The typical treaty of alliance pledges all the allies (other members of the alliance) of an attacked or threatened nation to go to war in its behalf. Thus, an alliance may help prevent war by making it clear that an attack on any member nation would be met by the combined forces of all the allies.

Modern alliances sometimes go beyond the signing of the agreement to the setting up of defense procedures and forces. Such precautions are useful; with today's weapons, an aggressor nation might otherwise be able to conquer a weaker country before its allies could effectively come to its aid.

Almost all alliances are defensive, or at least contain a clause stating that they are. For example, the Rome-Berlin-Tokyo Axis —the offensive alliance formed before World War II by Italy, Germany, and Japan—was purportedly intended for defense against Communism.

Since the rise of national states in 16th-century Europe, most alliances have been aimed at maintaining a balance of power so that no nation should be so much stronger than the others that it would be able to dominate them. (See BALANCE OF POWER.) The 15-member North Atlantic Treaty Organization is an example of an alliance that is designed to deter a potential aggressor through strength and preparedness. The Warsaw Pact, between Russia and its satellite nations in eastern Europe, was intended as a counterbalance to NATO.

Another type of alliance occurs when countries that are not pledged to give mutual assistance to one another are drawn into war against a common enemy. In World War I, for example, the United States was technically an "associated power," though commonly called one of the Allies.

In 1778, during the Revolutionary War, the United States signed a treaty of alliance with France, and French aid helped the United States win independence. But many people felt that the new nation should remain aloof from foreign politics. In 1796, in his Farewell Address, President George Washington stated, "It is our true policy to steer clear of permanent alliances with any portion of the foreign world." President Thomas Jefferson, in his First Inaugural Address (1801), cited "peace, commerce, and honest friendship with all nations—entangling alliances with none" as one of the guiding principles of the United States.

World War I and World War II, however, showed that the United States policy of isolationism could no longer be followed. In 1949 the United States entered NATO, its first peacetime alliance. A number of other alliances followed.

For further information, see:

ANZUS PACT
AXIS, THE
CENTRAL TREATY ORGANIZATION (CENTO)
NORTH ATLANTIC TREATY ORGANIZATION (NATO)
ORGANIZATION OF AMERICAN STATES (OAS)
QUADRUPLE ALLIANCE
SOUTHEAST ASIA TREATY ORGANIZATION (SEATO)
TRIPLE ALLIANCE
TRIPLE ENTENTE
WARSAW PACT

Books about Alliances

Naidu, M. V. *Alliances and Balance of Power* (St. Martin's Press, 1975).
Treaties and Alliances of the World, revised edition (Scribner's, 1974).

Alliance for Progress, an economic and social development program for Latin America promoted jointly by the United States and the nations of Latin America. The 10-year program was suggested by President John F. Kennedy and was established by the Organization of American States at Punta del Este, Uruguay, in August, 1961. The program concentrated on land and tax reform, better education and health services, housing development, better wages and working conditions, and monetary and fiscal reform. Most of the specific goals of the Alliance were not met, but the program did help to promote inter-American economic cooperation.

Allied Chemical Corporation, one of the largest chemical companies in the United States and in the world. There are eight operating divisions, a Canadian subsidiary, and an international marketing division. The corporation has more than 150 plants and makes more than 400 different products. Among these are sulfuric acid, alkalies, synthetic organic chemicals, plastics, resins, fibers, plant foods, and natural-gas liquids. Allied Chemical was formed in 1920. Headquarters are in New Jersey.

American Alligator
Florida State News Bureau

Allies. See ALLIANCE. For lists of allies in World War I and World War II, see WORLD WAR I, table *Nations Involved in World War I;* WORLD WAR II, table *Nations Involved in World War II.*

Alligator, ăl′ĭ-gā′tĕr, a large reptile that inhabits swamps, rivers, lakes, and marshes. Alligator skin makes a handsome, durable leather and is widely used for handbags, wallets, shoes, belts, and watch bands. Millions of alligators have been sold as pets, killed for their skins, or stuffed as souvenirs, bringing the species close to extinction. Game laws now protect alligators in the wild, and the animals are raised commercially on "farms."

Five-week-old Alligator
Philip Gendreau

There are two species of alligators. The *American alligator* is found from North Carolina south to Florida and west to central Texas. The *Chinese alligator* is found in the lower valley of China's Yangtze River. The Chinese alligator is smaller than the American, reaching a maximum length of five or six feet. Otherwise, the two species are similar. The alligator family is made up of alligators and *caimans.* Caimans are found in South and Central America and on the island of Trinidad. (See CAIMAN.)

Description

Alligators are closely related to crocodiles. Alligators have broad heads and rounded snouts; crocodiles, triangular-shaped heads and pointed snouts. Both of the enlarged teeth on each side of the crocodile's lower jaw are plainly visible when the mouth is closed. In the alligator, however, these teeth fit into a pit in the upper jaw, and are not visible when the mouth is closed. Crocodiles are known to attack people, but alligators rarely do so.

The average length of the American alligator is 6 to 12 feet. An adult male weighs about 250 pounds and a female about 115 pounds. The alligator has a long, thick tail that gradually tapers to a point; four short legs; and large, powerful jaws. The eyes, nostrils, and ears (which are behind the eyes, hidden under flaps of skin) are on the top of the snout. Alligators often float with only the nostrils, eyes, and ears above water.

A-320

The tough skin is made up of small, leathery plates. Only the skin of the belly and sides, which is free of underlying bony material, is used commercially. An adult is brownish-black to black with a white to yellowish-white belly. The young are black with yellow crossbands.

Habits

In the summer alligators sun themselves on land or float in water. They swim with their tails, and use their legs for walking. Their walk is awkward and slow, but they can run rapidly for short distances. In the winter they hibernate in mud burrows.

In the spring, the female buries 30 to 60 eggs (each about three inches long) in a nest made of decaying plant material. At the end of a 9- to 10-week incubation period, the unhatched young make a peeping noise and the female uncovers the nest. The young are 8 to 9 inches long at birth and grow rapidly until they reach adulthood (at about 10 years of age).

Alligators have large stomachs, and eat enormous amounts of food during the summer. Young alligators feed mainly on water insects and small water animals. Adults eat mostly fish, frogs, and snakes. Sometimes they eat larger animals, such as pigs, muskrats, and waterfowl.

Adult alligators occasionally make a short, grunting noise, which is repeated several times. Angry adults make a hissing noise and the males often bellow or roar, especially during mating season.

The American alligator is *Alligator mississipiensis;* the Chinese, *A. sinensis.* Alligators and caimans make up the alligator family, Alligatoridae.

Alligator Gar. See GAR.

Alligator Pear. See AVOCADO.

Alligator Snapping Turtle. See TURTLE, subtitle *Kinds:* Freshwater Turtles.

Allison, William Boyd (1829-1908), a United States political leader. He was a Republican party leader in the U. S. Senate for 35 years, earning a reputation as a moderate and a party harmonizer. Allison gave his name to the Bland-Allison Act of 1878. His amendment modified the Bland Bill (calling for increased coinage of silver) by specifying the amount to be coined.

Allison was born in Perry Township, Ohio, and was admitted to the bar in Ohio. In the 1850's he settled in Iowa. He served in the U. S. House of Representatives (1863-71), and in the Senate (1873-1908). Allison was chairman of the Appropriations Committee from 1881 until his death, except during 1893-95.

Alliteration, ă-lĭt'ĕr-ā'shŭn, the constant or frequent repetition of a letter or sound, usually at the beginning of a word. Alliteration, rather than rhyme or meter, was the distinguishing feature of Anglo-Saxon and early English poetry. The opening lines of William Langland's *The Vision Concerning Piers the Plowman,* written in 14th-century Middle English, illustrate its use:

In a *s*omer *s*eason when *s*oft was the *s*onne
I *sh*ope me in *sh*roudes as I a *sh*epe were.

(In a summer season when soft was the sun
I clothed myself in rough garments as though
  I were a shepherd.)

Alliteration persisted in English poetry, frequently in rhymed verse. An example is these lines from Tennyson's *The Princess:*

The *s*plendor falls on ca*s*tle walls
  And *s*nowy *s*ummits old in *s*tory;
The *l*ong *l*ight shakes across the *l*akes
  And the wild cataract *l*eaps in *gl*ory.

Excessive use of alliteration was satirized by Shakespeare and others. Swinburne, who used alliteration skillfully, mocked the device in these lines from *Nephelidia:*

From the *d*epth of the *d*reamy *d*ecline of the *d*awn through a *n*otable *n*imbus of *n*ebulous moonshine.

Allopathy. See HAHNEMANN, SAMUEL.

Allosaurus. See DINOSAUR, subtitle *Kinds of Dinosaurs:* Saurischians.

Allotropy, ă-lŏt'rŏ-pĭ; ăl'ŏ-trō'pĭ, the property that certain chemical elements have of existing in two or more different forms in the same physical state (gas, liquid, or solid). Some allotropic forms, or allotropes, arise from differences in the number of atoms in a molecule of the element, as in ordinary oxygen, O_2, and triatomic oxygen (ozone), O_3. Allotropy can also be caused by different arrangements of atoms in amorphous (noncrystalline) or crystalline structures of an element. Carbon, for example, exists in strikingly different crystalline allotropic forms as diamond and as graphite. The property of crystallizing in two or more forms is termed *polymorphism.*

A number of other elements, notably tin, iron, selenium, phosphorus, and sulfur, have allotropes resulting from different arrangements of their atoms. For a description of some of these allotropes, see the individual articles on these elements.

Allouez, ȧl'wā', **Claude Jean** (1622-1689), a French Jesuit missionary who explored the Lake Superior region and was called "apostle of the west." He came to Canada in 1658, and was appointed vicar general for all traders and natives of the northwest in 1663.

From 1665 to 1675, Allouez traveled among the Indians of the Lake Superior–Lake Michigan region and established missions, including that at De Pere (in what is now Wisconsin) in 1671. From 1676 until his death he worked among the Illinois and Miami Indians.

Alloy, ăl'oi, a substance with metallic properties that contains two or more chemical elements, at least one of which must be a metal. Totally pure metals are virtually never used commercially because it costs too much to remove all impurities. The almost-pure metals of commerce, however, are not considered alloys. In order for a substance to be called an alloy, the various elements it contains must be purposely included.

Alloying is done for a number of reasons. Among the characteristics that can be controlled by alloying are hardness, toughness, electrical resistance, workability, magnetic properties, melting point, tensile strength (the minimum stress that will cause a substance to break when it is pulled), resistance to corrosion, and resistance to expansion when heated.

The number of alloys is almost infinite, partly because a change in the percentages of an alloy's components produces a new alloy. For example, aluminum and copper can be combined to make a series of binary (two-component) alloys ranging from almost-pure aluminum to almost-pure copper. A similar variation can be found in other series of binary alloys. Most alloys, however, have more than two components and thus have an even greater range of variation.

The metal present in greatest quantity in an alloy is called the alloy *base.* The other components are called alloy *elements.* When an alloy is named according to its components, the base is named first. Thus, copper is the base in a copper-tin alloy. Iron-base alloys are called *ferrous alloys.* All alloys based on metals other than iron are called *nonferrous alloys.*

Alloys are usually formed by melting the various components, mixing them, and then letting the mixture cool and harden. The

solid formed can be a true chemical *compound* of metals, a solid *solution,* a *mixture* of metallic crystals, or some combination of these. Strictly speaking, the term *alloy* refers only to a solid solution of two or more metals; in common usage, however, it is applied to all of the types of substances just mentioned, provided they have the properties of a metal. (See CHEMISTRY, section "The Fundamentals of Chemistry," subtitle *Nature and Structure of Matter:* Compounds, and Mixtures; METAL; SOLUTION.)

Ferrous Alloys

All ferrous, or iron-base, alloys, contain carbon. In addition, they may include cobalt, silicon, manganese, chromium, molybdenum, nickel, phosphorus, sulfur, and other substances. Ferrous alloys are usually divided into three classes—wrought iron, cast irons, and steels. The ferrous alloys, particularly the steels, are considered the most important group of materials in the modern, industrial world. They have an almost unlimited range of structural, industrial, and ornamental uses.

For descriptions of the various ferrous alloys, see IRON AND STEEL, section "Iron Refining and Iron Products," subtitle *Iron Products,* and section "Steel Making and Steel Products," subtitle *Kinds of Steel.*

Nonferrous Alloys

Although nonferrous alloys are based on metals other than iron, some of them contain small percentages of iron as an alloy element. The most widely used base metals for nonferrous alloys are aluminum, copper, lead, magnesium, nickel, tin, and zinc.

Aluminum-base Alloys are generally lightweight and tough but considerably weaker than steel. Aluminum is frequently alloyed with manganese, silicon, magnesium, copper, and zinc. Aluminum-manganese alloys are highly resistant to corrosion and are used in the food-processing and chemical industries. Aluminum-silicon alloys are easily cast and are widely used for die and sand casting. Aluminum-copper alloys have relatively high strength and are easily machine-worked. Duralumin, for example, which contains about 95.5 per cent aluminum, 3 per cent copper, and lesser amounts of manganese and magnesium, is used in machinery and aircraft parts.

Copper-base Alloys include brass, bronze, and German silver. *Brasses,* which are alloys of copper and zinc, are used for such

SOME IMPORTANT ALLOYS

NAME	ALLOY BASE*	ALLOY ELEMENTS (with approximate percentages by weight†)
Ferrous Alloys		
Wrought Iron	Iron	Carbon (0.08), Manganese (0.01), Silicon (0.16), Phosphorus (0.06), Sulfur (0.01), Slag (1.2)
White Cast Iron	Iron	Carbon (3)
Gray Cast Iron	Iron	Carbon (3.5), Silicon (2.5)
Malleable Cast Iron	Iron	Carbon (2.5), Silicon (1), Manganese (0.25), Phosphorus (1.5), Sulfur (0.1)
Carbon Steel	Iron	Manganese (0.45), Silicon (0.25), Carbon (0.2)
Alloy Steel	Iron	Nickel (1.75), Manganese (0.8), Chromium (0.75), Carbon (0.3), Molybdenum (0.25)
Stainless Steel	Iron	Chromium (18), Nickel (9), Carbon (0.1)
Tool Steel (high-speed)	Iron	Tungsten (18), Chromium (4), Vanadium (2)
Nonferrous Alloys		
Babbitt Metal	Tin	Antimony (7), Copper (3)
Bell Metal	Copper	Tin (22)
Brass	Copper	Zinc (15)
Bronze	Copper	Tin (8.25), Phosphorus (0.15)
Duralumin	Aluminum	Copper (3), Manganese (1), Magnesium (0.5)
Gold (18 carat)	Gold	Silver (20), Copper (12)
Hastelloy	Nickel	Molybdenum (28), Iron (5)
Inconel	Nickel	Chromium (16), Iron (8)
Monel Metal	Nickel	Copper (33)
Nickel Silver (German Silver)	Copper	Zinc (34), Nickel (20)
Permalloy	Nickel	Iron (17), Molybdenum (4)
Pewter	Tin	Antimony (7), Copper (2)
Solder (soft)	Tin	Lead (40)
Sterling Silver	Silver	Copper (7.5)
Type Metal	Lead	Antimony (19), Tin (5), Copper (1)

*The alloy base is the predominant metal in the alloy.

†Most of the percentages in the list are for one typical member of a series of alloys known by one general name.

things as lamp fixtures, plumbing accessories, ornaments, and musical instruments. *Bronzes* are copper-tin alloys that sometimes contain smaller amounts of lead, zinc, silver, manganese, or other metals. The term "bronze" is often used commercially to designate a number of copper-base alloys with no tin but with properties similar to bronze, especially the typical bronze color. *Aluminum bronze* seldom contains tin. Bronze is used to make coins, bells, ship propellers, screws, bolts, and many other objects. *Nickel silver,* formerly called German silver, is a ternary (three-component) alloy of copper, nickel, and zinc used to make rivets, costume jewelry, and tableware.

See also BRASS; BRONZE.

Lead-base Alloys frequently contain either tin or antimony. Tin tends to increase the strength of lead, and antimony is added to lead to impart both strength and hardness. Lead-tin alloys are used for solder. Lead-antimony alloys are used for storage-battery plates and cable coverings.

Magnesium-base Alloys frequently have aluminum, zinc, thorium, or one of the rare-earth metals as the principal alloy elements. The alloys of magnesium are stronger and more resistant to high temperatures than pure magnesium. Magnesium-base alloys have numerous industrial and structural uses.

Nickel-base Alloys are usually highly resistant to corrosion. Elements that are frequently alloyed with nickel include chromium, copper, iron, molybdenum, silicon, aluminum, and manganese. *Inconel* alloys, which are nickel-chromium alloys containing small amounts of other elements, are used primarily in structures that must withstand high temperatures. The *monel* series of alloys, consisting primarily of nickel and copper, are corrosion-resistant and very strong.

Permalloy is a magnetic alloy of nickel (40-80 per cent) and iron that sometimes contains small amounts of other elements. It is very easily magnetized, and for this reason is used in such things as transformers, telephone receivers, and electric motors and generators. *Hastelloy,* a nickel-base alloy containing up to 30 per cent molybdenum, is a high-temperature alloy with exceptionally high strength.

See also MONEL METAL; PERMALLOY.

Tin-base Alloys include pewter and babbitt metal as well as several types of soft solders.

A-324

Alloys of tin with about 40 per cent lead are used for soldering electrical and electronic equipment because such alloys possess good electrical conductivity. Pewter, an alloy of tin, antimony, and copper, was once widely used for tableware. It is still used for some tableware and decorative items such as candlesticks. Babbitt metal, typically a tin-base alloy that contains antimony and copper, is used to make bearings. (Some forms of babbitt metal have a lead rather than a tin base.)

See also BABBITT METAL; PEWTER; SOLDER.

Zinc-base Alloys frequently contain copper, aluminum, and magnesium. Such alloys are frequently used for die castings of automobile carburetors and auto trim parts, and for a wide range of mechanical and decorative hardware items. An alloy of zinc with lead that can be etched evenly is used for photoengravers' plates. Zinc alloys with aluminum and magnesium are hard and strong. They are used for padlocks and hardware.

Other Alloys. See ALNICO; AMALGAM.

All's Well That Ends Well, a "bitter" comedy (or tragicomedy) by William Shakespeare, written between 1602 and 1604. Though William Hazlitt called it "one of the most pleasing of our author's comedies," it has been little produced in the 20th century. Shakespeare adapted the plot from a story by Boccaccio, probably by way of William Painter's *Palace of Pleasure* (1566-67). The existing play may be a revision of the lost comedy *Love's Labor Won.*

The King of France rewards Helena, who has cured him with a prescription inherited from her physician father, by compelling the Count of Rousillon to marry her. The count flees after the marriage, but Helena follows and wins him by disguising herself and substituting for another girl in a rendezvous with her husband. Helena is made memorable by her persistent devotion to her errant husband. Some effective satire goes into the character of Parolles, the count's boastful, conniving, and cowardly follower.

Allspice, or **Jamaica Pepper.** See PIMENTO.

Allston, Washington (1779-1843), a United States painter. Although his classical landscapes and Biblical paintings were highly regarded in his day, Allston now is remembered for his imaginative, Romantic

Moonlit Landscape
by Washington Allston
in 1819
oil on canvas
24 by 35 inches
(61 by 89 cm)
Museum of Fine Arts, Boston

landscapes. *Moonlit Landscape* and *Ship in a Squall,* his finest works, reveal skillful handling of color and light.

Allston was born on the family plantation in South Carolina, and graduated from Harvard in 1800. He studied art in London with Benjamin West at the Royal Academy and then lived in Rome, 1804-08. After three years in the United States, Allston again lived in England, painting such idyllic classical works as *Italian Landscape.* He returned to the United States in 1818 and lived in Boston and Cambridge. He was working on *Belshazzar's Feast,* a painting he thought would be his masterpiece, when he died.

Allusion. See FIGURE OF SPEECH, subtitle *Kinds of Figures.*

Alluvium, ă-lū′vĭ-ŭm, the silt, clay, sand, and other material transported and deposited by running water. The term excludes lake and ocean deposits and is usually restricted to geologically recent sediments. Alluvium is laid down in many places but occurs most extensively on flood plains (areas along streams that are subjected to flooding); in river deltas; and in alluvial fans, cones, and plains at the base of steep mountains. Some of the world's richest agricultural land consists of alluvial soil. Such regions are also among the most heavily populated on earth. Examples include the Nile River valley and the deltas of eastern and southeastern Asia.

Alma, äl′mà, a Russian river. It was the scene of the first battle of the Crimean War. The Alma rises in the Crimean Mountains in the Ukraine, and flows about 45 miles (72

km) into the Black Sea, 17 miles (27 km) north of Sevastopol. Along its lower course the allied armies of Britain, France, and Turkey defeated Russian forces on September 20, 1854.

Alma College. See UNIVERSITIES AND COLLEGES (table).

Alma Ata, äl′mä-ätä′, Soviet Union, the capital and largest city of the Kazakh S.S.R. It lies in Central Asia in the foothills of the Tien Shan mountains, about 1,850 miles (2,980 km) southeast of Moscow. The city is modern and attractively planned. Alma Ata has textile, leather, engineering, printing, and motion picture industries. It is also a food-processing and agricultural marketing center. The Kazakh Academy of Sciences, the Kazakh State University, and the state opera, ballet theater, and museum are here.

The city, first called Vernyy, was founded as a Russian military post in 1854. It grew as a trade center early in the 20th century. It acquired its present name in 1921 and became the capital of the republic in 1929.

Population: 910,000.

Almagro, äl-mä′grō, **Diego de** (1475?-1538), a Spanish soldier and explorer. During 1524-33, Almagro assisted Francisco Pizarro in the overthrow of the Inca empire of Peru. He was given none of the conquered lands, receiving instead territory to the south (now Chile and southern Bolivia). In 1535 Almagro led the first expedition to this area. When he found only hostile Indians and no gold, he was enraged and began a war with his partner Pizarro. Almagro was captured and put to death.

Almanac, ôl'má-năk, a pamphlet or book containing a calendar of days, weeks, and months. Is usually gives information about the time of sunrise and sunset, phases of the moon, religious and civil holidays, and miscellaneous facts. Jokes, riddles, recipes, medical advice, agricultural hints, and other entertaining or useful features became a part of almanacs issued by many commercial enterprises (frequently by patent medicine manufacturers) in the latter half of the 19th and early part of the 20th centuries. *The Old Farmer's Almanac,* founded by Robert B. Thomas in 1792, has changed very little.

Modern general almanacs include statistical data and other information on historical and current events. Examples are *The Hammond Almanac,* the *Information Please Almanac,* and the British *Whitaker's Almanack.* Examples of specialized almanacs include *American Ephemeris and Nautical Almanac* and *The American Nautical Almanac.* The German *Almanach de Gotha* gives details on the royal and titled families of Europe. It was published from 1764 to 1944, and revived in 1964.

Bickerstaff's *Boston Almanack* for 1773 featured a "furious wild beast" that supposedly had ravaged France.
Essex Institute, Salem

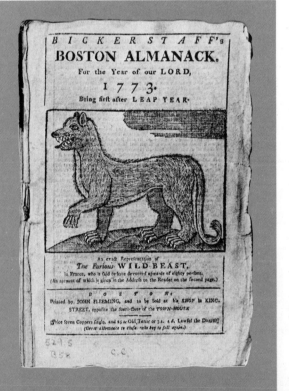

In the British Museum is an Egyptian almanac compiled in the 13th century B.C. It lists lucky and unlucky days, gives the dates of religious festivals, and makes various predictions. The *fasti* of ancient Rome were calendars posted in the forum for the information of the public. Almanacs that used astrology as the basis for predictions of coming events were long popular in Europe, particularly in France. *Poor Robin's Almanack* (1663-1775) was a British almanac notorious for its superstitious misinformation.

The first almanac in English America was *An Almanack for New England for the Year 1639,* compiled and published by William Pierce (or Peirce). Benjamin Franklin's *Poor Richard's Almanack* (1732-57) became famous for its homely wisdom and shrewd proverbs. The *American Almanac and Repository of Useful Knowledge,* begun in 1830, included information on world events, government activities, and politics.

Almandite. See GARNET.

Almeida-Garrett, äl-mā'ē-thá-gár-rĕt', **João Baptista da Silva Leitão** (1799-1854), a Portuguese dramatist, novelist, poet, and statesman. He did much to stimulate the Romantic movement and the modern drama in his native land. *Auto de Gil Vicente* (1838) is a representative historical play. *Camões* (1825) is an epic poem about Luis Vaz de Camoëns, author of *The Lusiads.* Almeida-Garrett was born in Oporto, but was brought up in the Azores. In 1820 he was exiled for revolutionary activities and went to England. Returning in 1826, he helped Dom Pedro gain the throne and was rewarded with the post of minister of the interior.

Almond, ä'mŭnd, the name of a fruit and the tree bearing it. The fruit is commonly called a nut, but botanically it is not a true nut but a *drupe.* Almond trees belong to the rose family and are closely related to peach trees. They are grown for their beauty and for the commercial value of the nuts. Almond trees reach a height of about 30 feet (9 m) and have pink or white blossoms. They blossom early—between January and April —and therefore are easily damaged by frost. They have been cultivated in the Mediterranean regions and central Asia for more than 4,000 years. Major almond producers are the United States (primarily California), Spain, Iran, Greece, Tunisia, and Turkey.

There are two kinds of almond trees. One produces a sweet, edible nut and the other a bitter, inedible nut. Sweet almonds are used as food or in food products, such as ice cream and candies. The oil of sweet almonds is used as a lubricant for delicate mechanisms, in cosmetic creams, and in medicine as a gentle laxative.

The oil of bitter almonds is used after the poisonous acid (prussic acid) that gives the bitter taste has been removed. Bitter-almond oil is used as a flavoring in foods and medicines and for aroma in perfumes and cosmetics.

Flowering almond shrubs are two related species that are grown as ornamental plants. *Green almond* is another name for the fruit of the pistachio tree; it is not an almond. (See PISTACHIO.)

See also NUT (color page).

The almond is *Prunus dulcis* or *P. Amygdalus*. The sweet almond is of the variety *dulcis;* the bitter, var. *amara.* Flowering almond shrubs are *P. glandulosa* and *P. triloba.* All belong to the rose family, Rosaceae.

Almshouse. See POOR LAWS.

Alnico, ăl′nĭ-kō, any of several magnetic alloys composed of iron, aluminum, nickel, and cobalt. Some alnicos also contain copper and titanium. A magnet made of alnico is many times stronger than one of similar size made of iron or steel. Alnico magnets are commonly used in magnetic compasses, telephone receivers, loudspeakers, and instruments that measure electric current.

Aloe, ăl′ō, a genus of perennial plants of the lily family. There are about 200 species, almost all native to Africa. Aloes are called *succulents* because they have thickened, juicy leaves that can store water. Most species of aloe are stemless.

The long, swordlike leaves have sharp points at their tips and generally have spines along the edges. The leaves grow in dense clusters, usually close to the ground. A flower stalk extends from the center of the cluster. Red or yellow flowers grow in compact, finger-shaped tufts at the end of the stalk. The individual flower is tubular and usually slightly curved.

Aloes grow easily in well-drained soil, and are often cultivated as decorative plants. Propagation is by seeds and leaf or root cuttings. Aloes grow from 4 inches (10 cm) to 60 feet (18 m) in height, depending on the species.

Aloes were used as medicinal herbs by the

California Almond Growers Exchange
Almond. *Top left,* a grove of trees; *top right,* fruit and nuts; *bottom,* a branch in flower.

Egyptians as early as 1600 B.C. The use of aloes in medicine has continued into modern times. The drug *aloes,* used as a mild laxative, is derived from various species of aloe plants. *Aloin,* also used as a mild laxative, is prepared from a mixture of juices found in several species of aloe plants. These drugs are obtained from the dried juices of the leaves. A gel extracted from the leaves is used to treat burns, soothe dry, chapped skin, and relieve peptic ulcers.

The *American aloe* is not an aloe but an agave (century plant). See AGAVE.

Aloe plants used in medicine include Zanzibar aloe, *Aloe perryi;* Cape aloe, *A. ferox;* and Barbados aloe, *A. vera* or *A. barbadensis.* Aloes belong to the lily family, Liliaceae.

Alopecia, or **Baldness.** See BALDNESS.

Aloysius Gonzaga, ăl′ō-ĭsh′ĭ-ŭs gŏn-dzä′gä, Saint (1568-1591), an Italian Jesuit and the official patron of Roman Catholic youth. He is extolled for his purity and sanctity. A brilliant youth of noble descent, Gonzaga renounced the succession to his family title to enter the Society of Jesus (Jesuits). He died in Rome at the age of 23 while caring for the sick during a plague. He was declared a saint in 1726. His feast day is June 21.

Alpaca, ăl-păk′à, a domesticated animal of the camel family found in southern and

Field Museum of Natural History

Alpaca

the other two stars appear as a single, very bright star to the unaided eye. Alpha Centauri is slightly more than four light-years from the sun. It is in the constellation Centaurus.

Alpha Particles. See RADIATION, subtitle *Nuclear Radiation.*

Alphabet, a set of letters, in a fixed order, with which a language is written. The word comes from the names for the first two letters of the Greek alphabet, *alpha* and *beta,* which in turn come from the Semitic *aleph* and *beth.* The letters of an alphabet are phonetic signs, each one standing for one or more individual speech sounds. An alphabet differs in this important respect from a *syllabary,* a set of characters each representing the sound of a syllable, and *picto-ideograms* (such as hieroglyphics), which represent objects and ideas rather than sounds.

The articles in this encyclopedia are arranged according to the English alphabet. The first article under each letter is the story of the letter itself. See, for example, the article on A, at the front of this volume.

Alphabetic writing is the most advanced system of writing known. Of the major civilizations of the past 2,000 years, only China failed to develop an alphabet. For earlier systems of writing, see WRITING.

Modern Alphabets

Hundreds of alphabets are in use in the world today. Many of them are direct descendants of the original alphabet, the Semitic alphabet, invented some 3,500 years ago. Others were invented in more recent times, such as the Korean (in the 15th century) and the Somali (in the 20th).

There are two main branches of development from the ancestral Semitic alphabet. One has no vowels, the vowel sounds being indicated (if at all) by small marks added to the consonants. The major alphabets of this type in use today are those of the Hebrew language, spoken in Israel and in Jewish religious observances; and of Arabic, spoken in most of the Moslem countries of the world. The alphabets of southern and southeastern Asia are believed to stem mainly from this vowelless branch.

Roman and Cyrillic Alphabets. The other branch that developed from the ancestral Semitic alphabet began with the Greek alphabet, the first to have full-fledged vowel signs. From it was derived the Roman al-

western South America. The name is applied also to the fabric made from the animal's hair. Alpacas are smaller than camels and do not have humps. They are grazing animals and live in semiarid regions from sea level to elevations of 15,000 feet (4,600 m). Alpacas are closely related to llamas and guanacos.

Alpacas are about 40 inches (1 m) tall at the shoulders. The head and neck resemble a camel's; the body, that of a sheep. The lustrous, straight, silky hair ranges in color from white to brown or black, and can grow up to 20 inches (50 cm) long. Strong and water-repellent, it is used especially in making coat fabrics. Alpacas have been bred for their wool since the time of the Incas, and are seldom used for food or as beasts of burden.

The *suri* is a breed of alpaca that produces a superior grade of wool. Its hair is somewhat curly and is longer, finer, and silkier than that of the common alpaca. The llama and the alpaca are occasionally interbred. (See also LLAMA.)

The alpaca is *Lama pacos* of the camel family, Camelidae.

Alpha and Omega, ăl'fȧ; ō-mē'gȧ, the first and last letters of the Greek alphabet. In the bible the phrase denotes "the beginning and the end." In Revelation the phrase is applied to God in 1:8 and to Jesus Christ in 22:13. The letters are often used in Christian symbolism, denoting God as the creative origin of the world and the ultimate end toward which it moves.

Alpha Centauri, a system of three stars, one of whose members—Proxima Centauri—is the star nearest the sun. Proxima can be seen only with a telescope;

HEBREW | ARABIC | GREEK | RUSSIAN

HEBREW Letter	HEBREW Name	ARABIC Letter	ARABIC Name	GREEK Letter (Capital and lower case)	GREEK Name	RUSSIAN Letter (Capital and lower case)	RUSSIAN Name†
א	aleph	ا	alif	A α	alpha	А а	ä
ב	beth		ba	B β	beta	Б б	bě
ג	gimel		ta	Γ γ	gamma	В в	vě
ד	daleth		tha	Δ δ	delta	Г г	gě
ה	he		jim	E ε	epsilon	Д д	dě
	waw		ha	Z ζ	zeta	Е е	yě
	zayin		kha	H η	eta	Ё ё	yô
	heth		dal	Θ θ	theta	Ж ж	zhě
	teth		dhal	I ι	iota	З з	zě
	yodh		ra	K κ	kappa	И и Й й	ē; short ē
	kaph		zay	Λ λ	lambda	К к	kä
	lamedh		sin	M μ	mu	Л л	ěl
	mem		shin	N ν	nu	М м	ěm
	nun		sad	Ξ ξ	xi	Н н	ěn
	samekh		dad	O ο	omicron	О о	ō
	ayin		ta	Π π	pi	П п	pě
	pe		za	P ρ	rho	Р р	ěr
	sadhe		ayn	Σ σ ς*	sigma	С с	ěs
	qoph		ghayn	T τ	tau	Т т	tě
	resh		fa	Y υ	upsilon	У у	ōō
	sin; shin		qaf	Φ φ	phi	Ф ф	ěf
	taw		kaf	X χ	chi	Х х	kä
			lam	Ψ ψ	psi	Ц ц	tsě
			mim	Ω ω	omega	Ч ч	chě
			nun			Ш ш	shä
			ha			Щ щ	shchä
			waw			Ъ ъ	hard sign
			ya			Ы ы	yě-rě′
						Ь ь	soft sign
						Э э	ě
						Ю ю	yōō
						Я я	yä

*Final letter   †The pronunciation symbols are the ones used throughout this encylopedia.

phabet, in wider use today than any other. With it are written the languages of the traditionally Roman Catholic and Protestant countries of Europe and the major languages of North and South America. It is used also for a number of African and some Southeast Asian languages (such as Vietnamese), and is the basis for alphabets designed for various American Indian and African tribal tongues. Turkey changed from the Arabic to the Roman alphabet in 1928.

Adoption of the Roman alphabet is under consideration by the Japanese, whose writing is partly in Chinese characters and partly syllabic. The Chinese governments, both Communist and Nationalist, are also studying the possibility of adopting the Roman alphabet.

The Roman alphabet offers a simple and relatively satisfactory means of recording sounds. As used for the English language, it has 26 letters. Two of them, *c* and *q*, duplicate the sounds of other single letters— *s* and *k*. The redundancy is partly a result of pronunciation changes, which take place gradually but continuously. The English alphabet, on the other hand, has not changed since two letters (*u* and *j*) were added in the 16th century.

English pronunciation and spelling, however, have many inconsistencies, and the 26 letters have to represent, by means of various combinations, at least 40 distinctive sounds. (See PRONUNCIATION; SPELLING, subtitle *Difficulties in English Spelling*.) The alphabet still serves the English language adequately, however, without the use of *diacritics* (small marks over, under, or through a letter to indicate a sound different from its customary one; the umlaut [such as ö] and cedilla [ç] and bar [ł] are examples).

Many foreign languages that are written with the Roman alphabet using diacritical marks may be read with more precise pronunciation than can English. In French, for example, *e* may be given different sounds by placing accent marks above it (*é*, *è*, and *ê*).

A foreign alphabet may lack letters included in the English alphabet but contain others unused in English. The Spanish alphabet has one more letter (*ñ*) than the English, while the Italian uses four English letters (*k, w, x, y*) only for foreign words. The Polish alphabet lacks three English letters, but has nine extra ones.

The Greek alphabet has another branch, the Cyrillic, used for writing certain Slavic languages. Of these, Russian Cyrillic is the most widespread. As simplified after the Russian Revolution of 1917, it has 32 letters. It is used in Soviet-dominated countries speaking Finno-Ugric and Turkic as well as Slavic languages.

Improved Phonetic Alphabets. Because of the vastly different sounds given the same letter in different languages, the alphabet for one will not serve to show how another is pronounced. "Nation," for example, is spelled the same in French as in English, but every letter except the first *n* has a different sound.

The International Phonetic Alphabet, with more than 100 characters, was introduced in 1888 and with various modifications is widely used for the phonetic transcription of speech in any language. However, even this alphabet cannot give all possible nuances of sound that are used in human speech, and it is cumbersome to use. As a result, some linguists, in their study of languages, prefer *phonemic* alphabets for each language, with the letters or symbols representing phonemes (distinctive sounds in that particular language). (See also LANGUAGE, subtitle *Structure of Language: Sound*.)

The English language is especially troublesome to write phonetically because of its inconsistencies in spelling and pronunciation. (The difference in the sound of *th* in "then" and "thin," and the different ways of representing an *f* sound in "fan," "phone," and "enough" are examples.) At least 40 phonemic symbols are needed to write it so it can be read without confusion. For teaching children, illiterates, and foreigners to read English, an improved phonetic alphabet in which no letter stands for more than a single sound has long been desired.

Three such systems were introduced in the 1960's. The Shavian alphabet, developed by Kingsley Read under the terms of the will of George Bernard Shaw, has 48 letters. The Initial Teaching Alphabet (ITA), developed by Sir James Pitman, who also assisted on the Shavian project, has 44. Unifon, developed by Chicagoan John R. Malone, has 40.

All three alphabets have separate letters for each of the *th* sounds and for other common phonemes such as *ch, sh,* and the sound represented by *s* in "television" and *z* in "azure." There are 18 letters for vowel sounds in the Shavian system, 16 in the ITA and Unifon. Experimental teaching programs for ITA were begun in Great Britain and for ITA and Unifon in the United States. Learning to read may be easier using these alphabets, but making the necessary later transition to the standard alphabet is difficult for many.

History of the Alphabet

The alphabet developed in ancient times from earlier systems of writing—picto-ideograms and syllabaries. By about 3000 B.C. the Egyptians were using 24 signs representing consonant sounds in combination with more than 400 picto-ideographic hieroglyphics. The cuneiform writing of Mesopotamia had sound signs for single vowels, but not for consonants except in syllables. (See also CUNEIFORM WRITING.) This system required separate characters for about 600 combinations. Sometime after 2000 B.C. one of the Semitic peoples living at the eastern end of the Mediterranean Sea made one of the most important discoveries in history— that a brief set of sound signs could be used to write all the words and names in a language.

It is not known where the discovery was made. Inscriptions in early syllabic-alphabetic writing have been found on the Sinai Peninsula of Egypt and in the regions of ancient Palestine and Phoenicia. The site of Byblos, a Phoenician city of high culture, has produced what are thought to be the oldest examples, dating from perhaps 1700 B.C.

The Egyptian sound signs are thought to have inspired the Semitic alphabet, which also consisted solely of consonants. Since the vowel sounds were implied rather than written, the system might be considered a pre-alphabet rather than a true alphabet. Many of the letter forms were evidently adapted from Egyptian characters; the source of others, however, is uncertain. The sound signs may have been selected arbitrarily with no regard for their previous identification.

There were slight variations in the Semitic alphabet as used in different regions. The number of letters ranged from perhaps 15 to 22. The Sinaitic and Palestinian, or Canaanite, letters had more resemblance to Egyptian forms than did those in northern alphabets. From one south Semitic alphabet, the Sabaean, came Ethiopic. Amharic, the modern script of Ethiopia, is the main surviving descendant of this branch.

The Alphabet in Europe. Sometime around 1000 B.C. the Greeks adopted a Semitic alphabet of 22 letters, probably from the Phoenicians, a Semitic people who traded throughout the Aegean area. The Greeks retained the Semitic names for the letters, modifying them to suit their own language. They also retained the 22 letters, although the Greek language did not require that many consonant sounds. When the Greeks gave vowel sounds to five of the unused consonant signs, they created the first true alphabet. The Classical Greek alphabet adopted by Athens in 403 B.C. had 24 letters; 19, or possibly 20, of them had been part of the original 22.

Initial Teaching Alphabet Publications, Inc.
Pitman's Initial Teaching Alphabet, with its 44 symbols and words illustrating the sounds represented by each symbol.

It was an earlier form of the alphabet that Greek colonists in southern Italy passed on to the Etruscans in the north. The Etruscans conquered Rome in the seventh century B.C. and left the alphabet as a legacy of their rule. The Classical Latin alphabet used in the time of the Roman Empire had 23 letters, formed as in the present Roman alphabet. I and J were both represented by I; U and V by V. W did not exist. Y and Z appeared only in loan words from the Greek.

Although in time the Roman alphabet spread throughout western Europe, in the early Middle Ages it had several rivals. Runic inscriptions, found in northern Europe mainly in the Scandinavian countries, were written with an alphabet that may have been derived from the Etruscan, or directly from Greek. The oghams, characters used for Celtic inscriptions in the western British Isles, were apparently a kind of stonemason's code for the letters of some existing alphabet, possibly Latin. (See also OGHAM; RUNE.)

A special version of the Roman alphabet was the Gothic, or Black Letter. (See HAND-

WRITING for illustration.) It began about the 12th century in northern Europe. The Black Letter alphabet was used in the British Isles until the Renaissance and in Scandinavia into the 19th century. It is particularly identified with Germany, where it was in general use until after World War II. The German Black Letter alphabet has 34 letters and letter combinations.

Greek was the official language of the Byzantine (Eastern Orthodox) Church and the Byzantine Empire. However, in the ninth century, when Saint Cyril went among the Slavic Moravians to convert them to Christianity, he preached in the Slavic language. In order to write Slavic, Cyril invented a new alphabet, called Glagolitic, from the Slavic for "word." The alphabet was adopted by the Bulgarians, who changed the letters to resemble Greek characters. The redesigned alphabet, introduced about 940, was named Cyrillic in Cyril's honor. It came to be used by all the Slavic countries of the Eastern Orthodox faith.

The Alphabet in Asia. The ancient Aramaeans had their own version of the early Semitic alphabet. When in the eighth century B.C. they were conquered and dispersed by the Assyrians, their language and alphabet came into use throughout the Middle East, displacing Old Hebrew, among others. The classical Hebrew, Syriac, and Arabic alphabets grew out of the Aramaic.

Evidence suggests that one or more versions of the Aramaic alphabet eventually reached India, where numerous offshoots developed. It is believed that one of these offshoots traveled farther eastward with the Buddhist religion and was adopted in Indochina, Indonesia, Tibet, and Mongolia. The Korean alphabet, invented in the 15th century, may have been inspired by one derived from the Aramaic.

See also BLINDNESS, subtitle *How the Blind "Read"*; PHONETICS.

Books about the Alphabet

Chappell, Warren. *The Living Alphabet* (University Press of Virginia, 1975).
Diringer, David, and H. A. Freeman. *A History of the Alphabet Throughout the Ages and in All Lands* (State Mutual, 1978).
Humez, Alexander and Nicholas. *Alpha to Omega: the Life and Times of the Greek Alphabet* (Godine, 1981).
Ogg, Oscar. *The 26 Letters*, revised edition (Crowell, 1971).

Alpheus. See ARETHUSA.

Alphonso. See ALFONSO.

Alpine Goat. See GOAT, subtitle *Domestic Goats*.

Alps, a mountain system of central Europe. Its lofty ranges stretch in a rough arc from the Riviera on the Mediterranean coast, across southeastern France and northern Italy, through most of Switzerland, Austria, and Liechtenstein, and into southern West Germany and northwestern Yugoslavia. The Alps are about 470 miles (760 km) long along the inner edge of the arc, and 810 miles (1,300 km) along the outer edge. Their width ranges from 80 to 150 miles (130-240 km). They cover approximately 85,000 square miles (220,000 km²). The Alps are part of a larger mountain system formed during relatively recent geologic time. Some principal parts of this system, aside from the Alps proper, are the Apennines of the Italian peninsula; the Pyrenees, between France and Spain; and the Dinaric Alps, which rise behind Yugoslavia's Dalmatian coast.

Alpine resorts, with their magnificent scenery and their facilities for mountain climbing, skiing, and other sports, are popular vacation spots. Tourists flock to such places as St. Moritz, Lucerne, and Interlaken, in Switzerland; Kitzbühel and Arlberg, Austria; and Cortina d'Ampezzo, Italy.

Geographical Divisions

A line running from Lake Constance up the Rhine Valley and across Splügen Pass to Lake Como divides the Alps into western and eastern sections.

The Western Alps consist of a high, narrow chain with many branches. Ranges here include the Maritime, Cottian, and Graian Alps and the Mont Blanc group. East of the French border, the chain widens to form parallel ranges. This section, lying mostly in Switzerland, has the highest average elevation. Main ranges here are the Pennine, Bernese, Lepontine, and Glarus Alps.

The Eastern Alps are generally lower and broader than the Western Alps. At the widest point, they are 150 miles (240 km) from north to south and have numerous ranges, separated mainly by tributaries of the Danube. The ranges include the Rhaetian, Bavarian, Tyrolean, and Carnic Alps, the Hohe and Niedere Tauern, the Dolomites, and the Julian Alps.

Glaciers, Lakes, and Rivers

During the last great Ice Age, the Alps were covered by massive mountain glaciers,

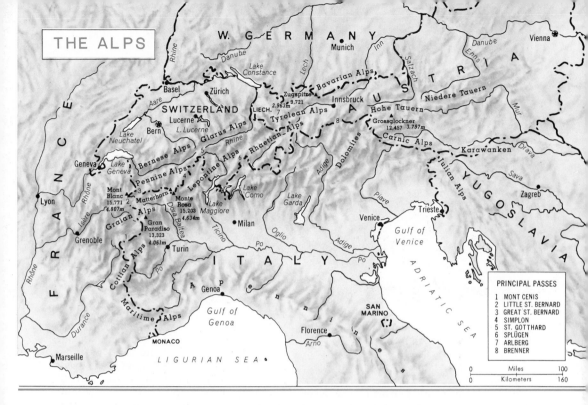

THE ALPS

PRINCIPAL PASSES
1 MONT CENIS
2 LITTLE ST. BERNARD
3 GREAT ST. BERNARD
4 SIMPLON
5 ST. GOTTHARD
6 SPLÜGEN
7 ARLBERG
8 BRENNER

remnants of which are found at high elevations. In the Bernese Alps is the Aletsch Glacier, with an area of 66 square miles (171 km²). Another large glacier is the Mer de Glace ("Sea of Ice") on the northern slope of Mont Blanc.

The Ice Age glaciers scooped out broad valleys. In some of these glacial depressions, large, deep lakes were formed. Among those on the northern edge of the Alps are Lakes Geneva, Lucerne, and Constance. On the southern side are Lakes Maggiore, Lugano, Como, and Garda.

Three of the largest rivers of Europe—the Rhine, Rhône, and Po—originate in the Alps. Major southern tributaries of the Danube originate here as well. There are also hundreds of small, swift streams, some with spectacular waterfalls.

Peaks

The Alps have hundreds of peaks more than 10,000 feet (3,000 m) high. Some of them are:

	HEIGHT	
NAME AND LOCATION	Feet	Meters
Mont Blanc, France	15,771	4,807
Monte Rosa, Switzerland-Italy	15,203	4,634
Matterhorn, Switzerland-Italy	14,690	4,478
Finsteraarhorn, Switzerland	14,022	4,274
Jungfrau, Switzerland	13,642	4,158
Gran Paradiso, Italy	13,323	4,061
Monte Viso, Italy	12,602	3,841
Grossglockner, Austria	12,457	3,797

Passes and Tunnels

Most Alpine passes higher than 6,000 feet (1,800 m) above sea level are blocked by ice and snow in winter. Rail and highway tunnels have been built under the principal passes, allowing continuous traffic the year round. An exception is the Brenner Pass, which at 4,508 feet (1,374 m) is low enough to be kept open all year.

Alpine tunnels were limited to rail traffic until 1964, when the Great St. Bernard auto tunnel was opened. The Mont Blanc Tunnel, opened in 1965, is the world's longest road tunnel; the Simplon, consisting of

Jungfrau, one of Switzerland's best-known peaks, attains a height of 13,642 feet (4,158 m) in the Bernese Alps. A railroad runs partway to the summit.

Swiss National Tourist Office

Tyrolean Landscape in the Kitzbühel Alps of Austria
Austrian National Tourist Office

tubes opened in 1905 and 1922, is one of the world's longest rail tunnels.

Climate

As in any mountain region, the higher the elevation, the colder the climate. Climate depends also on whether an area is shaded or is open to sunlight. Usually, slopes facing south have milder winters than do those facing north. Rain and snow are heavy nearly everywhere; snow falls on the high peaks most of the year.

Avalanches—masses of snow, mixed with earth and loose rock—frequently slide down mountain slopes into the valleys and villages below. A distinctive wind of the Alps is the *föhn* or *foehn,* a dry, warm, southerly wind that quickens the melting of snow in spring.

Plants and Animals

The lower mountainsides are covered with forests of oak, chestnut, and beech. Above these is a belt of evergreens, includ-

Mont Blanc, a 15,771-foot (4,807-m) peak in France and the highest in the Alps, is viewed here from across the border in Italy. A glacier is shown on the mountain's flank.
Italian Government Travel Office

ing spruce and fir. From 5,000 to 6,000 feet (1,500-1,800 m), the forests thin out, and are replaced by meadows and high pastures. Here grow such Alpine flowers as edelweiss and primrose. Above the snow line, at 8,000 to 10,000 feet (2,400-3,000 m), are only snow, ice, and bare rock. The term "Alpine" is used to describe roughly similar climate and vegetation in high mountainous areas in many parts of the world.

The chamois (an antelope) and the ibex (a wild goat) are native to the Alps, but are rare. Hunting is regulated strictly.

Agriculture and Industry

Population is generally sparse in the mountains, where cattle raising and dairying are chief occupations. Cultivation of crops is limited largely to valleys, foothills, and mild southern slopes, where wine grapes, fruits, grains, and hay are grown. The making of cheese and handicraft articles is traditional.

Rapidly flowing Alpine streams have been harnessed to provide hydroelectric power used for industrial purposes in Alpine valleys. The French Alps are a center of aluminum refining. Other industrial activities include the production of heavy machinery, small precision items, and chemicals. In many areas the tourist business provides the single largest source of income.

For further information, see:

Land

A-334

Water

ADIGE RIVER	LUGANO, LAKE
COMO, LAKE	MAGGIORE, LAKE
CONSTANCE, LAKE	RHINE
GARDA, LAKE	RHÔNE RIVER
GENEVA, LAKE	SAVA RIVER
LUCERNE, LAKE OF	

See also subtitles *Physical Geography* or *Physical Features* in the articles on Austria, France, Germany, Italy, Switzerland, and Yugoslavia.

Cities

INNSBRUCK	LUCERNE	ST. GALLEN

Miscellaneous

LIECHTENSTEIN	TYROL

Books about the Alps

Knight, Max, and Gerhard Klammet. *Return to the Alps* (Friends of the Earth, 1974).

National Geographic (periodical). *The Alps* (National Geographic Society, 1973).

Spring, Ira, and Harvey Edwards. *One Hundred Hikes in the Alps* (Mountaineers-Books, 1979).

Wyss, M. A. *The Alps* (Abrams, 1975).

Alsace-Lorraine, ăl′săs-lŏ-rān′, a historic region now part of France. It encompasses the departments of Haut-Rhin and Bas-Rhin (in Alsace) and Moselle (in Lorraine) in northeastern France. Alsace-Lorraine has an area of about 5,600 square miles (14,500 km²) and is bounded by Luxembourg, West Germany, and Switzerland. Among its major cities are Strasbourg and Metz. Because of its fertile land, rich mineral deposits, and central location, this region was for centuries a source of bitter conflict between France and Germany.

The Alsace-Lorraine region was part of Roman Gaul in the first century B.C. It was invaded by barbarians beginning in the fourth century A.D. and eventually was conquered by the Franks. In 843 the treaty of Verdun divided the empire of Charlemagne into three sections, the Alsace-Lorraine region becoming part of the Middle Kingdom of Lothair I. This kingdom (called Lotharingia) later broke up into a number of autonomous states, including Alsace and Lorraine. Both the east Frankish (or German) and the west Frankish (or French) kingdoms repeatedly tried to annex these states.

In the 10th century, Lorraine became a German duchy. Gradually, however, it came under the influence of France. In 1552 the bishoprics of Metz, Toul, and Verdun were seized by the French under Henry II. The rest of the area was governed by its own dukes until 1766, when France gained control of all Lorraine.

Alsace, part of the German duchy of Swabia from the 10th century, was divided into a number of feudal principalities in the 14th century. It remained a part of Germany until the 17th century, although a number of cities, including Strasbourg, were independent. Alsace was occupied by the French during the Thirty Years' War, 1618-48. By the peace of Westphalia, 1648, all Alsace except the bishopric of Strasbourg became French territory. Strasbourg was acquired by France in 1681.

In 1871, following the French defeat in the Franco-Prussian War, Germany annexed most of Alsace and part of Lorraine, forming Alsace-Lorraine. The annexation stirred strong opposition among the people, who resisted attempts to Germanize the region. France regained control in 1919, after World War I. Although the French agreed to respect local customs, they met resistance from some Alsatians who wanted autonomy. During World War II, Germany reoccupied Alsace-Lorraine, 1940-44. It was returned to France after the German defeat.

See also METZ; MOSELLE RIVER; STRASBOURG.

Alsatian Dog. See DOG, subtitle *Breeds of Dogs:* Working Dogs (German Shepherd), and color page.

Alsike Clover. See CLOVER.

Alsop, ôl′sŭp, the name of two United States journalists, noted as analysts of national and international affairs. They were born in Avon, Connecticut.

Joseph (Wright) **Alsop** (1910-   ), after graduation from Harvard in 1932, joined the staff of the New York *Herald Tribune*. He wrote a Washington political column with Robert E. Kintner, 1937-40. Following military service in World War II, Alsop and his brother Stewart wrote a syndicated political column for the *Herald Tribune*, 1945-58. Joseph Alsop continued writing a syndicated column alone.

Stewart (Johonnot Oliver) **Alsop** (1914-1974) graduated from Yale in 1936. He began his career in the publishing business; served in the British and United States armies during World War II; and wrote a Washington political column with his brother Joseph, 1945-58. He was an editor of *The Saturday Evening Post,* 1958-68, and a columnist for *Newsweek,* 1968-74.

Altai Mountains, ăl′tī; ăl-tī′, a mountain range of central Asia. It extends north-

Otto Wunderlich, Madrid
Altar in Cathedral at Toledo, Spain. Elaborate 16th-century decoration is seen behind the altar.

west-southeast for about 1,000 miles through parts of Russia, China, and the Mongolian People's Republic. In Siberia, where the range is extremely rugged, stands 14,783-foot-high Gora Belukha, the highest peak in the Altais. To the southeast the range becomes lower and increasingly barren, ending in the Gobi Desert. From the Altais flow Russia's Ob and Irtysh rivers. Mineral wealth is potentially great; known deposits include copper, gold, zinc, lead, silver, and mercury. Valleys and intermountain tablelands provide farmland for growing grain and raising livestock.

Altar in Chapel at an Air Force Base
Bolling Air Force Base, Washington, D. C.

Altaic. See LANGUAGE, subtitle *Language Families:* Ural-Altaic.

Altair, the brightest star in the constellation Aquila. It is the 12th brightest star in the sky, with an apparent magnitude of 0.77. Altair is about 10 times as luminous as the sun and is white in color. It is about 16 light-years from the earth. As seen from earth, Altair has a faint star on each side of it.

Altar, a raised structure on which religious sacrifices are offered or on which incense is burned in the worship of a deity. The word is from the Latin *altus,* "high." In common speech an altar is any structure or place used for sacrifice or worship. Altars are used in many religions, both ancient and modern. In Masonic lodges and other fraternal societies an altar is a piece of furniture used in rituals and ceremonies.

In the Roman Catholic Church the altar is the table of stone on which ·the sacrifice of Mass is offered. Mass may be offered outside a church or chapel on a portable altar, or *altar-stone.* An unconsecrated altar is also called an altar-stone. A fixed altar (or consecrated altar) must have at least three parts: the stone table or top of stone; the supports, which may be a solid mass or consist of a column or columns; and the sepulchre (a cavity for relics of martyrs). The altar sometimes has a dome-shaped roof, or *ciborium.* The *reredos* is an ornamented screen back of the altar (and sometimes attached to it).

In the Church of England and Episcopal Church the altar is of stone or wood. These churches use the word "altar," but also use the term "Holy Table," "Lord's Table," or "Table." Protestant churches generally do not have an altar, but may have a simple communion table below and in front of the pulpit. Protestants commonly refer to the pulpit platform or prayer rail as the altar.

The Old Testament tells of many altars. The Temple in Jerusalem had the great altar for burnt offerings. The first Christian altars were probably of wood. It is believed that the practice of using the tombs of martyrs as altars brought about the change to stone.

Altdorfer, ält'dôr'fĕr, **Albrecht** (1480?-1538), a German painter and engraver. He was one of the first artists to paint landscapes for their own sake, without human figures. *Landscape near Regensburg* is characteristic of his romantic interpretations of the Danube valley. In other works, such as *Battle of Alexander* and *St. George in the Forest,* he set small, detailed figures in elaborate landscape backgrounds. Altdorfer also did many drawings and etchings of the Bavarian forests. Little is known about his early life. He worked in Regensburg, where he was the city architect and a councilman.

Alternating Current. See ELECTRICITY, subtitle *The Nature of Electricity: Currents.*

Alternation of Generations. See REPRODUCTION OF LIVING ORGANISMS, subtitle *Alternation of Generations.*

Alternator. See ELECTRICAL MACHINERY, subtitle *Simple Generators.*

Altgeld, ŏlt′gĕld, **John Peter** (1847-1902), a United States political leader notable for his courage in opposing injustices in unpopular causes. Shortly after his election in 1892 as first Democratic governor of Illinois after the Civil War, he pardoned three anarchists convicted of conspiracy to incite to murder in connection with the Chicago Haymarket riot of 1886. In 1894 Altgeld protested President Cleveland's sending troops to maintain order during the Pullman strike in Chicago.

Illinois State Hist. Lib.
John P. Altgeld

Altgeld was born in Germany, and in infancy was brought by his parents to Richland County, Ohio. He had little formal education. Altgeld served briefly in the Civil War, studied law, and was state's attorney in Andrew County, Missouri, before coming to Chicago in 1875. He was judge of the Superior Court of Cook County, 1886-91. His book *Our Penal Machinery and Its Victims* (1884) was the beginning of a long fight for prison reforms. He ran for reelection as governor in 1896, but was defeated.

Althea. See ROSE OF SHARON.

Althing, äl′thĭng; ôl′thĭng, the national assembly of Iceland, believed to be the oldest legislature in the world. The Althing first met in 930. Its power declined after 1264, when Iceland came under the rule of the Norwegian king. The assembly was abolished in 1800 but restored in 1843.

See also ICELAND, subtitles *Government* and *History.*

Althouse, ôlt′hous, **Paul** (1889-1954), a United States tenor. He was the first United States singer to debut at the Metropolitan Opera (1913) without having had European training and experience. For more than 25 years, he sang leading tenor roles in *Aïda, I Pagliacci,* and Wagnerian operas. Althouse studied in his native Reading, Pennsylvania, and in New York City. In his later years he was a voice teacher. His pupils included Richard Tucker and Eleanor Steber.

Altimeter. See AIRPLANE, section "Parts of an Airplane," subtitle *Instruments.*

Altiplano. See ANDES, subtitle *Geographical Divisions:* The Central Andes; BOLIVIA, subtitle *Physical Geography.*

Altis. See OLYMPIA (in Ancient Greece).

Altitude, ăl′tĭ-tūd, the height or elevation of a point or object above a given reference level. In geography and aviation, the reference level is sea level, and altitudes are expressed in feet or meters. In astronomy, the reference level is the horizon, and altitudes are expressed in degrees, as angular distances. In geometry, "altitude" refers to the perpendicular distance from the base of a figure to its highest point. For example, the altitude of a triangle is the distance from its base to its vertex.

Sea level is calculated by averaging heights of the ocean near shorelines. The averages are taken over long periods of time. In the United States, a standard mean (average) sea level has been adopted for the measurement of altitudes. Countries having no shoreline generally use a sea level determined by a neighboring country.

An airplane's altitude is measured with an instrument called an *altimeter.* (See AIRPLANE, section "Parts of an Airplane," subtitle *Instruments.*) An astronomer can determine the altitude of a celestial body by pointing a telescope at it and measuring the angle between the telescope and the horizon. Measurements of angular distance can also be made with an instrument called a *sextant.* (See SEXTANT.)

Altitude Sickness. See AVIATION AND SPACE MEDICINE.

Alto. See VOICE, subtitle *Voice in Singing:* Women's Voices.

Altocumulus. See CLOUD, subtitle *Types of Clouds.*

Alton, ôl′t'n, Illinois, a city in Madison County. It lies on the Mississippi River near the mouths of the Missouri and Illinois rivers. The city is 69 miles south-southwest of Springfield (Illinois) and 18 miles north of St. Louis (Missouri). Alton's factories, many of which line the low-lying riverfront, produce glass, paperboard, tools, mining equipment, and brass and steel goods. Large oil refineries are nearby. Much of the city's residential section lies atop bluffs that overlook the river.

Alton was first settled in 1815. It grew as a river port and was incorporated in 1837. That same year Elijah P. Lovejoy, an abolitionist editor, was killed by a mob of local citizens. The last Lincoln-Douglas debate took place here in 1858.

Population: 34,171.

Altoona, ăl-tōō'nȧ, Pennsylvania, a city in Blair County. It is on the Little Juniata River about 85 miles (137 km) east of Pittsburgh. Altoona is a commercial and industrial center. Railway repair shops are here and the city produces electrical machinery, clothing and clothing patterns, processed foods, and shoes.

In Baker Mansion are museum exhibits of Blair County history. Near Altoona is scenic Horseshoe Curve, a railway route that crosses the Allegheny Front.

Altoona was first settled in 1849 as the base of operations for railway construction westward. A conference was held here in 1862 at which Northern governors pledged their support of President Lincoln.

Population: 57,078.

Alto-rilievo. See RELIEF, in sculpture.

Altostratus. See CLOUD, subtitle *Types of Clouds.*

Altrusa International, a service organization of executive and professional women. Altrusa seeks "to help resolve civic and social welfare problems within the commu-

Altrusa Emblem
Altrusa International

nity and the world." Its magazine is *International Altrusan.* The organization was founded in 1917. It has about 19,000 members in some 565 clubs in the United States and a number of other countries. Each club has only one representative from a specific business or profession. Headquarters are in Chicago.

Altus, ăl'tŭs, Oklahoma, the seat of Jackson County. It is about 120 miles (193 km) southwest of Oklahoma City. Altus is the marketing, processing, and trading center for an agricultural area that produces cotton, wheat, and livestock. Concrete blocks, asphalt, fertilizer, livestock feed, and oil made from cotton seeds are among the city's products. Nearby is Lake Altus, in Quartz Mountain State Park. Altus was settled and incorporated in 1891. It has the mayor-council form of government.

Population: 23,101.

Alum, ăl'ŭm, a chemical compound of two sulfates and water. (A sulfate is a compound of sulfur, oxygen, and one or more other elements.) One of the two sulfates usually contains aluminum, but it can be any other metal with a valence of 3, such as chromium or iron. The other sulfate usually contains an alkali metal, such as potassium, but can instead contain either another metal with a valence of 1 or ammonium (a group of atoms formed by combining ammonia and hydrogen). At ordinary temperatures, all alums are solids.

The most important commercial alums are potassium alum and ammonium alum. Other alums include sodium alum (soda alum), chrome alum, rubidium alum, and cesium alum. Potassium and ammonium alum are used in tanning leather, in the manufacture of paper, and in dye making. They are also ingredients of some baking powders. Certain types of fire extinguishers contain alum. Alums are also used in the purification of water and in the treatment of sewage. Alum is sometimes used to produce hardness and crispness in pickles (but too much alum will make the pickles bitter). It has also been used as a preservative.

Alum is an emetic (an agent that causes vomiting) and is used for this purpose to treat certain types of poisoning. However, large quantities of alum taken internally are poisonous. Alum is also used as an astringent (a substance that causes shrinkage of tissue).

The general formula for alum is $M_2(SO_4)_3 X_2SO_4 \cdot 24H_2O$, where M is aluminum or some other trivalent metal, and X is an alkali metal, some other univalent metal, or ammonium. Thus, potassium alum is $Al_2(SO_4)_3K_2SO_4 \cdot 24H_2O$; ammonium alum is $Al_2(SO_4)_3(NH_4)_2SO_4 \cdot 24H_2$.

Alumina. See ALUMINUM, section "Importance," subtitle *Aluminum Compounds,* and section "Production."

Aluminum,

Aluminum, *á-lū'mǐ-nǔm*, a silver-white, metallic chemical element; it is called *aluminium* in Europe and (sometimes) in Canada.

Aluminum is the most abundant metal on earth, and the third most abundant element (after oxygen and silicon). About 8 per cent of the earth's crust is made up of aluminum. However, aluminum is never found uncombined in nature because it is highly reactive chemically. Aluminum is a good conductor of heat and electricity. It is ductile and malleable, and therefore it can be drawn out into a wire and hammered and pressed without breaking. It is also an excellent reflector of light.

Importance of Aluminum

The Metal and Its Alloys

Aluminum metal is strong and lightweight. In contact with air, it forms a thin oxide coating that protects the metal from rusting. It will tarnish under some circumstances, however, unless the surface is given special treatment. Aluminum weakens at elevated temperatures and must be alloyed with other metals for uses that subject it to great heat.

Aluminum can be worked by most of the industrial metalworking processes. It can be rolled into plates and sheets. Continued rolling produces aluminum foil. Aluminum can also be cast, forged, extruded (shaped by being pushed through an opening in a mold), and drawn into wire. Various types of aluminum alloys can be worked either hot or cold. Aluminum can also be treated to give a variety of surface textures and finishes.

Aluminum and its alloys are used in many objects that are exposed to weathering and corrosion from the atmosphere. Examples are building exteriors, lamp posts, exterior trim on automobiles, and awnings and shutters on houses. Some strong aluminum alloys are used in structural parts of airplanes, automobiles, trains, and ships to reduce the over-all weight of these vehicles.

Aluminum and its alloys are used for cooking utensils, doorknobs, refrigerator accessories (such as ice trays), and screen and storm doors. The alloys are used to make

A-339

roofing and window frames. Aluminum foil is a common packaging material. Furniture, jewelry, camera parts, tableware, eyeglass frames, cans, and bottle caps are also made from aluminum. Mirrors used in reflecting telescopes are often coated with aluminum.

Aluminum cable is widely used in place of copper for carrying electric current. Because aluminum has only 62 per cent of the electrical conductivity of copper, an aluminum conductor must have a greater cross-sectional area than one of copper in order to carry the same amount of electricity. Even with this increase in cross section, however, an aluminum conductor is still lighter in weight than a copper conductor of the same current-carrying capacity. Aluminum cable is also less expensive than copper.

Aluminum Compounds

Aluminum forms many useful compounds. *Aluminum oxide,* or *alumina,* which has the

Mining Bauxite in Arkansas. The ore usually is near the surface and is mined with power shovels.

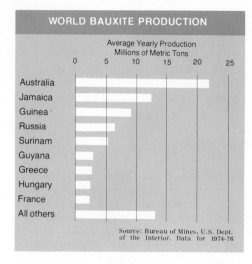

WORLD BAUXITE PRODUCTION

Average Yearly Production
Millions of Metric Tons

	0	5	10	15	20	25
Australia						
Jamaica						
Guinea						
Russia						
Surinam						
Guyana						
Greece						
Hungary						
France						
All others						

Source: Bureau of Mines, U.S. Dept.
of the Interior. Data for 1974-76

chemical formula Al_2O_3, is an extremely hard compound. *Corundum* and *emery* are forms of aluminum oxide used as abrasives. (See CORUNDUM; EMERY.) Aluminum oxide also occurs naturally as ruby and sap-phire, which are highly prized gem stones. In porous form, aluminum oxide is used as an *adsorbent,* to draw moisture from various gases.

Aluminum hydroxide, $Al(OH)_3$, is used as a mordant in dyeing fabrics. (A mordant is a substance that causes fabrics to accept dyes more readily.) Powdered aluminum hydroxide is used as a catalyst (a substance that influences the rate of a chemical reaction without itself being consumed) in certain chemical processes.

Aluminum sulfate, $Al_2(SO_4)_3$, is used in the manufacture of alum and paper. *Alum,* which is usually a double salt of aluminum and another metal, is used in the manufacture of baking powder and in the tanning of leather. (See ALUM.) *Aluminum chloride,* $AlCl_3$, is used as a catalyst in organic chemistry. Aluminum is also present in *kaolin,* a pure clay used for many pottery objects. Thermite, a mixture used to weld iron and steel, is composed of powdered aluminum and iron oxide. (See THERMITE.)

Production of Aluminum

Aluminum Ores

The primary aluminum ore is *bauxite,* a rock composed of various aluminum oxide minerals, such as gibbsite, diaspore, and boehmite. Bauxite also contains impurities such as iron oxide, silicon oxide, and ti-

Ore Processing. At this plant in Surinam bauxite is crushed and dried for shipment to a plant where it will be converted to alumina.
Alcoa

tanium oxide. It is a soft rock, basically white or gray, but the impurities can change its color to red, yellow, or brown. *Alunite,* a lower-grade ore, is sometimes used as a source of aluminum in regions where bauxite is not readily available.

Aluminum occurs in many other kinds of rocks, but these rocks are very seldom used as aluminum ores because the processes required to separate the aluminum from them are difficult and expensive. Ruby, sapphire, and a few other aluminum-containing minerals are more valuable in combined form than for the aluminum they contain.

Location of Bauxite Deposits. Bauxite deposits are formed from the weathering of alumina-rich rocks, such as nepheline syenite, schists, and shales. Many of the bauxite deposits are formed in areas that are subjected to an alternate wetting and drying cycle—as in the tropics, or where the water table rises and falls periodically. Bauxite deposits are not widespread, but some contain extremely high-grade ore.

The largest deposit of bauxite in the United States is in Arkansas. Most of the domestic supply of bauxite comes from this deposit. Other deposits worked in the United

Extraction of Alumina. *Left,* a crusher grinds the bauxite into powder as the first step in the Bayer process. *Right,* digester vessels heat powdered ore.

States are in Alabama, Mississippi, and Georgia. However, bauxite reserves in the United States are not sufficient for domestic consumption, and additional bauxite must be imported. The largest share of it comes from the Caribbean area and from South America.

The largest reserves of bauxite in the world occur in Australia, particularly along the eastern shore of the continent. Other large reserves are in Guinea, Jamaica, Hungary, Ghana, Surinam, French Guiana, Yugoslavia, and Russia. Smaller deposits are found in Greece, Guyana, and France. (The name *bauxite* comes from the French town of Les Baux, where bauxite was first discovered and identified early in the 19th century.) India, mainland China, Brazil, Indonesia, the Dominican Republic, and Haiti also have bauxite reserves.

Production of Bauxite. The world's leading producers of bauxite are shown by the graph on the previous page. Canada, one of the leading aluminum-producing countries, has no known bauxite deposits.

Since bauxite deposits are usually near the surface of the earth, strip-mining methods are generally used to remove the ore. (For a description of strip mining, see MINING, sub-title *Types of Mining:* Surface Mining.) The few deep deposits are mined by using underground shafts.

Extraction of Alumina

Bauxite cannot be converted directly into metallic aluminum. Bauxite contains oxides of other metals, such as iron and titanium, that are easier to reduce than aluminum oxide. If the bauxite were directly reduced, the result would be an undesirable aluminum alloy. Therefore, the bauxite is first converted into nearly pure alumina, or aluminum oxide. The alumina is then reduced to metallic aluminum by electrolysis.

When bauxite mines are located at great distances from alumina-producing plants, the ore is usually given some preliminary treatment at the mine. It is then the common practice to dry the ore in kilns, so that water is not shipped with the bauxite. Some bauxite is found mixed with clay, and is

Extraction of Alumina (continued). *Left,* filter presses remove impurities from the solution after it leaves settling tanks. It then goes to cooling towers and precipitators, where aluminum hydroxide crystals form. *Right,* kilns heat the crystals and free them from water, leaving nearly pure alumina.

Electrolysis. *Left,* a current passes through these electrolytic cells containing alumina powder mixed with cryolite. The resulting molten aluminum is siphoned from the bottom of a-cell by the spout of a crucible. *Right,* aluminum is poured from the crucible to form ingots.

washed to remove the clay particles. (Clay usually contains silicon dioxide, which interferes with the process used to treat high-grade ore.) The ore is then shipped to a plant for conversion to alumina. The two most common methods of producing alumina are the Bayer process (used for high-grade ore) and the lime-soda process (for low-grade ore).

Bayer Process. High-grade bauxite is ground up and placed in iron tanks, called *digesters,* with a solution of caustic soda (sodium hydroxide). This mixture is heated under pressure for several hours. The sodi-

um and aluminum oxide combine to form a solution of sodium aluminate. The impurities in the bauxite do not combine, but remain suspended in the liquid. The mixture is then transferred to settling tanks, where most of the impurities (called "red mud") settle to the bottom and are removed. The sodium-aluminate solution is then diluted and filtered.

As the next step, the sodium-aluminate solution is pumped through cooling towers and precipitators, and crystals of aluminum hydroxide are recovered. These crystals are then heated to about 1800° F. The heating process drives off the chemically combined water and leaves 99.6 per cent pure alumina powder.

Lime-soda Process. Low-grade ore containing large quantities of silicon dioxide cannot be used profitably in the Bayer process because insoluble aluminum silicate forms and becomes part of the red mud, thus reducing the amount of aluminum metal produced.

Ready for Manufacture. *Left,* three ingots, each weighing 8,333 pounds, are loaded for shipment to a sheet mill. *Right,* rolled sheets of aluminum await fabrication into finished products.

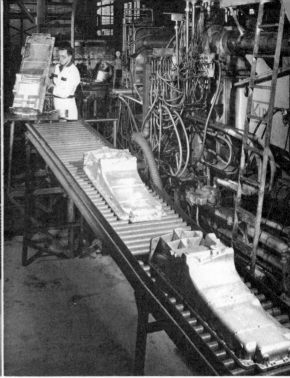

The lime-soda process, however, can be used to recover aluminum from ores rich in silicon dioxide and from the red mud produced by the Bayer process.

In the lime-soda process, limestone, soda ash (sodium carbonate), and low-grade ore or red mud are mixed together and finely ground. The ground mixture is then heated to about 2500° F. in a rotary kiln. The insoluble aluminum silicate is broken down, and sodium aluminate and insoluble calcium silicate are formed. This mixture is then treated with water to dissolve out the sodium aluminate. The dissolved sodium aluminate can then be treated by the Bayer process to produce alumina.

Electrolysis of Alumina

Virtually all commercial aluminum is produced from alumina by the *Hall-Héroult process*. In this process, alumina is dissolved in a bath of molten cryolite (sodium-aluminum fluoride). Electric current is then passed through the mixture, causing metallic aluminum to be electrolytically separated out. Large quantities of electric power are required. Between 8 and 9 kilowatt-hours of electricity are needed to produce one pound of aluminum. Many aluminum-producing plants are located near hydroelectric projects. Others are located where large quantities of fuel, such as coal, lignite, or natural gas, are available.

Making Aluminum Products. *Left,* a press forms bread pans from flat sheet blanks. *Right,* die-cast "crocodile snouts"—four-foot-long oil pans for diesel engines—are among the largest aluminum die castings made.

Electrolytic Equipment. Aluminum is produced in a series of electrolytic cells. Each cell is rectangular, about 18 feet long, 6 feet wide, and 3 or 4 feet deep. The cells, which are made of steel, are lined with insulating material that is coated on the inside with carbon mixed with pitch. The carbon resists the action of the molten cryolite, which is a powerful solvent. A single aluminum plant may have several hundred cells in operation

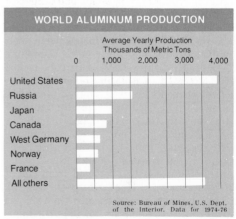

WORLD ALUMINUM PRODUCTION

Average Yearly Production
Thousands of Metric Tons

	0	1,000	2,000	3,000	4,000
United States					
Russia					
Japan					
Canada					
West Germany					
Norway					
France					
All others					

Source: Bureau of Mines, U.S. Dept. of the Interior. Data for 1974-76

Alcoa

Early Aluminum Extraction. This reduction pot in the original works of The Pittsburgh Reduction Company was tapped in 1888, marking the beginning of the aluminum industry in the United States.

Electrolytic Process. The powdered alumina is dissolved in the molten cryolite. The carbon anodes are lowered into the cryolite and the current is turned on. A direct current of 50,000 to 200,000 amperes is required for each cell. The current flows through the cryolite from the anodes to the bottom of the cell, where a layer of molten aluminum acts as the cathode. The alumina is broken down by the electric current into aluminum and oxygen.

The metallic aluminum collects at the bottom of the cell and is siphoned off periodically. The oxygen collects at the anodes and combines with the carbon, forming carbon monoxide and carbon dioxide. These gases escape from the top of the bath. When the alumina in the bath is depleted, more is added from the top. In practice, the process is continuous. The aluminum produced by the Hall-Héroult process is between 99.5 and 99.9 per cent pure.

The finished aluminum is cast in ingots. If the aluminum is to be alloyed, it is combined with the other metal or metals in a remelting process or directly in the electrolytic cells. (For a discussion of aluminum alloys, see ALLOY, subtitle *Nonferrous Alloys:* Aluminum-base Alloys.)

at one time. Natural cryolite, a mineral found only in Greenland, was originally used in the cells, but it has been replaced by synthetic cryolite.

Suspended above each cell is a series of carbon anodes (as many as 24). The anodes are produced from a mixture of petroleum, pitch, and coke, which has been baked for several hours. The anode is consumed in the production of aluminum (by combining with the oxygen).

History

Aluminum is the most recently discovered of the primary industrial metals. While copper and iron were known thousands of years ago, aluminum was not discovered until the 1800's. Aluminous clays had been used to make pottery since prehistoric times, and various aluminum compounds had been used in medicines and dyes for thousands of years. But because aluminum is so reactive, methods used to obtain other metals from their compounds did not work with aluminum. Even Sir Humphrey Davy, a British chemist who succeeded in isolating other highly reactive elements by electrolytic methods, failed when he tried to obtain aluminum the same way in 1807. He named the elusive metal "alumium" and later "aluminum," after the Latin name *alumen* for alum.

Oersted's Work

Aluminum was first isolated from one of its compounds by Hans Christian Oersted, a Danish physicist and chemist. In 1825, he obtained a small quantity of impure alumi-

num by combining heated potassium amalgam (an alloy of potassium and mercury) with anhydrous aluminum chloride. The potassium combined with the chlorine, leaving an aluminum amalgam. The mercury was then distilled from the amalgam, leaving metallic aluminum.

Friedrich Wöhler, a German chemist, tried to repeat Oersted's experiment in 1827 but failed. However, he devised a more successful method than Oersted's by substituting pure potassium for the potassium amalgam. There is still some disagreement as to whether Oersted or Wöhler was the first to isolate aluminum metal, but Oersted is generally given the credit.

Commercial Development of Aluminum

The first method of producing aluminum in sufficient quantity for commercial use was discovered by Henri Sainte-Claire Deville, a French chemist, in the 1850's. His process used sodium instead of potassium (used by Wöhler) to reduce aluminum chloride to metallic aluminum. Not only was it possible to produce larger quantities of aluminum by using sodium, but, because sodium was much cheaper than potassium, the cost was substantially less.

As a result of Deville's process, the price of aluminum, which had been more than $500 a pound in 1852, dropped to $17 a pound in 1859. At this price, aluminum was used for jewelry and expensive tableware. It had no industrial uses, however, because of its high price and the small quantities then available.

The process for producing commercial quantities of aluminum at reasonable cost was invented independently in 1886 by Charles Martin Hall in the United States and Paul Louis Toussaint Héroult in France. The two men applied for patents in their respective countries within seven weeks of each other. Héroult also applied for a United States patent. The original process worked out by Hall and Héroult included dissolving alumina in a molten cryolite bath. However, both originally used an externally heated furnace to melt the cryolite.

The internally heated electric furnace, in which the cryolite is melted by the same electric current that decomposes the alumina, is now used in all commercial production of aluminum. It was invented in 1884 by Eugene and Alfred Cowles. The Cowles furnace was used prior to Hall's and Héroult's discovery to produce an alloyed form of aluminum. It was then used by Hall to produce pure aluminum. Conflicting patent claims led to long lawsuits, some of which were won by the Cowles brothers and some by Hall.

Symbol: Al. Atomic number: 13. Atomic weight: 26.9815. Specific gravity: 2.70. Melting point: 1,220° F. (660° C.). Boiling point: 4,473° F. (2,467° C.). Aluminum has one stable isotope—Al-27. It belongs to Group III-A of the Periodic Table and has a valence of +3.

Books about Aluminum

Banks, F. E. *Bauxite and Aluminum: an Introduction to the Economics of Non-Fuel Minerals* (Lexington Books, 1979).

Selberg, C. A. *Foil* (Addison-Wesley, 1975).

Sinia, R. J. *Aluminum in Packaging* (Heinman, 1973).

Aluminum Bronze. See BRONZE.

Aluminum Company of America, or **Alcoa,** the world's leading producer of aluminum and one of the largest industrial corporations in the United States. It mines and processes bauxite, refines alumina from bauxite, smelts aluminum from alumina, processes aluminum and aluminum alloys into mill products and finished products, and recycles used aluminum products. The company was organized in 1888 as The Pittsburgh Reduction Company. The founders included Charles M. Hall, one of the inventors of the commercial aluminum-making process. The present name was adopted in 1907. Headquarters are in Pittsburgh, Pennsylvania.

See also HALL, CHARLES MARTIN.

Alva, ăl'vȧ (or **Alba**), Fernando Álvarez de Toledo, Third **Duke of** (1508-1582), a Spanish general and administrator. He was a harsh but able leader, fanatically loyal to Spain and the Roman Catholic Church. As military commander under Charles V, Holy Roman emperor and king of Spain, Alva led the forces that defeated the Protestant Schmalkaldic League in the Battle of Mühlberg (1547). As viceroy of Naples under Philip II, Alva in 1556 subordinated his loyalty to the Church to help defeat Pope Paul IV and Henry II of France, who had combined to drive the Spaniards from Italy.

Following the revolt of the Netherlands against Spanish rule in 1566, Philip sent Alva to suppress the rebellion with 10,000 Spanish troops. As governor of the Netherlands (1567-73), Alva carried out a reign of terror. His court for punishing suspected rebels and heretics became known as the "Council of Blood." Thousands were sentenced to death. The estates of those who failed to appear before the court were confiscated.

In 1568 Alva defeated an army led by William the Silent, forcing him to withdraw

Duke of Alva
by Titian
Art Reference Bureau

to Germany. New rebellion broke out when Alva levied taxes to raise money for his activities. He was replaced as governor in 1573. In 1580 Alva led the Spanish forces that enforced Philip's claim to the throne of Portugal.

Alvarado, äl'vä-rä'thŏ, **Pedro de** (1495?-1541), a Spanish soldier and explorer of Central America. Alvarado commanded a ship in the Spanish expedition to Yucatán, led by Juan de Grijalva, in 1518. From 1519 to 1521, he served as one of the principal lieutenants of Hernando Cortez in the conquest of the Aztec empire of Mexico. Left in command of the Aztec capital of Tenochtitlán (now Mexico City) in 1520, Alvarado provoked a brief but bloody revolt by his brutality toward the Indians. In the temporary retreat from the city, he distinguished himself by his daring in battle.

During 1523-27, Alvarado subdued the Mayas in Guatemala and the Pipils in what is now El Salvador. He was governor of the Captaincy General of Guatemala (all of Central America), 1530-34. In 1534 he led an unsuccessful expedition against Quito, northern capital of the Inca empire. Alvarado was killed during the Mixton War, an Indian uprising against the Spanish in western Mexico.

Alvarez, äl'vȧ-rĕz, the family name of two United States scientists, father and son.

Walter C. (Clement) **Alvarez** (1884-1978), physician, physiologist, and author, was a consultant in internal medicine at the Mayo Clinic for 25 years. An authority on digestive disorders and migraine, he was one of the first physicians to show that emotional and mental stress may produce symptoms of disease. Alvarez was born in San Francisco and received his M.D. degree from Cooper Medical College (a forerunner of Stanford University School of Medicine) in 1905. He was professor of medicine at the University of Minnesota from 1934 until his retirement in 1951. For many years afterwards he wrote a syndicated medical-advice column.

His books include: *Minds That Came Back* (1961); *Incurable Physician: an Autobiography* (1963); *Help Your Doctor to Help You* (1976).

Luis W. (Walter) **Alvarez** (1911-   ), the son, received the 1968 Nobel Prize in physics. The award was made for his contributions to elementary particle physics, in particular the discovery of a number of resonance states through his development of the hydrogen bubble chamber for recording the paths of nuclear particles. Alvarez also did valuable work in radar research, including the development of a ground-controlled approach system for landing aircraft and an improved method for controlling air traffic.

Alvarez was born in San Francisco. After receiving his Ph.D. degree from the University of Chicago in 1936, he joined the faculty of the University of California. He became professor of physics in 1945 and was associate director of the Lawrence Radiation Laboratory, 1954-59.

Alveoli. See LUNGS, subtitle *The Bronchial Tree.*

Alverno College. See UNIVERSITIES AND COLLEGES (table).

Alyssum, ȧ-lĭs'ŭm, a genus of perennial herbs of the mustard family. Members of this genus are more commonly called *madworts*. There are about 100 species of alyssums, all native to Europe and Asia. Sweet alyssum is a related plant. (See SWEET ALYSSUM.)

The flowers are usually white or yellow, and grow in dense clusters at the end of the stems. Most alyssums grow easily in ordinary garden soil and require very little cultivation. Alyssums are low-growing, and for this reason they are often planted in rock gardens. They seldom exceed 12 inches (30 cm) in height. Alyssums are also planted in flower borders and in window boxes. Propagation is by seeds and cuttings. The most popular species of alyssum is the *golden tuft,* or *gold dust.*

Golden tuft is *Alyssum saxatile.* Alyssums belong to the mustard family, Cruciferae.

Alzheimer's Disease. See BRAIN, subtitle *Disorders of the Brain:* Organic Disorders (Senility).

AM (Amplitude Modulation). See RADIO, section "How Radio Works," subtitle *Transmitting Radio Signals:* Modulation.

AMA. See AMERICAN MEDICAL ASSOCIATION.

Amadis of Gaul, ăm'ȧ-dĭs, the central figure of a medieval cycle of prose romances of chivalry. Amadis was a son of the king of Gaul and a princess of Brittany. The first account of his exploits known to be published was the Spanish version of Garci Rodríguez de Montalvo (1508), probably based on a lost Portuguese work of the 13th century. Its glorification of the ideals of chivalry and its emphasis on fantasy and the supernatural had a marked effect on 16th-century prose fiction.

Amagasaki, ä-mä-gä-sä-kė̇, Japan, a city in Hyogo Prefecture, on southwestern Honshu. It lies on Osaka Bay, an arm of the Inland Sea. The city is about four miles (6 km) northwest of downtown Osaka, of which it is an industrial suburb. Amagasaki's factories produce chemicals, machinery, textiles, glass, and fabricated iron and steel goods. The city suffered severe damage from Allied bombings during World War II. Population: 532,417.

Amahl and the Night Visitors, an opera in one act. Gian Carlo Menotti wrote the music and libretto. The first opera written specifically for television, *Amahl and the Night Visitors* was first produced by the NBC Opera Theater on Christmas Eve, 1951. It is one of the few operas in which a leading role is both acted and sung by a child.

Amahl, a crippled boy with a lively imagination, lives with his mother, a poor shepherdess. One night they are visited by the Three Kings who are on their way to visit the Christ Child. When Amahl adds his crutch—his most valuable possession—to their gifts, his crippled leg is healed. He then accompanies the Three Kings to Bethlehem.

Amalekites, ăm′á-lĕk-īts; á-măl′ĕ-kīts, in the Bible, a Semitic tribe often at war with the Hebrews. The Amalekites lived in the desert south of Canaan. They were descended from Amalek, Esau's grandson, and therefore related to the Hebrews (Genesis 36:12). After the Israelites fled from Egypt under Moses they defeated the Amalekites near Mount Sinai (Exodus 17). The Amalekites were a scourge of the Hebrews under the judges (Judges 6:33, 7:12), under King Saul (I Samuel 15), and under David (I Samuel 30:18), until the reign of Hezekiah (I Chronicles 4:43).

Amalgam, á-măl′găm, an alloy of mercury and one or more other metals. The substances thus combined are said to be *amalgamated*. Most metals will amalgamate with mercury. At ordinary temperatures amalgams may be either solid or liquid, depending on the percentage of mercury in them.

Amalgams are widely used in dentistry for filling teeth. Dental amalgams contain silver, copper, zinc, and tin, in addition to mercury. When first prepared by the dentist, dental amalgams are semiliquid, but they soon harden and become solid. Amalgams are also used as electrodes in some commercial electrolytic processes. The tendency of gold and silver to amalgamate with mercury is sometimes made use of in removing these metals from their ores.

Amalgamated Clothing and Textile Workers Union, an AFL-CIO union of workers in the garment and textile industries. The union was formed in 1976 by a merger of the Amalgamated Clothing Workers of America (ACWA) and the Textile Workers Union of America (TWUA).

The ACWA, founded in 1914, was one of the first unions organized on an industry-wide basis. It was also one of the first unions in the United States to establish a health-and-welfare plan for its members. Sidney Hillman, the union's president from 1914 to 1946, helped organize the Congress of Industrial Organizations (CIO) in the 1930's. The Textile Workers Union of America was founded in 1939.

The headquarters of the Amalgamated Clothing and Textile Workers Union are in New York City. For membership, see LABOR UNION (table).

Amalthea, ăm′ăl-thē′á, in Greek mythology, the goat that suckled the infant Zeus when he was left with the nymphs in a Cretan cave. Ambrosia and nectar flowed from her horns. When one of these was broken off, it was filled with fruits and given to Zeus. The Romans called it *cornucopia* (horn of plenty), and it became a symbol of abundance. Another story is that Amalthea was a nymph who fed the child with goat's milk, and that the cornucopia was a horn of Achelous (who had assumed the shape of a bull) that Hercules had broken off.

Amana Society, a cooperative community in Iowa, located northwest of Iowa City. It owns 25,000 acres (10,100 hectares) of land and includes seven settlements. There are about 1,000 members of the Amana Corporation and several hundred nonmembers living in the settlements. Farming is the chief industry. Craft and industrial products include smoked meats, woolens, furniture, and appliances.

The history of the group began in Germany in 1714 with the founding of a pietist religious group called The Community of True Inspiration. More than 800 members came to the United States in 1842, settling first in New York State, then going to Iowa in 1855. The group organized a communistic community, called Amana Society. The community flourished for many years, but in 1932 it was reorganized so that the economic and religious affairs were separated. The Amana Corporation was organized as a producing and marketing cooperative for profit. The Amana (Faithfulness) Church Society still retains many of its pietistic traditions.

Amanullah Khan (1892-1960). See AF-GHANISTAN, subtitle *History*.

Amaranth, ăm'à-rănth, the name of a family, as well as a genus, of plants found throughout the world except in polar regions. The family contains about 60 genera and 600 species of herbs, the majority of which grow as weeds. The individual flowers are usually small, but they often grow in dense, showy clusters. Some members of the amaranth family, such as tampala, are grown as vegetables; tampala, which is rich in vitamins and minerals, is a dietary stable in parts of South America. Other members of the family, such as cockscomb, are grown as ornamentals. Several species, including the globe amaranth, are popular everlastings (plants whose flowers retain their color when dry).

The amaranth genus consists of about 50 species of annual herbs. Garden amaranths that are grown for their colorful foliage and attractive flower clusters include love-lies-bleeding (or tassel flower), prince's-feather,

Globe Amaranth
George W. Park Seed Company

and Joseph's coat. Some species of pigweeds and tumbleweeds are of the amaranth genus.

Love-lies-bleeding is *Amaranthus caudatus;* prince's-feather, *A. hypochondriacus;* Joseph's coat, *A. gangeticus.* Tampala is *A. tricolor.* The globe amaranth is *Gomphrena globosa.* All belong to the amaranth family, Amaranthaceae.

See also COCKSCOMB; TUMBLEWEED.

Amarillo, ăm'à-rĭl'lō, Texas, a city in the northern part of the state. It is the seat of Potter County, but lies also in Randall County. The city was named Amarillo (which in Spanish means "yellow") for the yellow sands of Amarillo Creek.

Amarillo is sometimes called the Queen of the Panhandle because it occupies a leading position in the commerce, industry, and trade of northwestern Texas. The region is noted for its rich agricultural lands and valuable oil and gas fields. In Amarillo are meat-packing plants, flour mills, oil and gas refineries, and zinc smelting and synthetic rubber factories. One of the world's largest helium plants and a carbon-black plant are nearby.

Amarillo began in 1887 as a railway construction camp. It grew into a bustling cattle town and, in the 20th century, prospered with the development of the region's natural resources.

Population: 149,230.

Amaryllis, ăm'à-rĭl'ĭs, the name of a genus, as well as a family, of lilylike plants native to tropical regions. The genus *Amaryllis* consists of only one species, called the *belladonna lily.* However, the name amaryllis is commonly applied also to a number of plants belonging to related genera.

The belladonna lily has 3½-inch (9-cm) flowers growing in dense clusters at the end of long stalks that are often 18 inches (46 cm) tall. There are many varieties of this plant, which bear flowers ranging in color from white through shades of red to purple. Propagation is by bulbs.

The amaryllis family is made up of about 90 genera. Plants of more than 40 genera are cultivated in the United States as ornamentals. Some members of the amaryllis family, such as agave, are important sources of fibers used in making cord and rope. Others, such as narcissus and jonquil, are widely grown for their aromatic oils, used in perfumes and soaps. Vegetables, such as onions and chives, are grown for food and seasoning.

The belladonna lily is *Amaryllis belladonna*. Plants of the following genera are commonly called amaryllis: *Crinum, Hippeastrum, Brunsvigia, Sprekelia, Lycoris,* and *Vallota*. All belong to the amaryllis family, Amaryllidaceae.

For other members of the amaryllis family, see:

AGAVE	JONQUIL	SHALLOT
CHIVE	LEEK	SISAL
CRINUM	NARCISSUS	SNOWDROP
DAFFODIL	ONION	TUBEROSE
GARLIC		

Amateur Athletic Union of the United States (AAU), a national organization that promotes competition in amateur sports. Except where schools and colleges have jurisdiction, the AAU governs such sports as handball, racquetball, horseshoe pitching, long-distance running, volleyball, karate, and trampoline and tumbling, as well as adult competition in basketball and gymnastics. The AAU also runs the Junior Olympics program, which provides competition in some 20 sports for athletes 8 to 18. The Sullivan Award is given each year by the AAU to the person it designates as the nation's top amateur athlete.

The AAU was founded in 1888 as the governing body for all amateur sports. The National Collegiate Athletic Association (NCAA) withdrew from the AAU in 1960, and during the 1960's and 1970's participants in all the major amateur sports formed their own governing organizations. The AAU continued to take responsibility for the minor sports. Headquarters are in Indianapolis, Indiana.

Amateur Fencers League of America. See FENCING (concluding paragraph).

Amateur Radio. See RADIO, section "Uses and Regulation of Radio," subtitle *Amateur Radio.*

Amati, ä-mä′tĕ, the name of a family of violinmakers in Cremona, Italy. Their instruments rank with the Stradivari and Guarneri violins as the greatest ever made. Andrea Amati (1530?-1611?) is considered the designer of the modern violin. His amber-colored varnish came to be identified with the Amati violin. Other members of the family specialized in bass viols and cellos. Andrea's grandson, Niccolò (1596-1684), became the most famous member of the family. Antonio Stradivari and Andrea Guarneri were his pupils. Niccolò's son Girolamo (1649-1740) was the last famous Amati.

Amato, Pasquale (1878-1942), an Italian operatic baritone. He was known for his

A. B. Morse Company

Amaryllis. The flower shown belongs to the genus *Hippaestrum.* Hybrids of this genus are popular as both house and garden plants.

acting ability as well as for the exceptional power and range of his voice. Amato studied in his native Naples. He made his debut there as Germont in *La Traviata* in 1900. Eight years later he joined the Metropolitan Opera Company in New York City. There he created the role of sheriff Jack Rance in *The Girl of the Golden West* (1910) and the title role of Walter Damrosch's *Cyrano de Bergerac* (1913). After retiring from the Metropolitan Opera in 1921, Amato taught voice in New York City and directed opera at Louisiana State University.

Amatol. See EXPLOSIVE, subtitle *Demolition and Blasting Charges:* Amatol.

Amazon River, ăm′ȧ-zŏn, (*Portuguese and Spanish:* **Amazonas**), one of the great rivers of the world and the chief river of South America. With a length of about 4,000 miles (6,400 km), it is the second longest river in the world, exceeded only by the Nile. The Amazon's flow is by far the world's largest. On average, the river discharges some 4,200,000 cubic feet (119,000 m³) per second into the Atlantic Ocean—a volume of water roughly seven times as great as that discharged by the Mississippi River. The Amazon is also one of the world's deepest rivers. Downstream from Manaus there are numerous places with depths of more than 300 feet (90 m).

Course and Characteristics

The Amazon begins as the Huarco, a small stream high in the Andes of southern Peru, about 100 miles (160 km) from the Pacific Ocean. From there it flows northward, progressively becoming the Toro, Santiago, Ene, Tambo, Apurímac, and Ucayali. The Amazon proper begins at the junction of the Ucayali and the Marañón, south of Iquitos, Peru. From Iquitos the Amazon flows eastward through the Amazon Basin of Brazil, reaching the Atlantic Ocean through a wide estuary at the Equator. Most of the water enters the sea through several branches north of Marajó Island; some of the flow goes south of the island via the Pará River past the port city of Belém.

After leaving the Andes, the Amazon becomes increasingly wide and follows a gentle gradient, or slope, to the sea. In many areas there are numerous bordering lakes, marshy islands, and swamps. Although it carries silt in suspension, the Amazon's water, in a chemical sense, is amazingly pure, in places approaching the quality of distilled water. Unlike most rivers that flow into the ocean, the Amazon has not built a sizable delta. Instead, the river's enormous discharge moves far out to sea, where its silt is intercepted and carried northward by strong ocean currents. Tides occur in the estuary and a tidal bore, a wall of water that moves rapidly upstream, sometimes forms.

Tributaries and Basin

Thousands of rivers flow, directly or indirectly, into the Amazon, draining parts of Bolivia, Brazil, Colombia, Ecuador, Guyana, Peru, and Venezuela. The longest tributary is the 2,100-mile (3,380-km) Madeira River; other major tributaries include the Negro, Tapajós and Xingu. Many tributaries are interrupted by falls and rapids that impede navigation. The Amazon river system is joined to the Orinoco system by the Casiquiare River in Venezuela.

The Amazon Basin covers an area of about 2,720,000 square miles (7,040,000 km²)—almost 40 per cent of the total area of South America.

One of the world's largest forested tracts covers the Amazon Basin. Growing there is a profusion of different species of trees in various kinds of forests. Most widespread are the tropical rain forests, where trees reach heights of up to 200 feet (60 m) and form a dense canopy overhead. Because little sunlight reaches the forest floor, there is scant underbrush. There are also savanna grasslands in the basin.

The forests and rivers of the Amazon Basin teem with a wide variety of animal life. Carnivores such as pumas, jaguars, and ocelots prey on deer, monkeys, rodents and other animals. Reptiles include crocodiles, caimans, and such snakes as boa constrictors and anacondas. Hundreds of kinds of brightly colored birds and myriad species of insects fill the forests. The rivers abound with many species of fish, including piranhas and pirarucus.

The hot, humid climate, dense forests, and the virtual inaccessibility of the land long discouraged development of the basin. However, construction of new roads into and across the basin in Brazil, beginning in the 1970's, is aiding development, especially settlement, plantation agriculture, cattle ranching, and lumbering and mining operations.

Even the river itself, capable of carrying small ocean vessels as far as Iquitos, Peru, is little used. Most river traffic carries supplies to the various settlements, but brings little from them. The chief cities on the river are Iquitos and the Brazilian cities of Manaus, Macapá, and Santarém. Belém, the chief port, is on the Pará River. Elsewhere there are small riverside towns and settlements and aboriginal Indian communities.

A-350

History

The Spanish, arriving in the early 16th century, were the first Europeans to see the Amazon. Francisco de Orellana was the first white man to sail down the river. He is credited with naming it, for the legendary female warriors, after supposedly coming in contact with warlike women along the river. A few missions were established here, but serious settlement did not occur until the rubber boom of the 19th century. When Brazil lost its monopoly on rubber to Asian plantations, the industry declined rapidly.

See also BELÉM; JAPURÁ RIVER; MADEIRA RIVER; MANAUS; MARAJÓ; NAPO RIVER; ORELLANA, FRANCISCO DE; PURUS RIVER; PUTUMAYO RIVER; RIO NEGRO; TAPAJÓS RIVER; UCAYALI RIVER.

Albert J. Klee: The Aquarium
An Amazon River Settlement

Books about the Amazon River

Kelly, Brian, and Mark London. *The Amazon* (Harcourt Brace Jovanovich, 1983).
Lathrap, D. W. *The Upper Amazon* (Thames & Hudson, 1979).
Shoumatoff, Alex. *The Rivers Amazon* (Sierra Club Books, 1978).
Smith, N. J. *Man, Fishes, and the Amazon* (Columbia University, 1981).
Sterling, Tom. *The Amazon* (Time-Life Books, 1974).

For Younger Readers:

McConnell, Rosemary. *The Amazon* (Silver Burdett, 1978).

Amazons, ăm′*a*-zŏns, in Greek legend, a tribe of female warriors said to have lived in Asia Minor on the shores of the Black Sea. Men were not permitted to settle permanently in their domain, and male babies were killed at birth. Each Amazon would cut off her right breast so that it would not interfere with the use of the bow. Amazons were a popular subject of Greek art.

The Spanish conquistador Francisco de Orellana claimed to have observed female warriors while exploring the Amazon river in the early 16th century. He named them and the river after the legendary Greek warriors.

Ambassador, ăm-băs′*a*-dẽr, a diplomatic agent of the highest rank. *Ministers* are diplomatic agents of lower rank. Usually countries exchange ministers only when the relations between them are unfriendly or unimportant. Members of the British Commonwealth of Nations exchange *high commissioners* with the rank of ambassador. Vatican City has diplomatic relations with many countries; in the major countries it is represented by *nuncios* with ambassadorial rank.

The heads of most national delegations to the United Nations have the rank of ambassador. The principal United States representatives to other international organizations usually also have the rank of ambassador. Most countries follow this practice. Representatives to certain specialized United Nations agencies have the rank of minister.

The United States ambassador to each country is appointed by the President, with the advice and consent of the Senate, and serves at the pleasure of the President. Some ambassadors are career persons who have risen in the foreign service; others are appointed because of prominence in politics or business.

Types of Ambassadors

An *ambassador ordinary* lives in the foreign country to which he is assigned. His official premises are called an *embassy*. Normally, he has the power to perform routine duties only, and must await instructions from his government on important matters. He has less influence today than formerly, because improved communications allow heads of state to confer directly.

An *ambassador extraordinary,* sometimes called an "ambassador without portfolio" or "roving ambassador," is one who is sent on special missions only. An *ambassador plenipotentiary* is an ambassador ordinary or extraordinary who is given full power to conclude a treaty or conduct other important business.

Duties and Privileges

An ambassador is the official representative of his government. He deals with the

A-351

foreign minister of the host country, but may sometimes see the head of its government. His main duty is to report on what he observes and finds out in the foreign country. He entertains and is entertained, and maintains a wide variety of social contacts.

The ambassador, his family, and his staff are exempt from arrest in the country in which they serve. But if a diplomatic agent flouts local laws or is disrespectful or indiscreet in his acts or words, the foreign government may ask his home government to recall him, and it may even dismiss him.

See also DIPLOMATIC SERVICE; MINISTER.

Ambedkar, *ăm*-bād'kĕr, **Bhimrao Ramji** (1893-1956), an Indian statesman. He was a leader of India's untouchables (a class of people considered to be below the lowest caste) and a principal author of the 1949 Indian constitution. This document included an article that outlawed discrimination against untouchables. As minister of law in Jawaharlal Nehru's cabinet, 1947-51, he drafted a new legal code that legalized inter-caste marriages and in other ways modernized the social system.

Although Ambedkar was born an untouchable, he was able to receive an education under British colonial rule. After earning doctoral degrees from Columbia University and the University of London School of Economics, he became a spokesman for the untouchables. By appealing to the British, he advanced the untouchables' cause despite the resistance of Hindu leaders.

Amber, ăm'bĕr, a fossil resin. It was formed millions of years ago from a sticky fluid that oozed from the bark of evergreen trees, such as pine. Amber often contains the preserved bodies of insects that were caught and embedded in it. Amber is as hard as some kinds of stone, and is usually yellow, orange, or brown. Most amber is transparent or translucent and takes a fine polish. Attractive pieces of amber are used for jewelry, ornaments, and pipestems. Low-quality amber is used to make varnish. The world's major deposits of high-quality amber lie along the southern shores of the Baltic Sea.

When rubbed, amber acquires an electric charge and will attract bits of paper. The ancient Greeks called amber *elektron,* and from this comes the world *electricity.*

Ambergris, ăm'bĕr-grēs, a gray, yellow, or black waxlike substance formed in the intestine of the sperm whale. Ambergris was used long before the Christian Era in medicinal cure-alls, love potions, and perfumes by the Egyptians, Chinese, and others. In modern times, ambergris has been used primarily as a fixative in perfumes. In the United States, its use has now been largely discontinued because the sperm whale is an endangered species.

Lumps of ambergris weighing more than 100 pounds (45 kg) have been removed from dead sperm whales. Lumps of various sizes are sometimes found floating in the ocean or lying on ocean beaches.

Amberjack, the name of a group of fish found in temperate ocean waters throughout the world. Many amberjacks are popular game fish. The *common,* or *greater, amberjack* is found off the west coast of Europe, off the east coast of the United States, and in the Gulf of Mexico. It is most abundant south of Cape Hatteras and is often caught as a game fish in Florida waters. Its upper body is blue, the belly is silver, and the fins are yellowish-gray. The common amberjack can reach five to six feet (1.5-1.8 m) in length and more than 100 pounds (45 kg) in weight. The average weight, however, is 10 to 15 pounds (4.5-6.8 kg). The *Pacific amberjack* and the *Pacific yellowtail* are often caught off the southwestern coast of the United States.

Amberjacks make up the genus *Seriola.* The common amberjack is *S. dumerili;* the Pacific amberjack, *S. colburni;* the Pacific yellowtail, *S. dorsalis.* Amberjacks belong to the family Carangidae.

For record catch, see FISHING, table titled *Saltwater Fishing Records.*

Ambrose, ăm'brōz, Saint (340?-397), a saint of the early Christian Church. He bears the title of Doctor of the Church in recognition of his contributions to theology. Ambrose was born in Treves (Trier), Germany, into a noble family. He became governor of a Roman province with his capital in Milan. In 374 he was elected bishop of Milan by popular acclaim even though he had just been converted and had not yet been baptized. He became a great preacher, wrote hymns and many books, and founded the basilica of Sant' Ambrogio.

Ambrose took a strong stand against the heresy of Arianism and exerted a powerful influence in molding Christian theological orthodoxy. He converted Saint Augustine. His feast day is December 7.

Ambrosia, ăm-brō′zhĭ-å, in Greek mythology, the food of the Olympian gods. It was described as a fragrant kind of honey. Anyone who ate ambrosia became immortal. The goddesses used it as a beautifying lotion. The word often is applied to any fragrant or delicious food. For the drink of the gods, see NECTAR.

Ambulance, ăm′bū-lăns, a vehicle for carrying the sick and injured to and from a hospital. The word is from the French *hôpital ambulant,* which means "traveling hospital." About 1800 Dominique Jean Larrey (1766-1842), the chief surgeon in the French army under Napoleon, devised the first ambulance—a one-horse vehicle to carry the wounded from the field of battle. Trains, ships, and aircraft are used as ambulances, but the term usually refers either to an automobile that resembles somewhat a large station wagon or to a light truck with a box-like compartment at the rear.

Ambulances are equipped with stretchers, bandages and other first-aid supplies, and equipment for administering oxygen. Some ambulances—often called mobile trauma units or intensive care units—are staffed by paramedics. Paramedics are trained to use various types of electronic equipment, to administer drugs, and to perform such life-saving procedures as cardiopulmonary resuscitation (CPR). Equipment in these units includes defibrillators (machines that use electrical shock to restore heartbeat to victims of cardiac arrest), high-frequency radios for voice communication with a hospital, and heart-tone sets (devices that transmit the pattern of a patient's heartbeat to a hospital for analysis).

Ameba. See AMOEBA.

Amen, or **Amon.** See AMMON.

Amendment, a change in a document, record, proposal, or oral statement. The amendment may alter the original form by adding, taking away, or substituting words or statements.

A *constitutional amendment* is a formal change in the constitution of a country or state. The United States Constitution provides for the method of its amendment in Article V. Amendments may be proposed in either of two ways:

1. By a two-thirds vote of each house of Congress.

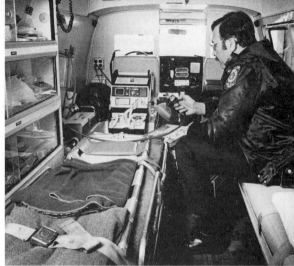

Rich Frishman, Chicago

Ambulance. A paramedic inspects life-saving equipment in a mobile trauma unit. Paramedics for such units are often policemen or firemen.

2. By a convention called by Congress at the request of the legislatures of two-thirds of the states.

In either case, proposed amendments become effective only after ratified by three-fourths of the states. The ratification is done either by the state legislatures or by state conventions, the method used being specified by Congress.

The Constitution has been amended 25 times. The 21st Amendment was the only one ratified by conventions. The method of proposing an amendment by convention has never been used.

In every state except New Hampshire amendments to the state constitution are proposed by the legislature. Proposals must be adopted by referendum vote of the people. Delaware's constitution can be amended by

Horse-drawn Ambulance of New York City's Department of Charities in the late 19th century

Chicago Public Library

a two-thirds vote of each house in two successive legislatures.

In *legislation,* amendments may change the effect of existing laws. During the law-making process amendments may be proposed when bills are under consideration.

In *parliamentary law,* amendments may be proposed when motions are being considered. See PARLIAMENTARY LAW.

In *judicial procedure,* an amendment is a correction, by permission of the court, of an error in the record of a case.

Amenhotep IV. See AKHNATON.

America, à-měr'ĭ-kà, the lands of the Western Hemisphere, including the continents of North America and South America and nearby islands. To the east lies the Atlantic Ocean, and to the west the Pacific. In the north, North America spreads out into many islands that extend into the Arctic. In the south, South America narrows to a tip pointing toward the Antarctic.

Each continent is shaped roughly like a triangle. Together they cover a greater distance from north to south than any other landmass—about 9,600 miles. Their total area is about 16,000,000 square miles, more than one-fourth of the earth's land surface. The two continents meet at the Panama-Colombia border, where the narrow Isthmus of Panama joins South America.

In popular terms, *Central America* refers to the part of North America that lies south of Mexico, while *Latin America* takes in Mexico and all independent countries of Central America, South America, and the West Indies that speak Latin, or Romance, languages (Spanish, French, or Portuguese).

Scientists believe the first inhabitants of America crossed Bering Strait from Siberia to Alaska perhaps 25,000 to 40,000 years ago. Although the Norsemen had settlements in North America about 1000 A.D., permanent European settlement came only after Christopher Columbus' voyage of 1492.

America was named after the Italian navigator Amerigo Vespucci. "America" first appeared on a map made in 1507 by a German, Martin Waldseemüller. "America" is often used to refer to the United States of America alone.

See also CENTRAL AMERICA; COLUMBUS, CHRISTOPHER; NORSEMEN; NORTH AMERICA; SOUTH AMERICA; VESPUCCI, AMERIGO.

"America," a patriotic hymn to the United States. The words, beginning "My

country, 'tis of thee," were written by Samuel Francis Smith of Boston and first published in 1832. The music is that of the British national anthem, "God Save the King" (or "God Save the Queen"), the composer of which is unknown.

"America the Beautiful." See BATES, KATHARINE LEE.

American Academy and Institute of Arts and Letters, an honorary organization that furthers literature and the fine arts. Membership is limited to 250 United States citizens outstanding in literature, art, and music. Persons of foreign citizenship may be elected to honorary membership. The academy confers awards and honors, holds exhibitions, and publishes an annual volume, *Proceedings.* The organization has a library, art gallery, and museum.

The organization was formed in 1976 through the merger of the National Institute of Arts and Letters (founded 1898) and the American Academy of Arts and Letters (1904). Headquarters are in New York City.

American Academy in Rome, an institution in Italy that offers to United States artists and scholars the opportunity for independent creative work or research. The academy is not a school in the usual sense and offers no courses, but grants fellowships in architecture, landscape architecture, literature, musical composition, painting, sculpture, history of art, and classical studies.

The American Academy in Rome was founded in 1894. It was chartered by Congress in 1905, and was consolidated with the American School of Classical Studies in Rome in 1913.

American Academy of Arts and Sciences, an honorary society that seeks "to cultivate every art and science which may tend to advance the interest, honor, dignity, and happiness of a free, independent, and virtuous people." There are two groups of members: fellows, who must be United States citizens or residents, and foreign honorary members. The membership includes persons notable in the arts and sciences, writers, educators, and men active in public affairs. The academy grants various prizes and awards, including the Rumford Prize and the Emerson-Thoreau Medal. The chief publication is *Daedalus,* a quarterly.

The Massachusetts legislature chartered the academy in 1780. Early members included John Adams, one of the society's founders and its second president, George Washington, Benjamin Franklin, and Thomas Jefferson.

The academy has about 2,300 members. Headquarters are in Boston.

American Academy of Political and Social Science. See SOCIAL SCIENCE.

American Advertising Federation. See ADVERTISING (concluding paragraph).

American Airlines, one of the largest airlines in the United States. It serves more than 20 states, the District of Columbia, Mexico, Canada, and the Caribbean. American carries more freight than any other domestic airline. Its history began in 1926 when a company was formed to carry mail between Chicago and St. Louis; Charles A. Lindbergh was the chief pilot. The present name was adopted in 1934. The main office is at the Dallas-Fort Worth Regional Airport in Texas.

American Alliance for Health, Physical Education, and Recreation. See PHYSICAL EDUCATION (end of article).

American Aloe. See AGAVE.

American Anthropological Association. See ANTHROPOLOGY.

American Arbitration Association. See ARBITRATION, subtitle *Commercial Arbitration.*

American Association for Higher Education, a national organization concerned with all phases of higher education. It was founded in 1870 and is associated with the National Education Association. Membership is about 7,500, and is composed of college and university administrators and teachers. It publishes *The Journal of Higher Education.* Headquarters are in Washington, D. C.

American Association for Marriage and Family. See MARRIAGE, subtitle *Marriage Counseling.*

American Association for the Advancement of Science (AAAS), the largest general scientific organization in the United States. AAAS objectives are to further the work of scientists, facilitate cooperation among scientists, improve the effectiveness of science in the promotion of human welfare, and increase public understanding and appreciation of the importance and promise of the methods of science in human progress. Its publications include the periodicals *Science* and *Science 80.*

The AAAS was founded in 1848. Membership includes more than 130,000 individuals (some of them nonscientists). About 330 societies and academies are affiliated with the AAAS. Headquarters are in Washington, D. C.

American Association of Advertising Agencies. See ADVERTISING (following history section).

American Association of Museums. See MUSEUM (final paragraph).

American Association of Retired Persons (AARP), a United States organization for persons over 55 years of age. Members need not be retired. AARP offers health insurance and a worldwide travel service and provides discount pharmacy services. The association maintains a nursing home at Ojai, California. *Modern Maturity* is a bimonthly publication and the *AARP News Bulletin* is a monthly. AARP was organized in 1958 and has about 12,000,000 members. Headquarters are in Washington, D.C.

American Association of School Administrators (AASA), a professional group that is an associated organization of the National Education Association of the United States (NEA). The AASA provides in-service education to members and disseminates research findings. *The School Administrator,* the official publication, is issued 13 times a year. The AASA was founded in 1865 as the National Association of School Superintendents. There are about 18,000 members. National headquarters are in Arlington, Virginia.

American Association of University Professors (AAUP), a national organization in the United States that serves the interests of all teachers and research scholars at institutions of higher learning. The AAUP seeks to maintain academic and professional standards, defends academic freedom and the principle of tenure, and tries to improve salaries and increase faculty participation in college and university government. *Bulletin of the AAUP* is published eight times a year. There are 70,000 members in approximately 1,200 institutions of higher education. Headquarters are in Washington, D. C.

American Association of University Women (AAUW), an organization of women graduates of colleges and universities. The association promotes the education and advancement of women and works for higher standards in education. Its program is designed to enable members to continue their lifelong learning and discharge their responsibility to society. Five Areas of Interest define the association's traditional concerns: Women, The Community, Cultural Interests, Education, and International Relations.

The AAUW awards about 70 fellowships to American women for postgraduate study and brings about 50 women to the United States from foreign countries each year for study. The *AAUW Graduate Woman* is published six times a year.

The organization was founded in 1882. Membership is more than 190,000, organized in some 1,930 branches throughout the United States. Headquarters are in Washington, D. C.

American Automobile Association (AAA), a national federation of state and regional motor clubs and associations. Its aim is to improve motoring and traveling conditions in general. It supplies members of its motor clubs with travel information, personal accident insurance, and bail bonds, and provides emergency repair service. Publications include maps and tour books. The association was organized in 1902. Total membership of its affiliated clubs is about 21,000,000. National headquarters are in Falls Church, Virginia.

AAA Emblem

Cemetery and Memorial, maintained by the American Battle Monuments Commission at Suresnes, France, honors American dead of both World Wars.
American Battle Monuments Commission

American Bankers Association. See BANKS AND BANKING (end of article).

American Bar Association (ABA), the principal organization of lawyers in the United States. Membership is open to any lawyer admitted to the bar of any state or United States possession. The ABA accredits law schools, seeks improvements in the administration of justice, and, through codes of conduct, promotes professional and judicial ethics. The *American Bar Association Journal* is published monthly. The ABA was founded in 1878. Membership is about 255,000. Headquarters are in Chicago.

American Basketball Association. See BASKETBALL, subtitle *Professional Basketball.*

American Battle Monuments Commission, an independent agency of the United States government. It is responsible for the construction and maintenance of military cemeteries and memorials built by the United States government on foreign soil and for some monuments in the United States.

For those who died in military service during World War I eight cemeteries are maintained in France, Belgium, and Great Britain. For World War II dead there are 14 cemeteries in France, Belgium, the Netherlands, Luxembourg, Great Britain, Italy, Tunisia, and the Philippines. The commission maintains a cemetery in Mexico City for 750 dead of the Mexican War. The agency is headed by a chairman. Some of the commission members are retired military men.

American Beauty Rose. See ROSE, subtitle *Garden and Commercial Roses.*

American Beech. See BEECH.

American Bible Society (ABS), a nonprofit, interdenominational organization that distributes Bibles throughout the world. It devotes much effort to Bible translation and revision. Braille editions are provided for the blind. The Bible Society *Record* is published 10 times a year. The society was founded in 1816. The ABS has a membership of about 290,000. Headquarters are in New York City.

American Bowling Congress. See BOWLING, subtitle *History.*

American Broadcasting Companies, Inc. (ABC), a major United States television and radio broadcaster and publisher. Its television network has about 205 affiliated stations, reaching virtually all populated areas of the United States. Its four radio networks have about 1,700 affiliated stations. ABC owns television stations in New York, Los Angeles, Chicago, Detroit, and San Francisco, and radio stations in those cities and in Houston and Washington, D.C. Its publishing division publishes trade and business books and special-interest magazines. ABC was formed in 1942; in 1953 it merged with United Paramount Theatres, Inc. Its present name was adopted in 1965. Headquarters are in New York City.

American Can Company, a leading United States producer of container and packaging products, paper products, and chemical products. It also has a commercial printing operation. Products include Northern brand towels, Dixie cups, and Vogue and Butterick sewing patterns. The company with its subsidiaries operates plants and sales offices throughout the United States and Canada. Overseas subsidiaries, affiliates, and licensees extend its operations to some 30 countries. The American Can Company was founded in 1901 through a merger of about 60 companies. Until 1956 its chief product was metal cans. Headquarters are in Greenwich, Connecticut.

American Cancer Society, a voluntary organization dedicated to the control and eradication of cancer. The society's long-range goal is to find a cure or preventive for cancer; its immediate goal is to save as many lives as possible and to diminish suffering. The society supports cancer research and conducts educational programs for both the medical profession and the general public. It operates through some 3,000 local units. The ACS was founded in 1913 and has headquarters in New York City.

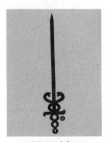

ACS Emblem

American Carpatho-Russian Orthodox Greek Catholic Church. See EASTERN ORTHODOX CHURCH, subtitle *Orthodox Branches in the United States.*

American Ceramic Society. See CERAMICS.

American Cheese. See CHEESE, table *Varieties of Cheese.*

American Chemical Society, an organization of chemists and chemical engineers. It is one of the world's largest societies devoted to a single science. Aims include the encouragement of research; the raising of the standards of professional ethics, education, and achievement; and the increase and spread of chemical knowledge. The numerous publications include *Chemical and Engineering News,* a weekly. The society was founded in 1876. Membership is more than 775,000 in the United States and Puerto Rico. Headquarters are in Washington, D.C.

American Civil Liberties Union (ACLU), a national, nonpartisan organization that works to protect individuals and organizations from being deprived of their basic freedoms as guaranteed by the Constitution—in speech, press, assembly, and religion. A guiding principle is the ACLU's belief that all persons and groups—even those espousing unpopular or antidemocratic causes—are entitled to due process of law and equality before the law. The ACLU supports test cases involving constitutional issues, opposes proposed legislation that it feels would limit constitutional freedoms, and makes public protests against what it perceives as violations of civil liberties.

The American Civil Liberties Union was organized in 1920. Membership is more than 200,000. Headquarters are in New York City.

American Colonial Life (1607-1776), the manner of living in the 13 colonies that became the United States. Most of the original settlers were English. In the region between New England and Virginia, however, were early colonists of two other nationalities—the Dutch in New York, and the Swedes along the Delaware River. Each nationality brought its own way of living— styles of architecture and clothing, types of food, agricultural methods, and social activities. All, however, learned many useful things from the Indians—especially about native foods—as well as from each other. By the end of the colonial period the differences among the colonies were not those of origin, but regional differences that had developed in America.

The 13 colonies are listed in a box accompanying this article. For the history of their settlement, see UNITED STATES, section "History of the United States," subtitle *Exploration and Settlement to 1763;* the *History*

Colonial Living Room and Kitchen. Toward the end of the 17th century, New England colonists had homes of several rooms. The main room, as shown in this model, was both kitchen and living room.

sections of the 13 original states and MAINE and VERMONT; and PLYMOUTH COLONY. See also PIONEER AND FRONTIER LIFE.

Economic Life in the 17th Century

The colonists' first regular work was raising food for themselves, and throughout the colonial period this was the main occupation of many families. A European company that sent colonists to America, however, expected a return on its investment. There were those among the settlers, also, who hoped to win a fortune in the New World. Consequently, commercial activities were an important part of colonial life.

Commerce and Industry. In Virginia, tobacco culture was begun in 1612. It proved so profitable that the colony went from near failure to permanent prosperity in only a few years. In Plymouth Colony, fur trade with the Indians was the first successful business. The Dutch, already engaged in the Hudson River fur trade, founded their colony, New Netherland, to expand it. A Swedish colony was settled on the Delaware River to develop the fur trade there.

The New England colonists soon found lumbering to be a profitable business, since England was running short of timber. Iron ore, another valued resource, was discovered, and in the 1640's a successful iron industry was started in Massachusetts. Commercial fishing, which had preceded permanent settlement, continued as an important occupation.

Servants and Slaves. The planters in Virginia were the first colonists to be able to afford servants. The original need was for farmhands to work in the tobacco fields. It was met by paying the passage of new colonists, who signed, or had signed for them by an official, *indentures*—contracts binding them

to work for a certain term of years to repay the planter.

Some of the indentured servants (also known as bondsmen and redemptioners) came to America of their own free will. Those who were forced to come included convicts, Negroes sold into slavery in Africa, and persons (especially children) kidnaped by ship's captains. Later, the Negroes were sold as slaves in America, generally in the South. Few New England farmers could afford indentured servants, but tradesmen and industrialists often could.

Transportation. Early transportation in the colonies was largely by water, in broad-bottomed boats called shallops. The Dutch used sailboats on the Hudson and Delaware rivers. The Indian canoe was not generally adopted by the Atlantic coast settlers.

On land, Indian trails were widely used. The first roads were for bringing timber from the forests and tobacco from the plantations to the waterways. Although colonial governments called for the laying out of highways, the road system was not adequate for carriage and stagecoach travel until the 18th century. (See also TRAILS.)

Domestic Life in the 17th Century

Homes. The English colonists built their first permanent dwellings in the cottage style they had known at home. The structures were of wood, with a framework of heavy, hand-hewn timbers. The frame for each wall was constructed flat on the ground; the frames were then raised into position and fastened together. The outside walls were covered with clapboards (called weatherboards in Virginia), the inside walls with wide vertical boards. The space inside a wall was filled with straw and clay or with bricks for insulation.

The few windows were at first of oiled paper or thin sheets of horn, later of small, diamond-shaped panes of glass. There was an attic under a steep-pitched roof, which in the early period was covered with thatch, later with boards and shingles.

In New England stones were used to build the walls of the cellar, which was a New World innovation that provided frost-free winter storage, and the fireplace and chimney. In a one-room house the fireplace was toward the corner at the end of the room. If there was a second room, it was on the other side of the fireplace, which then opened into both rooms. When more space was needed, a one-story lean-to was added across the back, and the main roof was continued down over it. The resulting shape was the origin of the so-called saltbox house, a popular New England style for many generations.

In Virginia, where stone was scarce, bricks were used for the chimney, built outside the end wall. Because of the distance from neighbors and the hostility of the Indians, plantation homes usually had shuttered windows and often had gun slits in the walls of upper rooms.

The settlers' homes in New Sweden were log cabins, a kind of structure common in the forested Scandinavian countries. Since whole logs were used for the walls, log cabins were much easier to build than the English cottages, for which it was necessary first to split the logs into timbers and planks. After New Sweden (as part of New Netherland) was absorbed into the English colonies, the log cabin was adopted by most settlers moving to the frontier. (See also PIONEER AND FRONTIER LIFE, subtitle *Log-cabin Pioneers:* Homes.)

In New Netherland the Dutch built high, narrow houses of brick, with steep red tile roofs. The windows had shutters and the doors opened in two sections, upper and lower. The homes of the Flemish who came to New Netherland were low and wide, with overhanging eaves, built of stone or wood with shingled roofs.

Furnishings. Furniture in the English colonies at first consisted largely of simple pieces that the settlers could make for themselves —a table, at least one chair for the head of the household, some stools and benches, chests for storage, and beds. As soon as possible, better furniture was imported from England, especially by the tobacco planters in the South. In New England, however, cabinetmakers were soon producing fine furniture. The Dutch settlers, well supplied by the Dutch West India Company with goods

The Thirteen Colonies
(The dates refer to the first permanent white settlements.)

Virginia (1607)—Established by the London Company.

New Jersey (1618)—Originally settled by the Dutch, but seized by the English in 1664.

Massachusetts (1620)—Founded as two colonies: Plymouth Colony (1620), settled by the Pilgrims; and Massachusetts Bay Colony (1630), by Puritans. They were united in 1691, and annexed Maine, which had been colonized by the New England Council in the 1620's.

New Hampshire (1622)—Originally part of Maine, then a colony from 1629 until annexed by Massachusetts, 1641-43. Became a separate colony again in 1679.

Pennsylvania (1623)—Originally settled by Dutch and Swedes. Came under English control in 1664 and was granted to William Penn in 1681.

New York (1624)—Founded as New Netherland by the Dutch West India Company. Seized by the English in 1664 and renamed.

Maryland (1634)—Granted to Lord Baltimore.

Connecticut (1635)—Founded by settlers from Massachusetts and other colonies. New Haven Colony, founded by settlers from Massachusetts in 1638, annexed to Connecticut in 1662, when the older colony was granted a royal charter.

Rhode Island (1636)—Settled by two groups from Massachusetts and united in 1644. Chartered by King Charles II in 1663.

Delaware (1638)—Settled by Swedes; seized by the Dutch in 1655 and by the English in 1664. Granted to William Penn in 1682.

North Carolina (1653)—Settled by pioneers from other colonies. Carolina separated from Virginia and granted to a private company in 1663; divided into two colonies in 1711. Made a royal province in 1729.

South Carolina (1670)—Originally part of Carolina Colony. Was separated from North Carolina in 1711 and became a royal province in 1729.

Georgia (1733)—Granted to a private company by George II in 1732 and settled a year later at Savannah.

Old Sturbridge Village
Candlemaking, one of the women's chores, is here reenacted in an authentic setting.

from home, had ornate furniture, pottery, pewter, and silverware from the beginning. (See also FURNITURE, subtitle *Period Styles of Furniture:* United States.)

Artificial light other than from the fireplace was obtained by burning hot fat or wax. A rushlight was a dried rush soaked in grease and held upright on a metal support. A betty lamp was a dishlike container of grease or oil with a wick. Candles, the least smoky type of light, were made of tallow or bayberry wax. Fire was started by the use of flint and steel. Making fire was neither quick nor easy, and an effort was made to keep the fireplace fire going always. (See also CANDLE; FIRE, illustration *Old Ways of Making Fire;* LAMP.)

Family Tasks. The English settlers in both New England and the Southern colonies lived at first as pioneers in a wilderness. In the early colonial period members of the household produced all of their own food, soap and candles, clothing, household lin-

Drop-leaf Table with pine top and maple frame is typical of the practical but attractive furniture made in the early colonial period.
National Gallery

ens, and bed coverings, as well as most of their utensils.

The men and boys farmed, fished, hunted for game, butchered the domestic animals, cured the meat that could not be eaten at once, tanned the hides, and made simple footgear. The many wooden items used by the family were made at home—trenchers (dish-platters), mugs, spoons, storage kegs and barrels, farm implements, and the family loom, among others. Breaking up the stalks of flax to extract the fibers for spinning was a man's work, and the men also assisted with such domestic jobs as boiling soap.

Preparation of food by the women and girls included the hand-grinding of grain into meal or flour. However, the greatest amount of women's time was used making textiles and clothing. Flax (linen) or wool fibers were combed clean, hand-spun into thread or yarn, dyed if desired, woven into cloth, and sewed by hand into garments or household articles. (Since the home-made looms were quite narrow, all sheets and blankets had to be seamed.) Girls began learning to spin at the age of five or six and were experts at the loom by the time they were married.

As towns developed, specialists in various crafts set up in business, and articles such as boots, felt hats, iron and pottery utensils, and barrels could be bought. The establishment of tanneries, gristmills, and sawmills further reduced the home labor of the families living within convenient distance of them. In rural areas the work load was lessened by itinerant craftsmen who traveled from one farm to another, staying as long as their services were needed. These welcome specialists included the shoemaker, the weaver, the tailor, the tinker (a tinsmith who repaired metal items), and the chandler (a candlemaker who also made soap).

Food and Drink. Food was plentiful in the colonies, although at times there was little variety. The forests were full of game and fowl, and seafood was abundantly available, especially in Virginia and Maryland. Cattle were imported from Europe at an early date. At first they were kept more for their hides and for breeding oxen than for food. The Dutch, however, used milk to make butter and cheese. Pigs were the most common meat animal.

When an animal was slaughtered, as much fresh meat as possible was eaten at once, and

A-360

the rest was preserved by salting or smoking it. Salt pork was the common meat of the poorer colonists. In the South, fresh cooked meat was sometimes kept in a crock sealed with fat.

Corn was the native grain used for food by the Indians, who taught the settlers how to grow it and eat it. It became the staple starch food of the English colonists. They ate corn as a fresh vegetable, as hominy, as boiled cereal, or as the main ingredient of bread, cake, and pudding. Wheat did not grow well in New England but was a successful crop in New Netherland. The Dutch were especially fond of fried cakes and waffles made of wheat flour.

Green vegetables were a seasonal item in New England, but available much of the year farther south. Root vegetables (but not including either sweet or white potatoes in the 17th century) were stored for winter use. Pumpkin could be stored, but was also dried. A popular type of bread was made of boiled, mashed pumpkin mixed with corn meal. Apple trees, imported from Europe, were widely grown to provide fruit for making cider.

Cider, usually fermented, and beer were the most popular drinks. The Dutch imported wine and brandy, and so did the prosperous planters. Everyone, including tiny children, drank alcoholic beverages. Water was considered dangerous, and because of ignorance about sanitation it often was. Milk was generally not used as a beverage. During the 17th century tea, coffee, and chocolate were introduced in Europe and became available in the colonies.

All cooking except baking was done in great open fireplaces. Some iron pots were hung over the fire; others had legs and long handles and were set on the hearth. Stews and porridges were the common food, although meat and game might be roasted before the open fire, turned on a spit by hand, generally by a child. Corn pone and pudding could be baked in a covered pot buried in embers, but a bake oven was required for raised bread. The oven was usually built into the side of the fireplace in Northern homes, but in the South it was often outdoors.

Food was eaten from wooden trenchers, two or more persons sharing a dish, with spoons and the fingers. Linen napkins were customarily provided for each meal. Table

Colonial Houses. *Top,* brick homes with dormer windows became Southern favorites. (This building was an inn, but its architecture is similar to that of Southern houses of the period.) *Middle,* in New York and Pennsylvania the Germans introduced dwellings of stone. *Bottom,* the clapboard saltbox house originated in New England, where it was long a popular style.

Top: Red Lion Inn, Williamsburg, Virginia. Photo from Colonial Williamsburg. Middle: Conrad Weiser homestead, Womelsdorf, Pennsylvania. Photo from Pennsylvania Historical and Museum Commission. Bottom: Solomon Richardson house in Old Sturbridge Village, Massachusetts. Photo from Old Sturbridge Village.

Water Transportation. In the early 1700's the New York-to-Brooklyn ferry was a rowboat (end of pier). Flatboats were commonly used by farmers. The four-story house is of typical Dutch style.

salt was imported at first, but maple sugar and honey were American products. The English did not spread their bread with butter; this custom was later learned from the Dutch.

Dress. As much as possible, the colonists dressed in the fashion prevailing in Europe. The planters in the South soon began to send back to England for fine clothes. Even the New England Puritans liked trimmings of silver and gold lace and silk dresses. Elegant apparel, however, was considered a sign of social status, and in several colonies there were laws against the wearing of finery by the poorer classes.

Cotton was an imported luxury. The common fabrics were wool and linen, or linsey-woolsey, a combination of the two fibers. Coarse linen, dyed blue with indigo, was the usual material of work shirts and women's

Land Transportation. Two-wheeled carts were well suited to both dirt roads and cobblestones. The building with the cupola in this 1765 view of Philadelphia is the College and Academy, later the University of Pennsylvania.

house dresses. Leather, especially deerskin, was used for workingmen's breeches as well as for jackets.

Women wore long, full skirts throughout the colonial period. Upper-class men customarily wore knee-length breeches while men of the lower classes frequently wore pantaloons. From the time children stopped wearing baby clothes they were dressed exactly like their elders. Head coverings were worn by all adults, inside the house as well as outside. Women wore small white linen caps, covering these when outdoors with the hoods attached to their cloaks (which were usually scarlet). Men wore wool work caps or felt hats.

In the early 17th century no such garment as a coat existed. Men's tunics sometimes had separate sleeves that were tied in with tapes or ribbons. By the end of the century the sleeved tunic had developed into a coat with a flared skirt. The custom of wearing silver and gold buckles on shoes apparently was introduced by the Dutch, who had a taste for ornate dress. Another style favored by the Dutch colonists, fluted ruffs around the neck, had been given up by the English settlers, who preferred the flat collar.

Community Life in the 17th Century

Religion. Sunday was a day of rest in all the colonies, and the church was an important center of community life. In New England, largely settled and completely ruled by Puritans, the church was the very core of existence. Only members of the church were citizens, permitted to vote for public officials. The governing body of the church laid down the secular law as well as religious regulations and saw to enforcement of both.

The Puritan outlook was stern; any kind of luxury and almost any kind of enjoyment was considered dangerous to piety. On Sunday attendance at church was compulsory, and the sermon long and full of threats to sinners. Even in the bitterest winter weather there was no heat in the church. Later, as customs became more relaxed, some persons carried small charcoal stoves to use as foot warmers.

See also BLUE LAWS; PURITAN, subtitle *History of Puritanism:* In New England.

Blown Glass was produced in the colonies from early days, but rarely at a profit. The sugar bowl is attributed to the first financially successful glassmaker, Caspar Wistar, who founded a factory in New Jersey in 1740. The enameled tumbler was probably made in the 1770's by Henry Stiegel of Pennsylvania, who successfully copied many European techniques.
Corning Museum of Glass

Education. An unusually high proportion of New England settlers were educated people. In 1640, about one in every 250 had attended university in England. Such a tradition, combined with the desire that everyone read the Bible and all ministers have a classical education, led to the quick establishment of schools. The first one was opened in Boston in 1635; the first college, Harvard, was founded in 1636. In the same year the first school was opened in New Netherland. In the Southern colonies, however, there was little concern for education, and no official action was taken until late in the century. The first Southern college, William and Mary, opened in 1693.

Generally girls were taught no academic subjects beyond reading and writing, but were instructed in sewing, embroidery, and good conduct. Arithmetic was included in elementary education for boys. For vocational training, they were apprenticed to artisans.

For details about colonial schools, see EDUCATION, subtitle *History of Education: Colonial America, 1607-1776.* See also APPRENTICE; HORNBOOK; NEW ENGLAND PRIMER; SAMPLER.

Recreation. In the New England colonies amusements were frowned on. However, any occasion that brought people together provided an opportunity for visiting and general sociability. Corn-huskings, house-raisings, and quilting parties were among the gayer occasions. Town meetings, elections, militia training days, and even the Thursday religious lectures and the Sunday services were social events also. The main Puritan holiday was Thanksgiving, which lasted about a week. (See also TOWN MEETING.)

In the Southern colonies there was no prohibition against entertainment. Dancing was one of the most popular recreations, enjoyed by adults and children, masters and servants. The wealthy planters were fond of horse racing and the gambling that accompanied it. They also bet on cock fights, shooting matches, athletic events, and card games. Christmas was a major holiday in the Southern colonies.

The Dutch enjoyed dancing also, along with skating, sleighing, and fishing. Bowls and ninepins were favorite games. There were numerous holidays in New Netherland, of which the most popular were New Year's Day and May Day.

The 18th Century

By the 18th century the Swedish colony had been absorbed by New Netherland, which in turn had been seized by the English and renamed New York. Although New York City was rapidly Anglicized, the Dutch influence remained strong in the Hudson Valley. New influences were making themselves felt in the region between New England and Chesapeake Bay. A Quaker colony, Pennsylvania, had been founded, with its capital at Philadelphia on the Delaware River. Offering low-priced land and religious freedom to colonists, Pennsylvania attracted thousands of German settlers. Large numbers of Scotch-Irish came also, settling mainly in frontier country.

Economic Developments. The Pennsylvania Quakers and Germans were not only industrious, but they had some of the most fertile land in the colonies. In the mountain areas were bountiful forests and plentiful deposits of iron ore. Agriculture and industry brought quick prosperity to Pennsylvania, while Philadelphia thrived on commerce and soon became the busiest port in the country.

Raleigh Tavern Bake Shop, Colonial Williamsburg

Bake Shop. Shops such as this were found in colonial cities; the small-town or rural family did its own baking. The brick oven was first heated by burning wood in it. The wood was then removed and the bread and cakes were placed inside where they were baked by the heat of the bricks.

New England, which could now import wheat and flour from the Middle Colonies, turned increasingly from subsistence farming to manufacturing. Shipbuilding became a major industry along the coast, vessels being constructed for both English and colonial owners. The cod-fishing fleets were joined by far-ranging whaling fleets and by increasing numbers of merchant vessels trading with the West Indies, Great Britain, and Africa. Rum, distilled from West Indian molasses, was an important New England product, as were salt and barrels. (See also WHALE, picture *Early-day Whaling*.)

Of the five colonial communities that ranked as cities, four were in the North— Philadelphia, Boston, New York, and Newport. (The fifth was Charleston.) Throughout the North population was dense enough that towns grew up in the midst of farmlands as well as in industrial regions. Life took on an increasingly urban character. More and more artisans set up shop and produced commercially articles that previously had been made at home or imported.

Tobacco continued as Virginia's main commercial crop, while rice and indigo were grown for export in the Carolinas and Georgia. The great size of the plantations made each one a community in itself, complete with all the necessary craftsmen, many of whom were indentured servants or slaves. With abundant slave labor for manual tasks, there was no incentive toward efficiency or invention. Although artisans' shops were to be found in Baltimore, Annapolis, Williamsburg, and Charleston, most luxuries were still imported from England.

A-364

Domestic Developments. The Germans introduced a new style of architecture—the narrow stone house and the great barn, in part of stone and often built into a hillside that formed a natural ramp to the hayloft. Brick homes became fashionable in the South, and brick began to be used throughout the colonies for fine mansions. Dormer windows, which permitted more use of the attic, came into style. (See also illustrations accompanying HOME [*Styles of Homes in the United States:* Historic] and MASSACHUSETTS [*House of Seven Gables*].)

House furnishings of prosperous families became more comfortable. Floors were covered with carpets and rugs, and walls were surfaced with wood paneling or imported wallpaper. The best candles were made of spermaceti, a wax extracted from whale oil, and were manufactured mainly in Newport. Handsome furniture was available from the cabinetmakers of Newport, New York, Philadelphia, and Baltimore. Colonial silversmiths and glassblowers produced luxury wares.

The introduction of potatoes and rice added important new staples to the diet. Rum became popular with the well-to-do, gin with the poorer classes. Fine china was imported from England, and some was produced in the colonies—but china plates were only for display, not for use. Food was eaten from silver plates in fine homes and pewter in most others, although woodenware still served the frontier family. Table knives and spoons were common implements, forks a novelty. Cooking was still done in the fireplace, although iron heating stoves began to be used in mid-century. (See also STOVE, subtitle *History*.)

Restrictions on elaborate dress were no longer enforced, and everyone emulated European styles as far as his means permitted. Among the gentry, men wore coats of fine imported broadcloth; breeches of silk, brocade, velvet, or plush; silk hose; and lace ruffles at wrist and throat. Wigs were immensely popular and were worn by servants and youngsters as well as the men of the household, especially in New England. For comfort, a man kept his head shaved and when at home exchanged the wig for a turban.

Women's overskirts were draped up in various ways, and in the 1730's hoop skirts came into fashion. Hair was still always covered with a cap, now usually frilled. In the 1760's women in the colonies began to wear the elaborate, towering coiffures then stylish in Europe. Later, fashionable women took to wearing wigs, also elaborate and towering. Shoes, too, became elaborate, with slender high heels.

Religion, Education, and Recreation. Religious belief in New England had become liberalized by 1700, and the church no longer ruled the community. In the 1720's, however, a revival known as the Great Awakening began in New Jersey. It was a highly emotional movement that during the next 10 years swept through all denominations throughout the colonies.

One of the results of the revival was the founding by church groups of four new colleges, bringing the total number in the colonies to nine. By the 18th century statutes calling for free elementary schools were on the books in most colonies, but little effort was made in some places to provide them. In cities and towns, however, most children received schooling.

The religious revival did not keep dancing from spreading to the North. Among the entertainments at the annual fairs held in many Northern communities were dancing and singing contests, as well as races, wrestling matches, and other sports. Another popular male recreation was membership in a social club, which often held its meetings in a public tavern. The social clubs helped to bring the colonial period to an end, as the exchange of news and views centered increasingly on America's grievances against Great Britain. From the clubs grew the patriotic societies of the Revolutionary War such as the Sons of Liberty.

See also MONEY, subtitle *History of Money:* Early U. S. Monetary System; NEWSPAPER, subtitle *Development of Newspapers to 1800:* Colonial Papers; POST OFFICE, subtitle *History of Postal Service:* Mail Service in Colonial America; STAGECOACH.

American Colonization Society, a private organization created in 1816 to transport free Negroes from the United States to Africa. Its efforts resulted in the creation of the Republic of Liberia in 1847. The society sent about 6,000 Negroes to Africa, but after 1867 it had little importance. It was dissolved in 1912.

See also LIBERIA, subtitle *History.*

American Copper Butterfly. See BUTTERFLIES AND MOTHS, subtitle *Kinds of Butterflies:* The Gossamer Wings.

American Council of Learned Societies (ACLS), a federation of national scholarly organizations concerned with the humanities and with the humanistic aspects of the social sciences. The objective is to advance humanistic studies in all fields of learning and to maintain and strengthen the relations among the societies devoted to such studies. The ACLS awards post-doctoral fellowships and grants-in-aid to promote research in the United States and abroad. The *Dictionary of American Biography* is prepared and published under its auspices. The council was organized in 1919. Headquarters are in New York City.

American Council on Education, an organization of national and regional education associations and institutions of higher learning. The council is "a center of co-operation and co-ordination for the improvement of education at all levels, with emphasis on higher education." The council's periodicals include *A Fact Book on Higher Education* and *The Educational Record,* both quarterlies, and *Higher Education and National Affairs,* a weekly. It also publishes two directories—*American Universities and Colleges* and *American Junior Colleges.*

The council was founded in 1918. Members include 234 national and regional associations and organizations and 1,294 in-

Books about American Colonial Life

Asimov, Isaac. *The Shaping of North America* (Houghton Mifflin, 1973).
Boorstin, D. J. *The Americans: the Colonial Experience* (Random House, 1958).
Canfield, Cass. *Samuel Adams's Revolution, 1765-1776* (Harper & Row, 1976).
Catton, Bruce and W. B. *The Bold and Magnificent Dream: America's Founding Years, 1492-1815* (Doubleday, 1978).
Hofstadter, Richard. *America at 1750: a Social History* (Knopf, 1971).
Schlesinger, A. M. *Birth of the Nation: a Portrait of the American People on the Eve of Independence* (Knopf, 1968).
Simmons, R. C. *The American Colonies: from Settlement to Independence* (McKay, 1976).
For Younger Readers:
Buske, M. R., editor. *Significant American Colonial Leaders* (Childrens Press, 1976).
Farr, Naunerle. *The New World, 1500-1750* (Pendulum Press, 1977).
Ingraham, Leonard. *Album of Colonial America* (Watts, 1969).
Lazarus, Lois. *With These Hands They Built a Nation* (Messner, 1971).
Tunis, Edwin. *Colonial Living* (Crowell, 1976).

American Dental Association
American Dental Association Building

stitutions of higher learning. Headquarters are in Washington, D. C.

American Defense Service Medal. See DECORATIONS AND MEDALS, subtitle *United States Awards:* Service Medals.

American Dental Association, the national professional organization of dentists in the United States. Its aims are to improve dental health and promote high professional standards. Through the Council on Dental Education it evaluates and accredits dental schools and dental-hygiene schools. Its *Journal* is a monthly. It also publishes *Dental Abstracts* (monthly), *Journal of Oral Surgery* (bimonthly), and *ADA News* (weekly). The association was founded in 1859. Membership is more than 133,000 and includes most practicing dentists in the United States. Headquarters are in Chicago.

American Dialect Society. See DIALECT.

American Drama. See DRAMA, subtitle *Drama in the United States.*

A-366

American Eagle. See EAGLE, subtitle *Sea Eagles:* The Bald Eagle, or American Eagle.

American Economic Association, an organization of economists, business executives, governmental administrators, and others interested in economics and its applications to present-day problems. The aims are to encourage historical and statistical research into the actual conditions of industrial life and to provide a nonpartisan forum for economic discussion. Publications include the *American Economic Review* and the *Journal of Economic Literature,* both quarterlies.

The American Economic Association was organized in 1885. Membership is more than 18,000. Headquarters are in Nashville, Tennessee.

American Eel. See EEL, subtitle *Common Eels:* The American Eel.

American Ethical Union. See ETHICAL CULTURE.

American Expeditionary Forces (A.E.F.), the official designation for United States troops serving in Europe in World War I. John J. Pershing, with the temporary rank of general, National Army, commanded the A.E.F. throughout its service. He was ordered to France on May 26, 1917, and was followed shortly by elements that formed the First Division. Eventually 2,-000,000 men were sent to Europe. There were 42 divisions, of which 29 were in combat.

The First Army was set up on July 24, 1918, effective August 10, under Pershing's personal command, which he retained until organization of the Second Army on October 15. Lieutenant Generals Hunter Liggett and Robert L. Bullard then took command of the two armies. The Third Army, which was being organized at the time of the Armistice, became the Army of Occupation. Nine corps were organized, of which seven were in combat, including the Second Corps, serving with British forces. Small contingents of the A.E.F. served in Italy and at Archangel and Murmansk, Russia.

The A.E.F. came to an end in 1919 when American troops were withdrawn from Europe.

See also WORLD WAR I, section "The War in 1917," subtitles *The United States Enters the War* and *The Western Front, 1917;* section "The War in 1918," subtitles *The Crisis of the War* and *The Western Front, 1918;* and section "Aerial and Colonial Warfare, 1914-18," subtitle *Aerial Warfare.*

American Express Company, a travel and financial service corporation. It books tours, makes reservations and arrangements for tourists, sells money orders and travelers checks, and issues credit cards. The company also runs an international banking division and owns Fireman's Fund, a group of life and property insurance companies. American Express operates offices in more than 100 countries. The company was founded as an express company in 1850, but sold all its shipping interests during World War I. Headquarters are in New York City.

American Falls. See NIAGARA FALLS, subtitle *General Description.*

American Farm Bureau Federation (AFBF), the largest general farm organization in the United States. It promotes the study of agricultural problems and carries on educational, legislative, marketing, and service programs to benefit farmers. The AFBF is a federation of county farm bureaus. Membership is on a family basis. The first county bureaus were organized in 1912-14 to work with county agricultural agents. The national organization was founded in 1919.

About 2,700,000 farm families are represented in the AFBF through membership in county farm bureaus in all 50 states and Puerto Rico. National headquarters are in Park Ridge, Illinois.

American Federation of Arts (AFA), an organization of about 500 art institutions and 2,500 individuals interested in fostering art appreciation. The AFA organizes traveling exhibitions of art and film programs for museums and art centers in the United States and foreign countries. Works are lent by museums, galleries, and private collections. The federation publishes the *American Art Directory* and *Who's Who in American Art*. The AFA was organized in 1909. Its headquarters are in New York City.

A. E. F. Arriving in France. Units of the First Division debark at St. Nazaire in June, 1917, three months after the United States entered the war.

Wide World

American Federation of Government Employees. See LABOR UNION (table).

American Federation of Labor and Congress of Industrial Organizations (AFL-CIO), the largest federation of labor unions in the United States. It came into being in 1955 when the American Federation of Labor and the Congress of Industrial Organizations merged.

The AFL-CIO is composed of national and international unions in various occupations and industries. Individuals do not belong directly to the AFL-CIO. They belong to labor unions that in turn belong to the larger organization.

The AFL-CIO seeks to bring unorganized workers into its unions; to settle disagreements among member unions, including jurisdictional disputes (in which two unions claim the right to organize the same group of workers); and to get laws passed that are beneficial to labor and the labor movement. It also deals with national and international problems of special interest to labor.

Structure

The AFL-CIO is a federation of autonomous unions. The number of these member unions changes from time to time, and the number of workers belonging to the unions also changes. No exact figure of membership is valid for very long. At the time of the merger in 1955, there were 136 national or international unions in the AFL-CIO, with a total membership of about 15,000,000 workers. In the early 1980's the number of member unions was 106 while the total membership was about what it had been at the time of the merger.

The local union is the basic unit in the American labor movement. There are about 60,000 locals represented in the AFL-CIO. Most of them are chartered by one of the national or international unions, although several hundred are directly affiliated to the federation. In large cities, locals of various unions are united into central councils. There are also statewide federations of AFL-CIO unions, one in each state. In addition, the AFL-CIO contains nine trade and industrial departments, each made up of unions in closely related trades or industries.

The basic policies of the AFL-CIO are set by its convention, which is its highest governing body. The convention meets every two years, although a special convention may be called at any time to consider a particular problem. Each national and international union is entitled to send delegates to the convention, the number of delegates being determined by the size of the union. Other affiliated organizations are entitled to be represented by one delegate each.

The governing body between conventions is the executive council, which is made up of the federation's president, secretary-treasurer, and a number of vice presidents, all elected by the convention. The executive council carries out policies set by the convention and deals with whatever issues arise between conventions.

The executive officers of the AFL-CIO are its president and secretary-treasurer. They are responsible for supervising the day-by-day affairs of the federation. The president appoints a number of standing committees on legislative, political, educational, and other subjects. Staff departments are established as needed to carry on the federation's activities. A separate department of organization, under the direction of the president, furthers organizing of new union groups.

The general board of the AFL-CIO meets to consider policy questions referred to it by the executive officers or the executive council. It consists of the executive council members plus a principal officer of each affiliated national and international union and each trade and industrial department.

The AFL-CIO receives a portion of the dues paid by each member of each local union. This money is used to carry on the administrative and staff work. The AFL-CIO owns the building at 815 Sixteenth St. N.W. in Washington, D.C., where it has its principal offices. Many member unions also own headquarters buildings.

The national organization publishes a weekly newspaper, the *AFL-CIO News,* and a monthly magazine, *The American Federationist.* Some departments of the AFL-CIO issue specialized publications.

History

Most early unions in the United States were local, but national unions began to appear around 1850. In the 1870's the Knights of Labor (founded in 1869) began to expand and become one vast nationwide union including all workers of every type and skill. Although it flourished for more than 10 years, the Knights of Labor finally collapsed because its organization was rigid and cumbersome.

AFL Founded. Meanwhile, Samuel Gompers (1850-1924) and other trade unionists began to see that real strength lay in uniting workers according to craft, skill, or trade so that members would have the same interests. These leaders organized the Federation of Organized Trades and Labor Unions of the United States and Canada in November, 1881, at Pittsburgh. The name was changed to American Federation of Labor in 1886.

The basic principle of the new organization, which Gompers called "the principle of voluntarism," was that the local union best understood its own problems and should therefore have the power to solve them. The national unions and the federation were to help, but not control, the local groups.

Gompers served as president of the federation from 1886 until his death in 1924, except for one year. The organization grew steadily. By 1890 it had 500,000 members; by 1920, more than 4,000,000. William Green (1873-1952) succeeded Gompers as president in 1924 and continued in office until his death.

The CIO Split. In the early 1930's differences arose regarding the most effective way to bring unionism to workers in mass production industries. On one side were William Green and other old-time leaders who emphasized the traditional organization along craft, skill, and trade lines. On the other side was a group that favored organization by industries. Among this group were John L. Lewis of the United Mine Workers, Sidney Hillman of the Amalgamated Clothing Workers, and David Dubinsky of the International Ladies' Garment Workers. This difference of opinion created a split in the executive council and conventions.

In 1935 the heads of eight unions, representing 900,000 members, formed the Committee for Industrial Organization. It was expected to work within the framework of the AFL. In 1936, however, the executive council suspended the CIO unions, and the CIO operated as a separate and rival organization. The following year, all unions supporting the Committee for Industrial Organization were expelled from the AFL.

The Committee for Industrial Organization changed its name in 1938 to Congress of Industrial Organizations and adopted a constitution and elected officers. Lewis, the first president, withdrew in 1940, and Philip Murray (1886-1952) was elected president.

United Press International

The CIO Split. Leaders of the CIO are shown in 1936, shortly before being expelled from the AFL. *Center*, John L. Lewis, first president of the CIO. *Right*, Philip Murray, who succeeded Lewis in 1940. *Left*, Lee Pressman, attorney for the CIO.

He served until his death, being succeeded by Walter Reuther of the United Auto Workers. William Green, who also died in 1952, was succeeded by George Meany, formerly secretary-treasurer of the AFL.

The AFL-CIO. The first successful step toward reuniting the rival groups came in 1953 when they agreed not to raid each other's membership. The actual merger came in 1955. The AFL then had about 10,000,-000 members and the CIO 5,000,000. George Meany was elected president of the AFL-

Merger. George Meany, *left*, president of the AFL, and Walter Reuther, president of the CIO, open the 1955 convention that merged the two organizations. Thirteen years later Reuther led his United Auto Workers out of the AFL-CIO.

United Press International

American Fur Company Traders, their wagons laden with manufactured goods to trade for furs, leave St. Louis in a caravan, about 1830. Painted by William Henry Jackson.

CIO, and Walter Reuther became a vice president of the federation.

A number of unions remained independent of the AFL-CIO. The federation later lost the nation's two largest unions—the Teamsters, expelled in 1957 on charges of corruption, and Reuther's United Auto Workers, which withdrew in 1968 after suspension for nonpayment of dues. The UAW action climaxed a policy dispute in which Reuther accused the federation of failing to adapt to changing needs of the labor movement. The UAW returned to the federation in 1981.

For list of articles on individual AFL-CIO unions, see cross references following LABOR UNION. See also the table in that article titled *Largest Unions in the United States.* For leaders, see cross references following LABOR.

American Federation of Musicians of the United States and Canada, a trade union of professional instrumental musicians. The union's major aim is to promote the interests of musicians. The federation was chartered in 1896 and is affiliated with the AFL-CIO. *International Musician* is a monthly. Headquarters are in New York City. For membership, see LABOR UNION (table).

American Federation of State, County and Municipal Employees, a labor union of public employees. It seeks to promote job security and to win the right to collective bargaining. The union publishes *Public Employee Newspaper,* a monthly. The federation was founded in 1936 and is affiliated with the AFL-CIO. Headquarters are in

Washington, D.C. For membership, see LABOR UNION (table).

American Federation of Teachers, an AFL-CIO union of teachers in the United States. It works for higher salaries and pensions, job security, smaller teaching loads, academic freedom, better professional standards, and federal aid to education. The union publishes the *American Teacher* newspaper monthly from September through May. The American Federation of Teachers was organized in 1916. Headquarters are in Washington, D.C. For membership, see LABOR UNION (table).

American Federation of Television and Radio Artists. See ACTING (end of article).

American Folklore Society. See FOLKLORE, subtitle *American Folklore.*

American Forest Institute. See LUMBERING (end of article).

American Foresty Association. See FOREST (end of article).

American Foundation for the Blind. See BLINDNESS, subtitle *Opportunities for the Blind:* Rehabilitation of Adults.

American Foxhound. See DOG, subtitle *Breeds of Dogs:* Hounds (Foxhound, American).

American Friends Service Committee. See FRIENDS, THE RELIGIOUS SOCIETY OF, subtitle *History of the Friends.*

American Fur Company, a United States fur-trading company founded by John Jacob Astor in 1808. The company operated at first in the Upper Great Lakes region, trading with Canadian companies. In 1810 Astor organized a subsidiary, the Pacific Fur

Company, which founded a post, Astoria, at the mouth of the Columbia River. The plan was to carry otter skins to China, Oriental wares to Europe, and European goods back to the United States. A ship disaster and the War of 1812 forced the sale of Astoria to the North West Fur Company.

In 1817 Ramsay Crooks became a partner, and the American Fur Company established a Northern Department based at Mackinac Island. With a virtual monopoly on the Great Lakes trade, the company entered the trade on the upper Mississippi and Missouri rivers and in the Rocky Mountains. A Western Department, set up in 1822 with headquarters at St. Louis, absorbed the Columbia Fur Company in 1827, but met serious competition from the Rocky Mountain Fur Company in 1832. Beaver was becoming scarce. In 1834 Astor sold the Western Department to its St. Louis agent, the Chouteau company. The Northern Department, retaining the firm name, was bought by Crooks and remained in business until 1842.

American Gas Association. See GAS (fuel) (end of article).

American Gem Society. See GEM (concluding paragraph).

American Geographical Society, the oldest geographical society in the United States. Its objectives are to encourage research in geography and to spread geographical knowledge. It has sponsored research projects and was associated with many early Arctic explorations. Publications include *Geographical Review,* a scholarly quarterly, and *Focus,* a bimonthly. The society was founded in 1852. Membership is about 2,400. Headquarters are in New York City.

American Gold Star Mothers. See GOLD STAR MOTHERS, AMERICAN.

American Heart Association (AHA), a voluntary health agency that combats heart and blood-vessel diseases, the leading causes of death in the United States. Funds are devoted chiefly to research, education, and community service. Resources come from voluntary contributions, mostly during the annual Heart Fund campaign in February. AHA has affiliates in all 50 states and has more than 100,000 members. It was founded in 1924 as a professional organization, but in 1948 membership was opened to persons other than physicians. Headquarters are in Dallas, Texas.

American Historical Association, an organization of professional historians and others interested in promoting historical studies and the collection and preservation of historical manuscripts. The association awards a number of annual prizes for historical research. It publishes the *American Historical Review.* The association was organized in 1884 and incorporated by an act of Congress in 1889. Membership is more than 14,000. Headquarters are in Washington, D.C.

American History. See UNITED STATES, section "History."

American Hospital Association. See HOSPITAL (end of article).

American Hotel and Motel Association. See HOTEL (end of article).

American Humane Association. See HUMANE SOCIETIES.

American Indians. See INDIANS, AMERICAN.

American Institute of Aeronautics and Astronautics (AIAA), a national organization of aerospace scientists and engineers. It provides interchange of information through its publications and meetings. Its chief publication is *Astronautics & Aeronautics,* a monthly. The AIAA was formed in 1963 by merger of the American Rocket Society (founded in 1930) and the Institute of the Aerospace Sciences (founded in 1932). Membership is about 25,000. Headquarters are in New York City.

American Institute of Architects (AIA), a professional society that promotes excellence in architecture and urban design; conducts programs to educate the public in these fields; and fosters ethical standards of practice. The society provides architectural scholarships and fellowships and grants awards, prizes, and medals for meritorious work in architecture. It publishes *AIA Journal,* a monthly. The AIA was founded in 1857. Membership is about 26,000 in more than 200 local chapters. Headquarters are in Washington, D.C.

American Institute of Biological Sciences. See BIOLOGY (last paragraph).

American Institute of Certified Public Accountants. See ACCOUNTING (end of article).

American International College. See UNIVERSITIES AND COLLEGES (table).

American Iron and Steel Institute, an organization of the iron and steel industry. It promotes the use of iron and steel, collects statistics concerning the industry, engages in investigation and research, and provides a forum for the exchange of information and discussion of problems. There are some 75 company members and about 2,500 individual members. The institute was founded in 1908. The institute's headquarters are in Washington, D.C.

American Jewish Congress, an organization that works to strengthen Jewish life and advance human rights. It seeks to oppose all forms of discrimination and bigotry; to defend civil rights, civil liberties, and church-state separation; and to protect Jewish security abroad. The American Jewish Congress was founded in 1918. It helped organize the World Jewish Congress in 1936 to give aid to persecuted Jews overseas. Both organizations, strongly pro-Zionist, supported the new state of Israel. The American Jewish Congress has a membership of 50,000 families. Its headquarters are in New York City.

American Kennel Club. See DOG, subtitle *The American Kennel Club and Dog Shows.*

American Labor Party (ALP), a political party in New York State, formed in 1936 and dissolved in 1956. It had little strength outside New York City, but it elected one congressman, Vito Marcantonio, who served 12 years in the U. S. House of Representatives (1939-51). The ALP elected a few local officials and state legislators and influenced other election contests by giving support to favored nominees of the two major parties (usually Democratic).

The ALP was formed by labor leaders, liberals, and socialists who wanted to support the reelection of President Franklin D. Roosevelt, but outside the Democratic party. In 1944, after a Communist-dominated faction won control of the party, many leaders withdrew to form the Liberal party. In 1948 the ALP drew 509,000 votes for Henry A. Wallace, the Progressive candidate for President. Thereafter it declined rapidly.

American League. See BASEBALL, subtitle *Organization of Professional Baseball: Major Leagues.*

American Legion, a national organization of veterans of World War I, World War II, the Korean Conflict, and the Vietnamese War. Any man or woman who served honorably in the U. S. Army, Navy, Air Force, or Coast Guard during one of these conflicts is eligible for membership. Major aims of the American Legion are to further the interests of veterans and their families, to promote national security, to improve educational and recreational services for all citizens, and to support the expression of American ideals.

Activities

Veterans' Affairs. The Legion sponsors federal and state legislation on medical, insurance, claims, pension, and compensation benefits to veterans. It took the lead in organizing the United States Veterans' Bureau, which was reorganized in 1930 as the Veterans Administration. Through its rehabilitation program, the Legion works for the expansion of federal hospital services to veterans. During World War II it began a campaign that resulted in the Servicemen's Readjustment Act of 1944. This was the "GI Bill of Rights" that gave World War II, Korean, and Vietnam veterans opportunities for education, home and business loans, and other benefits.

Children and Youth. The American Legion Children and Youth program gives direct assistance, promotes child welfare laws, and provides public information.

American Legion Parade. "The Spirit of '76" was the theme of this Legion float.
American Legion

National Security. A broad program of education and legislative support for military and civil defense preparedness is carried on by the Legion.

Americanism. The Legion backs legislation to fight the Communist party and other groups opposed to the American political and economic systems. It campaigns for the increased display of the American flag as a symbol of liberty. The Legion sponsors American Legion Baseball, for youths through age 18; Boy Scout troops; and a national high school oratorical contest. It sponsors Boys State and Boys Nation. (See BOYS STATE.) The Legion's Americanism work is done through its National Americanism Commission.

Organization

The basic unit of the American Legion is the local *post.* Many posts have clubhouses

Legion Emblem

with meeting and recreation rooms. In many small towns, the American Legion post is the center of community social life. There are more than 16,000 posts. They are organized into districts and the districts into departments. The 58 departments represent the 50 states, the District of Columbia, and seven foreign countries.

Resolutions originate in the local posts and are then considered at the annual district, department, and national conventions. The national commander of the Legion is elected annually.

The official publication is *The American Legion Magazine,* a monthly. National headquarters are in Indianapolis, Indiana. An office building in Washington, D. C., houses some of its divisions and sections. Membership is about 2,700,000.

The American Legion Auxiliary grew out of provisions adopted by the 1919 national convention of the Legion. The first national convention of the Auxiliary met in 1921.

The Auxiliary includes mothers, wives, daughters, granddaughters, and sisters of Legion members or of deceased servicemen. Women who served in the armed forces are eligible for membership in both the Legion and the Auxiliary. The Auxiliary sponsors Girls State. (See GIRLS STATE.) Membership is about 1,000,000.

The Sons of the American Legion, founded in 1932, is for male descendants of Legion members or of veterans who were eligible for membership. There are about 31,000 members.

History

The American Legion was organized at a caucus of the American Expeditionary Forces, March 15-17, 1919, in Paris, France. It was chartered by Congress on September 16, 1919.

In 1942 Congress amended the charter to open the Legion to veterans of World War II, and it acted again in 1950 to admit veterans of the Korean Conflict. In 1966 Legion membership was opened to veterans of the Vietnamese War.

American Legion Auxiliary. See AMERICAN LEGION, subtitle *Organization.*

American Library Association (ALA), an organization of librarians, library trustees, and friends of libraries. It is the oldest and largest national library association in the world, and the chief spokesman of the modern library movement in North America. Its object is "to extend and improve library service and librarianship in the United States and throughout the world."

The ALA has 12 divisions organized in two groups: (1) type-of-library divisions, such as the American Association of School Librarians; and (2) type-of-activity divisions, such as the Reference and Adult Services Division.

The organization conducts many special projects through foundation and government grants. It gives out many medals, awards, and citations, including the Newbery and Caldecott medals for writers and illustrators of children's books. Publications, in addition to professional books, include *American Libraries,* monthly, and *The Booklist,* semimonthly.

The ALA was founded in Philadelphia in 1876. It has about 35,000 members in the United States, Canada, and other countries. Headquarters are at 50 East Huron Street, Chicago, Illinois 60611. The ALA also has an office in Washington, D. C.

American Literature. See LITERATURE, AMERICAN.

American Lotus. See WATER LILY.

American Loyalists, or **Tories,** the American supporters of Great Britain during the Revolutionary War, 1775-83. A large number of Americans (estimated at one-

Library of Congress

American Loyalist about to be tarred and feathered by patriots during the Revolutionary War, from an 18th-century engraving titled "The Tory's Day of Judgment"

fourth to one-third of the colonial population of about 2,500,000) opposed the Revolution and its objectives. They represented all classes of society and all sections of the country. Loyalism, however, was strongest among the more prosperous and conservative classes and in the Middle Atlantic region and the lower South.

Many Loyalists contributed supplies, money, and information to the British, and some 30,000 or more served in the British army. Patriots considered Loyalists internal enemies. In a number of states, they were denied the right to vote and their property was confiscated. About 100,000 eventually fled to Great Britain, the West Indies, and Canada. (See also UNITED EMPIRE LOYALISTS.) The others chose to remain in the United States and accepted the American victory. Compensation for confiscated Loyalist property was an issue in the treaty negotiations at the end of the war. (See also REVOLU-

A-374

TIONARY WAR, AMERICAN, subtitle *The End of the War:* Treaty of Paris.)

American Lung Association. See TUBERCULOSIS (concluding paragraph).

American Lutheran Church. See LUTHERANS, subtitle *Lutheran Churches in the United States.*

American Management Associations, a nonprofit organization of executives in industry, commerce, government, education, and other fields. A number of associations constitute divisions in the organization. Its purpose is to help executives improve their management skills. The AMA provides for the exchange of information through courses, conferences, seminars, and publications and conducts research into the principles of management. Its publications include *The Management Review.* The organization was founded in 1923. Membership is more than 60,000. Headquarters are in New York City.

American Marketing Association. See MARKETING, subtitle *History.*

American Mathematical Society. See MATHEMATICS (concluding paragraphs).

American Meat Institute. See MEAT PACKING (end of article).

American Medical Association (AMA), an organization of physicians of the United States. Its objective is "to promote the science and art of medicine and the betterment of public health." The AMA works to help physicians keep up-to-date on every phase of modern medicine, to improve medical education, to fight medical quackery, to provide information on new drugs, to encourage adherence to the highest standards of medical ethics, and to educate the public on health matters.

The AMA is a federation of 55 state and territorial associations, which in turn are composed of more than 1,900 medical societies. The weekly *Journal of the American Medical Association* is the most widely circulated medical journal in the world. Monthly periodicals include several specialty journals and *Prism,* a general-interest magazine for doctors. *American Medical News* is a weekly publication.

The AMA was founded in 1847. It has more than 200,000 members. National headquarters are in Chicago.

American Meteorological Society, a scientific, educational, and professional society of meteorologists and others interested in the atmospheric sciences. Its objectives are the development and spreading of knowledge of meteorology in all its phases and applications and to advance its professional ideals. The society conducts national meetings and specialized conferences, issues numerous publications, and grants awards, citations, and scholarship aid. It was organized in 1919. There are about 9,700 members. Headquarters are in Boston.

American Motors Corporation (AMC), a United States automobile manufacturing company. AMC makes several passenger models and the Jeep. The company was created in 1954 by merger of the Hudson Motor Car Company and the Nash-Kelvinator Corporation. AMC's best-known car was the Rambler, introduced in 1950 as the Nash Rambler, the first modern compact car. (For photo, see AUTOMOBILE, section "History" [picture page].) It was discontinued in 1969. AMC purchased Kaiser Jeep Corporation in 1969. AMC general offices are in Southfield, Michigan, but the main automotive plants are in Kenosha, Wisconsin; Toledo, Ohio; and Brampton, Ontario.

American Museum of Natural History, an institution in New York City devoted to public education and research in the natural sciences and anthropology. It is the largest museum of its kind in the world, consisting of interconnected buildings that cover more than 20 acres (8 hectares) and contain more than 40 exhibition halls. Among its exhibit halls are the Gardner D. Stout Hall of Asian Peoples, the museum's largest anthropological hall; the Arthur Ross Hall of Meteorites, which contains the 31-ton (28,000-kg) Ahnighito meteorite, the largest ever unearthed; the Hall of Reptiles and Amphibians; and the Hall of Minerals and Gems, which contains the famed Star of India sapphire.

Other exhibits include those on fossil reptiles, Mexican and Central American cultures, African cultures, early mammals, primates, oceanic birds, North American and African mammals, Plains Indians and Indians of the Northwest Coast, and ocean life.

The American Museum-Hayden Planetarium was built in 1935 through the generosity of Charles Hayden (1870-1937). It presents the motion of the celestial bodies on a 75-foot (23-m) dome by means of a special projector.

The museum staff has included many

well-known scientists. The staff conducts exploration and research as well as a variety of educational programs. Field stations for research are maintained in other parts of the United States. The museum publishes the magazine *Natural History* and several scientific and technical journals.

The museum was founded in 1869. It is maintained by appropriations from city funds, interest on the endowment, and gifts from members and friends.

American Music. See BLUES; COUNTRY AND WESTERN MUSIC; FOLK MUSIC; JAZZ; MUSIC, subtitle *Music in the United States;* MUSICAL; RAGTIME; SPIRITUAL.

American Muslim Mission. See BLACK MUSLIMS.

American National Red Cross. See RED CROSS, subtitle *American Red Cross.*

American National Standards Institute (ANSI), an organization that promotes the development of standards of measurement, quality, safety, and terminology for products and projects. A federation of 215 societies and about 1,000 companies, the ANSI coordinates efforts at voluntary standardization. It is the United States member of two international standards bodies. It was organized in 1918 as the American Engineering Standards Committee and was later

American Museum of Natural History has a display of dinosaurs from the Cretaceous Period, which ended 65,000,000 years ago. Here are skeletons of *Tyrannosaurus Rex* and *Triceratops.*
American Museum of Natural History

American Philosophical Society

American Philosophical Society has met in Philosophical Hall on Independence Square, Philadelphia, since 1789. Towers mark Independence Hall (left) and Supreme Court Building (right).

called the American Standards Association. Headquarters are in New York City.

American Newspaper Publishers Association. See NEWSPAPER, subtitle *United States Newspaper Organizations.*

American Numismatic Association. See NUMISMATICS (end of article).

American Numismatic Society. See NUMISMATICS (end of article).

American Occupational Therapy Association. See OCCUPATIONAL THERAPY (end of article).

American Optometric Association. See OPTOMETRY.

American Ornithologists' Union, a society of ornithologists and amateur students of birds. Publications include a checklist of North American birds, monographs on birds of the Americas, and *The Auk,* a quarterly. The society was founded in 1883. Headquarters are in Washington, D.C.

American Osteopathic Association. See OSTEOPATHY.

American Party, in United States history, the name of several minor political parties, the most important of which was often called the Know-Nothing party. The parties were all anti-Catholic. In the 1840's there was a heavy immigration of Roman Catholics, mostly Irish, and feelings against them gave rise to the Native American party. This party elected mayors in New York City and Boston and several members of Congress, but by 1849 it had virtually disappeared.

The movement continued in various secret societies. Members became known as "Know-Nothings" because when asked about their

societies they replied they knew nothing. Soon these societies joined to form the American party. It attracted many Whigs, whose party was then breaking up. In 1854 the new party won elections in several New England states and elsewhere and elected many members to Congress. The Know-Nothings hoped to keep the foreign-born out of office and to make naturalization difficult.

In 1856 the American party nominated Millard Fillmore for President. He won more than one-fifth of the total votes but carried only one state, Maryland. The party then declined because it evaded the slavery issue; in the North its support went mostly to the new Republican party. In 1860 most of the remaining members joined the Constitutional Union party.

In 1888 another political organization sprang up under the name of American party. Its Presidential candidate received only 1,591 votes. The last party by the name appeared in 1924 with Ku Klux Klan support, but it won very few votes.

American Petroleum Institute. See PETROLEUM (end of article).

American Pharmaceutical Association. See PHARMACY (end of article).

American Philosophical Society, the oldest learned society in the United States. Most members are elected to represent the mathematical and physical sciences, geological and biological sciences, social sciences, and humanities. Some members are elected for their involvement in their professions or in public affairs. Membership is limited to 500 citizens and residents of the United States, plus 100 scholars in foreign countries.

The society's library, near its historic building on Independence Square in Philadelphia, specializes in the history of American science and culture and the American Indian. It includes papers of Benjamin Franklin and Charles Darwin. Chief publications are *Transactions, Proceedings,* and *Year Book* (all annuals) and *Memoirs* (monographs). Many research grants are given.

The society was founded in 1743 by Benjamin Franklin, who modeled it after the Royal Society of London. (He used the word *philosophy* in its meaning of "love of knowledge.") The new society soon became inactive but in 1769 was revived and merged with the American Society (formed in 1750 on the pattern of Franklin's Junto of 1727). After 1769 the society met every year, except 1777-78, when Philadelphia was occupied by the British. For many years it was virtually a national academy of science.

American Physical Therapy Association. See PHYSICAL THERAPY.

American Podiatry Association. See PODIATRY.

American Printing House for the Blind, the oldest national agency for the blind in the United States. The agency is private but is the United States' official manufacturer of learning materials for the blind, and receives an annual grant from Congress for this purpose. It produces materials in Braille; talking books and recorded tapes; books with large type; and learning aids such as relief maps. The agency was chartered by Kentucky in 1858, and was first granted aid by Congress in 1879. Its plant is in Louisville, Kentucky.

American Psychiatric Association. See PSYCHIATRY (end of article).

American Psychological Association. See PSYCHOLOGY (end of article).

American Public Welfare Association, an organization of public welfare agencies, professional welfare workers, and others interested in welfare work. The organization promotes improvement in social welfare programs. The association was founded in 1930. Membership is about 9,000. Headquarters are in Washington, D.C.

American Racing Pigeon Union. See PIGEON (end of article).

American Radio Relay League. See RADIO, section "Uses and Regulation of Radio," subtitle *Amateur Radio.*

American Railway Union. See DEBS, EUGENE VICTOR.

American Red Cross. See RED CROSS, subtitle *American Red Cross.*

American Retail Federation. See RETAIL TRADE (end of article).

American Revolution. See REVOLUTIONARY WAR, AMERICAN.

American Sable. See MARTEN.

American Saddle Horse. See HORSE, section "Breeds of Horses," subtitle *Important Breeds:* Light Horses.

American Samoa, să-mō'ă, an island territory of the United States in the South Pacific Ocean, 2,500 miles (4,000 km) southwest of Hawaii. It shares the Samoa Islands with independent Western Samoa and consists of Tutuila and Aunuu islands, the three Manua islands, and two small atolls. The total area is 77 square miles (199 km²). Tutuila is the largest and most populous island. The climate, although tropical and rainy, is pleasant because of the ocean's moderating effect.

Samoans, who are of Polynesian stock, make up most of the population. Many work in agriculture, raising coconuts, taro, breadfruit, and other tropical crops; copra is a principal export. Tourism and the canning of fish, primarily tuna, are also important. Pago Pago, on Tutuila, is the capital.

American Samoa has a constitution; the governor and legislature are both elected by the people.

Although the Samoa Islands were discovered in 1722, few territorial claims were made until the late 19th century. By agreement in 1899, Germany and Great Britain renounced their claims to the islands east of 171° West longitude in favor of the United States. Formal cession by Samoan chiefs took place in 1900 and 1904.

Population: 32,297.

American Society for the Prevention of Cruelty to Animals. See HUMANE SOCIETIES.

American Society of Composers, Authors and Publishers (ASCAP), an organization of writers and publishers of music. The society safeguards the legal rights of its members to secure compensation when their copyrighted musical works are performed publicly for profit, and grants licenses and collects royalties. ASCAP was founded in 1914. Membership is about 27,000. Headquarters are in New York City.

American Society of Interior Designers. See INTERIOR DECORATION (end).

American Society of Newspaper Editors. See NEWSPAPER, subtitle *United States Newspaper Organizations.*

American Sociological Association. See SOCIOLOGY.

American Stock Exchange. See STOCK EXCHANGE.

American Telephone and Telegraph Company (AT&T), the world's largest communications system and one of the world's largest corporations, with more than 3,000,000 shareholders. It manufactures telephone and other communications equipment and computers through the Western Electric Company, and sells telecommunications equipment and services through AT&T Information Systems, both subsidiaries. AT&T also provides long-distance connections for more than half the telephones in the United States. Bell Telephone Laboratories is AT&T's research and development organization.

AT&T was organized in 1885 to build long-distance lines for the American Bell Telephone Company. In 1900 AT&T took over the assets of the parent company, including several regional companies providing local service and wiring. As wholly-owned subsidiaries of AT&T, these companies formed a network known as the Bell System. In 1984 they became independent of AT&T and each other as part of the settlement of a federal antitrust suit against AT&T.

Main offices are in New York City.

American Temperance Society. See TEMPERANCE MOVEMENT.

American Tragedy, An (1925), a novel by Theodore Dreiser. Clyde Griffiths falls in love with a society girl through whom he could realize his ambitions for wealth and social standing. When Roberta Alden, a factory worker he has seduced, announces she is pregnant and demands he marry her, he plans to murder her. He takes Roberta rowing on a secluded lake, but lacks the courage to carry out his plan. The boat overturns by accident, and he lets her drown. Clyde is accused of murder, tried, convicted, and put to death. Dreiser places the real blame not on Clyde, but on industrial society with its false values and ambitions, restricted opportunities, and double standards of morality.

The book appeared in two volumes. It was an immediate success. Although sometimes criticized as slow-moving and formless, it is generally considered Dreiser's masterpiece. Dreiser based the work on an actual murder case of 1906.

American Trucking Associations. See TRUCK, subtitle *Trucking in the United States*.

American University, a private, coeducational institution of higher learning in Washington, D.C., affiliated with the United Methodist Church. The university has colleges of arts and sciences, business administration, law, and public and international affairs. It also has a school of nursing and a division of continuing education.

Under the Washington Semester Program, students from more than 200 colleges spend a semester at American University studying various aspects of national government, journalism, or the arts. The university was chartered in 1893 and opened in 1914.

For enrollment, see UNIVERSITIES AND COLLEGES (table).

American Veterans Committee (AVC), an organization of veterans of World Wars I and II, the Korean Conflict, and the Vietnamese War. It was founded in 1944. The motto "Citizens first, veterans second" was adopted to indicate that the AVC would help veterans obtain legitimate benefits from the government but would oppose lobbying for special privileges. The AVC publishes *The Bulletin,* a quarterly. There are about 25,000 members. Headquarters are in Washington, D.C.

American Veterans of World War II, Korea, and Vietnam. See AMVETS.

American Veterinary Medical Association. See VETERINARY MEDICINE AND SURGERY (end of article).

American Water Ski Association. See WATER SKIING.

American Water Spaniel. See DOG, subtitle *Breeds of Dogs:* Sporting Dogs (Spaniel, American Water).

American Youth Hostels. See HOSTEL.

Americanization, the cultural process (called *assimilation*) by which immigrants to the United States gradually adopt American speech, ideals, traditions, and ways of life. The term also refers to the movement promoting the process of assimilation. The United States has been called a *melting pot,* that is, a place where people of many nations and cultures have been blended into one.

Before 1900 the Americanization of immigrants—especially the Irish, Germans, and Scandinavians—tended to take place without planning and conscious thought. After 1900 with the great increase in immigration from many countries people began to fear that assimilation had halted, or was proceeding too slowly. During World War I there was concern about divided loyalties among the foreign-born. Americanization became a national crusade as public and private agencies cooperated in setting up classes in English, civics, and history. After immigration was restricted in 1921 the need for such classes gradually declined.

Americanization classes have continued,

but since World War II the term itself has been little used. There is a new emphasis on the rich heritage of the United States as a nation of many nations and on the value of cultural diversity, rather than uniformity.

"American's Creed, The," a statement of political faith compiled in 1917 by William Tyler Page (1868-1942) from ideas expressed by famous Americans. In 1918 the U.S. House of Representatives adopted the creed on behalf of the people of the United States. The text is as follows:

> I believe in the United States of America as a Government of the people, by the people, for the people; whose just powers are derived from the consent of the governed; a democracy in a republic; a sovereign Nation of many sovereign States; a perfect union, one and inseparable; established upon those principles of freedom, equality, justice and humanity for which American patriots sacrificed their lives and fortunes.
>
> I therefore believe it is my duty to my country to love it; to support its Constitution; to obey its laws; to respect its flag; and to defend it against all enemies.

Americans for Democratic Action (ADA), a national organization that promotes liberal domestic and foreign policies for the United States. ADA objectives are to reject totalitarianism, whether Communist or Fascist, and to strengthen liberal tendencies and oppose conservative policies within the major political parties. The ADA was founded in 1947. It has about 65,000 members in 50 local groups. Headquarters are in Washington, D.C.

***America's* Cup.** See SAILING, subtitle *Sailboat Racing* (and table).

America's Dairyland, a nickname for Wisconsin.

Americium, ăm′ẽr-ĭsh′ĭ-ŭm; ăm′ẽr-ĭs′ĭ-ŭm, a radioactive chemical element. In pure form, it is a silvery metal. Americium does not occur in nature; it is man-made. Its most easily manufactured isotope, americium 241, is produced by bombarding plutonium with neutrons. Americium 241 has a half-life of about 450 years. It is used in radiochemical research and as a source of ionization for smoke detectors. The longest-lived isotope is americium 243, which has a half-life of about 7,400 years.

Americium was first produced in 1944 by Glenn T. Seaborg, Ralph A. James, Leon O. Morgan, and Albert Ghiorso at the University of Chicago. Seaborg named the element americium after the Americas.

Symbol: Am. Atomic number: 95. Atomic weight:

243. Specific gravity: 13.67. Americium has 11 isotopes: Am-237 through Am-247. Melting point: about 1,821° F. (994° C.). Boiling point: 4,725° F. (2,607° C.). Americium is a transuranium element belonging to the actinide series of the Periodic Table and can have a valence of +2, 3, 4, 5, or 6.

Americus Vespucius, or Amerigo Vespucci. See VESPUCCI, AMERIGO.

Ames, Fisher (1758-1808), a United States statesman, political writer, and orator. Ames was a leading member of the Federalist party and a staunch supporter of Alexander Hamilton's policies. He favored a strong national government administered by an aristocracy of talent and virtue.

Ames was born in Dedham, Massachusetts. He graduated from Harvard in 1774 and was admitted to the Massachusetts bar in 1781. His pro-Federalist essays, written for Boston papers during 1786-87, led to his election to the U.S. House of Representatives. He served from 1789 to 1797, helping to formulate Federalist legislation. His speeches in the House earned him a place among America's great orators.

Ames, Oakes. See CRÉDIT MOBILIER OF AMERICA.

Ames, Iowa, a city in Story County. It is about 30 miles (50 km) north of downtown Des Moines. Iowa State University of Science and Technology is here. The city was first settled in 1864.

Population: 45,775.

Amethyst, ăm′ẽ-thĭst, a variety of semiprecious quartz that is colored violet-blue or purple by manganese. Amethyst is much used for charms, seals, and rings. Amethyst crystals are found in mineral veins and in cavities that occur in agate and certain rocks. The finest amethysts are found in Uruguay, Brazil, and Siberia. Beautiful amethysts are obtained along the shores of Lake Superior. Amethysts are also found in Arizona. The *amethystine sapphire,* a gem of great beauty and brilliance, is often called *oriental amethyst.* It is a violet or purple sapphire, and much more valuable than amethyst. The amethyst is the birthstone for

Fisher Ames

A-379

French Cathedrals by Martin Hurlimann: Houghton Mifflin
Cathedral of Notre Dame at Amiens. It was begun in 1220. Its rose window dates from the 16th century.

February and carries the sentiment of sincerity.

See also GEM (color page).

Amherst, ăm'ẽrst, Jeffrey Amherst, First **Baron** (1717-1797), a British army officer. Amherst was born in Kent County, England. After serving in the War of the Austrian Succession and in the Seven Years' War, he was sent to America as a major general. Amherst won the first British victory in the French and Indian War, at Louisbourg in 1758. Replacing James Abercromby as commander in chief, he captured Ticonderoga and Crown Point in 1759, and directed the capture of Montreal in 1760.

Amherst was governor of Virginia, 1759-68, although his duties were performed by a deputy. He was also governor general of British North America, 1760-63; Pontiac's Rebellion occurred during his last year in that post. After returning to England, Amherst was created a baron in 1776. From 1772 to 1795 he served almost continuously as commander in chief of the British armed

A-380

forces. He was made field marshal in 1796. His *Journal* was published in 1931.

Amherst College. See UNIVERSITIES AND COLLEGES (table).

Amiens, ăm'ĭ-ĕnz, France, the capital of Somme Department. It lies on the Somme River, about 70 miles (110 km) north of Paris. Amiens is an industrial and commercial center. Since the Middle Ages it has been known for the manufacture of cotton, woolen, and linen textiles. Other products include machinery, chemicals, clothing, and processed food. The Cathedral of Notre Dame is the largest cathedral in France and is regarded as one of the finest examples of Gothic architecture.

Amiens, settled first by Celtic people, was conquered by the Romans in 51 B.C. It was made a bishopric in the fourth century. Amiens came under the French crown in the late 12th century, and from then until 1790 it was the capital of the historic province of Picardy. The Peace of Amiens, which provided a short pause in the Napoleonic Wars, was signed here in 1802. In 1918 Allied forces defeated German troops in the Battle of Amiens, a turning point in World War I.

Population: 131,120.

Amiens, Peace of (1802). See GREAT BRITAIN, subtitle *History of Great Britain, 1707-1837:* The Younger Pitt; NAPOLEON I, subtitle *The Consulate (1800-04).*

Amine, ă-mēn'; ăm'ĭn, an organic compound derived from ammonia. In an amine molecule, at least one of the hydrogen atoms of the ammonia molecule (NH_3) is replaced by an organic *radical* (a group of atoms that acts as a single element). In a *primary* amine, one of the hydrogen atoms is replaced; in a *secondary* amine, two; and in a *tertiary* amine, all three. Most amines are poisonous, and are basic rather than acidic. The most important amine is *aniline,* from which dyes and other chemicals are produced. (See ANILINE.)

Amino Acids, ă-mē'nō, chemical compounds produced by living organisms. Many amino acids are the structural units of proteins. These compounds are called amino acids because each of them contains at least one amino group (an atom of nitrogen and two atoms of hydrogen bonded together chemically).

Importance

Although more than 100 amino acids have been identified, only some 25 serve as "building blocks" of proteins. Protein molecules consist of about 50 to more than 3,000 amino acid molecules linked together. When proteins are digested, they are broken down into their constituent amino acids. Proteins differ from one another because of the kinds, number, and arrangement of their amino acids. (See also PROTEIN.)

Amino acids are used by the body to make tissues, enzymes, hormones, and other vital body substances, and are necessary for the growth, maintenance, and repair of tissues. Most plants are able to produce all the amino acids they need. Animals cannot manufacture all the amino acids they require and must obtain the remainder from their food.

Amino acids that are not produced by animal bodies but that are necessary for proper nutrition are called *essential* amino acids. Human beings produce only about 15 of the amino acids they need. Among the essential amino acids required by man are isoleucine, leucine, lysine, methionine, phenylalanine, threonine, tryptophan, and valine. Many amino acids can be obtained in pure form, either by isolating them from proteins or by synthesizing them. They are used as dietary supplements and for experimental studies in nutrition.

Structure

Amino acids occur principally in chains consisting of several amino acid molecules linked together. These chains are called *polypeptides*. Some amino acid molecules, however, occur singly or attached to other organic molecules, such as carbohydrates. Pure amino acids are usually colorless, water-soluble crystals.

Amino acids have properties of both bases and acids. Each amino acid molecule contains at least one amino group (NH_2) and at least one carboxyl group (COOH). The amino group gives the amino acid its basic properties, and the carboxyl group provides the acidic properties. In most amino acids, these two groups are attached to a central carbon atom. In addition, a hydrogen atom (H) and another atom or group of atoms (R), which varies with each amino acid, are attached to the central carbon atom. Thus, the generalized formula for an amino acid is RCH (NH_2) COOH. For example, glycine, the simplest amino acid, is HCH (NH_2) COOH.

Amis, ā′mĭs, **Kingsley** (William) (1922-), an English author. His best-known works—such as his first novel, *Lucky Jim* (1954)—are comic satires of modern society. His writings also include verse and nonfiction. Amis was born in London. After

A-381

serving in World War II, he attended Oxford University, graduating in 1947. He taught English before becoming a full-time writer.

His other books include: Novels—*That Uncertain Feeling* (1955); *One Fat Englishman* (1964); *The Green Man* (1969); *The Riverside Vallas Murder* (1973); *Ending Up* (1974); *Jake's Thing* (1979). Verse —*Bright November* (1947); *A Case of Samples* (1956); *Poems* (1968); *Collected Poems, 1944-1978* (1978). Nonfiction—*New Maps of Hell: a Survey of Science Fiction* (1956); *The James Bond Dossier* (1965); *What Became of Jane Austen* (1971).

Amish, ăm′ĭsh; ä′mĭsh, a group of Protestant Christians, the strictest and most conservative sect of the Mennonites. The Amish avoid modern conveniences and regard education beyond the eighth grade as a threat to their way of life. The U.S. Supreme Court has exempted the Amish from compulsory school attendance laws after the eighth grade, on the grounds that such laws interfere with their constitutional right to free expression of their religion. The Amish are skilled farmers. Large Amish communities are found in Pennsylvania, Ohio, Indiana, Illinois, Iowa and Ontario.

The sect was founded about 1693 by Jacob Ammann, a Swiss Mennonite bishop who insisted on strict adherence to Mennonite beliefs and practices. The largest body, the Old Order Amish Church, has about 33,000 members.

The Amish shun modern inventions such as automobiles and still travel by horse and buggy.

Mel Horst, Witmer, Pa.

Amistad National Recreation Area. See NATIONAL PARKS, section "United States."

Amman, ăm-măn′, Jordan, the nation's capital and largest city. It is about 45 miles (72 km) east-northeast of Jerusalem. Amman is the commercial and industrial center of Jordan. Cement, textiles, processed foods, and tobacco and leather goods are produced. The city has a number of ancient ruins. The modern section has wide boulevards and streets lined with stores· and government buildings, including the king's palace. The University of Jordan and an agricultural college are here.

Prehistoric man occupied the site of Amman as early as 3500 B.C. By 1300 B.C. it had become the chief city of the Ammonites. It was taken over about 300 B.C. by the Hellenistic rulers of Egypt, who named it Philadelphia, and then by the Romans (30 B.C.). Under Moslem rule from the mid-seventh century A.D., the city declined. It revived after 1920, when it was made the administrative center of Transjordan, and especially after 1946, when it became the capital of newly independent Jordan.

Population: 711,850.

Ammanati, äm′mä-nä′tĕ, **Bartolommeo** (1511-1592), a Florentine architect and sculptor. Ammanati worked in the Mannerist style, which linked the classicism of the Renaissance and the flamboyancy of the Baroque. This style can be seen in the Collegio Romano, Rome; the *cortile* (interior courtyard) of the Pitti Palace, Florence; and in his other buildings. The Fountain of Neptune in the Piazza della Signoria, Florence, is his most important sculpture. (For color picture, see ITALY.) His Santa Trinità bridge in Florence was destroyed during World War II, but was rebuilt according to his design.

Ammann, Jacob. See AMISH.

Ammann, äm′än, **O. H.** (Othmar Hermann) (1879-1965), a United States civil engineer. A master bridge builder, Ammann designed the George Washington and Verrazano-Narrows bridges in New York City, and the three bridges connecting Staten Island and New Jersey—Bayonne Bridge, Goethals Bridge, and Outerbridge Crossing. He also designed New York's Triborough, Bronx-Whitestone, and Throgs Neck bridges. Ammann was born in Switzerland and graduated from the Swiss Federal Polytechnic Institute in 1902. He came to the United States in 1904.

Ammeter. See GALVANOMETER.

Ammon, ăm′ŏn, the Greek and Roman name for the ancient Egyptian god Amen, ä′mĕn. The name is also written Amon and Amun. Ammon originally was a local deity in Thebes. However, when the local princes of Thebes became masters of all Egypt about 2000 B.C., Ammon became a national god worshipped throughout Egypt. Gradually his name was joined with that of the Egyptian sun-god Re as Amen-Re. He also became the god of oracles, with his principal shrine at an oasis in the Libyan desert. Ammon sometimes is pictured as a ram or as a man with a ram's head.

Ammonia, ă-mō′nĭ-à; ă-mōn′yà, an industrially important chemical compound of nitrogen and hydrogen. At ordinary temperatures and pressures, ammonia is a colorless gas about three-fifths as heavy as air. It is poisonous and has a strong, choking odor. Ammonia dissolves readily in water, alcohol, and ether. In solid form, it is white and crystalline.

The most widely used method of producing ammonia commercially is the *Haber process,* in which nitrogen from the air is combined with hydrogen in the presence of a catalyst. (See HABER PROCESS.) Ammonia can also be obtained from coal or from animal protein matter, such as horns, hooves, and dung. When these materials are heated, ammonia gas is given off.

Plants use ammonia in the soil as a source of nitrogen, which is needed to build proteins that are essential to their life. (See NITROGEN CYCLE.) Many commercial fertilizers, such as urea and ammonium sulfate, are produced from ammonia. In some cases, pure ammonia is added to the soil as a fertilizer.

Ammonia is used as a solvent for organic compounds and for some metals, such as the alkali metals. It is used in the manufacture of dyes, explosives, plastics, drugs, nitric acid, and many other chemicals. Ammonia dissolved in water forms *ammonium hydroxide.* Diluted ammonium hydroxide is "household ammonia," which is used for many types of cleaning.

Ammonia is easily liquefied by being cooled under pressure. When liquid ammonia vaporizes, it absorbs large quantities of heat without changing its temperature. For these reasons, ammonia is widely used as a refrigerant. It is used both for industrial refrigeration and in refrigerators of the gas type. (See REFRIGERATION, diagram *How a Gas Refrigerator Works*.)

Ammonium Salts

When ammonia reacts chemically with an acid, an *ammonium salt* is formed. *Ammonium carbonate* (formed from ammonia and carbonic acid) is used as an ingredient of smelling salts. *Ammonium chloride,* or *sal ammoniac,* (from ammonia and hydrochloric acid) is used in dry-cell batteries. Several salts are important as fertilizers, especially *ammonium nitrate, ammonium phosphate,* and *ammonium sulfate*. The nitrate is also used in explosives, the phosphate in flame-proofing wood and textiles, and the sulfate in water treatment and tanning.

In a water solution, an ammonium-salt molecule breaks up to form an *ammonium ion* (a positively charged group of atoms consisting of one nitrogen and four hydrogen atoms) and an acid ion (a negatively charged acid molecule).

Ammonia has the chemical formula NH_3. The ammonium ion is NH_4^+. Ammonium hydroxide is NH_4OH; ammonium carbonate, $(NH_4)_2CO_3$; ammonium chloride, NH_4Cl; ammonium nitrate, NH_4NO_3; ammonium sulfate, $(NH_4)_2SO_4$.

Ammonite, ăm′ō-nīt, any one of a group of shelled sea animals that became extinct millions of years ago. Ammonites were mollusks whose shells ranged in size from about one-half inch (13 mm) to more than six feet (1.8 m) in diameter. They are known today only from the fossilized remains of their shells. Ammonite shells resemble the shells of the pearly nautilus, a living sea creature, in that they consist of a succession of chambers, with the animal occupying the outermost chamber. Ammonites flourished during the Triassic and Jurassic periods, and became extinct about 65 million years ago, at the end of the Cretaceous period.

The name "ammonite" comes from the fact that many of the shells resemble the horns of the ancient Egyptian god Ammon, who sometimes was represented as a man with a ram's head.

Ammonites make up the suborder Ammonoidea of the class Cephalopoda, phylum Mollusca.

Ammonites, an ancient Semitic people often at war with the Hebrews. They lived east of the Jordan River. Their capital was Rabbath Ammon—the Philadelphia of Roman times, now Amman, capital of Jor-

Jurassic Ammonite
American Museum
of Natural History

dan. According to the Bible, the Ammonites were descendants of Lot, and were therefore related to the Hebrews (Genesis 19:30-38). They were defeated by the Hebrews under Jephthah and under King Saul, and were conquered by David. Later they regained their independence, continuing as a separate people until about the third century B.C.

Ammonium. See AMMONIA.

Ammunition, ăm′ū-nĭsh′ŭn, projectiles fired from guns, including their fuzes, primers, and propellant charges. It is used in warfare, for target shooting and hunting, and for ceremonial purposes. In a broad sense, self-contained explosive weapons are also ammunition; they are not discussed in this article, however, but are covered in the articles BOMB; GRENADE; MINE; MISSILES AND ROCKETS; TORPEDO. Also excluded from this article are fireworks and nuclear weapons. (See FIREWORKS; NUCLEAR WEAPONS.)

Small-arms Ammunition

Small arms are firearms of .50 caliber (having a barrel with an inside diameter of one-half inch [12.7 mm]) or less—including rifles, pistols, revolvers, and machine guns —and shotguns of all gauges.

A *round,* or single piece, of fixed ammunition is called a *cartridge*. It usually consists of a *case,* a *projectile* (bullet), a *propellant* (explosive that propels the bullet), and a *primer* (explosive that sets off the propellant). It is called *fixed ammunition* because the case and projectile are attached to each other (fixed) during manufacture and remain so until the round is fired.

The cartridge case, usually of brass or other metal, is a hollow tube that contains smokeless powder or some other propellant. The front end of the case holds the bullet. At the rear is the primer, which in *center-fire* cartridges is a cap sunk into the center at the rear, and in *rimfire* cartridges encircles the outer edge of the case. (Some cartridges are made without a case. A caseless cartridge

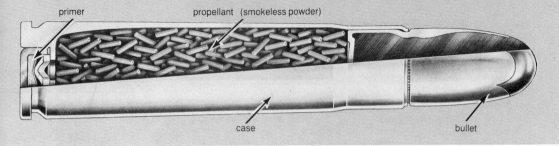

Remington Arms Co.

A Center-fire Rifle Cartridge, about 3 times actual size

consists of a molded propellant charge with a bullet affixed to one end and a primer to the other.)

The propellant is a relatively slow-burning powder. (An explosive that burns too fast could burst the gun barrel.) Its burning is started by a spark from the primer, which ignites when struck by the firing pin.

The projectile, or bullet, is the part of the cartridge that is fired at the target. Rapidly expanding gases from the burning powder break the bullet loose from the case and propel it through the barrel at high speed. Inside the weapon's barrel are spiral grooves (called *rifling*) that cause the bullet to spin, increasing its stability in flight.

Bullets are made of lead, of lead alloyed with tin or antimony, or of a lead core jacketed with a harder metal. Lead gives the bullet weight while the jacket prevents the soft lead from deforming in flight or upon hitting the target. *Armor-piercing* bullets have a core of extremely hard material, such as tungsten carbide. *Tracer* bullets contain a chemical that burns and gives off light, aiding the gunner in correcting his aim. *Blank ammunition,* used in training and for salutes, has a paper, wax, or plastic wad or pellet instead of a bullet.

Bullets used for hunting have hollow points or points made of soft lead. When they strike they expand, and kill game quickly. Expanding (or dumdum) bullets are banned from warfare by international treaties, as are wooden bullets and white-

phosphorus bullets. (See DUMDUM BULLET.)

A cartridge for a shotgun is called a *shell.* The most common type of shell contains *shot*—round pellets of lead or steel—instead of a single projectile. The shot is held in a paper or plastic case and separated from the propellant by a wad of paper, plastic, or felt. Some shotgun cartridges use a lead slug instead of shot.

Artillery Ammunition

Artillery includes guns, howitzers, mortars, recoilless rifles, and missile launchers. (See ARTILLERY.)

Fixed ammunition, made like the cartridges for small arms, is used in some guns with bore diameters up to 105 millimeters (about 4 inches). In *semi-fixed ammunition,* used in some guns of calibers from 75 mm to 120 mm (about 5 inches) and in some 5-inch (127-mm) and 6-inch (152-mm) naval guns, the projectile fits loosely in the case and can be removed to increase or decrease the powder charge. With *separate-loading ammunition* the projectile is placed in the gun, followed either by a case containing propellant and primer, or by cloth bags of powder and a separate primer.

Projectiles. An artillery projectile made of solid metal is called *shot.* Several types, known as kinetic-energy projectiles, are designed for penetrating armor plate. These projectiles are made of a dense metal (or with a core of dense metal) and are fired from guns at a very high velocity.

An artillery projectile that contains an explosive charge is called a *shell.* A *high-explosive shell* inflicts damage by the force of the explosion itself, as well as by fragments of the shell casing that scatter widely. One type of projectile designed for use against troops contains bundles of small dartlike fragments called *flechettes* that scatter in all directions with great force when the shell explodes. *Smoke shells* contain a chemical used to produce smoke screens.

A Shotgun Shell, about ¾ actual size

Remington Arms Co.

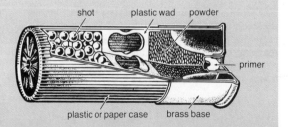

A-384

AMMUNITION

Chemical shells, used in World War I, contained poison gas that was released on impact. (See POISON GAS.) *Illuminating,* or *star, shells* contain flares attached to parachutes to illuminate targets at night.

An *armor-piercing shell* does not explode until a fraction of a second after impact, thus permitting the shell to penetrate the target. The *shaped-charge shell* has in its nose a cavity that extends into the explosive charge. This concentrates the explosive force, allowing the shell to penetrate thick armor.

Charges and Fuzes. The explosive charge in an artillery projectile is usually TNT, amatol, a picric-acid compound, or ammonium picrate. (See EXPLOSIVE, subtitle *Demolition and Blasting Charges.*)

The explosive charge is set off by a fuze. The rotation of the projectile in the gun barrel unlocks the fuze mechanism so that it is "armed" and ready to set off the main charge. The fuze may act directly on the main charge, or, more generally, it may detonate a small quantity of another explosive, such as lead azide. A series of two to four successive split-second explosions (called the *explosive train*) takes place in the firing of many types of rounds.

Impact fuzes are designed to detonate the projectile on striking an object. Some fuzes contain a short delay element (normally compressed black powder) which allows the shell either to penetrate the target or to ricochet into the air for a fraction of a second before bursting. *Time fuzes* explode the shell at a preset time after it leaves the gun. Some time fuzes use a mechanical watchlike device; others are operated by the slow burning of a train of compressed black powder. The *proximity fuze* contains an electronic device that explodes the projectile at a preset distance from the target. Other types of fuzes may be set to detonate the explosive charge at a given altitude.

See also FUSE (fuze is the military spelling).

Primers and Propellants. Artillery is fired by friction primers, in which a strip of metal is drawn through mercury fulminate or some other priming material; by electric primers, ignited by a spark; and by percussion primers like those used on small-arms ammunition.

The propellant is usually a slow-burning smokeless powder. Smokeless powders are

A-385

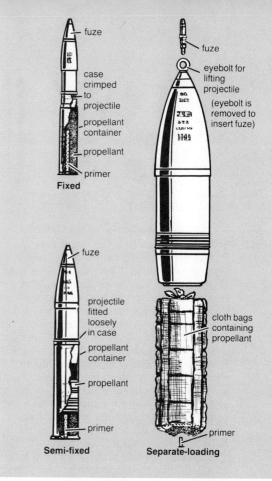

Artillery Ammunition

forms of nitrated cellulose. (See EXPLOSIVE, subtitle *Propellants.*)

The ammunition used in recoilless rifles has a perforated case to allow part of the propellant gases to escape to the rear of the gun, thus eliminating recoil, or "kick."

History

Early Artillery Ammunition. Gunpowder, a mixture of sulfur, saltpeter, and charcoal, was known in China as early as the 10th century, but was used mainly in firecrackers. It was being used in war in Europe by the early 14th century, when it was loaded in small cannon to propel stones or the metal darts that had been used in crossbows.

Recoilless Round for 57-mm Gun. Perforations in the case allow some of the gases to escape.

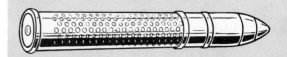

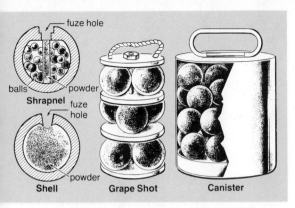

fuze hole

balls — powder
Shrapnel fuze hole

powder
Shell **Grape Shot** **Canister**

Artillery Ammunition of the Civil War

About 1350, balls cast of lead, bronze, or iron came into use. Experiments were made in loading cannon with large numbers of small balls that would scatter over the battlefield. *Case shot,* or *canister,* consisted of projectiles of this type placed in a case or can for loading. Canister was in use as early as 1439. It was particularly effective against infantry and cavalry at distances up to 350 yards (320 m). A later form of canister was *grape shot,* which was effective at ranges up to 1000 yards (900 m). Grape shot consisted of from 9 to 60 iron balls grouped around a frame that would break up and scatter the balls at some distance from the gun.

Both canister and grape were used extensively during the period from the French Revolution through the American Civil War. The mainstay of artillery fire, however, was the cannon ball of solid iron.

Explosive shells were used as early as the 14th century. In the simplest form a cord fuze was inserted in a hole bored in a hollow iron ball. The hollow was filled with gunpowder, the fuze was ignited when the gun was fired, and the bursting charge scattered fragments of the shell. In 1804 Henry Shrapnel, of England, invented spherical case shot—a sphere filled with balls and an explosive charge set off in midair by a time fuze. Spherical case shot came to be called *shrapnel.* During World War I shrapnel shells were widely used and accounted for most of the wounds inflicted by artillery fire. Although shrapnel has not been in general use since, injuries from shell fragments are still commonly called shrapnel wounds.

Until the mid-19th century all cannon were discharged by applying fire to the powder through a *touchhole* (a hole bored in the base of the gun's barrel). During the American Civil War a friction primer was

introduced. The friction primer was inserted into the touchhole and activated by pulling a lanyard—a long cord attached to the movable part of the primer. Late in the century smokeless powder replaced gunpowder as the propellant for artillery ammunition.

Early Small-arms Ammunition. Ammunition for early small arms consisted of gunpowder and lead balls. It was loaded through the *muzzle,* or front end, of the barrel. A charge of gunpowder was poured down the barrel and then the ball was pushed down the barrel with a *ramrod.* With rifled weapons, a small patch of cloth, paper, or leather was placed over the muzzle after the powder was poured in and was rammed down together with the ball. (The patch made the ball fit snugly in the barrel and, when the gun was fired, caused the ball to be spun by the rifling in the barrel.)

Riflemen would carry powder in a flask made of metal or in a horn (usually a cow's horn). They would carry bullets in a pouch and usually have a mold for casting their own bullets from lead. For soldiers, ammunition was often supplied in *paper cartridges.* Each cartridge contained a bullet and enough powder for one shot. The soldier would tear open a cartridge with his teeth and empty the contents into the barrel.

In firing a gun, gunpowder in the barrel was set off by means of a flash produced by an external priming charge. In early muskets, the priming charge consisted of a small amount of gunpowder placed in a pan located near an opening, or vent, leading to the rear of the barrel. In muskets called *matchlocks,* which date from the early 1500's, the priming charge was ignited with a mechanism that brought the smoldering end of a taper, or wick, into the pan. In later weapons, such as the *wheel lock* and *flintlock,* the powder in the pan was ignited by sparks produced by a mechanism that struck flint against steel. These weapons were replaced in the mid-1800's with guns that were fired with a *percussion cap.* The cap contained mercury fulminate, an explosive. It was placed over a nipple on a tube leading to the vent. The cap was made to explode by striking it with a moving part called a hammer. The percussion cap was invented in 1807 by Alexander John Forsyth, a Scottish clergyman.

Development of Modern Ammunition. Claude Étienne Minié of France in 1849 produced

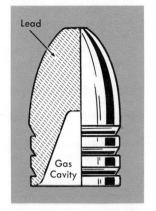

Lead

Gas Cavity

Civil War
Period
Minié Ball
Caliber .69

an elongated bullet—called the *Minié ball*—that had a hollow base. When the bullet was fired from a gun, the explosion of the propellant forced the sides of the base to expand and tightly grip the rifling as the bullet passed through the barrel. The Minié ball helped increase the accuracy of small arms. Fixed ammunition was developed in the mid-19th century as firearms that were loaded through the *breech,* or rear of the barrel, became practical. The first smokeless powder practical for military use was developed by Paul Marie Eugène Vieille, a Frenchman, in 1887.

Several high explosives were produced by chemists in the 19th century, but because of the dangers in handling, their application to military purposes was slow. Guncotton was invented by Christian Schönbein, a German chemist, in 1846. It became a basic ingredient of smokeless powders. At about the same time Ascanio Sobrero, an Italian, discovered nitroglycerin. It was unsafe to handle until Alfred Nobel of Sweden in 1866 combined it with absorbents to form dynamite. The United States used a "dynamite gun" in the Spanish-American War. Nobel also invented ballistite, a kind of smokeless powder. (See NOBEL, ALFRED BERNHARD.) Picric acid was produced by P. Woulfe in 1771 but was not used as a military explosive until the 1880's.

World War I and After. TNT was first made in 1863 but did not find military use until World War I, when it largely replaced the picric-acid explosives. It is still the most important military explosive.

After World War I a great deal of attention was devoted to the design and composition of projectiles and to the composition of propellants to improve range and accuracy. Many changes were minor—for example, adoption of a "boat-tailed" bullet for .30

caliber rifle ammunition that had less tendency to tumble in flight.

Explosives that became important during World War II include cyclonite, or RDX, and ammonium picrate, or Explosive D. This war also marked the beginnings of the recoilless rifle, the proximity fuze, missile development, and nuclear weapons.

Through the years the trend in the design of ammunition has been toward smaller calibers, permitting lighter-weight weapons. At the same time the goal has been to increase the penetrating power of small-arms ammunition and the destructiveness of artillery ammunition; this has been done through improving propellants, explosive charges, and the metals used for casings and projectiles.

The ball for muzzle-loading rifles was usually of .69 caliber. Early breech-loaders had a caliber of .45 and the rifles used by the U.S. Army in the two World Wars were of caliber .30. After World War II the United States adopted a 7.62 mm rifle cartridge, which is slightly smaller and lighter than the .30 caliber but has greater penetrating power. A high-velocity cartridge of 5.56 mm (about .22 caliber) was designed for the lightweight M-16 rifle, which was adopted by United States military forces in the mid-1960's. The caseless cartridge was also introduced in the 1960's.

See also BALLISTICS; CALIBER; GUNPOWDER.

Amnesia, ăm-nē′zhǐ-à, a partial or complete loss of memory. Amnesia can result from physical causes, such as an injury to the head, a brain tumor, arteriosclerosis, or senility. It can also be brought about by certain kinds of emotional shock or stress. Amnesia is usually temporary, but can be permanent when there is severe brain damage. Sufferers from emotionally caused amnesia are sometimes helped by psychiatric treatment.

Amnesty, ăm′něs-tǐ, a proclamation by a sovereign power or government declaring that certain offenses have been officially forgotten or overlooked. The word comes from the Greek, meaning "a forgetting." Amnesty is usually granted to large numbers of offenders or classes of persons at one time to free them from prosecution for political offenses, such as treason, sedition, or rebellion. It is similar to a pardon except that amnesty erases all legal record of the offense.

A pardon merely releases an individual convicted of a crime from all or part of the punishment.

The U.S. Constitution gives the President power "to grant reprieves and pardons for offenses against the United States" (Article II, Section 2). Although the term "amnesty" is not expressed, the Supreme Court has ruled that it falls under the definition of pardon as used in the Constitution. Also, by practice, the President's power to grant amnesties has become well established. In addition, the court has held that Congress may enact amnesty laws.

Amnesty in History

The earliest known example of amnesty occurred in Athens in 403 B.C. Thrasybulus granted a general amnesty to supporters of the Council of Thirty, the government that he had overthrown.

When the monarchy was restored in England in 1660, Charles II granted amnesty to all involved in the Great Rebellion except those who had had a part in putting his father, Charles I, to death. In 1778, during the American Revolution, the British offered amnesty to all men of the colonial forces who would lay down their arms.

The broadest use of amnesty in United States history took place during and after the Civil War. In the Amnesty Proclamation of 1863, President Lincoln offered amnesty to all Confederates except high civil and military leaders. After the war, President Andrew Johnson granted hundreds of amnesty petitions. The Amnesty Act of 1872, which offered amnesty to all but a few hundred former Confederates, was the first general Congressional amnesty.

After World Wars I and II, Presidential amnesties were granted to some draft evaders and others convicted of wartime offenses. Following the Vietnamese War, a conditional amnesty was offered to draft evaders and deserters. This was not a true amnesty, however, because hospital work or some other humanitarian type of alternative service was required of offenders before release from legal penalties.

Amnesty International. See POLITICAL PRISONER.

Amniocentesis. See PREGNANCY, subtitle *Prenatal and Childbirth Care:* Prenatal Detection of Congenital Diseases.

Amoeba, á-mē′bá, a protozoan (one-celled animal) noted for the simplicity of its body structure. Amoebas (or amoebae) are widely distributed over the world in fresh and salt water, damp soil, moist vegetation, and the bodies of other animals. Most of the amoebas that live in animal bodies do no apparent harm, but one species in man causes *amoebic dysentery,* a serious and often fatal disease. Most amoebas are of microscopic size, but the two species known as the *common amoeba* and *giant amoeba* can sometimes be seen with the unaided eye. Living amoebas—especially the common amoeba—are often studied in biology classes because they are easily obtained, and because they are easily observed through a microscope.

The amoeba is a jellylike mass of protoplasm (living matter) that is constantly changing its shape. A *cell membrane* encloses a thin outer layer of transparent protoplasm called the *ectoplasm* and a granular inner mass called the *endoplasm.* The endoplasm contains the *cell nucleus,* which controls the amoeba's life processes. In most species, the endoplasm also contains a water bubble, called the *contractile vacuole,* that regulates the amoeba's water content. Within the endoplasm there are also bits of food enclosed in *food vacuoles.*

Amoeba, greatly enlarged

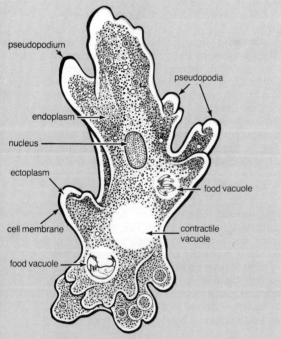

pseudopodium

pseudopodia

endoplasm

nucleus

ectoplasm

food vacuole

cell membrane

contractile vacuole

food vacuole

The amoeba does not have permanent body parts to perform its various functions. It moves by pushing out temporary extensions called *pseudopodia* (false feet) from any part of its surface. The entire body of the amoeba flows into one pseudopodium, and the animal then puts out another. The amoeba changes direction by putting out a pseudopodium on another side of its body. It captures food—algae and microscopic animals—by extending pseudopodia to surround the food particle, which is then digested within a food vacuole. Body wastes are excreted by diffusion through the cell membrane and by means of the contractile vacuole. Most amoebas reproduce by fission.

Amoebas make up the order Amoebozoa of the class Sarcodina. The common amoeba is *Amoeba proteus;* the giant amoeba, *Pelomyxa carolinensis.* The amoeba that causes dysentery is *Entamoeba histolytica.*

Amoebic Dysentery. See DYSENTERY.

Amon. See AMMON.

Amorites, ăm′ŏ-rīts′, an ancient Semitic people who moved from the desert into the Fertile Crescent about 2500 B.C. Along the Mediterranean coast they mingled with prior settlers to form the Canaanites. On the east side of the crescent the Amorites conquered the Akkadians and Sumerians about 2000 B.C. and subsequently founded the Old Babylonian Empire.

See also BABYLONIA, subtitle *History.*

Amortization, ăm′ĕr-tĭ-zā′shŭn; á-môr′-tĭ-zā′shŭn, an accounting term that has four commonly used meanings:

1. Payment of a long-term debt such as a mortgage by making direct, periodic, partial payments during the life of the debt.
2. Provision for the future payment of a debt, such as the maturity of a bond issue, by the periodic setting aside of sums in a *sinking fund* so that the fund will equal the amount of the debt at maturity (see BOND).
3. Periodic reduction of the *book value* (value as shown in the accounting records) of an asset (usually an intangible asset such as a patent) until it is zero.
4. Periodic reduction or increase of the book value of a bond bought at a *premium* (a price above the face value) or *discount* (a price below the face value) so that the book value at maturity equals the face value.

Amory, ā′mŏ-rĭ, **Cleveland** (1917-   ), a United States social historian. *The Proper Bostonians* (1947) is a slightly impudent history of Back Bay "first families" from the colonial period to the 1940's. *The Last Resorts: a Portrait of American Society at Play* (1952) describes the social elite in summer resorts of the late 19th century. *Who Killed Society?* (1960) is about the lowering of standards in fashionable society.

Amory was born in Nahant, Massachusetts, and graduated from Harvard in 1939. After serving in World War II, he was an editor and journalist. In 1967 he founded the Fund for Animals, a humane organization devoted to protecting animals from abuse and neglect.

His other books include *Home Town* (1950), a novel; *Man Kind? Our Incredible War on Wildlife* (1974); *The Trouble with Nowadays* (1979).

Amos, ā′mŏs, in the Bible, a Hebrew prophet who lived about 750 B.C.

The Book of Amos denounces in vivid language the luxuries of his times, condemns the rich for the injustice toward the poor, and proclaims that religion is not ritual—it is social righteousness. Amos considered God to be the God of all nations, not of the Hebrews alone. He proclaimed that since Israel had broken the covenant with God it would be punished. Amos did his preaching in the northern kingdom of Israel.

Amosite. See ASBESTOS, subtitle *Asbestos Minerals.*

Amoy, ämoi′, or **Hsiamen (Xiamen),** shyä′mŭn′, China, a city in Fukien (Fujian) province. It lies on a coastal island in the Formosa Strait, about 1,060 miles (1,710 km) south of Peking. Nearby are the Quemoy Islands, outposts of the Nationalist Chinese government on Taiwan. Amoy is a seaport and the base for a large fishing fleet. Its few manufacturing industries produce mainly chemicals and paper. A railway causeway links the city with the mainland. Amoy was one of the first Chinese ports opened to foreign trade in 1842 and remained a treaty port for 100 years. It was taken by the Communists in 1949 and has since become an important military base.

Population: 224,300.

Ampère, André Marie (1775-1836), a French mathematician and physicist, noted for his work in electromagnetism. He discovered that electric currents in two wires exert magnetic forces on each other—two parallel currents flowing in the same direction attract each other, while two parallel currents flowing in opposite directions repel each other. As a result of experiments conducted between 1820 and 1825, Ampère developed a mathematical formula (Ampère's Law) for calculating the magnetic force caused by an electric current. He also helped develop the galvanometer, an instrument that measures electric current. The ampere, a unit of electric current, was named for him.

Ampère became professor of mathematics at the École Polytechnique, Paris, in 1809 and, later, professor of physics at the Collège de France. His *Collection of Electrodynamical Observations* was published in 1822.

Ampere. See ELECTRICITY, subtitle *Units of Electricity.*

Amphetamine, ăm-fĕt'á-mēn, a chemical substance used in several drugs that stimulate the central nervous system. Amphetamine or its derivatives, such as amphetamine sulfate and amphetamine phosphate, are the active ingredients of these stimulant drugs, which are also called "amphetamines" and "pep pills." Amphetamines are usually taken orally in tablet form. Benzedrine, Dexedrine, and Edrisal are three of the most widely used amphetamines.

Amphetamines are prescribed to stimulate mildly depressed persons, to curb appetite, to treat alcoholism, to counteract sleepiness, and to relieve mental fatigue. Paradoxically, amphetamines have also been used successfully in treating hyperkinetic, or hyperactive children. Among frequent side effects are insomnia and elevated blood pressure. Amphetamines are potentially habit-forming, and overuse can result in excessive nervousness, hallucinations, and impairment of judgment.

The chemical formula is $C_9H_{13}N$.

See also BENZEDRINE.

Amphibian, ăm-fĭb'ĭ-ăn, one of a large class of cold-blooded *vertebrates* (animals with backbones). The name comes from Greek words meaning "dual life," because most amphibians spend the early part of their life cycle in water and the later part on land. Amphibians include frogs, toads, and salamanders. There are nearly 2,500 living species of amphibians. They are widely distributed over the world, mostly in fresh water or moist places. A few kinds of toads live in deserts. Amphibians vary in size from a species of toad less than an inch long to a species of salamander nearly six feet long.

Amphibians *respire* (take in oxygen and let out carbon dioxide) through the skin. They also have other organs of respiration, including gills in the young of all species and the adults of some species, and lungs in the

adults of many species. Some amphibians can also respire through the mucous membranes of the mouth.

Most amphibians lay their eggs in water, where they hatch out as larvae and develop into adults through a process called *metamorphosis.* Some amphibian larvae eat only live water animals, such as small insects, mollusks, crustaceans, and worms. Others feed on algae or dead animal matter. Adult amphibians may eat live water animals, or even small birds and mammals. Some amphibians can regrow lost tails or legs during the larval stage, and some even shortly after metamorphosis.

Amphibians make up the class Amphibia. Orders of the class are:

1. **Apoda**—the caecilians. Limbless, worm-like; found in the tropics.

2. **Urodela**—salamanders, including newts, mud puppies, and axolotls. Tailed; four-legged. See AXOLOTL; MUD PUPPY; NEWT; SALAMANDER.

3. **Anura**—includes toads and frogs. Tailless; four-legged; hind legs adapted for jumping. See FROG; SPADEFOOT TOAD; TOAD.

Books about Amphibians

Breen, J. F. *Encyclopedia of Reptiles and Amphibians* (T.F.H. Publications, 1974).

King, F. W., and John Behler. *The Audubon Society Field Guide to North American Reptiles and Amphibians* (Knopf, 1979).

Smith, H. M. *Amphibians of North America* (Golden Press, 1978).

For Younger Readers:

Fichter, G. S. *Keeping Amphibians and Reptiles as Pets* (Watts, 1979).

Amphibian Plane. See AIRPLANE, section "Types of Airplanes," subtitle *Classification by Landing Gear:* Amphibian.

Amphibious Warfare, military campaigns of combined land and sea forces. Since no military action of any size would be undertaken without also using air power, the word *triphibious,* meaning use of land, sea, and air forces, has been suggested, but is not commonly used. A successful amphibious assault against a well-defended beach requires a unified command, control of the air, and an efficient supply system.

A typical amphibious assault begins with air attacks on enemy airfields, defenses, and lines of supply. Under cover of the air bombing, warships move in and open fire on shore batteries and defenses. This phase is called "softening up." Sometimes swimmers, called *underwater demolition teams* or *frogmen,* go in at night to locate or remove underwater obstacles.

Spotted Salamander
(Ambystoma maculatum)
6" — 7¾"

Great Crested Newt
(Triturus cristatus)
about 6"

Eastern Spotted Newt
(Notophthalmus viridescens)
ADULT 2⅞" — 4"

JUVENILE (Red Eft) 1⅜" — 3⅜"

Hellbender Salamander
(Cryptobranchus alleganiensis)
11½" — 20"

Great Plains Toad
(Bufo cognatus)
1⅞" — 3½"

Pickerel Frog
(Rana palustris)
1¾" — 3"

AMPHIBIANS

Fowler's Toad
(Bufo fowleri)
2" — 3"

Green Frog
(Rana clamitans)
2¼" — 3½"

wm blackmun

Amphibious Warfare. Once a beachhead is seized, huge quantities of supplies must be landed. The scene is Iwo Jima during World War II.

After hours, days, or even weeks of aerial and naval bombardment, the amphibious assault is launched from large amphibious warfare ships, which carry landing craft, tanks, helicopters, troops, and supplies. First troops are landed on the beaches by helicopters and by landing craft, some of which are tracked to operate on land as well as water. Sometimes parachutists are dropped and troops are landed inland by helicopters to secure key enemy positions.

Tanks and artillery are brought in soon after the troop landings. The soldiers try to move rapidly inland so that more men, tanks, and supplies can be landed in comparative safety. Some shallow-draft amphibious ships unload right onto the beaches or with the aid of portable causeways, and some unload via landing craft. For information on U.S. Navy amphibious vessels, see NAVY, U.S., subtitle *Ships and Aircraft:* Combatant Ships (Amphibious Warfare Ships, Landing Craft).

As ground is gained inland and the battle has shifted away from the beachhead, the action is no longer amphibious, and specialists in amphibious warfare are relieved by regular troops.

History

Amphibious warfare has existed since the beginning of warfare. It presented few special problems, however, until comparatively recent times (about the 16th century), when land and sea warfare became complicated and highly specialized arts.

James Wolfe's capture of Quebec in the French and Indian War and the Yorktown campaign of the American Revolution are classic examples of 18th-century amphibious warfare. The British assault at Abukir Bay (1801) against the army Napoleon had aban-

doned in Egypt displayed the principles and techniques of this kind of warfare to perfection. A high degree of cooperation was developed by General U. S. Grant and Admiral David Dixon Porter in Civil War campaigns along the Mississippi River.

The British Gallipoli campaign in World War I was an amphibious operation that ended in failure. This failure convinced most European nations that a successful assault against a beach defended by modern weapons was impossible. The U.S. Marine Corps, however, felt that the British would have succeeded had they not made many mistakes. Beginning with a thorough study of Gallipoli, the Marines by 1934 had drawn up principles that were applied with great success in World War II.

Amphibious warfare was widely used on all fronts in World War II. The British trained specialists (called Commandos) for quick raids. Similar were the U.S. Army's Rangers. United States Marines were highly trained amphibious specialists, and organizations as large as a corps were built around the Marines. The landings in North Africa, Sicily, Italy, and France were large-scale amphibious operations. Guadalcanal, the Philippines, Iwo Jima, and Okinawa were notable in the Pacific campaign, which was largely amphibious. The landing at Inchon in 1950, during the Korean Conflict, was a brilliantly successful amphibious action.

In the Falkland Islands War (1982), which began after Argentina seized the Falkland Islands from Great Britain, a well-executed nighttime amphibious operation by the British made possible their retaking of the islands.

See also GALLIPOLI CAMPAIGN; KOREAN CONFLICT, subtitle *United Nations Counterattack;* QUEBEC, BATTLE OF; VICKSBURG, SIEGE OF; WORLD WAR II, section "The War with Germany and Italy, 1942-45," subtitles *African Invasion, 1942-43* and *Operation Overlord, 1944,* and section "The War with Japan, 1941-45."

Amphibole. See ASBESTOS, subtitle *Asbestos Minerals;* HORNBLENDE; JADE.

Amphictyonic Council, ăm-fĭk'tĭ-ŏn'ĭk, or **Amphictyonic League,** an association of neighboring city-states in ancient Greece. The councils, of which there were several, were originally organized to coordinate religious festivals in honor of certain gods. Later the councils became loose political confederations of states allied for mutual defense against foreigners.

The Delphic amphictyony was one of the earliest confederations of Greek states. It was centered around the temple of Apollo at Delphi and concerned itself with public welfare and the maintenance of peace among members. One of Philip of Macedon's first steps toward supremacy in Greece was to force admission of his country to a seat in the amphictyony at Delphi. When he united Greece under the League of Corinth in 338 B.C., he designated the council to serve as the supreme court.

Amphion, ăm-fī′ŭn, in Greek mythology, a king of Thebes who ruled jointly with his twin brother Zethus. Antiope was their mother by Zeus, who had approached her in the form of a satyr. Fleeing her father's home in disgrace, she bore twin sons whom she left in charge of a shepherd on Mount Cithaeron. The god Hermes gave Amphion a lyre, which he learned to play with great skill. Zethus became a shepherd and hunter.

Grown to manhood, the twins went to Thebes, where they found their mother being cruelly treated by King Lycus and his wife, Dirce. They punished Dirce, killed Lycus, and seized the throne. (For a depiction of Dirce's punishment, see FARNESE BULL.) Amphion was married to Niobe.

When the brothers built the walls of Thebes, Amphion was able to move huge stones in place merely by playing his lyre. Zethus, though stronger, had to toil and sweat to place his share of the stones.

Amphioxus, ăm′fī-ŏk′sŭs, or **Lancelet,** lăns′lĕt, a small marine animal found in shore waters in temperate and tropical regions. There are about 30 species of amphioxuses. The animal is seldom more than two inches (5 cm) long; the American species of the Pacific coast, however, sometimes grows to four inches (10 cm) in length. The amphioxus is rather fishlike in appearance. On the back it has a fin that runs almost the entire length of the body; on the underside near the tail it has a short fin. The sharp-edged body gave it the name amphioxus ("double edged"), and the lance-shaped tail the name lancelet.

The amphioxus is an intermediate form between *invertebrates* (animals without backbones) and *vertebrates* (animals with backbones). Instead of a backbone, the amphioxus has a *notochord*—a firm, flexible rod of cartilage-like material that extends from the tip of its head to the tip of its tail. It has a nerve cord lying above and parallel to the notochord, but has no specialized brain.

The amphioxus swims well, but spends most of its time buried tail down in coarse, clean sand or gravel in shallow water. It feeds on microscopic organisms, which it strains from the seawater through its gill slits.

Amphioxuses make up the subphylum Cephalochordata of the phylum Chordata. The amphioxus of the American west coast is *Branchiostoma californiense;* that of the east coast, *B. virginiae.*

Amphipolis, ăm-fĭp′ō-lĭs, an ancient Greek city on the Strimon River just inland from the north shore of the Aegean Sea. It was founded by Athenians in the mid-fifth century B.C. to serve as a military outpost, a trade center, and a base for mining gold from the nearby Pangaion Mountains. During the Peloponnesian War (431-404 B.C.) Amphipolis was captured by Sparta, and then was made autonomous. In 357 B.C. Philip of Macedon seized the city to gain control of the coast and of the gold mines. After a few centuries the gold gave out and Amphipolis sank into obscurity.

Amphitheater, ăm′fĭ-thē′à-tēr, an oval, circular, or semicircular building, used especially for entertainment. The spectators' seats rise in tiers around a central stage or arena. Modern amphitheaters are generally used for sporting events, and sometimes for political conventions and indoor circuses.

In architecture the term amphitheater is applied to the circular or oval Roman buildings that were used for gladiatorial contests and sometimes were flooded for naval exhibitions. One of the first Roman amphitheaters was built at Pompeii in 70 B.C. The Colosseum of Rome (completed 82 A.D.) was the largest and most famous amphitheater of ancient times. Ruins of other Roman amphitheaters are at Verona and Capua, Italy, and Nîmes and Arles, France.

See also COLOSSEUM; STADIUM.

Amphitryon, ăm-fĭt′rĭ-ŏn, in Greek mythology, a king of Tiryns. Zeus fell in love with Alcmene, Amphitryon's wife, and while Amphitryon was away visited her in the form of her absent husband. Alcmene bore twins: Hercules by Zeus and Iphicles by Amphitryon.

Plautus, Molière, and Dryden are among the many writers who based comedies on the story. A modern version is Jean Giraudoux's *Amphitryon 38* (1929).

Amplifier, ăm'plĭ-fī'ẽr, a device that magnifies (amplifies) electrical signals, usually through the use of electron tubes or transistors. The electrical signals can come from a microphone, antenna, phonograph pickup, telephone cable, magnetic tape, electric guitar, the tuner section of an AM or FM radio, or some other source. A well-designed amplifier produces at its output an undistorted enlargement of the signals received at its input.

The heart of an amplifier consists of one or more electron tubes or transistors that amplify the electrical signals passing through them. (See ELECTRONICS, section "Some Basic Electronic Devices and Circuits," subtitle *Amplifiers.*) Resistors, capacitors, and (in most amplifiers) transformers are needed to regulate current flow and furnish the voltage levels required for proper operation of the tubes or transistors. In amplifiers that are powered by alternating current, rectifiers (of either the tube type or the solid-state type) are needed to convert the alternating current to direct current.

Modern amplifiers use transistors instead of electron tubes. In contrast to an electron-tube amplifier, an all-transistor amplifier requires no warmup period, generates less heat, is more compact, and is likely to need fewer repairs.

Audio Amplifiers

An audio amplifier sends its enlarged electrical signals directly into a loudspeaker, which converts the signals to sound waves. It is the most common type of amplifier found in the home. Audio amplifiers are designed to amplify the power of electrical signals in the audio range of frequencies; that is, the range of frequencies that can be detected by a normal human ear. The audio range is usually defined as extending from 20 to 15,000 hertz (cycles per second).

The loudness of the sound produced by a loudspeaker varies with the output power of the amplifier driving it. The greater the amplifier power, the louder the sound. Some high-quality audio amplifiers can produce more than 100 watts of output power without distortion. An electronic device called a *preamplifier* is sometimes necessary to make a very weak signal, such as that produced by a magnetic phonograph pickup, strong enough to be handled by an audio amplifier.

Audio amplifiers can be either integral

parts of the equipment with which they are used, or they can be separate units. Every television set and complete radio for example, contains an audio amplifier. In some high-fidelity, or *hi-fi*, systems, the audio amplifier is separate from the preamplifier, radio tuner, and record-playing equipment. Other hi-fi arrangements are built around the *receiver,* or *tuner-amplifier,* which consists of an AM-FM radio tuner, preamplifier, and audio amplifier in one cabinet. A record turntable or tape player can be connected by electrical wires to the receiver.

Audio amplifiers in modern hi-fi systems are designed for stereophonic recordings and broadcasts. Such amplifiers are essentially two identical amplifiers in one enclosure. These amplify the two channels of the stereophonic signal from an FM tuner or from a recording. Some hi-fi amplifiers can also handle quadraphonic (four-channel) broadcasts and recordings. (For an explanation of stereophonic and quadraphonic sound reproduction, see HIGH FIDELITY, subtitles *Stereophonic Sound* and *Quadraphonic Sound.*)

Other Amplifiers

In a radio or television receiver, an *r-f* (radio-frequency) *amplifier* is used to amplify electrical signals from an antenna in the range of frequencies extending from about 100 to 1,000,000 kilohertz (kilocycles per second). An r-f amplifier is a *tuned amplifier;* that is, it is designed to amplify signals in a specified, narrow band of frequencies. (An audio amplifier, in contrast, is a *broad-band amplifier;* it amplifies over a wide range of frequencies.)

The *resonant frequency* (frequency of maximum amplification) of an r-f amplifier is chosen by the listener as he moves a dial or channel selector. By means of "gang" tuning, whereby two or more tuning elements (usually variable capacitors) are controlled by a single dial, the listener selects from the antenna the carrier frequency of the desired station and at the same time tunes the r-f amplifier to that frequency. (See RADIO, section "How Radio Works," subtitle *Receiving Radio Signals.*)

In an *i-f* (intermediate-frequency) *amplifier,* which is used after the r-f stage in radio, radar, and television receivers to amplify internally produced signals, the resonant frequency remains constant. Most AM radio receivers use an intermediate frequency of

Royal Palace and Dam Square, Amsterdam

455 kilohertz, while the intermediate frequency of FM receivers is 10.7 megahertz (megacycles per second). A *video amplifier* is a broad-band amplifier used to amplify the electrical signals that form the picture in a television receiver.

Microwave amplifiers amplify signals in a microwave range of frequencies (1 to 100 gigahertz [1,000 to 100,000 megacycles per second]), and are used with radar equipment, television relay towers, and radio telescopes. A *maser* is a type of microwave amplifier, while a *laser* is similar to a maser except that it uses light rather than microwaves. (See LASER).

The voltage amplification, or *gain*, of an electronic amplifier is defined as the ratio of its output voltage to its input voltage at a specified frequency, and can range up to 1,000,000 or more. Gain is sometimes defined in terms of power rather than voltage. Thus, the power gain of an amplifier is

$$\frac{\text{output watts}}{\text{input watts}}.$$

The variation of gain with frequency is known as *frequency response*. Most hi-fi amplifiers have controls for adjusting both gain (the "volume" control) and frequency response.

The gain of an amplifier is usually expressed in *decibels* (abbreviation *db*). The decibel gain is given by:

$$20 \log \left(\frac{\text{output voltage}}{\text{input voltage}} \right).$$

Thus, an amplifier that increases the strength of a signal from 0.001 volt at its input to 10 volts at its output has a gain of

$$20 \log \left(\frac{10}{0.001} \right) = 20 \log (10,000) = 80 \text{ db}.$$

If the frequency response of an amplifier is specified as "± 2 db, 20-20,000 Hz" by the manufacturer, the voltage gain of the amplifier should not vary by more than 2 decibels within the frequency range of 20 to 20,000 hertz. (Two decibels is about the smallest variation that the human ear can detect.)

Amplitude. See WAVES, subtitle *How Waves Are Described.*

Amplitude Modulation. See RADIO, section "How Radio Works," subtitle *Transmitting Radio Signals:* Modulation.

Amputation, ăm'pŭ-tā'shŭn, the removal of a part of the body through surgery. The term refers most commonly to removal of all or part of an arm or leg, but may refer to removal of any external part of the body, such as an ear.

Gangrene (the death or decay of tissue, resulting from infection or lack of blood) often makes amputation of the affected part of the body necessary. Amputation can also be performed to prevent a severe infection or cancer from spreading. An embolus (a mass of clotted blood or foreign matter) in an artery or vein of an arm or leg can necessitate amputation. (Decrease of the limb's blood supply can lead to gangrene. Another danger is that the embolus might be transported to another part of the body and lead to serious illness or death; for example, see STROKE.)

Amritsar, ŭm-rĭt'sẽr, India, a city in Punjab state, near the Pakistan border, about 255 miles (410 km) northwest of New Delhi. Amritsar has long been the religious and commercial center of the Sikhs. The Golden Temple, surrounded by a small lake called the Pool of Immortality, is their most sacred shrine. Textiles and carpets are notable products of the city's handicraft industry. A wide variety of food products and other consumer goods are manufactured here.

Amritsar was founded in 1577 by Ram Das, the fourth guru (leader) of the Sikhs. With the building of the temple, begun under Ram Das, the city grew as a stronghold of Sikhism. Early in the 20th century it was the scene of numerous outbreaks against British authority. In 1919 British troops fired on a public meeting, killing 400 persons. The Amritsar Massacre, as it is sometimes called, spurred the nationalist movement throughout India.

Population: 407,628.

Amsterdam, ăm'stẽr-dăm, Netherlands, the largest city, a seaport, and the official capital of the nation. It is in Noord (North) Holland Province, 25 miles (40 km) northeast of The Hague, seat of the government. Amsterdam's name stems from a 13th-century dam built on the Amstel River. This short canalized stream flows through the city to the IJ, an arm of the IJsselmeer (formerly Zuider Zee).

Amsterdam's main canals—such as Singel, Prinsen, Keizers, and Heren—are intersected by numerous short waterways, dividing the city into about 90 islands that are linked by more than 600 bridges. The city is often called "the Venice of the North."

Damrak, a bustling thoroughfare, runs south from the IJ to the Dam, or town square, site of the Royal Palace (built 1648-65). North across the square is Nieuwe Kerk (New Church), the coronation church of Holland. Office buildings and fashionable shops, restaurants, and theaters line the streets radiating from the Dam. Along many of the streets and canals are narrow, steep-gabled houses of medieval and Renaissance merchant princes; they are now used chiefly as warehouses. Beyond the old city are modern industrial and residential suburbs.

Points of Interest

Amsterdam is the cultural center as well as one of the many educational centers of the Netherlands. The University of Amsterdam and the Amsterdam Free University are the chief institutions of higher learning.

In the Rijksmuseum are collections of paintings by such renowned Dutch artists as Rembrandt and Vermeer. A separate museum, the Rijksmuseum Vincent van Gogh, is devoted to works by Van Gogh. In the Tropical Museum are exhibits of life in the tropics. The Concertgebouw symphony orchestra is internationally renowned. Amsterdam maintains beautifully landscaped parks and zoological and botanical gardens.

Economy

Amsterdam is the nation's hub of commerce, industry, and finance. Its port, with excellent warehouse, shipbuilding, and repair facilities, is one of the busiest in Europe.

Manufacturing industries include the making of machinery, fabricated steel goods, aircraft, ships, beer, chemicals, clothing, and railway and bridge equipment. Since the mid-19th century Amsterdam has been the world center of the diamond-cutting industry. The city is important in national and international finance.

Amsterdam is a major crossroads of transportation. It is connected to the North Sea by the North Sea Canal. The Amsterdam-Rhine Canal accommodates barge traffic between the city and the Rhine River delta. The city is served by numerous express highways and railroads. Schiphol Airport,

seven miles (11 km) southwest of downtown Amsterdam, is one of Europe's busiest airfields.

History

There was only a fishing village on the site of Amsterdam until the 13th century, when feudal lords built a castle there and a dam across the mouth of the Amstel River to keep out the sea. A shipping community grew up rapidly, and in 1369 Amsterdam joined the Hanseatic League.

In the 16th century many Flemish Protestant merchants and Spanish and Portuguese Jewish diamond cutters fled to Amsterdam because of religious persecution by the Spanish. In the Peace of Westphalia (1648), commercial advantage for the newly independent Netherlands was assured by closing the sea outlet of Amsterdam's rival port, Antwerp, which was still held by Spain. Amsterdam became the trading and financial center of western Europe.

Under Napoleon Bonaparte Amsterdam was made capital of the Kingdom of Holland. It continued as the capital city of the independent Kingdom of the Netherlands founded in 1815. The gradual silting up of the channel to the Zuider Zee (now the IJsselmeer) threatened the city's future. During the 19th century, three canals were built to connect Amsterdam with the North Sea and the Rhine River.

Population: 733,593.

Amsterdam, New York, a city in Montgomery County. It is on the Mohawk River, about 30 miles (48 km) northwest of Albany. Amsterdam is a leading carpet and rug manufacturing center. Other products include clothing and electrical equipment. Nearby is a section of the original Erie Canal. Amsterdam was first settled in 1783 and was incorporated in 1885. It has the mayor-council form of government.

Population: 21,872.

Amtrak, the popular name for the National Railroad Passenger Corporation, an independent agency of the United States government. It directs intercity rail passenger service as a coordinated nationwide system. Trains are owned by Amtrak, but not rail facilities; the trains are operated by the railroads. Amtrak functions at a financial loss; its deficits are met by congressional appropriation. Amtrak was created in 1970, and most of the nation's railroads chose to participate in the corporation by purchasing stock. Directors are named in part by the President and in part by participating railroads.

Amu Darya, ä′mōō där′yȧ, a river in Central Asia known as the Oxus in ancient times. It is formed by the Vakhsh and Pyandzh rivers, which flow from the lofty Pamirs. Measured from its most distant headstream to its delta in the Aral Sea, the Amu Darya is about 1,600 miles (2,580 km) long. It flows generally northwestward, mainly in the Soviet Union. Part of its course marks the Soviet-Afghanistan border. The Amu Darya is navigable by barge in its lower course and is important for irrigation.

Amulet. See CHARM.

Amundsen, ä′mōōn-sĕn, **Roald** (1872-1928), a Norwegian polar explorer. Amundsen was the first man to reach the South Pole, to sail a ship completely through the Northwest Passage, and to fly a dirigible over the North Pole.

Amundsen was born in Borge. After studying medicine for two years, he went to sea on a Norwegian freighter. From 1897 to 1899 he served as first mate on a Belgian ship, the *Belgica,* which was the first to winter in the Antarctic.

From 1903 to 1906 Amundsen commanded the *Gjöa* in the first complete navigation of the Northwest Passage between the Atlantic and Pacific oceans. (See also NORTHWEST PASSAGE.)

Polar Expeditions

Returning to Norway, Amundsen prepared to drift from the Bering Strait towards the North Pole in Fridtjof Nansen's ship, the *Fram.* Interest in the project died, however, after Robert E. Peary reached the Pole in 1909.

In 1910 Amundsen sailed south from Norway in the *Fram.* The public expected the ship to sail to the Bering Strait by way of Cape Horn around South America; Amundsen, however, headed for the South Pole. On October 19, 1911, he and four companions began the overland trip with four sledges and 52 dogs. They raised the Norwegian flag at the South Pole on December 14, 1911, about one month before the arrival of Robert F. Scott's British expedition.

After World War I, Amundsen planned to drift from the Bering Strait towards the North Pole in the *Maud.* Taking the Northeast Passage to the Bering Strait (1918-20), he became the second man (the first was Nils

Roald Amundsen
NEW STANDARD
Collection

Nordenskjöld) to sail along the whole northern coast of Europe and Asia. In 1922 as the *Maud* began its drift, Amundsen left the ship to make a flight across the North Pole. However, damage to the plane forced him to cancel the trip.

In 1925 Amundsen and Lincoln Ellsworth, his American financial supporter, tried to reach the North Pole in two seaplanes. They did not reach the Pole, but their flight was the first of any real extent over the Arctic Ocean. In May, 1926, they finally crossed the North Pole in the semirigid dirigible *Norge,* built and piloted by Umberto Nobile. They were not first, however; Richard E. Byrd had flown over the Pole a few days earlier.

In 1928, Nobile was forced down in the dirigible *Italia* while on an arctic expedition. Amundsen lost his life at sea while flying to assist in Nobile's rescue.

Books by Amundsen include *Amundsen's Northwest Passage* (1908); *The South Pole* (1913); *Our Polar Flight* (with Ellsworth, 1925); *First Crossing of the Polar Sea* (with Ellsworth, 1927); *My Life As an Explorer* (1927).

Amundsen Sea, an arm of the South Pacific Ocean. It lies off the coast of Antarctica's Marie Byrd Land. The sea was explored and named in 1929 by Nils Larsen, a Norwegian.

Amur River, ä-mōōr′, a river in northeast Asia. The Chinese call it Heilung Kiang, or Heilong Jiang, meaning "Black Dragon River." Measured from the junction of its main headstreams, the Shilka and Argun rivers, the Amur is about 1,800 miles (2,900 km) long. With the Shilka and Onon, the system measures about 2,700 miles (4,350 km) in length. More than 1,000 miles (1,600 km) of its course forms the boundary between the Soviet Union and China. From its source the Amur winds generally southeastward and then northeastward until it empties into the Tatar Strait, which connects the Sea of Japan and the Sea of Okhotsk.

The Amur's main tributaries are the Zeya, Bureya, and Ussuri rivers of the Soviet Union and the Songhua River of China. During the ice-free season (May-November) the Amur is navigable by barge in its lower course. It flows through important mining and lumbering regions. Rich fishing grounds lie near its mouth. Blagoveshchensk, Khabarovsk, Komsomolsk, and Nikolayevsk, all in the Soviet Union, are the chief cities on the Amur.

AMVETS (American Veterans of World War II, Korea, and Vietnam), a national organization of United States war veterans. Its aims are "to promote peace, to preserve America's way of life, and to help veterans help themselves." Membership is open to all citizens who served honorably in any branch of the armed services during World War II, the Korean Conflict, or the Vietnamese War. *The National AMVET* is a bimonthly newspaper.

The American Veterans of World War II was organized in 1944. The shortened form of the name was adopted later. Congress chartered the organization in 1947 and in 1950 granted permission to the organization to admit veterans of the Korean Conflict. Vietnam veterans became eligible for membership in 1966.

There are about 200,000 members in 1,100 local posts. Headquarters are in Lanham, Maryland.

Amyl Acetate. See BANANA OIL.

Anabaptists, ăn'á-băp'tĭsts, the nickname given to various groups of radical Protestants during the 16th-century Reformation. Their enemies called them Anabaptists ("rebaptizers") because they practiced adult baptism—which for most new members meant being baptized a second time. They called themselves generally "Christian Brethren" and denied they were rebaptizers since they regarded infant baptism as not valid.

The Anabaptists believed the Reformation did not go far enough. They were not interested in reforming the church; they wanted to restore the church of New Testament days. Defining the church as the community of the redeemed, they insisted on separating the church from the state. The Anabaptists refused to bear arms for the state, and they shunned politics and public affairs.

There were four main centers of the

movement: Zurich, Switzerland; southern Germany; the Rhineland, especially Strasbourg; and Austria, including the Tyrol and Moravia. Anabaptism was a movement of the people, and it became intertwined with social discontent. In Germany occurred the bloody Peasants' War of 1524-26, in 'which the Anabaptist leader Thomas Münzer took part. The revolt was put down with terrible slaughter. In 1534 in Münster, Germany, a group of fanatics led by Jan Bockelson (or John of Leyden) set up a "Kingdom of the Saints." John made himself king, legalized polygamy, and established communal ownership of property. Münster was besieged and captured, and the defenders were massacred or tortured to death.

Protestants and Catholics joined to persecute the Anabaptists. The movement was crushed, but remnants survived. In the Netherlands Menno Simons took over the leadership of a group that later took the name Mennonites. In Austria Jacob Hutter organized another sect, now called Hutterian Brethren, or Hutterites.

The modern Baptists, while of independent origin, took over some of the Anabaptist beliefs, especially that of adult (or believers') baptism. Protestantism in the United States supports two Anabaptist principles: separation of church and state and voluntary church membership.

See also HUTTERIAN BRETHREN; MENNONITES; PEASANTS' WAR; REFORMATION.

Anabasis. See XENOPHON.

Anableps, ăn'á-blĕps, a genus of freshwater and marine fish found in tropical America from Yucatán to equatorial Brazil. Though commonly called "four-eyed fish," the anableps has only one pair of eyes, with each eye divided into two sections. The fish swims near the surface with the upper portion of each eye protruding above the waterline. The upper section of the eye is used for seeing objects in air; the lower section is for underwater vision. Average length of these fish is between six and eight inches (15 and 20 cm).

There are three species of anableps, the most common of which is *Anableps anableps*. All belong to the family Anablepidae.

Anabolism. See METABOLISM.

Anaconda, ăn'á-kŏn'dá, or **Water Boa,** bō'á, a water snake of Central and tropical South America. Anacondas are not poisonous. They kill their prey—birds and small

Anaconda

reptiles and mammals—by squeezing them until they suffocate, or by drowning them. Anacondas are *ovoviviparous* (the female retains her fertilized eggs in her body until they hatch). A large number of young are produced at one time.

There are two species of anacondas. The *giant anaconda* averages about 17 feet (5 m) in length, but some individuals grow to more than 30 feet (9 m) long and are 3 feet (90 cm) around the middle. The giant anaconda is olive green with round black spots. The *yellow anaconda* is smaller than the giant anaconda. It is yellow-green with irregular black markings.

Anacondas belong to the family Boidae. The giant anaconda is *Eunectes murinus;* the yellow, E. *notaeus.*

Anacreon, *à*-năk′rē-ŏn (572?-488? B.C.), a Greek lyric poet. His characteristic poems are lively and witty tributes to love and drinking. He also wrote hymns to Eros, Artemis, and Dionysus. Only fragments of Anacreon's works have survived. A few lyrics in a collection of 60 published under his name in 1554 are believed to be authentic.

Anacreon was born in the Ionian city of Teos in Asia Minor. He fled with his fellow townsmen before the invading Persians in about 545 B.C., and settled at Abdera in Thrace. Anacreon lived at the court of the tyrant Polycrates in Samos, about 537 to 522, and later moved to Athens.

Anacreon's short poems are called *Anacreontics,* a name sometimes applied to other brief and sprightly poems celebrating love and wine. The typical Anacreontic stanza has four lines with alternate rhyme. Anacreontics were very popular in Europe during the 17th and 18th centuries. The Irish poet Thomas Moore was noted for his Anacreontics. The tune of "The Star-Spangled Banner" is from an old English Anacreontic drinking song, "To Anacreon in Heaven."

Anaerobic Bacteria. See BACTERIA, subtitle *Life and Growth of Bacteria.*

Anaesthetic. See ANESTHESIA.

Anagram, ăn′*à*-grăm, a word or group of words formed by transposing the letters of another word or group of words and bearing some relation in meaning to the original. For example, the sentence *Flit on, cheering angel* is an anagram of the name *Florence Nightingale.* Miss Nightingale was known as the "Angel of the Crimea" for her work as a nurse during the Crimean War. For a related form of word play, see PALINDROME.

The ancient Greeks believed that the anagram of a person's name had some occult or mystical influence over his life and destiny. Anagrams were popular throughout Europe during the Middle Ages and later. King Louis XIII of France (1601-1643) was so fond of them that he employed a court anagrammatist.

Anaheim, ăn′*à*-hīm, California, a city in Orange County. It is 23 miles (37 km) southeast of downtown Los Angeles. Anaheim was long a center of fruit growing and processing before it became an industrial city. It manufactures electronic equipment, including computers, and hardware. The city became a leading tourist center after Disneyland, a huge amusement park, was opened here in 1955. (See DISNEYLAND.) Anaheim is the home of the California Angels, an American League baseball team. Anaheim was settled in 1857.

Population: 219,494.

Analgesic, ăn′ăl-jē′sĭk, any drug that eliminates or reduces pain without causing loss of consciousness. The salicylates, such as aspirin, are the most widely used analgesics; they are taken primarily to relieve headaches and muscular aches. Most narcotics, when taken in regular doses, can act as analgesics; a few, notably cocaine, are used as local anesthetics. Some narcotics, such as morphine, are used to relieve extreme pain; others, such as codeine, to relieve mild to moderate pain. The acetanilids are occasionally used to relieve minor pains. Under certain circumstances, barbiturates can act as analgesics, but barbiturates are used primarily as sedatives.

See also ACETANILID; ANESTHESIA, subtitle *Local Anesthesia;* BARBITURATES; NARCOTIC; SALICYLIC ACID.

Analog Computer. See COMPUTER, subtitle *Analog Computers.*

Analytic Geometry. See GEOMETRY, subtitle *Kinds of Geometry.*

Ananias, ăn'á-nī'ăs, in the Bible, the name of two Christians in the early church. Ananias and his wife Sapphira lied about the amount of their gifts to the church at Jerusalem and were struck dead (Acts 5:1-10). The other Ananias baptized Saul (or Paul) after his conversion on the road to Damascus (Acts 9:1-19).

Anapest. See POETRY, subtitle *Rhythm and Meter.*

Anaphase. See CELL, subtitle *Cell Division.*

Anaphylaxis. See ALLERGY, subtitle *How Allergic Reactions Occur.*

Anarchism, ăn'ár-kĭz'm, a political theory that advocates the abolition of all government. It was also, in the 19th and 20th centuries, a political movement. Anarchists regard political organization as an evil and look upon government as a means by which the powerful oppress the weak. They argue that man is good and that, if there were no government, injustice would collapse. Cooperation, they say, would replace coercion. People would work together voluntarily in a network of free associations, some formed according to localities and regions, others to meet economic needs. *Anarchy* is the condition (absence of government) desired by the anarchists. This word is also used to refer to a condition of social chaos, but anarchists dispute this meaning.

Anarchists, like socialists, believe that there should be no private ownership of business. Unlike socialists, anarchists do not want any form of government control over industry; they believe that production should be controlled solely by workers' associations. In France and certain Latin countries many anarchists have been *syndicalists,* who proposed to use labor unions ("syndicates") as instruments in the revolutionary struggle for a new society. (See SYNDICALISM.)

The Frenchman Pierre Joseph Proudhon (1809-1865) made anarchism a popular movement. His followers believed in establishing anarchist principles by peaceful means. The Russian Mikhail Bakunin (1814-1876) proposed the use of violence to destroy rule by governments; he tried to gain control of the European Communist movement, but was defeated by Karl Marx. During the late 19th and early 20th centuries, revolutionary anarchists assassinated such heads of government as President Carnot of France, Empress Elizabeth of Austria, King

Humbert of Italy, and President McKinley of the United States.

The anarchist movement dwindled rapidly in the 20th century, except in Spain. In the Spanish Civil War, anarchists fought for the Loyalists, who were defeated by General Franco. The movement as a political force then ended. Anarchistic ideas, however, were revived in the 1960's by student radicals and other revolutionaries, and old anti-anarchist laws were used to prosecute them.

See also KROPOTKIN, Prince PETER ALEXEVICH; PROUDHON, PIERRE JOSEPH.

Anasazi, ă-ná-sä'zĭ, a prehistoric American Indian people. The name comes from a Navaho word meaning "ancient ones." Their remains are found mainly in the Four Corners region, where Arizona, New Mexico, Colorado, and Utah meet. The Anasazi are also called Basketmakers, for one of their early products, later largely replaced by a distinctive pottery. They are also known for their early dwellings—pit houses, which developed into the *kiva* (underground ceremonial chamber) of the Pueblo Indians, in large part their descendants. The Anasazi period began about the first century A.D. and blended into the cliff-dwelling and pueblo periods. (See also CLIFF DWELLERS; MESA VERDE NATIONAL PARK.)

Anastasia, ăn'ăs-tā'shĭ-á (1901-1918?), youngest daughter of Nicholas II, the last czar of Russia. Nicholas and his immediate family were killed by the Bolsheviks in Ekaterinburg (now Sverdlovsk) in July, 1918, but rumors spread that Anastasia had been only wounded, and had been saved. Several women later claimed to be Anastasia, but none produced enough evidence to receive the Romanov fortune, estimated at 25 to 100 million dollars. Anastasia has been the subject of books, plays, and films.

See also NICHOLAS (czars), for picture.

Anatolia. See ASIA MINOR.

Anatomy, á-năt'ô-mĭ, the science that deals with the form and structure of organisms. The word comes from the Greek for a "cutting up," or dissection. Although the term "anatomy" can refer to the structure of any plant or animal, it usually refers to the structure of the human body only.

A knowledge of anatomy is essential in medicine. As part of his training, a medical student is required to dissect a human cadaver (corpse) and study its tissues under a microscope. Physicians must be thoroughly

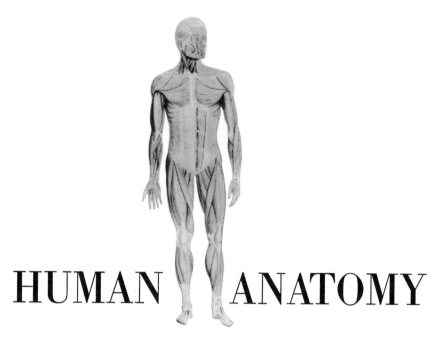

HUMAN ANATOMY

ILLUSTRATIONS BY RONALD KELLER

Prepared in consultation with
Charles N. Berry, Ph.D.
Seton Hall College of Medicine and Dentistry

This section on human anatomy is presented to help you to form a conception of the structure of the human body. The various structures of the body may be seen in their exact locations and in relation to the other structures. By the use of the transparencies one can determine these relationships in three dimensions—horizontally, vertically, and also in depth. In this way an understanding can be developed about the systems of the body and, therefore, about the total human organism.

Plate A shows the inside of the rib cage looking toward the front, while Plate F shows the inside of the skeleton looking toward the back. On the front of the first transparency (Plate B) most of the organs of the respiratory and digestive systems can be seen as viewed from the front. These organs include the trachea, the lungs, the intestines, pancreas, liver, and gall bladder. The thyroid gland (a part of the endocrine system) and the domelike diaphragm muscle are also seen. The back view of these organs is found on the reverse side of the transparency (Plate C). In Plate D are shown the principal parts of the circulatory system, plus the kidneys, adrenals, and parts of the excretory system as seen from the front. In Plate E a back view of the same systems is shown.

A drawing of the human skeleton with the various bones labeled is found in this encyclopedia with the article SKELETON. The muscles are shown in an illustration with the article MUSCLE.

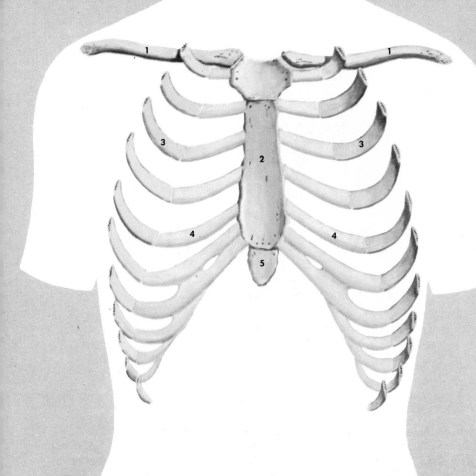

1. Collarbone (clavicle)
2. Sternum
3. Rib
4. Cartilage of the rib
5. Xiphoid process

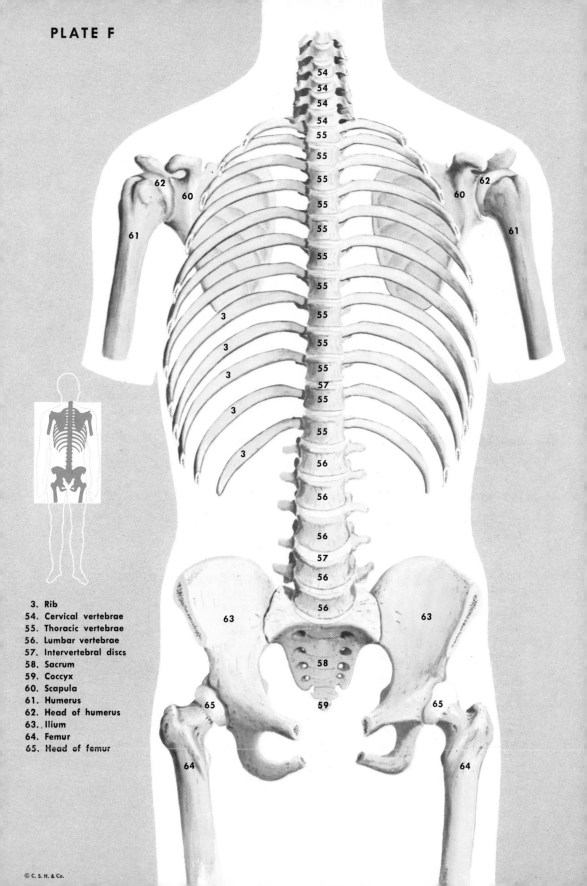

PLATE F

3. Rib
54. Cervical vertebrae
55. Thoracic vertebrae
56. Lumbar vertebrae
57. Intervertebral discs
58. Sacrum
59. Coccyx
60. Scapula
61. Humerus
62. Head of humerus
63. Ilium
64. Femur
65. Head of femur

© C. S. H. & Co.

INDEX

familiar with the normal relationships and appearances of tissues, bones, and organs, so that they can recognize diseased or injured parts. A surgeon's knowledge of anatomy tells him where to make an incision and what to look for inside the patient's body.

Fields of Anatomy

The study of anatomy is divided into several broad fields. These include:

Comparative Anatomy, the study of the similarities and differences in body structures of man and other animals.

Microscopic Anatomy, the study of the tissues and cells that make up organs. The study of tissues is called *histology,* the study of cells *cytology.*

Gross Anatomy, the study of the structures visible to the unaided eye.

Embryology, the study of the structural development of an organism from its earliest stage to its mature form.

Pathological Anatomy, the study of the effects of disease on body tissue.

Other Branches of anatomy, dealing with specific organs or types of organs, include: neurology (nerves), osteology (bones), and myology (muscles).

History

The ancient Egyptians and Greeks knew little about anatomy because dissection of the human body was against their religious principles. What little they did know was learned mostly from dissecting other animals. Hippocrates (460?-377? B.C.), the Greek "father of medicine," understood the basic structure of little but the skeleton. The philosopher Aristotle (384-322 B.C.) did not know much more than Hippocrates about human anatomy, but he conducted many experiments on animals other than man and obtained significant information about their anatomy.

Herophilus of Chalcedon (about 300 B.C.), a Greek physician, is regarded as the founder of anatomy. He made many contributions to the understanding of several parts of the human body, such as the brain and eyes, and was the first to make a distinction between arteries and veins and between nerves and tendons.

Galen (130?-201? A.D.), another Greek physician, made more contributions to anatomy than any other man of ancient times. He greatly increased the knowledge of the circulatory system and the nervous system, devoting particular emphasis to the spinal cord. Although his conclusions were often misleading and sometimes inaccurate, until the 16th century the study of anatomy depended almost entirely on Galen's works.

Leonardo da Vinci (1452-1519), the Italian artist-scientist, made many studies of the human body—especially its proportions and its muscles. His discoveries did not add to the anatomical knowledge of his period, however, because his notebooks were not published.

Andreas Vesalius (1514-1564), a Belgian physician, corrected Galen's works and dissected human bodies to obtain material for his studies of physiology and anatomy. He published the first accurate textbook, launching the modern study of anatomy.

The English physician and anatomist William Harvey (1578-1657) discovered the circulation of blood. Thomas Bartholin (1616-1680), a Danish physician, discovered the lymphatic system. From that time on, progress in anatomy was rapid. Marcello Malpighi (1628-1694), an Italian physician, and Anton van Leeuwenhoek (1632-1723), a Dutch naturalist, made important contributions by using the microscope to study human anatomy. Comparative anatomy became a distinct study in the 1800's through the efforts of Georges Cuvier (1769-1832), a French naturalist.

The development and refinement of microscopes, microscopic techniques, and new methods of dissecting, such as the cutting of extremely thin sections of tissue, led to the development of histology and cytology. The discovery of X rays in 1895 gave anatomists and physicians an opportunity to study the internal structures of living human bodies and to diagnose abnormalities. In the first half of the 20th century the development of X-ray microscopy and electron microscopy opened still another field—submicroscopic, or molecular, anatomy.

Modern anatomy draws on other branches of science, including electronics, physics, and chemistry, to further the understanding of the body. New methods are constantly being developed to learn more about the normal and abnormal structures of such complicated organs as the eyes, heart, brain, and central nervous system.

For further information, see:

Parts of the Body

ABDOMEN	ARM	CAPILLARIES
ACHILLES'	BLADDER	CARTILAGE
TENDON	BLOOD	CELL
ADENOIDS	BONE	CHEST
ANKLE	BRAIN	CILIA
APPENDIX	BURSA	COLLARBONE

COLON
DIAPHRAGM
EAR
ESOPHAGUS
EYE
FACE
FOOT
GALL
  BLADDER
GLAND
HAIR
HAND
HEAD
HEART
HIP
INTESTINE
JOINT
KIDNEYS
KNEECAP

LARYNX
LEG
LIGAMENT
LIVER
LUNGS
LYMPH
MAMMARY
  GLANDS
MASTOID
  PROCESS
MEMBRANE
MOUTH
MUSCLE
NAIL
NERVOUS
  SYSTEM
NODE
NOSE
ORGAN

PANCREAS
PITUITARY GLAND
PORE
PROSTATE GLAND
RIB
SINUS
SKELETON
SKIN
SKULL
SOLAR PLEXUS
SPLEEN
STOMACH
TEETH
THROAT
THYROID GLAND
TISSUE
TONGUE
TONSILS
TRACHEA

Related Subjects

MAN, subtitle *Man's*
  Body
MEDICINE

PATHOLOGY
PHYSIOLOGY
SURGERY

Biographies

ARISTOTLE
CUVIER, BARON
GALEN
GOLGI, CAMILLO
HARVEY, WILLIAM
HIPPOCRATES
HUNTER, JOHN

LEEUWENHOEK,
  ANTON VAN
MALPIGHI, MARCELLO
MORGAGNI,
  GIOVANNI B.
VESALIUS, ANDREAS
VINCI, LEONARDO DA

Books about Anatomy

Bruck-Kan, R. M. *Introduction to Human Anatomy* (Harper & Row, 1969).

Goss, C. M., editor. *Gray's Anatomy of the Human Body,* 29th edition (Lea & Febiger, 1973).

For Younger Readers:

Gilbert, Sara. *Feeling Good: a Book About You and Your Body* (Four Winds Press, 1978).

Klein, A. E. *You and Your Body* (Doubleday, 1977).

Rayner, Claire. *The Body Book* (Barron's, 1979).

Anatomy of Melancholy, The. See BURTON, ROBERT.

Anaxagoras, ăn'ăk-săg'ô-răs (500?-428 B.C.), a Greek philosopher and scientist. He introduced philosophy to Athens, and was the first to suggest that mind (*nous*) is the primary cause of changes in the physical world. Anaxagoras believed that all natural objects are composed of tiny particles, or "seeds," which contain a mixture of all properties of things and which the mind brings together into an orderly world. As a scientist he was the first to explain eclipses of the sun. He contended the sun is made up of burning rock and that the moon merely reflects light from the sun.

Anaxagoras was born in a Greek colony in Asia Minor, near present-day Izmir (Smyrna), Turkey. He spent most of his adult life

A-402

as a teacher in Athens. His pupils included Pericles, Euripides, and possibly Socrates. Only fragments of his book *On Nature* survive. Anaxagoras was accused of impiety because his theories on the sun and moon contradicted religious ideas. He was forced to leave Athens and died in Asia Minor.

Anaximander of Miletus, *ȧ*-năk'sĭ-măn'dĕr; mī-lē'tŭs (611?-547? B.C.), a Greek philosopher and astronomer. He was a student of Thales, who taught that water is the original substance of nature. Anaximander believed the primary substance to be something formless, indefinite, and immortal (he called it "the boundless") containing two sets of opposites—wetness and dryness; and cold and heat. According to his theory the universe evolved from the eternal motion of the boundless, which separated the opposites; thus living creatures evolved from a sort of sea urchin, which developed from wetness being evaporated by the sun.

Anaximander is believed to have made the first map and the first sundial, and to have been the first to observe that the earth is a sphere.

Anaximenes of Miletus, ăn'ăk-sĭm'ĕ-nēz, a Greek philosopher of the late sixth century B.C. He belonged to the Milesian school, which was founded by Thales and continued by Anaximander. Anaximenes believed air to be the primary substance of nature. The air, he said, is in eternal motion, and thus it forms the universe by two opposite processes: condensation and expansion. As air is condensed it grows cold and forms —by successive degrees—wind, clouds, water, earth, and stones. As air is expanded it grows hot and becomes fire, which is borne upward to form the heavenly bodies. His theory explained everything in the universe by a material cause and by a physical law.

Ancestor Worship, worship of the spirits of dead ancestors. It is based upon the belief that the ancestral spirits are immortal and have the power to help or harm the living. Rites are performed to appease the spirits or to persuade them to use their power to benefit the living. By strengthening the bond between the living and the dead, ancestor worship emphasizes the continuity of life.

Ancestor worship occurs in both primitive and civilized societies. It is most important among some of the Sudanese and Bantu tribes of Africa. Ancestor worship is also found in China, where it has existed since the Shang Dynasty (about 1523-1028 B.C.); and in Japan (as part of Shintoism), Melanesia, and Polynesia. (See SHINTO.) It was a minor cult among the Romans. (See MANES.)

Kinds of Ancestor Worship

Ancestral spirits may be worshiped as individuals or as a group, and by a single descendant or by a family, clan, tribe, or nation. Ritual activities may be simple or elaborate and assume varying degrees of importance in the religion of a people.

Every adult male among the Manus, a primitive Melanesian fishing people, worships the spirit of one of his recently deceased relatives. The Manus believe that ancestral spirits have the power to cause illness or death. Each man preserves the skull of the relative who became his ancestral spirit and makes offerings to it. In return the spirit protects him from the anger of other ancestral spirits. If the man is the head of a household, his ancestor's spirit protects all living members of the household and punishes them with illness for wrongdoing. After a man's death, his spirit becomes the protector of one of his surviving relatives and his ancestral skull is discarded.

Among the Bakongo of west Africa, each village, occupied by a single clan, worships its *Bakulu,* the spirits of ancestors who led good lives. The Bakongo believe that the Bakulu have the power to give or withhold the good things of life—food, health, children, good luck. The head of the village visits the ancestor shrine in the cemetery every fourth day to hold a small service. Special offerings are made for good hunting. Occasionally each village honors its Bakulu by holding a major series of ceremonies, the Feast of the Dead.

Ancestor worship is a widespread practice in China. Most Chinese believe that the living and dead members of a family influence each other. Families notify their ancestors of important occasions and make offerings of food, flowers, and incense to them before household shrines or in ancestral temples. Chinese ancestor worship also involves elaborate funeral rites, frequent memorial ceremonies, and regular care of the graves.

Ancestry. See GENEALOGY; HEREDITY.

Anchises, ăn-kī′sēz, in Greek legend, a young shepherd so handsome that Aphrodite descended from Mount Olympus to make love to him. She bore Anchises a son, Aeneas.

Anchises then was blinded by lightning for telling of the love affair. Virgil's *Aeneid* tells how Aeneas carried his aged father out of burning Troy, but does not mention that Anchises was blind at the time. Aeneas later persuaded the Cumaean sibyl to accompany him to the underworld, where he sought the advice of Anchises. Anchises revealed to Aeneas the future of Troy and foretold the founding of the Roman state by Aeneas's son Ascanius (or Iulius).

See also AENEID (picture).

Anchor, ăng′kẽr, a heavy weight that can be lowered into the water by cable from a ship or other floating structure to prevent drifting. Anchors of different sizes and designs are used to prevent drifting of warships, commercial vessels, pleasure craft, and buoys. They are also carried aboard barges, dredges, and ferries. Anchors weigh from several pounds to 10 tons or more.

The principal parts of a common anchor are the *flukes,* metal prongs that hook into the floor of the ocean or harbor; and a vertical bar called a *shank.* Some anchors also contain a horizontal bar called a *stock.* The stock helps to hold the anchor at such an angle that the fluke will dig into the bottom.

A ship is said to be *at anchor* when its anchor is on the bottom. To *weigh anchor* is to lift the anchor. An anchor cable of nylon, wire rope, manila rope, or steel or iron chain is attached to a ring in the top of the anchor shank. On deck, the other end of the cable is wound once around a cylindrical device called a *capstan* or *windlass.* The anchor is raised or lowered by turning the

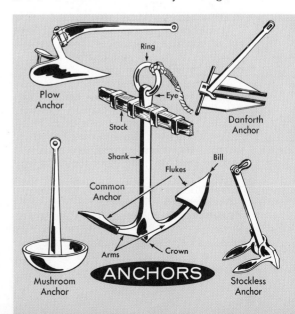

Plow Anchor

Ring

Eye

Danforth Anchor

Stock

Shank

Bill

Flukes

Common Anchor

Mushroom Anchor

Arms

Crown

ANCHORS

Stockless Anchor

U.S. Fish & Wildlife Svc.

Anchovy

capstan or windlass to wind or unwind the cable. Hoisting power is supplied by hand (on small boats) or by a motor.

A *sea anchor* is sometimes used when the ocean is too deep for a conventional anchor to reach bottom. It consists of a bag, usually of canvas, to which is attached a line. When thrown overboard the bag is held fairly steady by the weight of the water that fills it. During storms, a sea anchor is sometimes used to keep the craft's bow into the wind and to reduce rolling.

Prehistoric sailors used anchors made of heavy stones, tied with thongs or crude rope. By 750 B.C., the Greeks and Syrians had developed an anchor with two hooked arms and a stock. This was the basic design of the common anchor until the 1800's. More recent types are the *stockless* anchor, introduced in 1821; the *mushroom,* 1850; the *plow* anchor, 1933; and the *Danforth,* 1939.

Anchorage, Alaska, a seaport and the state's largest city. It lies at the mouth of Knik Arm, a branch of Cook Inlet, about 570 miles (920 km) west-northwest of Juneau, the state capital. Anchorage is the commercial, trade, and transportation center of south-central Alaska. The city has large sawmills, fish canneries, food processing plants, and railway repair shops. Elmendorf Air Force Base and the Army's Fort Richardson are here. There are rail and highway connections to other parts of Alaska and an international airport.

At Anchorage are a campus of the University of Alaska, a historical museum with collections of Indian and Eskimo artifacts, and a natural history museum.

Anchorage was settled in 1915 as the base of operations for building the Alaska Railway. Settlement of the Matanuska Valley in 1935 and establishment of defense facilities during World War II led to the city's rapid growth. Anchorage suffered severe earthquake damage in 1964. (For a picture, see ALASKA.)

Population: 174,431.

Anchorite. See HERMIT.

Anchovy, ăn-chō′vĭ; ăn′chŏ-vĭ, a small, silver-blue food fish found in warm and temperate sea waters in many parts of the

A-404

world. A few species enter freshwater streams. The anchovy is 2 to 10 inches (5-25 cm) long, with a pointed head and a snout that projects over its large mouth. The *common European anchovy,* abundant along the Atlantic coast and in the Mediterranean Sea, is extensively caught and processed for export. The *anchoveta,* or *Peruvian anchovy,* inhabits the South Atlantic Ocean from Peru to Chile. The anchoveta is high in protein and is ground into fishmeal for use in livestock feeds. Anchoveta oil is an important export of Chile and Peru.

Anchovies make up the family Engraulidae. The common European anchovy is *Engraulis encrasicholus;* the anchoveta, *E. ringens.*

Ancient History. See HISTORY.

Ancona, äng-kō′nå, Italy, a seaport, the capital of Ancona province, and the chief city of Marches region. It lies in the foothills of the Apennine Mountains on the Adriatic Sea, about 130 miles (210 km) northeast of Rome. Ancona is a commercial and industrial center. A white marble arch built in 113 A.D. in honor of the Roman emperor Trajan is one of the city's attractions. Ancona was settled in 400 B.C. by exiles from Greece.

Population: 108,466.

Ancona. See POULTRY, subtitle *Kinds of Chickens* (Mediterranean Class).

Andalusia, ăn′då-lōō′zhå, a region in southern Spain. It extends from the Sierra Morena south to the coast and encompasses the fertile valley of the Guadalquivir River. The region is divided into the provinces of Almería, Granada, Jaén, Córdoba, Málaga, Cádiz, Seville, and Huelva—all named for their capital cities. The Mediterranean coast between Algeciras and Málaga is a resort area called the Costa de Sol (Sunny Coast).

In ancient times Andalusia attracted Phoenicians, Greeks, Carthaginians, and Romans. The Moorish conquest of the eighth century was the beginning of a brilliant cultural era in Andalusia. Many fine examples of Moorish architecture survive.

Andalusian. See HORSE, section "Breeds of Horses," subtitle *Important Breeds:* Light Horses.

Andaman and Nicobar Islands, ăn′då-măn; nĭk′ŏ-bär, a union territory of India, consisting of two island groups. They lie south of Burma, between the Andaman Sea on the east and the Bay of Bengal on the west. The islands stretch generally north-south for about 490 miles.

The Andamans have a total area of 2,500 square miles. Five of the largest islands— Baratang, Rutland, and North, Middle, and South Andaman—lie close together and are known as the Great Andamans. Another main island, Little Andaman, is separated from the cluster by a narrow channel of water. There are also some 200 smaller islands in the Andaman group. The Nicobars, with a total area of 635 square miles, are separated from the Andamans by Ten Degree Channel. Two large islands, Great Nicobar and Little Nicobar, and 16 smaller islands make up the group.

The rolling hills of the Andaman and Nicobar islands are the weathered crests of partly submerged mountains. The maximum elevation above sea level is 2,402 feet, on North Andaman. Tropical rain forests are widespread, and mangrove swamps fringe much of the coasts. The islands have a hot, humid climate. The mean annual temperature is 85° F. Rainfall measures as much as 138 inches annually; most of it falls during the monsoon.

Cultivated areas on the Andamans are used for growing rice, coffee, coconuts, and Manila hemp and sisal. Timber is also a major product. Coconut is the chief product of the Nicobars. Port Blair on South Andaman, with a population of about 14,000, is the territory's largest town; it is also the administrative center.

Both island groups were settled many centuries ago by primitive immigrants from Indochina: the Nicobars by people of Mongoloid stock and the Andamans by Negrito pygmies. There was little contact with the outside world until the mid-19th century, when the British took control of the islands. Until India became independent (1947), the Andamans were used as a penal colony. The Japanese held both island groups during World War II. Since 1951 the government of India has resettled peasant farmers from the mainland on the Andamans in an effort to develop agriculture.

In 1971 the population of the union territory was 115,090.

Andaman Sea, an arm of the Indian Ocean. It is bordered by upper Burma on the north, the Malay Peninsula on the east, Sumatra on the south, and Andaman and Nicobar Islands on the west. The sea is about 850 miles long (north-south) and up to 420 miles wide. Rangoon, Burma, is the

leading port. The Irrawaddy, Salween, and Sittang are the chief rivers emptying into the sea.

Andersen, Hans Christian (1805-1875), a Danish writer. Though a poet and novelist, he is most famous for his fairy tales. He has delighted young readers of all lands with his sometimes simple, always imaginative stories of fir trees and flowers, storks, swans, and nightingales, and princes, princesses, and soldiers.

Andersen took traditional tales and themes and by his sympathetic understanding of human emotions and qualities gave them deeper moral and symbolic meaning than they had possessed originally. Some of these tales are based on stories told by the common people among whom he spent his childhood. Others are mainly products of his imagination, though strongly colored by folk themes and settings.

Andersen's sunny nature would not permit him to use bitter satire, but he sometimes

Hans Christian Andersen. This photograph was taken in 1869 in the garden at Roligheden, country estate of his friends Moritz G. and Dorothea Melchior, where he wrote many of his fairy stories.

mocked people's frailties in a gentle way, as in "The Emperor's New Clothes." Often there is a tinge of sadness, as in "The Ugly Duckling." Andersen is said to have considered this story, which tells of an awkward young swan at first mistaken for a duckling, an allegory of his own life.

A Struggle for Fame

Hans Christian Andersen was born in Odense, the son of a poor shoemaker. His ugliness made him shy, and he was treated rudely by other children in school. When he was 11, his father died and Hans quit school to work in a factory. He amused himself at home by reading plays and acting them out with puppets in a toy theater he had built.

When he was 14, Hans left home for Copenhagen. There he tried everything to get into the theater—write, act, sing, dance. He did attract the attention of influential persons and was sent to a government school. Although 17 years old, Hans had to enter a class for small boys. His unhappiness continued, but he remained in school for five years. He then left to try his hand at poetry, travel books, farce, and fiction.

Success

Andersen's first novel, *The Improvisatore* (1835), was received enthusiastically, and his financial troubles were at an end. In the same year the first installment of his fairy tales was published. The book, which began with "The Tinder Box" and "Little Claus and Big Claus," was reviewed unfavorably by all the critics but one. Andersen agreed with this general opinion, for he considered his adult works of more importance. Nevertheless, he kept on writing fairy tales until his health began to fail in 1872. He died of cancer three years later.

Andersen's more than 160 fairy tales include such favorites as "The Red Shoes," "The Snow Queen," and "The Little Match Girl." His tales have been translated into 80 languages. *In Spain* (1863), a travel book, is one of his most successful adult works.

Anderson, Alexander (1775-1870), a United States engraver. His illustrations for *The Looking Glass of the Mind* (1794) were the first wood engravings made in the United States. Anderson was born in New York City. A self-taught engraver, he made his first prints when he was 12 years old. Anderson also studied medicine and in 1795 became a licensed physician. His illustrations appeared in many magazines and in such books as *Emblems of Mortality* (1800), *Sal-*

magundi (1814), and *Historical Collections of New Jersey* (1868).

Anderson, Carl David (1905-   ), a United States physicist noted for his studies of gamma rays and cosmic rays. Anderson

California Inst. of Tech.
Carl D. Anderson

shared the 1936 Nobel Prize in physics for his discovery in 1932 of the positron, a positively charged atomic particle with the mass of an electron. In 1936 he and Seth Neddermeyer announced they had discovered the mesotron (now called meson), an atomic particle larger than an electron but smaller than a proton.

Anderson was born in New York City. He received his Ph.D. degree in 1930 from the California Institute of Technology, where he became professor of physics in 1939.

Andersón, Elizabeth Garrett (1836-1917), the first English woman physician and a leader in the women's rights movement. She determined to study medicine after a meeting in 1859 with Dr. Elizabeth Blackwell, the first United States woman physician, who had been permitted to practice in England. Through private study, a few classes she was permitted to attend at medical schools, and employment as a surgical nurse, Elizabeth Garrett acquired her medical training. She was not permitted, however, to take the examination for a physician's license in England.

Licensed as a pharmacist, she took up work at a London dispensary for women, which she helped to develop into a hospital (given her name in 1918). In 1870 she received an M.D. degree from the Sorbonne in Paris. Her marriage the next year to James S. Anderson did not halt her medical practice. With Dr. Blackwell she helped to establish the London School of Medicine for Women in 1875, and to obtain the right in 1877 for women to be granted medical degrees in England.

Anderson, Judith, the stage name of Dame Frances Margaret Anderson (1898-   ), an Australian-born actress known for her performances in tragic roles. She was especially praised for her portrayal of the queen in *Hamlet* (1936) and Lady Macbeth in *Macbeth* (1937). In 1947 she triumphed in the title role of Robinson Jeffers' *Medea*. She appeared frequently in motion pictures and television plays. She was born in Adelaide, and made her debut in Sydney in 1915. After 1918 she spent much of her time in the United States. In 1960 she was made a Dame of the British Empire.

Anderson, Leroy (1908-1975), a United States conductor, composer, and arranger of popular music. "Sleigh Ride," "Blue Tango," "The Syncopated Clock," and "Fiddle-Faddle" are among his works. Anderson was born in Cambridge, Massachusetts. He was graduated from Harvard University in 1929, and was director of its band, 1932-35. From 1936 to 1950 Anderson was arranger and guest conductor for the Boston Pops Orchestra. He organized his own orchestra in 1950.

Other works include *Irish Suite, A Suite of Carols,* and the musical *Goldilocks* (1958).

Anderson, Marian (1902-   ), a United States contralto. The resonant low tones and natural beauty of her voice brought her wide acclaim as a singer of spirituals, *lieder,* and arias. After many years of success on the concert stage, she became the first Negro to join the Metropolitan Opera Company. She made her debut as Ulrica in *A Masked Ball* in 1955.

Marian Anderson was born in Philadelphia, and studied voice with Giuseppe Boghetti. In 1925 she won first prize in a vocal competition that led to an appearance with the New York Philharmonic in Lewisohn Stadium. Scholarships enabled her to continue her study in Europe. She made her Berlin debut in 1930 and her London and Paris debuts in 1934. Then came tours in the United States and many other countries. National attention was focused on Miss Anderson in 1939 when the Daughters of the American Revolution refused to let her sing in Constitution Hall in Washington, D. C. Through the efforts of Eleanor Roosevelt and others, she sang before 75,000 people from the steps of the Lincoln Memorial.

Marian Anderson
National Archives

Miss Anderson toured India and the Far East for the State Department in 1957, and in 1958 became a delegate to the United Nations. She gave a series of farewell concerts in 1964-65, retiring from the concert stage. *My Lord, What a Morning* (1956) is her autobiography.

Anderson, Maxwell (1888-1959), a United States dramatist. He was one of the few 20th-century American playwrights to use blank verse. His historical plays in that form include *Elizabeth the Queen* (1930), *Mary of Scotland* (1933), *Valley Forge* (1934), *Joan of Lorraine* (1946), and *Anne of the Thousand Days* (1948).

The blank-verse tragedy *Winterset* (1935) is based on the Sacco-Vanzetti case of the 1920's. Like several other Anderson plays, it stresses inner moral conflict and the power of conscience. Mio, the central character, seeks revenge for the electrocution of his anarchist father for a murder Mio is sure he did not commit. Anderson adapted *Winterset* from *Gods of the Lightning* (1928), a prose play which he had written with Harold Hickerson.

Anderson wrote two musical comedies with scores by Kurt Weill: *Knickerbocker Holiday* (1938), about the early Dutch in New York; and *Lost in the Stars* (1949), based on Alan Paton's novel of South Africa, *Cry the Beloved Country* (1948). *Both Your Houses,* a satire on corrupt politics, won the Pulitzer Prize in 1933.

Anderson was born in Atlantic, Pennsylvania, the son of a Baptist clergyman. He was raised in various parts of the Midwest where his father held pastorates. He was graduated from the University of North Dakota in 1911, and received his master's degree from Stanford University in 1914. Anderson worked on North Dakota and California newspapers before going to New York City in 1918. There he was on the staff of the *Evening Globe,* the *Morning World,* and the magazine *New Republic.*

Anderson's first Broadway play, *White Desert* (1923), had little success. *What*

Maxwell Anderson
Wide World

A-407

Price Glory? (1924), a realistic drama of World War I written with Laurence Stallings, made him famous and prosperous. In his latter years he wrote television dramas.

His other plays include: *Saturday's Children* (1927); *High Tor* (1937); *Key Largo* (1939); *The Eve of St. Mark* (1942); *Barefoot in Athens* (1951); *The Bad Seed* (1955). *You Who Have Dreams* (1925) is a volume of lyric verse. *The Essence of Tragedy* (1939) and *Off Broadway* (1947) are collections of critical essays.

Anderson, Robert (1805-1871), a United States army officer. In the first military action of the American Civil War (April 12-13, 1861), Major Anderson defended Fort Sumter in South Carolina against Confederate bombardment for 34 hours before surrendering. (See also FORT SUMTER.) He was born near Louisville, Kentucky, and graduated from West Point in 1825. Anderson fought in the Black Hawk, Seminole, and Mexican wars. He was promoted to major in 1857 and to brigadier general in 1861.

Anderson, Sherwood (1876-1941), a United States author of short stories and novels about life in the Middle West. His recognition as a Naturalist came with *Winesburg, Ohio* (1919), a series of short stories about a small town much like Clyde, Ohio, where Anderson lived as a boy. He called the characters in the sketches "grotesques" because of their grotesque eccentricities.

Most of the Winesburg stories are psychological portraits of the town's people as seen through the eyes of George Willard, an adolescent reporter groping for "the sadness of sophistication" as he rebels against Winesburg's social and moral narrowness. The frustrations and secret yearnings of various townspeople are described in simple, forthright language with a touch of lyricism.

The style, technique, and subject matter of *Winesburg, Ohio* had a strong influence on younger writers of the naturalistic-realistic school. Two of these were Er-

A-408

nest Hemingway and William Faulkner, both of whom received advice and encouragement from Anderson in their beginning days. Both began by imitating Anderson to some extent. Both later parodied him: Hemingway in *The Torrents of Spring* and Faulkner in *Mosquitoes.*

Anderson, particularly in his earlier novels, voiced a kind of ingenuous primitivism which exalted simple life and unsophisticated people over materialistic society and its attendant industrialization. *Poor White* (1920) is about an inventor for whom industrial success means disenchantment and the spiritual blight of his home town. In *Many Marriages* (1923) a businessman tries to escape from a humdrum existence. *Dark Laughter* (1925) contrasts the uninhibited enjoyments of Negroes with the neurotic concerns of white people cursed by the complexities of a mechanized age. In *Perhaps Women* (1931), a nonfiction work, Anderson wonders if female leaders might not be able to rescue our culture from the sterility induced by mechanization.

Anderson's Life

Sherwood Anderson was born in Camden, Ohio. His schooling was irregular; he had to take odd jobs to help support the family. When he was 14, his mother died. Young Sherwood then began his wanderings. In 1896 he went to Chicago and worked as a laborer. After a brief interlude of soldiering in the Spanish-American War, he spent several years writing advertising copy in Chicago. He then married and settled in Ohio, where for some time he operated a paint factory in Elyria. Faced with bankruptcy and dissatisfied with his dull lot, he fled from family and business to Chicago and advertising again. He was encouraged by Theodore Dreiser and other members of the Chicago literary group to write his first novel, *Windy McPherson's Son* (1916). This story

Sherwood Anderson
Harcourt, Brace and World, Inc.

of a boy who moves from poverty to financial success, but eventual disillusionment, approximates the author's own story.

After touring Europe in 1921, Anderson lived in New Orleans and New York City. In 1924 he moved to a farm near Marion, Virginia. He bought and edited two Marion newspapers—one Democratic and the other Republican. Anderson died while on a South American tour.

His other books include: Poems—*Mid-American Chants* (1918). Novels—*Beyond Desire* (1931); *Kit Brandon* (1936). Short stories—*The Triumph of the Egg* (1921); *Horses and Men* (1923); *Death in the Woods* (1933). Autobiography—*A Story Teller's Story* (1924); *Tar: A Midwest Childhood* (1926); *Memoirs* (1942). Anderson's letters were published in book form in 1953. *The Buck Fever Papers,* a collection of his newspaper columns, was published in 1971.

Anderson, Indiana, the seat of Madison County. It is on the White River, about 33 miles (53 km) northeast of downtown Indianapolis. Anderson is an industrial city with factories producing automotive parts, packaging machinery, tools, and containers. The city serves as a trade center for the surrounding agricultural area. Anderson College is here.

Anderson was first settled in 1823. It was chartered as a city in 1865. Between 1887 and 1900 development of nearby natural-gas reserves spurred the city's growth.

Population: 64,695.

Anderson, South Carolina, the seat of Anderson County. It is about 95 miles (153 km) northwest of Columbia. Anderson's products include clothing, textiles, and fiberglass. The city also serves as a trade center for the surrounding agricultural area, in which cotton, pimentos, and cattle are produced. Nearby Hartwell Reservoir is a tourist attraction. Anderson was first settled in 1826.

Population: 27,638.

Anderson College. See UNIVERSITIES AND COLLEGES (table).

Andersonville National Historic Site. See NATIONAL PARKS, section "United States."

Andersonville Prison, a Confederate military prison for captured Union Army soldiers, located at Andersonville, Georgia. It was used as a prison from February, 1864, to April, 1865. It was planned to accommodate 10,000 men but at one time held over 30,000. It was an open stockade without barracks. Overcrowding, poor food, pollut-

ed water, and inadequate medical care caused the deaths of about 13,000 prisoners. After the war Captain Henry Wirz, the prison superintendent, was convicted of murdering his prisoners by neglect and was hanged. Historians believe that the verdict was unjustified, since Wirz could not obtain adequate supplies from the impoverished government.

MacKinlay Kantor's *Andersonville* (1955), although fiction, gives a realistic picture of life in the prison.

Andes, ăn′dēz, (*Spanish:* **Cordillera de los Andes,** kôr′thĕ-yā′rä thä̊ lôs än′däs), the great mountain system of South America. It extends near the continent's Pacific coast for more than 4,000 miles (6,400 km), running through Venezuela, Colombia, Ecuador, Peru, Bolivia, Chile, and Argentina. After the towering Himalayan system of Asia, the Andes are the highest mountains in the world.

Along much of its length, the system divides into two, sometimes three, roughly parallel chains. These are the *Cordillera Occidental,* the western chain; the *Cordillera Central;* and the *Cordillera Oriental,* the eastern chain. Various local names are used to designate parts of these chains.

Geographical Divisions

The Andes are a geologically young and complex series of folded and faulted mountains. There are major volcanic areas, especially in southern Colombia and Ecuador, from southern Peru to northern Argentina, and in the south-central part of Chile. The entire Andean region is an active earthquake zone.

The Northern Andes begin in Venezuela and Colombia, where the mountain ranges rise almost directly from the Caribbean sea. In Colombia, deep river valleys divide the Andes into the three distinct cordilleras. Farther south, in Ecuador, the mountains consist of two chains, separated by a deep rift valley. Dotting the chains are numerous volcanoes, including Chimborazo and Cotopaxi. The Andes reach their narrowest point in Ecuador, where the crests of the ranges are as little as 20 miles (32 km) apart.

The Central Andes begin in northern Peru and broaden into high plateaus, on which are mountain ranges and volcanic peaks. As in the northern section, there are two or three major ranges depending on location.

In southern Peru and western Bolivia,

CARIBBEAN SEA

Cristóbal Colón
18,947'
5.775 m
Lake Maracaibo
Caracas

TRINIDAD
AND
TOBAGO

PANAMA
Panamá

Pico Bolívar
16,427'
5.007 m

Orinoco

VENEZUELA

Georgetown

Medellín

Magdalena

Llanos

GUYANA

Bogotá

Cali

COLOMBIA

Orinoco

Huila
18,865'
5.750 m

Quito

Equator

Negro

Japurá

ECUADOR

Chimborazo
20,702'
6.310 m

Guayaquil

Marañón

Solimões

Amazon

Ucayali

Juruá

BRAZIL

P

E

R

U

A

N

D

E

S

Madeira

Huascarán
22,205'
6.768 m

Lima

PACIFIC

Coropuna
21,079'
6.425 m

Lake Titicaca

BOLIVIA

El Misti
19,098'
5.822 m

La Paz

Altiplano

Illimani
21,201'
6.462 m

Sajama
21,463'
6.542 m

Sucre

Atacama

Puno

Chaco

PARAGUAY

Tropic of Capricorn

Antofagasta

Bartholomew
Depth
−26,160'
−7,974 m

Atacama Desert

Llullaillaco
22,057'
6.723 m

Gran

Asunción

Ojos del Salado
22,572'
6.880 m

Bonete
22,546'
6.872 m

A

R

G

E

N

T

I

N

A

Salado

Paraná

Aconcagua
22,834'
6.960 m

Santiago

Uspallata
Pass

Pampas

Buenos
Aires

C

H

I

L

E

Concepción

Colorado

A

N

D

E

S

ATLANTIC

OCEAN

San Valentín
13,238'
4.035 m

Patagonia

Falkland Islands

ANDES

⊛ Capitals

0   Miles   400

0   Km   400

Tierra del
Fuego

Cape Horn

---

the ranges enclose an area of high intermontane basins called the *Altiplano* (high plain). Most of this area lies at elevations of more than 12,000 feet (3,600 m). To the southeast, along the eastern margin of the Andes, is a high, dry region called the *Puna*. The Andes are at their widest in Bolivia, where the eastern and western ranges are as much as 400 miles (640 km) apart.

As the Andes narrow in northern Argentina and Chile, they form a single principal range. Here are the highest mountains of the Americas, including many volcanoes.

The Southern Andes stretch from central Chile to the tip of the continent at Cape Horn. In general, they are lower than the ranges to the north, although there are high, isolated volcanic peaks. The mountains have been heavily glaciated, especially in the extreme south, where large glaciers still exist. For much of their course the Southern Andes plunge directly into the sea, creating a rugged, indented shoreline, with many offshore islands.

Rivers and Lakes

Except in Venezuela, where all rivers flow to the Atlantic Ocean, the Andes form the divide between Atlantic and Pacific drainage. Hundreds of large rivers flow eastward to the Atlantic. Most are either headstreams or tributaries of the great Orinoco, Amazon, and Paraná systems. No large rivers flow westward to the Pacific.

There are few lakes, other than glacial ones in southern Chile. Lake Titicaca, on the Altiplano between Peru and Bolivia, is South America's largest freshwater lake. It is also the highest navigable lake in the world. The only other large lake is Lake Poopó, also on the Altiplano.

Peaks

More than 20 Andean peaks rise to elevations above 20,000 feet (6,100 m). Among them are:

NAME AND LOCATION	ELEVATION Feet	Meters
Aconcagua, Argentina	22,834	6,960
Ojos del Salado, Argentina-Chile	22,572	6,880
Bonete, Argentina.	22,546	6,872
Huascarán, Peru	22,205	6,768
Llullaillaco, Argentina-Chile	22,057	6,723
Sajama, Bolivia	21,463	6,542
Illimani, Bolivia	21,201	6,462
Chimborazo, Ecuador	20,702	6,310

Passes and Transportation

Passes through the Andes are high and difficult to approach, but several are used by

In the Andes. Lake Todos los Santos is in the mountains of south-central Chile. Mount Tranador, in the background, is on the border between Chile and Argentina, and rises to 11,660 feet (3,554 m) above sea level.
Panagra

railways, roads, or both. Uspallata Pass on the Chile-Argentina border is followed by the Pan American Highway. Railroads have been built at great heights in the Andes to bring out valuable minerals, especially in Peru, Bolivia, and Chile. Most traffic in the mountains, however, is carried on unpaved roads and trails, mainly by burros and llamas. Principal cities are linked by airlines.

Climate and Vegetation

Since the Andes stretch from about 10° North latitude to 55° South, there is a wide climatic range. In the low equatorial foothills, temperatures average about 80° F. (27° C.) the year long. In contrast, the cold, wet, almost uninhabitable areas of the extreme south have average temperatures a little over 40° F. (4° C.). The effects of increasing elevation, and consequent lower temperatures, are felt everywhere. The highest mountains are mantled with snow throughout the year even near the Equator.

In the tropical areas, climate and vegetation depend chiefly on elevation. The foothills, up to about 3,000 feet (900 m) above sea level, are called the *tierra caliente* (hot land), an area of tropical rain forests. Above this zone, extending to about 6,500 feet (2,000 m), is the *tierra templada* (temperate land), with mixed deciduous trees and grasslands. Still higher, up to about 10,000 feet (3,000 m), is the *tierra fría* (cold land), with coniferous forests, hardy grasses, and shrubs. Still higher, there are Alpine pastures, called *páramos,* that extend above the tierra fría to the snow line.

Agriculture

Because of rough terrain and high elevations, very little of the Andes is suitable for agriculture. Most of the people live by subsistence farming. However, there are small areas of the tierra caliente where tropical cash crops are raised. The most valuable are bananas, sugar, and cotton. Coffee is the chief commercial crop on the tierra templada, especially in Colombia.

Subsistence farming extends through the middle and highland zones. On the tierra templada, corn and temperate fruits and vegetables are grown; on the tierra fría, hardy strains of wheat and barley. At high elevations Indians raise llamas and alpacas. These animals, unique to the Andes, produce wool and milk and are agile pack animals. Llamas are also used for meat.

Mining

Some of the world's richest copper mines are in the high mountains of Peru and Chile. Bolivia has long been one of the world's leading tin producers. Peru and Bolivia, as in the days of Spanish rule, are major producers of silver. Platinum, tungsten, vanadium, molybdenum, bismuth, lead, zinc, and gold are also mined in the Andes. Colombia is famous for its gem emeralds.

The People

Indians are the native peoples of the Andes. The chief group is the Quechua, the dominant people of the great Inca empire. Their language, also called Quechua, is widely spoken by Indians in Peru, Bolivia, Ecuador, Chile, and Argentina. Other groups are the Chibcha of Colombia and the Aymará of Bolivia and Peru. People of Spanish descent and *mestizos* (people of mixed Spanish-Indian culture) live mainly in the cities.

Books about the Andes

Benson, Elizabeth, and William Conklin. *Museums of the Andes* (Newsweek Books, 1981).

Guidoni, Enrico, and Roberto Magni. *The Andes* (Grosset & Dunlap, 1977).

MacKinnon, Jack. *The Andes* (Time-Life Books, 1976).

Meish, Lynn. *A Traveler's Guide to El Dorado and the Inca Empire* (Penguin Books, 1977).

Morrison, Tony. *Land Above the Clouds: Wildlife in the Andes* (Universe Books, 1974).

Andesite, ăn'dě-zīt, a fine-grained rock that is widely distributed in the earth's crust. Andesite reaches the surface as lava from volcanoes. As it cools it forms gray to grayish-black sheets, often in thick accumulations. Andesite consists chiefly of feldspar minerals mixed with smaller amounts of iron and magnesium. It was named for the Andes of South America, where it is widely found. Andesite is used for building stone and monuments.

Andorra, ăn-dôr'à, or **Valleys of Andorra,** a semi-independent country high in the Pyrenees between France and Spain. It covers only 175 square miles (453 km²) and is nowhere more than 20 miles (32 km) across. Scenic valleys and rugged mountains that crest at elevations up to about 10,000 feet (3,000 m) make up most of the terrain. The chief river is the Valira, which flows southward into Spain. Winters are cold, with deep snow lasting for months; summers are warm and relatively dry.

Tourism is probably the most important part of the economy. Many foreigners visit Andorra to vacation and to buy imported merchandise at low cost—Andorra does not impose customs duties. The raising of livestock and hardy crops, for centuries the main economic activity, remains impor-

tant. Manufacturing consists almost entirely of the making of a few consumer goods, including handicraft items. Hydroelectric power is generated and sold to Spain and France. Good roads link Andorra with its neighbors; there are no railways or airports.

Andorra's population in 1979 was about 31,000; that of Andorra (or Andorra la Vella), the capital, 12,000. Catalan is the official language; Spanish and French are also used. Virtually all the people are Roman Catholics. Andorra maintains schools up to the lower secondary level, but attendance is not required provided parents instruct their children up to the age of 14.

Andorra is a principality with the President of France and the Bishop of Urgel in Spain as co-princes. They are charged with the conduct of foreign affairs, defense, and the judicial system. Legislative power is vested in a council consisting of four popularly elected members from each of Andorra's seven districts.

Because of its small size and isolated location, Andorra has remained outside the mainstream of European history. Its present boundaries and political status were established in 1278, when the Spanish Bishop of Urgel and the French Count of Foix agreed to rule as co-princes, ending a long dispute. French rights passed eventually to the presidents of France. In 1978 Andorra's co-princes met for the first time in 700 years.

See also FLAG (color page).

Andover Academy. See PHILLIPS ACADEMY (Andover).

Andrada e Silva, ănn-drà'thà ĕ sĭl'vả, **José Bonifácio de** (1763?-1838), a Brazilian statesman, scientist, and poet, known as his country's "Patriarch of Independence." Andrada was born in Santos, Brazil. He studied in Portugal, where he became a noted geologist. Returning to Brazil in 1819, Andrada became active in the independence movement.

As adviser and chief minister to Dom Pedro, regent of Brazil, Andrada influenced his decision to declare independence from Portugal in 1822. After Dom Pedro was proclaimed constitutional emperor as Dom Pedro I, Andrada became minister of the interior and of foreign affairs. He was exiled in 1823 after a disagreement with the emperor, but allowed to return in 1829. From 1831 to 1833 he tutored Dom Pedro II.

Andradite. See GARNET.

Andrássy, ŏn'drä-shĭ, the family name of two Hungarian statesmen, father and son.

Count Gyula Andrássy (1823-1890) was a leading figure in the unsuccessful revolt of 1848-49 against Hungary's Austrian rulers. After helping to form the Dual Monarchy of Austria-Hungary in 1867, Andrássy served as the first constitutional premier of Hungary, 1867-71. As foreign minister of Austria-Hungary, 1871-79, he represented his government at the Congress of Berlin in 1878 and signed the Dual Alliance with Germany in 1879.

Count Gyula Andrássy (1860-1919), the son, served as Hungary's minister of the interior, 1906-10, and as foreign minister of Austria-Hungary in 1918. He joined an attempt to restore the Hungarian monarchy in 1921. Later he led the opposition to the government of Admiral Miklós Horthy and Count Stephen Bethlen.

André, än'drā, **John** (1751?-1780), a British army officer who was hanged as a spy during the American Revolution. In September, 1780, André met with Benedict Arnold at West Point to arrange the details of Arnold's planned betrayal of this important American fortress to the British. He was returning to New York City disguised as a civilian when he was seized by American militiamen near Tarrytown. Arnold's secret dispatches were discovered in his boots. André was brought before a court martial, condemned as a spy, and hanged near Tappan, New York.

André was born in London of Swiss-French parentage. He joined the British army at the age of 20 and served in Canada, 1774-75. André was captured by the Americans in 1775 and released in a prisoner exchange the following year. He then fought at Brandywine, Germantown, and Monmouth. In 1778 he was made adjutant to the British commander Sir Henry Clinton, with the rank of major.

In 1821 André's remains were taken to England and buried in Westminster Abbey.

Andrea Chénier, an opera in four acts by Umberto Giordano. Luigi Illica wrote the libretto, which is in Italian. *Andrea Chénier* was first produced at La Scala, Milan, in 1896. "Un di all' azzurro spazio" and "Come un bel di di Maggio" are among favorite arias. The story takes place in Paris during the Revolution and Reign of Terror. Principal characters are Andrea Chénier, an ide-

The Apostle Saint Andrew
by El Greco, 16th century
oil on canvas, 28 x 21½"
(71.1 x 54.6 cm)
Los Angeles County Museum of Art

White Island in September. The last diary entry was dated October 6.

Andreev, Leonid N. See ANDREYEV, LEONID NIKOLAYEVICH.

Andrew, Saint, one of the 12 apostles of Jesus Christ. Originally a disciple of John the Baptist, he became the first follower of Jesus. Andrew's brother was Simon Peter (Saint Peter), and it was through Andrew that Peter first met Jesus. Andrew also brought others to Jesus, and has been called the first Christian missionary.

According to Christian traditions, Andrew became a missionary in the Black Sea region. Legends tell of his martyrdom at Patrae (Patrai) in Greece. He is said to have been crucified on an X-shaped cross, now called the cross of Saint Andrew. Saint Andrew became the patron saint of both Russia and Scotland. The white cross of Saint Andrew on a blue field forms the national flag of Scotland. The cross is combined with the crosses of Saint George (England) and Saint Patrick (Ireland) in the Union Jack of Great Britain.

The principal Biblical references to Andrew are John 1:40, 6:8, and 12:22 and Mark 13:3. His feast day is November 30.

Andrew, John Albion (1818-1867), a United States political leader. He was noted for his opposition to slavery and for his support of the abolitionist John Brown in 1859. He was governor of Massachusetts, 1861-66. In 1863 he obtained the consent of the War Department to organize one of the first Negro army units, the 54th Massachusetts Regiment.

Andrew was born in Windham, Maine. After graduation from Bowdoin College (1837) he settled in Boston and became a lawyer. He joined the short-lived Free Soil party and became a Republican after it went out of existence in 1856.

Andrew Johnson National Historic Site. See NATIONAL PARKS, section "United States."

Andrews, Charles McLean (1863-1943), a United States historian. He was awarded the 1935 Pulitzer Prize in history for the first volume of his four-volume *Colonial Period*

alistic poet; Madeleine, a member of the nobility; and Charles Gérard, a former servant and official of the revolutionists. Giordano's fame rests almost entirely on this opera.

Andrea del Sarto. See SARTO, ANDREA DEL.

Andrea della Robbia. See ROBBIA, DELLA.

Andreanof Islands. See ALEUTIAN ISLANDS.

Andrée, àn-drā', **Salomon August** (1854-1897), a Swedish explorer. On July 11, 1897, Andrée and two companions set out on the first flight to the North Pole, from Spitsbergen (Svalbard) in the well-equipped balloon *Ornen* (Eagle). Except for one pigeon and two buoys carrying messages, Andrée and his companions were never heard from again.

In 1930 their remains were discovered on White Island, east of Spitsbergen. Andrée's diary revealed that the balloon had been forced down on July 14, 1897, about 500 miles (800 km) from the Pole. The men attempted to return to Spitsbergen, reaching *of American History* (1934-38). Andrews was born in Wethersfield, Connecticut. He received his Ph.D. degree from Johns Hopkins University in 1889 and was a professor of American history at Yale University from 1910 to 1931.

His books include: *Fathers of New England* (1919); *Colonial Folkways* (1919); *The Colonial Background of the American Revolution* (1924).

Andrews, Roy Chapman (1884-1960), a United States naturalist, explorer, and author. He was a leading authority on whales and proved that Central Asia was one of the chief centers of early mammal and reptile life. Andrews was born in Beloit, Wisconsin, and graduated from Beloit College in 1906. He went to New York City to work for the American Museum of Natural History, becoming assistant curator of the department of mammals in 1911. On his early expeditions for the museum, 1908-14, Andrews studied whales and other water mammals along the coasts of Alaska and Asia. He received his M.A. degree from Columbia University in 1913.

As leader of the museum's Asiatic expeditions, 1916-32, Andrews explored Central Asia and worked extensively in Mongolia. He discovered one of the world's richest fossil fields in the Gobi desert, containing the first known dinosaur eggs and the remains of the long-extinct Baluchitherium, the largest known land mammal. His expeditions also discovered previously unknown geological strata and mapped new areas of the Gobi. Andrews became director of the museum in 1935 and retired as an honorary director in 1942.

Among his numerous books are *Whale Hunting with Gun and Camera* (1916); *On the Trail of Ancient Man* (1926); *The New Conquest of Central Asia* (1932); *This Amazing Planet* (1940); *Under a Lucky Star* (autobiography, 1943); *Meet Your Ancestors* (1945); *Heart of Asia* (1951); *Nature's Ways* (1951); and *Beyond Adventure* (1954).

Andrews University. See UNIVERSITIES AND COLLEGES (table).

Andreyev (or **Andreev**), ŭn-dryä′-yĕf, **Leonid Nikolayevich** (1871-1919), a Russian short-story writer and dramatist. His first work was realistic and often moral in tone, but he later emphasized the symbolical and became deeply pessimistic and negative. *The Red Laugh* (1904) is a story depicting a soldier driven mad by the horrors of war. In *The Life of Man* (1906), a morality play, the characters are mere abstractions

with names like Man and His Wife. Revolutionaries condemned for plotting an assassination are pictured sympathetically in *The Seven That Were Hanged* (1908). Andreyev's most popular play was *He Who Gets Slapped* (1915), a tragic melodrama about a circus clown. The circus serves as a symbolical environment for life and society.

Andreyev graduated in law from the University of Moscow, but turned to writing at Maxim Gorky's advice. A bitter foe of the Bolsheviks, he died in self-imposed exile in Finland.

Andrič, ăn′drĭch; ăn-drĕch′, **Ivo** (1892-1975), a Yugoslav novelist. He was awarded the 1961 Nobel Prize for literature for *The Bridge on the Drina* (1945) and other novels about his native Bosnia. Andrič was a revolutionary in his youth, when his country was controlled by Austria-Hungary. After World War I he served in diplomatic posts for what became Yugoslavia. The Germans kept him under house arrest in Belgrade during World War II. After the war he was a deputy in the Yugoslav parliament.

Androcles, ăn′drŏ-clēz, or **Androclus,** ăn′drŏ-clŭs, a Roman slave of the first century A.D. According to Aulus Gellius, a Latin writer of that period, Androcles ran away from his cruel master in Africa and hid in a cave. There he found a lion suffering from a thorn in its paw, and removed the thorn. He eventually was captured and, as punishment for running away, was sent into the arena with a hungry lion. The lion, instead of eating Androcles, licked his hand. It was the lion he had befriended. Man and lion were then set free.

George Bernard Shaw in his play *Androcles and the Lion* (1912) uses the story as a basis for satirical comment on the early Christian movement and its martyrs. Androcles is made a docile Greek tailor who has been converted to Christianity.

Andromache, ăn-drom′á-kĕ, the wife of the Trojan hero Hector. The description of her parting with Hector as he goes to battle in the Trojan War is a touching passage in Homer's *Iliad*. After Hector was slain by Achilles and Troy had fallen to the Greeks, she was assigned as a captive to Achilles' son Neoptolemus (Pyrrhus). Andromache bore Neoptolemus a son and narrowly escaped being murdered by Neoptolemus' wife Hermione. Andromache later married Hector's brother Helenus.

Yuri Andropov
Wide World

Andromache is the central figure in Euripides' *Andromache* and appears in his *The Trojan Women*. Racine's play *Andromaque* (1667) is another version of her story.

Andromeda Galaxy, a spiral galaxy that is larger than the Milky Way (the galaxy to which earth belongs) but similar to it in structure. (A galaxy is a large concentration of stars, dust, gas, and other material. See GALAXY.) The Andromeda galaxy is the only galaxy beyond the Milky Way that can be seen with the unaided eye from the middle latitudes of the Northern Hemisphere. It appears as a hazy spot in the constellation Andromeda.

The Andromeda galaxy is about 2.2 million light-years from earth. It is estimated to be about 160,000 light-years in diameter and to contain more than 200,000,000,000 stars. The galaxy is wheel-shaped, but the view from earth is nearly edge on, making it appear to be elongated. Because of the similarities between it and what astronomers have been able to map of the Milky Way, information obtained on the Andromeda galaxy helps man understand the structure of his own galaxy.

After the invention of the telescope in the 17th century, the Andromeda galaxy was called the *Great Nebula of Andromeda* (a name that is still sometimes used) and was thought to be a cloud of dust within the Milky Way. In the 19th century, some astronomers theorized that the Andromeda galaxy was not a dust cloud, but a huge group of stars so far away that telescopes of the time could not separate the individual stars. This theory was upheld in 1923 when Edwin Hubble, an American astronomer, discovered some variable stars in the edges of the Andromeda galaxy. In 1944 Walter Baade, a German-American astronomer, was able to identify individual stars in the central portion of the galaxy.

Andropov, ŭn-drŏ'pŏv, **Yuri Vladimirovich** (1914-   ), a Soviet political leader. He emerged as the most powerful figure in the Soviet Union in 1982, when he became general secretary of the Communist party following the death of Leonid Brezhnev. In 1983 he also became President of the Soviet Union. Earlier, during 1967-82, he headed the KGB, the Soviet secret police.

Andropov was born in Nagutskoye in the Ukraine, the son of a railroad worker. He attended a technical school and later Petrozavodsk University, and worked for a few years as a telegraph operator. He joined the Communist party in 1939 and for many years was an organizer for the Young Communist League, both in the Soviet Union and in Finland. He served as ambassador to Hungary during 1954-57. Andropov was elected to the party's Central Committee in 1962 and became a voting member of the Committee's ruling group, the Politburo, in 1973.

Andros, ăn'drŏs, Sir **Edmund** (1637-1714), an English colonial administrator in America. He was a capable, honest official, but his manner was overbearing and he repeatedly came into conflict with the colonists over government policy.

In 1674 Andros was appointed governor of New York, which had been taken in 1664 from the Dutch, but the Dutch settlers forced his recall in 1681.

Andros returned to America in 1686 to serve as governor of the new union of colonies decreed by James II and named the Dominion of New England. (It consisted at first of only New England but later New York and New Jersey were included.) For a variety of economic, political, and religious reasons, the union was unpopular with the colonists, especially the New England Puritans. When word was received in 1689 of the Glorious Revolution of 1688 in England, the colonists deposed Andros and dissolved the dominion.

In 1692, under William and Mary, Andros returned again, to serve as governor of Virginia. Here he aroused the anger of Dr. James Blair, founder of the College of William and Mary, by opposing a program of church reform. Dr. Blair caused him to be recalled in 1697.

See also CHARTER OAK.